Antique Trader®
Pottery & Porcelain
Ceramics
PRICE GUIDE
6th Edition

©2009 by Krause Publications, Inc., a subsidiary of F+W Media, Inc.

Published by

kp krause publications

A subsidiary of F+W Media, Inc.

700 East State Street • Iola, WI 54990-0001
715-445-2214 • 888-457-2873
www.krausebooks.com

Our toll-free number to place an order or obtain
a free catalog is (800) 258-0929.

Library of Congress Control Number: 2008937718

ISBN 13-digit: 978-0-89689-933-9
ISBN 10-digit: 0-89689-933-0

Designed by Wendy Wendt
Edited by Kyle Husfloen

Printed in China

ON THE COVER: Front left: Bavarian porcelain teapot with gold decoration, marked
"Barvaria," ca. 1930s, 7" h. - $40-$80; center back: Weller Pottery "Glendale" pattern 14"
vase, ca. 1915, $1,000-$1,500; front right: Japanese porcelain 10" d. plate decorated with
birds & flowers on a red ground, marked "Japan," ca. 1920s - $75-$150.

Antique Trader®
Pottery & Porcelain
Ceramics
PRICE GUIDE
6th Edition

Kyle Husfloen

More Great Books in the Antique Trader® Series

Antiques & Collectibles Price Guide
Book Collector's Price Guide
Bottles Identification & Price Guide
Collectible Paperback Price Guide
Furniture Price Guide
Guide to Fakes & Reproductions
Indian Arrowheads Price Guide
Jewelry Price Guide
Kitchen Collectibles Price Guide
Limoges Price Guide
Perfume Bottles Price Guide
Radio & Television Price Guide
Royal Doulton Price Guide
Salt and Pepper Shaker Price Guide
Stoneware and Blue & White Pottery Price Guide
Teapots Price Guide
Tools Price Guide
Vintage Clothing Price Guide
Vintage Magazines Price Guide

TABLE OF CONTENTS

Introduction 6

Photography Credits 7

Special Contributors 7

Collecting Guidelines. 11

Market Survey - Ceramics 2008-2009. 13

Typical Ceramic Shapes 22

Price Listings. 25

Appendix I - Ceramics Clubs &
Associations 755

Appendix II - Museums & Libraries with Ceramics
   Collections 758

Appendix III - References to Pottery and
   Porcelain Marks 759

Appendix IV - English Registry Marks 760

Glossary of Selected Ceramics Terms 763

Index 766

Introduction

Impressive is the *6th edition of the Antique Trader Pottery & Porcelain Ceramics Price Guide* on many levels— the fantastic photography, incredible pottery and porcelain pieces, the breadth and depth of the material, accuracy of information and low retail price for such an authoritative book. Back in 1994, when I compiled the first edition of the popular identification and price guide, I couldn't have imagined how quickly 14 years would fly by! But I've compiled this material in 2008 and you'll be reading the new guide in early 2009!

A lot of changes have been made to the title over the years, all for the better. Today it is much larger than the 1994 guide and the photographs are now in full color. We still include the helpful appendices that appeared back in that first edition, including a glossary of ceramics terms, a list of collecting clubs and associations, a list of museums and libraries with ceramics collections, and another list of references to pottery and porcelain marks.

We even include a special appendix illustrating and explaining English registry marks. In addition to these sections, our new edition also includes an illustrated list of marks found on pottery and porcelain. At the front of the book we again include a feature on collecting guidelines and have followed this with my in-depth market survey that offers a comprehensive survey of the current state of the ceramics marketplace. All of these features and lists combine to bring you the most comprehensive and educational guide to the wide world of ceramics collecting.

Whether your favorite collectible is a mid-century modern ceramic line, lovely Victorian porcelains or the many variations of fine art pottery, you'll find them covered here. I have gathered the most current pricing information using auction results and contributions from many specialist collectors and dealers. Keep in mind that the prices included here reflect current replacement values, in other words, what you might expect to pay if you were to purchase comparable pieces.

This is important to remember because if you are trying to sell similar items, you may or may not receive a matching dollar amount. Many factors, including condition, rarity and local demand, will affect the price you may receive for your ceramic prize. Over the decades some "hot" ceramics categories have cooled down as other categories have gained in popularity. The listings will reflect many of the market trends, and I take special pride in our detailed descriptions of listed pieces.

Antique Trader Pottery & Porcelain Ceramics Price Guide gives you all the pertinent factors that influence the value of a specific piece of pottery or porcelain. The over 10,000 listings included here are highlighted by more than 4,300 full-color photos and cover all the most popular categories of ceramics, from the 18th century through the late 20th century. Whatever your collecting preference, you'll find it covered in the following pages. This up-to-date and informative guide should become an important part of any antiques reference library.

I hope you enjoy our efforts and I'll be happy to hear your comments. Meanwhile, happy hunting!

Kyle Husfloen, Editor

Please note: *Although our descriptions, prices and illustrations have been double-checked to ensure accuracy, neither the editor, publisher nor contributors can assume responsibility for any losses that might be incurred as a result of consulting this guide, or of typographical or other errors.*

Photography Credits

There are many other companies and individuals I must also thank. Among the photographers who have contributed to this edition are: Charles Casad, Monticelo, Ill.; Neva Colbert, St. Clairsville, Ohio; Susan N. Cox, El Cajon, Calif.; Susan Eberman, Bedford, Ind.; Mary Ann Johnston, New Cumberland, W. V.; Ann Kerr, Sidney, Ohio; Vivian Kromer, Bakersfield, Calif., and Pat McPherson, Ramona, Calif.

For other photographers, artwork, data or permission to photograph in their shops, we sincerely express appreciation to the following auctioneers, galleries, individuals and shops: Alderfers, Hatfield, Pa.; Charlton Hall Galleries, Columbia, S.C.; Christie's, New York; Cincinnati Art Galleries, Cincinnati; Copake Country Auction, Copake, N.Y.; William Doyle Galleries, New York; Early Auction Company, Milford, Ohio; Garth's Auctions, Delaware, Ohio; Glass-Works Auctions, East Greenville, Pa.; and Green Valley Auctions, Mt. Crawford, Va.

Also to Harris Auction Center, Marshalltown, Iowa; Jackson's International Auctioneers, Cedar Falls, Iowa; James D. Julia, Fairfield, Maine; McMasters Harris Auctions, Cambridge, Ohio; Neal Auction Company, New Orleans; New Orleans Auction Galleries, New Orleans; Northwest Auctions, Portsmouth, N.H.; Dave Rago Arts & Crafts, Lambertville, N.J.; Seeck Auctions, Mason City, Iowa; Skinner, Inc., Bolton, Mass.; Treadway Gallery, Cincinnati; Bruce & Vicki Waasdorf, Clarence, N.Y.; and Wood Auctions, Douglass, Kan.

Special Contributors

ABC Plates

Joan M. George, Ed.D
67 Stevens Ave.
Old Bridge, NJ 08857
e-mail: drjgeorge@nac.net

Abingdon

Elaine Westover
210 Knox Highway 5
Abingdon, IL 61410-9332

American Painted Porcelain

Dorothy Kamm
10786 Grey Heron Ct.
Port St. Lucie, FL 34986
e-mail: dorothykamm@adelphia.net

Amphora-Teplitz

Phil and Arlene Larke
O.S.A.R. Antiques
1505 Black Oaks Place
Minneapolis, MN 55447
(763) 473-0394
e-mail: imalark@aol.com

Amphora Collectors International
21 Brooke Dr.
Elizabethtown, PA 17022
e-mail: tombeaz@comcast.net

Bauer Pottery

James Elliot-Bishop
500 S. Farrell Dr., S-114
Palm Springs, CA 92264
e-mail: gmcb@ix.netcom.com

Beatrix Potter Figurines

Reg G. Morris
2050 Welcome Way
The Villages, FL 32162
e-mail: modexmin@comcast.net

Bellaire (Marc) Ceramics

Donald-Brian Johnson
3329 South 56th St., #611
Omaha, NE 68106
e-mail: donaldbrian@webtv.net

Belleek (Irish)

Del E. Domke
16142 N.E. 15th St.
Bellevue, WA 98008-2711
(425) 746-6363
Fax: (425) 746-6363
e-mail: delyicious@comcast.
netWeb site: The Beauty and Romance of Irish Belleek

Blue and White Pottery

Steve Stone
12795 W. Alameda Pkwy.
Lakewood, CO 80225
e-mail: Sylvanlvr@aol.com

Blue Ridge Dinnerwares

Marie Compton
M & M Collectibles
1770 S. Randall Rd., #236
Geneva, IL. 60134-4646
ebay name: brdoll

Blue Willow (see Willow Wares)

Sascha Brastoff

Susan N. Cox
800 Murray Dr.
El Cajon, CA 92020
e-mail: antiquefever@aol.com

Donald-Brian Johnson
3329 South 56th St., #611
Omaha, NE 68106
e-mail: donaldbrian@webtv.net

Brayton Laguna Pottery

Susan N. Cox
800 Murray Dr.
El Cajon, CA 92020
e-mail: antiquefever@aol.com

Buffalo Pottery

Phil Sullivan
P.O. Box 69
So. Orleans, MA 02662-0069

Caliente Pottery

Susan N. Cox
800 Murray Dr.
El Cajon, CA 92020
e-mail: antiquefever@aol.com

Catalina Island Pottery

James Elliot-Bishop
500 S. Farrell Dr., S-114
Palm Springs, CA 92264
e-mail: gmcb@ix.netcom.com

Ceramic Arts Studio of Madison

Tim Holthaus
CAS Collectors Association
P.O. Box 46
Madison, WI 53701-0046
e-mail: CAScollectors@
Ameritech.net

Donald-Brian Johnson
3329 South 56th St., #611
Omaha, NE 68106
e-mail: donaldbrian@webtv.net

Cleminson Clay

Susan N. Cox
800 Murray Dr.
El Cajon, CA 92020
e-mail: antiquefever@aol.com

Cowan

Tim & Jamie Saloff
P.O. Box 339
Edinboro, PA 16412
e-mail: tim.saloff@verizon.net

deLee Art

Susan N. Cox
800 Murray Dr.
El Cajon, CA 92020
e-mail: antiquefever@aol.com

Doulton & Royal Doulton - Bunnykins

Reg. G. Morris
2050 Welcome Way

The Villages, FL 32162
e-mail: modexmin@comcast.net

East Liverpool & Related Potteries

William A. & Donna J. Gray
2 Highland Colony
East Liverpool, OH 43920
e-mail: harkermate@comcast.net

Florence Ceramics

David G. Miller
1971 Blue Fox Dr.
Lansdale, PA 19446-5505
(610) 584-6127
Florence Ceramics Collectors
Society
e-mail: FlorenceCeramics@aol.
com

Flow Blue

K. Robert and Bonne Hohl
47 Fawn Dr.
Reading, PA 19607

Franciscan Ware

James Elliot-Bishop
500 S. Farrell Dr., S-114
Palm Springs, CA 92264
e-mail: gmcb@ix.netcom.com

Frankoma Pottery

Susan N. Cox
800 Murray Dr.
El Cajon, CA 92020
e-mail: antiquefever@aol.com

Geisha Girl Porcelain

Elyce Litts
P.O. Box 394
Morris Plains, NJ 07950
(908) 964-5055
e-mail: memories@worldnet.att.net

Gonder Pottery

James R. & Carol Boshears
e-mail: Gondernut@aol.com

Hadley Pottery

Donna Rand
905 Ahland Road
Louisville, KY 40207
(502) 592-1009
e-mail: derbyfan@bellsouth.net

Hall China

Marty Kennedy
4711 S.W. Brentwood Rd.
Topeka, KS 66606

(785) 554-5837
(785) 273-4981
e-mail: martykennedy@cox.net
Web site: http://www.inter-ser-
vices.com/HallChina

Harker Pottery

William A. and Donna J. Gray
2 Highland Colony
East Liverpool, OH 43920-1871
e-mail: harkermate@comcast.net

Haviland

Nora Travis
13337 E. South St.
Cerritos, CA 90701
(714) 521-9283
e-mail: Travishrs@aol.com

Hull

Joan Hull
1376 Nevada SW
Huron, SD 57350

Hull Pottery Association
11023 Tunnel Hill N.E.
New Lexington, OH 43764

Ironstone

Bev Dieringer
P.O. Box 536
Redding Ridge, CT 06876
e-mail: dieringer1@aol.com

Tea Leaf Ironstone

Tea Leaf Club International
P.O. Box 377
Belton, MO 64012
Web site: www.tealeafclub.com

Jewel Tea - Autumn Leaf

Jo Cunningham
535 E. Normal
Springfield, MO 65807-1659
(417) 831-1320
e-mail: hlresearcher@aol.com

Kitchen Collectibles

Cow Creamers:

LuAnn Riggs
1781 Lindberg Dr.
Columbia, MO 65201
e-mail: artichokeannies@bessi.net

Eggcups:

Joan M. George, Ed.D
67 Stevens Ave.
Old Bridge, NJ 08857
e-mail: drjgeorge@nac.net

Napkin Dolls, Reamers:

Bobbie Zucker Bryson is the co-author, with Deborah Gillham and Ellen Bercovici, of the pictorial price guide *Collectibles for the Kitchen, Bath & Beyond, 2nd Edition*, published by Krause Publications. It covers a broad range of collectibles including napkin dolls, stringholders, pie birds, figural egg timers, razor blade banks, whimsical whistle milk cups and laundry sprinkler bottles. Bryson can be contacted via e-mail at Napkindoll@aol.com.

String Holders, Egg Timers, Pie Birds:

Ellen Bercovici
360-11th Ave. So.
Naples, FL 34102

Limoges

Debby DuBay, Ret. USAF
Limoges Antiques Shop
20 Post Office Avenue
Andover, MA 01810
(978) 470-8773
e-mail: dlimoges@flash.net
Web: www.limogesantiques.com
<http://www.limogesantiques.com>

Lotus Ware

William A. and Donna J. Gray
2 Highland Colony
East Liverpool, OH 43920-1871
email: harkermate@comcast.net

Majolica

Michael G. Strawser Auctions
P.O. Box 332
Wolcottville, IN 46795
(260) 854-2859
Web: www.majolicaauctions.com

McCoy Pottery

Craig Nissen
P.O. Box 223
Grafton, WI 53024-0223
(414) 377-7932
e-mail: McCoyCN@aol.com

Mettlach

Gary Kirsner
863 Northridge Dr.
Prescott, AZ 86301
(928) 227-3723
e-mail: gkirsner@cableone.net

Andre Ammelounx
P.O. Box 136
Palatine, IL 60078
(847) 991-5927

Monmouth - Western Stoneware

Gail Peck
2121 Pearl St.
Fremont, NE 68025
e-mail: gpeck1@neb.rr.com

Morton Potteries

Burdell Hall
201 W. Sassafras Dr.
Morton, IL 61550
(309) 263-2988
e-mail: bnbhall@mtco.com

Mulberry Ware

K. Robert Hohl
47 Fawn Dr.
Reading, PA 19607-9736

Nicodemus Pottery

Susan N. Cox
800 Murray Dr.
El Cajon, CA 92020
e-mail: antiquefever@aol.com

Betty Lou Nichols

Donald-Brian Johnson
3329 South 56th St., #611
Omaha, NE 68106
e-mail: donaldbrian@webtv.net

Nippon

Jackson's International Auctioneers & Appraisers
2229 Lincoln St.
Cedar Falls, IA 50613
(319) 277-2256
(319) 277-1252 (fax)
Web: www.jacksonsauction.com

Noritake

Janet and Tim Trapani
7543 Northport Dr.
Boynton Beach, FL 33437
e-mail: ttrapani1946@yahoo.com

Old Ivory

Alma Hillman
197 Coles Corner Rd.
Winterport, ME 04496
e-mail: oldivory@roadrunner.com

Other

Louise Irvine
England - (020) 8876-7739
email: louiseirvine@blueyonder.co.uk

Pascoe and Company
253 SW 22nd Ave.
Miami, FL 33135
email: sales@pascoeandcompany.com

Oyster Plates

Michael G. Strawser Auctions
P.O. Box 332
Wolcottville, IN 46795
(260) 854-2859
Web: www.majolicaauctions.com

Pacific Clay Products

Susan N. Cox
800 Murray Dr.
El Cajon, CA 92020
e-mail: antiquefever@aol.com

Pennsbury Pottery

Mark and Ellen Supnick
7725 NW 78th Ct.
Tamarac, FL 33321
email: Saturdaycook@aol.com

Phoenix Bird Porcelain

Joan Collett Oates
1107 Deerfield St.
Marshall, MI 49068
(269) 781-9791

Pierce (Howard) Porcelains

Susan N. Cox
800 Murray Dr.
El Cajon, CA 92020
e-mail: antiquefever@aol.com

Quimper

Sandra V. Bondhus
16 Salisbury Way
Farmington, CT 06032
email: nbondhus@pol.net

Red Wing

Gail Peck
2121 Pearl St.
Fremont, NE 68025
email: gpeckl@neb.rr.com

Robj Décorative Ceramics

Donald-Brian Johnson
3329 South 56th St., #611
Omaha, NE 68106
email: donaldbrian@webtv.net

Royal Bayreuth

Mary McCaslin
6887 Black Oak Ct. E.
Avon, IN 46123
(317) 272-7776
e-mail: maryjack@indy.rr.com

Royal Copley

Donald-Brian Johnson
3329 South 56th St., #611
Omaha, NE 68106
email: donaldbrian@webtv.net

Rozart Pottery

Susan N. Cox
800 Murray Dr.
El Cajon, CA 92020
e-mail: antiquefever@aol.com

R.S. Prussia

Mary McCaslin
6887 Black Oak Ct. E.
Avon, IN 46123
(317) 272-7776
e-mail: maryjack@indy.rr.com

Schoop (Hedi) Art Creations

Susan N. Cox
800 Murray Dr.
El Cajon, CA 92020
e-mail: antiquefever@aol.com

Shawnee

Linda Guffey
2004 Fiat Ct.
El Cajon, CA 92019-4234
e-mail: Gufantique@aol.com

Shelley China

Mannie Banner
126 S.W. 15th St.
Pembroke Pines, FL 33027
(954) 443-2933

Janice Dodson
P.O. Box 957
Bloomfield Hills, MI 48303

Edwin E. Kellogg
4951 N.W. 65th Ave.
Lauderhill, FL 33319

Curt Leiser
National Shelley China Club
12010 – 38th Ave. NE
Seattle, WA 98125
(206) 362-7135
e-mail: curtpleiser@cs.com

Gene Loveland
11303 S. Alley Jackson Rd.
Grain Valley, MO 64029

Steins

Gary Kirsner
863 Northridge Dr.
Prescott, AZ 86301
(928) 227-3723
e-mail: gkirsner@cableone.net

Andre Ammelounx
P.O. Box 136
Palatine, IL 60078
(847) 991-5927

Stoneware Pottery

Vicki & Bruce Waasdorp
P.O. Box 434
Clarence, NY 14031
(716) 759-2361
e-mail: waasdorp@antiques-stone-ware.com

Harris Strong Designs

Donald-Brian Johnson
3329 South 56th St., #611
Omaha, NE 68106
e-mail: donaldbrian@webtv.net

Vernon Kilns

Pam Green
You Must Remember This
P.O. Box 822
Hollis, NH 03049
e-mail: ymrt@aol.com
Web: www.ymrt.com

Warwick

John Rader Sr.
780 S. Village Dr., Apt. 203
St. Petersburg, FL 33716
(727) 570-9906

Watt Pottery

Jan & Jim Seeck
Seeck Auctions
P.O. Box 377
Mason City, IA 50402
(641) 424-1116
Web site: www.seeckauction.com

Willow Wares

Jeff Siptak
4013 Russellwood Dr.
Nashville, TN 37204
e-mail: WillowWare@aol.com

Russel Wright Designs

Kathryn Wiese
Retrospective Modern Design
P.O. Box 305
Manning, IA 51455
e-mail: retrodesign@earthlink.net

Zeisel (Eva) Designs

Kathryn Wiese
Retrospective Modern Design
P.O. Box 305
Manning, IA 51455
email: retrodesign@earthlink.net

Zsolnay

Federico Santi / John Gacher
The Drawing Room Antiques
152 Spring St.
Newport, RI 02840
(401) 841-5060
email: drawrm@hotmail.com
Web: www.drawrm@hotmail.com

Collecting Guidelines

Whenever I'm asked about what to collect, I always stress that you should collect what you like and want to live with. Collecting is a very personal matter and only you can determine what will give you the most satisfaction. With the wide diversity of ceramics available, everyone should be able to find a topic they will enjoy studying and collecting.

One thing that every collector should keep in mind is that to get the most from your hobby you must study it in depth, read everything you can get your hands on, and purchase the best references available for your library. New research material continues to become available for collectors and learning is an ongoing process.

It is also very helpful to join a collectors' club where others who share your enthusiasm will support and guide your learning. Fellow collectors often become your best friends and sources for special treasures to add to your collection. Dealers who specialize in a ceramics category are always eager to help educate and support collectors, and many times they become a mentor for a novice who is just starting out on the road to the "advanced collector" level.

With the very ancient and complex history of ceramic wares, it's easy to understand why becoming educated about your special interest is of paramount importance. There have been collectors of pottery and porcelain for centuries, and for nearly as long collectors have had to be wary of reproductions or "reissues." In Chinese ceramics, for instance, it has always been considered perfectly acceptable to copy as closely as possible the style and finish of earlier ceramics and even mark them with period markings on the base. The only problem arises when a modern collector wants to determine whether his piece, "guaranteed" antique, was produced over 200 years ago or barely a century ago.

With European and, to some extent, American wares, copying of earlier styles has also been going on for many decades. As far back as the mid-19th century, copies and adaptations of desirable early wares were finding their way onto the collector market. By the late 19th century, in particular, revivals of 18th century porcelains and even some early 19th century earthenwares were available, often sold as decorative items and sometimes clearly marked. After 100 years, however, these early copies can pose a real quagmire for the unwary.

Even more troublesome for collectors is the flood of reproductions that have been produced during the past 30-40 years. Not only are high end early wares copied but even more modern, collectible wares have fallen victim to this problem. For instance, McCoy pottery, never an expensive line, has seen a large number of copies hit the market. A few years ago an entrepreneur "copyrighted" the McCoy trademark (something that had never been done by the original company owners). He now has the right to manufacture all sorts of copies of McCoy pieces, especially cookie jars, and market them with the original impressed company mark. Cookie jars, in fact, have been one of the hardest hit areas of ceramics collectibles with not only McCoy cookie jars out there but also many of the Shawnee Pottery jars, as well as some from other cookie jar makers of the past. In addition, the popular Little Red Riding Hood and other figural pieces made by Shawnee are being offered. With a little checking you can find many of these copies on web sites.

Many of the patterns made by Roseville Pottery have also been widely reproduced in recent years. For at least 20 years porcelain pieces carrying "Hand-Painted Nippon" fake marks have been offered by reproduction wholesalers. When first manufactured, these pieces and the misleading marks were fairly easy to identify. Sadly, recently much better quality reproductions with "realistic" markings are offered.

Some of the most expensive American pottery sold today is from famous firms established in the late 19th and early 20th century. Some of their best examples can sell for tens of thousands of dollars, which has spurred a market for reproduction pieces. All the major potteries of the past, including Rookwood, Cowan, Fulper, Grueby, Ohr and Van Briggle, have now fallen victim to this trend. Fortunately for all collectors and dealers, novice or advanced, the American Art Pottery Association web site has a link to a page offering up-to-date information on these fakes and forgeries.

Other specialized collecting clubs, such as the International Nippon Collectors'

Club and the McCoy Pottery Collectors' Society, also offer great information on reproductions on their web sites. Another excellent source can be found on the web under "At Pottery Collector's Groups & Info." This site has an alphabetical listing of collecting groups of nearly all collectible ceramics categories.

Again, education is the key. As you're building your store of knowledge and experience, buy with care from reliable sources.

Another area that calls for special caution on the part of collectors, especially the tyro, is that of damaged or repaired pieces. A wise collector will always buy the best example he/she can find, and it is a good policy to save up to buy one extra fine piece rather than a handful of lesser examples. You never want to pass up a good buy. But, in the long run, a smaller collection of choice pieces will probably bring you more satisfaction (and financial reward) than a large collection of moderate quality.

Purchasing a damaged or clearly repaired piece is a judgment only the collector can make. In general I wouldn't recommend it unless the piece is so unique that another example is not likely to come your way in the near future. For certain classes of expensive and rare ceramics, especially early pottery that has seen heavy use, a certain amount of damage may be inevitable and more acceptable. The sale price, however, should reflect this fact.

Restoration of pottery and porcelain wares has been a fact of life for many decades. Even in the early 19th century before good glues were available, "make-do" repairs were sometimes done to pieces using small metal staples, and today some collectors seek out these quaint examples of early recycling. Since the early 20th century, glue and repainting have been common methods used to mask damages to pottery and porcelain, and these repairs can usually be detected today with a strong light and the naked eye.

The problem in recent decades has been the ability of restorers to completely mask any sign of previous damages using more sophisticated repair methods. There is nothing wrong with a quality restoration of a rare piece as long as the eventual purchaser is completely aware such work has been done.

It can take more than the naked eye and a strong light to detect some invisible repairs today, and that's where the popular black light, using ultraviolet rays, can be of help. Many spots of repair will fluoresce under the black light. I understand, however, that newer glues and paints are becoming available that won't show up under the black light. The key then, especially for the beginner, is know your ceramic or your seller and be sure you have a money-back guarantee when making a major purchase.

I certainly don't want to sound too downbeat and discourage anyone from pursuing what can be a wonderfully fun and fulfilling hobby, but starting from a position of strength, with confidence and education, will certainly payoff in the long run for every collector.

Ceramics, in addition to their beauty and charm, also offer the collecting advantage of durability and low maintenance. It's surprising how much pottery and porcelain from two centuries ago is still available to collect. There were literally train cars full of it produced and sold by the late 19th century, and such wares are abundantly available and often reasonably priced. Beautiful dinnerwares and colorful vases abound in the marketplace and offer exciting collecting possibilities. They look wonderful used on today's dining tables or gracing display shelves.

A periodic dusting and once-a-year washing in mild, warm water is about all the care they will require. Of course, it's not recommended you put older pottery and porcelains in your dishwasher where rattling and extremely hot water could cause damage. And, of course, it's more satisfying to hold a piece in your hand in warm soapy water in a rubber dishpan (lined with towels for added protection) and caress it carefully with a dishrag. The tactile enjoyment of holding the object brings a new dimension to collecting.

Whatever sort of pottery or porcelain appeals to you most, whether it is 18th century Meissen or mid-20th century California-made pottery, you can take pride in the fact that you are carrying on a collecting tradition that goes back centuries. Back to the days when only the crowned heads of Europe could vie for the finest and rarest ceramics with which to accent their regal abodes.

Kyle Husfloen, Editor

MARKET SURVEY – CERAMICS 2008-2009

By Kyle Husfloen, Editor

In the world of collectible ceramics, which includes both pottery and porcelain pieces, there is something available to fit every budget and aesthetic preference.

For over a century American collectors have been searching out decorative old ceramics. Of special interest to pioneering Eastern collectors was the ware we refer to as "Historic Staffordshire Ware." Produced in England in the early 19th century, these earthenwares were transfer-printed in shades of very dark blue on white and featured a central design showing an early American building or location. They, of course, were meant to appeal to the American market of the 1820s and 1830s, but by the 1890s their primitive charm was attracting collectors.

Other types of early English earthenware were produced especially for the American market. The so-called "Liverpool jugs" or pitchers were widely exported to the young United States in the late 18th and early 19th century. These pieces once again were printed with scenes that would appeal to Americans. A wide variety of designs, including portraits of our Revolutionary War heroes or naval scenes, were available. These pieces also caught the interest of pioneer American collectors and they have never lost there appeal. These two classes of wares I include among a category I'll call "Country Wares" because in today's collecting market, examples generally appeal to those who love the "country" look.

As the 20th century moved forward, other very charming and somewhat primitive "country" pottery also gained in popularity. Today choice examples of redware, slipware and stoneware produced by American artisans of the past are highly prized. There is quite an abundance of such wares on the collecting market, so in many instances pieces can be purchased for modest prices, often under $100. However, the very rarest and most unique examples can bring astronomical prices, some in the five-figure range.

In the last few decades another type of earthenware that has been rediscovered by collectors is colorful 19th century majolica. Produced widely in England, the United States, France and Germany, there is a huge variety of designs to be found. Again, nice pieces can be found at modest prices, but very rare forms in top condition can break the $10,000 level.

Although the range of collectible ceramics has skyrocketed in the last half century, the rules that governed collectors of 50 or 100 years ago still hold true: Know your topic and purchase the best examples in your favorite collecting category. These are constants that all serious collectors should keep in mind. On the other hand, if you find a charming, less expensive piece that you love, go ahead and add it to your collection, but just be aware that there is much less chance of market appreciation in the near term.

In addition to the country ceramics I've touched on above, I have divided the world of ceramics collecting into several sub-categories in the following pages. I can then more clearly illustrate how diverse the ceramics marketplace has become in recent years.

As early as the 1890s pioneering American collectors were traveling the highways and byways of rural New England searching for historic Blue & White Staffordshire such as this serving dish decorated with the "Arms of North Carolina." Not long ago this piece sold at auction for over $5,000.

This Liverpool earthenware 12" jug-form pitcher, ca. 1800, features a transfer-printed black scene of the ship "The America" on one side and a scene showing "Death of Wolfe" on the other. Made for the American market, this example was also trimmed with polychrome colors. Today it sells for over $5,200.

Old American redware pottery is fairly abundant on the market, however this 8-1/2" tall covered pitcher is quite a rarity. With a glossy green streaked with brown glaze, it sold at auction a few years ago for $4,300.

American stoneware pottery is among the hottest areas in ceramic collecting today. This 5-3/4" tall crock, unsigned but attributed to James Morgan, Jr. of New Jersey, ca. 1790, sold at a Waasdorp American Pottery Auction in 2007 for $19,800.

Although more common examples of American-made slipware pottery can be found in the $200-500 range, extremely rare examples will sell for thousands. This unique 12-1/4" d. charger has the yellow slip spelling out "Norwalk feb'y the 13 1854" and is attributed to the Smith Pottery of Norwalk, Connecticut. A very rare dated piece, this charger sold for $19,975 at auction a few years ago.

This rare stoneware 6-gallon crock features a rare blue-slip design of a phoenix bird. It is marked "N. Clark & Co., Rochester, New York," ca. 1850. It was sold in a Waasdorp American Pottery Auction for $72,600 in 2007.

Art Nouveau Ceramics

The Art Nouveau (literally "new art") originated in Paris in the 1890s. The naturalistic motifs often feature flowing whiplashes and sinuous figures of maidens with flowing long hair as well as other undulating designs drawn from nature. It soon became the rage for all types of decorative arts, and ceramics were no exception. Some extraordinary early pieces were manufactured in Europe, but this school of design was a bit slower to reach American shores. In the period between 1900 and 1910 quite a few Art Nouveau inspired ceramic designs were coming from more commercial American potteries such as Weller, Roseville, Owens and others. Although these American ceramic designs didn't prove all that popular, you'll find Art Nouveau themes showing up on many other American-made decorative wares including metalwares, jewelry, glassware and even some furniture. Today the best examples of European or American Art Nouveau ceramics can bring stratospheric sums, and the market has remained strong for the past quarter century.

Some fabulous Art Nouveau pottery pieces were produced at the Zsolnay Pottery of Pecs, Hungary. This large 28" tall Zsolnay vase features a scene of an Art Nouveau maiden in a forest setting and is covered with a fine iridescent glaze. Manufactured around 1900, today this piece would sell in the $25,000-$35,000 range.

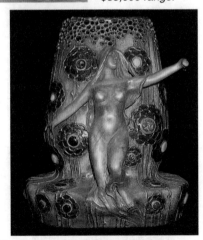

The Teplitz region of Bohemia (later Czechoslovakia) was home to several potteries that made some superb Art Nouveau pieces. This massive 18-1/4" tall vase is highlighted at the front by a large figure of a nude Art Nouveau maiden. Also highlighted by decorative "jewels." It is marked "Amphora – Austria" and is valued in the $45,000-$50,000 range.

The American Weller Pottery was one of the first to offer some truly unique Art Nouveau-inspired lines. They even had one line called "L'Art Nouveau." Probably their choicest line, featuring Art Nouveau designs covered with fine iridescent glazes, is Sicardo. Only produced between 1902 and 1907, today the best examples will bring prices in the thousands. This 11" tall vase with a bold molded Art Nouveau floral design sold not too long ago for over $10,000.

Arts & Crafts Ceramics

Another school of design that had its origins in England in the second half of the 19th century is known as Arts & Crafts. This movement was a reaction against fussy Victorian design and cheap mass-produced furniture and decorative arts. Hand-craftsmanship was stressed and soon caught on with many American potteries whose wares today are classed under "art pottery."

One of the pioneer American potteries was the Rookwood Pottery of Cincinnati, Ohio, founded in the 1880s. They used top designers and decorators over the years. Most of their late 19th century pieces have a more Victorian sensibility and feature dark shaded wares with their glossy "Standard" glaze. Early in the 20th century this firm moved quickly into manufacturing fine Arts & Crafts designs with wonderful new glazes. Rookwood remained the premier American art pottery for many years, but in the early 20th century they the early 20th century they competed with many new potteries including Marblehead, Grueby, Van Briggle, Newcomb College and Pewabic, among many others. Most of these companies were not in business all that long and thus produced much less pottery than Rookwood. However, today their choicest pieces can sell for astounding prices.

The Arts & Crafts theme also filtered down to the more commercial potteries such as Roseville and Weller, who also entered the market with Arts & Crafts inspired lines in the teens and 1920s.

The collecting of American art pottery really took off about 35 years ago and it remains a very strong area of collecting today. Depending on your taste and pocketbook, there's a huge range of pieces to choose from.

To see how "small details" can greatly affect the market value of two similar pieces, compare this Rookwood advertising tile, decorated with bright fall colors, to the same piece decorated in shades of rich blue and green. This example, with the bright fall colors, sold at a Cincinnati Art Galleries 2008 auction for $41,300.

A nice example of Rookwood Arts & Crafts design, this 12-1/4" tall vase features a Painted Mat glaze decorated with red poppies on a coffee-colored ground. Decorated by Albert Valentien in 1901, it sold for $40,120 at the Cincinnati Art Galleries auction in 2007.

Here is the same Rookwood tile design in shades of blue and green that sold at a 2007 Cincinnati Art Galleries auction for $97,750, over twice as much as the tile in fall colors.

Many "commercial" American potteries also produced some unique Arts & Crafts designs.

This unusual "Minerva" line two-part jardinière was made by the Weller Pottery, ca. 1915. It sold at a 2007 Cincinnati Art Galleries auction for $5,546.

Roseville Pottery also manufactured a number of lines inspired by the Arts & Crafts movement.

This Roseville "Sunflower" pattern jardinière and pedestal, ca. 1930, sold a few years ago for $4,140.

Another big name in fine American Arts & Crafts art pottery is Newcomb College. This large 12" Newcomb College vase decorated with incised trees in shades of blue under a glossy glaze dates from 1902. Newcomb pieces with glossy glazes are much scarcer than matte glazed pieces. The Cincinnati Art Galleries sold this rare piece in 2008 for $29,500.

Art Deco Ceramics

One of the first truly "modern" design movements, the Art Deco style derived its name from the Exposition Internationale des Arts Decoratifs et Industriels Modernes held in Paris, France in 1925. In contrast to the sinuous, naturalistic designs of Art Nouveau, Art Deco stressed very angular geometric designs often in bold contrasting colors.

During the late 1920s and through the 1930s, Art Deco was featured in diverse fields including architecture (the Chrysler Building in New York City), industrial design (kitchen appliances to cameras) and all areas of decorative arts, including ceramics, glassware and furniture.

The French were the leading proponents of Art Deco design, and the finest and most expensive pieces came from their factories. However, Art Deco soon trickled down to influence commercial production in the United States and around the world. Since this style tended to be a bit "avant garde" for American middle class tastes of the time, it wasn't always a big hit on the commercial market (Roseville's "Futura" line, for example). However, Art Deco still strongly influenced a wide range of household items from ashtrays and dresser sets to cocktail shakers, costume jewelry and souvenir items (Chicago's "Century of Progress" exposition, 1932-33; New York World's Fair, 1939-40).

Several American potteries of the 1930s did produce some outstanding Art Deco designs, including Roseville Pottery, Weller Pottery and Cowan Pottery, among many others. Since the late 1960s there has been a strong interest in Art Deco design that continues to the present. There are many relatively inexpensive pieces available to collectors, but the finest and rarest examples can sell for thousands of dollars. It is definitely a collecting field with something for every taste and budget.

The penultimate example of Art Deco ceramics is the "Jazz" bowl produced by the Cowan Pottery in 1931. Designed by Viktor Schreckengost, it features classic motifs of Art Deco design: bold angular designs and contrasting colors. Originally commissioned by Eleanor Roosevelt, it has remained an icon of the era ever since. In 2004 an example sold for $254,400.

Foreign-made Art Deco pottery is also highly valued today. This 19-7/8" tall vase produced by Boch Freres of Belgium was sold in 2007 by the Cincinnati Art Galleries for $11,505.

Cowan Pottery produced many Art Deco designs. Some of the favorite forms with collectors are its nude female figurines and figural flower frogs. This Cowan dancing lady figurine, Shape No. 687, stands 11-3/4" tall. Today it is valued at $675.

The Japanese also featured Art Deco designs on many of their 1930s exports. The Noritake Company in particular produced some delightful Art Deco porcelain pieces. This 8-3/4" d. wall plaque with a silhouetted scene of a lady is today valued at $840.

Modern Designs in Commercial Ceramics

After World War II, the 1930s Art Deco style gradually evolved into a still-streamlined style often referred to as "Moderne." These streamlined, modernist themes were a big hit during the 1950s and 1960s. Once again every facet of the decorative arts was influenced, including commercially produced American ceramics. In some instances, noted designers of the era developed specific ceramic lines for American potteries. Especially notable were the Russel Wright "American Modern" dinnerware line made by the Steubenville Pottery Company and "Casual" dinnerware made by the Iroquois China Company. Designer Eva Zeisel has been responsible for even more "Modernist" designs in dinnerwares since the late 1940s: Castleton "Museum Ware," Hyalyn "Z Ware," Hall China Company's "Hallcraft – Century Dinnerware" and "Town and Country Dinnerware" for Red Wing Potteries. Many pieces in these Russel Wright and Eva Zeisel lines are still available to collect at modest prices, but values continue to rise.

General Commercial Wares

In addition to the style discussed above, there is a myriad of pottery and porcelain pieces produced by commercial companies throughout the 20th century. Many of these may reflect some of the design influences discussed above but many more are considered traditional designs. Novelty designs and American country motifs have been very popular in the United States for over a century and continue to have wide appeal today. Dozens and dozens of American and foreign potteries have churned out a huge volume of diverse wares and many of these pieces are still available to collectors at modest prices. In nearly every case, however, there will be rarities that the discerning buyer should keep an eye open for. Again, it is very important to become knowledgeable about the specific collecting field that appeals to you in order to build a worthwhile collection. Never forget the factors such as condition and size, as well as rarity and local demand, have a major influence on the value of any piece. Age alone does not denote "value" as many choice pieces from the 1950s and 1960s can and do sell for much more than common pieces a century or more old.

Since the collecting field for pottery and porcelain is so vast it becomes even more important for a person to specialize whenever possible. By narrowing your focus you can become an informed and careful buyer. Always buy what you like first but also be armed with knowledge and an eye for detail. That way you'll never regret a purchase and will build a collection that you love and that will likely appreciate in value over the decades.

Although many pieces in Russel Wright's "Casual China" dinnerware line will sell for under $50, this rare carafe in the oyster grey color can go for over $900.

Eva Zeisel has had a long and productive career in design. Her "Town & Country" line for Red Wing Pottery is very sought after today with many pieces selling in the $25-$75 range. However, rarities such as this teapot with a bronze glaze go for much more. Today this piece can sell in the $550 range.

Fiesta Ware, one of the first pottery lines to focus on "casual" dining, was introduced in the 1930s and is still being produced today. There is a huge variety of pieces and colors available so you must learn what is common and what is rare. The covered cream soup bowl in Fiesta is a rare form with many examples selling in the $700-$800 range. However, this extremely rare turquoise blue example has sold for $8,000.

McCoy Pottery produced a huge range of inexpensive pottery wares over the years. Until a few years ago they tended to be quite inexpensive. Today many of McCoy's whimsical items can sell in the $50-$100 range, however, its wide range of cookie jars tends to sell for much more. One of its rarest cookie jars is this "Christmas Tree" design, ca. 1959, which today sells for over $1,000.

The Hall China Company has been producing attractive and durable utilitarian kitchenwares since the early 20th century. They are especially famous for their wide range of teapots, some with unique designs. Many Hall teapots will sell in the $50-$150 range but rare examples bring much more. This "Auto" style teapot in Chinese Red today sells in the $650 range.

A truly unique piece of McCoy Pottery is this one-of-a-kind "Robin Hood" design planter. Similar in design to other common McCoy planters, this rarity sold for $11,500 at Green Valley Auctions a few years ago.

Country style Watt Pottery kitchenwares were widely popular during the 1950s and early 1960s. Examples of these hand-painted pieces will often sell in the $50-$100 range today. However, these unique "Apple" pattern teapots are rarities. The one on the right in this photo is Model No. 122 valued at $1,400 while the one on the left, Model No. 505, is even rarer, going for around $4,700.

Japanese early "Nippon Era" (1891-1921) porcelains are very collectible today. Nippon china can be found in a wide range of pieces of varying quality. Average quality common pieces can be found for well under $100. However, large and elaborate pieces will bring extraordinary prices. This ornate 21" tall Nippon urn features a unique hand-painted scene of a Native American hunter standing in a marshland setting and carrying a goose he has shot. It is also heavily trimmed with elaborate gold designs, adding to the appeal. This piece sold in a 2005 Jackson's Auctioneers sale for $20,563.

Blue and white Japanese-made "Phoenix Bird" porcelain dinnerwares were widely exported beginning in the early 20th century. Originally an inexpensive dime store ware, common older pieces can still be found for under $20. However rare items have steadily grown in value. This unique coffee biggin and dripolater sold at auction in early 2008 for $500.

Cooling Off?

Not all vintage pottery lines are as "hot" today as they were a few years ago. Although still selling, prices appear to have leveled off except for the rarest examples.

*English Chintz China: Decorated with colorful overall floral designs the rare early teapots can still sell for over $500, but many older pieces will be found for under $50.

*American Pennsbury Pottery: Hand-painted tablewares decorated with Pennsylvania Dutch designs, many old pieces are on the market for under $20.

*German Hummel figurines: Wildly popular and over-produced during the 1970s and 1980s, today these charming figurines of German children are getting hard to sell. Pieces carrying an early mark (pre-1950) or that are especially large and ornate will still draw collector interest.

Typical Ceramic Shapes

The following line drawings illustrate typical shapes found in pottery and porcelain pitchers and vases. These forms are referred to often in our price listings.

Pitcher - Barrel-shaped

Pitcher - Jug-type

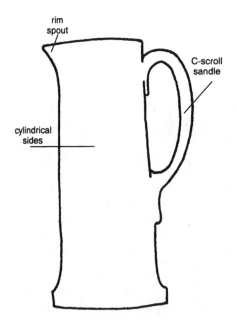

rim
spout

C-scroll
sandle

cylindrical
sides

Pitcher - Tankard-type with cylindrical sides, C-scroll handle, and rim spout.

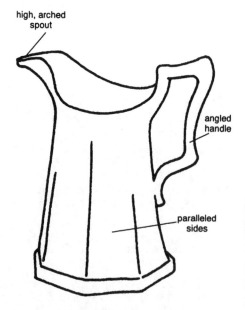

high, arched
spout

angled
handle

paralleled
sides

Pitcher - Tankard-type with panelled (octagonal) sides, angled handle and high, arched spout.

Vases

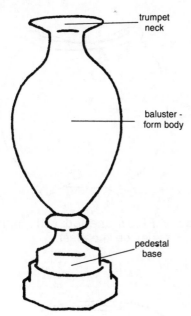

trumpet
neck

baluster -
form body

pedestal
base

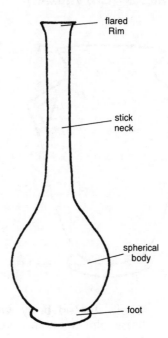

flared
Rim

stick
neck

spherical
body

foot

Vase - Baluster-form body with trumpet neck on a pedestal base.

Vase - Bottle-form — Spherical footed body tapering to a tall stick neck with flared rim.

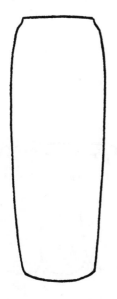

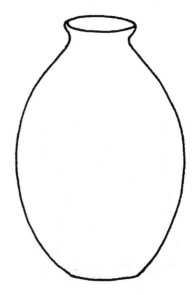

Vase - Cylindrical

Vase - Ovoid body, tapering to a short, flared neck.

Vases (Continued)

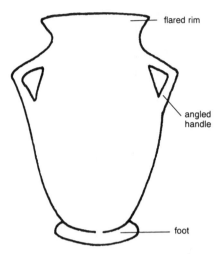

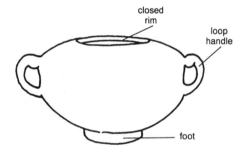

Vase - Pillow-shaped with molded rim; on knob feet.

Vase - Ovoid, footed body with flared rim & angled handles.

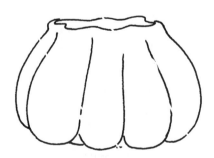

Vase or bowl vase - Spherical, footed body with closed rim and loop handles.

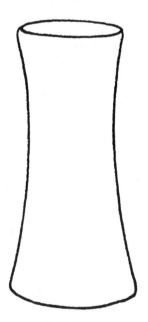

Vase - Waisted cylindrical form.

Vase - Squatty bulbous body with lobed sides.

Marks

Abingdon

Various Amphora-Teplitz Factory -. 1880s-1930s

Austrian

Bauer

BEATRIX POTTER'S
"Mr Jackson"
F. Warne & Co. Ltd.
© Copyright 1974
BESWICK ENGLAND

© F. Warne & Co. 1988
Licensed by Copyrights
John Beswick
Studio of Royal Doulton
England

ROYAL ALBERT ®
ENGLAND

BESWICK
MADE IN ENGLAND

BESWICK
MADE IN ENGLAND

Beatrix Potter Backstamps

Blue Ridge
Hand Painted
Underglaze
Southern Potteries Inc.
MADE IN U.S.A.

Blue Ridge Dinnerwares

Boch Freres Mark

Brayton Laguna

Buffalo Pottery

MADE
IN   351
CALIFORNIA USA

Caliente

NEAR
CUT

TUSCAN

Cambridge

Catalina Island Pottery

Ceramic Arts Studio

Clarice Cliff

Cleminson

Clewell Wares

Clifton

Cowan

deLee Art

Derby & Royal Crown Derby

Fiesta

Franciscan

Frankoma

Fulper

Gallé Pottery

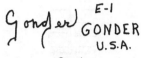 E-1
GONDER
U.S.A.

Gonder

Jugtown Pottery

GRUEBY

Grueby Pottery

Lenox China

Hall

Longwy

J.S.T.&CO.
KEENE. NH.

 Hampshire pottery

HAMPSHIF

Hampshire

McCoy

Harker

Meissen

H&C° Haviland & Co Limoges

Haviland

Mettlach

Hull

Minton

MOORCROFT

Moorcroft

Newcomb College Pottery

Niloak Pottery

Noritake

North Dakota School of Mines

GEO. E. OHR
BILOXI, MISS.

Ohr Pottery

Owens Pottery

   S.E.G.

Paul Revere

ZANEWARE
MADE IN U.S.A.

Peters & Reed

Pickard

HOWARD
PIERCE   Howard Pierce   HP
Pierce   Claremont, Calif

Howard Pierce

 HENRIOT QUIMPER

Quimper

R.S. Prussia & Related

Red Wing

Rookwood

Royal Worcester

Rosenthal

Hedi Schoop
HOLLYWOOD CAL.
HEDI SCHOOP
HOLLYWOOD, CALIF.

Schoop

Roseville

Sèvres

Royal Bayreuth

U.S.A.

Shawnee

 ROYAL DOULTON

Royal Doulton

Shelley

Royal Dux

Stangl

Royal Vienna

Teco

Tiffany Pottery

Early Van Briggle Pottery

Vernon Kilns

Warwick

Watt Pottery

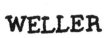

Early Wedgwood

Weller

Wheatley

Zsolnay

ABC Plates

Early Prattware Plate with Sphinx Image

3 3/4" d., Prattware, a molded central scene of a sphinx, molded border w/blue wash, England, late 18th c. (ILLUS.) **$450**

"The Serious Boy" ABC Plate

4 1/2" d., "The Serious boy," dark green transfer-printed scene showing a mother seated in a chair & her son nearby looking out a window, framed by a pious verse, ca. 1830s-40s, rare smalll size (ILLUS.) **$350**

"A Present for a Friend" ABC Plate

5" d., "A Present for a Friend" black transfer-printed inscription within an oval

wreath, molded letters & black border bands (ILLUS.) **$350**

"A Walk Before Breakfast" ABC Plate

5" d., "A Walk Before Breakfast," dark blue transfer-printed scene of a girl & boy walking in a woodland & watching a man race past on horseback, short verse around the scene (ILLUS.) **$250**

Early "Christmas Day" ABC Plate

5" d., "Christmas Day," black transfer-printed scene of a young boy enjoying Christmas dinner, red vitruvian scroll border band (ILLUS.) **$400**

"Diligence" Motto ABC Plate

5" d., "Diligence is the Mother of good luck...," black transfer-printed color-tinted scene showing a girl holding a basket & looking at beehives, mid-19th c. (ILLUS.) .. **$225**

"Going to School" ABC Plate

5" d., "Going to School," black transfer-printed scene wearing long pants & fancy collars on the way to school, one carries a lunch pail (ILLUS.).................................. **$225**

Comical "Laughing" ABC Plate

5" d., "Laughing," brown transfer-printed scene w/added colors showing the head of a mirthful lady (ILLUS.) **$300**

"Playfellows" Early ABC Plate

5" d., "Playfellows," early black transfer-printed scene showing a young boy & his dog, ca. 1840 (ILLUS.)............................... **$425**

"The Happy Children" ABC Plate

5" d., "The Happy Children," black transfer-printed scene of a seated Victorian mother w/her children within a pious verse border (ILLUS.) **$350**

Bone China Aesop's Fables ABC Plate

5" d., "The Husband and the Stork," part of an Aesop's Fables series, green transfer-printed center scene, quality bone china w/a scalloped rim (ILLUS.)......................... **$300**

"The Morning Walk" ABC Plate

5" d., "The Morning Walk," early black transfer scene of a mother & daughter on a morning stroll, surrounded by a verse the describes the scene (ILLUS.)............... **$350**

"The Nosegay" ABC Plate

5" d., "The Nosegay," black transfer-printed color-tinted scene of a young woman walking & holding a small bouquet of flowers (ILLUS.) **$225**

Early Printed & Colored Football Plate

5 1/4" d., "Football," center w/transfer-printed & colored scene of children playing football, mid-19th c. (ILLUS.) **$250**

Early Girl with Pitcher ABC Plate

5 1/4" d., "Girl with a Pitcher," center w/early transfer-printed scene of a girl getting a

pitcher of water from a stream, first half 19th c. (ILLUS.)....................................... **$300**

"Peg Top" ABC Plate

5 1/4" d., "Peg Top," black transfer-printed scene tinted in color, a group of boys playing a game w/a top (ILLUS.)............... **$250**

"The Thrasher" ABC Plate

5 1/4" d., "The Thrasher," black transfer-printed scene of two men threshing grain, color-tinted poem (ILLUS.)........................ **$250**

Early Motto ABC Plate

5 1/2" d., motto-type, an oval wreath encloses a motto telling how to run a successful business, black transfer (ILLUS.).............. **$230**

"Quizzing" ABC Plate with Lady Portrait

6" d., "Quizzing," sepia transfer-printed scene w/added colors showing an amusing head of a 18th c. matron looking through a monocle (ILLUS.) **$300**

ABC Plate with Sluggard Scene

Early Sign Language ABC Plate

Comical "Snuffing" ABC Plate

"The Blind Girl" ABC Plate

6" d., Sign Language plate, black transfer-printed scene of early wooden dolls framed by a printed border of hands showing positions for various letters, embossed alphabet border (ILLUS.) **$300**

6" d., "Sluggard," black transfer-printed scene of a man waking up & stretching w/a verse about the sluggard, rare design (ILLUS., top next column) **$225**

6" d., "Snuffing," a black transfer-printed scene tinted in color, shows a bust portrait of a comical gentleman in 18th c. dress taking snuff (ILLUS., middle next column) **$300**

6" d., "The Blind Girl," transfer-printed & color-tinted scene of Victorian children giving alms to a seated blind girl by a gate, late 19th c. (ILLUS., bottom next column) .. **$175**

"Ball Game" ABC Plate

6 1/4" d., "Ball Game," red transfer-printed scene of three young Victorian men playing catch, mid-19th c. (ILLUS.).................. **$200**

Boy Crossing a Stile ABC Plate

6 1/4" d., boy crossing a stile, transfer-printed sepia & color-tinted scene of a young man stepping across a stile (ILLUS.) **$175**

"David and Goliath" ABC Plate

6 1/4" d., "David and Goliath," red transfer-printed center scene based on biblical story (ILLUS.) **$175**

"Dr. Franklin's Maxims" ABC Plate

6 1/4" d., "Dr. Franklin's Maxims," mulberry transfer-printed center scene showing a woman yelling at a dog who has knocked over a pail of milk, a house, mill & men in the background, sayings by Benjamin Franklin surround the scene, green-printed alphabet border, bone china (ILLUS.) .. **$250**

Girls & Dog in Garden ABC Plate

6 1/4" d., girls & a dog scene in purple transfer printing, shown in a formal garden setting of the early 19th c. (ILLUS.) **$225**

"Jump Little Nag Tail" ABC Plate

6 1/4" d., "Jump Little Nag Tail," brown transfer-printed scene tinted in color, a row boys playing leap-frog (ILLUS.)........... **$200**

English "Cricket" ABC Plate

6 3/4" d., "Cricket," black transfer-printed center scene of boys playing cricket, scene found in other colors, 19th c. (ILLUS.) **$225**

Rare Queen Victoria & Prince Albert Plate

6 3/4" d., "Queen Victoria and Prince Albert of Saxe Coburg," black transfer-printed bust portraits of the queen & prince, commemorating their wedding in 1840 (ILLUS.) **$500**

Hunting Theme ABC Plate

6 3/4" d., hunting scene printed in brown, hunters in wide fields w/their dogs (ILLUS.) .. **$175**

"Highland Dance" ABC Plate

7" d., "Highland Dance," black transfer-printed color-tinted scene of a young man & two ladies dancing outside w/a flute player in the background, a house in the distance, mid-19th c. (ILLUS.) **$175**

"I is for Isobel" ABC Plate

6 3/4" d., "I is for Isobel," green transfer-printed scene of a young girl riding a donkey w/a man standing along side (ILLUS.) **$225**

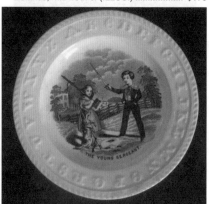

"The Young Sergeant" ABC Plate

7" d., "The Young Sergeant," black transfer-printed color-tinted scene of a boy holding up a sword and commanding a young lady holding a broom over her shoulder as a rifle, mid-19th c. (ILLUS., previous page) **$175**

Rare "Abraham Lincoln" ABC Plate

7" d., "Abraham Lincoln," brown transfer-printed center scene showing a bust portrait of Lincoln, ca. 1865, a companion plate shows a portrait of George Washington (ILLUS.) **$500**

"Frolics of Youth" ABC Plate

7" d., "Frolics of Youth - The Fall of China," a play on words w/a blue transfer-printed scene of two Victorian boys, one shooting a sling shot to knock down a stack w/a china vase & toys (ILLUS.) **$250**

7" d., "Leopard," a square brown transfer-printed center scene w/added colors showing a leopard in a tree, scattered letters around the borders, part of the Wild Animal series by Brownhills Pottery, England, late 19th c. (ILLUS., top next column) **$350**

7" d., "The Old Grandpa," a black transfer-printed scene tinted in color, shows an elderly gentleman greeting two children (ILLUS., middle next column) **$220**

"Leopard" ABC Plate from an Animal Series

"The Old Grandpa" ABC Plate

"The Royal Children" ABC Plate

7" d., "The Royal Children," black transfer-printed scene showing three of Queen Victoria's young children, one riding a pony, broken & carefully repaired w/staples, mid-19th c. (ILLUS.) **$350**

CERAMICS

Also see Antique Trader Pottery & Porcelain - Ceramics Price Guide, 5th Edition

Abingdon

From about 1934 until 1950, Abingdon Pottery Company, Abingdon, Illinois, manufactured decorative pottery, mainly cookie jars, flowerpots and vases. Decorated with various glazes, these items are becoming popular with collectors who are especially attracted to Abingdon's novelty cookie jars.

Abingdon Mark

Abingdon Round Ashtray

Ashtray, round, turquoise, No. 555, 1941-46, 8" d. (ILLUS.) **$25**
Book ends/planters, model of dolphin, No. 444D, blue glaze, 5 3/4" h., pr..................... **$80**
Candleholder, double, No. 479, Scroll patt., 4 1/2" h... **$15**

Bamboo Candleholders & Console Plate

Candleholders, Bamboo patt., No. 716, pr. (ILLUS. left & right w/console plate)............ **$50**
Candleholders, Sunburst, in the form of three ribbed connected semicircles, rose, No. 447, 1938, 8" l., pr. (ILLUS. right & left w/window box, bottom of page)............. **$80**
Console bowl, No. 532, Scroll patt., 14 1/2" l.. **$20**
Console plate, Bamboo patt., No. 715, 10 1/2" d. (ILLUS. w/candleholders, top of page).. **$125**
Cookie jar, Baby, No. 561, 11" h. ...... **$750-$1,000**
Cookie jar, Clock, No. 563, 9" h. **$130**
Cookie jar, Floral/Plaid, No. 697, 8 1/2" h. .... **$150-$250**
Cookie jar, Humpty Dumpty, No. 663, 10 1/2" h.. **$275**
Cookie jar, Miss Muffet, No. 662D, 11" h. **$275**

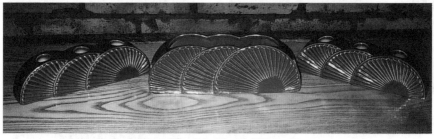

Sunburst Candleholders & Window Box

Mother Goose Cookie Jar

Cookie jar, Mother Goose, No. 695D, 1950, 12" h. (ILLUS.) **$425**

Wigwam Cookie Jar

Cookie jar, Wigwam, No. 665D, 11" h. (ILLUS.).. **$750-$1,000**

Pineapple Cookie Jar

Cookie jar, Pineapple, No. 664, 1949-50, 10 1/2" h. (ILLUS.) **$200**
Cookie jar, Pumpkin, No. 674D, 8" h. **$550**
Cookie jar, Windmill, No. 678, 10 1/2" h. **$500**

Scarf Dancer Figure

Figure, Scarf Dancer, No. 3902, 13" h. (ILLUS.).. **$800 up**

Abingdon Flower Boat & Fruit Boat

Various Abingdon Flowerpots

Flower boat, Fern Leaf, oblong ribbed leaf shape, pink, No. 426, 1937-38, 13 x 4" (ILLUS. left w/fruit boat, top of page) **$100**

Flowerpots, Nos. 149 to 152, floral decoration, 3" to 6" h., each (ILLUS. of three, second from top of page) .... **$15-$30**

Fruit boat, Fern Leaf, oblong ribbed leaf shape, white, No. 432, 1938-39, 6 1/2 x 15" (ILLUS. right w/flower boat, top of page) **$100**

Abingdon Lamp Base

Lamp base, No. 254, draped shaft, 13" h. (ILLUS.) **$200**

Model of heron, No. 574, tan glaze, 5 1/4" h. **$68**

Model of peacock, No. 416, turquoise glaze, 7" h. **$96**

Model of penguin, white, 3" h. **$50**

Planter, model of a puppy, No. 652D, 6 3/4" l. **$75**

String holder, Chinese head, No. 702, 5 1/2" h. **$500**

Vase, 5" h., No. B1, whatnot type.................. **$100**

Vase, 5" h., white floral decoration on blue ground, small handles, No. 567D, 1942-46 (ILLUS. right w/window box No. 570D, page 42) **$40**

Vase, 5 1/2" h., No. 142, Classic line **$40**

Vase, 7" h., No. 171, Classic line **$40**

Vase, 7 1/4" h., Fern Leaf, ribbed leaf-style sides flaring to bowl-style opening, green, No. 423, 1937-38 (ILLUS. right w/taller Fern Leaf vase, bottom of page 41) **$100**

Abingdon Delta Vase

Vase, 8" h., Delta, handles, ribbed base, rose, No. 108, 1938-39 (ILLUS., previous page) **$40**

Abingdon Scroll Vase

Abingdon Gamma Vase

Vase, 8" h., Gamma, short bulbous base connected to tall slightly flaring lobed neck by applied side handles, turquoise, No. 107, 1938-39 (ILLUS.) **$40**

Vase, 8" h., Scroll, bulbous body, neck w/four handles tapers out at top, green, No. 417, 1937-38 (ILLUS., top next column) **$125**

Vase, 8 1/4" h., Swedish, handled, white, No. 314, 1934-36 (ILLUS., middle next column) **$85**

Vase, 10 1/4" h., Fern Leaf, tall ribbed leaf-shape sides taper out to top opening, blue, No. 422, 1937-39 (ILLUS. left w/smaller Fern Leaf vase, bottom of page) **$95**

Abingdon Swedish Vase

Abingdon Fern Leaf Vases

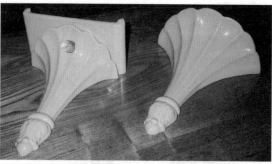

Abingdon Acanthus Wall Bracket & Wall Pocket

Abingdon Window Box & Vase

Wall bracket, Acanthus, pink, No. 589, 1947, 7" h. (ILLUS. left w/wall pocket, top of page) **$65**

Wall pocket, Acanthus, pink, No. 648, 1948, 8 3/4" h. (ILLUS. right w/wall bracket, top of page) **$65**

Wall pocket, figural butterfly, No. 601, 8 1/2" h. **$150**

Window box, oblong, scalloped rim, white floral decoration on blue ground, No. 570D, 1942-46, 10" l. (ILLUS. left w/vase No. 567D, second from top of page) **$35**

Window box, Sunburst, in the form of three connected ribbed semicircles, rose, No. 448, 1938-39, 9" l. (ILLUS. center w/Sunburst candleholders, bottom page 38) **$85**

American Painted Porcelain

During the late Victorian era, American artisans produced thousands of hand-painted porcelain items including tableware, dresser sets, desk sets, and bric-a-brac. These pieces of porcelain were imported and usually bear the marks of foreign factories and countries. To learn more about identification, evaluation, history and appraisal, the following books and newsletter by Dorothy Kamm are recommended: American Painted Porcelain: Collector's Identification & Value Guide, Comprehensive Guide to American Painted Porcelain, and Comprehensive Guide to American Painted Porcelain and Painted Porcelain Jewelry and Buttons: Identification & Value Guide.

Thanks to Pineapple Patti's, Red Rooster Attic, Treasure Coast Antique Mall and Richard E. McGlenn, all of Fort Pierce, Florida, for graciously allowing me to photograph their pieces. - Dorothy Kamm

Bowl, 8" w., hexagonal, decorated w/clusters of wild roses on alternating panels, mother-of-pearl lustre ground, marked "MZ - Altrolau - CM-R - Czechoslovakia," ca. 1918-39 .... **$45**

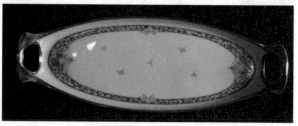

Painted & Signed Celery Tray

Celery tray, long oval, double-handled, decorated w/conventional floral border in enamel & burnished gold, burnished gold rim & handles, marked "Vignaud - Limoges" & signed "N. A. Ray," stamped "N.A. Ray Studio, Monesdale, PA," ca. 1911-38, 15" l. (ILLUS., bottom previous page) **$95**

Creamer & open sugar bowl, double-handled, yellow lustre ground, decorated w/enameled & gilded design of scrolls & flowers, burnished gold handles, marked "T&V Limoges - France," ca. 1892-1907, the set **$45**

Signed Demitasse Cup & Saucer

Demitasse cup & saucer, decorated w/conventional design, burnished gold rim & handle, signed "D.D. Portez, 1916," the set (ILLUS.) **$15**

Cup & Saucer from Dessert Set

Dessert set: 4 7/8 x 5 1/2" double-handled spoon tray & pair of cups & saucers; each decorated w/pink wild roses, signed "G.B. Shantz," tray marked "Made in Japan," cups & saucers w/a crown & wreath mark & "Epiag, Made in Czechoslovakia," ca. 1920-35, the set (ILLUS. of cup & saucer)............................ **$70**

Cake Plate from Czech Dessert Set

Dessert set: 9 1/2" d. double-handled cake plate & five cups & saucers; decorated w/a conventional border of paint, enamel & burnished gold, marked "Epiag, Aich - Czechoslovakia," ca. 1920-30, some wear, the set (ILLUS. of cake plate)............. **$80**

Dish, hexagonal, decorated w/violets, burnished gold rim, marked "MZ Altrohlau - CM-R - Czecholslovakia," signed "A. Denniston," ca. 1918-39, 5 1/4" w................ **$35**

Fruit Bowl Decorated with Currants

Fruit bowl, ribbon handle, decorated w/currants, burnished gold rim & handle, illegible signature, marked "Hutschenreuther, Selb," ca. 1880-1910, some wear, 10 1/2" l. (ILLUS.)...................................... **$105**

Grape juice set: jug-form pitcher & five tumblers; decorated w/clusters of grapes, burnished gold rims, marked "T&V Limoges," ca. 1892-1907, some wear, the set (ILLUS., top next page) **$399**

Decorated Limoges-made Grape Juice Set

Jam jar, cov., doubled-handled, decorated w/blackberries, burnished gold handles, marked "HR" in circle & "Favorite - Hutschenreuther, Selb, Bavaria," stamped "Wm. Macleod, Erie, PA," ca. 1905-20, 5" h. **$70**

Nut set: 5 x 7" footed nut bowl & six 2 7/8" d. individual footed cups; mother-of-pearl lustre interior, ivory exterior, burnished gold foot & rims, bowl marked "B & Co. Limoges, France," cups marked "Noritake, Nippon," ca. 1920-30, the set **$69**

Haviland Plate Decorated with Pears

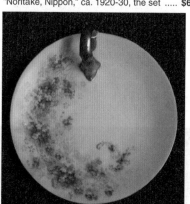

Ring-handled Olive Dish with Flowers

Olive dish, ring-handled, decorated w/forget-me-nots, burnished gold rim & handle, signed "Sandwich," marked "Favorite Bavaria," ca. 1908-18, some wear, 6 5/8" d. (ILLUS.) **$30**

Plate, decorated w/pink & ruby roses, burnished gold rim, marked w/a crown & crossed scepters & "R.C. Bavaria," ca. 1901-33 .... **$14**

Plate, 6" d., decorated w/hawthorn, marked w/a shield & "Thomas Bavaria," ca. 1908-20 .... **$12**

Plate, 6 1/2" d., decorated w/yellow wild roses, signed "Luken Studios," Chicago, ca. 1895-1926 .... **$15**

Plate, 8 3/4" d., decorated w/pears, burnished gold rim, signed "Floyd," marked "Haviland France," ca. 1894-1915 (ILLUS., top next column) **$30**

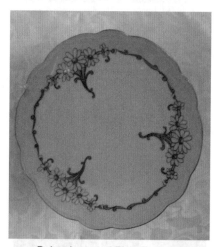

Daisy-decorated Plate From Set

Plates, 7" d., decorated w/a conventional border design of daisies, burnished gold scalloped rim, marked w/a crown & double-headed eagle & "M.Z. Austria," ca. 1884-1909, some wear, set of 4 (ILLUS. of one) **$90**

A Plate Decorated with Grape Clusters

Plates, 8 1/2" d., decorated w/a conventional design of grape clusters & whiplash vines, burnished gold banding, signed "C. Ludwig," marked w/a shield & "Thomas Bavaria," ca. 1908-20, set of four (ILLUS. of one)... **$120**

Fancy Scroll-handled Ring Stand

Ring stand, decorated w/forget-me-nots, oblong shallow dished shape w/fancy central scroll handle, burnished gold rim & stem, marked "UNO-IT Favorite Bavaria," ca. 1910-20, 3 1/2" d., 3 1/2" h. (ILLUS.).. **$40**

Ring Stand with Forget-me-nots

Ring stand, round w/central tree-form ring holder, decorated w/forget-me-nots, burnished gold rim & handle, signed "M.L. Nobbe," marked "GDA/France," ca. 1900-41, 5 7/8" l. (ILLUS.) **$59**

Salt & Pepper Shakers with Floral Borders

Salt & pepper shakes, bulbous ovoid body w/bulbous top, decorated w/a border band of enameled flowers on a burnished gold ground, burnished gold tops, unmarked, ca. 1915-25, 3" h., pr. (ILLUS.) **$60**

Iris-decorated Salt & Pepper Shakers

Salt & pepper shakes, upright slightly flaring cylindrical shape w/an in-body twist, decorated w/a border design of conventional iris, yellow lustre ground w/scattered burnished gold leaves, burnished gold bands & tops, no mark, ca. 1912-25, 2 1/2" h., pr. (ILLUS.) **$60**

Rose-decorated Salt & Pepper Shakers

Salt & pepper shakes, upright waisted cylindrical shape w/a flaring scalloped base, decorated w/pink & yellow roses, burnished gold tops, marked w/a crown & crossed scepters & "R.C. Bavaria," ca. 1901-33, gold worn, 2 3/4" h., pr. (ILLUS.) **$30**

Spoon tray, double-handled, decorated w/yellow poppies, marked w/a wreath, "R.S. Germany" & signed "SMP," ca. 1904-38, 8 1/4" l. **$30**

Limoges Stein Decorated with Currants

Stein, decorated w/currants, burnished gold rim, marked "JP/L France," ca. 1891-1932, some wear, 5" h. (ILLUS.) **$50**

Trivet, round, decorated w/a bucolic landscape, golden yellow lustre rim, marked "Japan," ca. 1915-25, 6" d. **$15**

Jewelry

Brooch, oval, decorated w/forget-me-nots on a pale yellow center w/pale blue border, gold-plated bezel, signed "A. Jibbing," ca. 1900-20, 1 3/8 x 1 1/2" **$75**

Brooch, round, decorated w/a conventional-style trillium w/raised paste & burnished gold pistils & burnished gold background, brass-plated bezel, ca. 1910-15, 1 9/16" d. **$55**

Brooch/pendant, heart shape, decorated w/daisies on a light shading to dark blue ground, gold-plated bezel, ca. 1900-20, 1 13/16 x 2" **$55**

Brooches, oval, decorated w/forget-me-nots on a pale pink & blue ground w/white enamel highlights on petal edges, burnished gold rims, gold-plated bezels, gold wear, ca. 1900-20, 13/16 x 1", pr. **$75**

Handy pin, crescent-shaped, decorated w/pink & ruby roses & green leaves on an ivory ground, w/white enamel highlights & one burnished gold tip, gold-plated bezel, ca. 1890-1915, 2 3/16" w. **$45**

Hatpin, circular head, decorated w/a conventional geometric design in raised paste dots & scrolls, covered w/burnished gold, turquoise enamel jewels, cobalt blue flat enamel, gold-plated bezel, ca. 1905-20, 1" d., 6 3/8" shaft **$110**

Hatpin, circular head, decorated w/pink roses & greenery on a pale blue & yellow ground, burnished gold border, gold-plat-ed bezel, ca. 1890-1920, some gold wear, 1" d., 7 3/4" shaft **$125**

Hatpin Head with Ruby Roses

Hatpin, circular head, decorated w/ruby roses & green leaves, embellished w/burnished gold scrolls, gold-plated bezel, head 1 3/8" d., shaft 7 3/4" l. (ILLUS. of head) **$125**

Unusual Portrait Shirtwaist Button

Shirtwaist button, round w/shank, decorated w/the bust portrait of a young blonde-haired girl, wearing a pale blue dress, against a shaded yellow to black ground, 1 3/8" d. (ILLUS.) **$90**

Shirtwaist buttons, heart-shaped, decorated w/pink roses, raised paste scrolled border covered w/burnished gold, ca. 1890-1910, 1 1/8 x 1 3/16", pr. **$85**

Shirtwaist buttons, round, each decorated w/a geometric pinwheel design in light blue, black & gold trimmed w/burnished gold dots & a center turquoise "jewel," on a burnished gold ground, two 1" d., three 7/8" d., the set (ILLUS., top next page) **$125**

Shirtwaist set: oval cuff links & three round buttons w/shanks; decorated w/clusters of violets on pale yellow ground, burnished gold rim, gold-plated bezel on cuff links, ca. 1900-15, cuff links 3/4 x 1 1/4", buttons 1 1/4" d., the set **$175**

Shirtwaist Buttons with Pinwheels

Amphora - Teplitz

The Amphora Company began in the country village of Turn, in the Teplitz region of Bohemia. The Teplitz region supported the highest concentration of ceramic production, not only in Bohemia, but throughout all of the Austro-Hungarian Empire.

Amphora's aim was always to produce richly ornamented porcelain luxury items. In addition to American exports there were sales to European dealers. Through world exhibitions and international trade shows, Amphora's collections received numerous significant awards and certificates.

By 1900 Amphora was at the pinnacle of its success. After World War I in 1918, Czechoslovakia was established. The company continued production until the end of the 1930s.

Prices vary according to rarity, design, quality and size. The variety of art produced by Amphora Company provides something for everyone. For more information on Amphora, two books serve as excellent resources: Monsters & Maidens - Amphora Pottery of the Art Nouveau Era, by Byron Vreeland and Ceramics from The House of Amphora, 1890-1915 by Richard Scott. - Phil and Arlene Larke.

Early Amphora Figural Owl Lamp

Various Amphora-Teplitz Factory Marks - 1880s-1930s

Boudoir amp, figural, kerosene-type, the porcelain base modeled as an owl w/amber glass eyes, brown trim on ivory ground, red rose transfer mark of Alfred Stellmacher, impressed "1003 - A," painted "27," 1876 (ILLUS., top next column)
.... **$1,500**

Amphora Fates Series Candlestick

Candlestick, Fates Series, ivory porcelain, the tapering cylindrical shaft molded in low-relief w/women's heads & moths, applied flower buds under the rim & two whirling women's heads form the socket opening, clear glaze w/underglaze hatching in cobalt blue & grey, soft mother-of-pearl lustre, matte yellow relief, mark of Riessner, Stellmacher & Kessel Company, Fate seal, red "RStK" transfer, impressed numbers "2006.41," inked numbers "601- 1530," 1900, 11" h. (ILLUS., previous page) **$3,600**

Fine Amphora Figural Fairy Candlestick

Candlestick, figural, porcelain, an Art Nouveau full-figure fairy resting against a column forming the base of the candlestick, at the top between her hands is a molded owl head, w/a violet lustre & matte green patina, the figure w/matte gilding & green patina, mark of Ernst Wahliss Company & "EW," a printed crown & impressed "4781" & free-hand numbers over-glaze "4781 - 298 -7," 1900, 9 1/2" h. (ILLUS.) **$4,900**

Amphora Jeweled Compote

Compote, open, 11" d., 9" h., the round footed w/colored jeweled trim supporting a pair of curved legs centered by a tree trunk leg holding the wide shallow

bowl w/round flower heads inset w/jewels around the exterior, mottled mauve, rose & green ground, signed "Made in Czechoslovakia - Amphora," early 20th c. (ILLUS.) **$1,320**

Tall Amphora Dragon-handled Ewer

Ewer, footed bulbous ovoid body tapering to a tall pierced cylindrical neck w/a high arched & ruffled spout, a long figural curling dragon handle in green & rose trimmed w/gold, the neck & base in pink & the body h.p. w/a cobalt blue medallion among a field of red poppies, gold rose transfer mark of Alfred Stellmacher, Turn, Teplitz, printed "744" & impressed "25," 1884, 13 1/4" h. (ILLUS.) **$1,900**

Extremely Rare Amphora Maiden Figure

Figure of an Art Nouveau maiden, the standing maiden emerging from the sea w/her arms extended & resting on two large aquatic plant leaves, at her feet the head of another maiden w/her hair flowing, decorated in blues & gold, mark of E. Stellmucher, impressed "Amphora 775/2," firing crack running from bottom up, 19 1/2" h. (ILLUS.) **$9,315**

Large Model of a Crowing Rooster

Model of a rooster, larger-than-life crowing rooster designed by Berwiel & glazed in mottled golden brown, this example found in Germany, another reported to be in a Scandinavian art museum, incised "Berwiel 08" on the side, impressed "Amphora" & "Austria" in oval, a crown, "Imperial - Amphora - Turn" in a circle & 8237/37, 26" h. (ILLUS.) .... **$10,500-$11,000**

Amphora Planter with Goose Girl

Planter, figural, designed as a two-level fountain-planter mounted in front w/the figure of a young Dutch girl looking down at two geese, oblong rockwork base, decorated in pastel shades of brown, green & cream, impressed Amphora marks, 9 3/4" h. (ILLUS.) **$316**

Planter, figural, low flaring buttress base below the long oblong bowl w/incurved sides molded at each end w/figural dragon handles w/their wings wrapped back over the sides, each side w/a pale blue hammered ground incised w/yellow grapes flanking an oval wreath panel enclosing a sailing ship scene, ink stamped double oval mark w/"Made in Czecho-

Large Amphora Dragon-handled Planter

Slovakia - Amphora," impressed "5174 - 25," inked "734 - 264 -4," ca. 1918-1939, 16" l., 16 1/4" h. (ILLUS.) **$1,800**

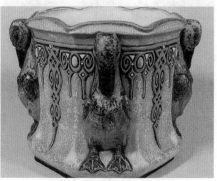

Unusual Amphora Duck Planter

Planter, figural, the deep octagonal container w/a dark yellow speckled round & a scalloped rim trimmed in blue, the half-figure of a duck in dark blue & gold alternating on four panels w/ornate molded blue circle & scroll w/pendant bands, ink-stamped double oval mark w/"Czecho-Slovakia - Amphora," printed letter "F," ca. 1920, 8" h. (ILLUS.) **$1,500**

Rare Amphora Gres - Bijou Planter

Planter, Gres - Bijou Series, known as the "Lightning Bolt" decoration, hard earthenware, yellowish body, the mid-section double-walled w/a wide band of ornamental piercing & greyish-green marblizing, matte gilding, obliquely grooved ringlets w/applied colored "stones" & relief web of thick threads, underglaze painting in green & cobalt blue, greenish glaze spotted w/dark breen & rose frits, matted metallic gloss, marked w/ovals enclosing "Amphora - Austria," impressed crown & "3790," ca.   1918-1939,   12 1/4" d., 8 1/4" h. (ILLUS.) **$21,000**

Dramatic Statue of Bear & Bull

Statue, porcelain, modeled as bear attacking a large bull, animals in cream w/tan highlights, posed on a dark brown rockwork base, signed "Jarl 1907" on the side, impressed crown & "Austria - Amphora," ca. 1907, 15 1/4" h. (ILLUS.) **$2,500**

Fine Amphora Portrait Vase

Vase, 5 3/8" h., gourd-form w/a wide squatty bulbous lower body tapering to a slender neck w/bulbed top, decorated w/a large portrait of an Art Nouveau maiden in shades of gold, white & blue w/a mottled green ground, impressed Amphora mark (ILLUS.) **$1,840**
Vase, 5 3/4" h., figural, elegantly executed Paul Dachsel creation w/a greenish cast & numerous vertical ribs extending up from the base, four intertwined gold-bodied

dragonflies form a reticulated top, immediately below a series of smaller dragonflies encircle the vase, two multilayered handles within handles complete the design, stamped over glaze w/intertwined "PD - Turn - Teplitz," impressed "104"... **$3,500-$4,000**

Amphora Vase with Gnarled Tree Scene

Vase, 5 3/4" h., wide squatty bulbous base tapering sharply to a neck w/four molded buttress handles, decorated w/a stylized scene in tans & greys of the setting sun behind a black gnarled tree, trimmed in muted gilt, base marked "Amphora - AB" & the name of a retail outlet in St. Louis, Missouri, late 19th - early 20th c. (ILLUS.)........ **$578**

Double-gourd Amphora Vase with Rabbits

Vase, 6 3/8" h., double-gourd form w/a wide squatty bulbous lower body in green decorated w/molded light green leaves & a pair of rabbits in mottled blue & tan, slip-marked "Amphora - Austria - Turn" w/partial Amphora label, few minor glaze nicks, one leaf mended (ILLUS.) **$920**

Fine Amphora Ibis Vase

Vase, 9" h., hard earthenware, Ibis design, footed squatty bulbous lower body below tapering long lappet panels to the wide flaring triangular rim above the molded ibis heads forming long handles, yellowish body, painting in matte gold on the rim & neck shading to a rich reddish rose at the base, impressed "Amphora- Austria" in ovals, a crown, imperial circle & "15006 - 57," 1904-1906 (ILLUS.) **$3,500**

Paul Dachsel Pine Tree Vase

Vase, 9" h., hard earthenware, pine tree design, tapering fluted good shape w/green relief tree trunks up the sides, applied pine cones branching at the neck, ochre underglaze painting, transparent matte glaze, brown frit on pine cones, patches of dark green frit on trunks, grey patina & matte

gilding, Kunstkeramik Paul Dachsel Company, marked w/a black "PD" transfer, impressed "2037-12," 1908-1909 (ILLUS.) .. **$7,300**

Amphora Marabella Poppies Vase

Vase, 9" h., Marabella Series, hard earthenware, bulbous ovoid body tapering to a tiny flared neck, the greyish body decorated w/an irregular relief web of strong threads, whitish & greenish base glaze, dark green & rose frit glaze w/matellic lustre on the relief, cobalt blue & black underglaze painting of peonies on a wide middle band, matte gold sponging, red "RStK" transfer mark, impressed oval w/"Amphora - 3271," ink-printed "50," ca. 1903-04 (ILLUS.) **$2,900**

Amphora Carved Ivory-like Vase

Vase, 9 3/4" h., carved-type, porcelain, designed as an ivory tusk deeply carved w/an Oriental figure emerging from a large pot in an Asian landscape w/a seated figure below, from the period when Alfred Stellmacher developed a technique to produced pottery that resembled ivory, on a plinth-form base, bottom marked w/"A.S." in a rose transfer, impressed "1012," 1884 (ILLUS.) **$1,200**

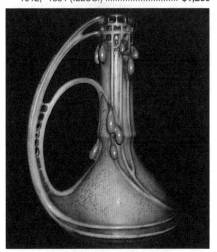

Abstract Paul Dachsel Vase

Vase, 9 7/8" h., a Paul Dachsel abstract design w/a reticulated geometric top & a reticulated handle within a reticulated handle sweeping in an arc from the top to the bottom w/abstract tendrils extending around the bottom of the body & back of the handles, several high-glazed green pods resembling teardrops of various sizes hang from the abstract handle, vines & a center funnel, the top rim & top of handle finished in gold, rare, stamped over glaze w/intertwined "PD - Turn - Teplitz" (ILLUS.)...................................... **$7,000-$7,500**

Vase, 10" h., a Paul Dachsel abstract architectural style w/a geometric design consisting of a rounded bottom from which four handles begin flush & extend to the top of the rim where they flare open, each handle suggests an abstract candelabrum w/charcoal flames rising from each, finished in iridescent gunmetal grey w/charcoal black sheen touches, gold wash on top, modern in all respects even though produced in the 1904-10 period, rare form, stamped over glaze w/intertwined "PD - Turn - Teplitz," impressed "1049".. **$8,500-$9,000**

Vase, 10 1/4" h., hard earthenware, Gres - Bijou Series, wide cylindrical body w/an angled shoulder to the short neck, yellowish body applied overall w/stone "jewels" & a relief cell design of thick threads, brown & carmine underglaze painting, glossy transparent mother-of-pearl frit dust glaze, matte & glossy gilding, mark of Riessner & Kessel Company w/impressed ovals enclosing "Austria - Amphora - 3672 - 60," 1904-1906 (ILLUS., top next column) **$3,600**

Jeweled Gres - Bijou Series Amphora Vase

Bulbous Footed Amphora Vase with Jays

Vase, 10 1/2" h., porcelain, bulbous body w/molded rim band & raised on four incurved block legs, the body h.p. w/a winter forest scene w/two jars, Asian influence on the four legs decorated w/Asian-like designs w/similar designs around the rim, mark of Ernst Wahliss Company w/red transfer "EW" in a shield topped w/a crown, impressed "9308," inked "9308/9340," ca. 1899-1909 (ILLUS.) **$2,800**

Amphora Vase with Molded Florals

Vase, 11 3/4" h., tall gently tapering body w/a reticulated rim flanked by long slender leaf handles, molded overall w/stylized flowers & leaves in shades of green & tan, marked w/the Wahliss logo & numbers 5698-2710 (ILLUS.)........................... **$748**

Czech Vase with Figural Dragon

Vase, 12" h., a wonderful & colorful dragon hugs the circumference of the top w/its huge, detailed wings draping along the sides, detailed claw-like feet decorated in two glazes, one predominately blue, the other predominately tan, a Czechoslovakian creation w/no Austrian counterpart, stamped over the glaze "Amphora - Made in Czech-slovakia" in an oval (ILLUS.) **$6,000**

Amphora Figural Cockatoo Vase

Vase, 12" h., figural, three standing cockatoos, fully feathered, extend around the body of the vase, their plumes rising over the rim, very detailed w/glossy glaze, subtle color mix of blues, greens & tans w/brown streaks, semi-rare, impressed "Amphora" & "Austria" in ovals, a crown & Imperial circle & "11986 - 56" (ILLUS.) .... **$4,500-$5,000**

Amphora Vase with Figural Farmer

Vase, 12 3/4" h., hard earthenware, figural, upright shape crudely molded of leafy trees, a seated Brittany grain farmer seated holding his scythe on one side, decorated in earthtones, impressed crown & ovals w/"Amphora - Austria - 4889 - 98 - G," ca. 1909-1910 (ILLUS.) .. **$1,000**

Vase, 13" h., stoneware, Campina Series, bulbous ovoid body w/a wide rounded shoulder centered by a small neck flanked by low angled handles, the sides incised & painted w/a large wood ground, a yellowish body w/impressed contours, the colorful wood grouse posed on a pine bough, repeating wave-like band in dark yellow & cobalt blue around the base, bright cloisonne enamels, stylized plant designs on the back, designed by Max Von Jungwirth, impressed crown & ovals w/"Amphora - Austria, Campina rectangle, imperial circle & "11611," ca. 1909-1910 .... **$1,500**

Dachsel "Enchanted Forest" Vase

Vase, 13" h., wide-shouldered tapering cylindrical body, a fantasy design by Paul Dachsel worthy of the description "enchanted forest," the design consists of slender molded abstract trees extending from the narrow base to the bulbous top, lovely heart-shaped leaves extend in clusters from the various branches, trees in muted green, the leaves in pearlized off-white w/gold framing, the symbolic sky in rich red extending between the trees from the bottom to the top, rare, intertwined "PD" mark rubbed off (ILLUS.) .... **$9,500-$10,000**

Vase, 14" h., figural, a fantasy dragon featuring two flaring wings, one extending practically from the top to the bottom of the body, the other well above & beyond the rim, creature w/a convoluted tail, spine & teeth, the head w/open mouth positioned at top of the vase, bluish green gold iridescence, glazes vary from a flat tan to a variety of very iridescent colors, made in 14" & 17" size, impressed "Amphora" in oval, illegible numbers, large size w/better glazes, $6,500, 14" size w/drab glazes..................... **$9,500-$10,000**

Unusual Tubular Amphora Vase

Vase, 14 1/4" h., unusual multi-spouted design, a small round dark blue base w/yellow blossoms supporting four curved tubes meeting at the base & at the top below the ringed neck in dark blue w/small yellow blossoms, each tube topped by a small cylindrical spout, the mottled yellow & blue ground on the tubes centered by a long almond-shaped dark blue reserve enclosing yellow Macintosh roses & green leaves, possibly inspired by Paul Dachsel, impressed crown & ovals w/"Amphora - Austria," number obscured by glaze, ca. 1906-1907 (ILLUS.) **$1,000**

Large Floral-decorated Amphora Vase

Vase, 14 5/8" h., tall gently tapering ovoid form w/a closed rim, the upper half w/a cream background decorated w/tall stems of stylized gold flowers, the lower half in dark green decorated w/a repeating band of tight scrolls in light green, marked "Turn Teplitz Bohemia - R St & K - Made in Austria - Amphora - 630" (ILLUS.).................. **$1,840**

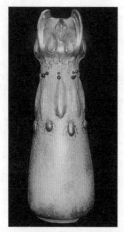

Tall Amphora Vase with Insects

Vase, 14 3/4" h., tall gently tapering ovoid body w/a swelled top, decorated w/eight three-dimensional iridescent indigo blue insects of varying sizes crawling up the side toward a series of leaves adorned w/berries, above the berries is a four-handled 3" h. heavily gilded top, the rest of the body in iridescent light blue w/gold highlights, rare, impressed "Amphora" & "Austria" in ovals, a crown & 3987/58 (ILLUS.) .... **$9,000-$9,500**

Flower-decorated Art Nouveau Vase

Vase, 15" h., bulbous squatty base tapering to a slender neck w/fanned rim, unique Art Nouveau design w/an open flower blossom tinged in gold at the top, two curved vine handles extend from the neck to the base, the base relief-molded w/detailed leaves, found in numerous color variations & glazes, the most magnificent being a bronze glaze, value depends on the glaze w/bronze being the rarest, impressed "Amphora" & "Austria" in oval, a crown & 3852/42 (ILLUS.) .... **$4,500-$5,500**

Amphora Vase with Golden Grapes

Vase, 15 1/2" h., cascades of golden grapes stream down on all sides between four funnel necks, the central funnel projecting skyward, this funnel design suggests Paul Dachsel, especially desirable because the piece is viewable from any angle, metallic purplish glaze w/metallic gold highlights containing numerous little gold circles, marked "Amphora" & "Austria" in ovals, a crown & "3680" (ILLUS.) .... **$4,000-$4,500**

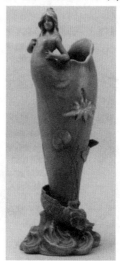

Tall Figural Amphora Vase

Vase, 16 1/2" h., figural, tall ovoid body w/the wave-molded base wrapped by a figural sea serpent, the tall lily-form vase molded at the rim w/an Art Nouveau maiden extending above the rim, impressed mark "BB 3749," some crazing (ILLUS.).. **$1,093**

Tall Maiden & Calla Lily Amphora Vase

Vase, 24 3/4" h., figural, porcelain, standing maiden w/calla lily, the neck applied w/lily leaves against which the maiden stands, lily-shaped mouth, vivid blue & green underglaze painting, figure w/matte gilding & gold accents throughout, Ernst Wahliss Company, impressed "Made in Austria - 4695-5," 1890-1900 (ILLUS.) **$9,900**

Rose-decorated Teplitz Water Jug

Water jug, spherical double-spouted form w/large arched & bead-trimmed gold handles from the cylindrical neck to the shoulder w/tiny arched handles above them, decorated w/a large teardrop-form reserve decorated w/long-stemmed white roses on leafy gold stems on a dark green ground, a wide center body band w/matching roses, textured background

in mottled light green & gold w/tiny dotted florals, marked "Turn Teplitz - Made in Austria - PD (Paul Dachsel) - 1165," 8 1/8" h. (ILLUS.) **$1,955**

Austrian

Numerous potteries in Austria produced good-quality ceramic wares over many years. Some factories were established by American entrepreneurs, particularly in the Carlsbad area, and other factories made china under special brand names for American importers. Marks on various pieces are indicated in many listings.

Austrian Mark

Austrian Porcelain Fancy Teapot

Teapot, cov., ruffle-footed ribbed baluster-form body w/a domed cover & ring finial, serpentine spout & ornate C-scroll handle, gold trim, Imperial Crown China, Vienna, Austria, ca. 1890s (ILLUS.)............... **$45**

Ornate Austrian Porcelain & Metal Urn

Urn, an elongated inverted pear-shaped body h.p. w/a large oblong reserve showing a standing lady wearing a blue gown standing in a landscape & reaching down to a cherub, the maroon & light blue background, raised on a square gilt-metal plinth foot & slender colorfully enameled pedestal & fitted w/a slender trumpet-shaped colorfully enameled metal neck w/gilt-metal gadrooned leaf band, artist-signed, 9 1/2" h. (ILLUS., previous page) **$403**

Fine Austrian Vase with Semi-Nude Girl

Vase, 9 1/4" h., gently tapering cylindrical body w/a rounded shoulder & tiny flared neck, the body h.p. w/a wide band showing a semi-nude Moroccan girl carrying an amphora in an exotic landscape, neck & shoulders in iridescent maroon decorated w/ornate gilt enamel scrolls, artist-signed, late 19th c. (ILLUS.) **$2,820**

Ornate Flower-decorated Austrian Vase

Vase, cov., 25" h., tall ovoid urn-form body raised on a gold-trimmed molded scrolling foot, pierced long scroll-molded handles w/gold trim, the high domed cover w/a high gold flame-form finial & h.p. w/flower sprigs, the body h.p. w/large bouquets of colorful flowers, illegible impressed mark, late 19th c., some minor professional repair & chips (ILLUS.) .... **$400-$800**

Bauer

The Bauer Pottery was moved to Los Angeles, California, from Paducah, Kentucky, in 1909 in the hope that the climate would prove beneficial to the principal organizer, John Andrew Bauer, who suffered from severe asthma. Flowerpots made of California adobe clay were the first production at the new location, but soon they were able to resume production of stoneware crocks and jugs, the mainstay of the Kentucky operation. In the early 1930s, Bauer's colorfully glazed earthen dinnerwares, especially the popular Ring-Ware pattern, became an immediate success. Sometimes confused with its imitator, Fiesta Ware (first registered by Homer Laughlin in 1937), Bauer pottery is collectible in its own right and is especially popular with West Coast collectors. Bauer Pottery ceased operation in 1962.

Bauer Mark

Batter bowl, Ring-Ware patt., green, 1 qt **$125**
Beater pitcher, Ring-Ware patt., red, 1 qt. **$85**
Bowl, berry, 5 1/2" d., Ring-Ware patt., yellow **$25**
Bowl, 13" d., Cal-Art line, green **$35**
Butter dish, cov., Ring-Ware patt., 1/4 lb., cobalt blue **$200**
Cake plate, Monterey patt., yellow **$185**
Casserole, cov., individual, Ring-Ware patt., cobalt blue, 5 1/2" d. **$300**
Casserole, cov., individual, Ring-Ware patt., orange/red, 5 1/2" d. **$200**
Coffee carafe, cov., Ring-Ware patt., copper handle, orange/red **$150**
Cookie jar, cov., Monterey Moderne patt., chartreuse **$100**

Monterey Midget Creamer

Creamer, midget, Monterey patt., orange/red (ILLUS.) **$20**

Creamer & cov. sugar bowl, Ring-Ware
patt., orange, pr. $75
Cup, Jumbo, cobalt blue, 3 3/8" h. .... $125-$150
Cup, Jumbo, orange, 3 3/8" h. $260
Flowerpot, Speckleware, flesh pink,
8 1/4" d., 6 1/2" h. $40
Gravy boat, Ring-Ware patt., burgundy $145
Mixing bowl, nesting-type, Ring-Ware
patt., No. 18, chartreuse $75

Bauer Oil Jar

Oil jar, No. 100, orange, 16" h. (ILLUS.) $1,000
Oil jars, No. 100, white, 12" h., pr. $3,000
Pitcher, Ring-Ware patt., orange, 1 qt. $85
Pitcher, cov., jug-type, ice water, Monterey
patt., turquoise $325
Plate, 9" d., Ring-Ware patt., grey $65
Plate, 10 1/2" d., dinner, Ring-Ware patt.,
cobalt or delph blue, each $95
Plate, chop, 12" d., Ring-Ware patt., white $230
Plate, chop, Monterey Moderne patt., yellow ... $45
Punch bowl, Ring-Ware patt., three-footed,
jade green, 14" d. $550
Salt & pepper shakers, beehive-shaped,
Ring-Ware patt., orange/red, pr. $60
Sugar shaker, Ring-Ware patt., jade green ... $350
Teapot, cov., Ring-Ware patt., burgundy, 2-
cup size $325

Vase, 8" h., Hi-Fire line, deep trumpet-
shaped form w/widely flaring sides fluted
on the exterior, yellow $90

Matt Carlton Line Vase

Vase, 8" h., ovoid base w/widely flared rim,
twist shoulder handles, orange, Matt Car-
lton Artware line (ILLUS.) $650
Vase, 13" h., ovoid base w/widely flared rim,
twist shoulder handles, jade green, Matt
Carlton Artware line $1,200
Vase, 14" h., crimped fan shape, Matt Carl-
ton line, Chinese yellow $750

Bavarian

*Ceramics have been produced by various pot-
teries in Bavaria, Germany, for many years.
Those appearing for sale in greatest frequency
today were produced in the 19th and early 20th
centuries. Various company marks are indicated
with some listings here.*

Plates, 11" d., dinner, broad lightly scalloped emerald green border, the interior
centered by a bright h.p. polychrome
bouquet of spring flowers within a gold inner band, lion shield mark of Carl
Schumann, ca. 1900, set of 12 (ILLUS.,
bottom of page) $748

Elegant Green-bordered & Flower-decorated Plates

Fancy Bavarian Porcelain Teapot

Teapot, cov., a flaring ruffled foot below the squatty bulbous ribbed body tapering to a flaring ruffled neck & domed cover w/knob finial, serpentine spout & fancy C-scroll handle, overall delicate scrolling vine decoration, Jollio, Bavaria, Germany, early 20th c. (ILLUS.) **$60**

Beatrix Potter Figurines

The John Beswick factory in Longton, Stoke on Trent, celebrated its 100th anniversary in 1994. Originally, it produced earthenware household items and decorative ornaments. With the passage of time, the product line became more diverse and the decorations more ornate and attractive. Moreover, small domestic, farmyard and wild animal figurines were added to the product lines. Beswick was a family-owned and family-run pottery. As the owners neared retirement, they realized there were no next of kin to carry on the business. They sold the company to Royal Doulton in 1969 but Doulton later sold off the line.

Beatrix Potter is known the world over. Generations of children since the early 1900s have been fascinated by the antics of her coterie of small animals in her series of illustrated children's "Tales of Peter Rabbit and Friends." These storybook characters have been produced as small china figurines since the 1920s, but it was not until 1947 that Beswick gained copyright approval from the Frederick Warne Co., the Peter Rabbit book publisher, to manufacture and market them. Upon acquisition of the manufacturing rights, Royal Doulton continued to promote and sell the Beatrix Potter figures using the Beswick trademark until 1989, when it switched to a "Royal Albert" under print. Royal Albert was another of its famous product lines and had greater brand recognition in the United States. The backstamp change was not well received by the global collector community. Within a decade, the Beswick backstamp was reintroduced and used on the Beatrix Potter figurines until the end of 2002, when the Warne license expired. The old Beswick factory was closed.

All the Beatrix Potter figurines were assigned a "P" or production model number. Although these "P" numbers do not appear on the figures themselves, they are used extensively by collectors to uniquely identify a particular figure.

Many varieties of backstamp exist. They indicate a period of manufacture and influence sec-ondary market values. The basic types of backstamp are shown. If collectible subtypes exist, a range of market values is given for the basic type. Many special backstamps were used in the 1990s to promote sales. These details are outside the scope of this compendium.

Basic Beatrix Potter Backstamps

Aunt Pettitoes, P2276, crown backstamp, 1970-93 .... **$75**

Aunt Pettitoes Figure

Aunt Pettitoes, P2276, gold circle/oval backstamp, 1970-93 (ILLUS.) **$650**
Benjamin Bunny, P1105, ears in, shoes in, crown backstamp, 1980-2000 .... **$35**
Benjamin Bunny, P1105, ears in, shoes in, Beswick Ware backstamp, 1980-2000 .... **$35**

Benjamin Bunny Figure

Benjamin Bunny, P1105, ears in, shoes in, gold circle/oval backstamp, 1980-2000 (ILLUS., previous page) **$80**

Benjamin Bunny, P1105, ears in, shoes in, John Beswick script backstamp, 1980-2000 .... **$175**

Christmas Stocking Figural Group

Christmas Stocking, P3257, crown backstamp, 1991-94 (ILLUS.) **$250**

Cousin Ribby, P2284, brown line backstamp, 1970-93 .... **$65**

Cousin Ribby, P2284, crown backstamp, 1970-93 .... **$75**

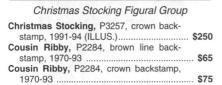

Cousin Ribby Figure

Cousin Ribby, P2284, gold circle/oval backstamp, 1970-93 (ILLUS.) **$625**

Fierce Bad Rabbit, P2586, feet in, light brown rabbit, brown line backstamp, 1980-97 .... **$100**

Goody & Timmy Tiptoes, P2957, brown line backstamp, 1986-96 (ILLUS., top next column)... **$300**

Goody & Timmy Tiptoes, P2957, crown backstamp, 1986-96................................. **$100**

Goody Tiptoes, P1675, brown line backstamp, 1961-67 .... **$75**

Goody & Timmy Tiptoes

Goody Tiptoes, P1675, crown backstamp, 1961-67 .... **$45**

Goody Tiptoes Figure

Goody Tiptoes, P1675, gold circle/oval backstamp, 1961-67 (ILLUS.) **$300**

Hunca Munca Spills the Beads

Hunca Munca Spills the Beads, P3288, crown backstamp, 1992-96 (ILLUS.) **$70**

Hunca Munca Sweeping, P2584, brown dustpan, Beswick Made in England backstamp, 1977-2002 .... **$35**
Hunca Munca Sweeping, P2584, brown dustpan, brown line backstamp, 1977-2002 .... **$90**

Hunca Munca Sweeping

Hunca Munca Sweeping, P2584, brown dustpan, crown backstamp, 1977-2002 (ILLUS.) **$35**
Hunca Munca Sweeping, P2584, brown dustpan, John Beswick script backstamp, 1977-2002 .... **$150**

Jemima Puddle-Duck Made a Feather Nest

Jemima Puddle-Duck Made a Feather Nest, P2823, brown line backstamp, 1983-97 (ILLUS.) **$60**
Jemima Puddle-Duck Made a Feather Nest, P2823, crown backstamp, 1983-97 .... **$40**
Jemima Puddle-Duck Made a Feather Nest, P2823, John Beswick script backstamp, 1983-97 .... **$150**
Jemima Puddle-Duck with Foxy Whiskered Gentleman, P3193, Beswick Made in England backstamp, 1990-99 .... **$80**
Mrs. Rabbit, P1200, umbrella in, crown backstamp, 1975-2002 (ILLUS., top next column) **$45**
Mrs. Rabbit, P1200, umbrella in, John Beswick script backstamp, 1975-2002 .... **$100**
Mrs. Rabbit & Bunnies, P2543, brown line backstamp, 1976-97 (ILLUS., middle next column) **$100**

Mrs. Rabbit Figure

Mrs. Rabbit & Bunnies

Mrs. Rabbit & Bunnies, P2543, crown backstamp, 1976-97 .... **$60**
Mrs. Rabbit & Bunnies, P2543, John Beswick script backstamp, 1976-97 .... **$145**

Mrs. Rabbit Cooking

Mrs. Rabbit Cooking, P3278, Beswick
Made in England backstamp, 1992-99
(ILLUS., previous page) $45
Mrs. Rabbit Cooking, P3278, crown back-
stamp, 1992-99 .... $35
Mrs. Tiggy-Winkle, P1107, plaid dress, Be-
swick Made in England, backstamp,
1972-2000 .... $35
Mrs. Tiggy-Winkle, P1107, plaid dress,
brown line backstamp, 1972-2000 .... $100

Mrs. Tiggy-Winkle

Mrs. Tiggy-Winkle, P1107, plaid dress,
crown backstamp, 1972-2000 (ILLUS.)........ $35
Mrs. Tiggy-Winkle, P1107, plaid dress,
gold circle/oval backstamp, 1972-2000 ..... $225
Mrs. Tiggy-Winkle, P1107, plaid dress,
John Beswick script backstamp, 1972-
2000 .... $140

No More Twist

No More Twist, P3325, crown backstamp,
1992-97 (ILLUS.)... $65

The Old Woman Who Lived in a Shoe Knitting

**Old Woman Who Lived in a Shoe Knitting
(The),** P2804, Beswick Made in England
backstamp, 1983-2002 (ILLUS.).................. $35
**Old Woman Who Lived in a Shoe Knitting
(The),** P2804, brown line backstamp,
1983-2002 .... $225
**Old Woman Who Lived in a Shoe Knitting
(The),** P2804, crown backstamp, 1983-
2002 .... $40
Peter Rabbit, P1098, brown line backs-
tamp, 1948-80 .... $110

Peter Rabbit Figure

Peter Rabbit, P1098, gold circle/oval backstamp, 1948-80 (ILLUS.)............................ $300
Peter Rabbit, P1098, light blue jacket,
crown backstamp, 1980-2002 .... $35

Peter Rabbit in Light Blue Jacket

Peter Rabbit, P1098, light blue jacket, brown line backstamp, 1980-2002 (ILLUS.) **$70**

Peter Rabbit, P1098, light blue jacket, Beswick Made in England backstamp, 1980-2002 .... **$35**

Peter Rabbit, P1098, light blue jacket, John Beswick script backstamp, 1980-2002 ...... **$135**

Peter with Postbag, P3591, Beswick Made in England backstamp, 1996-2002 .... **$45**

Poorly Peter Rabbit

Poorly Peter Rabbit, P2560, brown line backstamp, 1976-97 (ILLUS.) **$120**

Poorly Peter Rabbit, P2560, crown backstamp, 1976-97 .... **$55**

Poorly Peter Rabbit, P2560, John Beswick script backstamp, 1976-97 .... **$145**

Ribby & the Patty Pan, P3280, crown backstamp, 1992-98 (ILLUS., top next column) **$50**

Ribby & the Patty Pan

Simpkin Figure

Simpkin, P2508, brown line backstamp, 1975-83 (ILLUS.) **$600**

Squirrel Nutkin

Squirrel Nutkin, P1102, red-brown squirrel, brown line backstamp, 1983-89 (ILLUS.)..... **$95**

Squirrel Nutkin, P1102, red-brown squirrel, gold circle/oval backstamp, 1983-89 . **$250-$300**

Tabitha Twitchit & Miss Moppet, P2544, brown line backstamp, 1976-93 .... **$235**

Belleek

American Belleek

Pitchers, Creamers and Ewers

American Belleek Pitcher & Four Vases

Willets, 15 1/2" h, tankard-type, tall slightly tapering body w/a long squared handle, h.p. color scene of Cavaliers in a tavern (ILLUS. second from right with four vases, top of page) **$690**

Vases

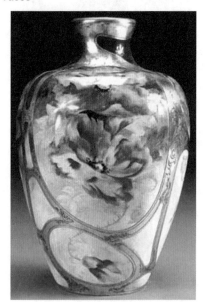

Fine Silver-Overlaid CAC Porcelain Vase

Ceramic Art Company, bulbous ovoid body tapering to a small trumpet neck, decorated w/large & small panels h.p. w/large reddish orange poppies & green & yellow leaves & stems, overlaid w/sterling silver chased w/scrolling acanthus leaves made by the Gorham Mfg. Co., artist-signed, palette mark, ca. 1900, 14 1/2" h. (ILLUS.) **$1,763**

Lenox, 10 1/2" h., gently flaring cylindrical body w/a rounded shoulder to the low, wide rolled rim, h.p. decoration of tall white & black egrets against a shaded pale blue, grey & white ground (ILLUS. far right with pitcher & three other vases, top of page) **$633**

Lenox, 11" h., tall slender cylindrical body tapering slightly to the flat rim, h.p. by the Pickard Studio w/a large cluster of pink & red roses w/green leaves against a shaded dark green to yellow ground, serpentine gold bands at the top & base, artist-signed (ILLUS. far left with pitcher & three other vases, top of page) **$1,495**

Willets, 15 1/2" h., large simple ovoid form w/a flat rim, h.p. around the upper half w/a wide band of large yellow, red & pink roses among leafy branches (ILLUS. third from left with pitcher & three other vases, top of page) **$920**

Willets, 15 1/2" h., tall wide cylindrical body tapering slightly at the top to a wide flat rim, h.p. w/large red & pink roses on green leafy vines against a pale green to yellow ground (ILLUS. second from left with the pitcher & three other vases, top of page) **$748**

Tall Slender Willets Urn-form Vase

Willets, 18 1/2" h., tall slender urn-form w/a round pedestal base in green w/gold bands, the slender ovoid body h.p. w/a long bouquet of small pink & red roses among green leaves against a white-white ground, the slender widely flaring trumpet neck in dark green w/gold bands, high ornate arched & scrolled gold shoulder handles continuing down the sides (ILLUS.) **$1,150**

Miscellaneous
Ceramic Art Company, loving cup, footed bulbous ovoid body w/a flat rim & three large loop handles in green & cream, the white body decorated w/two color scenes based on "The Song of Hiawatha" & a third panel w/a Longfellow poem, artist-signed & dated 1897, CAC-Belleek mark #1, 6 1/2" h. **$470**

Irish Belleek

Belleek china has been made in Ireland's County Fermanagh for many years. It is exceedingly thin porcelain. Several marks were used, including a hound and harp (1865-1880), and a hound, harp and castle (1863-1891). A printed hound, harp and castle with the words "Co. Fermanagh Ireland" constitutes the mark from 1891. The earliest marks

were printed in black followed by those printed in green. In recent years the marks appear in gold.

The item identification for the following listing follows that used in Richard K. Degenhardt's reference Belleek - The Complete Collector's Guide and Illustrated Reference, first and second editions. The Degenhardt illustration number (D...) appears at the end of each listing. This number will be followed in most cases by a Roman numeral "I" to indicate a first period black mark while the Roman numeral "II" will indicate a second period black mark. In the "Baskets" section an Arabic number "1" indicates an impressed ribbon mark with "Belleek" while the numeral "2" indicates the impressed ribbon with the words "Belleek - Co. Fermanagh." Both these marks were used in the first period, 1865-1891. Unless otherwise noted, all pieces here will carry the black mark. A thorough discussion of the early Belleek marks is found in this book as well as at the Web site: http://home.com-cast.net/~belleek_website/index.html.

Prices for items currently in production may also be located at this site, especially via the 1983 Suggested Retail Price List. Prices given here are for pieces in excellent or mint condition with no chips, cracks, crazing or repairs, although, on flowered items, minimal chips to the flowers is acceptable to the extent of the purchaser's tolerance. Earthenware pieces often exhibit varying degrees of crazing due to the primitive bottle kilns originally used at the pottery.

(1) Photographs used with permission, Rod Kearns, Photographer, rkearnsbak.rr.com.

Belleek Triple Shell Menu Holder

Triple Shell menu holder, D535-II (ILLUS.) .. **$400**

Basket Ware
Basket, four-lobed form w/widely flared rims, D1693-1 (ILLUS., bottom of page) **$3,000**

Four-lobed Belleek Basket

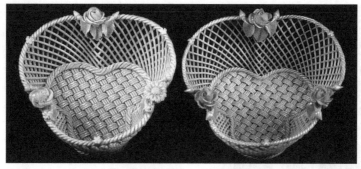

Two Belleek Shamrock Baskets

Large Henshall's Twig Basket

Basket, Henshall's Twig Basket, large size,
D120-1 (ILLUS.) **$4,200**

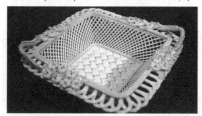

Belleek Melvin Basket

Basket, Melvin Basket, painted blossoms,
D1690-5 (ILLUS.) **$800**
Basket, round, center arched handle, flat-
tened rim w/applied colored blossoms,
flat rod, D1274-1 (ILLUS., top next col-
umn) **$6,200**
Basket, Shamrock basket, three different
flowers around the rim, small size, D109-
1, each (ILLUS. of two, top of page) **$520**

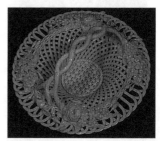

Round Belleek Handled Basket

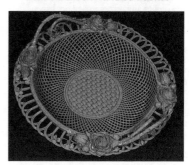

Large Sydenham Twig Basket

Basket, Sydenham Twig Basket, large size,
D108-1 (ILLUS.) **$4,400**
Basket, cov., oval, small size (D114-I) **$6,000**
Box, cov., Forget-Me-Not trinket box, flower
blossoms on the cover (D111-III) **$600**
Brooch, flowered (D1525-II) **$400**

Two Views of the Rare Spider's Web Cake Plate

Cake plate, Spider's Web cake plate, D1279-3 (ILLUS. of plate & close-up of spider, bottom previous page)................ **$5,400**

Flower bouquet, hand-formed in green ware, features samples of all flower styles used on Belleek wares, mounted in a shadowbox frame, marked with two ribbons & "Belleek (R) Co. Fermanagh," ca. 1955-79 .... **$2,200**

Unique Belleek Woven Mirror Frame

Frame, woven mirror frame, oval, unique, Second Period Mark II (ILLUS.) **$5,000**

Very Rare Belleek Frame

Frame, photo or mirror, oblong w/two oval picture openings, ornately applied w/flowers overall, D66-II (ILLUS.) **$6,200**

Woven Flowered Jewel Stand

Jewel stand, Woven Flowered Jewel Stand, D1575-II (ILLUS.) **$1,400**

Menu holder, decorated w/applied flowers, various designs, D275-II, each **$600**

Comports & Centerpieces

Cherub Candelabra

Candelabra, Cherub Candelabra, w/drip cups, D341-II (ILLUS.) **$6,000**

Bird Nest Stump Vase-Centerpiece

Centerpiece, Bird Nest Stump Vase, w/eggs in nest, D57-II (ILLUS.) **$3,200**

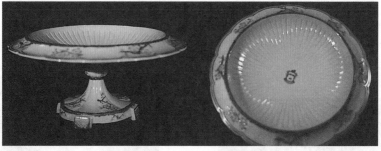

Belleek Thorn Comport & Top View

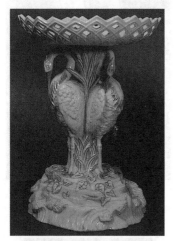

Rare Belleek Bittern Comport

Comport, Bittern Comport, figural tall birds
form pedestal, gilt trim, D6-II (ILLUS.)... **$10,000**

Boy on Swan Figural Comport

Comport, Boy on Swan Comport, beetle
flies on base, D33-I (ILLUS.)................. **$10,000**
Comport, Thorn Comport, D36-II, 4 1/2" h.
(ILLUS. of two views, top of page) **$1,400**
Comport, Tri Dolphin & Shell Pedestal
Comport, painted, D1149-I (ILLUS., top
next column)... **$4,200**
Comport, Trihorse Comport, impressed "Bel-
leek Co. Fermanagh," D37-I (ILLUS., mid-
dle next column)..................................... **$3,400**

Belleek Tri Dolphin & Shell Comport

Irish Belleek Trihorse Comport

Earthenware

Earthenware Bowl with Inscription

Bowl, deep sides, Celtic inscription that
translates "Friendship is Better than
Gold," D857-II (ILLUS.) **$400**

Chamber Pot with Gladstone

Chamber pot, printed portrait of William
Gladstone on the inside bottom, D2082-I
(ILLUS.)... **$1,600**
Jelly mold, deep slightly flaring rounded
sides, design on the interior (D880-I) **$460**
Mug, cylindrical, scenic transfer-printed
decoration (D858-II) **$360**

Transfer-printed Belleek Plate

Plate, 10" d., black transfer-printed pottery
scene in the center, a crest on the flanged
rim, D887-I (ILLUS.)................................... **$400**

Belleek Earthenware Serving Dish

Serving dish, open, oval, embossed end
handles, pedestal base, D915-II (ILLUS.) .. **$400**
Toothbrush tray, cov., found w/various
transfer-printed designs (D932-I) **$440**

Floral-decorated Earthenware Tray

Tray, oval, brown transfer-printed floral design, D900-I (ILLUS.) **$400**

Belleek Earthenware Decorated Trivet

Trivet, round, decal & hand-painted decora-
tion, D1057-I (ILLUS.) **$800**

Hand-painted Earthenware Trivet

Trivet, round, h.p. w/lily-of-the-valley,
D1057-I (ILLUS.)...................................... **$1,000**

Religious Items & Lithophanes
Figure of the Blessed Virgin Mary, large
size (D1106-II) **$1,800**

Belleek Cherub Head Water Font

Holy water font, Cherub head w/spread
wings, D1110-VI (ILLUS.) **$100**
Holy water font, Coral & Shell (D1111-V) **$100**

Sacred Heart Holy Water Font #4

Holy water font, Sacred Heart font, #4, D1115-III (ILLUS.) **$260**

Holy water font, Sacred Heart font, #8 (D1114-II) **$320**

Lithophane, Madonna, Child & Angel (D1544-III) **$3,200**

Lithophane, Madonna, Child & Angel (D1544-VII) **$600**

Child Looking in Mirror Lithophane

Lithophane, round, child looking in mirror, D1539-VII (ILLUS.) **$480**

Tea Ware - Common Patterns (Harp Shamrock, Limpet, Hexagon, Neptune, Shamrock & Tridacna)

Harp Shamrock butter plate, D1356-III (ILLUS., top next column) **$200**

Harp Shamrock Butter Plate

Harp Shamrock Butter Plate

Harp Shamrock butter plate, D1356-VI (ILLUS.) **$100**

Belleek Harp Shamrock Teakettle

Harp Shamrock teakettle, overhead handle, large size, gilt trim, D1359-III (ILLUS.) **$660**

Belleek Hexagon Breakfast Set

Hexagon breakfast set: small cov. teapot, open sugar & creamer, two plates & two cups & saucers, h.p. floral decoration, no tray, D396-II (ILLUS., bottom previous page) **$3,200**

Hexagon Pattern Belleek Teapot

Hexagon teapot, cov., large size, D407-II (ILLUS.) **$600**

Shamrock Souvenir Mug

Mug, cylindrical, Shamrock, souvenir-type, h.p. Irish scene, D216-II (ILLUS.) **$300**
Neptune biscuit jar, cov. (D531-II) **$460**
Neptune creamer & open sugar bowl, green tint, pr. (D416-II & D417-II) **$400**

Neptune Pattern Cup & Saucer

Neptune teacup & saucer, green tint, D414-II (ILLUS.) **$240**
Neptune teapot, cov., medium size, green tint (D415-II) **$480**
Neptune tray, green tint (D418-II) **$1,200**
Shamrock bread plate, round w/loop handles (D379-III) **$180**
Shamrock eggcup, footed (D389-II) **$120**
Shamrock marmalade jar, cov., barrrel-shaped, D1561-IV (ILLUS. right with marmalde & mustard, bottom of page) **$100**
Shamrock marmalade jar, cov., cup marmalade, D1323-III (ILLUS. center with mustard & marmalade, bottom of page) **$100**

Shamrock Marmalades & Mustard

Shamrock Large & Name Mugs

Shamrock mug, large size, D216-II (ILLUS.
right, top of page) **$120**
Shamrock mug, Name Mug, impressed
reserve for name, small size, D216-II
(ILLUS. left, top of page) **$140**
Shamrock mustard jar, cov., footed spher-
ical form, D298-III (ILLUS. left with marmalades, bottom previous page) **$100**
Shamrock pitcher, milk, jug-form (D390-II)... **$320**

Shamrock Low-Shape Cup & Saucer

Shamrock teacup & saucer, low shape,
D366-III (ILLUS.) **$160**

Tridacna Boat-shaped Creamer

Tridacna creamer, boat-shaped, D247-VI
(ILLUS.)... **$60**

Large Tridacna Gilt-trimmed Sugar

Tridacna sugar bowl, open, gilt-trimmed,
large size, D472-I (ILLUS.) **$440**

**Tea Ware - Desirable Patterns (Echinus,
Limpet [footed], Grass, Hexagon, Holly,
Mask, New Shell & Shell)**
Echinus creamer & open sugar bowl,
decorated (D647-I & D648-I), pr. **$1,000**
Echinus cup & saucer, egg shell, crested
(D358-I)... **$500**
Echinus eggcup, footed (D666-I)................. **$400**
Echinus teapot, cov., pink tint w/gold trim,
small size (D659-I) **$900**
Grass coffeepot, cov., large size (D1402-I) . **$1,600**
Grass creamer & covered sugar bowl,
middle size, D748 & D748-I, pr. **$800**

Grass Eggcup with Crest

Grass eggcup, footed, crested decoration, D754-I (ILLUS., previous page) **$600**

Grass honey pot, cover & stand, model of a beehive on a low table-form base, the set (D755-I) **$1,000**

Grass mustache cup & saucer (D739-I) **$620**

Grass teakettle, cov., large size, D751-I (ILLUS. at right with teapot & tray) **$1,000**

Grass Teapot, Kettle & Tray

Grass teapot, cov., small size, D750-I (ILLUS. left with kettle & tray) **$800**

Grass tray, round, D736-I (ILLUS. with teapot & teakettle) **$2,000**

Mask powder bowl, small size, D1548-III **$160**

Tea Ware - Museum Display Patterns (Artichoke, Chinese, Finner, Five O'Clock, Lace, Ring Handle Ivory, Set #36 & Victoria)

Bone china bread plate, heavy pink ground & gilt trim, D844-I (ILLUS. left with teacup & saucer, bottom of page) **$680**

Bone china teacup & saucer, heavy pink ground & gilt trim, D848-I (ILLUS. right with bread plate, bottom of page).............. **$620**

Chinese creamer w/dragon head spout & open sugar bowl, decorated (D485-I & D486-I), pr. **$1,400**

Chinese tea urn, figural cover, ornate winged dragon spout, twisted rope-form overhead handle, large winged dragon support on round base w/paw feet, decorated (D482-I)...................................... **$18,000**

Chinese Pattern Teacup & Saucer

Chinese teacup & saucer, decorated, D483-I (ILLUS.)...................................... **$800**

Chinese teapot, cov., small size, decorated (D484-I)... **$2,000**

Lace Pattern Belleek Teapot

Lace teapot, cov., medium size, D800-II (ILLUS.)... **$1,000**

Lace tray, round, decorated (D803-I) **$6,000**

Bone China Bread Plate & Teacup and Saucer

Artichoke Tea Ware Muffin Dish

Muffin dish, cov., Artichoke Tea Ware, gilt trim, D720-I (ILLUS., top of page) **$2,000**

Ring Handle Ivory Ware Belleek Plate

Plate, Ring Handle Ivory Ware plate, h.p. Irish scene, unsigned but from the School of Eugene Sheerin, 7 1/2" d., D823-II (ILLUS.) **$1,800**
Ring Handle bread plate, Limoges decoration (D824-I) **$1,400**

Tea Ware - Rare Patterns (Aberdeen, Blarney, Celtic (low & tall), Cone, Erne, Fan,

Institute, Ivy, Lily (high & low), Scroll, Sydney, Thistle & Thorn)

Aberdeen breakfast set: cov. teapot, creamer, open sugar & cups & saucers; no tray, D494-II (ILLUS., bottom of page) **$2,200**

Low Celtic Candlestick

Celtic Candlestick, Low, painted & gilt, 4 3/4" h., D1511-VI (ILLUS.) **$340**

Belleek Aberdeen Pattern Breakfast Tea Set

Celtic Design Bread Plate

Celtic Design bread plate, Celtic Design tea ware, multicolored & gilt, D1425-III (ILLUS.).. **$600**

Celtic Design Creamer

Celtic Design creamer, Celtic Design tea ware, tall shape, multicolored, ('mystery'

mark, 1st Period over Celtic Scroll, probably a transition from 1st to 2nd period), 4 1/2" h., D1442-II (ILLUS.)........................ **$400**
Celtic fruit dish, round, D1512-II **$1,200**
Celtic teacup & saucer, low shape, painted (D1456-III & D1457-III)................................ **$400**
Cone teacup & saucer, pink tint (D432-II) **$440**

Fan Pattern Teacup & Saucer

Fan teacup & saucer, decorated, D694-II (ILLUS.).. **$600**
Institute plate, 6" d., pink tint (D724-I) **$160**

Institute Decorated Sugar Bowl

Institute sugar bowl, cov., decorated, D728-I (ILLUS.)... **$600**

Thorn Brush Tray & Scent Bottles

Thorn brush tray & scent bottles, turquoise & gilt decoration, D333-I & D335-I (ILLUS.) **$2,200**

Low Lily Tea Set with Green Tint & Gold Trim

Thorn creamer & open sugar bowl, small
size (D760-I & D761-I), pr. **$1,000**
Thorn teapot, cov., small size, decorated
(D759-I) **$800**
Thorn tray, oval, decorated (D762-I) **$2,600**

Tea Wares

Tea set: cov. teapot, open sugar & creamer
& two cups & saucers; Low Lily patt.,
green tint w/gold trim, 2nd period, creamer & open sugar, $400-$500; cup & saucer, $260-$320; teapot only (ILLUS. of
set, top of page) .... **$700-$800**

Tea urn, Chinese (Dragon) patt., fancy dark
pink, black & heavy gold trim, 17" h., 1st
period (ILLUS.)........................ **$18,000-$25,000**

*Extremely Rare Decorated Chinese Pattern
Tall Tea Urn*

Tea urn, Chinese (Dragon) patt., fancy pale
pink, black & heavy gold trim, 17" h., 1st
period (ILLUS.)........................ **$18,000-$25,000**

Another Version of the Rare Chinese Tea Urn

Grass Pattern Teakettle with Multicolored Decoration

Teakettle, Grass patt., multicolored decoration w/gold, 1st period (ILLUS.)...... **$600-$1,000**

Gold-trimmed Ringhandle Teakettle

Teakettle, Ringhandle patt., undecorated except gold trim, 3rd period (ILLUS.)
.... **$1,000-$1,400**

Aberdeen Pattern Teapot with Cob Decoration

Teapot, Aberdeen patt., Cob decoration, 2nd period (ILLUS.).......................... **$700-$800**

Decorated Artichoke Pattern Teapot

Teapot, Artichoke patt., green decoration w/gold trim, 1st period (ILLUS.) ..... **$800-$1,000**
Teapot, Bamboo patt., undecorated, 1st period (ILLUS. right with decorated Echinus teapot, top next page) .... **$800-$1,000**

Blarney Pattern Teapot with Green Tint & Gold Trim

Teapot, Blarney patt., green tint & gold trim, 2nd period (ILLUS.).......................... **$700-$800**

Rare Chinese Pattern Decorated Teapot

Teapot, Chinese (Dragon) patt., multicolored decoration with gold, 1st period (ILLUS.)
.... **$1,600-$2,800**

Cone Pattern Teapot with Orange Tint & Gold Trim

Teapot, Cone patt., orange tint & gold trim, 2nd period (ILLUS.).......................... **$600-$800**

A Decorated Echinus and Undecorated Bamboo Teapot

Teapot, Echinus patt., footed, blue & pink decoration w/gold trim, 1st period (ILLUS. left with Bamboo teapot, top of page) .... **$800-$1,200**

Early Echinus Teapot with Pink Tint & Gold Trim

Teapot, Echinus patt., footed, pink tint & gold trim, 1st period (ILLUS.) .... **$700-$800**

Fan Pattern Teapot with Pink Tint & Gold Trim

Teapot, Fan patt., pink tint & gold trim, 2nd period (ILLUS.) .... **$600-$1,000**

Multicolored Finner Pattern Teapot

Teapot, Finner patt., multicolored decoration, 2nd period (ILLUS.) .... **$1,000-$1,400**

5 O'Clock Pattern Teapot with Green Decoration

Teapot, (Five) 5 O'Clock patt., green decoration, note the unique "5 O'clock-shaped" handle (ILLUS.) .... **$1,200-$2,000**

Grass Pattern Teapot with Color Decoration

Teapot, Grass patt., multicolored decoration, 1st period (ILLUS.) .... **$600-$800**

High Lily Teapot with Green Tint

Teapot, High Lily patt., green tint, 2nd period (ILLUS.) .... **$700-$800**

Lace Pattern Teapot with Chocolate & Gold Decoration

Teapot, Lace patt., chocolate decoration & gold trim, 2nd period (ILLUS.) ..... **$1,000-$1,400**

Early Undecorated Lace Pattern Teapot

Teapot, Lace patt., undecorated, 1st period (ILLUS.) .... **$800-$900**

Limpet Footed Pink Tint 2nd Period Teapot

Teapot, Limpet patt., footed, pink tint, 2nd period (ILLUS.) .... **$600-$800**
Teapot, Limpet patt., pink tint w/gold trim, 3rd period .... **$300-$400**

Limpet Shape Irish Belleek Teapot

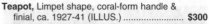

Teapot, Limpet shape, coral-form handle & finial, ca. 1927-41 (ILLUS.) **$300**

Low Celtic Pink Tint Teapot

Teapot, Low Celtic patt., pink tint, 3rd period (ILLUS.) .... **$800-$1,200**

Undecorated Mask Pattern Teapot

Teapot, Mask patt., undecorated, 3rd period (ILLUS.) .... **$400-$500**

Neptune Pattern Teapot with Pink Tint

Teapot, Neptune patt., pink tint, 2nd period (ILLUS.) .... **$400-$600**

Ringhandle Teapot with Celtic Decoration

Teapot, Ringhandle patt., Celtic decoration, 3rd period (ILLUS.) .... **$800-$1,000**

Shamrock-Basketweave Teapot with Standard Decoration

Teapot, Shamrock-Basketweave patt., standard decoration, 3rd period (ILLUS.) .... **$400-$500**

Shell Pattern Teapot with Pink & Gold Decoration

Teapot, Shell patt., footed, pink & gold decoration, 1st period (ILLUS.) .... **$800-$1,000**

Sydney Pattern Teapot with Pink Tint

Teapot, Sydney patt., pink tint, 2nd period (ILLUS.) .... **$600-$800**

Early Undecorated Thistle Pattern Teapot

Teapot, Thistle patt., undecorated, 1st period (ILLUS.) .... **$600-$800**

Gold-trimmed Thorn Pattern Teapot

Teapot, Thorn patt., gold trim, 1st period (ILLUS.) .... **$600-$1,000**

Early Tridacna Teapot with Gold Trim

Teapot, Tridacna patt., gold trim, 1st period (ILLUS.) .... **$400-$600**

Vases & Spills
Aberdeen vases, left & right, flowered, medium size (D58-II), pr. **$1,600**
Celtic Vase-J, D1199-III, each **$460**

Clam Shell & Griffin Belleek Vase

Clam Shell & Griffin vase, pink tint, D140-I (ILLUS.) **$2,200**

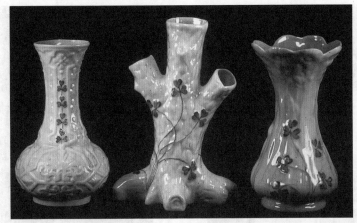

Daisy & Shamrock Spills

Double Fish vase, painted, D1204-I, 11 1/2" h. (ILLUS.) **$2,400**

Belleek Coral and Shell Vase

Coral and Shell Vase, D133-II (ILLUS.) **$880**
Daisy spill, D178-III (ILLUS. right with Shamrock spills, top of page).................... **$220**

Belleek Flowered Spill

Flowered Spill, raised on twig feet, large size, D45-III (ILLUS.) **$380**

Belleek Figural Frog Vase

Frog vase, model of frog w/head up & mouth open, large size, D181-II (ILLUS.)
.... **$1,000**
Ivy Stump spill (D147-I) **$420**

Irish Belleek Double Fish Vase

Belleek Marine Jug Vase

Marine Jug Vase, coral designs, ruffled
foot, D134-II (ILLUS.) **$800**
Prince Arthur Vase, flowered (D1218-II) **$920**

Belleek Ram's Head Flower Holder

Ram's Head Flower Holder, figural,
D1180-I (ILLUS.) **$1,400**

Belleek Rathmore Flowerpot

Rathmore flowerpot, bulbous w/flaring
scalloped rim & applied flowers, D43-II
(ILLUS.) **$2,200**

Belleek Ribbon Vase

Ribbon Vase, flowered, D1220-III (ILLUS.) ... **$340**

Seahorse and Shell Flower Holder

Seahorse and Shell flower holder, rectan-
gular base, D129-I (ILLUS.) **$1,200**
Shamrock spill, D191-III (ILLUS. left with
Daisy spill, top previous page) **$220**
Shamrock Tree Stump spill, D1224-III
(ILLUS. center with Daisy spill, top pre-
vious page) **$240**

Irish Belleek Specimen Holder

Specimen holder, composed of small ball-
shaped vases, large size, D185-I,
5 1/2" h. (ILLUS.) **$1,200**
Triple Fish Vase, painted (D1231-I) **$4,600**

Cardium on Shell Dish & Sycamore and Worcester Plates

Celtic bowl of roses, h.p. colors of dark pink, yellow & green, D1510-VII (ILLUS.) **$2,600**

Cleary salt dip, oblong, pink tint & gilt trim (D295-II) **$100**

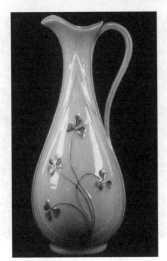

Belleek Typha Jug Spill

Typha Jug Spill, decorated w/shamrocks, D1790-VI (ILLUS.) **$120**

Tea Wares - Miscellaneous
Items produced, but with NO matching tea set pieces.

Cardium on Shell dish, Size 2, pink tint, D261-I (ILLUS. center with Sycamore & Worcester plates, top of page) **$180**

Decorated Belleek Flask

Flask, ovoid form, gilt Harp, Hound & Castle logo at the center in gold, D1523-I (ILLUS.) **$2,200**

Greek Dessert Plate with Scene

Greek dessert plate, tinted & gilt-trimmed, h.p. center scene titled "Eel Fishery on the Erne," by E. Sheerin, D29-I (ILLUS.) **$3,600**

Hand-painted Celtic Bowl of Roses

Irish Pot Creamer & Open Sugar Bowl

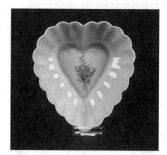

Flower-decorated Heart Plate

Heart plate, scalloped edges, Size 2, h.p. flowers, D635-III (ILLUS.).......................... **$120**

Irish Pot creamer & open sugar bowl, Size 2, D232-II, pr. (ILLUS., top of page)... **$240**

Model of Irish Harp

Model of Irish Harp, small size, D77-II (ILLUS.) **$400**

Armorial Souvenir Loving Cup

Loving cup, three-handled, armorial souvenir, D1503-I (ILLUS.) **$400**

Shell-shaped Nautilus Creamer

Nautilus creamer, shell-shaped, pink tint, D279-I (ILLUS.)... **$600**

Scenic Celtic Commemorative Plate

Plate, pottery, Scenic Celtic Commemorative Plate, painted & gilded, D1553-V (ILLUS.).... **$800**

Scenic Plate with Fancy Gilt Border

Plate, scenic center of Irish peasant homes w/ornate gilt scroll border, h.p. by former pottery manager Cyril Arnold, artist-signed & w/what appears to be "15 PA" following the signature, 8 1/2" d., D1527-IV (ILLUS.) **$1,200**

Ring Handle Decorated Plate

Ring Handle plate, 6" d., Limoges Decoration, D822-I (ILLUS.) **$600**
Shell creamer, large size (D601-I) **$720**

Belleek Oblong Shell Jelly

Shell jelly, oblong, painted, D798-I (ILLUS.) **$520**
Shell plateau, bowl-shaped, medium size, D792-I (ILLUS., bottom of page) **$380**

Bowl-shaped Shell Plateau

Two Large Swan Creamers

Swan creamer, figural, large size, D254-III
(ILLUS. left, top of page) **$320**
Swan creamer, figural, large size, D254-VI
(ILLUS. right, top of page) **$120**
Sycamore plate, leaf-shaped, Size 2, pink
tint, D642-II (ILLUS. right with Cardium
on Shell dish, top of page 88) **$120**
Toy creamer & open sugar bowl, Cleary
patt. (D249-III), pr. **$160**
Toy creamer & open sugar bowl, Ivy patt.,
small size (D241-I), pr. **$240**

Belleek Shamrock Wedding Cup

Wedding cup, three-handled, Shamrock
patt., h.p. trim, D2105-II (ILLUS.) **$640**
Worcester plate, Size 2, D682-II (ILLUS.
left with Cardium on Shell dish) **$120**

Bennington

*Bennington wares, which ranged from stone-
ware to parian and porcelain, were made in Bennington, Vermont, primarily in two potteries, one
in which Captain John Norton and his descen-
dants were principals, and the other in which
Christopher Webber Fenton (also once associated
with the Nortons) was a principal. Various marks
are found on the wares made in the two major potteries, including J. & E. Norton, E. & L. P. Norton,
L. Norton & Co., Norton & Fenton, Edward*

*Norton, Lyman Fenton & Co., Fenton's Works,
United States Pottery Co., U.S.P. and others.*

*The popular pottery with the mottled brown on
yellowware glaze was also produced in Bennington, but such wares should be referred to as
"Rockingham" or "Bennington-type" unless they
can be specifically attributed to a Bennington,
Vermont factory.*

Round Waisted Bennington Cuspidor

Cuspidor, short round waisted shape
w/side hole, Flint Enamel glaze, Type A
impress mark on base, mid-19th c., 8" d.,
3 3/4" h. (ILLUS.) **$144**

Bennington Rockingham Toby Pitcher

Toby pitcher, figural seated Mr. Toby, dark
brown mottled Rockingham glaze, un-
marked, 6" h. (ILLUS.) **$259**
Wash pitcher, footed octagonal tapering
ovoid ribbed body w/a high, wide arched
spout & high angled handle, streaky dark
brown & blue Flint Enamel glaze, oval impressed mark of Lyman Fenton & Co.,
1849, 11 3/4" h. **$863**

Berlin (KPM)

The mark KPM was used at Meissen from 1724 to 1725, and was later adopted by the Royal Factory, Konigliche Porzellan Manufaktur, in Berlin. At various periods it has been incorporated with the Brandenburg scepter, the Prussian eagle or the crowned globe. The same letters were also adopted by other factories in Germany in the late 19th and early 20th centuries. With the end of the German monarchy in 1918, the name of the firm was changed to Staatliche Porzellan Manufaktur and though production was halted during World War II, the factory was rebuilt and is still in business. The exquisite paintings on porcelain were produced at the close of the 19th century and are eagerly sought by collectors today.

Oval KPM Plaque with Family Scene

Plaque, oval, a colorful scene of a Middle Eastern family showing a mother, father, son & daughter sitting on an upholstered sofa, within an ornately scrolling gilt gesso oval frame, plaque impressed on the back "KPM - T," 7 1/2 x 9 1/4" (ILLUS.) **$960**

Rare KPM Oval Portrait Plaque

Plaque, oval, decorated w/a bust portrait of a lovely young woman w/a red flower in her long flowing brown hair, a deep yellow off-the-shoulder shawl, in an ornately

molded oval gilt-plaster frame, KPM mark on the back, late 19th c., plaque 8 1/2 x 10 1/2", overall 15 x 18" (ILLUS.) **$11,155**

KPM Plaque with Portrait of Woman

Plaque, oval, finely painted w/the head of a lovely young woman w/long curly brown hair gazing upward, bright blue eyes, back w/impressed KPM mark, two small scratches in the background, slight frame damage, late 19th c., plaque 8 x 11" (ILLUS.) **$2,243**

Berlin Plaque of Young Beauty

Plaque, oval, titled "Meditation," bust-length portrait of a brunette beauty w/a red flower in her hair, diaphonous white & pale blue drapery around her shoulders, artist-signed, impressed monogram & sceptre marks, late 19th - early 20th c., unframed, 6 5/8 x 8 7/8" (ILLUS.) **$7,800**

KPM Plaque with Semi-Nude Woman

Plaque, rectangular, a three-quarters length standing portrait of a semi-nude young woman w/long brown hair & a red robe around her waist, artist-signed, unframed, flake to one corner, 6 3/8 x 9 3/8" (ILLUS.)............................ **$4,025**

KPM Plaque with Scene of Nude Woman & Monk

Plaque, rectangular, h.p. w/a color scene of a nude woman lying helpless at the waters edge w/a distressed monk at her side gazing up to the heavens, back impressed "KPM - W - i - 255," late 19th c., in walnut shadowbox frame, plaque 7 x 9 1/2" (ILLUS.) **$5,175**

Plaque of Pretty Young Girl

Plaque, rectangular, three-quarter length portrait of a young girl seated in a woodland setting winding thread for her embroidery, impressed monogram & sceptre mark, late 19th - early 20th c., in giltwood frame, 8 3/4 x 10 3/4" (ILLUS.) **$7,200**

Plaque with Women and Child

Plaque, rectangular, titled "Bonheur Maternal," depicting an interior scene w/two young women rocking a child in a hammock accented in gold, impressed monogram & sceptre mark, early 20th c., in giltwood frame, 7 1/2 x 10" (ILLUS.)............ **$6,000**

Part of a Set of Vegetable-decorated Salad Plates

Rare Plaque of Woodland Beauty

Plaque, rectangular, titled "Fruhling," a bust-length portrait of a dark haired beauty w/white blossoms in her hair in a wooden background of blossoming trees, wearing diaphanous white draped gown, artist-signed, impressed monogram & sceptre mark, late 19th - early 20th c., in giltwood frame, 10 1/4 x 12 3/8" (ILLUS.) **$12,000**

Plates, salad, 8 1/2" d., each finely painted at the top w/a still-life of vegetables, herbs & grains, titled in German on the back, the lobed rim trimmed in gold, blue sceptre & iron-red orb marks, late 19th c., set of 12 (ILLUS. of part, top of page)... **$60,000**

Betty Lou Nichols Ceramics

Although Betty Lou Nichols (1922-1995) created a wide variety of ceramic figurines, she's best known for her distinctive line of "lady head vases." From the 1940s well into the 1960s, such vases, many sporting oversized hats with openings in the crown to accommodate small bouquets, were popular with florist shops and consumers. Today "Betty Lou's" are among the most sought-after head vases. They're immediately recognizable by their darkly-fringed, three-dimensional eyelashes, oversized hair bows and coiled ceramic curls.

A California native, Nichols immersed herself in art from an early age, later studying at Fullerton Junior College under noted ceramist Mary Hodgedon. After marriage and initial employment as a photographer, Nichols opened her first ceramics studio in 1945, in the backyard of her parents' La Habra home. As with many mid-1940s ceramics firms, the timing was right since overseas imports of decorative objects had been cut off during World War II.

Nichols' initial acclaim came with a series of "Gay 90s" figurines created for Bullock's of Los Angeles. The idea for her lady head vases is credited to noted sales representative Ruth Sloan (who also represented Kay Finch). With the introduction of head vases, success came quickly; in 1949 Betty Lou Nichols Ceramics relocated to a larger La Habra factory, eventually employing over 30 workers.

Betty Lou Nichols Ceramics remained in operation until 1962. In addition to head vases, planters and figurines, production items included decanters, plates, mugs and other decorative ware. The firm also took on special contracted projects such as ceramic figures based on characters from the Walt Disney movie "Fantasia," and containers for products from California's Knott's Berry Farm. After her retirement from ceramic work, Nichols embarked on a successful second career as a painter, specializing in portraits and landscapes.

Abundant ruffles and flourishes contribute to the appeal and value of Betty Lou Nichols ceramics, but also contribute to their fragility. It's rare today to find a Betty Lou in pristine condition, with all eyelashes, curls and bodice trim intact. Fortunately, Betty Lou repair has become a booming cottage industry and restoration experts are readily available to bring back the bloom to these glamour girls.

Advisor/photographer for this category is Donald-Brian Johnson, an author and lecturer specializing in mid-twentieth century design. Reference material courtesy of Maddy Gordon, author of Head Vases, Etc.: The Artistry of Betty Lou Nichols (Schiffer Publishing, Ltd., 2002).

Dick Planter, Holly Figurine & Tom Planter

"Adele," Gay 90s figurine, 9" h. ...... **$1,000-$1,200**

Anna Figurine and Fritz Planter

"Anna," figurine, 9" h. (ILLUS. right with Fritz planter) .... **$75-$100**
"Dick," planter, 5" h. (ILLUS. right with Holly figurine & Tom planter, top of page) .. **$50-$75**
"Ermyntrude," head vase, 8 1/2" h. ..... **$500-$600**

Nichols "Florabelle" Head Vase

"Florabelle," head vase, 10" h. (ILLUS.)
.... **$950-$1,000**
"Fritz," planter, 9 1/2" h. (ILLUS. left with Anna figurine, previous column) .... **$75-$100**
"Holly," figurine, 7" h. (ILLUS. center with Dick planter & Tom planter, top of page)
.... **$50-$75**

Nichols "Madonna" Planter

"Madonna," planter, 8" h. (ILLUS.)......... **$75-$100**

Nichols "Margot" Planter

"Margot," planter, 9 1/2" h. (ILLUS., previous page) .... **$150-$175**

Nichols "Mary Lou" Head Vase

"Mary Lou," head vase, 5 1/2" h. (ILLUS.)
.... **$200-$225**

"Santa" Figurine and "Mrs. Santa" Figurine/Planter

"Mrs. Santa," figurine/planter, 9" h. (ILLUS.
right with Santa figurine) .... **$100-$125**
"Nora," figurine, 10" h. (ILLUS., top next
column) .... **$200-$225**
"Olga the Flower Vendor & Tina," planter,
11" l. (ILLUS., middle next column)... **$450-$475**
"Portia Piggy Bank," 8" h. .... **$150-$175**
"Santa," figurine, 9 1/2" h. (ILLUS. left with
Mrs. Santa, middle this column)........ **$100-$125**
"Singing Angel," figurine, 8" h. (ILLUS.,
bottom next column).............................. **$50-$75**
"Tom," planter, 6" h. (ILLUS. left with Dick
planter & Holly figurine, top previous
page) .... **$50-$75**
"Tom Cat Nodder," nodding-head figurine
.... **$100-$125**
"Valerie," head vase, 6" h..................... **$350-$400**

Nichols "Nora" Figurine

Nichols "Olga the Flower Vendor & Tina" Planter

Nichols "Singing Angel" Figurine

Fine Bisque Figure of a Reclining Nude

Bisque

Bisque is biscuit china, fired a single time but not glazed. Some bisque is decorated with colors. Most abundant from the Victorian era are figures and groups, but other pieces, from busts to vases, were made by numerous potteries in the United States and abroad. Reproductions have been produced for many years, so care must be taken when seeking antique originals.

Fine Bisque Figure of a Seated Nude

Tall Bisque Classical Maiden Figure

Figure of a classical maiden, standing wearing a shear robe w/pink & yellow drapes at her waist, pouring from a small jug, blue anchor mark, 19th c., 16 1/2" h. (ILLUS.).. **$259**

Figure of a nude woman, reclining on her stomach w/her head raised, painted hair & facial features, marked on the bottom "1627 Germany," early 20th c., 6" l. (ILLUS., top of page)...................... **$1,035**

Figure of a nude woman, seated w/her legs extended & her hands clasped under her chin, h.p. facial features w/smiling mouth, brown mohair wig & scarf, base marked "406R," Germany, early 20th c., 3 1/4" l., 3" h. (ILLUS., top next column).. **$805**

Bisque Figures of Young Couple

Figures of a Colonial lady & man, she seated with one hand raised & wearing a creamy flower-decorated gown trimmed in pink; he seated facing her wearing a floral-decorated coat, vest & breeches & high pink boots, w/later wooden chairs, unmarked, ca. 1900, 11" h., pr. (ILLUS.) .... **$175-$200**

Cute Bisque Victorian Children

Figures of a young Victorian girl & boy, she standing on a rockwork base wearing a high-fronted blue bonnet, tight-fitting knee-length dress w/blue neck scarf & pink ruffle trim; he standing on a rock-work base wearing a straw boater hat, blue jacket & pink tie above pink knee-breeches, long white stockings & pink shoes, facing pair, R-in-Diamond mark, possibly Rudolstadt, Germany, ca. 1900, 14 1/2" h., pr. (ILLUS.) .... **$150-$200**

Fancy Regency Posed Couple in Bisque

Figures of lady & gentleman in Regency costume, each standing on a low circular fluted brown base, she wearing an Empire gown in pale green decorated w/red floral sprigs, elbow-length gloves & holding a huge open pink fan behind her head; he wearing a pale blue cockade hat, pink cape, pale green jacket, ruffled cravat & pink vest over pink-striped pale green kneebreeches, holding up one arm to look through a monocle, marked "Heubach -

Made in Germany," early 20th c., minor base flakes, 14" h., facing pr. (ILLUS.) **$489**

German Bisque Regency Girl & Boy

Figures of Regency girl & boy, she standing on a domed scroll-trimmed tan base, wearing a tall shell-shaped bonnet framing her tightly curled brown hair, also a high-waisted pale green pink-trimmed dress w/a long shawl, holding a small brown & white dog in one hand & a long basket at her other shoulder; he standing on a matching base, wearing a very high-brimmed hat & a very long overcoat w/flaring lapels & collar in pale blue & pink, a coral-colored cravat, white shirt & flower-painted pale yellow kneebreeches, a sack in one hand, a cane in the other, attributed to Heubach, Germany, 13 1/2" h., pr. (ILLUS.) **$230**

Fashionable Bisque Regency Couple

Figures of Regency lady & gentleman, each standing on a tall cylindrical pale green & yellow leafy scroll & blossom base, she wearing a high-fronted yellow bonnet, a long-sleeved gown w/a tight bodice & decorated in shades of light & dark yellow, one hand lifting the hem of the gown; he standing wearing a large scallop & feather-decorated yellow cockade hat, a long buttoned jacket in light & dark yellow & matching kneebreeches, holding a small floral bouquet, impressed mark of Heubach, Germany, ca. 1900, 15" h., facing pr. (ILLUS.) **$288**

German Bisque Girl & Boy Figures

Figures of Victorian girl & boy, she standing on a rockwork base, wearing a high blue bonnet, green & white dress w/pink ribbon belt, carrying a basket over her arm; he standing on a rockwork base, wearing a pink & white long jacket over striped blue kneebreeches, a blue tam w/a pink ribbon, carrying a rectangular basket in one hand, Germany, ca. 1900, 14" h., pr. (ILLUS.) **$184**

Bisque Figures of Peasant Children

Figures of young peasant girl & boy, she standing on a rockwork base wearing a long dress decorated w/clover designs, balancing a small book on her head & carrying a jug in one hand; he standing on a rockwork base wearing a hat, shirt & clover-decorated rolled-up pants, playing a small lute, attributed to Heubach, Germany, ca. 1900, 15 1/2" h., pr. (ILLUS.) **$259**

Bisque 18th C. Couple in Fancy Dress

Figures of young woman & man in fancy 18th c. dress, she standing on a scrolled base, wearing a pale blue riding hat, pale blue swirled gown w/puffed shoulders & tight sleeves, large bow at her neck, leaning on a scroll pedestal holding a closed fan; he standing on a matching base w/scroll pedestal, wearing a pale blue tricorn hat w/feather, long pale blue jacket w/ruffled cravat, gold & sprig-decorated pale blue vest & kneebreeches, probably German, ca. 1900, 13" h., facing pr. (ILLUS.) ...... **$175-$200**

Blue Ridge Dinnerwares

The small town of Erwin, Tennessee, was the home of the Southern Potteries, Inc., originally founded by E.J. Owen in 1917 and first called the Clinchfield Pottery.

In the early 1920s Charles W. Foreman purchased the plant and revolutionized the company's output, developing the popular line of handpainted wares sold as "Blue Ridge" dinnerwares. Freehand painted by women from the surrounding hills, these colorful dishes in many patterns continued in production until the plant's closing in 1957.

Blue Ridge
Hand Painted
Underglaze
Southern Potteries Inc.
MADE IN U.S.A.

Blue Ridge Dinnerwares Mark

Ashtray, advertising for Clinchfield Railroad $75

Blue Ridge Fall Colors Ashtray

Ashtray, individual, Fall Colors patt. (ILLUS.)..... $25
Ashtray, individual size, Butterfly patt............. $25
Ashtray, regular type, Staccato patt. $15
Basket, aluminum frame holding a Colonial
    shape bowl in the Red Flower patt.............. $15
Boston eggcup, Skyline shape, Becky patt. $10
Bowl, 5 1/4" d., Piecrust shape, Green Briar
    patt. $8
Bowl, child's, Astor shape, Blue Pig patt........ $100
Bowl, 5 1/4" d., cereal, Candlewick shape,
    Quaker Apple patt. $5
Bowl, 6" d., cereal, Candlewick shape,
    Quaker Apple patt. $10
Bowl, 7" l., tab-handled, Colonial shape,
    Wild Strawberry patt...................................... $25
Bowl, 10" d., salad-type, Candlewick
    shape, Mount Vernon patt............................ $30
Butter dish, cov., Skyline shape, Plantation
    Ivy patt... $25
Cake lifter, Berry Delicious patt. $35
Cake lifter, Berry Delicious patt., 9" l. $25
Cake plate, 11" d., Candlewick shape,
    Bleeding Heart patt. $35
Cake plate, footed, Antique Leaf patt.............. $25

Blue Ridge Fruit Fantasy Cake Plate

Cake plate, handled, Fruit Fantasy patt.,
    9 x 10 1/2" (ILLUS.)...................................... $75
Cake plate, handled, Yellow Nocturne patt...... $50
Cake plate, round, Candlewick shape,
    Bleeding Heart patt., 11 1/2" d. $30
Candy box, cov., Dogtooth Violet patt. $200
Casserole, cov., Colonial shape, Ridge Dai-
    sy patt. $45
Celery dish, leaf-shaped, Easter Parade
    patt., 11" l. $22
Celery dish, oval, Skyline shape, Forest
    Fruit patt.. $10
Chocolate pot, cov., china, Chintz patt.,
    9 1/2" h... $165
Chocolate pot, cov., Fall Colors patt. $350
Cigarette box, cov., Ridge Rose patt. $100
Cigarette box, cov., square, Butterfly patt.,
    4 1/4" w.. $110

Rare Mariner Pattern Blue Ridge Coaster

Coaster/butter pat, Astor shape, Mariner
    patt., 4" d. (ILLUS.) $150
Coaster/butter pat, Gum Drop Tree patt........ $50
Coaster/butter pat, Mariner patt. $100
Coffeepot, cov., Ovide shape, Wild Straw-
    berry patt... $150
Creamer, demitasse size, Astor shape, For-
    get-Me-Not patt. $45
Creamer, open, large size, Colonial shape,
    Red Nocturne patt... $20
Creamer, pedestal base, Chintz patt. $75
Creamer, regular size, Candlewick shape,
    Mountain Ivy patt.. $15
Creamer & sugar bowl, pedestal-based,
    Rose of Sharon patt., the set $95
Creamer & sugar bowl, regular size, Colo-
    nial shape, Garden Lane patt., the set........ $35
Cup & saucer, demitasse size, Colonial
    shape, Peony patt., saucer 5" d., the set $55
Cup & saucer, demitasse-type, Colonial
    shape, Peony patt., cup 2 1/8" h., the set .. $100
Cup & saucer, jumbo size, Colonial shape,
    Red Apple patt., cup 3 3/4" h., the set $100
Cup & saucer, jumbo size, Colonial shape,
    Red Apple patt., saucer 7 1/2" d., the set .. $100
Cup & saucer, regular size, Candlewick
    shape, Bluebell Bouquet patt., saucer
    6" d., the set $17
Cup & saucer, regular size, Colonial shape,
    Christmas Tree patt. $50

Cup & saucer, regular size, Colonial shape, Rock Rose patt... $15

Eggcup, double, Brittany patt......................... $100

Egg plate, Rooster patt.................................... $85

Feeding dish, child's, Flower Children patt. .. $150

Gravy boat, Colonial shape, Wrinkled Rose patt., 7 1/2" l... $25

Mug, child's, Yellow Bunny patt., 2 3/4" h.
.... $225-$250

Pie baker, round, Triplet patt., 10" d. $30

Pitcher, 4" h., miniature, Virginia shape, Sheree patt... $300

Pitcher, 4 1/2" h., Alice shape, Romance patt... $65

Pitcher, 5 1/2" h., Chick shape, Flora patt. $100

Pitcher, 5 1/2" h., china, Chick shape, Flora patt.. $110

Pitcher, 5 5/8" h., Clara shape, Galore patt. $80

Pitcher, 5 3/4" h., Antique shape, Tulip Row patt.. $150

Pitcher, 5 3/4" h., Helen shape, Sea Mist patt... $100

Pitcher, 5 7/8" h., earthenware, Abby shape, See Green patt............................... $40

Pitcher, 6" h., china, Martha shape, Sea Green patt... $85

Pitcher, 6" h., earthenware, Abby shape, yellow $40

Pitcher, 6 1/8" h., Martha shape, Buttermilk patt... $65

Pitcher, 6 1/8" h., Spiral shape, Tralee Rose patt.. $40

Blue Ridge China Anniversary Song Pitcher

Pitcher, 6 1/2" h., china, Swirl shape, Anniversary Song patt. (ILLUS.)........................ $175

Pitcher, 6 1/2" h., earthenware, Martha shape, Blue Beauty patt. $65

Pitcher, 6 3/4" h., Sculptured Fruit shape, decorated w/blue grapes........................... $100

Pitcher, 6 3/4" h., Sculptured Fruit shape, decorated w/yellow grapes......................... $75

Pitcher, 7" h., Sculptured Fruit shape, decorated w/purple grapes........................... $50

Pitcher, 8 1/8" h., Betsy shape, Anniversary Song patt.. $250

Pitcher, 8 1/4" h., Rebecca shape, Whig Rose patt.. $150

Plate, child's, Flower Children patt................ $100

Plate, 6" d., bread & butter, Colonial shape, Paper Roses patt. $8

Plate, 7" d., dessert, Piecrust shape, Magnolia patt... $15

Plate, 7" d., round, dessert-type, Colonial shape, Orchard Glory patt........................... $10

Plate, 7" w., square, Apple Trio patt............... $25

Plate, 7" w., square, Poinsettia patt. $25

Plate, 8" d., round salad-type, Colonial shape, Garden Flowers patt...................... $25

Plate, 8" d., round salad-type, Colonial shape, Tiger Lily patt................................ $15

Plate, 8" d., salad, Colonial shape, Orchard Glory patt... $13

Plate, 8" d., salad, Skyline shape, Windmill patt... $60

Plate, 9" d., luncheon, Colonial shape, Big Apple patt... $12

Plate, 9" d., luncheon, Skyline shape, Red Barn patt... $35

Plate, 9" d., round, dinner-type, Candlewick shape, Bluebell Bouquet patt.................... $15

Plate, 9" d., round dinner-type, Skyline shape, Stanhome Ivy patt. $8

Plate, 10" d., dinner, Colonial shape, Christmas Tree with Mistletoe patt. $75

Plate, 10" d., dinner, Colonial shape, Iris Anne patt... $28

Plate, 10" d., round, dinner-type, Colonial shape, Christmas Tree patt......................... $85

Plate, 10" d., round dinner-type, Colonial shape, Wrinkled Rose patt........................... $20

Plate, 10" d., round, dinner-type, Skyline shape, Christmas Doorway patt.................... $90

Plate, 10" d., round dinner-type, Skyline shape, Red Barn patt.................................. $35

Platter, 11 1/2" l., Candlewick shape, Dahlia patt.. $25

Platter, 11 1/2" l., Colonial shape, Polka Dot patt... $25

Platter, 12" d., Colonial shape, Berryville patt... $30

Platter, 13" d., Candlewick shape, Blue Moon patt.. $30

Platter, 13" l., Colonial shape, Apple Trio patt... $30

Platter, 14" l., Colonial shape, Pristine patt.
.... $35

Platter, 15" l., Skyline shape, Loretta patt........ $18

Relish dish, deep shell shape, Ridge Rose patt., 9 x 9"... $95

Relish dish, four-part w/center handle, Ridge Daisy patt., 8 1/2" w...................... $45

Salad fork, Fruit Fantasy patt. $50

Salad spoon, Fruit Fantasy patt. $50

Salt & pepper shakers, Barrel shape, Paper Roses patt., pr. $75

Salt & pepper shakers, Blossom Top shape, one w/a red flower & yellow center, other w/colors reversed, pr. $30

Salt & pepper shakers, Bud Top patt., one w/yellow bud top, other w/pink bud top, pr.. $75

Salt & pepper shakers, china, Chintz patt., 5 3/4" h., pr.. $74

Salt & pepper shakers, Dominecker shape, one decorated w/a rooster, the other a hen, pr... $110

Blue Ridge Mardi Gras Range Set

Salt & pepper shakers, Range shape, Mardi Gras patt., pr. $30

Salt & pepper shakers, range-size, Mardi Gras patt., 4 3/8" h., pr. (ILLUS., top of page) $25

Salt & pepper shakers, short, Skyline shape, Cheerio patt., 2 1/2" h., pr. $15

Salt & pepper shakers, Skyline shape, Breakfast Bar patt., pr. $20

Salt & pepper shakers, Tall China shape, Chintz patt., pr. $100

Snack plate w/cup well, Skyline shape, Spiderweb Blue patt. $15

Snack set: plate w/cup well & matching cup; Colonial shape, Garden Lane patt., 8" d., the set $30

Snack tray, Martha shape, Garden Lane patt. $100

Soup bowl, tab-handled, Colonial shape, Mickey patt., 7" d. $15

Soup bowl, tab-handled, Candlewick shape, Bluebell Bouquet patt., 6" d. $15

Soup plate, flanged rim, Colonial shape, Mardi Gras patt., 8" d. $15

Soup plate, flanged rim, Candlewick shape, Sweet Clover patt., 8" d. $15

Spoon rest, Apple patt. $15

Spoon rest, Apple patt., 6 1/2" l. $18

Sugar bowl, cov., regular size, Candlewick shape, Mountain Ivy patt. $20

Sugar bowl, open, demitasse size, Astor shape, Forget-Me-Not patt., 1 7/8" h. $45

Sugar bowl, open, large, Colonial shape, Polka Dot patt. $20

Sugar bowl, pedestal base, Chintz patt. $75

Teapot, cov., china, Mini Ball shape, Dogtooth Violet patt., 5 1/2" h. $225

Teapot, cov., Colonial shape, Becky patt., 8"h. $110

Teapot, cov., Colonial shape, Crab Apple patt., 8 1/2" h. $175

Teapot, cov., demitasse size, Astor shape, Hollyberry patt., 6 1/2" h. $350

Tidbit tray, one-tier, Colonial shape, Carol's Roses patt. $30

Tidbit tray, two-tier, Colonial shape, Northstar Cherry patt. $45

Toast dish, cov., Jonquil patt. $110

Toast plate, cov., Astor shape, Jonquil patt. .. $150

Tray, demitasse size, Candlewick patt., Rosebuds patt. $90

Vase, 5 1/8" h., Bulbous shape, Hibiscus patt. $80

Vase, 5 1/4" h., Bud shape, Helen patt. $150

Vase, 8" h., boot-shaped, Summertime patt. .... $75-$100

Blue Ridge China Stephanie Vase

Vase, 8" h., china, ornate loop shoulder handles, Stephanie patt. (ILLUS.) $65

Vase, 8" h., Handled shape, Stephanie patt. .. $105

Vase, 9 1/4" h., ruffle-top style, Delphine patt. .... $75-$125

Vase, 9 1/4" h., Ruffled Top shape, Melody
patt. $30

Vegetable bowl, oval, Candlewick shape,
Brunswick patt., 9" l. $20

Vegetable bowl, oval, Colonial shape,
Poinsettia patt., 7 x 9" $26

Vegetable bowl, round, Colonial shape,
Fruit Punch patt., 9" d. $30

Vegetable bowl, round, Colonial shape,
Fruit Punch patt., 9" d. $35

Vegetable bowl, round, Colonial shape,
Savannah patt., 9" d. $25

Blue & White Pottery

*The category of blue and white or blue and
grey pottery includes a wide variety of pottery,
earthenware and stoneware items widely produced in this country in the late 19th century
right through the 1930s. Originally marketed as
inexpensive wares, most pieces featured a white or
grey body molded with a fruit, flower or geometric
design and then trimmed with bands or splashes
of blue to highlight the molded pattern. Pitchers,
butter crocks and salt boxes are among the
numerous items produced, but other kitchenwares
and chamber sets are also found. Values vary
depending on the rarity of the embossed pattern
and the depth of color of the blue trim; the darker
the blue, the better. Some entries refer to several
different books on blue and white pottery. These
books are: Blue & White Stoneware, Pottery &
Crockery by Edith Harbin (1977, Collector Books,
Paducah, KY); Stoneware in the Blue and White
by M.H. Alexander (1993 reprint, Image Graph-
ics, Inc., Paducah, KY); and Blue & White Stoneware by Kathryn McNerney (1995, Collector
Books, Paducah, KY).*

Baking dish, embossed Peacock patt.,
round w/heavy egg-and-dart-molded rim
over gently curved sides, Brush-McCoy
Pottery Co., 9" d. (ILLUS., top next col-
umn) $800

Bean pot, cov., nearly spherical body
w/small loop shoulder handle, inset flat
cover w/knob finial, relief-molded label
"Boston Baked Beans," blue Swirl patt.,

6 3/4" h. (ILLUS. right with Brickers
Cookie Jar, bottom of page) $250

Embossed Peacock Baking Dish

Wesson Oil Red Wing Beater Jar

Beater jar, cylindrical w/molded rim, blue
band & printed advertising "Wesson Oil -
For Making Good Things to Eat," Red
Wing Pottery, 5 1/2" h. (ILLUS.) $100

Boston Baked Bean Pot & Brickers Cookie Jar

Diffused Blue Beater Jar & Plain 8" Pitcher

Beater jar, cylindrical w/narrow rim band, Diffused Blue, 4 3/4" h. (ILLUS. right with plain Diffused Blue 8" h. pitcher, top of page) **$125**

Embossed Greek Key Bowl

Bowl, 6" to 12" d., embossed Greek Key patt., Red Wing Pottery Co., depending on size (ILLUS. of one) .... **$100-$170**
Brush vase, Rose decal, ovoid body w/forked flaring rim, Western Stoneware, 5 1/2" h. (ILLUS. second from left with

Rose decal soap dish, shaving mug & hot water pitcher, bottom of page) **$175**

Red Wing Daisy Pattern Butter Crock

Butter crock, cov., embossed Daisy patt., Red Wing Pottery Co., found in three sizes, 3 1/2" h. (ILLUS.)................................. **$395**

Rose Decal Brush Vase, Soap Dish, Shaving Mug and Hot Water Pitcher

Two Greek Key Butter Crocks

Butter crock, cov., embossed Green Key border patt., Diffused Blue, no advertising, Western Stoneware Co., 4 1/4" h. (ILLUS. right with marked butter crock, top of page) **$150**

Butter crock, cov., embossed Green Key border patt., Diffused Blue, printed blue advertising, Western Stoneware Co., 4 1/4" h. (ILLUS. left with unmarked butter crock, top of page) **$295**

Butter crock, cov., stenciled Dutch Scene patt., Brush-McCoy Pottery Co., 6 3/4" d., 5" h. **$325**

Scroll Pattern Labeled Butter Crock

Diffused Blue Butter Crock with Advertising

Butter crock, cover & wire bail handle w/wooden grip, cylindrical w/flaring rim, Diffused Blue, printed black oval w/Kansas advertising, Western Stoneware Co., 6" h. (ILLUS.) **$750**

Butter crock, cover & wire bail handle w/wooden grip, cylindrical w/flaring rim, Diffused Blue, Scroll patt., printed blue frame around "Butter," Western Stoneware Co., found in various sizes (ILLUS., top next column)... **$150**

Red Wing Butter Crock with Advertising

Small & Large Embossed Willow Crackers Canisters

Butter crock, cover & wire bail handle w/wooden grip, cylindrical w/molded rim, printed rectangular panel w/advertising for the Hazel Pure Food Company, Red Wing Pottery (ILLUS., previous page) **$450**

Canister, cov., embossed Willow (Basketweave & Morning Glory) patt., "Crackers" (short), Brush-McCoy Pottery Co. (ILLUS. left with tall canister, top of page) **$550**

Canister, cov., embossed Willow (Basketweave & Morning Glory) patt., "Crackers" (tall), Brush-McCoy Pottery Co., average 6 1/2 to 7" h. (ILLUS. right with short canister, top of page) **$1,000**

Canister, cov., stenciled Vines patt., "Oat Meal," A.E. Hull Pottery Co., 7 1/4" h. (ILLUS. left with smaller "Rice" canister, top next column) **$400**

Canister, cov., stenciled Vines patt., "Rice," A.E. Hull Pottery Co., 5 1/2 to 6" h. (ILLUS. right with larger "Oat Meal" canister, top next column) **$250**

Two Stenciled Vines Canisters

Casserole, cov., embossed Flying Bird patt., A.E. Hull Pottery Co., 9 1/2" d. (ILLUS., bottom of page) **$600**

Embossed Flying Bird Casserole & Cover

Willow Chamber Pot & Slop Jar

Light Diffused Blue Swirl Coffeepot & Dark Diffused Blue Oval Coffeepot

Chamber pot, cov., embossed Willow (Basketweave & Morning Glory) patt., Brush-McCoy Pottery Co., 9 1/2" d., 8" h. (ILLUS. right with Willow slop jar, top of page)... **$325**

Coffeepot, cov., cylindrical w/side spout & long angled handle, inset domed cover w/large knob finial, metal bottom plate, dark blue Diffused Blue Oval patt., 11" h. (ILLUS. left with light blue Swirl pattern coffeepot, second from top of page) **$2,700**

Coffeepot, cov., light blue Swirl patt., tapering ovoid body w/a pointed rim spout, heavy C-form handle w/thumb rest, inset lid w/acorn finial, tin base w/bottom plate, 11 1/2" h. (ILLUS. right with dark blue Diffused Blue Oval pattern coffeepot, second from top of page) **$1,225**

Coffeepot, cov., embossed Bull's-Eye patt., w/bottom plate (ILLUS., next column) **$3,250**

Rare Bull's-Eye Pattern Coffeepot

Swirl Pattern Tapering Coffeepot

Marked Cookie Jar with Maple Leaves

Coffeepot, cov., dark blue Swirl patt., tapering ovoid body w/a pointed rim spout,
heavy C-form handle w/thumb rest, inset
lid w/acorn finial, tin base w/bottom plate,
11 1/2" h. (ILLUS.) **$1,225**

Cookie jar, cov., bulbous flat-bottomed
shape w/inset cover, Diffused Blue, printed in blue "Cookie Jar - Brickers," 8" d.
(ILLUS. left with Boston Baked Beans
pot, bottom of page 98) **$750**

Diffused Blue Cruet

Cruet, no stopper, spherical body w/a small
cylindrical neck w/a small rim spout, long
loop handle, Diffused Blue, 4" h. (ILLUS.) .. **$500**

Diffused Blue Western Cookie Jar

Cookie jar, cov., wide cylindrical shape
w/base bands & a flared rim w/inset cover, Diffused Blue, printed in black on the
front "Cookies," Western Stoneware Co.
(ILLUS.) **$600**

Cookie jar, cov., wide cylindrical shape
w/base bands & a flared rim w/inset cover,
Diffused Blue, printed in large black Gothic letters flanked by maple leaves "Cookies," Western Stoneware Co. (ILLUS., top
next column) **$800**

Banded Stoneware Egg Bucket

Diffused Blue Sta-Hot Foot Warmer

Egg bucket, cylindrical w/wire bail handle & wooden grip, decorated w/thin blue & white bands, 5" h. (ILLUS., previous page)............ **$200**

Embossed Beaded Rose Ewer & Basin Set

Ewer & basin set, embossed Beaded Rose patt., A.E. Hull Pottery Co., the set (ILLUS.) **$750**

Foot warmer, paneled cylindrical shape, metal stopper in end, Diffused Blue, blue printed logo for Sta-Hot, printed "Pat. Apl'd For" on back, loop side handle (ILLUS., top of page) **$250**

Hot water pitcher, 7" h., Rose decal, bulbous lobed body w/wide flaring rim, loop handle, Western Stoneware (ILLUS. far right with Rose decal brush vase, soap dish & shaving mug, bottom of page 99) ... **$200**

Lard bucket, cov., cylindrical w/molded rim, Diffused Blue, no advertising on the front, missing bail handle, Western Stoneware, 5" h. **$325**

Diffused Blue Advertising Lard Bucket

Lard bucket, cov., cylindrical w/molded rim, Diffused Blue, printed advertising on the front, missing bail handle, Western Stoneware, 5" h. (ILLUS.) **$425**

Western Stoneware Marked Lard Bucket & Stupid Pitcher

Barrel-shaped Shaded Blue Mug & Pitcher

Lard bucket, cover & wire bail handle w/wooden grip, cylindrical, Diffused Blue, printed in large Gothic letters "Lard" flanked by maple leaves, Western Stoneware, 5" h. (ILLUS. left with Stupid pitcher, bottom previous page) **$325**

Red Wing Hazel Brand Lard Bucket

Lard bucket, cover & wire bail handle w/wooden grip, cylindrical w/molded rim, large printed blue rectangular panel w/advertising for Hazel Brand Pure Leaf Lard, Red Wing Pottery (ILLUS.) **$450**

Mug, barrel-shaped, shaded dark to light blue, 4 1/2" h. (ILLUS. left with matching pitcher, top of page) **$100**

Peanut butter crock with wooden lid, cylindrical w/molded rim, printed in a blue rectangle "Bishop's Peanut Butter - 32 Pounds Net Weight" (ILLUS., top next column) **$550**

Bishop's Peanut Butter Crock

American Beauty Rose 10" Pitcher

Stenciled Wildflower Hall Boy Pitchers

Both Sides of a Stenciled Conifer Pitcher

Pitcher, 10" h., 7" d., embossed American Beauty Rose patt., Burley-Winter Pottery Co. (ILLUS., previous page)...................... **$475**

Pitcher, 6 3/4" h., stenciled Wildflower patt., hall boy-type w/cylindrical body & five stencils per side, Brush-McCoy Pottery Co. (ILLUS. right with other Wildflower hall boy, top of page)................................. **$550**

Pitcher, 6" h., stenciled Wildflower patt., hall boy-type w/waisted body & five stencils per side, Brush-McCoy Pottery Co. (ILLUS. left with other Wildflower hall boy, top of page)... **$750**

Pitcher, 5" h., stenciled Conifer Tree patt., printed advertising on the reverse, Brush-McCoy Pottery Co. (ILLUS. of both sides, second from top of page)......... **$350**

Pitcher, 6 1/2" h., tapering bulbous body, Diffused Blue, printed advertising below the spout (ILLUS.)..................................... **$285**

7 1/2" Embossed Dainty Fruit Pitcher

Pitcher, 7 1/2" h., embossed Dainty Fruit patt., A.E. Hull Pottery Co. (ILLUS.).......... **$650**

Pitcher, 8" h., barrel-shaped, shaded dark to light blue, (ILLUS. right with matching mug, top of previous page) **$250**

Bulbous Diffused Blue Pitcher

Banded Diffused Blue Pitcher with Oval

Pitcher, 8" h., cylindrical w/thin molded base & rim rings, Diffused Blue w/oval in center of side (ILLUS.) **$175**

Pitcher, 8" h., plain footed simple cylindrical shaped w/small rim spout & pointed loop handle, Diffused Blue (ILLUS. left with Diffused Blue beater jar, top of page 99) ... **$175**

9" Embossed Cosmos Pitcher

Stenciled Acorn 8" Pitcher

Pitcher, 8" h., stenciled Acorn patt., Brush-McCoy Pottery Co. (ILLUS.)...................... **$300**

Pitcher, 8" h., Stupid patt., diffused blue bands (ILLUS. right with Western Stoneware lard bucket, page 104)...................... **$450**

Pitcher, 9" h., 6 1/2" d., embossed Cosmos or Wild Rose patt., w/overall blue sponging, Nelson McCoy Sanitary Stoneware Co. **$750**

Pitcher, 9" h., 6 1/2" d., embossed Cosmos or Wild Rose patt., w/advertising, Nelson McCoy Sanitary Stoneware Co. (ILLUS., top next column)...................................... **$2,500**

8" Stenciled Wildflower Waisted Pitcher

Pitcher, 8" h., stenciled Wildflower patt., tall waisted body w/long spout, five stencils per side, Brush-McCoy Pottery Co., also found in 8 1/2" h. size (ILLUS.) **$800**

Embossed Daisy on Snowflake Salt Box

Salt box, cov., embossed Daisy on Snowflake patt., unknown maker, 6" d., 4" h. (ILLUS., previous page) **$250**

Embossed Raspberry Salt Box

Salt box, cov., embossed Raspberry patt., Brush-McCoy Pottery Co., 6" d., 4" h. (ILLUS.) **$175**

Diffused Blue Salt Crock with Advertising

Salt crock, hanging-type, no lid, Diffused Blue, printed Iowa advertising on the front, Western Stoneware co., 6" d., 4 1/4" h. (ILLUS.) **$600**

Simple Diffused Blue Salt Crock

Salt crock w/wooden lid, hanging-type, Diffused Blue, printed "Salt," 4" h. (ILLUS.) **$150**

Salt crock w/wooden lid, hanging-type, stenciled Nautilus patt., printed Gothic script "Salt," A.E. Hull Pottery Co., 6" d., 4 1/4" h. (ILLUS. right with bulbous vase, bottom of page) **$225**

Shaving mug, Rose decal, bulbous lobed body w/loop handle, Western Stoneware, 3 3/4" h. (ILLUS. second from right with Rose decal brush vase, soap dish & hot water pitcher, bottom of page 99) **$150**

Stenciled Nautilus Salt Crock & Vase

Rare Diffused Blue Scuttle Shaving Mug

Shaving mug, scuttle-style, Diffused Blue,
6" h. (ILLUS.) **$1,250**

Slop jar, cov., embossed Willow (Basketweave & Morning Glory) patt., Brush-
McCoy Pottery Co., 9 1/2" d., 12 1/2" h.
(ILLUS. left with chamber pot, top of page
102) **$350**

Soap dish, cover & drainer, Rose decal,
squatty bulbous form w/domed cover &
loop handle, Western Stoneware,
5 1/4" d., 2" h. (ILLUS. far left with Rose
decal brush vase, shaving mug and hot
water pitcher, bottom of page 99) **$350**

Tall Two Stags Umbrella Stand

Umbrella stand, embossed Two Stags
patt., tall trees & large oak leaves &
acorns, solid blue, Logan Pottery Co.,
21" h. (ILLUS.) **$2,250**

Vase, 6" h., stenciled Nautilus patt., bulbous
form, A.E. Hull Pottery Co. (ILLUS. left
with Nautilus salt crock, bottom previous
page) **$325**

Swirl Pattern Spherical Teapot

Teapot, cov., Swirl patt., spherical body
w/row of relief-molded knobs around the
shoulder, inset cover w/knob finial, swan's-
neck spout, shoulder loop brackets for wire
bail handle w/turned wood grip, metal bot-
tom plate, 6" d., 6" h. (ILLUS.) **$800**

Diffused Blue Ovoid Handled Vase

Vase, 11" h., Diffused Blue, wide ovoid
body w/short flared neck & pointed shoul-
der handles (ILLUS.) **$325**

Blue Iris Pattern Wall Pocket

Wall pocket, long pointed shape, h.p. blue iris decoration & blue rim bands, 11" l. (ILLUS.).. **$250**

Very Rare Wildflower Water Cooler

Water cooler, cov., stenciled Wildflower patt., domed cover w/button knob atop a tall cylindrical section above the wider cylindrical base section w/a "3" in a circle above the metal spigot, 3 gal. (ILLUS.)... **$4,500**

Barrel-shaped Blue Banded Water Cooler

Water cooler, cover & metal spigot, barrel-shaped, decorated w/narrow blue bands & printed "5" above the spigot, Robinson Clay Products - Robinson Ransbottom Pottery, 5 gal. (ILLUS.) **$350**

Diffused Blue Whipped Cream Crock

Whipped cream crock, cov., swelled cylindrical body w/a flared rim & tab handles, domed cover w/button finial, dark blue Diffused Blue, 7" h. (ILLUS.) **$700**

Boch Freres

The Belgian firm, founded in 1841 and still in production, first produced stoneware art pottery of mediocre quality, attempting to upgrade their wares through the years. In 1907, Charles Catteau became the art director of the pottery, and slowly the influence of his work was absorbed by the artisans surrounding him. All through the 1920s wares were decorated in distinctive Art Deco designs and are now eagerly sought along with the hand-thrown gourd-form vessels coated with earthtone glazes that were produced during the same time. Almost all Boch Freres pottery is marked, but the finest wares also carry the signature of Charles Catteau in addition to the pottery mark.

Boch Freres Mark

Bold Art Deco Boch Freres Box

Box, cov., rounded square w/domed top, colorful Art Deco design w/alternating tapering stripes of black & green up the sides with every other black stripe painted w/a stylized oval & loop design in maroon, orange & yellow, marked "Boch Freres La Louviere," 1930s, 4 5/8" w., 2 7/8" h. (ILLUS.) **$288**

Boch Freres Floral Art Deco Vase

Vase, 7 3/4" h., bulbous baluster-form w/a flat mouth, creamy white body decorated around the shoulder w/a wide pale yellow band highlighted by clusters of white & raspberry Art Deco flowers, thin black stripes down the sides, blue logo mark on the base (ILLUS.) **$230**

Fine Boch Fres. Catteau Antelope Vase

Vase, 9" h., wide bulbous body tapering to a short cylindrical neck, Charles Catteau design of four antelope in various poses along w/leaves & grasses all done in shades of blue, green & black against a white crackle ground, marked "Keramis made in Belgium D 943 Ch. Catteau," 1930s (ILLUS.) **$1,725**

Boch Catteau Vase with Two Antelope

Vase, 9 1/4" h., bulbous ovoid body w/a short cylindrical neck, a Charles Catteau design w/a grazing antelope on each side painted in shades of blue & black against a white crackled ground, marked "D 943 made in Belgium," 1930s (ILLUS.) **$1,265**

Rare Boch Fres. Penguin Vase

Vase, 14 1/2" h., 13 1/2" d., wide bulbous body w/a small molded mouth, decorated w/a tall band of stylized penguins in black & light green against a white crackle ground, a wide geometric base band composed of black & light green triangles, black in mark & number "D 1104," ca. 1930 (ILLUS.)......................... **$9,400**

Metal-mounted Boch Oxblood Vases

Vases, 11 1/2" h., ovoid oxblood-glazed bodies mounted on a stamped metal foot & fitted w/metal blossom & stem handles flanking the mouth, one marked w/com-

pany logo, each drilled in the base, pr. (ILLUS.)... **$375**

Brayton Laguna Pottery

In the 1940s California saw an influx of pottery companies; however, it was Durlin Brayton who earlier, about 1927, began his enterprise. During these previous years Brayton created an assortment of products along with many beautiful glazes, honing his skills before other artists arrived. He married his second wife, an artist, Ellen Webster Grieve, in 1936 and together they became very successful. Durlin Brayton's talent caught the eye of Walt Disney, who bestowed on him the honor of being the first pottery licensed to create ceramic copies of some of Disney's most famous characters. Brayton did this from 1938 until 1940. Ellen Grieve Brayton died in 1948 and Durlin Brayton followed shortly after in 1951. The pottery continued to operate until 1968.

Brayton collectors need to familiarize themselves with the marks, lines and glazes produced by this firm. There are as many as a dozen marks, however, not all Brayton is marked. Hand-turned pieces were the first used and many were marked with Durlin Brayton's handwriting with "Brayton Laguna" or "Brayton Tile." These items have become scarce. Assorted lines include: African-American figures, animals, Art Deco designs, Blackamoors, Calasia (a design of circles and feathers), Children's Series, Circus Series, Disney Characters, Gay Nineties, Hillbilly Shotgun Wedding, kitchen items, sculptures, tiles, Webtonware and the Wedding Series, plus a few others.

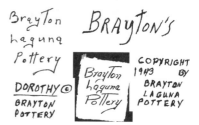

Brayton Laguna Marks

Circus Series Clowns Book Ends

Book ends, Circus Series, clowns sitting w/legs outstretched, white clothes w/green & red ruffles at sleeve & leg cuffs & collar, red hats, 1940s walk-a-dog & pots stamp mark "Brayton," 6" h. (ILLUS.)................ **$295**

Bowl, 10" d., 2" h., Calasia line, feather design in bottom, scalloped rim w/raised circles on inner rim, pale green **$90**

Box, cov., round, white base w/red strawberries, one white flower & green leaves on cover, marked "Copyright 1943 by Brayton Laguna Pottery," 5 1/2" d., 5" h. **$30**

Box, cov., trinket-type, pale blue w/darker blue flowers on the cover & base, marked "Brayton Laguna," 4 x 5", 2" h. **$35**

Bust of woman, chin down w/head slightly turned, white or black crackle glaze, incised "Brayton's Laguna, Beach, Calif. F-1P," 13 1/4" l., 12" h. **$700**

Bust of woman, White Crackle glaze, 12" h. **$510**

Candleholder, figural, three choirboys **$180**

Candleholders, figural Blackamoor, pr. **$250**

Cigarette box, cov., black flecked glossy red, stamp mark "Brayton Calif. U.S.A.," 3 1/4 x 5", 2" h. **$63**

Cookie jar, cov., light brown matte body w/overall honeycomb texture, dark brown straight tree branches w/five partridges around body in pale blue, yellow & orange, glossy white interior, pale blue lid, Model No. V-12, Mark 2, 7 1/4" h. (ILLUS.) .. **$268**

Cookie jar, cov., model of a chicken, brilliant glazes of blue, red, green & yellow, hard to find, 10" h. **$750**

Cookie jar, figural Mammy, burgundy base & turquoise bandanna, rare early version **$1,475**

Cookie jar, figural Provincial Lady, textured woodtone stain w/high-gloss white apron & scarf tied around head, red, green & yellow flowers & hearts motif on clothing, being reproduced so must be marked, "Brayton Laguna Calif. K-27," 13" h. **$550**

Cookie jar, figure of Swedish Maid (Christina), produced 1941, incised mark, 11" h. **$610**

Creamer, figural cat **$68**

Brayton Calico Kitten Creamer

Creamer, figural, model of a seated calico kitten w/a white body decorated w/pink, mauve & blue flowers & brown stitching, blue ribbon around neck, glossy glaze, ink-stamped "Copyright 1942 by Brayton Laguna Pottery," 6 1/2" h. (ILLUS.) **$65**

Creamer & sugar bowl, figural, in the form of a sprinkler can & wheelbarrow, w/floral pale pinks & blues on a white ground, 3" h., pr. **$43**

Creamer & sugar bowl, in the form of a sprinkler can & wheelbarrow, w/floral design in pale pinks & blues on white ground, stamp mark "1948," 3" h., pr. (ILLUS., top of next page) **$80**

Creamer & sugar bowl, individual, eggplant, unglazed bottom, created by Durlin Brayton, incised mark "Brayton Laguna Pottery," pr. **$270**

Creamer & sugar bowl, round, eggplant glaze, created by Durlin Brayton, incised mark on unglazed bottom "Brayton Laguna Pottery," 2 1/2" h., pr. **$85**

Rare Brayton Laguna Mammy Cookie Jar

Cookie jar, cov., figural black Mammy, bright blue dress, white apron w/yellow, black, green & blue trim, red bandana on head, yellow earrings, rare early version, stamped "Brayton Calif. U.S.A.," 12 5/8" h. (ILLUS.) **$850**

Brayton Laguna Cookie Jar

Garden Motif Creamer & Sugar

Provincial Line Cup with Tea Bag Holder

Cup w/tea bag holder, Provincial line, brown bisque stain w/white & yellow flowers & green leaves outside, gloss yellow inside, marked "Brayton Laguna Calif. K-31," 1 3/4" h. (ILLUS.) **$26**

Figure, African-American baby w/diaper, seated, green eyes, 3 3/4" h. **$172**

Figure, baby on all fours **$110**

Figure, baby sitting up **$110**

Figure, Blackamoor, kneeling & holding open cornucopia, heavily jeweled w/gold trim, 10" h. **$260**

Figure, Blackamoor, kneeling, jeweled trim, 15" h. **$330**

Figure, Blackamoor, walking & carrying a bowl in his hands, glossy gold earrings, white bowl & shoes, burgundy scarf, shirt & pantaloons, 8 1/4" h. **$249**

Figure, boy, Alice in Wonderland, not Walt Disney, marked "R," designer Frances Robinson, 3 3/4" h. **$325**

Children's Series "Ann" Figure

Figure, Children's Series, "Ann," girl seated w/legs apart, knees bent, 4" h. (ILLUS.) **$148**

Figure, Children's Series, "Ellen," girl standing w/pigtails & a hat tied at neck, arms bent & palms forward, one leg slightly twisted, 7 1/4" h. **$98**

Figure, Children's Series, "John," boy w/horn **$140**

Figure, Children's Series, "Jon," boy standing & carrying a basket in one hand, rooster in other, 8 1/4" h. **$126**

Figure, peasant woman w/basket at her side in front & basket at her left in back, blue dress, yellow vest, incised mark "Brayton Laguna Pottery," 7 1/2" h. **$110**

Figure, sailor boy holding a gun **$336**

Figure, woman w/two wolfhounds, one on each side, woman w/red hair & wearing a long yellow dress, 9 1/2" h. **$152**

Figure, woman wearing a blue dress & bonnet & holding a book **$140**

African-American Boy & Girl

Figure group, African-American boy & girl, boy holding basket of flowers in each hand, black shoes, yellow socks, barefoot girl, created by L.A. Dowd, early 1940s, paper label, 4 1/4" base, boy 7" h., girl 5 1/2" h. (ILLUS.) **$540**

Figure group, an abstract sculpture of a man & a cat, black glaze, ca. 1957, 21" h. .. **$835**

Figure group, an African-American boy & girl on a single base, boy holding a basket of flowers in each hand, created by L.A. Dowd, ca. 1942, paper label, scarce, base 4 1/4" d., girl 5 1/2" h., boy 7" h. **$850**

Figure group, Bride & Groom, the bride standing on the left w/white dress & pink flowers w/green leaves & pink hat, bouquet in left hand, her right hand on the groom's shoulder, man seated wearing striped trousers, black jacket, brown shoes & brown hat in left hand, black hair & mustache, stamp mark, 4 3/4" l., 8 1/2" h. **$217**

Figure group, "One Year Later," mother seated on left w/green dress holding baby in white dress, man standing w/striped trousers, black hair, mustache, jacket & shoes, stamp mark, 4" l., 8 1/4" h. **$199**

Figure group, "Seashore Honeymoon," a woman & man w/man wearing a red & white-striped top & red swimming trunks, the woman w/a pale blue swin-dress, white hat w/blue polka dots, "Laguna Beach Calif. 1895" printed in black around a life preserver on the back, part of the "Wedding Series," stamped mark "copyright 1943 by Brayton Laguna Pottery," 9" h.. **$250**

Baby from Hillbilly Series

Figure of a baby, standing w/hands on hips, wearing swimming trunks, Hillbilly Shotgun Wedding series designed by Andy Anderson, ca. 1938, three pots & dog walker stamp mark, scarce, 4 1/4" h. (ILLUS.)... **$325**

Figure of a boy, blond hair, standing on a round base, wearing white pajamas trimmed in blue, created by Durlin Brayton, ca. 1935, 5 1/2" h......................... **$225**

Figure of a boy, "Eugene," Children's Series, standing w/hat on head, handkerchief pinned at his chest, arms behind his back holding a flower, stamped mark "Eugene" above the line & "Brayton Pottery" below the line, 7" h. (ILLUS. right with figure of Ellen, top next column) **$105**

Eugene & Ellen from Children's Series

Brayton Laguna Seated Clown Figure

Figure of a clown, sitting w/feet crossed, hands behind back, white clothing w/red dots, blue, red, green & yellow ruffles on neck collar, wrists & ankles, black shoes, ink stamped w/three pots on left & dog-walker on right, 5 1/4" l., 6" h. (ILLUS.) **$165**

Brayton Laguna Dutch Boy & Girl

Figure of a Dutch boy, standing wearing dark blue pants, light blue jacket, red cap & yellow wooden shoes, designed by Frances Robinson, ca. early 1940s, 8" h. (ILLUS. right with Dutch girl, previous page) $110

Figure of a Dutch girl, standing wearing a white apron w/blue trim, light blue blouse, white cap & yellow wood shoes, holding a flower in one hand, designed by Frances Robinson, ca. early 1940s, 7" h. (ILLUS. left with Dutch boy, previous page) $115

Figure of a girl, "Ellen," Children's Series, standing w/pigtails & hat, tied at the neck w/a large polka dot bow, arms bent at elbows & palms forward, one leg slightly twisted w/right toes on top of left foot, stamped mark "Ellen" above the line & "Brayton Pottery" below the line, 7 1/2" h. (ILLUS. left with figure of Eugene, previous page) $115

Brayton Laguna African-American Choir Boy

Figure of African-American choir boy, standing holding a hymnal, flowers on irregular base, gold sticker w/"Brayton Laguna Pottery," hard to find, 5" h. (ILLUS.) $110

Figure of an opera singer, standing woman wearing a long necklace, green dress, marked w/three pots & dog walker, 8" h. ... $195

Figure of Geppetto, standing, pensive pose, from the Disney movie "Pinocchio," ca. 1939, 8 1/4" h. $925

Figure of woman, Gay Nineties Series, holding parasol, unglazed bottom, incised mark "Brayton Laguna Pottery," 9 1/2" h. $240

Figure of woman, standing & carrying a brown basket on each arm, long green dress & red scarf over her head, marked "Brayton Calif. U.S.A.," 11" h. (ILLUS., top next column)... $125

Figures, African-American boys on hands & knees playing dice, w/original die, 4 3/4" l., 3 1/2" h., 3 pcs. $295

Woman with Baskets Brayton Figure

Figures, Children's Series, "Eric" & "Inger," Swedish boy & girl, pr. $230

Figures, dice players w/dice, the African-American soldiers on hands & knees, attached pottery die show a "4" & a "3," dice 1" w., pink glaze, players 4 3/4" l., 3 1/2" h., set of three $200

Figures, dice players w/dice, the African-American soldiers on hands & knees, attached pottery die show a "4" & a "3," dice 1" w., white glaze, players 4 3/4" l., 3 1/2" h., set of three $275

Figures, Hillbilly Shotgun Wedding series, 8 pcs. $1,975

Flower holder, figural, "Francis," girl standing & holding small planter in front, White Crackle glossy glaze dress, yellow pot, brown hair w/blue ribbon, brown-stained face & arms, bluebird on right arm, 6 1/2" h. $73

Model of a dog, "Pluto" from Walt Disney, in a sniffing pose, 5 3/4" l., 3 1/2" h. $150

Model of a giraffe, white-glazed spots over wood-like bisque, designed by Walter Bringhurst, 8 1/4" h. $200

Model of a turtle, ca. 1934, gold sticker reading "Brayton Laguna Pottery," 4 1/2" l., 2" h... $150

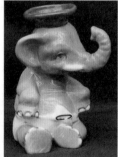

Brayton Laguna Seated Elephant Figure

Model of an elephant, seated, trunk up, head turned slightly, lilac ground w/white diaper & tusks, royal blue opening on head to serve as a bud vase, marked w/three vases & dog walker, 5" h. (ILLUS.) .. $155

Pair of Brayton Laguna Quails

Models of quails, brown w/black speckles on white breasts, black & white feather details on wings, incised mark "Brayton's Laguna Beach," 9" & 11" h., pr. (ILLUS.) ... **$165**

Mug, w/pretzel-shaped handle, raised pretzel shapes on gold, stamp mark "Brayton Calif. U.S.A.," 5" h. **$34**

Pencil holder, figural, gingham dog................. **$90**

Planter, in the form of a peasant man w/flower cart, assorted glazes, unmarked, 6 x 11", 11" h............................... **$169**

Salt & pepper shakers, figural, gingham dog & calico cat, pr....................................... **$90**

Salt & pepper shakers, figural mammy & chef, 5 1/2" h., pr.. **$150**

Salt & pepper shakers, figural peasant couple, Provincial patt., pr........................... **$73**

Teapot & cover on stand, Provincial patt., tulip stand, the set..................................... **$138**

Tile, chartreuse & yellow bird, turquoise, yellow & white flowers, black background incised mark, "Laguna Pottery," 7 x 7" **$495**

Brayton Laguna Tile

Tile, square, w/scene of man in sombrero napping under palm tree, man dressed in white serape & cobalt blue pants & sombrero, cacti & palm tree in greens & turquoises, pale green ground, unglazed back, created by Durlin Brayton, incised mark, "Brayton Laguna Pottery," 6 3/4" sq. (ILLUS.)... **$585**

Vase, 5 1/2" h., model of grey elephant wearing diaper & open blue hat, 1940s walk-a-dog & pots stamp mark "Brayton"... **$172**

Vase, 5 1/2" h., round foot flaring to a scalloped rim, created by Durlin Brayton in the early period, turquoise glaze rising to a deeper turquoise, incised mark "Brayton Laguna Pottery," 7" sq. **$450**

Vase, 7 1/4" h., 7" w., 7" l., pillow shape w/feather design on each side & raised circles on recessed short base, fern green... **$93**

Rare Mexican Theme Brayton Tile

Tile, square, decorated in bold colors w/a Mexican woman followed by two children & a dog w/a palm tree & cactus in the background, incised mark "Brayton Tile," 7" sq. (ILLUS.).. **$700**

Sea Horse Vase

Vase, 8 1/2" h., model of a sea horse, white body w/pink, yellow & turquoise accents, stamp mark underglaze "Brayton Calif. U.S.A." (ILLUS.)...................................... **$312**

Vase, 9" h., figure of a gypsy woman's head, beads around her neck, ca. 1939, incised mark "Brayton Laguna Pottery" **$300**

Vase, 9" h., round foot w/raised circles, Calasia patt., slightly bulbous body w/feathered design, flaring gently at rim, light blue w/lighter blue inside, Model No. A-7..... **$95**

Russian Woman Wall Plaque

Wall plaque, figure of woman, arms above head, Russian dress, Webton Ware mark, hard to find, 13 1/2" h. (ILLUS.) **$230**
Wall plaque, model of a large zebra, black & gold **$130**

Brayton Figural Man Wall Pocket

Wall pocket, figure of a standing man w/his arms above his head, wearing a long white robe w/pink socks, belt & hat, Webton Ware mark, hard to find, 13" h. (ILLUS.).. **$175**

Webton Ware Wall Pocket Bowl

Wall pocket, model of a bowl w/shaped rim, two holes for hanging, Webton Ware mark on unglazed back, 2 3/4" w., 4 1/4" h. (ILLUS.) **$125**

Buffalo Pottery

Incorporated in 1901 as a wholly owned subsidiary of the Larkin Soap Company, founded by John D. Larkin of Buffalo, New York, in 1875, the Buffalo Pottery was a manufactory built to produce premium wares to be included with purchases of Larkin's chief product, soap.

In October 1903, the first kiln was fired and Buffalo Pottery became the only pottery in the world run entirely by electricity. In 1904 Larkin offered its first premium produced by the pottery. This concept of using premiums caused sales to skyrocket and, in 1905, the first Blue Willow pattern pottery made in the United States was introduced as a premium.

The Buffalo Pottery administrative building, built in 1904 to house 1,800 clerical workers, was the creation of a 32-year-old architect, Frank Lloyd Wright. The building was demolished in 1953, but many critics considered it to be Wright's masterpiece.

By 1910 annual soap production peaked and the number of premiums offered in the catalogs exceeded 600. By 1915 this number had grown to 1,500. The first catalog of premiums was issued in 1893 and continued to appear through the late 1930s.

John D. Larkin died in 1926, and during the Great Depression the firm suffered severe losses, going into bankruptcy in 1940. After World War II the pottery resumed production under new management, but its vitreous wares were generally limited to mass-produced china for the institutional market.

Among the pottery lines produced during Buffalo's heyday were Gaudy Willow, Deldare, Abino Ware, historical and commemorative plates, and unique handpainted jugs and pitchers. In the 1920s and 1930s the firm concentrated on personalized wares for commercial clients including hotels, clubs, railroads, and restaurants.

In 1983 Oneida Silversmiths bought the pottery, an ironic twist since, years before, Oneida silver had been featured in Larkin catalogs. The pottery has now ceased all domestic production of ceramics. - Phillip M. Sullivan.

Buffalo Pottery Mark

Abino Ware (1911-1913)
Author;s Note: Today this is a seller's market with prices escalating rapidly.

Candlestick, Nautical design, 9" h............. **$1,200**
Matchbox holder w/ashtray **$2,000**

Rare Abino Ware Tankard-form Mug

Mug, tankard-type, windmill scene, 1912, marked w/number 264, signed by R. Stuart, white interior, not in the Altman book, 7" h. (ILLUS.) **$2,000**
Pitcher, 7" h., octagonal jug-type, Portland Head Light scene .... **$2,800+**

Very Rare Abino Ware 9" Pitcher

Pitcher, 9" h., octagonal jug-type, windmill decoration, 1912, bears number 220 &

signed by C. Harris, not in Altman book (ILLUS.)... **$3,250**
Pitcher, 10 1/2" h., tankard-type **$2,100**
Saucer, windmill decoration **$200**
Teacup, windmill decoration **$400**
Vase, 8" h., seascape decoration............. **$2,200+**

Blue Willow Pattern (1905-1916)
Author's Note: Pieces dated 1905 and marked "First Old Willow Ware Manufactured in America" are worth double the prices shown here.

Chop plate, scalloped edge, 11" d................ **$275**

Very Rare Blue Willow Cuspidor

Cuspidor, full Willow decoration, dated 1911, not in Altman book, 7 1/4" d. top, 5" h. (ILLUS.) **$500**
Match safe, 2 3/4 x 6" **$250**
Oyster tureen, notched cover....................... **$600**

Blue Willow Wash Pitcher

Pitcher, wash-type (ILLUS.)........................... **$750**
Pitcher, jug-type, "Hall Boy," 6 1/2 oz., 3 pts. **$325**
Pitcher, cov., jug-type, 3 1/2 pts. **$450**
Pitcher, jug-type, "Chicago," 4 1/2 pts. **$450**
Salad bowl, square, 9 1/4" w........................ **$275**
Sauceboat w/attached stand, oval, double-handled, 1 pt. **$400**
Teapot, cov., square, 2 pts., 5 1/2 oz............ **$400**
Teapot, cov., individual size, 12 oz. **$300**
Vegetable dish, cov., square, 7 1/2 x 9 1/2" .. **$300**

Deldare "Fallow Field Hunt" Plates

Deldare Ware (1908-1909, 1923-1925)

Author's Note: "Fallowfield Hunt" and "Ye Olden Days" scenes are similarly priced for the equivalent pieces in this line.

Calendar plate, 1910, 9 1/2" d. .... **$2,800+**

Calling card tray, round w/tab handles, "Ye Olden Days" scene, 7 3/4" d. .... **$450+**

Candleholder, shield-back style, "Ye Olden Days" scene, 7" h. .... **$2,000+**

Candlestick, "Ye Olden Days" scene, 9 1/2" h. **$750**

Dresser tray, rectangular, "Dancing Ye Minuet" scene, 9 x 12" **$900**

Fruit bowl, 9" d., 3 3/4" h.,"Ye Village Tavern" scene, 1909 .... **$600**

Humidor, cov., octagonal, 7" h. **$1,400**

Pitcher, 12 1/2" h. tankard-type, double-decorated w/"The Great Controversy" scene on one side & "All You Have To Do To Teach a Dutchman English" scene on the other side, artist-signed, 1908 .... **$1,250+**

Plate, 6 1/4" d., salesman's sample .... **$2,400+**

Plates, 9 1/4" d., "The Fallow Field Hunt - The Start," artist-signed, set of 4, each (ILLUS., top of page) **$300**

Punch bowl, footed, 14 3/4" d., 9 1/4" h. ... **$7,000+**

Relish dish, oblong, 6 1/2 x 12".................... **$500**

Salad bowl, 12" d., 5" h. **$600**

Vase, 8 1/2" h., 6" d., footed tapering ovoid body w/a flaring rim, "Ye Olden Days" scene, black ink mark .... **$1,300+**

Vase, 9" h., tall waisted cylindrical form, "Ye Olden Days" scene, 1909 .... **$1,400**

Wall plaque, 12" d. **$1,000**

Emerald Deldare (1911)

Candlestick, Bayberry decoration, 9" h. **$1,000**

Very Rare Deldare Jardiniere & Base

Jardiniere & garden seat pedestal base, "Ye Lion Inn" scenes on jardiniere, two "Ye Olden Days" scenes on base, 1908, jardiniere 9" h., base 13 1/2" h., the set (ILLUS.)... **$12,000**

Pitcher, 8" h., octagonal, "Ye Olden Days" scene... **$850**

Emerald Deldare Chocolate Pot

Coffee/chocolate pot, cov., tall tapering hexagonal form w/pinched spout & angled D-form handle, inset lid w/blossom finial, stylized symmetrical designs highlighted w/white flowers on body & lid, band just under spout w/stylized moths & large butterfly, decorated by L. Newman, ca. 1911, artist's name in green slip, ink stamp logo & "7," 10 1/2" h. (ILLUS.) **$3,000**

Very Rare Emerald Deldare Pitcher

Pitcher, 8 3/4" h., octagonal, angled handle, color scene of "Dr. Syntax Setting Out to the Lakes," signed by M. Gerhardt, dated 1911 (ILLUS.)................................ **$2,000**

"Dr. Syntax" Emerald Deldare Plate

Plate, 7 1/4" d., h.p. floral border & center scene, "Dr. Syntax Soliloquizing," by E. Missel, marked w/Emerald Deldare logo, "1911" & "4" (ILLUS.) **$1,400**
Plate, 8 1/4" d., stylized floral & geometric decoration **$750**

Another Rare Emerald Deldare Pitcher

Pitcher, 9" h., octagonal, angled handle, color scene of "Dr. Syntax Setting Out to the Lake,s (sic)," signed by R. Stuart, dated 1911 (ILLUS.)..................................... **$1,900**
Plaque, round, "Friday," scene of monks at a long table eating fish on Friday, 12" d. .... **$2,000+**
Plaque, round, "Lost," scene of herd of sheep in blizzard, 13 1/2" d.................. **$2,200+**

Emerald Deldare Saucer & Teacup

Saucer, round, "Dr. Syntax and the Bookseller," 1911 (ILLUS. with teacup)............. **$350**
Teacup, tapering cylindrical body w/angled handle, "Dr. Syntax at Liverpool," 1911 (ILLUS. with saucer) **$400**
Vase, 8" h., 6 1/2" d., ovoid w/a wide shoulder tapering to a short flaring neck, olive green ground decorated in shades of green & white w/a kingfisher & iris, signed by J. Gerhardt, 1911................... **$1,800**

Rare Tall Emerald Deldare Vase

Vase, 13" h., 5 3/8" d., tall waisted cyindrical shape, decorated w/Art Nouveau style geometric & floral designs, 1911 (ILLUS.) **$2,100**

Gaudy Willow (1905-1916)

Author's Note: Pieces dated 1905 and marked "First Old Willow Ware Manufactured in America" are worth double the prices shown here. This line is generally priced five times higher than the Blue Willow line.

Bone dish, 3 1/4 x 7 1/4" **$225**
Boston eggcup, 7 oz. **$350**
Butter dish, cover & insert, the set, 7 1/4" d. **$750**
Cake plate, double-handled, 10 1/4" d. **$600**
Creamer, round, 1 pt., 2 oz. **$500**
Gravy/sauceboat, 14 1/2 oz. **$450**
Pickle dish, square, 4 1/2 x 8 1/4" **$350**
Plate, dinner, 10 1/2" d. **$275**

Large Display of Gaudy Willow Pottery

Platter, 18" l., oval .... **$1,000+**
Saucer, 6 1/2" d. **$50**
Sugar bowl, cov., round, 24 1/4 oz. **$500**
Teacup, 10 oz. **$200**

Jugs and Pitchers (1906-1909)

Jug, "George Washington," blue & white, 1907, 7 1/2" h. **$700**
Jug, "Mason," brown/beige colors, 1907, 8 1/2" h. .... **$1,100+**
Pitcher, 8 3/4" h., bone china, melon-shaped, white, 1909 .... **$1,200**
Pitcher, "Art Nouveau," gold & blue, 1908, 9 1/2" h. .... **$1,200+**
Pitcher, "Buffalo Hunt," jug-form, Indian on horseback hunting buffalo, dark bluish green ground, 6" h. **$350**
Pitcher, "Chrysanthemum," dark green, 1908, 7 1/2" h. **$500**
Pitcher, "Cinderella," jug-type, ca. 1907, marked w/Buffalo transfer logo & date, "Cinderella" & "1328," 6" h. .... **$700+**
Pitcher, "Gloriana," blue on white, ca. 1908, 9" h. (ILLUS. right, bottom of page) **$900**

"Holland" & "Gloriana" Pitchers

Pitcher, "Holland," decorated w/three colorful h.p. scenes of Dutch children on the body w/band near the rim decorated w/a rural landscape, ca. 1906, marked w/Buffalo transfer logo & date, "Holland" & "9," overall consistent staining, 5 3/4" h. (ILLUS. left with Gloriana Pitcher, bottom previous page) **$750**
Pitcher, "John Paul Jones," blue & white, 1908, 8 3/4" h. .... **$1,250+**
Pitcher, "Marine Pitcher, Lighthouse," blue & white, 1907, 9 1/4" h. .... **$1,250+**
Pitcher, "New Bedford Whaler - The Niger," bluish green, 1907, 6" h. **$900**
Pitcher, "Pilgrim," brightly colored, 1908, 9" h. **$1,100**
Pitcher, "Robin Hood," multicolored, 1906, 8 1/4" h. **$700**
Pitcher, "Roosevelt Bears," beige, 1906, 8 1/4" h. **$3,400**
Pitcher, "Sailor" patt., waisted-tankard form, decorated in blues w/the heads of two seamen above scenes of sailing ships, opposite side w/a lighthouse & rocky coastline, 1906, 9 1/4" h. .... **$1,250+**
Pitcher, "Whirl of the Town," brightly colored, 1906, 7" h. **$700**

Plates - Commemorative (1906-1912)

Rare Hadley's Anniversary Plate

Buffalo Pottery Niagara Falls Plate

Niagara Falls, dark blue w/Bonrea pattern border, ca. 1907, 7 1/2" d. (ILLUS.) **$150**
Richest Hill in the World, Butte, Montana, deep bluish green, 7 1/2" d. **$175**
State Capitol, Helena, Montana, deep bluish green, 7 1/2" d. **$175**

Great Falls, Montana Plate

B. & M. Smelter, and the largest smokestack in the world. Great Falls, Montana, deep green, ca. 1909, 7 1/2" d. (ILLUS.) **$150**
Gen. A.P. Stewart Chapter, United Daughters of the Confederacy, No. 81, Richmond, Virginia, blue & white, 1907, 10 1/2" d. **$350**
George Washington & Martha Washington, deep bluish green, 7 1/2" d., each **$275**
Hadley's 40th Anniversary Sale, Pioneer, Ohio - 1868-1908, deep bluish green w/three vignettes, not in Altman book, 7 1/2" d. (ILLUS., top next column) **$200**
Improved Order of the Redman, green border w/multicolored design, 7 1/2" d. **$200**
Locks (The), Lockport, New York, deep bluish green, 7 1/2" d. **$150**
New Bedford, Massachusetts, blue & white, 1908, 10 1/2" d. **$200**

W.C.T.U. Commemorative Plate

World's & National Woman's Christian Temperance Union, center view of a house & vignettes around the border, blue & white, ca. 1908, 9" d. (ILLUS.) **$400**

Plates - Historical - Blue or Green (1905-1910)

Capitol Building, Washington, D.C., 10" d. **$95**

Faneuil Hall, Boston, 10" d. **$95**

Independence Hall, Philadelphia, 10" d. **$95**

Mount Vernon, 10" d. **$95**

Niagara Falls, 10" d. **$95**

White House, Washington, 10" d. **$95**

Miscellaneous Pieces

Boston Eggcup Made for a Hotel

Boston eggcup, white w/Blue Lune liner, a small blue picture of the ship Mayflower on the side, inside base reads "Made Expressly for The Mayflower - Washington, D.C. - Buffalo China," undated, not in Altman book, 3 1/2" d., 3 3/4" h. (ILLUS.) **$100**

First Buffalo China Christmas Plate

Christmas Plate, 1950, first of a series of annual plates ending in 1962, 9 1/2" d. (ILLUS.)... **$75**

Marine Corps Demitasse Cup

Cup, demitasse size, white w/red band & logo of the Marine Corps, Ye Olde Ivory, bottom marked "Buffalo China - Made in U.S.A. C-10," not in Altman book, 2 1/2" h. (ILLUS.) **$75**

Cup & saucer, Bluebird patt, china mark, set **$75**

Feeding dish, child's, alphabet border, color center scene of Dolly Dingle children signed by Grace Drayton **$175**

Dutch Children Feeding Dish

Feeding dish, child's, alphabet border, Dutch children at play in center, ca. 1916, 7 3/4" d. (ILLUS.) **$125**

Gravy boat, Seneca patt., 8 1/2" l.................... **$45**

Mugs, decorated w/various color transfer scenes of friars in a shaded brown to white ground, white interior, gold-rimmed tops, originally part of a mug & pitcher set, 5 1/2" h., each (ILLUS. of two, below) **$150**

Two Buffalo Pottery Friar-decorated Mugs

Large & Small Geranium Pitchers

Pitcher, Geranium patt., blue & white, small size (ILLUS. front row, right with other Geranium pitchers, top of page)................. **$275**

Pitcher, Geranium patt., pale green & brown on white, small size, 1906-1909 (ILLUS. front row, left with other Geranium pitchers, top of page) **$175**

Rare York Pattern Pitcher

Pitcher, York patt., white body w/blue & red flowers, 1910, rare, 7 1/2" h. (ILLUS.)........ **$650**

Pitcher, 9" h., flattened ovoid body tapering to a wide arched spout, printed in red w/the Larkin Company logo, possibly used in the Larkin Company cafeteria in Buffalo, printed on the base "Vitreous (above a buffalo) Buffalo Pottery," undated, ca. 1908, 10 cup size, not in Altman book (ILLUS., top next column)....... **$1,000**

Pitchers, Geranium patt., large sizes, multicolored design or dark blue & white,

1906-1909, each (ILLUS. in back row, top of page).. **$400**

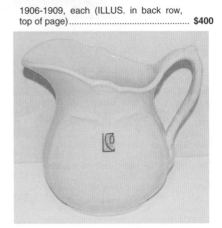

Rare Larkin Company Pitcher

Plate, 6 1/2" d., Bluebird patt., china mark **$75**

Plate, 6 3/8" d., bread & butter, made for the New York, New Haven & Hartford Railroad, ca. 1935 (ILLUS. right, bottom of page).. **$95**

Plate, 8 3/8" d., luncheon, made for the New York, New Haven & Hartford Railroad, ca. 1935 (ILLUS. center with other railroad plates, bottom of page) **$150**

Plate, 9" d., dinner, Hotel Robert Fulton service, Buffalo China **$250**

Plate, 9" d., Multifleur patt., Buffalo China...... **$300**

Plate, 9 1/2" d., Bing Crosby portrait, Buffalo China **$600**

Plate, 9 1/2" d., dinner, Roycroft Inn service .. **$400**

NY, NH & H Railroad Plates

Rare Buffalo China Turkey Platter

Plate, 9 3/4" d., dinner, made for the New York, New Haven & Hartford Railroad, ca. 1935 (ILLUS. left with other railroad plates, bottom previous page) **$175**

Plate, 10" d., New York World's Fair, 1939 ... **$550**

Plate, 10 1/4" d., dinner, Bangor patt., eagle backstamp, 1906 .... **$600**

Plate, 10 1/4" d., dinner, Japan patt., multi-colored, 1906 .... **$250**

Plate, 10 1/2" d., Stuyvesant Hotel service, green & gold.. **$250**

Plate, 10 3/4" d., Jack Dempsey photo-graph, Buffalo China **$500**

Plate, 10 3/4" d., Pere Marquette Hotel ser-vice, Ye Olde Ivory..................................... **$300**

Plate, 11" d., Breakfast at the Three Pi-geons, Fallowfield Hunt line, on Colorido Ware.. **$750**

Plate, 11" d., George Washington portrait, gold-embossed border band, made for the Chesapeake & Ohio Railroad, 1932..... **$750**

Platter, 13 1/4 x 18 1/2", Turkey patt., large colorful turkey in landscape in center, fall landscape border scenes, Colorido Ware, 1937, Buffalo China (ILLUS., top of page) .... **$3,200+**

Portland vase, reproduced in 1946, 8" h. ... **$1,000**

Salt & pepper shakers, from the Roycroft Inn, pr. **$800**

Teapot, cov., tea ball-type w/built-in tea ball, Argyle patt., blue & white, 1914 .... **$300**

Tom & Jerry set: punch bowl & 12 cups; Colorido Ware, the set .... **$1,000+**

Vase, 6 3/4" h., 3 3/8" d., cylindrical waisted shape, h.p. scene similar to a village scene of bygone days as used on Del-dare, marked "Buffalo China Rouge Ware," not in the Altman book (ILLUS., top next column)..................................... **$1,500**

Vase, 10 1/2" h., 2 3/4" d. base, tall ovoid body tapering to a widely flaring trumpet neck w/gently fluted rim, long angular shoulder handles, a wide white body band decorated w/large blossoming branches w/green & brown leaves, shoulder & base bands w/stylized natu-ral design in brown & white, brown neck & handles, from the 1906 Premium cat-alog, dated 1906, not in the Altman book (ILLUS., bottom next column) **$600**

Rare Buffalo Pottery Rouge Ware Vase

Tall Decorative Buffalo Pottery Vase

Caliente Pottery

In 1979 the pottery world lost a man who used his talents to create satin matte glazes and blended colors. Virgil Haldeman's career got its start after he graduated from the University of Illinois in 1923. In 1927 he moved to Southern California and it was there that he and his partner opened the Haldeman Tile Manufacturing Company in Los Angeles. The business was sold just a few years later and Haldeman went to work for the Catalina Clay Products Company on Catalina Island. When Virgil quit his job as ceramics engineer and plant superintendent three years later he opened the Haldeman Pottery in Burbank, California.

In the early years, the word "Caliente" was used as a line name to designate flower frogs, figurines and flower bowls. Collectors now use the Caliente name almost exclusively to indicate all products made at the Haldeman pottery.

At best, items were randomly marked and some simply bear a deeply impressed "Made in California" mark. However, in 1987 Wilbur Held wrote a privately printed book titled Collectable Caliente Pottery, which aided tremendously in identifying Caliente products by a numbering system that the Haldeman Company used. According to Held, molded pieces usually are numbered in the 100s; handmade pieces, 200s; mostly animals and fowl, 300s; dancing girls, 400s; continuation of handmade pieces, 500-549; and molded pieces with roses added, 550 and above. Stickers were also used and many are still firmly attached to the items.

Caliente Marks

Basket, round, footed rim w/rope handle, green, Model No. 222, incised "Handmade Calif.," 7" l. (ILLUS., top next column) **$48**

Rope-handled Green Caliente Basket

Caliente Pottery Basket

Basket, w/hand-coiled center handle, yellow, Model No. 221, 5" l. (ILLUS.) **$29**

Bowl, 4 3/4" h., bulbous ivy-type, satin matte white gloss, two pink applied roses & one rosebud w/two green leaves, Model No. 560 (ILLUS. center with two vases, bottom of page) **$70**

Bowl, 8" d., 2 1/2" h., green, rolled edge, Model No. 14-1, early ware (ILLUS. right w/handled vases, top of page 130) **$154**

Candy dish, figural, swan w/head bent at neck serving as handle, pink inside, white outside, Model No. 64, 9" l., 6" h. **$82**

Ewer, w/handles, ivory base & lower half of body darkening to pink w/overall pink inside, applied w/two ivory leaves, one pink rose & one white rose & white rosebud, marked "558 Handmade Cal.," 9 1/2" h. **$89**

Caliente Pottery Bowl & Vases

Caliente Dancing Girl Figures

Ewer, w/handles, yellow gloss ground w/applied two white roses & three yellow leaves in relief, incised mark "554 U.S.A.," 5 1/2" h. **$48**

Figure of a dancing girl, arms outstretched w/each hand holding up tip of skirt, right foot visible, head bent far to the right touching right shoulder, pale green, impressed mark "Made in California," Model No. 408, 6 1/2" h. (ILLUS. left, top of page) **$184**

Figure of a dancing girl, head bent w/right hand to shoulder, left hand holding dress up, kicking left leg, pale pink, impressed mark "Made in California," Model No. 407, 7" h. (ILLUS. right, top of page) **$135**

Figure of dancing girl in bloomers, a scarf in each hand draping to the floor, head bent & slightly tilted, face features indistinct, left hand resting on waist, Model No. 406, very hard to find, 6 1/2" h. (ILLUS.) **$170**

Figure of woman standing, holding lower section of long dress away from body exposing legs, head tilted slightly w/hat on her head, impressed mark "Made in California" in block letters, Model No. 405, 6 1/4" h. (ILLUS. center, top of page) **$125**

Caliente Dancing Girl in Bloomers

Caliente Pottery Floater

Floater, blue inside, white outside, floral design in relief, 12" l. (ILLUS.) **$57**

Floater, flat & shallow dish to float flowers, oval w/two overlapping rim cuts w/candle rings in two rose petals & four inward rim bends, script-incised mark, Model No. 509, 16" l. **$68**

Floater, pink inside, white outside, Model No. 205 14" l. **$41**

Flower frog, model of a sailboat, satin matte white glaze, Model No. 73, 5" h. **$69**

Caliente Rooster & Hen

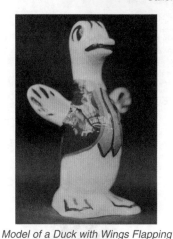

Model of a Duck with Wings Flapping

Model of a duck, wings up, details brush painted, well marked w/sticker, incised Model No. 334 & in-mold mark, 4" h. (ILLUS.) **$122**

Model of a hen, standing on round base, unusual hand-decorated, brown body w/darker brown highlights, green & white base incised "336" & "USA," 3 1/2" h. (ILLUS. left, top of page) **$83**

Model of a pointer dog, on oval base, walking position, tail & head up, white base & lower portion of dog's body, upper half caramel gloss, Model No. 360, 6 3/4" l., 4" h. **$90**

Model of a rooster, seated on round base, unusual hand-decorated brown body w/darker brown highlights, green & white base, incised "306" & "USA," 3 3/4" h. (ILLUS. right w/hen, top of page) **$83**

Model of an egret, white, Model No. 369, 4 1/4" h. (ILLUS., top next column) **$78**

Planter, model of a Dutch shoe w/one rose & leaves, green glaze w/pink, unmarked, Model No. 555, 5" l., 2 1/2" h. **$41**

Sign, Caliente Pottery dealer, unnumbered, 3 1/4" h., 9 1/2" l. **$439**

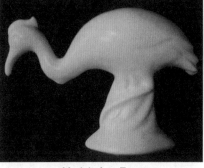

Model of an Egret

Vase, 3 3/4" h., one handle, yellow, Model No. 37 (ILLUS. second from left w/handled vases & bowl, top next page) **$42**

Vase, 7" h., footed w/ring at shoulder & two handles at top, orange, Model No. 9 (ILLUS. left w/handled vases & bowl, top next page) **$195**

Vase, 7" h., urn-shaped w/three rings around base, pale pink body w/applied white rose & pink leaves, script incised mark, Model No. 581 (ILLUS. right w/bowl & vase, bottom of page 127) **$89**

Vase, 8" h., flat front & back w/curved sides, slightly scalloped rectangular opening, one applied green rose & leaves blending to gold top w/two applied rosebuds, one rose & one leaf, "Model No. 570" & "Calif." etched into glazed bottom, a hard-to-find glaze combination (ILLUS. left w/bowl & vase, bottom of page 127) **$96**

Vase, 9" h., two small handles at top, green early ware, Model No. 1-1 (ILLUS. second from right w/handled vases & bowl, top next page) **$230**

Wall pocket, heart-shaped w/piecrust edge & applied rose & leaves at center top, Model No. 7, 7" h. **$77**

Wall pocket, three plumes w/bow near bottom, satin matte white glaze, incised mark, Model No. 6, 6 1/2" h. **$89**

Caliente Handled Vases & Bowl

Cambridge Art Pottery

The Cambridge Art Pottery was incorporated in Cambridge, Ohio, in 1900 and began production of artwares in early 1901. Its earliest lines, Terrhea and Oakwood, were slip-decorated glossy-glazed wares similar to the products of other Ohio potteries of that era.

In 1902 it began production of an earthenware cooking ware line called Guernsey that featured a dark brown exterior and porcelain white lining. This eventually became its leading seller, and in 1909 the name of the firm was changed to The Guernsey Earthenware Company to reflect this fact. In 1907 the company introduced a matte green-glazed art line it called Otoe, but all production of its art pottery lines ceased in 1908. The company eventually became part of The Atlas Globe China Company, which closed in 1933.

TUSCAN

Various Cambridge Marks

Cambridge Oakwood Line Cruet

Cruet, Oakwood line, footed bulbous body tapering to a tall cylindrical neck w/wide spout, small looped shoulder handle, streaky mottled tan & green to dark brown & brick red glossy glaze, impressed on the bottom "Oakwood 34," 5 1/4" h. (ILLUS.) $70

Cambridge Oakwood Line Vase

Vase, 7 3/4" h., Oakwood line, simple baluster-form body tapering to a small flaring neck, overall drippy black, brown & yellow glaze, marked on base "Oakwood - 200," bruise at rim, stilt pull on base (ILLUS.) $81

Canton

This ware has been decorated for nearly two centuries in factories near Canton, China. Intended for export sale, much of it was originally inexpensive blue-and-white hand-decorated ware. Late-18th and early-19th century pieces are superior to later ones and fetch higher prices.

Bowl, 10" d., 2 1/4" h., wide shallow shape w/a flaring scalloped rim, orange peel glaze bottom, 19th c. (ILLUS., next page) $460

Nice Large Scalloped Canton Bowl

Scarce Canton Candlesticks

Canton Bowl with Cut Corners

Bowl, 10 1/2" w., 4 3/4" h., squared w/cut corners, simple island landscape in the center bottom, 19th c. (ILLUS.) **$881**

Candlesticks, slender tapering cylindrical form w/flattened socket rim, 19th c., rim chip, 7 1/2" h., pr. (ILLUS., top next column) **$2,233**

Large Canton Charger

Charger, wide round shape w/dished rim, large round central landscape, small edge fleck, 19th c., 14 3/4" d. (ILLUS.) **$403**

Plates, 7" d., round w/flanged rim, set of 8 (ILLUS., bottom of page)........................... **$322**

Set of Eight Canton Plates

Set of Seven Old Canton Plates

Plates, 7 1/4" d., shallow dished shape, 19th c., one w/a repaired edge, set of 7 (ILLUS.).. **$316**

Set of Ten Old Canton Plates

Plates, 8 1/2" d., shallow dished shape, 19th c., two w/small chips, one w/spider cracks, one w/very old tight hairline, set of 10 (ILLUS.)... **$575**

Large Early Canton Platter

Platter, 10 1/4 x 13", rectangular w/cut corners, large Chinese landscape in the center, decorative floral & scroll border band, first half 19th c. (ILLUS.) **$863**

Platter, 16 1/2 x 20", oblong w/cut-corners, deep curved sides, 19th c. (ILLUS., top next column)... **$748**

Punch bowl, narrow footring below deep rounded sides, early 19th c., 13 1/4" d., 5 1/2" h. (ILLUS., second from top next column) **$3,055**

Large Oblong Canton Platter

Fine Early Canton China Punch Bowl

Large Early Canton Serving Dish

Serving dish, cov., rectangular foot w/rectangular flaring sides w/rounded corners, high domed cover w/a pine cone finial, 19th c., 10 x 11", 6" h. (ILLUS.) **$633**

Fine Large Canton Soup Tureen

Soup tureen, cov., flared base band below the deep oval canted sides w/figural boar head end handles, long low domed cover w/figural helmet finial, 19th c., 8 3/4 x 12", 9" h. (ILLUS.) **$1,265**

Canton Lighthouse-shape Teapot

Teapot, cov., tapering cylindrical lighthouse-shape, straight spout, double strap handle, domed cover w/snail-like finial, small spout nick & tip of finial, 19th c., 8 1/2" h. (ILLUS.)................................... **$690**

Canton Tureen, Cover & Undertray

Tureen, cover & undertray, oblong w/beveled corners, molded boar's head handles on base & molded stem handle on the cover, 19th c., overall 12 5/8" l., 9" h., the set (ILLUS.)...................................... **$1,998**

Unusual Canton China Warming Platter

Warming platter, oval w/flanged rim, small tab handle at one end & filling hole at other end, 19th c., 15 3/4" l., 2 1/2" h. (ILLUS.) **$441**

Capo-di-Monte

Production of porcelain and faience began in 1736 at the Capo-di-Monte factory in Naples. In 1743 King Charles of Naples established a factory there that made wares with relief decoration. In 1759 the factory was moved to Buen Retiro near Madrid, operating until 1808. Another Naples pottery was opened in 1771 and operated until 1806 when its molds were acquired by the Doccia factory of Florence, which has since made reproductions of original Capo-di-Monte pieces with the "N" mark beneath a crown. Some very early pieces are valued in the thousands of dollars but the subsequent productions are considerably lower.

Large Fancy Capo-di-Monte Box

Box, box., rectangular waisted shaped w/beveled corners, conforming gilt-metal hinged fittings w/matching low domed cover, the sides molded & colored w/scenes of putti & nudes in landscapes, molded scene of female nudes in a landscape on the cover, signed on the bottom w/the blue "N" & crown mark, slight flake at rim, late 19th - early 20th c., 8 x 10 3/4", 5" h. (ILLUS.) **$360**

Ornate Molded Capo-di-Monte Ewer

Ewer, Baroque-style, the pedestal base composed of brightly colored molded scrolls & mounted with two figures of child mermaids blowing horns & w/a dolphin, the tall cylindrical body ornately molded w/ nude figures w/leafy trim &

oval blue reserves all in bold colors, the wide shoulder w/fancy molded details includingt a seated bearded merman w/his arms wrapped around the arched spout & grasping the horns of a grostesque seat creature, the ornate S-scroll handle down his back, blue mark on base, late 19th - early 20th c., 16 3/4" h. (ILLUS.) **$920**

Capo-di-Monte Teapot with Scenes

Teapot, cov., three gold paw feet supporting the spherical body decorated w/two large round reserves w/colorful landscapes w/naked frolicking figures, a cobalt blue background & inset cover w/ball finial, pink ribbed serpentine spout & ornate pink-trimmed C-scroll handle, late 19th - early 20th c., 9 1/2" w., 6 1/4" h. (ILLUS.) .. **$374**

Capo-di-Monte Campana-form Urns

Urns, campana-form, a gilded square foot supporting a bell-shaped base w/a red & white band below a green & yellow leaf band, the large urn w/large green & yellow leaves around the swelled base w/double mask head gold handles below the tall cylindrical sides & wide rolled rim w/red trim, the sides molded in bold relief w/semi-nude classical figures decorated in bright colors, blue mark on base, late 19th - early 20th c., 6" w., 8" h., pr. (ILLUS.) **$489**

Urns, cov., a tripartite plinth base supporting three incurved legs & a rounded dish all in white w/gold trim, the base supporting a large bulbous urn-form body molded in bold relief w/a continuous scene of knights in battle & decorated w/polychrome, the incurved shoulder w/reticulated panels below the gilt rim supporting a high domed matching reticulated cover topped w/a crown-form finial in gold & dark blue, late 19th - early 20th c., crown finials restored, 12" h., pr. (ILLUS., top next column) **$489**

Pair of Ornate Capo-di-Monte Urns

Carlton Ware

The Staffordshire firm of Wiltshaw & Robinson, Stoke-on-Trent, England, operated the Carlton Works from about 1890 until 1958, producing both earthenwares and porcelain. Specializing in decorative items like vases and teapots, it became well known for its lustre-finished wares, often decorated in the Oriental taste. The trademark Carlton Ware was incorporated into its printed mark. Since 1958, a new company, Carlton Ware Ltd., has operated the Carlton Works at Stoke.

Carlton Ware Moonlight Cameo Teapot

Teapot, cov., tall waisted cylindrical shape w/an angled gold handle & serpentine spout, low cover w/pointed gold finial, Moonlight Cameo patt., black matte ground w/a large oval flame lustre medallion on each side showing dancing maidens blowing bubbles under a full moon, marked "2944 - 0/608" w/crown & bird mark (ILLUS.) **$300**

Catalina Island Pottery

The Clay Products Division of the Santa Catalina Island Company produced a variety of wares during its brief ten-year operation. The brainchild of chewing-gum magnate William Wrigley Jr., owner of Catalina Island at the time, and business associate D.M. Retton, the plant was established at Pebbly Beach, near Avalon, in 1927. Its twofold goal was to provide year-round work for the island's residents and to produce building material for Wrigley's ongoing development of a major tourist attraction at Avalon. Early production consisted of bricks and roof and patio tiles. Later, art pottery, including vases, flower bowls, lamps and home accessories, were made from a local brown-based clay; in about 1930, tablewares were introduced. These early wares carried vivid glazes but had a tendency to chip easily, and a white-bodied, more chip-resistant clay imported from the mainland was used after 1932. The costs associated with importing clay eventually caused the Catalina pottery to be sold to Gladding, McBean & Company in 1937. Gladding McBean continued to use the Catalina name and molds for are ware and dinnerware for products manufactured on the mainland until 1942. After 1942, some of the molds were sold to and used by Weil of California. Gladding, McBean items usually have an ink stamped mark and can be distinguished from Island ware by the glaze and clay as well.

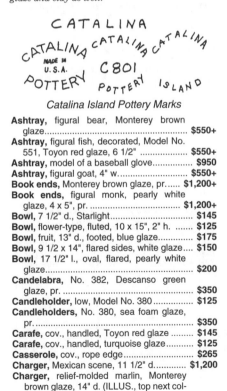

Catalina Island Pottery Marks

Charger with Marlin

Charger, relief-molded swordfish, Descanso green glaze, 14" d. .... **$1,200+**
Charger, rolled edge, Toyon red glaze, 14 1/2" d. **$225**
Coaster **$75**
Coffee server, cov. **$250**
Compote, footed, w/glass liner, Toyon red glaze **$225**
Console bowl, fluted .... **$225+**
Creamer, rope edge **$85**
Creamer, 6" h. **$250**
Cup, demitasse **$45**
Cup & saucer, rope edge **$75**
Custard cup **$45**
Flask, model of a cactus, Descanso green, 6 1/4" h. .... **$600+**
Flower frog, model of a pelican **$550**
Flower frog, model of a stork, 7" h. **$550**
Flowerpot, 4 1/2" h. **$145**
Indian bowl, rare **$650**
Lamp base, basketweave design, Descanso green glaze **$2,200**
Model of clamshell, pearly white glaze **$600**
Mug, 6" h. **$55**
Oil jar, No. 351, Toyon red glaze, 18" h. **$1,200**
Pipe holder/ashtray, figural napping peon, No. 555, Descanso green or blue glaze, each **$650**
Pitcher, 7 1/2" h., Toyon red glaze **$350**
Planter, model of a cat, cactus planter, Catalina **$475**
Plate, Moorish design decoration **$1,200**
Plate, 8 1/2" d., salad, rope edge **$55**
Plate, 10 1/2" d., dinner, rope edge................. **$65**
Plate, chop, 11" d., Descanso green glaze **$95**
Plate, 11 1/4" d., painted desert scene **$1,100**
Plate, chop, 12 1/2" d., Toyon red glaze **$145**
Plate, chop, 13 1/2" d., rope edge.................. **$120**
Plate, 14" d., submarine garden decoration **$1,250**
Relish tray, handled, clover-shaped, sea foam glaze (ILLUS., next page) **$1,300**
Salt & pepper shakers, figural senorita & peon, Toyon red & yellow glaze, pr........... **$245**
Salt & pepper shakers, gourd-shaped, pr. ... **$125**

Ashtray, figural bear, Monterey brown glaze.. **$550+**
Ashtray, figural fish, decorated, Model No. 551, Toyon red glaze, 6 1/2" .... **$550+**
Ashtray, model of a baseball glove............... **$950**
Ashtray, figural goat, 4" w........................... **$550+**
Book ends, Monterey brown glaze, pr...... **$1,200+**
Book ends, figural monk, pearly white glaze, 4 x 5", pr. .... **$1,200+**
Bowl, 7 1/2" d., Starlight............................... **$145**
Bowl, flower-type, fluted, 10 x 15", 2" h. **$125**
Bowl, fruit, 13" d., footed, blue glaze............. **$175**
Bowl, 9 1/2 x 14", flared sides, white glaze.... **$150**
Bowl, 17 1/2" l., oval, flared, pearly white glaze... **$200**
Candelabra, No. 382, Descanso green glaze, pr. **$350**
Candleholder, low, Model No. 380 .... **$125**
Candleholders, No. 380, sea foam glaze, pr. **$350**
Carafe, cov., handled, Toyon red glaze **$145**
Carafe, cov., handled, turquoise glaze........... **$125**
Casserole, cov., rope edge........................... **$265**
Charger, Mexican scene, 11 1/2" d............. **$1,200**
Charger, relief-molded marlin, Monterey brown glaze, 14" d. (ILLUS., top next column) .... **$1,200+**

Clover-shaped Relish Tray

Salt & pepper shakers, model of cactus,
pr... **$145**

Salt & pepper shakers, model of tulip, blue
glaze, pr. **$125**

Shot tumbler, nude figure, "Bottoms Up,"
3 1/4" h... **$195**

Sugar bowl, cov., rope edge........................... **$85**

Tea tile, 8" w... **$295+**

Tile, Spanish design, 6 x 6" sq. .... **$295+**

Tile Plaque with Macaw

Tile plaque, depicting green macaw,
12 x 18" (ILLUS.)................................... **$2,500+**

Tortilla Warmer

Tortilla warmer, cov., Monterey brown
glaze (ILLUS.) **$750**

Tumbler **$50**

Vase, 5" h., handled, Model No. 612, Man-
darin yellow glaze **$225**

Vase, 5" h., stepped, handled, turquoise
glaze **$350**

Vase, bud, 5" h., Model No. 300, Descanso
green glaze **$170**

Vase, 5 1/2" h., Model No. 600, tan glaze..... **$150**

Vase, 6" h., ribbed body, blue glaze............. **$175**

Vase, 7 1/2" h., trophy-form, handled, Toy-
on red glaze **$900**

Vase, 7 3/4" h., Model No. 627, blue glaze **$225**

Vase, 9" h., experimental multicolored glaze .. **$800**

Vase, 10" h., fluted **$225**

Vase, 10" h., pearly white glaze **$225**

Vinegar bottle w/stopper, gourd-shape **$165**

Wall pocket, basketweave design, 9" l. **$450**

Wall pocket or vase, seashell form, white
clay... **$350+**

Ceramic Arts Studio of Madison

During its 15 years of operation, Ceramic Arts Studio of Madison, Wisconsin, was one of the nation's most prolific producers of figurines, shakers, and other decorative ceramics. The studio began in 1940 as the joint venture of potter Lawrence Rabbitt and entrepreneur Reuben Sand. Early products included hand-thrown bowls, pots, and vases, exploring the potential of Wisconsin clay. However, the arrival of Betty Harrington in 1941 took CAS in a new direction, leading to the type of work it is best known for. Under Mrs. Harrington's artistic leadership, the focus was changed to the production of finely sculpted decorative figurines. Among the many subjects covered were adults in varied costumes and poses, charming depictions of children, fantasy and theatrical figures, and animals. The inventory soon expanded to include figural wall plaques, head vases, salt-and-pepper shakers, self-sitters, and "snuggle pairs."

Metal display accessories complementing the ceramics were produced by another Reuben Sand firm, Jon-San Creations, under the direction of Zona Liberace (stepmother of the famed pianist). Mrs. Liberace also served as the studio's decorating director.

During World War II, Ceramic Arts Studio flourished, since the import of decorative items from overseas was suspended. In its prime during the late 1940s, CAS produced over 500,000 pieces annually, and employed nearly 100 workers.

As primary designer, the talented Betty Harrington is credited with creating the vast majority of the 800-plus designs in the Studio inventory--a remarkable achievement for a self-taught artist. The only other CAS designer of note was Ulle Cohen ("Rebus"), who contributed a series of modernistic animal figurines in the early 1950s.

The popularity of Ceramic Arts Studio pieces eventually resulted in many imitations of lesser quality. After World War II, lower-priced imports began to flood the market, forcing the studio to close its doors in 1955. An attempt to continue the enterprise in Japan, using some of the Madison master molds as well as new designs, did not prove successful. An additional number of molds and copyrights were sold to Mahana Imports, which released a series of figures based on the CAS originals. Both the Ceramic Arts Studio-Japan and Mahana pieces utilized a clay both whiter and more lightweight than that of Madison pieces. Additionally, their markings differ from the "Ceramic Arts Studio, Madison Wis." logo, which appears in black on the base of many studio pieces. However, not all authentic studio pieces were marked (particularly in pairs); a more reliable indicator of authenticity is the "decorator tick mark." This series of colored dots, which appears at the drain hole on the bottom of every Ceramic Arts Studio piece, served as an in-house identifier for the decorator who worked on a specific piece. The tick mark is a sure sign that a figurine is the work of the studio.

Ceramic Arts Studio is one of the few figural ceramics firms of the 1940s and '50s that operated successfully outside of the West Coast. Today, CAS pieces remain in high demand, thanks to their skillful design and decoration, warm use of color, distinctively glossy glaze, and highly imaginative and exquisitely realized themes.

Many pieces in the Ceramic Arts Studio inventory were released both as figurines and as salt-and-pepper shakers. For items not specifically noted as shakers in this listing, add 50 percent to the shaker price estimate.

Complete reference information on the studio can be found in Ceramic Arts Studio: The Legacy of Betty Harrington by Donald-Brian Johnson, Timothy J. Holthaus, and James E. Petzold (Schiffer Publishing Ltd., 2003). The official Ceramic Arts Studio collectors group, "CAS Collectors," publishes a quarterly newsletter, hosts an annual convention, and can be contacted at www.cascollectors.com. The studio also has an official historical site, www.ceramicartsstudio.org. Photos for this category are by John Petzold.

Ceramic Arts Studio Marks

Accordion Lady, 8 1/2" h. .... **$500-$600**
Adam & Eve (one piece), extremely rare, 12" h. (ILLUS., bottom of page) .... **$10,000+**

Rare Adonis & Aphrodite Figures

Adonis & Aphrodite, 7" h. & 9" h., pr. (ILLUS.) .... **$500-$700**

Ceramics Arts Studion Extremely Rare Adam & Eve Figure Group

Al the Hunter & Kirby the Setter Figures

Al the Hunter & Kirby the English Setter,
7 1/2" h. & 2" l., pr. (ILLUS.)............. **$275-$375**
Angel Trio (Praying, Star & Singing),
4 1/2" h., 6 1/2" h. & 3 1/2" h., the set
.... **$300-$360**
Angel with Candle, 5" h. .... **$65-$75**
Arched Window with Cross metal accessory, 14" h. .... **$100-$120**

Baby Chick & Nest Snuggle Pair

Baby Chick & Nest snuggle pair, 1 1/4" h.
& 1 3/4" h., pr. (ILLUS.)..................... **$160-$200**
Bali Boy, shelf-sitter, 6" h...................... **$220-$250**
Bali Girl, shelf-sitter, 6" h. .... **$220-$250**
Bali-Hai & Bali-Lao, 7 3/4" h. & 8 1/2" h.,
pr.. **$180-$220**
Bali-Kris, carrying dagger, 8 1/4" h....... **$120-$140**
Balinese Woman lamp, Moss Mfg., scarce
.... **$350-$375**
Balky Colt, 3 3/4" h. .... **$100-$125**

Ceramic Arts Ballerina Quartet Set

Ballerina Quartet, left to right: 5" h. Rose,
6" h. Daisy, 3 1/2" h. Violet & 6" h. Pansy, the set (ILLUS.) .... **$1,040-$1,120**

Man & Woman Ballet Dancers Shelf-Sitters

Ballet Dancers, man & woman, shelf-sitters, 7" & 6 1/2" h., pr. (ILLUS.) .... **$120-$150**
Bamboo bowl, 2 1/2" h........................... **$25-$30**
Bass Viol Boy, 5" h. (ILLUS. second from
right with other child musicians, bottom of
page)... **$120-$140**
Big Dutch Boy & Girl, 4" h., pr............... **$30-$40**
Billy with ball down, shelf-sitter, 4 1/2" h.
.... **$240-$270**
Blackamoor salt & pepper shakers, an "S"
on one, a "P" on the other, 4 3/4" h., pr.
.... **$140-$160**
Bonnie head vase, 7" h........................ **$125-$150**

Group of Child Musician Figures

Boy & Puppy & Girl & Kitten Shelf-Sitters

Boy with Puppy & Girl with Kitten, shelf-sitters, 4 1/4" h., pr. (ILLUS.)............. **$150-$200**

Ceramic Arts Bride & Groom

Bride & Groom, 4 3/4" h. & 5" h., pr. (ILLUS.)
.... **$250-$300**
Bruce & Beth, 6 1/2" h. & 5" h., pr.......... **$80-$100**
Burmese Man, Woman & Chinthe,
4 3/4" h. & 5" h., the set (ILLUS., top next column) .... **$425-$620**
Carmen & Carmelita, 7 1/4" h. & 4 1/4" h., pr... **$300-$350**
Chinese Boy & Girl on Bamboo Planters,
5" h... **$60-$70**
Chinese Boy with Kite, 6" h................. **$400-$500**

Burmese Man, Woman & Chinthe

Chinese Emperor & Empress, 7" h., pr.
.... **$1,600-$2,000**
Chivalry lamp, 11" h............................ **$650-$700**
Chubby St. Francis, 9" h...................... **$180-$200**
Cockatoo plaques, A & B, 8" & 8 1/4" h., pr.
.... **$180-$220**
Comedy & Tragedy Mask plaques,
5 1/4" h., pr...................................... **$180-$220**
Daisy Donkey, 4 3/4" h. (ILLUS. right with Elsie Elephant, bottom of page).......... **$85-$100**
Dance Moderne Man & Woman, 9 1/2" h., pr... **$140-$220**

Dawn Abstract Female Figure

Dawn, abstract female figure, 6 1/2" h. (ILLUS.).. **$175-$200**

Daisy Donkey & Elsie Elephant

Small & Large Fighting Leopards Pairs

Deer plaque, stylized, 5 1/2" l. .... **$1,000-$1,200**
Duck Vase, two-sided, 4" h. .... **$225-$250**

Dutch Love Boy & Dutch Love Girl

Dutch Love Boy & Dutch Love Girl, 5" h.,
  pr. (ILLUS.)... **$120-$140**
Elf Sitting, 2 1/2" h. .... **$25-$30**
Elsie Elephant, 5" h. (ILLUS. left with Dai-
  sey Donkey, bottom previous page).... **$85-$110**
En Pose & En Repose shelf-sitters,
  4 3/4" h., pr...................................... **$100-$140**
Encore Man & Woman, 8 1/2" & 9" h., pr.
  .... **$200-$250**
Fighting Leopards, large, 6" h., 8" l., pr.
  (ILLUS. back with small pair of Fighting
  Leopards, top of page).................. **$900-$1,000**
Fighting Leopards, small size, 3 1/2" h.,
  6 1/4" l., pr. (ILLUS. front, left & right, with
  large Fighting Leopards, top of page) **$180-$250**
Fire Man & Fire Woman, dark red,
  11 1/4" h., pr. (ILLUS., top next column)
  .... **$400-$450**
Fish up on tails, A & B., 4" h., pr............. **$40-$70**
Flute Girl, 4 1/2" h. (ILLUS. second from
  left with other child musicians, bottom of
  page 138)... **$140-$160**

Dark Red Fire Man & Fire Woman

Fox & Goose Ceramic Arts Figures

Fox & Goose, 3 1/4" h., 2 1/4" h., pr. (ILLUS.)
  .... **$300-$350**
Frisky Colt, 3 3/4" h. .... **$100-$125**
Goosey Gander plaque, 4 1/2" h. .... **$140-$160**
Grapes teapot, miniature, 2 1/2" h. .... **$65-$85**
Hansel & Gretel, one-piece, 3" h. .... **$125-$150**

Lotus & Manchu Head Vases

Harlequin Boy & Girl with Mask Figures

Harlequin By & Girl with Masks, 8 1/2" &
8 3/4" h., pr. (ILLUS.) .... **$1,800-$1,900**
Harmonica Boy, shelf-sitter, 4" h. .... **$120-$140**
Heart Shape metal shelf, 11 1/2" h. ...... **$100-$120**

Ceramic Arts Hippo Ashtray

Hippo ashtray, 3 1/2" h. (ILLUS.) .... $100-$120
Honey Spaniel, 5 3/4" h. .... $200-$225
Horsehead server, miniature, 2 1/2" l.
.... $60-$70
Isaac, 10" h. .... $70-$100
Jim & June, 4 3/4" h. & 4 1/2" h., pr. ...... $80-$100
Kitten Scratching, 2" h. .... $50-$60
Kitten Sleeping (A), 2" h. .... $50-$60
Kitten Washing (A), 2" h. .... $50-$60
Kitten with Ball, 2" h. .... $50-$60
Little Jack Horner #2, 4" h. .... $75-$100
Little Miss Muffet #2, 4" h. .... $75-$100
Lotus & Manchu, head vases, 7 1/2" h. &
7 3/4" h., pr. (ILLUS., top of page) .... $150-$200
Lotus wall plaque, 8 1/2" h. .... $200-$225

Ceramic Arts M'amselle Figure

M'amselle, kneeling girl, all-white, 7" h.
(ILLUS.) .... $250-$350
**Manchu & Lotus Standing Lantern Man &
Woman,** 9" h., pr. .... $80-$120
Manchu wall plaque, 8 1/2" h. .... $200-$225
Masquerade Man & Woman plaques,
8" h., pr. .... $1,600-$2,000

Mei-Ling Head Vase

Mei-Ling head vase, 5" h. (ILLUS.)...... **$150-$175**
Mexican Boy with cactus, 6 3/4" h......... **$70-$85**
Mexican Girl, 6 1/4" h. .... **$70-$85**
Miss Lucindy, 7" h.................................. **$40-$50**
Modern Collie, reclining, 4 1/2" l.......... **$400-$500**

Modern Doe & Fawn Figures

Modern Doe & Fawn, designed by Rebus,
3 3/4" h. & 2" h., pr. (ILLUS.)............. **$175-$225**
Modern Fox, 6 1/2" l. .... **$120-$150**

Purple Mother & Calf Snugglers

Mother Cow & Calf snugglers, in purple,
5 1/4" h. & 2 1/2" h., pr...................... **$100-$300**
Musical Score metal shelf, Jon-San Cre-
ations, 12 x 14" .... **$85-$100**
One-Piece Scotties, 2 3/4" h............... **$100-$125**
Our Lady of Fatima, 9" h...................... **$260-$285**
Peek-A-Boo Pixie Tray, 4 1/2" .... **$125-$150**
Peter Rabbit, 3 1/2" h. .... **$100-$125**
Petrov & Petrushka, Russian boy & girl, 5"
& 5 1/2" h., pr. .... **$120-$150**
Pierrot & Pierette shelf-sitters, 6 1/2" h.,
pr... **$140-$200**
Pixie Riding Snail, 2 3/4" h. .... **$40-$50**
**Praise Angel (hand up) & Blessing Angel
(hand down),** 6 1/4" h. & 5 3/4" h., pr.
.... **$180-$240**
Rebekah, 10" h. .... **$70-$100**

Robins on Tree Trunk Planter

Robins on Tree Trunk planter, Ceramic
Arts Studio (Japan), 8" l. (ILLUS.)......... **$35-$45**

Very Rare Ceramic Arts Salome Figure

Salome, 14" h. (ILLUS.) .... **$1,800-$2,000**
Saxophone Boy, 5" h. (ILLUS. far right with
other child musicians, page 138) ...... **$140-$160**
Shadow Dancer A & B plaques, 8" h. &
7 3/4" h., pr... **$60-$80**
Siamese Cat & Kitten, 4 1/4" & 3 1/4" h.,
pr.. **$60-$75**

The Four Seasons Ceramic Arts Figures

Smi-Pi, chubby man carrying basket, scarce, 6 1/4" h. .... $350-$450
Sonny Spaniel, 5 3/4" h. .... $200-$225
St. Francis a Pace, 9 1/2" h. .... $125-$150
Summer Belle, 5 1/4" h. .... $100-$120

Swan Lake Man & Swan Lake Woman

Swan Lake Man & Swan Lake Woman, 7" h., pr. (ILLUS.) .... $1,800-$1,900
Swan teapot, miniature, 3" h. .... $60-$75
Tall Ballerina, 11" h. .... $350-$400
The Four Seasons, Autumn Andy, 5" h. (ILLUS. far right with three other figures, top of page) .... $160-$190
The Four Seasons, Spring Sue, 5" h. (ILLUS. second from left with three other figures, top of page).. $140-$170
The Four Seasons, Summer Sally, 3 1/2" h. (ILLUS. second from right with three other figures, top of page)........ $100-$130
The Four Seasons, Winter Willie, 4" h. (ILLUS. far left with three other figures, top of page)...................................... $90-$120
Tom Cat, shelf-sitter, 4 3/4" h.................... $50-$60
Wee Chinese Boy & Girl, 3" h., pr. .... $30-$40
Wee Eskimo Boy & Girl salt & pepper shakers, 3 1/4" h. & 3" h., pr. .... $50-$70
Wee French Boy & Girl salt & pepper shakers, 3" h., pr. .... $80-$90

Wee Piggy Boy & Girl Shakers

Wee Piggy Boy & Girl salt & pepper shakers, 3 1/4" h. & 3 1/2" h., pr. (ILLUS.) ... $50-$70

Wing-Sang & Lu-Tang on Bamboo Vases

Wing-Sang & Lu-Tang on Bamboo Vases, scarce, 6 1/4" h., pr. (ILLUS.)........ $90-$100
Winter Belle bell, 5 1/4" h. .... $75-$85
Young Camel, 5 1/2" h. .... $125-$150

Young Love Boy & Girl Shelf-Sitters

Young Love Boy & Girl, shelf-sitters, 4 1/2" h., pr. (ILLUS.) .... **$90-$100**

Chinese Export

Large quantities of porcelain have been made in China for export to America from the 1780s, much of it shipped from the ports of Canton and Nanking. A major source of this porcelain was Ching-te-Chen in the Kiangsi province, but the wares were also made elsewhere. The largest quantities were blue and white. Prices fluctuate considerably depending on age, condition, decoration, etc.

ROSE MEDALLION and CANTON export wares are listed separately.

Set of Chinese Export Covered Cups

Cups, cov., footed ovoid body w/a twined strap handle, low domed cover w/gold figural nut finial, decorated around the sides & cover w/a colorful flowering tree design w/an orange top rim band, 19th c., overall 3 1/2" h., set of 7 (ILLUS.) **$977**

Unusual Famille Rose Export Pitcher

Pitcher, 6 1/2" h., Famille Rose palette, slightly swelled cylindrical shape w/a deeply scalloped rim & pointed rim spout, jagged arched handle, the sides decorated w/large colorful panels of flowers, minor rim chips, 19th c. (ILLUS.) **$863**

Fitzhugh Pattern Plates

Plates, 9 3/4" d., blue Fitzhugh patt., early 19th c., pr. (ILLUS.) **$575**

Famille Rose Well-and-Tree Platter

Platter, 13 1/4 x 16 3/4" oval, well & tree-type, Famille Rose palette, the top decorated w/six large triangular panels of colorful florals, some minor gold loss, mid-19th c. (ILLUS.) **$978**

Punch Bowl for the American Market

Punch bowl, a deep footring & deep rounded sides, made for the American market & decorated on the sides w/a spread-winged eagle w/shield on the front & back, a gilt carnation on each side & repeated in the interior beneath a border matching the exterior grisaille & gilt lines, ca. 1800, 11 1/2" d. (ILLUS.) **$2,640**

Punch Bowl with Arms of New York State

Punch bowl, a deep footring & deep rounded sides, made for the American market & decorated on the sides w/the Arms of New York State in red, white, blue & gold on each side, narrow wavy blue line rim band, a pink peony sprig in the interior bottom, ca. 1795, 11 1/2" d. (ILLUS.) **$3,840**

Fine Rose Famille Export Punch Bowl

Punch bowl, Famille Rose palette, deep rounded & gently flaring sides, the exterior & interior w/the wide lower band filled w/colorful floral clusters, the exterior w/a wide gold band separating the lower section w/a densely painted floral rim band that continues to the inside rim, mid-19th c., 12 3/4" d., 5 1/2" h. (ILLUS.) **$1,265**

Late Chinese Export Punch Bowl

Punch bowl, green Fitzhugh patt., narrow footring below the deep rounded & gently flaring sides, the exterior & interior decorated w/large squared panels of design, bottom marked "Made in China," early 20th c., 11" d., 4 1/2" h. (ILLUS.) **$403**

Rose Mandarin Export Sauce Tureen

Sauce tureen, cov., Rose Mandarin design, a deep flaring foot supporting the squatty bulbous oblong body w/double loop end handles, the high domed & stepped cover w/a largber large gold flower finial, 19th c., 8" l., 6" h. (ILLUS.) **$1,265**

Fine Tall Export Umbrella Stand

Umbrella stand, Famille Rose palette in a Mandarin design, the tall cylindrical ribbed body decorated up the sides w/three bands containing alternating figural & floral panels, 19th c., 24 3/4" h. (ILLUS.) **$4,025**

Chintz China

There are over fifty flower patterns and myriad colors from which Chintz collectors can choose. That is not surprising considering companies in England began producing these showy, yet sometimes muted, patterns in the early part of the 1900s. Public reception was so great that this production trend continued until the 1960s.

Chintz Majestic Pattern Breakfast Set

Tea set: breakfast set: cov. teapot, cup, creamer, open sugar bowl, toast rack & oblong paneled tray w/end handles; Majestic patt., Countess shape, Royal Winton, the set (ILLUS.)................... **$1,750-$2,000**

Florence Pattern Stacking Tea Set

Tea set: stacking-type, cov. creamer, sugar & teapot; Florence patt., Delamere shape, Royal Winton, the set (ILLUS.) .... **$1,750-$2,000**

DuBarry Pattern Chintz Teapot

Teapot, cov., DuBarry patt., Diamond shape, James Kent, Ltd. (ILLUS.) .... **$950-$1,000**

Joyce-Lynn Ascot Shape Teapot

Teapot, cov., Joyce-Lynn patt., Ascot shape, Royal Winton (ILLUS.) .... **$1,300-$1,500**

Royal Winton Summertime Pattern Teapot

Teapot, cov., Summertime patt., Ajax shape, Royal Winton (ILLUS.) **$950**

Clarice Cliff Designs

Clarice Cliff was a designer for A.J. Wilkinson, Ltd., Royal Staffordshire Pottery, Burslem, England when it acquired the adjoining Newport Pottery Company, whose warehouses were filled with undecorated bowls and vases. In about 1925 her flair with the Art Deco style was incorporated into designs appropriately named "Bizarre" and "Fantasque" and the warehouse stockpile was decorated in vivid colors. These hand-painted earthenwares, all bearing the printed signature of designer Clarice Cliff, were produced until World War II and are now finding enormous favor with collectors.

Author's Note: Reproductions of the Clarice Cliff "Bizarre" marking have been appearing on the market recently.

Clarice Cliff Mark

Large Colorful Clarice Cliff "Latona" Pattern Bowl

Bowl, 16 3/8" d., a wide flat bottom & wide flaring sides, Latona patt., decorated around the exterior w/a polychrome scene of stylized trees in shades of red, orange, green, blue, black & cream, printed Bizarre Ware backstamp, surface wear to interior center, ca. 1930 (ILLUS., top of page) **$1,645**

cream-colored handle, printed Bizarre Ware backstamp, ca. 1930 (ILLUS.) **$1,880**

Clarice Cliff Patina Country Pitcher

Fine Clarice Cliff Blue Chintz Pitcher

Pitcher, 11 5/8" h., jug-form, the ovoid ribbed body tapering to a flat rim, decorated in the Fantasque Blue Chintz patt. in shades of blue, rose red, green & cream,

Vase, 9 3/4" h., simple ovoid form tapering to a wide flat rim, decorated in color in the Patina Country patt. in shades of green, purple, red, yellow & blue on a mottled light yellow ground, printed Bizarre Ware backstamp, ca. 1930 (ILLUS.) **$1,293**

Cleminson Clay

Betty Cleminson, a hobbyist, began working in her Monterey Park, California garage in 1941. She called the business Cleminson Clay. However, the business proved so successful that two years later Betty was forced to make several key decisions: She moved to El Monte, California and built a large factory; hired over fifty employees including many artists; and changed the name to "The California Cleminson." Later, another major decision was made to encourage her husband, George, to join the company. He had taught school but was also proficient at handling the financial affairs. He also oversaw the construction of the new building. At one point during the later years, the Cleminsons had about 150 employees. Due to the competition from imports, Betty, like so many American potters, was forced to close her operation in 1963. She died on Sept. 30, 1996 at the age of 86.

The Cleminsons created a variety of gift wares including butter dishes, canisters, cookie jars, salt and pepper shakers and string holders. An assortment of hand painted plates, wall plaques and other items with novelty sayings were a big hit with collectors. Distlefink was a highly successful dinnerware line when it was introduced. However, today the light brown ground is not nearly as popular as the white ground. Galagray was a small line consisting of mostly trays, serving dishes and flowerpots with a country theme.

The incised, stylized "BC" mark signifies Betty Cleminson. It was the first mark used. Another mark was a facsimile of a plate with a ribbon at the top and the words "The California" over "Cleminson" with the initials "bc" in the center, along with a boy and girl, one on each side of the plate. The words "hand painted" appear below the plate. This mark is the most familiar to collectors and can be found with or without the boy and girl. - Susan Cox

Most commonly found stamped mark with or without boy & girl on the sides. Early Betty Cleminson incised mark with her initials. Sometimes confused with the copyright symbol.

Ashtray, round w/six cigarette rest, three feet, decorated w/abstract designs, 1950s, 8 1/4" d., 3 3/4" h. **$50**

Bank, figural hanging-type, modeled as a stocking in red & white stripes, coin slot in top, mark w/boy & girl outside circle & Cleminson inside, 8 1/2" h. **$25**

Galagray Line Bowl

Bowl, 3" d., 2 3/4" h., straight 1/4" base rising to a lightly flared rim, Galagray line, grey ground w/red gloss inside & red abstract leaves around the outside center (ILLUS.)... **$36**

Butter dish, cov., figural, model of a Distlefink sitting on an oblong base, bird's head turned toward back, brown glossy glaze w/dark brown & rust accents, 7 1/2" l., 5 3/4" h. (ILLUS. bottom right with other Distlefink pieces, bottom of page)... **$65**

Grouping of Cleminson Distlefink Pieces

Butter dish, cov., figural, round model of a pudgy woman w/her skirt forming the lid & her upper body forming the handle, green dish w/cover in white gloss w/dark & light green, dark brown & black glazes, 7" h... **$155**

Cleminson Cheese Keeper, Cookie Jar & Salt Box

Cheese keeper, cov., figural, the cover modeled as a round pudgy woman w/a wide domed skirt, in dark & light green, dark brown, black & white glossy glaze, on a green round dish base, 6 1/2" h. (ILLUS. bottom right with cookie jar & salt box) **$160**

Cleminson Cleanser Shaker

Cleanser shaker, figure of a woman standing, yellow hair, pink scarf over head, pink & white dress w/grey trim, five holes in top of head, originally included a card around her neck w/a poem explaining that she was a cleanser shaker, marked w/copyright symbol & the plate w/a girl & boy on each side, 6 1/2" h. (ILLUS.) **$55**

Cleanser shaker, figure of woman standing, yellow hair, brown scarf, white & brown apron over yellow dress, blue accents, very common, 6 1/2" h........................ **$40**

Cookie jar, cov., cylindrical w/peaked cover w/knob handle, the sides in white h.p. w/red cherries, green leaves & brown branches encircling "Cookies," 9" h. (ILLUS. bottom left with cheese keeper and salt box, previous column)...... **$75**

Cookie jar, cov., heart-shaped cover w/two lovebirds forming handle, yellow ground w/white center, w/wording "The Way To A Man's Heart," in blue, black & pink, California Cleminsons in circle & copyright symbol mark, 9 1/4" h. **$255**

Cotton ball holder, figural, a baby's head w/one tooth, pale pink ground, brown eyes, blue collar bow, hard to find, 4" h. **$95**

Cleminson Clay Creamer

Creamer, figural, model of rooster, white w/green & pink accents, stamped mark, 5 1/2" h. (ILLUS.) **$59**

"For A Good Egg" Eggcup

Eggcup, boy's face on front, "For A Good Egg" on reverse, no mark, 3 3/4" h. (ILLUS.).. **$55-60**

Egg timer, Humpty-Dumpty head, yellow hat w/blue band, blue nose, yellow bow tie w/blue dots, black smile & eyes looking upward, glass w/sand attached to his back, marked w/a circle w/California Cleminson inside, scarce, 3 1/2" h. **$90**

Gravy boat, Distlefink patt., white ground w/green, purple, blue & black decorations, 10 1/2" l. **$28**

Mug with Head of Man & Woman

Mug, cylindrical w/loop handle, colored heads of a mustached brown-haired man & blonde-haired lady along with the wording "Now Is The Hour," 4 1/2" h. (ILLUS.) **$30**

Mug, girl & boy drinking on front, "Now Is The Hour" on reverse, stamped mark, 3 1/4" h. **$35**

Cleminson Clay Laundry Sprinkler

Laundry sprinkler, figural, Oriental man, hat forms metal top, stamped mark, 9" h. (ILLUS.) **$106**

Match holder, white ground w/a yellow bird on a branch w/blue flowers below, flowers on both sides w/blue & yellow trim, marked w/boy & girl, 6 1/2" h. **$125**

Juvenile Mug

Mug, juvenile, round knobs on sides, scene of Native American boy & his dog playing on front, stamped mark, 4 1/4" h. (ILLUS.) **$69**

"Morning After" Mug

Mug, cov., irregular shape w/front showing man's face w/hung-over expression, model of water bag forms lid, "Morning After" on reverse & "Never Again" on inside bottom, stamped mark, 5" h. (ILLUS.) **$60**

Cleminson Clay Pie Bird

Pie bird, figural, model of a bird, white body decorated in pink, blue & green, early mark, 1941, 4 1/2" h. (ILLUS.) **$90**

Bathtub-shaped Cleminson Planter

Pitcher, 10 1/2" h., figural, model of a Distlefink, beak forms spout, tail is handle, white body w/brown & green accents (ILLUS. bottom left with other Distlefink pieces, page 148) **$63**

Pitcher, 6 1/2" h., Galagray line, handle rises above the rim, country theme w/a boy & girl in red & grey **$45**

Planter, figural, modeled as an old-fashioned claw-foot bathtub, white interior & claw feet, exterior in light blue w/h.p. pink roses & green leaves, 7" l., 3 1/4" h. (ILLUS., top of page) **$40**

Plate, 6 1/2" d., pale blue background w/white & black silhouette, woman standing & churning butter **$40**

Plate, 6 1/2" d., pale blue ground w/a white & black silhouette scene of a woman sitting at a spinning wheel, two holes for hanging **$43**

Plate, 7" d., ecru ground w/stylized fruit in center w/green leaves, blue rectangles around verge, two factory-drilled holes for hanging **$22**

Cleminson Plate with Woman Singing

Plate, 7 1/4" d., blue rim w/pink stylized flowers, center w/h.p. profile bust of a lady singing, mark w/Cleminson in circle & boy & girl outside circle (ILLUS.) **$28**

Razor blade bank, model of a man's face, w/hand holding razor, slot in top for used blades, unglazed bottom w/stamped mark, 3 1/4" h. **$64**

Recipe holder, small footed oblong base rising to scalloped sides & rim, hearts & flowers motif, "Recipe holder" in brown & black, 4" l., 3" h. **$41**

Fluted Plate with Flowers & Butterflies

Plate, 7" d., fluted body & scalloped rim, decorated w/flowers & butterflies on a blue shaded to white ground, two holes for hanging, stamped mark (ILLUS.) **$38**

Cleminson Clay Ring Holder

Ring holder, figural, model of a dog w/tail straight up to hold jewelry, white body w/tan & dark brown accents, marked w/copyright symbol & plate w/a boy & girl on either side, 3" l., 2 3/4" h. (ILLUS., previous page) $49

Ring holder, figural, model of a hand, palm facing forward, large flower covers the wrist, 3" h. $58

Salt box w/hinged wooden cover, cylindrical w/high arched back crest w/hanging hole decorated w/an apple on a branch, the sides w/scrolls & small leaves below "Salt," maroon & green, 7 1/2" h. (ILLUS. top right with cheese keeper & cookie jar, page 149) $75

Salt box w/hinged wooden lid, figural bucket, white ground w/"Salt" in maroon & green & maroon leaves, cherry fruit & leaves at top near drilled hole for hanging, 8" h. $75

Salt & pepper shakers, figural, a man & woman artist, each holding a palette in one hand, the woman's palette w/"Salt" & the man's with "Pepper," each w/black ties, 6" h., pr. $70

Salt & pepper shakers, figural man & woman on square bases, Galagray line, red & grey colors, 6" h., pr. $48

Salt & pepper shakers, model of the Distlefink, 6 1/4"h., pr. (ILLUS. top with Distlefink butter dish & pitcher, page 148).. $30-$50

Serving dish, Galagray line, grey ground w/muted red country motif, scalloped rim on one edge, stamped mark w/boy & girl & the words "Galagray Ware" underneath along w/copyright symbol, 8 1/4" l............... $15

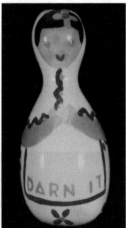

Cleminson Woman Sock Darner

Sock darner, white ground w/h.p. woman's face & brown hair, blue & maroon accents, words "Darn It" on front near bottom, feet on bottom unseen from standing position, 5" h. (ILLUS.) $79

Spoon rest, elongated quatrefoil w/gloss grey & orange, dark grey & tan leaves & blossoms, 8 1/2" l.. $32

String holder, heart-shaped $66

String holder-wall pocket, figural, a model of a house w/a red base & chimney & yellow trim around the door & brown roof, wording reads "Friends From Afar and Nearabout Will Find Our Latchstring Always Out".. $95

Tea bag holder, model of a teapot w/"Let Me Hold The Bag" in center, stamped mark, 4 1/4" w. $25

Vase, model of a watering can $33

Wall plaque, figural, model of a key printed w/"Welcome Guest" on a white ground w/the edge trimmed in yellow, yellow ground w/a green & rust stripe, 7" h............. $38

Wall Plaque with Applied Flowers

Wall plaque, oval w/scalloped rim trimmed in brown on inside edge, applied flowers & leaves in center w/h.p. background flowers, green gloss leaves, pink flower bud & two pink flowers w/yellow centers, two factory holes for hanging, boy & girl mark, 6 3/4" h. (ILLUS.) $51

Cleminson Clay Wall Plaque

Wall plaque, oval w/scalloped rim trimmed in brown on inside edge, applied pansy-like flowers & leaves in center, one in pinks, one yellow & blue, h.p. background flowers, green gloss leaves, two factory holes for hanging, 6 3/4" h. (ILLUS.) $51

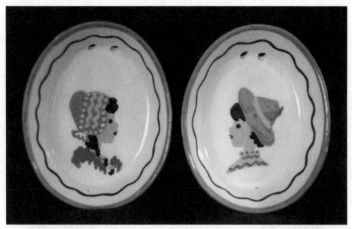

Cleminson Clay Wall Plaques

Wall plaques, oval, white ground, blue rims, scalloped brown line inside rims, centers w/bust profiles of boy in blue Alpine-type hat & girl in blue & pink bonnet, both w/brown hair & eyes, each plaque w/two holes for hanging, bc mark, 4 1/4" h., pr (ILLUS., top of page).................................... **$38**

Wall pocket, figural, model of a teapot w/bail handle w/black ceramic center w/painted flowers, black cover & cobalt blue glazed body w/a beige heart-shaped center, printed in the center "A Kitchen Bright & A Singing Kettle Make a Home The Place You Want To Settle," 8 1/4" h... **$30**

Wall pocket, model of a frying pan w/design on bottom, "Them that works hard eats hearty," hole in handle for hanging, ink stamp mark, 11 3/8" l. including handle **$54**

Wall pocket, model of a scoop, white body w/blue & red flowers & green leaves, second mark without boy & girl on each side, marked "hand painted" & copyright symbol, 9" l. (ILLUS.)... **$52**

Wall pocket, model of a teapot, wire & wood handle painted w/flowers, blue & brown glazes w/heart-shaped motif w/"Kitchen bright & a singing kettle make home the place you want to settle," marked w/boy & girl, 9" d., 6" h................... **$50**

Wall pocket, slightly flared top & bottom w/top showing "Let's pay off the Mortgage" & bottom showing a house & trees, gloss rose, 7" h. **$47**

Wall pocket, white ground w/scalloped blue edge, "Once burned" at top, "Twice shy" at bottom, woman holding spoon facing away from a black wood-burning kitchen stove, ink stamp mark, 5 1/4" sq. **$48**

Clewell Wares

Although Charles W. Clewell of Canton, Ohio, didn't operate a pottery, he is responsible for a category of fine art pottery through his development of a unique metal coating placed on pottery blanks obtained from Owens, Weller and others. By encasing objects in a thin metal shell, he produced copper- and bronze-finished ceramics. Later experiments led him to chemically treat the metal coating to attain the bluish green patinated effect associated with copper and bronze. Although he produced metal-coated pottery from 1902 until the mid-1950s, Clewell's production was quite limited, for he felt no one else could competently re-create his artwork, therefore operated a small shop with little help.

Wall Pocket in Form of Scoop

Clewell Wares Mark

Fine Clewell Table Lamp

Lamp, table-type, a hammered brass ringed foot supporting to tall baluster-form body w/a fine crusty bluish green finish, hammered copper cap & electrical fittings at the top, bottom signed "Clewell 277-6" & w/old paper label under the cap reads "$45.00," lamp body 15 3/4" h. (ILLUS.)..................................... **$978**

Small Bulbous Clewell Vase

Vase, 4 1/2" h., footed wide bulbous ovoid body w/a short wide flaring rim, original shaded & mottled dark brown to green patina, marked, No. 417-206 (ILLUS.) **$570**

Slender Footed Clewell Vase

Vase, 8" h., round cushion foot supporting the very tall slener waisted body, dark brown to green patina, marked, No. 424-26 (ILLUS.).. **$600**

Clifton Pottery

William A. Long, founder of the Lonhuda Pottery, joined Fred Tschirner, a chemist, to found the Clifton Art Pottery in Newark, New Jersey, in 1905. Crystal Patina was its first art pottery line and featured a subdued pale green crystalline glaze later also made in shades of yellow and tan. In 1906 its Indian Ware line, based on the pottery made by American Indians, was introduced. Other lines the pottery produced include Tirrube and Robin's-egg Blue. Floor and wall tiles became the focus of production after 1911, and by 1914 the firm's name had changed to Clifton Porcelain Tile Company, which better reflected its production.

Clifton Mark

Teapot, cov., a tall tapering cylindrical base below the squatty bulbous pot w/a short, wide angled spout & large ring handle, a low domed cover w/a button finial, overall medium green crystalline glaze, 6 1/2" h. (ILLUS., next page).................................... **$150**

Unusual Clifton Pottery Tall Teapot

Bulbous Fish-molded Clifton vase

Vase, 3 1/2" h., 3 1/2" d., miniature, spherical body tapering to a tiny neck, deeply molded overall w/stylized swirling fish, dark green mottled glaze, signed & dated 1906, No. 180 (ILLUS.) **$300**

Cowan

R. Guy Cowan opened his first pottery studio in 1912 in Lakewood, Ohio. The pottery operated almost continuously, with the exception of a break during the First World War, at various locations in the Cleveland area until it was forced to close in 1931 due to financial difficulties.

Many of this century's finest artists began with Cowan and its associate, the Cleveland School of Art. This fine art pottery, particularly the designer pieces, are highly sought after by collectors.

Many people are unaware that it was due to R. Guy Cowan's perseverance and tireless work that art pottery is today considered an art form and found in many art museums.

Cowan Marks

Ashtray, model of a ram, green, designed by Edris Eckhardt, 5 1/4" l., 3 1/2" h. (ILLUS. lower left with chick ashtray/nut dish, bottom this column) **$275**

Ashtray, center relief-molded unicorn decoration, caramel glaze, designed by Waylande Gregory, w/footed foliate metal stand, Shape No. 925, 3/4 x 5 1/2" **$150**

Ashtray, three-section base w/figural leaping gazelle & foliage on edge, Oriental Red glaze, designed by Waylande Gregory, 5 3/4" h. (ILLUS. lower right with horse bookend & boy & girl bookends, page 157) **$350**

Ashtray/nut dish, ivory glaze, Shape No. 769, 1" h. **$25**

Cowan Clown Ashtrays & Vases

Ashtray/nut dish, figural clown Periot, blue or ivory glaze, designed by Elizabeth Anderson, Shape No. 788, 2 1/2 x 3", each (ILLUS. lower center) **$125**

Cowan Ashtrays, Flower Frog & Vase

Ashtray/nut dish, model of a chick, green glaze, Shape No. 768, 3 1/2" h. (ILLUS. bottom center) **$75**

Cowan "Monk"/Readers Bookends

Bookends, figural, "Monk"/Readers, No. 522, pine green glaze, 6 3/8" h., pr. (ILLUS. of one, left with mustard yellow Monk bookend) **$900**

Gregory "Kicking Horse" Bookends

Bookends, "Kicking Horse," modeled as a wild horse w/rear legs raised, on a rectangular base, gunmetal black glaze, No.

#E-1, designed by Waylande Gregory, 9 1/4" h., pr. (ILLUS.) **$2,400**
Bookends, figural, model of a fish, Oriental Red glaze, Shape No. 863, 4 5/8" h., pr. ... **$750**
Bookends, figural Art Deco-style elephant, push & pull, tan glaze, designed by Thelma F. Winter, one Shape No. 840 & one Shape No. 841, 4 3/4" h., pr....................... **$850**

Cowan Bookends & Model of Horse

Bookends, figural, model of a seated polar bear, front paws near face, ivory glaze, designed by Margaret Postgate, 6" h., pr. (ILLUS. left)... **$1,250**
Bookends, figural, a nude kneeling boy & nude kneeling girl, each on oblong bases, creamy white glaze, designed by Frank N. Wilcox, Shape No. 519, Marks 8 & 9, ca. 1925, 6 1/2" h., pr. (ILLUS. with Cowan ashtray & kicking horse bookend, next page) **$400**
Bookends, figural, a little girl standing wearing a large sunbonnet & full ruffled dress, verde green, designed by Kat. Barnes Jenkins, Shape No. 521, 7" h., pr. .. **$325**
Bookends, figural, model of a unicorn, front legs raised on relief-molded foliage base, orange glaze, designed by Waylande Gregory, Shape No. 961, mark No. 8, 7" h., pr. (ILLUS. left, bottom of page) **$850**

Variety of Cowan Animal Pieces

Bookends, figural, model of a ram, black, thick rectangular base w/slanted top, Shape No. E-3, designed by Waylande Gregory, 7 1/2" h., pr............................. **$1,750**

Elephant Bookends & Paperweights

Bookends, figural, modeled as a large rounded stylized elephant w/trunk curved under, standing on a stepped rectangular base, overall Oriental Red glaze, designed by Margaret Postgate, Shape No. E-2, 7 1/4" h., pr. (ILLUS. top center & lower left)... **$1,800**

Cowan Bookends & Ashtray

Bookends, model of a stylized horse, back legs raised in kicking position, black, designed by Waylande Gregory, Shape No. E-1, 9" h., pr. (ILLUS. of one, with ashtray & boy & girl bookends) **$2,400**

Bowl, miniature, 2" d., footed, flared body, Shape No. 514, mark No. 5, orange lustre **$45**

Cowan Bowl & Vases

Bowl, 5 1/4" d., individual, green & black, designed by Arthur E. Baggs (ILLUS. right) **$2,500**

Cowan Bowl with Abstract Decoration

Bowl, 7 1/2" d., 4" h., wide cylindrical body w/flaring rim, hand-applied abstract decoration in black on a white to pale green ground, impressed mark, crazing (ILLUS.) .. **$345**

Bowl, 7 1/2" w., octagonal, the alternating side panels hand-decorated w/floral design, brown & yellow glaze, Shape No. B-5-B **$300**

Bowl, 2 1/2 x 9 1/4", Egyptian blue glaze, designed by R.G. Cowan, Shape No. B-12 .... **$75**

Bowl, w/drip, 3 x 9 1/2", blue lustre finish, Shape No. 701-A **$100**

Bowl, 2 1/4 x 10 1/4", blue pearl finish **$125**

Bowl, 3 x 11 1/4", designed to imitate hand molding, two-tone blue glaze, Shape No. B-827 .... **$260**

Bowl, 3 x 10 x 11 1/2", leaf design, ivory & green, designed by Waylande Gregory **$195**

Bowl, 3 x 9 1/4 x 12 1/4", copper crystal glaze, Shape No. B-785-A **$150**

Bowl, 3 x 6 x 12 1/2" oblong, caramel w/light green glaze, Shape No. 683 .... **$50**

Bowl, 2 3/4 x 11 1/2 x 15", Oriental Red glaze, designed by Waylande Gregory, Shape No. B-4 .... **$225**

Various Cowan Pieces

Buttons, decorated w/various zodiac designs, by Paul Bogatay, 50 pcs. **$450**

Candelabrum, "Pavlova," porcelain, two-light, Art Deco style, a footed squatty tapering central dish issuing at each side a stylized hand holding an upturned cornucopia-form candle socket, the center fitted w/a figure of a nude female dancer standing on one leg w/her other leg raised, her torso arched over & holding a long swirled drapery, Special Ivory glaze, stamped mark, 10" l., 7" h. (chip under rim of one bobeche) **$475**

Candleholder, flaring base w/flattened rim, black & silver, Shape No. 870, 1 1/2" h. **$45**

Candleholder, figural, model of a Viking ship prow, green glaze, Shape No. 777, 5 1/4" h. **$30**

Candleholders, Etruscan, Oriental Red glaze, Shape No. S-6, 1 3/4" h., pr. **$70**

Candleholders, ivory glaze, Shape No. 692, 2 1/4" h., pr. **$30**

Candleholders, footed, designed by R.G. Cowan, ivory, Shape No. 811, 2 3/8" h., pr. **$35**

Candleholders, blue lustre finish, Shape No. 528, 3 1/2" h., pr. **$30**

Candleholders, semicircular wave design, white glaze, Shape No. 751, 4 3/4" h., pr. .. **$125**

Candlestick, flared base below twisted column, blossom-form cup, green & orange drip glaze, Shape No. 625-A, 7 3/4" h. (ILLUS. far right, top of page) **$125**

Candlestick, figural, Byzantine figure flanked by angels, golden yellow glaze, designed by R.G. Cowan, 9 1/4" h. (ILLUS. left, top next column) **$300**

Candlestick, figural, Byzantine figure flanked by angels, salmon glaze, designed by R.G. Cowan, 9 1/4" h. (ILLUS. right, top next column) **$400**

Candlestick, two-light, large figural nude standing w/head tilted & holding a swirling drapery, flanked by blossom-form candle sockets supported by scrolled leaves at the base, matte ivory glaze, designed by R.G. Cowan, Shape No. 745, 7 1/2" w., 9 3/4" h. (ILLUS., bottom next column) **$850**

Byzantine Angel Candlesticks

Cowan Figural Nùde Candlestick

Cowan Figural Nude Candlestick

Candlestick, figural, seminude female standing before figural branches on round base w/flared foot, one arm across her body & the other raised overhead, shaded tan & green glaze, designed by R.G. Cowan, Shape No. 744-R, 12 1/2" h. (ILLUS.) **$1,000**

Candlestick/bud vase, tapering cylindrical shape w/flared foot & rim, blue lustre, Shape 530-A, 7 1/2" h. **$50**

Candlesticks, curled form, royal blue, 1 1/2" h., pr. **$70**

Candlesticks, figural grape handles, ivory glaze, 4" h., pr. **$80**

Candlesticks, w/loop handle, green, Shape No. 781, 4" h., pr. **$50**

Candlesticks, figural sea horse w/flared base, green, Shape No. 716, 4 3/8" h., pr. **$40**

Candlesticks, "The Girl Reserve," designed by R.G. Cowan, medium blue, Shape No. 671, 5 1/2" h., pr. **$250**

Cowan Candlesticks & Vase

Candlesticks, model of a marlin on wave-form base, verde green, designed by Waylande Gregory, 8" h., pr. (ILLUS. right) **$1,500**

Centerpiece set, 6 1/4" h. trumpet-form vase centered on 8" sq. base w/candle socket in each corner, Princess line, vase Shape No. V-1, Mark No. 8, candelabra Shape No. S-2, Mark No. 8, black matte, 2 pcs., together w/four nut dishes/open compotes, green glaze, Shape No. C-1, Mark No. 8, the set **$550**

Charger, "Polo" patt., incised scene w/polo players & flowers under a blazing sun, covered in a rare glossy brown & cafe-au-lait glaze, designed by Victor Schreckengost, mark Nos. 8 & 9, Shape No. X-48, impressed "V.S. - Cowan," 11 1/4" d. **$850**

Charger, wall plaque, yellow, 11 1/4" d. **$65**

Charger, octagonal, hand-decorated by Thelma Frazier Winter, 13 1/4" **$1,250**

Cigarette holder, w/wave design, Oriental Red glaze, designed by Waylande Gregory, Shape No. 927-J, 3 1/4" **$65**

Cigarette/match holder, sea horse decoration, pink, No. 726, 3 1/2 x 4" **$45**

Cigarette/matchholder, flared foot w/relief-molded sea horse decoration, orange glaze, Shape No. 72, 3 1/2" h. **$25**

Clip dish, green, 3 1/4" d. (part of desk set, Shape PB-1) **$20**

Comport, footed, square, green & white glaze, Shape No. 951, 4 1/2" sq., 2 1/4" h. **$25**

Console bowl, octagonal, stand-up-type, verde green, Shape No. 689, 3 x 8 x 8 1/2" **$75**

Console bowl, footed, low rounded sides w/incurved rim, orange lustre, Shape No. 567-B, 2 3/4 x 9 3/4" **$45**

Console bowl, footed, flaring fluted sides, white glaze exterior, blue glaze interior, Shape No. 713-A, 3 1/2 x 7 1/4 x 10 1/2" **$70**

Console bowl, April green, Shape No. B-1, 11 1/2" l., 2 1/4" h. **$70**

Console bowl, turquoise & dark matte blue, Shape No. 690, 3 1/2 x 8 x 16" **$75**

Console bowl, ivory & pink glaze, Shape No. 763, 3 1/4 x 9 x 16 1/2" **$55**

Console bowl, w/wave design, verde green, designed by Waylande Gregory, 2 3/4 x 9 x 17 1/2" **$225**

Console bowls, 3 3/4 x 4 1/2 x 11", two-handled, footed, widely flaring fluted sides, verde green, Shape No. 538, pr. **$185**

Console set: 6 1/2 x 10 1/2 x 17" bowl & pr. of candleholders; footed bowl w/figural bird handles, lobed sides, designed by Alexander Blazys, Shape No. 729, mottled blue glaze, the set **$375**

Console set: 9" d. bowl & pair of 4" h. candleholders; ivory & purple glaze, Shape Nos. 733-A & 734 .... **$125**

Cowan Decanters & Wine Cups

Decanter w/stopper, figural King of Clubs, a seated robed & bearded man w/a large crown on his head & holding a scepter, black glaze w/gold, designed by Waylande Gregory, Shape E-4, 10" h. (ILLUS. left) **$650**

Decanter w/stopper, figural Queen of Hearts, seated figure holding scepter & wearing crown, Oriental Red glaze, designed by Waylande Gregory, Shape No. E-5, 10 1/2" h. (ILLUS. right with King of Clubs decanter, above) **$625**

Desk set, w/paper clip dish, Oriental Red glaze, Shape PB-1, 2 1/2 x 5 1/2", the set **$45**

Cowan "Chinese Horse" & Jockey Figures

Figurine, "Chinese Horse," standing on a rectangular base, Egyptian blue glaze, designed by Ralph Cowan w/instruction from Waylande Gregory, 9" h. (ILLUS. left with Jockey/Fox Hunter) **$1,500**

Figurine, "Introspection," angular Modernist bird w/a black gunmetal glaze, designed by A.D. Jacobson, sold as a single sculpture or a pair as bookends, 8 1/4" h., each (ILLUS., top next column) **$2,100**

Figurine, "Jockey/Fox Hunter," standing man in riding gear, Shadow White glaze (white w/black highlights), designed by Waylande Gregory, 8 1/2" h. (ILLUS. right with Chinese Horse figurine, above) **$330**

Two Cowan "Introspection" Figurines

Very Rare "Mary" Figurine in a Terra Cotta Glaze

Figurine, "Mary," a kneeling female holding the end of a long pleated robe, on a stepped rectangular base, terra cotta glaze, sculpture limited to an edition of 50, designed by Margaret Postgate, 14 1/2" l., 10 1/4" h. (ILLUS.) **$6,000**

Figurine, "Nautch Dancer," female dancer w/long swirling dress, Shadow White glaze (white w/black highlights), designed by Waylande Gregory, 17 1/2" h. (ILLUS. right with matching figurine with a metallic silver glaze, next page) **$5,500**

Figurine, "Nautch Dancer," female dancer w/long swirling dress, special silver (metallic silver) glaze, designed by Waylande Gregory, from the artist's own family w/Cleveland show provenance, 17 1/2" h. (ILLUS. left with Shadow White Nautch Dancer, next page) **$6,500**

Two Versions of the "Nautch Dancer"

Two Cowan "Pelican" Figurines/Bookends

Figurine, "Pelican," stylized head of a bird in gunmetal black, bronze & silver glazes, sold as a single piece or as pairs for bookends, designed by A.D. Jacobson, limited edition, each (ILLUS. of two) **$3,800**

"Spanish Dancer" in Two Variations

Figurine, "Spanish Dancer," female wearing a long dress in an angled pose, in a special ivory glaze, designed by Eliza-

beth Anderson, 8 1/2" h. (ILLUS. left with polychrome version).................................. **$575**

Figurine, "Spanish Dancer," female wearing a long dress in an angled pose, polychrome hand-decorated glazes, designed by Elizabeth Anderson, 8 1/2" h. (ILLUS. right with ivory version, bottom previous column)...................................... **$850**

Fine Cowan "Torso" Figurine

Figurine, "Torso," female figure w/a terra cotta crackle glaze, designed by Waylande Gregory, 17" h. (ILLUS.)............... **$3,000**

Fine "Woodland Nymph" Figurine

Figurine, "Woodland Nymph," nude young female seated on a tree stump, special ivory glaze, designed by Waylande Gregory, 14" h. (ILLUS.) **$3,000**

Flower frog, figural, Art Deco dancing nude woman leaning back w/one leg raised & the ends of a long scarf held in her outstretched hands, overall white glaze, impressed mark, 7 1/2" h. $275

Flower frog, figural, Art Deco style, two nude females partially draped in flowing scarves, each bending backward away from the other w/one hand holding the scarf behind each figure & their other hand joined, on an oval base w/flower holes, ivory glaze, designed by R.G. Cowan, Shape No. 685, 7 1/2" h. (ILLUS. lower right with "Repose" flower frog, on page 163)... $575

Flower Frogs No. 698 & "Awakening"

Flower frog, figural, Art Deco-style nude dancing woman in a curved pose, standing on one leg & trailing a long scarf, ivory glaze, designed by Walter Sinz, Shape No. 698, 6 1/2" h. (ILLUS. left with Awakening flower frog) $175

Flower frog, figural, "Awakening," an Art Deco woman draped in a flowing scarf standing & leaning backward w/her arms bent & her hands touching her shoulders, on a flower-form pedestal base, ivory glaze, designed by R.G. Cowan, Shape No. F-8, impressed mark, 1930s, 9" h. (ILLUS. right with flower frog No. 698) $325

Flower frog, figural, "Diver," waveform base w/tall wave supporting nude female figure, back arched & arms raised over head, ivory glaze, designed by R.G. Cowan, Shape No. 683, 8" h. (ILLUS. right, top next column) $700

Flower frog, figural, "Fan Dancer," a standing seminude Art Deco woman, posed w/one leg kicked to the back, her torso bent back w/one arm raised & curved overhead, the other arm curved around her waist holding a long feather fan, a long drapery hangs down the front from her waist, on a rounded incurved broad leaf cluster base, overall Original Ivory glaze, designed by R.G. Cowan, Shape No. 806, stamped mark, 4" w., 9 1/2" h. $1,750

Cowan Female Form Flower Frogs

Flower frog, figural, "Marching Girl," Art Deco style, a nude female partially draped w/a flowing scarf standing & leaning backward w/one hand on her hip & the other raising the scarf above her head, on an oblong serpentine-molded wave base w/flower holes, ivory glaze, designed by R.G. Cowan, Shape No. 680, 8" h. (ILLUS. lower left with "Repose" flower frog, on page 163) $275

Flower frog, figural, nude female, one leg kneeling on thick round base, head bent to one side & looking upward, one arm resting on knee of bent leg w/the other hand near her foot, ivory glaze, designed by Walter Sinz, 6" h. (ILLUS. left with Diver flower frog, top this column)................. $375

Figural Nude with Scarf Flower Frog

Flower frog, figural, nude woman w/long flowing scarf, ivory, designed by R.G. Cowan, Shape No. 687, 11 3/4" h. (ILLUS., previous page) **$675**

Flower frog, figural, Pan sitting on large toadstool, ivory glaze, designed by W. Gregory, Shape No. F-9, 9" h. (ILLUS. with ram & chick ashtrays, on page 155) ... **$675**

Various Cowan Flower Frogs

Flower frog, figural, "Repose," Art Deco style, a seminude sinewy woman standing & slightly curved backward, her arms away from her sides holding trailing drapery, in a cupped blossom-form base, ivory glaze, designed by R.G. Cowan, Shape No. 712, 6 1/2" h. (ILLUS. lower center, above) **$375**

Flower frog, figural, "Scarf Dancer," Art Deco-style nude dancing woman in a curved pose standing on one leg & holding the ends of a long scarf in her outstretched hands, ivory glaze, designed by R.G. Cowan, Shape No. 686, 7" h. (ILLUS. top with "Repose" flower frog, above) **$275**

"Swirl Dancer" Flower Frog

Flower frog, figural, "Swirl Dancer," Art Deco nude female dancer standing & leaning to the side, w/one hand on hip & the other holding a scarf which swirls

about her, on a round lobed base w/flower holes, ivory glaze, designed by R.G. Cowan, Shape No. 720, 10" h. (ILLUS.) **$1,150**

Flower frog, figural, "Triumphant," figure of a standing seminude Art Deco woman w/one leg raised, leaning back w/one arm raised above her head & the other on her hip, a clinging drapery around her lower body, standing on a round incurved leaf cluster base, overall Original ivory glaze, stamped mark, 4 1/2" w., 15" h. **$1,850**

Flower frog, figural, "Wreath Girl," figure of a woman standing on a blossom-form base & holding up the long tails of her flowing skirt, ivory glaze, designed by R.G. Cowan, Shape No. 721, 10" h. (ILLUS. center with Diver flower frog, previous page) **$475**

Flower frog, fluted flower-form base centered by relief-molded stalk & leaves supporting the figure of a female nude standing w/one leg bent, knee raised, leaning backward w/one arm raised overhead & the other resting on a curved leaf, ivory glaze, designed by R.G. Cowan, Shape No. F-812-X, 10 1/2" h. **$775**

Flower frog, model of a deer, designed by Waylande Gregory, ivory glaze, Shape No. F-905, 8 1/4" h. (ILLUS. right with unicorn bookends, bottom of page 156) **$425**

Flower frog, model of a flamingo, orange glaze, designed by Waylande Gregory, Shape No. D2-F, 11 3/4" h. **$575**

Flower frog, model of a reindeer, designed by Waylande Gregory, polychrome finish, Shape No. 903, 11" h. (ILLUS. center with unicorn bookends, bottom of page 156) **$1,250**

Flower frog, model of an artichoke, light green, Shape No. 775, 3" h. **$55**

Ginger jar, cov., blue lustre, Shape No. 513, 6 3/4" h. **$195**

Ginger jar, cov., orange lustre, Shape No. 583, 10" h. **$275**

Cowan Figural "Aztec" Table Lamp

Lamp, "Aztec," table model, figural, a stylized standing man in an angular Art Deco
form, special ivory glaze, designed by
Waylande Gregory, 13" h. (ILLUS., previ-
ous page) **$1,800**

Lamp, candlestick-form, a disk foot & spiral-
twist standard w/a flaring molded socket
fitted w/an electric bulb socket, overall
marigold lustre glaze, impressed mark,
11" h. **$125**

"Cat" Lamp by Waylande Gregory

Lamp "Cat," table model, figural, designed
as a seated angular Art Deco style cat,
special ivory glaze, designed by Way-
lande Gregory, 9 3/4" h. (ILLUS.).............. **$480**

Lamp, foliage decoration, 9" h........................ **$250**

Lamp, girl w/deer decoration, ivory, 18" h. **$725**

Lamp, moth decoration, blue, w/fittings,
13" h., overall 22" h. **$375**

Lamp base, Art Deco style, angular, green,
designed by Waylande Gregory, Shape
No. 821, 8 3/8" h. **$300**

Cowan Lamp Base

Lamp base, round domed base below Modernist teardrop-shaped body decorated
w/nude female figure, ivory & brown
glaze, designed by Waylande Gregory,
11" h. (ILLUS.) **$1,500**

Bird on Wave Model

Model of bird on wave, Egyptian blue, designed by Alexander Blazys, Shape No.
749-A, 12" h. (ILLUS.)............................. **$1,400**

Model of elephant, standing on square
plinth, head & trunk down, rich mottled
Oriental Red glaze, designed by Margaret Postgate, ca. 1930, faint impressed
mark on plinth & paper label reading
"X869 Elephant designed by M....et P....,"
10 1/2" h... **$2,500**

Model of horse, standing animal on an oblong base, Egyptian blue glaze, designed by Viktor Schreckengost,
7 3/4" h. (ILLUS. right with polar bear
bookends, page 156)............................... **$4,500**

Model of ram, Oriental Red glaze, designed
by Edris Eckhart, 3 1/2" h.......................... **$250**

Paperweight, figural, modeled as a large
rounded stylized elephant w/trunk
curved under, standing on a stepped
rectangular base, ivory glaze, designed
by Margaret Postgate, Shape No. D-3,
4 3/4" h. (ILLUS. lower center with ele-
phant bookends, page 157) **$250**

Paperweight, figural, modeled as a large
rounded stylized elephant w/trunk
curved under, standing on a stepped
rectangular base, blue glaze, designed
by Margaret Postgate, Shape No. D-3,
4 3/4" h. (ILLUS. lower right with ele-
phant bookends, page 157) **$300**

Paperweight, figural, modeled as a large
rounded stylized elephant w/trunk curved
under, standing on a stepped rectangular
base, overall Oriental Red glaze, designed by Margaret Postgate, Shape No.
D-3, 4 3/4" h. (ILLUS. top right with elephant bookends, page 157) **$350**

Pen base, maroon, Shape No. PB-2, 3 3/4"
.... **$55**

Cowan Lakeware Urn & Vases

Plaque, hand-decorated by Arthur E. Baggs, Egyptian blue, artist-signed "AEB," 2 1/2 x 12 1/2" **$2,500**

Plaque, seascape decoration, designed by Thelma Frazier Winter, 11 1/2" d. **$750**

Plaque, terradatol, designed by Alexander Blazys, Egyptian blue, Shape No. 739, 15 1/2" **$850**

Strawberry jar w/saucer, light green, designed by R.G. Cowan, Shape No. SJ-6, 6" h., 2 pcs. **$225**

Strawberry jar w/saucer, Oriental Red glaze, designed by R.G. Cowan, Shape No. SJ-1, mark No. 8, 7 1/2" h., 2 pcs........ **$325**

Trivet, round, center portrait of young woman's face encircled by a floral border, white on blue ground, impressed mark & "Cowan," 6 5/8" d. (minor staining from usage) **$175**

Urn, classical form w/trumpet foot supporting a wide bulbous ribbed body w/a wide short cylindrical neck flanked by loop handles, overall Peacock blue glaze, stamped mark, 8" d., 9 1/2" h...................... **$75**

Cowan Urn w/Figural Grape Handles

Urn, cov., black w/gold trim & figural grape cluster handles, Shape No. V-95, 10 1/4" h. (ILLUS.) **$325**

Urn, Lakeware, blue, Shape V-102, 5 1/2" h. (ILLUS. left with vases, top of page)... **$85**

Vase, 3 1/4" h., footed, baluster-form, Feu Rouge glaze, Shape No. 533 .... **$125**

Vase, 4" h., bulbous ovoid tapering to cylindrical neck, Jet Black glaze, Shape No. V-5 (ILLUS. center w/urn, top of page) **$275**

Vase, 4" h., waisted cylindrical body w/bulbous top & wide flaring rim, mottled orange glaze, Shape No. 630 (ILLUS. second from left w/No. 625-A candlestick, top of page 158).. **$85**

Vase, 4 1/4" h., mottled green, Shape No. V-54 .... **$70**

Vase, 4 3/4" h., bulbous body w/horizontal ribbing, wide cylindrical neck, green glaze, Shape No. V-30 (ILLUS. lower left with clown ashtrays, page 155).................... **$60**

Vase, 4 3/4" h., bulbous body w/horizontal ribbing, wide cylindrical neck, mottled turquoise glaze, Shape No. V-30 .... **$85**

Vase, 4 3/4" h., waterfall, designed by Paul Bogatay, maroon, hand-decorated, Shape No. V-77 .... **$925**

Vase, 4 3/4" h., wide tapering cylindrical body, mottled orange, brown & rust, Shape No. V-34 (ILLUS. second from right w/No. 625-A candlestick, top of page 158)... **$55**

Vase, 5" h., fan-shaped, designed by R.G. Cowan, golden yellow, Shape No. V-801 .... **$55**

Vase, 5 1/4" h., Lakeware, melon-lobed shape **$55**

Vase, 5 1/2" h., footed wide semi-ovoid body w/flaring rim, dark bluish green, Shape 575-A, mark No. 4 .... **$55**

Vase, 5 1/2" h., Lakeware, bulbous base w/wide shoulder tapering to wide cylindrical neck, blue glaze, Shape No. V-72.......... **$50**

Vase, 5 1/2" h., orange lustre, Shape No. 608 .... **$45**

Vase, 6 1/4" h., experimental, polychrome, designed by Arthur E. Baggs, Shape No. 15-A, artist signed "AEB"........................ **$1,750**

Vase, 6 1/4" h., six-sided w/stepped neck, blue rainbow glaze, Shape No. 546 .... **$50**

Vase, bud, 6 1/4" h., flaring domed foot below ovoid body tapering to cylindrical neck w/flaring rim, plum glaze, Shape No. 916... **$85**

Vase, 6 1/2" h., blue & green, Shape No. V-55 .... **$85**

Cowan Decorated Vases

Vase, 6 1/2" h., bulbous body w/short molded rim, black w/Egyptian blue bands & center decoration, designed by Whitney Atchley, Shape No. V-38 (ILLUS. right) **$1,750**

Vase, 6 1/2" h., footed, squatty bulbous base w/trumpet-form neck, flattened sides w/notched corners, green glaze, Shape No. V-649-A (ILLUS. right w/urn, top of page 165) **$85**

Vase, 6 1/2" h., mottled dark blue & green, Shape No. V-55....................................... **$150**

Vase, 6 1/2" h., spherical body w/flaring cylindrical neck flanked by scroll handles, Egyptian blue, designed by Viktor Schreckengost, Shape No. V-99 (ILLUS. center w/bowl, top of page 157) **$450**

Vase, 6 1/2" h., wide bulbous body, yellow glaze, Shape V-91.................................... **$225**

Vase, cov., 6 1/2" h., wide bulbous body, blue glaze, Shape V-91 .... **$250**

Vase, 6 5/8" h., bright yellow glaze, Shape No. 797... **$85**

Vase, 6 3/4" h., footed bulbous ovoid body w/wide tapering cylindrical neck, Jet Black glaze, Shape V-25........................... **$300**

Vase, 7" h., fan-shaped w/scalloped foot & domed base decorated w/relief-molded sea horse decoration, pink glaze, Shape No. 715-A **$50**

Vase, 7" h., footed bulbous base, the narrow shoulder tapering to a tall wide cylindrical neck, Oriental Red glaze, Shape No. V-79... **$175**

Vase, 7" h., Lakeware, bulbous base w/trumpet-form neck, Oriental Red glaze, Shape No. V-75....................................... **$100**

Vase, bud, 7" h., blue lustre glaze.................. **$50**

Vase, 7 1/4" h., footed slender ovoid body w/flaring rim, Oriental Red glaze, Shape No. V-12 .... **$125**

Vase, 7 1/2" h., baluster-form w/trumpet-form neck, blue rainbow lustre, Shape No. 631 .... **$85**

Vase, 7 1/2" h., flared foot below paneled ovoid body, orange lustre glaze, Shape No. 691-A, mark No. 6 .... **$65**

Vase, 7 1/2" h., footed, tapering cylindrical body, green drip over yellow glaze, Shape No. 591, 8" h. (ILLUS. far right with clown ashtrays, page 155)................. **$275**

Vase, 7 1/2" h., tall slender ovoid body w/short cylindrical neck, orange lustre, Shape No. 552 (ILLUS. lower right with chick & ram ashtrays, page 155) **$100**

Vase, 5 1/4 x 7 3/4", flared tulip-shaped body, squared feet, blue **$75**

Vase, 8" h., blue lustre, Shape No. 615 .... **$75**

Vase, 8" h., bulbous body tapering to cylindrical neck w/flaring rim, verde green, Shape No. V-932 .... **$125**

Vase, 8" h., bulbous body tapering to cylindrical neck w/flaring rim, gold, Shape No. V-932 (ILLUS. far left w/No. 625-A candlestick, top of page 158).......................... **$150**

Vase, 8" h., bulbous body tapering to cylindrical neck w/flaring rim, Feu Rouge (red) glaze, Shape No. V-932............................. **$225**

Vase, 8" h., bulbous body tapering to cylindrical neck w/flaring rim, black drip over Feu Rouge (red) glaze Shape No. V-932 (ILLUS. top with clown ashtrays, page 155)... **$350**

Vase, 8" h., cylindrical body, black w/overall turquoise blue decoration, triple-signed (ILLUS. left with bulbous vase, top previous column) **$650**

Vase, 8" h., footed bulbous body w/trumpet-form neck, yellow shading to green drip glaze, Shape No. 627 (ILLUS. top center w/No. 625-A candlestick, top of page 158)... **$275**

Cowan "Squirrel" Vase by W. Gregory

Vase, 8 1/2" h., "Squirrel," bulbous ovoid body molded on one side w/a squirrel among leaves, a heron & pheasant among leaves also around the body, Mother-of-Pearl glaze, designed by Waylande Gregory, Shape No. V-19 (ILLUS.) **$1,440**

green glossy glaze, impressed mark, crazing (ILLUS.) **$345**

Cowan "Amazon" Vase by T. Frazier

Vase, 9 3/4" h., "Amazon," nearly spherical body w/a cylindrical neck, incised w/a continuous band of stylized dancing nude Amazon women, in charcoal grey & Shadow White glazes, designed by Thelma Frazier (ILLUS.).............................. **$2,100**

Vase, 10 1/2" h., footed bulbous ovoid body, Star patt., decorated w/relief-molded foliage, orange glaze, designed by Waylande Gregory, Shape V-32, mark No. 8 & 9 .... **$475**

Vase, 13 1/2" h., baluster-form body w/flaring rim, light blue glaze, Shape No. 563 (ILLUS. left w/marlin candlesticks, page 159) **$350**

Tall Slender Green Cowan Vase

Vase, 13 7/8" h., tall slender swelled cylindrical melon-ribbed body w/a narrow shoulder & tall trumpet-form neck, teal

Large Covered Cowan Vase

Vase, cov., 14" h., bulbous ovoid body in an Egyptian blue glaze w/separate cover & base in gunmetal black glaze, designed by Viktor Schreckengost, Shape No. V-90 (ILLUS.)... **$825**

Wine cups, Oriental Red glaze, Shape No. X-17, 2 1/2" h., each (ILLUS. of two, front left with decanter, page 160)..................... **$40**

deLee Art

Delores and Lee Mitchell, owners of deLee Art based in Los Angeles, California, seem to have quite accidentally enveloped themselves and their products in obscurity. While the Mitchells seemed to do everything possible to make deLee a household name, little is known about this company except that the products created are popular with collectors today. Almost all pieces are marked in some fashion. The Mitchells even gave names to their figurines, animals and so forth. Stickers with a silver background and black lettering have been found, often with the proper names of many items. Perhaps realizing that the stickers might be destroyed, the same pieces can be identified with an underglaze mark with the name deLee Art and might also include the name of the figurine and the date it was produced. Adding to this you can also find a deLee Art sticker. However, collectors do find deLee pieces void of any permanent mark and if the deLee sticker has been destroyed, there is no mark to indicate the maker. Knowing the products made by the Mitchells along with glazes helps immensely in identifying their unmarked products.

Today their skunk line is probably the least desirable among collectors. This could be because so many, in varied positions, were created. Two exceptions are the boy skunk figurine with blue hat and the matching girl skunk with her large, wide-brimmed blue hat. These skunks were produced in the late 1940s. Many deLee pieces bear a 1935 or 1938 mark and some have been found marked with a 1944 date so researchers have speculated that deLee was in business from the early to mid-1930s through the 1940s.

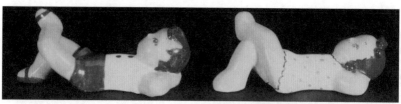

deLee Art Figures of Reclining Boy & Girl

de Lee Art
© 1938   *delee Art*

deLee Art Marks

Bank, figural, model of chicken w/black feathers & green bonnet, no mark, 6" h. ... **$144**

Bank, "Money Bunny," figural rabbit, ears up, pink w/blue purse w/flower on purse, silver w/black lettering sticker, "deLee" sticker & incised underglaze "deLee," 9" h **$140**

Cookie jar, model of boy chef, head down, eyes closed, arms folded over chest w/spoon in hands, colorful flowers on sleeves, apron forms bulbous bottom, marked "deLee Art 1944," 12 1/2" h. .. **$410**

Figure of African American boy, "8 Ball," incised mark "deLee Art © 40 USA - A Walter Lantz Creation," 4 1/2" h. **$180**

Figure of angel, standing, head tilted slightly to right, eyes closed, arms together in front at waist, overall glossy white glaze w/brown & blue tiny flowers & scallops on dress front & at wrist & neck, 6 1/2" h. **$60**

Figure of boy, lying on his stomach, head up, arms folded under his chest, 2 3/4" l. **$100**

Figures of boy & girl, lying on their backs w/legs crossed, boy w/dark green short pants, white shirt w/green buttons, brown hair, soles & straps of shoes, girl w/brown hair, blue eyes, white dress w/blue polka-dots, barefooted, both pieces marked w/a black & silver paper label "deLee Art, California, Hand decorated," 2 1/2" l., pr. (ILLUS., top of page).................................. **$219**

Figures of Latino dancers, black & white w/gold accents, incised "deLee Art, U.S.A.," 11 1/2" & 12 1/2" h., pr. **$335**

Bunny Hug Figure of Bunny

Model of bunny, "Bunny Hug" on sticker, ears up, white ground w/tan on ears, colorful small flowers on top of head & chest, marked "deLee," 6" h. (ILLUS.) **$48**

Model of elephant, seated on back legs, trunk up, head bent to right touching shoulder, white ground w/small pink & blue flowers w/green leaves, 4 3/4" h. **$76**

Model of skunk, "Phew," standing w/tail up, black gloss glaze w/white, wide stripe from top of head to middle of tail, white & black eyes, pink nose, paper label, 4 1/2" l **$35**

Models of elephants, "Happy & Lucky," trunks up, pastel floral on white, "Lucky" standing w/back leg up, "Happy" sitting on back legs, deLee stickers on both, name sticker on "Happy," no mark, 5" h., pr. (ILLUS., bottom of page) **$137**

"Happy & Lucky" Elephants

deLee Art "Jerry & Tom" Lambs

Models of lambs, "Tom & Jerry," "Tom" has blue bell, "Jerry" has blue flower, no marks, 4" h., pr. (ILLUS.)...................... **$105**

"Grunt & Groan" deLee Art Pigs

Models of pigs, "Grunt & Groan," "Groan" sitting & "Grunt" standing, no marks, 4 1/4" h. & 3 1/2" h., pr. (ILLUS.) **$128**

"Daisy" Figural Planter

Planter, "Daisy," figural, girl dressed in white w/blue & pink flowers, small bonnet w/flowers, planter in front formed by dress folds, incised mark "deLee Art © 1946, L.A., U.S.A.," 8" h. (ILLUS.) **$68**

Figural deLee Girl Planter

Planter, figural, girl dressed in white w/blue polka-dots, brown piping at edge of apron & collar of dress, large blue bow at waist in back, eyes closed w/brown eyelashes, holds up apron to form small planter in front, incised underglaze mark "deLee Art, 1938, Irene," 6" h. (ILLUS.) **$69**

"Hopalong" Bunny Planter

Planter, "Hopalong," model of a bunny w/closed eyes, planter w/bow at side, deLee sticker, incised "deLee Art," 6" h. (ILLUS.)... **$66**

"Mr. Skunk" Figural Planter

Planter, "Mr. Skunk" on sticker, model of skunk w/black body & white upright tail, pink mouth & nose, white eyes & hair, blue derby hat, tiny planter is formed where tail meets back, marked "deLee Art 1940 ©," 6" h. (ILLUS.) **$56**

Planter, "Nina," figural, girl dressed in white w/blue & pink flowers, head scarf, apron is double planter, no mark, 7" h. (ILLUS., top next column).. **$56**

Planter, "Sahara Sue," model of a camel seated w/front hoofs crossed, head up & slightly tilted to right, pale pink gloss w/caramel glaze highlights on hoofs, mouth & ears, flowers between neck, open hump forms small planter, 5 1/2" h. .. **$146**

"Nina" Figural Planter

Salt & pepper shakers, "Salty & Peppy," baby chicks w/chef hats, sitting in egg-shells, no mark, 5" h., pr. **$95**

Wall pocket, "Mr. Stinkie," model of a skunk, gloss black w/white, colorful flow-ers at left shoulder, small opening near stomach for matches, marked "deLee Art," 7 1/4" h. **$44**

Delft

In the early 17th century Italian potters settled in Holland and began producing tin-glazed earthenwares, often decorated with pseudo-Orien-tal designs based on Chinese porcelain wares. The city of Delft became the center of this pottery pro-duction and several firms produced the wares throughout the 17th and early 18th century. A majority of the pieces featured blue on white designs, but polychrome wares were also made. The Dutch Delftwares were also shipped to England, where eventually the English copied them at potteries in such cities as Bristol, Lam-beth and Liverpool. Although still produced today, Delft peaked in popularity by the mid-18th century.

Bottle, blue & white, footed bulbous ovoid body tapering to a tall slender cylindrical neck w/a flaring cupped rim, decorated w/medallions of large flowers trimmed w/small flowers & leaves, elongated scroll-work up the neck, London, England, 18th c., 9" h. (very slight rim glaze chips) **$1,175**

Bowl, 6 3/4" d., blue & white, a deep foot-ring supporting the deep rounded sides, decorated w/floral sprays on the interior & exterior w/crosshatching & dot borders, Lambeth, England, 18th c. (typical rim glaze chips)... **$470**

Bowl, 8 5/8" d., 2" h., scalloped rim on low lobed body, h.p. w/blue stylized flowers on a powder blue ground, England, mid-18th c., minor rim chips & glaze wear (ILLUS., next page) **$470**

Group of Three Colorful Delft Chargers

Lobed English Delft Bowl

Bowl, 10 1/4" d., blue & white, a small deep footring supporting the very deep rounded sides, the exterior & interior decorated w/flowers, insects & leafy vines surrounding central interlocking rectangles, England, probably Bristol (slight rim line, footrim chip, typical rim glaze chips) **$881**

Charger, round shallow dished form w/a flanged rim, the center w/large color medallions w/flowers, foliage & dragonflies, the border w/scrolled foliage between dragonfly medallions, Bristol, England, 18th c., two rim chips, glaze chips to rim, 13" d. (ILLUS. right with two other Delft chargers, top of page) **$1,645**

Charger, shallow dished center w/a wide flanged rim, decorated in polychrome w/a floral border w/a flower garden & fence in the center, Bristol, England, 18th c., 13 1/4" d. (rim hairline, two rim chips, typical glaze chipping on rim)...................... **$1,058**

Charger, round shallow dished form w/a wide flanged rim, the center h.p. w/a half-length portrait of Prince William flanked by "W" & "R," lobed border decorated in yellow & blue w/fruit & floral designs, Holland, 18th c., faint rim line, minor glaze chips at rim, 13 1/2" d. (ILLUS. center with two other Delft chargers, top of page) **$3,055**

Charger, round shallow dished form w/a wide flanged rim, the center h.p. in color

w/fenced flower garden, stylized floral blossom border, Bristol, England, 18th c., rim chip, heavy glaze chipping on rim, 13 7/8" d. (ILLUS. left with two other Delft chargers, top of page)............................... **$940**

![Large Dutch Delft Floral Charger]

Large Dutch Delft Floral Charger

Charger, round shallow dished form w/a narrow flanged rim, the center w/a large rounded panel-sided reserve h.p. w/leafy scrolls around a round center w/a stylized leafy blossom, the border band decorated w/small oval reserves decorated w/scrolls & squiggles, a blue initial or X under the bottom, various glaze & rim chips, Holland, 18th c., 13 3/4" d. (ILLUS.) **$460**

Pill slab, shield-shaped w/two top hanging holes, decorated in dark blue w/a coat-of-arms, possibly representing an apothecary, probably London, England, ca. 1770, typical glaze chips, 11"l. (ILLUS. right with Delft vase, top next page)........ **$8,225**

Plate, 8 1/2" d., blue & white, shallow w/wide flanged rim, the rim decorated w/a large cartouche framed w/two winged horses, a crown above & tassels & mask below, initials & dated "GP I 1688," England, ca. 1688, several small glaze chips to rim, circular glaze lines to surface **$2,703**

Old Delft Vase and Pill Slab

Urn-decorated Dutch Delft Plate

Plate, 8 3/4" d., shallow dished form w/a wide flanged rim, the center h.p. in dark blue w/a large urn filled w/fruit & fanned & feathery leaves & flowers, the border h.p. in dark blue w/wide half-leaves alternating w/squiggle bands, Holland, 18th c., tight hairline from rim nearly to center, small rim chip (ILLUS.) **$230**

Plate, 12 3/8" d., round, h.p. in dark blue w/the Peacock patt. in the center & round the flanged rim, Netherlands, first half 18th c. (minor rim chips) **$558**

Large Scenic Delft Tile

Tile, rectangular, decorated in blue & white w/a seaside scene w/women standing on the shore & sailing ships heading out to sea, after a painting by Hendrik Willem Mesdag, marked w/Delft & other painted & impressed marks, late 19th - early 20th c., 7 7/8 x 10" (ILLUS.) **$500**

Vase, 10" h., bulbous baluster-form w/a short cylindrical neck, the upper body h.p. w/Chinese figures in a landscape, the lower body w/an acanthus leaf border, England, 18th c., typical glaze chipping, slight rim hairline, missing cover (ILLUS. with Delft pill slab) **$1,528**

Wall pocket, blue & white, fluted cornucopia shape w/raised & decorated peony border, England, 18th c., probably Liverpool, 7 5/8" l. (rim chip, repair to knop, glaze rim chips) **$705**

Derby & Royal Crown Derby

William Duesbury, in partnership with John and Christopher Heath, established the Derby Porcelain Works in Derby, England about 1750. Duesbury soon bought out his partners and in 1770 purchased the Chelsea factory and six years later, the Bow works. Duesbury was succeeded by his son and grandson. Robert Bloor purchased the business about 1814 and managed successfully until illness in 1828 left him unable to exercise control. The "Bloor" Period, however, extends from 1814 until 1848, when the factory closed. Former Derby workmen then resumed porcelain manufacture in another factory and this nucleus eventually united with a new and distinct venture in 1878 which, after 1890, was known as Royal Crown Derby.

A variety of anchor and crown marks have been used since the 18th century.

Derby & Royal Crown Derby Marks

Quality Royal Crown Derby Modern Teapot

Early Derby Bisque Figure Group

Pretty Pink & Gold Royal Crown Derby Vase

Figure group, bisque, modeled as two Classical maidens by a flowering tree pointing down at the sleeping figure of Cupid, his head resting on his quiver, his bow on the ground at his side, rockwork base w/scattered blossoms, incised Derby crown mark, crossed batons & "D" mark w/triangle, incised Model No. 195, attributed to J.J. Spengler, ca. 1775, 12 1/4" h. (ILLUS.) **$3,824**

Teapot, cov., Old Avesbury (gold Avesbury) patt., oblong cylindrical body w/narrow angled shoulder, domed cover w/flower finial, straight spout, angled scrolled handle, modern, part of Royal Doulton Tableware, Ltd., England (ILLUS., top of page) **$1,350**

Vase, cov., 6 1/2" h., a wide squatty bulbous body w/a wide shoulder centered by a small ringed cylindrical neck fitted w/a ball stopper & flanked by gold scroll handles, the pink ground ornately decorated w/floral swags & fruiting vines w/lattice panels around the shoulder, printed mark, 1891 (ILLUS., top next column) **$646**

Doulton & Royal Doulton

Doulton & Company, Ltd., was founded in Lambeth, London, in about 1858. It was operated there until 1956 and often incorporated the words "Doulton" and "Lambeth" in its marks. Pinder, Bourne & Company Burslem was purchased by the Doultons in 1878 and in 1882 became Doulton & Company Ltd. It added porcelain to its earthenware production in 1884. The "Royal Doulton" mark has been used since 1902 by this factory, which is still in operation. Character jugs and figurines are commanding great attention from collectors at the present time.

John Doulton, the founder, was born in 1793. He became an apprentice at the age of 12 to a potter in south London. Five years later he was employed in another small pottery near Lambeth. His two sons, John and Henry, subsequently joined their father in 1830 in a partnership he had formed with the name of Doulton & Watts. Watts retired in 1864 and the partnership was dissolved. Henry formed a new company that traded as Doulton & Company.

In the early 1870s the proprietor of the Pinder Bourne Company located in Burslem, Stafford-

shire, offered Henry a partnership. The Pinder Bourne Company was purchased by Henry in 1878 and became part of Doulton & Company in 1882.

With the passage of time the demand for the Lambeth industrial and decorative stoneware declined whereas demand for the Burslem manufactured and decorated bone china wares increased.

Doulton & Company was incorporated as a limited liability company in 1899. In 1901 the company was allowed to use the word "Royal" on its trademarks by Royal Charter. The well known "lion on crown" logo came into use in 1902. In 2000 the logo was changed on the company's advertising literature to one showing a more stylized lion's head in profile.

Today Royal Doulton is one of the world's leading manufacturers and distributors of premium grade ceramic tabletop wares and collectibles. The Doulton Group comprises Minton, Royal Albert, Caithness Glass, Holland Studio Craft and Royal Doulton. Royal Crown Derby was part of the group from 1971 until 2000 when it became an independent company. These companies market collectibles using their own brand names.

ROYAL DOULTON

Royal Doulton Marks

Animals & Birds
Bird, Bullfinch, blue & pale blue feathers, red breast, HN 2551, 1941-46, 5 1/2" h. **$80**

Siamese Cat

Cat, Siamese, seated, glossy cream & black, DA 129, 4" h. (ILLUS.) **$30**
Dog, Airedale Terrier, K 5, 1931-55, 1 1/4 x 2 1/4" **$275**

Benign of Picardy Alsatian Figurine

Dog, Alsatian, "Benign of Picardy," dark brown, HN 1117, 1937-68, 4 1/2" (ILLUS.) .. **$250**
Dog, Bulldog, HN 1044, brown & white, 1931-68, 3 1/4" h **$250**

Standing Bulldog HN 1074 Figurine

Dog, Bulldog, HN 1074, standing, white & brown, 1932-85, 3 1/4" (ILLUS.) **$195**
Dog, Bulldog Puppy, K 2, seated, tan w/brown patches, 1931-77, 2" **$85**

Yawning Character Dog HN 1099

Dog, character dog yawning, white w/brown patches over ears & eyes, black patches on back, HN 1099, 1934-85, 4" h. (ILLUS., previous page) **$75**

Greyhound in White with Brown Patches

Dog, Greyhound, white w/dark brown patches, HN 1077, 1932-55, 4 1/2" (ILLUS.) **$575**
Dog, Irish Setter, Ch. "Pat O'Moy," reddish brown, HN 1054, 1931-60, 7 1/2" h. **$725**
Dog, Labrador, standing, black, DA 145, 1990-present, 5" h. **$55**

Pekinese Biddee of Ifield Figurine

Dog, Pekinese, Ch. "Biddee of Ifield," golden w/black highlights, HN 1012, 1931-85, 3" (ILLUS.) **$95**

Albourne Arthur Scottish Terrier

Dog, Scottish Terrier, Ch. "Albourne Arthur," black, HN 1015, 1931-60, 5" (ILLUS.) **$315**
Dog, Springer Spaniel, "Dry Toast," white coat w/brown markings, HN 2517, 1938-55, 3 3/4" **$175**
Dogs, Cocker Spaniels sleeping, white dog w/brown markings & golden brown dog, HN 2590, 1941-69, 1 3/4" h. **$105**

Terrier Puppies in Basket Figurine

Dogs, Terrier Puppies in a Basket, three white puppies w/light & dark brown markings, brown basket, HN 2588, 1941-85, 3" h. (ILLUS.) **$105**
Duck, Drake, standing, green, 2 1/2" **$50**
Duck, Drake, standing, white, HN 806, 1923-68, 2 1/2" h. **$105**

Elephant with Trunk in Salute Figurine

Elephant, trunk in salute, grey w/black, HN 2644, 1952-85, 4 1/4" (ILLUS.) **$175**
Horses, Chestnut Mare and Foal, chestnut mare w/white stockings, fawn-colored foal w/white stockings, HN 2522, 1938-60, 6 1/2" h. **$695**
Kitten, licking hind paw, brown & white, HN 2580, 2 1/4" (ILLUS., next page) **$75**
Kitten, on hind legs, light brown & black on white, HN 2582, 1941-85, 2 3/4" **$75**
Monkey, Langur Monkey, long-haired brown & white coat, HN 2657, 1960-69, 4 1/2" h. **$255**
Penguin, grey, white & black, green patches under eyes, K 23, 1940-68, 1 1/2" h. **$170**

Kitten Licking Hind Paw Figurine

Shetland Pony

Pony, Shetland Pony (woolly Shetland mare), glossy brown, DA 47, 1989 to present, 5 3/4" (ILLUS.) **$45**

Tiger, crouching, brown w/dark brown stripes, HN 225, 1920-36, 2 x 9 1/2" **$575**

Tiger on Rock Doulton Figurine

Tiger on a Rock, brown, grey rock, HN 2639, 1952-92, 10 1/4 x 12" (ILLUS.) **$1,150**

Bunnykins Figurines

Airman, DB 199, limited edition of 5000, 1999 .... **$75**

Astro, Music Box, DB 35, white, red, blue, 1984-89 .... **$300**

Aussie Surfer, DB 133, gold & green outfit, white & blue base, 1994 .... **$115**

Banjo Player, DB 182, white & red striped blazer, black trousers, yellow straw hat, 1999, limited edition of 2,500 .... **$150**

Bath Night Bunnykins

Bath Night, DB 141, tableau RDICC exclusive, limited edition of 5,000, 2001 (ILLUS.) **$160**

Be Prepared, DB 56, dark green & grey, 1987-96 .... **$60**

Bedtime, DB 63, second variation, red & white striped pajamas, 1987, limited edition **$425**

Bogey, DB 32, green, brown & yellow, 1984-92 .... **$150**

Boy Skater, DB 152, blue coat, brown pants, yellow hat, green boots & black skates, 1995-98 .... **$45**

Bunnykins Bride

Bride, DB 101, cream dress, grey, blue & white train, 1991 to 2001 (ILLUS.) **$45**

Busy Needles, DB 10, white, green & maroon, 1973-88.. **$75**

Carol Singer, DB 104, dark green, red, yellow & white, 1991, UK backstamp, limited edition of 700... **$250**

Cavalier, DB 179, red tunic, white collar, black trousers & hat, yellow cape, light brown boots, 1998, limited edition of 2,500.. **$265**

Choir Singer, DB 223, white cassock, red robe, 2001, RDICC exclusive...................... **$45**

Cinderella, DB 231, pink & yellow, RDICC exclusive, 2001 .... **$70**

Clown, DB 129, white costume w/red stars & black pompons, black ruff around neck, 1992, limited edition of 250 .... **$1,500**

Collector Bunnykins

Collector, DB 54, brown, blue & grey, 1987, RDICC (ILLUS.) **$550**

Cowboy, DB 201, 1999, limited edition of 2,500.. **$125**

Cymbals, DB 25, red, blue & yellow, from the Oompah Band series, 1984-90 .... **$115**

Day Trip, DB 260, two Bunnykins in green sports car, 2002, limited edition of 1,500 ... **$175**

Dodgem Car Bunnykins, DB 249, red car, 2001, limited edition of 2,500 .... **$175**

Dollie Bunnykins Playtime, DB 80, white & yellow, 1988, by Holmes, limited edition of 250 .... **$225**

Double Bass Player, DB 185, green & yellow striped jacket, green trousers, yellow straw hat, 1999, limited edition of 2,500..... **$150**

Drum-Major, DB 109, dark green, red & yellow, Oompah Band series, 1991, limited edition of 200.. **$525**

Drummer, DB 89, blue trousers & sleeves, yellow vest, cream & red drum, Royal Doulton Collectors Band series, 1990, limited edition of 250 .... **$525**

Drummer, DB 108, dark green & red, white drum, Oompah Band series, 1991, limited edition of 200 .... **$525**

Eskimo, DB 275, yellow coat & boots, orange trim, Figure of the Year, 2003 .... **$65**

Federation, DB 224, blue, Australian flag, limited edition of 2,500 .... **$165**

Fisherman, DB 170, blue hat & trousers, light yellow sweater, black wellingtons, 1997-2000... **$45**

Bunnykins Footballer

Footballer, DB 119, red, 1991, limited edition of 250 (ILLUS.)................................... **$650**

Fortune Teller, DB 218, red, black & yellow, white ball, 2000 .... **$65**

Gardener, DB 156, brown jacket, white shirt, grey trousers, light green wheelbarrow, 1996-98.. **$50**

Goalkeeper, DB 120, yellow & black, 1991, limited edition of 250 .... **$650**

Grandpa's Story, DB 14, burgundy, grey, yellow, blue & green, 1975-83 .... **$350**

Halloween, DB 132, orange & yellow pumpkin, 1993-97... **$80**

Harry the Herald, DB 115, yellow & dark green, 1991, Royal Family series, limited edition of 300 .... **$1,000**

Hornpiper, DB 261, brown, 2003 Special Event... **$43**

Jack & Jill, DB 222, tableau, brown pants, yellow & white dress, 2000 .... **$125**

Jogging, Music Box, DB 37, yellow & blue, 1987-89.. **$275**

Judy, DB 235, blue & yellow, 2001, limited edition of 2,500 .... **$180**

King John, DB 91, purple, blue & white, Royal Family series, 1990, limited edition of 250... **$550**

Liberty Bell, DB 257, green & black, 2001, limited edition of 2,001 .... **$125**

Little John, DB 243, brown cloak, 2001 .... **$60**

Magician, DB 159, black suit, yellow shirt, yellow table cloth w/red border, 1998, limited edition of 1,000 (ILLUS., next page).. **$695**

Master Potter, DB 131, blue, white, green & brown, 1992-93, RDICC Special............... **$250**

Limited Edition Magician

Minstrel, DB 211, 1999, limited edition of
2,500 .... **$105**
Mountie, DB 135, red jacket, dark blue trou-
sers, brown hat, 1993, limited edition of
750 .... **$800**
Mr. Bunnykins at the Easter Parade, DB
18, red, yellow & brown, 1982-93................ **$85**
Mrs. Bunnykins at the Easter Parade, DB
19, pale blue & maroon, 1982-96................ **$75**

Bunnykins Mystic

Mystic, DB 197, green, yellow & mauve,
1999 (ILLUS.)... **$55**
Old Balloon Seller, DB 217, multicolored,
1999, limited edition of 2,000 .... **$195**
Oompah Band, DB 105, 106, 107, 108,
109, green, 1991, limited edition of 250,
the set **$2,750**

Out for a Duck, DB 160, white, beige &
green, 1995, limited edition of 1,250 .... **$315**
Piper, DB 191, green, brown & black, 1999,
limited edition of 3,000 .... **$150**
Prince Frederick, DB 48, green, white &
red, Royal Family series, 1986-90 .... **$125**
Princess Beatrice, DB 93, yellow & gold,
Royal Family series, 1990, limited edition
of 250... **$465**
Ringmaster, DB 165, black hat & trousers,
red jacket, white waistcoat & shirt, black
bow tie, 1996, limited edition of 1,500....... **$500**
Rock and Roll, DB 124, white, blue & red,
1991, limited edition of 1,000 .... **$395**
Sands of Time, DB 229, yellow, 2000, limited order period of three months.................. **$60**
Saxophone Player, DB 186, navy & white
striped shirt, blue vest, black trousers,
1999, limited edition of 2,500 .... **$180**
Scotsman (The), DB 180, dark blue jacket
& hat, red & yellow kilt, white shirt, spor-
ran & socks, black shoes, 1998, limited
edition of 2,500 .... **$185**
Sousaphone, DB 86, blue uniform & yellow
sousaphone, Oompha Band series,
1990, limited edition of 250 .... **$500**
Susan, DB 70, white, blue & yellow, 1988-
93 .... **$125**

Bunnykins Sweetheart

Sweetheart, DB 174, white & blue, pink
heart, 1997, limited edition of 2,500
(ILLUS.).. **$205**
Tally Ho!, DB 12, burgundy, yellow, blue,
white & green, 1973-88.............................. **$105**
Touchdown, DB 29B (Boston College), ma-
roon & gold, 1985, limited edition of 50
.... **$2,000**
Touchdown, DB 99 (Notre Dame), green &
yellow, 1990, limited edition of 200 .... **$625**
Tyrolean Dancer, DB 246, black & white,
2001 .... **$60**
Will Scarlet, DB 264, green & orange, 2002 .... **$60**
Wizard, DB 168, brown rabbit, purple robes
& hat, 1997, limited edition of 2,000.......... **$400**

Rare Large Royal Doulton Footed Bowl with Tulips

Burslem Wares

Early Doulton Advertising Ashtray

Ashtray, earthenware, advertising-type, low squared white shape w/rounded corners w/notches for cigarettes, the rounded sides printed w/advertising for De Reszke Cigarettes, Burslem, ca. 1925, 5 1/2" w. (ILLUS.) **$250**

Flower-decorated Titanian Ware Bowl

Bowl, 5 1/4" d., Titanian Ware, shallow rounded shape h.p. on the interior w/flowers, designed by Percy Curnock, ca. 1920 (ILLUS.) **$750**

Bowl, 8 7/8" d., 3 3/4" h., wide shallow rounded form, interior w/transfer-printed polychrome fox hunt scenes, green vintage border w/gilt trim, early 20th c. **$125**

Bowl, 16" d., 9" h., a wide round pedestal base in brown & green supporting a wide, deep curved bowl decorated w/a continuous band of large bright yellow tulips on dark green leaves & stems, ca. 1910 (ILLUS., top of page) **$3,600**

Cabinet plates, 10 1/4" d., each w/a different English garden view within a narrow acid-etched gilt border, transfer-printed & painted by J. Price, ca. 1928, artist-signed, green printed lion, crown & circle mark, impressed year letters, painted pattern numbers "H3587," set of 12 .... **$2,750**

Vellum Centerpiece with Dragon Handle

Centerpiece, Vellum Ware, low oblong floral-decorated dish w/crimped & ruffled sides curving up at one end to form a high curved handle molded w/a figural gold dragon, designed by Charles Noke, ca. 1895 (ILLUS.) **$2,000**

Chocolate set: 8" h. cov. chocolate pot, 6 1/2" h. cov. water pot, creamer, sugar bowl & eight cups & saucers; bone china, each enamel decorated w/relief-molded fox in various poses, crop-form handles, 20th c., England, the set **$650**

Colorful Bewick Birds Cracker Jar

Cracker jar, cov., Bewick Birds Series, barrel-shaped w/a low molded rim & inset cover, the sides decorated w/a design of Bewick birds perched in a leafy branch, done in the print & tint technique in shades of brown, blue, yellow, rose red, green & pale blue, Burslem, ca. 1905 (ILLUS.) **$500**

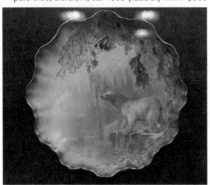

Polar Bear Scene on Bone China Plate

Dessert plate, bone china, rounded w/low ruffled rim, h.p. scene of a polar bear by a river, ca. 1890 (ILLUS.) **$300**

Tinworth Tribute "Tug of War" Figural

Figure group, earthenware, limited edition tribute to George Tinworth, the oval brown base inscribed "The Tug of War," a green grassy mound w/three dark blue frogs pulling against three brown mice, Model No. LW2, one of 150, designed by Martyn Alcock, Burslem, 2005, 5 1/2" l. (ILLUS.) **$600**

Yellow Ginger Jar with Bird & Flowers

Ginger jar, cov., bulbous nearly spherical body w/a domed cover, bright yellow ground painted in colorful enamels w/a long-tailed bird-of-paradise flying among stylized pendent flowers & fruiting branches, Model No. 1256C, date code for December 1925, 10 3/4" h. (ILLUS.) **$1,315**

Bone China Mephistopheles Match Holder

Match holder, bone china, figural, an upright oblong shape molded on one side w/the smiling face of Mephistopheles & on the other side w/his frowning face, the sides in blue inscribed w/a motto, designed by Charles Noke, Burslem, ca. 1900 (ILLUS.) **$1,000**

Set of Flower-decorated Napkin Rings

Napkin rings, each decorated w/applied hand-made colorful flowers, ca. 1935, a boxed set of 4 (ILLUS.) **$400**

Ruby Lustre Pitcher in de Morgan Style

Pitcher, Ruby Lustre, wide bulbous body tapering to a short cylindrical wide neck w/spout, simple loop handle, h.p. design of stylized dragons in the style of William de Morgan, ca. 1890 (ILLUS.) **$1,500**
Pitcher, 11" h., Poplars at Sunset patt. **$175**
Plate, 9 1/8" d., Peony patt., dark blue floral center w/rectangular panels around the border, trimmed w/reddish rust & beige, ca. 1900 .... **$65**

Plates, 9" d., slightly dished w/scalloped rim, gilt-trimmed rim w/polychrome leafy vines bordering brown enameled Shakespearean sites, retailed by Theodore B. Starr, New York City, Doulton, Burslem, late 19th c., set of 12 .... **$450**

Small Footed Doulton Salt Dip

Salt dip, small gilded ball feet supporting the squatty bulbous dish decorated w/flowers on a pale blue ground, gilt rim band, w/a salt spoon, ca. 1900 (ILLUS.).... **$400**

Rare Royal Doulton Bone China Teapot

Teapot, cov., bone china, hand-painted w/images of exotic birds & heavy gilt scroll trim, painted by Joseph Birbeck, ca. 1910 (ILLUS.)...................... **$2,000**
Teapot, cov., figural Norman and Saxon model, designed by Anthony Cartlidge, limited edition of 1,500, introduced in 2003 (ILLUS. of both sides, bottom of page).. **$300**

Two Views of the Norman & Saxon Royal Doulton Teapot

Two Views of the Doulton Pirate and Captain Teapot

Royal Doulton Old Salt Teapot

Teapot, cov., figural Old Salt model, the body in the image of a sailor mending a net, a mermaid forming the handle, designed by William K. Harper, introduced in 1989 (ILLUS.) **$300**

Teapot, cov., figural Pirate and Captain model, designed by Anthony Cartlidge, limited edition of 1,500, introduced in 2003 (ILLUS. of both sides, top of page) ... **$300**

Royal Doulton Teapot with Band of Polar Bears

Teapot, cov., Polar Bear Series, footed very wide squatty low body tapering to a flat rim & conical cover w/disk finial, short angled spout & loop handle, overall crackled background w/a center band of walking polar bears, ca. 1920s (ILLUS.) **$90**

Early Royal Doulton Floral Teapot

Teapot, cov., footed wide squatty bulbous body w/a wide flat neck & inset cover w/button finial, serpentine spout & C-form handle, decorated w/floral clusters, England, early 20th c. (ILLUS.) **$90**

Large Floral-decorated Doulton Tray

Tray, earthenware, rectangular w/rounded corners & tab end handles, a tan border & scattered pink & yellow floral clusters around the interior, ca. 1895, 17" l. (ILLUS.) **$400**

Doulton Vellum Tyg with Figural Handles

Tyg (three-handled mug), Vellum Ware, ornately scroll-molded cylindrical body decorated w/a large panel of Spanish Ware floral decoration, three figural cherub handles, ca. 1895 (ILLUS., previous page) **$800**

Doulton Bone China Man & Dog vase

Vase, bone china, footed gently flaring cylindrical body w/a flat rim, h.p. scene of a man & his dog in an autumnal landscape, designed by Harry Allen, ca. 1910 (ILLUS.) **$800**

Doulton Bone China Vase with Swans

Vase, bone china, footed tapering ovoid body w/a small trumpet-form neck, dark blue ground h.p. w/white swans & trimmed w/raised paste gold, designed by Fred Hodkinson, ca. 1910 (ILLUS.).... **$1,000**

Cobalt Blue Vase with Floral Bouquet

Vase, bone china, tall pedestal foot supporting the slightly tapering cylindrical body w/a flared & ruffled rim, gold loop handles at the lower body, h.p. white reserve w/a colorful floral bouquet within a raised gilt border, the cobalt blue background further trimmed w/ornate gold, ca. 1910 (ILLUS.) **$600**

Doulton Vellum Exhibition Vase

Vase, cov., Vellum exhibition-type, round foot & ringed pedestal in gold supporting the wide bulbous body w/a small cylindrical gold neck w/flaring rim & a low domed cover w/knob finial, decorated in the Spanish style w/colorful florals, ca. 1895 (ILLUS.) **$1,000**

Doulton Burslem Foliage Ware Vase

Vase, 5 7/8" h., Natural Foliage Ware, tapering gourd-form body, decorated
w/scattered brown leaves on a mottled
green & yellow ground, impressed mark,
Shape No. 7669 (ILLUS.).......................... **$173**

Bone China Vase with Bear Scene

Vase, 7" h., bone china, footed bulbous
ovoid body tapering to a flaring trumpet-
form neck flanked by gold loop
handles, h.p. in shades of blue w/the
scene of a large bear standing beside a
rocky shoreline, ca. 1910 (ILLUS.).......... **$1,200**

Doulton Bone China Vase with Bird

Vase, 6" h., bone china, footed ovoid body
w/a short trumpet neck, dark yellow
ground h.p. w/a large bird perched on a
blossoming branch, designed by Arthur
Eaton, ca. 1920 (ILLUS.)........................... **$400**

Titanian Ware Vase with Birds

Vase, 7" h., Titanian Ware, bulbous ovoid
body w/flared foot & wide flat
mouth, h.p. scene of two large perched
birds, designed by Edward Raby, ca.
1920 (ILLUS.) **$1,000**

Fine Doulton Vase with Pastoral Scene

Vase, 18 1/2" h., bulbous tulip-shaped body on a fluted pedestal base, the sides of the body finely h.p. w/a continuous pastoral & wooded landscape, high flaring & fluted mouth w/a ruffled rim matches the base & molded to resemble folds of cloth w/gilt-trimmed dark green panels alternating w/gilt-trimmed pale green panels, attributed to Arthur Eaton, ca. 1880 (ILLUS.)... **$4,560**

Vellum Vases with Molded Designs

Vases, Vellum Ware, buff-colored, a scalloped foot below the wide bell-shaped body molded w/a decoration of a frog & a mouse, a slender ringed neck w/cupped rim, small loop shoulder handles, pr. (ILLUS.)........... **$1,000**

Doulton Art Deco Style Vases

Vases, 8" h., earthenware, cylindrical foot supporting the swelled cylindrical body w/a wide flat mouth, printed w/colorful stylized Art Deco florals hanging from the rim, ca. 1935, pr. (ILLUS.)......................... **$400**

Figural Bell Whisky Pottery Decanter

Whiskey decanter w/stopper, figural bell, shaded dark to light brown, advertising Bells Whisky (sic), 1955, 10 1/2" h. (ILLUS.) **$150**

Character Jugs

Apothecary, small, D 6574, 4" h...................... **$65**
Aramis, small, D 6454, 3 1/2" h. **$48**
'Arriet, miniature, D 6250, 2 1/4" h. **$65**
Cap'n Cuttle "A", small, D 5842, 4" h. **$95**
Dick Turpin, horse handle, small, D 6535, 3 3/4" h.. **$60**
Don Quixote, miniature, D 6511, 2 1/2" h....... **$55**
Falstaff, small, D 6385, 3 1/2" h...................... **$45**
Fortune Teller (The), miniature, D 6523, 2 1/2" h.. **$375**
Gondolier, small, D 6592, 4" h. **$395**
Henry VIII, small, D 6647, 3 3/4" h................. **$65**
Jarge, small, D 6295, 3 1/2" h....................... **$135**
Jockey, second version, small, D 6877, 4" h... **$55**
John Peel, small, D 5731, 3 1/2" h. **$60**
Lobster Man, small, D 6620, 3 3/4" h. **$50**
Long John Silver, large, D 6335, 7" h........... **$90**
Lumberjack, small, D 6613, 3 1/2" h. **$55**
Merlin, miniature, D 6543, 2 3/4" h. **$50**
Mine Host, large, D 6468, 7" h....................... **$105**
Mr. Micawber, miniature, D 6138, 2 1/4" h. **$60**
Mr. Pickwick, miniature, D 6254, 2 1/4" h. **$55**
Mr. Quaker, large, D 6738, 7 1/2" h. **$650**
Night Watchman, large, D 6569, 7" h. (ILLUS., next page)... **$130**
North American Indian, small, D 6614, 4 1/4" h.. **$45**
Old Charley, tiny, D 6144, 1 1/4" h. **$75**
Old Salt, miniature, D 6557, 2 1/2" h. **$50**

Night Watchman

Paddy

Paddy, large, D 5753, 6" h. (ILLUS.).............. $120
Parson Brown "A", small, D 5529,
3 1/4" h. $63
Pearly Queen, small, D 6843, 3 1/2" h............. $60
Pied Piper, large, D 6403, 7" h. $75
Poacher (The), small, D 6464, 4" h.................. $45
Porthos, large, D 440, 7 1/4" h. $90
Red Queen (The), large, D 6777, 7 1/4" h. $125

Rip Van Winkle

Rip Van Winkle, large, D 6438, 6 1/2" h.
(ILLUS.)... $115
Robin Hood, 1st version, miniature, D
6252, 2 1/4" h.. $50
Robin Hood, large, D 6205, 6 1/4" h. $125
Robinson Crusoe, small, D 6539, 4" h. $60
Sairey Gamp, miniature, D 6045, 2 1/8" h. $40

Sam Weller

Sam Weller, large, D 6064, 6 1/2" h. (ILLUS.) $80
Sancho Panza, large, D 6456, 6 1/2" h. $85
Sancho Panza, small, D 6461, 3 1/4" h. $60
Santa Claus, reindeer handle, large, D
6675, 7 1/4" h.. $265
Scaramouche, small, D 6561, 3 1/4" h. $525
Sir Francis Drake, large, D 6805, 7" h. $105
Sleuth (The), miniature, D 6639, 2 3/4" h. $65
Snooker Player (The), small, D 6879, 4" h. $55
Tam O'Shanter, small, D 6636, 3 1/4" h. $70
Toby Philpots, small, D 5737, 3 1/4" h........... $60
Trapper (The), large, D 6609, 7 1/4" h........... $125
Ugly Duchess, small, D 6603, 3 1/2" h. $395
Veteran Motorist, miniature, D 6641,
2 1/2" h... $135
Viking, small, D 6502, 4" h............................. $150
Walrus & Carpenter (The), miniature, D
6608, 2 1/2" h.. $175
Winston Churchill pitcher, large, D 6907,
7" h... $135
Witch (The), large, D 6893, 7" h. $290

Figurines
Adele, HN 2480, flowered white dress,
1987-92.. $175
Affection, HN 2236, purple, 1962-94............. $115
Ajax, HN 2908, red, green & gold, 1980, lim-
ited edition of 950.. $475
Amy, HN 3316, blue & rose, Figure of the
Year series, 1991 .... $950
An Old King, HN 2134, purple, red, green &
brown, 1954-92 .... $450
April, HN 2708, white dress w/flowers,
Flower of the Month series, 1987............... $225
Artful Dodger, M 55, black & brown, Dick-
ens Miniatures Series, 1932-83 .... $75
Auctioneer (The), HN 2988, black, grey &
brown, 1986, R.D.I.C.C. Series (ILLUS.,
next page) $195
August, HN 3165, white & blue dress
w/poppies, Flower of the Month Series,
1987 .... $275

The Auctioneer

Autumn Breezes, HN 2147, black & white, 1955-71 .... **$350**
Ballad Seller, HN 2266, pink, 1968-73 .... **$250**
Beat You To It, HN 2871, pink, gold & blue, 1980-87 .... **$475**

Bedtime

Bedtime, HN 1978, white w/black base, 1945-97 (ILLUS.).. **$80**
Belle, HN 2340, green dress, 1968-88 .... **$70**
Biddy, HN 1513, red dress, blue shawl, 1932-51 .... **$180**

Blithe Morning, HN 2021, mauve & pink dress, 1949-71 .... **$295**
Bonnie Lassie, HN 1626, red dress, 1934-53 .... **$575**
Boy from Williamsburg, HN 2183, blue & pink, 1969-83 .... **$215**
Bridget, HN 2070, green, brown & lavender, 1951-73... **$280**
Broken Lance (The), HN 2041, blue, red & yellow, 1949-75.................................... **$450**
Bunny's Bedtime, HN 3370, pale blue, pink ribbon, 1991, RDICC Series, limited edition of 9,500 .... **$175**
Buttercup, HN 2309, green dress w/yellow sleeves, 1964-97................................... **$185**
Captain Cuttle, M 77, yellow & black, 1939-82 .... **$65**
Catherine, HN 3044, white, 1985-96 .... **$75**
Catherine of Aragon, HN 3233, green, blue & white dress, 1990, limited edition of 9,500 .... **$695**

Charlotte

Charlotte, HN 3813, brown figure, ivory dress, 1996-97 (ILLUS.)............................ **$225**
Chloe, HN 1765, blue, 1936-50 .... **$450**
Christmas Time, HN 2110, red w/white frills, 1953-67 .... **$545**
Claribel, HN 1951, red dress, 1940-49 .... **$400**
Clown (The), HN 2890, gold & grey, 1979-88 .... **$425**
Cup O' Tea, HN 2322, dark blue & grey, 1964-83... **$175**
Dainty May, M 67, pink skirt, blue overdress, 1935-49... **$625**
Easter Day, HN 1976, white dress, blue flowers, 1945-51 .... **$650**
Eventide, HN 2814, blue, white, red, yellow & green, 1977-91 .... **$275**
Fair Maiden, HN 2211, green dress, yellow sleeves, 1967-94.................................... **$80**
Farmer's Wife, HN 2069, red, green & brown, 1951-55 .... **$250**
Friar Tuck, HN 2143, brown, 1954-65 .... **$595**
Frodo, HN 2912, black & white, Middle Earth Series, 1980-84 .... **$175**

Golfer, HN 2992, blue, white & pale brown, 1988-91 .... $275

Good King Wenceslas, HN 2118, brown & purple, 1953-76 .... $275

Goody Two Shoes, M 80, blue skirt, red overdress, 1939-49 .... $115

Grand Manner, HN 2723, lavender-yellow, 1975-81 .... $245

Gypsy Dance, HN 2230, lavender dress, 1959-71 .... $275

Happy Anniversary, HN 3097, style one, purple & white, 1987-93 .... $205

Harmony

Harmony, HN 2824, grey dress, 1978-84 (ILLUS.) $225

Hazel, HN 1797, orange & green dress, 1936-49 .... $550

Hilary, HN 2335, blue dress, 1967-81 .... $195

Honey, HN 1909, pink, 1939-49 .... $525

Hornpipe (The), HN 2161, blue jacket, blue & white striped trousers, 1955-62 .... $750

Ibrahim, HN 2095, brown & yellow, 1952-55 .. $625

Invitation, HN 2170, pink, 1956-75 .... $215

Isadora, HN 2938, lavender, 1986-92 .... $350

Jack, HN 2060, green, white & black, 1950-71 .... $175

Janet, HN 1537, red dress, 1932-95 .... $125

Janice, HN 2022, green dress, 1949-55 .... $715

Joker (The), HN 2252, white, 1990-92 .... $250

Judith, HN 2278, yellow, 1986-89 .... $225

Karen, HN 1994, red dress, 1947-55 .... $450

Kate, HN 2789, white dress, 1978-87 .... $150

Katrina, HN 2327, red, 1967-69 .... $275

Lady April, HN 1958, red dress, 1940-49 ...... $425

Lady Betty, HN 1967, red, 1941-51 .... $450

Lady Pamela, HN 2718, purple, 1974-81 ...... $260

Laura, HN 2960, pale blue & white w/yellow flowers, 1984-94 .... $300

Lawyer (The), HN 3041, grey & black, 1985-95 .... $225

Lily, HN 1798, pink dress, 1936-71 .... $225

Lobster Man (The), HN 2317, blue, grey & brown, 1964-94 .... $275

Lunchtime, HN 2485, brown, 1973-80 .... $250

Make Believe

Make Believe, HN 2225, blue dress, 1962-88 (ILLUS.) $180

Mary Had a Little Lamb, HN 2048, lavender, 1949-88 .... $150

Maxine, HN 3199, pink & purple, 1989-90 ..... $215

Mayor (The), HN 2280, red & white, 1963-71 .... $275

Melanie, HN 2271, blue, 1965-81 .... $215

Midinette, HN 2090, blue dress, 1952-65 ...... $395

Miss Demure, HN 1402, lavender & pink dress, 1930-75 .... $250

Modesty, HN 2744, white, 1987-91 .... $225

Mr. Micawber, M 42, yellow & black, 1932-83 .... $80

Omar Khayyam, HN 2247, brown, 1965-83 .. $195

Paisley Shawl, HN 1987, cream dress, red shawl, 1946-59 .... $475

Pantalettes, M 15, shaded blue dress, red hat, 1932-45 .... $400

Parisian, HN 2445, blue & grey, matte glaze,1972-75 .... $150

Parson's Daughter (The), HN 564, red, yellow & green, 1923-49 .... $600

Pearly Boy, HN 1482, red jacket, 1931-49 .... $325

Pearly Boy, HN 2767, black, white & blue, 1988-92 .... $300

Penny, HN 2338, green & white dress, 1968-95 .... $75

Pensive, HN 3109, white w/yellow flowers on skirt, 1986-88 .... $175

Pensive Moments, HN 2704, blue dress, 1975-81 .... $300

Pied Piper (The), HN 2102, brown cloak, grey hat & boots, 1953-76 .... $275

Polka (The), HN 2156, pale pink dress, 1955-69 .... $295

Polly Peachum, HN 550, red dress, 1922-
49 .... **$750**
Potter (The), HN 1493, multicolored jugs &
jars, dark brown & red robe & hood, 1932-92 .. **$500**
Premiere, HN 2343, hand holds cloak,
green dress, 1969-79 .... **$195**

Pride & Joy

Pride & Joy, HN 2945, brown, gold & green,
RDICC, 1984 (ILLUS.) **$275**
Priscilla, M 24, red, 1932-45......................... **$600**
Prized Possessions, HN 2942, cream, pur-
ple & green, RDICC, 1982 .... **$650**
Puppetmaker, HN 2253, green, brown &
red, 1962-73... **$495**
Queen Elizabeth I, HN 3099, red & gold,
1987, Queens of the Realm Series, limit-
ed edition of 5,000.................................... **$650**
Rebecca, HN 2805, pale blue & lavender,
1980-96... **$450**
Regal Lady, HN 2709, turquoise & cream,
1975-83... **$195**
Rest Awhile, HN 2728, blue, white & pur-
ple, 1981-84 .... **$275**
Rosemary, HN 2091, red & blue, 1952-59..... **$600**

Rosemary

Rosemary, HN 3698, mauve & yellow,
1995-97 (ILLUS.) **$315**
Sairey Gamp, HN 2100, white dress, green
cape, 1952-67... **$475**
Sam Weller, M 48, yellow & brown, 1932-81 .... **$65**
Samwise, HN 2925, black & brown, Middle
Earth Series, 1982-84 .... **$725**
Sandra, HN 2275, gold, 1969-97 .... **$225**
Sara, HN 2265, red & white, 1981 to present .. **$250**
Sharon, HN 3047, white, 1984-95 .... **$90**
Shore Leave, HN 2254, 1965-79 .... **$295**
Silversmith of Williamsburg, HN 2208,
green jerkin, 1960-83 .... **$250**
Simone, HN 2378, green dress, 1971-81 ...... **$135**
Skater (The), HN 2117, red & white dress,
1953-71... **$485**
Soiree, HN 2312, white dress, green over-
skirt, 1967-84 .... **$175**
Spring, HN 2085, 1952-59............................. **$395**
Summer's Day, HN 2181, 1957-62 .... **$275**
Taking Things Easy, HN 2677, blue, white
& brown, 1975-87...................................... **$275**
Teatime, HN 2255, 1972-95........................... **$250**
Thanksgiving, HN 2446, blue overalls,
1972-76... **$250**
This Little Pig, HN 1793, red robe, 1936-95 .... **$85**
Top o' the Hill, HN 1834, orange dress,
green & red scarf, 1937 to present **$400**
Uriah Heep, HN 2101, black jacket, green
trousers, 1952-67 .... **$425**
Uriah Heep, HN 554, black jacket & trou-
sers, 1923-39.. **$525**
Votes For Women, HN 2816, 1978-81.......... **$325**
Winsome, HN 2220, red dress, 1960-85 .... **$220**
Writing, HN 3049, flowered yellow dress,
1986, limited edition of 750, Gentle Arts
Series.. **$1,150**

Flambé Glazes

Animals & Birds

Rouge Flambé Comical Bear Figure

Bear, comical seated pose, Rouge Flambé
glaze, Model 58, ca. 1918, 5" h. (ILLUS.) .. **$2,500**

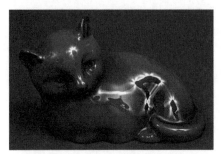

Reclining Cat Rouge Flambé Figure

Cat, reclining curled up w/head slightly raised to the side, Rouge Flambé glaze, Model 70, ca. 1920, 3 1/2" h. (ILLUS.).... **$1,600**

Small Rouge Flambé Chick Figure

Chick, small bird, Rouge Flambé glaze, Model 1163 B, designed by Charles Noke, ca. 1908, 2 1/4" h. (ILLUS.) **$1,000**

Flambé Alsatian on Pin Tray Rim

Dog, Alsatian seated on the rim of an oval alabaster pin tray, Rougle Flambé glaze, Model 497A, ca. 1930, 5" h. (ILLUS.) **$1,600**

Rouge Flambé English Setter Figure

Dog, English Setter, Rouge Flambé glaze (ILLUS.)... **$2,000**

Rouge Flambé Pekinese

Dog, Pekinese, Rouge Flambé, Model 544, ca. 1927, 2 1/2" h. (ILLUS.)............. **$1,500**

Rouge Flambé Raised Head Dragon

Dragon, head raised high, wings up & tail curled, Rouge Flambé glaze, Model HN3552, designed by Robert Tabbenor, 1993, 5 1/4" h. (ILLUS.) **$400**

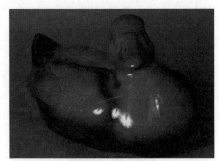

Rouge Flambé Duck Preening Figure

Duck, preening pose, Model 4, Rouge Flambé glaze, ca. 1912, 1 1/2" h. (ILLUS.) **$600**

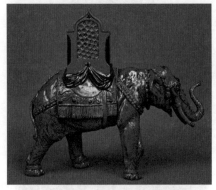

Rouge Flambé Shanxi Elephant Figure

Elephant, Shanxi, w/howdah on back, Rouge Flambé glaze, Model BA 42, designed by Alan Maslankowski, limited edition of 250, 2004, 11 1/2" l. (ILLUS.) .. **$1,700**

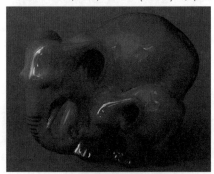

Elephant & Young in Rouge Flambé

Elephant & young, Rouge Flambé glaze, HN3548, designed by Eric Griffiths, 1990-96, 3 1/4" h. (ILLUS.) **$400**

Fish, Rouge Flambé, leaping fish raised on a pedestal support, prototype, ca. 1985.. **$1,600**

Seated Fox Rouge Flambé Variation

Fox, seated looking up, Rouge Flambé glaze color variation, Model 14, ca. 1912-96, 4 1/2" h. (ILLUS.) **$300**

Fox dish, elongated stalking pose, red monochrome glaze w/silver rim band, Model 20, ca. 1920, 12 1/2" l. (ILLUS., bottom of page)...................................... **$1,500**

Test Market "Going Home" Figure

Geese, two flying together, "Going Home," Rouge Flambé glaze, designed by Adrian Hughes, test market only, 1982, 6 1/4" h. (ILLUS.) **$1,200**

Monochrome Red Stalking Fox Dish

Monkey, Suzhou model, long monkey climbing on a branch, Rouge Flambé glaze, Model BA 40, limited edition of 250, designed by Martyn Alcock, 2004, 8 3/4" l. (ILLUS.).. **$800**

Rouge Flambé Hebei Goat Figure

Hebei goat, long-horned stag standing on rock, Rouge Flambé glaze, Model BA 63, limited edition of 250, designed by Alan Maslankowski, 10 1/4" h. (ILLUS.) **$500**

Early Rouge Flambé Model of Owlet

Owl with owlet, Rouge Flambé, Model 71, ca. 1912, 4 3/4" h. (ILLUS.).............. **$3,000**
Penguin, Rouge Flambé, standing animal w/head tilted to side, prototype **$1,250**

Prototype Figure of Flambé Kittens

Kittens, two kittens curled up together, Rouge Flambé, 2 1/2" (ILLUS.) **$600**

Early Rouge Flambé Pig

Pig, Rouge Flambé, fat squatty animal, Model 72, ca. 1912, 2" h. (ILLUS.)............ **$850**
Pigs at trough, Rouge Flambé, two animals, Model 81, ca. 1931, 2 1/2" h.......... **$2,400**

Rouge Flambé Model 1165 Rabbit

Rabbit, Rouge Flambé, seated animal w/one long ear to side, Model 1165, 1913-96, 2 1/2" h. (ILLUS.) **$250**

Rouge Flambé Suzhou Monkey Figure

Rouge Flambé Limited Tang Horse

Tang horse, Rouge Flambé, based on ancient Chinese model, Model BA 25, limited edition of 250, designed by Alan Maslankowski, 2002, 10 1/4" h. (ILLUS.)... **$1,800**

Rouge Flambé Modern Tortoise

Tortoise, Rouge Flambé, 1920-46, 2" h. (ILLUS.).. **$2,000**

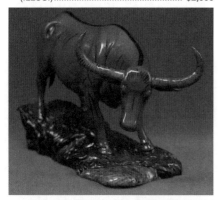

Limited Rouge Flambé Water Buffalo

Water buffalo, standing on an oblong base, Rouge Flambé, Model BA 59, limited edition of 150, designed by Martyn Alcock, 2005, 7" h. (ILLUS.) **$1,500**

Miscellaneous Pieces

Bowl, Mottled Flambé glaze, squatty bulbous shape w/a closed rim, the upper rim decorated w/small stylized red & blue flowers above the dark blue lower sides w/light blue speckled glaze, ca. 1955 ..... **$1,200**

Rouge Flambé Floral Band Bowl

Bowl, Rouge Flambé, round shallow shape w/inner bands of stylized flowers in black on a red ground, black border band, ca. 1930 (ILLUS.).. **$3,000**
Bowl, Rouge Flambé, shallow round shape w/a flanged rim, decorated in black w/a rural landscape w/a cottage, ca. 1945 .... **$1,000**

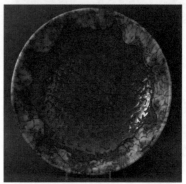

Doulton Wenzhou Flambé Bowl

Bowl, Wenzhou model, round shallow shape, Flambé glaze w/red speckles on black in the center w/a streaky border band in white, red & black, Model BA 13, limited edition of 250, 2000, 15" d. (ILLUS.) **$1,000**
Bowl, 5" d., Sung Ware glaze, footed deep rounded & flaring shape, dark black speckled w/red & blue on exterior, ca. 1930 .... **$1,000**

Sung Ware Bowl with Rabbit Band

Bowl, 9" d., Sung Ware glaze, black ground w/a red border band decorated w/rabbits & meandering berry vines, ca. 1930 (ILLUS., previous page) **$3,000**

Box, cov., miniature, Mottled Flambé glaze, flared foot supporting the flaring rounded box w/a low domed cover, designed by Charles Noke & Fred Moore, ca. 1955, 2 3/4" h. **$1,000**

Flambé Canton Ginger Jar

Sung Ware Inscribed Deer Charger

Charger, Sung Ware glaze, deep round center w/a wide flat flanged rim, the center decorated w/a large stylized stag & vines, the rim inscribed in black "Many a Race is Lost Ere Ever a Step is Taken," ca. 1925 (ILLUS.)...................... **$6,000**

Bold Chang Ware Glazed Vase

Vase, Chang Ware glaze, swelled cylindrical body tapering to a rounded shoulder & tiny trumpet neck, boldly contrasting colors, ca. 1955 (ILLUS.) **$3,000**

Rouge Flambé Fuzhou Buddha Figure

Figure of Buddha, seated, Fuzhou model, Rouge Flambé glaze, Model BA 46, limited edition of 100, 2004, 6 1/2" h. (ILLUS.) **$875**

Ginger jar, cov., Canton model, bulbous ovoid body w/small domed cover, Flambé glaze, Model BA 102, limited edition of 250, 1999, 7" h. (ILLUS., top next column).. **$800**

Pharoah character jug, Rouge Flambé, ca. 1920, 2 1/2" h. **$800**

1950s Mottled Flambé Tall Vase

Vase, Mottled Flambé, tall slightly tapering cylindrical body w/a rounded shoulder & small trumpet neck, ca. 1955 (ILLUS.).... **$1,500**

Woodland Scene Rouge Flambé Vase

Large Veined Sung Ware Vase

Vase, 8" h., Rouge Flambé, footed bulbous lower body tapering to cylindrical sides & a flaring rim, decorated w/a woodland landscape, ca. 1945 (ILLUS.)..................... **$500**

Vase, 9" h., Sung Ware glaze, footed bulbous ovoid body tapering to a short flaring neck, bold glazed shading from black to deep red to deep streaky blue & black at the base, decorated overall in black w/a scene of swimming fish among water plants, designed by Charles Noke & Fred Allen, 1929 .... **$2,000**

Vase, 9 1/4" h., Rouge Flambé Veined, footed spherical body tapering to a stick neck, frothy blue texture on lower body, stamped logo, Shape No. 1618 .... **$500**

Rouge Flambé Veined Tall Vase

Rouge Flambé Veined Doulton Vase

Vase, 10 3/4" h., Rouge Flambé Veined, ovoid body tapering to a tiny trumpet neck, Shape No. 1619 (ILLUS.) **$748**

Vase, 11 3/4" h., Veined Sung Ware glaze, bulbous body tapering to a tall trumpet neck, bold streaked dark blue & red glaze, ca. 1955 (ILLUS., top next column)................. **$2,500**

Vase, 13 1/8" h., Rouge Flambé Veined, slender swelled cylindrical body tapering to a slender stick neck, Shape No. 1617 (ILLUS., middle next column).................... **$345**

Vase, 13 1/2" h., Rouge Flambé Veined, slender swelled cylindrical body tapering to a slender stick neck, Shape No. 1617 (ILLUS., bottom next column) **$345**

Tall Rouge Flambé Veined Doulton Vase

Vase, 16" h., Chang Ware glaze, nearly spherical lower body w/a tall cylindrical neck, small angled handles on the shoulder bold mottled glaze, ca. 1930 .... **$5,000**

Pair of Doulton Flambé Vases

Vases, 6 1/4" h., footed ovoid body tapering sharply to a slender neck w/flared rim, red, gold & black flambé glaze, stamped mark, pr. (ILLUS.)....................................... **$288**

Sung Ware Flying Peacock Vases

Vases, 11" h., Sung Ware glaze, tall gently swelled cylindrical body w/a low flared mouth, decorated w/colorful flying peacock against a swirled red, black & yellow ground, ca. 1985, pr. (ILLUS.)................. **$4,000**

Kingsware

This line of earthenware featured a very dark brown background often molded with scenes or figures trimmed in color and covered with a glossy glaze. All pieces in this line were designed by the leading Royal Doulton designer, Charles Noke.

Ashtray, shallow round shape, center molded bust portrait of an old Fisherman, silver rim band, ca. 1904 (ILLUS., top next column) **$700**
Creamer, cylindrical w/a small rim spout & silver rim band, pointed angled handle, molded Pied Piper scene, 1905 (ILLUS., middle next column) **$400**

Kingsware Fisherman Ashtray

Kingsware Pied Piper Scene Creamer

Kingsware Dewars Arkwright Flask

Flask, baluster-shaped tapering to a small neck & high arched rim spout, C-form handle, molded oval reserve w/a bust portrait of a man in 18th c. within a wreath, titled "Richard Arkwright - 1732-1792," produced for Dewars Whisky, 1906, 9" h. (ILLUS.) **$1,200**

Kingsware Bacchus Figural Flask

Flask, figural, man wearing a top hat seated astride a large barrel, known as the Bacchus model, 8 1/2" h. (ILLUS.) **$3,000**

Kingsware Bill Sykes Flask

Flask, flat-bottomed bulbous ovoid body tapering to a figural neck modeled as the head of Bill Sykes, based on the Dickens character, 1905, 7 1/4" h. (ILLUS.) **$1,500**

Flask, footed bulbous ovoid body w/an off-center small top neck & spout & looped shoulder handle, molded portrait of Mr. Micawber from Dickens, 1910, 7" h. (ILLUS., top next column).. **$500**

Kingsware Mr. Micawber Flask

Kingsware Tony Weller Portrait Flask

Flask, footed tall ovoid body tapering to a small neck & spout, small shoulder loop handle, ball stopper, molded portrait of Tony Weller from Dickens, made for Dewars Whiskey, 8" h. (ILLUS.)............. **$1,000**

Flask, simple ovoid body tapering to a small neck & spout, D-form shoulder handle, silver stopper, molded portrait of Chadband, inspired by a character in Bleak House by Dickens, 8" h. (ILLUS., next page) **$1,800**

Kingsware Chadband Portrait Flask

Kingsware Quince Design Pitcher

Pitcher, jug-type, Quince design, flared foot
& swelled cylindrical body w/a flaring rim
w/spout, long D-form handle, molded w/a
half-length portrait of a man smoking a
long pipe, ca. 1905 (ILLUS.) **$1,000**

Kingsware Huntsman Loving Cup

Loving cup, cylindrical form w/flared rim &
long pointed loop handles, molded bust
portrait of the Huntsman, 1907, 7" h.
(ILLUS.) **$1,000**

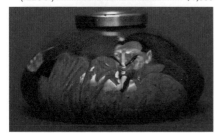

Kingsware Mephisto Match Holder

Match holder, wide low squatty bulbous
shape tapering to a small silver rim band,
molded Mephisto scene w/half-length
portrait of the devil, ca. 1902 (ILLUS.) **$850**

Kingsware Francis Drake Pitcher

Pitcher, 9" h., baluster-form body w/small
rim spout, C-form handle w/thumbrest,
molded scene of Sir Francis Drake, 1938
(ILLUS.)... **$1,500**

Kingsware Monk Shaving Mug

Kingsware Lynton Witch Tea Set

Shaving mug, ovoid body w/a flared rim & projecting brush spout, molded Friar portrait (ILLUS., previous page) **$1,500**

Tea set: cov. teapot, creamer & open sugar; rectangular bodies w/loop handles, molded Lynton Witch scene, 1902, the set (ILLUS., top of page) **$1,000**

Kingsware Darby & Joan Teapot

Teapot, cov., nearly spherical body w/a short shoulder spout, fitted cover w/knob finial, D-form handle, molded portraits of Darby & Joan, 1907 (ILLUS.) **$800**

Kingsware Dickens Figures Tobacco Jar

Tobacco jar, cov., wide cylindrical jar w/molded base & rim band, the sides molded in full-relief w/characters from Dickens, inset flat cover w/large bulbous knob (ILLUS.) **$2,000**

Kingsware Monks Vase

Vase, swelled cylindrical form w/a low slightly flaring rim, molded Monks scene (ILLUS.) **$550**

Tall Kingsware Falstaff Vase

Vase, 11" h., footed slightly tapering cylindrical body w/a flaring rim, long pointed loop handles down the sides, standing portrait of Falstaff, 1905 (ILLUS.)............ **$1,000**

Kingsware Whiskey Barrel with Scene

Whiskey barrel, model of barrel w/a tavern scene molded on the sides, 1928, 7" l. (ILLUS.).. **$1,300**

Lambeth Art Wares

Stoneware Ashtray with Card Suits

Ashtray, stoneware, short cylindrical form w/four notches around the rim, the dark blue sides applied w/four shields each enclosing a different suit symbol (ILLUS.) **$600**

Bottle, stoneware, miniature, simple cylindrical body w/angled shoulder to the bulbed neck, mottled brown glaze, ca. 1920 (ILLUS., top next column) **$150**

Bowl, stoneware, figural, modeled as a long narrow stylized pike-like fish w/molded fins, decorated overall in mottled dark & light blue, designed by Mark Marshall, ca. 1890 (ILLUS., bottom of page) .... **Rare**

Miniature Simple Stoneware Bottle

Small Slip-Decorated Doulton Bowl

Bowl, 4 1/4" d., stoneware, widely flaring rounded sides, brown base band below the white-glazed sides decorated in raised slip w/wave-like scroll designs, blue interior, ca. 1920 (ILLUS.) **$300**

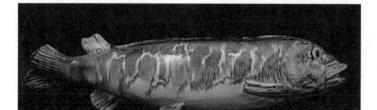

Doulton Long Fish-shaped Stoneware Bowl

Ringed Cachepot with Blue Flowerheads

Cachepot, stoneware, wide squatty bulbous body w/a wide short neck, a cobalt blue base & shoulder band molded w/small pointed leaves, the tan body w/a finely ringed ground applied w/two rows of small blue flowerheads connected by thin brown stems, ca. 1885 (ILLUS.) **$500**

Early Doulton Stoneware Candlesticks

Candlesticks, stoneware, funnel-shaped base tapering w/a flaring drip pan centered by a tall cylindrical shaft w/looped base handles, decorated w/incised de-

signs trimmed in blue & brown, ca. 1872, 11" h., pr. (ILLUS.) **$2,000**

Doulton Spherical Stoneware Clock

Clock, stoneware, spherical case enclosing a round dial w/Arabic numerals, ca. 1900 (ILLUS.)... **$1,200**

1930s Doulton Stoneware Cracker Jar

Cracker jar, cov., gently tapering cylindrical shape in lightly mottled brown trimmed w/brown ring bands, squared overhead caned bail handle, ca. 1935 (ILLUS.)......... **$200**

Doulton Stoneware Case Decanters in a Basket

Carrara Ware Ewers with Children

Decanters, stoneware, case-style w/square upright bodies in matte brick red & rounded shoulders w/a short neck & loop handle in glossy dark brown, set of four in a wicker basket holder, ca. 1880, each 8" h., the set (ILLUS., bottom previous page).......... **$1,500**

Doulton Eggcup with Raised Dots

Eggcup, stoneware, a ringed pedestal base in brown & dark blue, the dark blue cup molded overall w/small graduated raised dots, silver rim band, late 19th c. (ILLUS.) **$400**

Ewer, faience, ovoid body w/a swelled shoulder band below the trumpet neck, long brown handle, the pale tan ground h.p. overall w/colorful wildflowers & green leaves, designed by an unrecorded artist "WG," 1877, 12" h. (ILLUS., top next column) **$1,200**

Doulton Faience Ewer with Wildflowers

Ewers, Carrara Ware, tall ovoid body tapering to a cylindrical divided neck w/a tall vertical spout & high arched shoulder handle, cream ground, the body decorated overall w/large bluish green swirling leafy floral vines centered by oval medallions painted in color w/charming scenes of Victorian children, designed by Ada Dennis, Arthur Pearce & Josephine Durtnall, ca. 1890, 12" h., pr. (ILLUS., top of page).. **Rare**

Small Harradine Dutch Woman Figure

Figure of a Dutch woman, slip-cast stoneware, standing figure carrying a small basket, pale blue & white, designed by Leslie Harradine, Model H9, 1912, 4 1/2" h. (ILLUS.) **$1,500**

Doulton Stoneware Banded Ice Bucket

Ice bucket, stoneware, wide slightly tapering cylindrical form, molded w/two narrow body bands decorated w/small diamonds, the two wide body bands incised w/ornate leafy scrolls in light & dark green & cobalt blue, ca. 1880 (ILLUS.) **$800**

Inkwell, stoneware, figural, figure of a chubby standing baby wearing a long apron & dress w/ruffled shoulders, the dress in streaky green & tan, the ruffles in blue & the head in dark brown, designed by Leslie Harradine, ca. 1910, 3 1/2" h. (ILLUS., top next column) **$1,200**

Stoneware Brown-headed Baby Inkwell

Ornately Decorated Stoneware Isobath

Isobath, stoneware, a round domed foot supporting a wide cylindrical cup-shaped body w/a side cup spout & a conical cover w/knob finial, brown w/blue band rim, the body & cover decorated w/ornate large cream-colored floral & scrolling leaf panels, made for Thos. de la Rue, ca. 1893, 6" h. (ILLUS.) **$500**

Stoneware Jardiniere with Swimming Fish

Jardiniere, stoneware, squatty bulbous shape w/a wide, low cylindrical neck, molded in high-relief w/stylized long fish in green & brown swimming through large scrolling brown, grey & tan waves, designed by Mark Marshall, ca. 1900, 9" h. (ILLUS., previous page) **$2,000**

Realistic Copper Ware Riveted Jug

Jug, Copper Ware, footed tapering cylindrical body w/a pointed angled handle, glossy copper glaze molded w/riveted seams & simulated dents, ca. 1895, 6" h. (ILLUS.) **$650**

Banded Scroll-incised Stoneware Jug

Jug, stoneware, footed bulbous ovoid body tapering to a tall slender cylindrical neck w/a long handle from the rim to the shoul-

der, the body divided into wide bands, the bottom band decorated w/swirled ribs below molded narrow blue bands flanking a wide body band decorated w/incised tightly scrolling leafy branches dotted w/small applied florettes, a ribbed shoulder band applied w/a narrow flowering vine & the upper neck incised w/another band of swirled ribs, silver rim band, designed by Arthur Barlow, 1874, 10 1/2" h. (ILLUS.) **$800**

Miniature Doulton Stoneware Jug

Jug w/stopper, stoneware, miniature, footed squatty bulbous body w/a slender cylindrical neck w/a disk stopper & angled brown handle, buff ground applied around the body & shoulder w/bands of blue flowerheads, ca. 1880, 3 1/2" h. (ILLUS.).... **$500**

Unusual Doulton Liquor Spigot Measure

Liquor spigot measure, stoneware, two-section cylindrical shape w/a rounded bottom w/a button finial, a short cylindrical spigot on the lower front & a threaded projection at the top back, metal fitting & handle at the top, decorated in pale mottled green applied w/a spade-shaped brown Art Nouveau leaf, ca. 1910, 6" l. (ILLUS.) **$500**

Silicon Ware Decorated Match Holder

Match holder, cov., stoneware, Silicon Ware, flaring base & cylindrical sides w/a domed cover, light brown ground decorated around the sides w/a wide band composed of light blue small leaves flanking a band composed of pairs of white scrolls w/blue dots, white dot bands around the cover & base, ca. 1880, 3 1/4" h. (ILLUS.) **$350**

Doulton Stoneware Match Holder

Match holder & striker, stoneware, domed wide foot supporting a slightly tapering cylindrical ribbed striker w/open top for holding matches, the base decorated w/a blue band decorated w/an Art Nouveau design of a band of spade-shaped brown leaves, ca. 1910 (ILLUS.)........................... **$500**

Model of a sea lion, stoneware, the animal perched on a rocky outcrop, overall tan lustre glaze, designed by Richard Garbe, 1931, 8" h. (ILLUS., top next column) **$1,250**

Mustard pot, cov., stoneware, footed squatty bulbous shaped w/a molded rim fitted w/a metal band, C-form handle, brown ground incised w/a band of small double blue arches, ca. 1880, 2 1/2" h. (ILLUS., middle next column)..................... **$400**

1930s Tan Lustre Model of a Sea Lion

Squatty Doulton Stoneware Mustard Pot

Doulton Mustard Pot with Florette Band

Mustard pot w/silver rim & hinged cover, stoneware, footed squatty spherical brown body w/loop handle decorated w/a band of white-dotted rings enclosing a large molded blue florette, cobalt blue neck band, ca. 1885 (ILLUS., previous page) **$500**

Doulton Pepper Shaker with Swag Band

Pepper shaker, stoneware, footed waisted cylindrical body in streaky bluish green below the brown domed top, molded around the top of the neck w/a leafy swag band, ca. 1912, 4" h. (ILLUS.).................... **$500**

Unique Doulton Figural Chicken Pitcher

Pitcher, stoneware, jug-form, figural, modeled as a squatty bulbous chicken w/the head forming the spout, boldly glazed in browns, black & white, designed by Mark Marshall, ca. 1895 (ILLUS.) .... **Rare**

Tall Tankard Pitcher by G. Tinworth

Pitcher, stoneware, tankard-style, flared base ring below the tall cylindrical body w/a neck ring & short neck w/rim spout, C-form handle, the main body applied & incised w/a stylized scrolling blue & green foliate design, designed by George Tinworth, ca. 1880 (ILLUS.) **$1,500**

Doulton Stoneware Soccer Players Pitcher

Pitcher, 6" h., jug-style, stoneware, footed cylindrical body swelled at the bottom & flaring at the rim w/a small rim spout, long C-form handle, mottled brown ground applied around the bottom w/a blue leaf band & around the rim w/a thin blossom band, the main body applied w/a repeating design of applied light blue socker players in action, attributed to Harry Barnard, 1883 (ILLUS.) **$600**

Early Stoneware Medallion Motto Pitcher

Pitcher, 7 1/2" h., stoneware, jug-form, the ovoid body w/a short flaring neck w/a rim spout & a high arched handle, the buff body decorated w/large bold-relief sun-flower-shaped medallions each enclosing a different classical portrait, each medallion ringed by a motto written in black, ca. 1885 (ILLUS.)............................. **$500**

Hannah Barlow Lambethware Pitcher

Pitcher, 11" h., Hannah Barlow Doulton Lam-bethware, design of hounds chasing fox, 1875, vertical hairline crack (ILLUS.)......... **$1,250**

Doulton Faience Portrait Plaque

Plaque, faience, h.p. bust portrait of a lady w/curly blonde hair, border band in dark blue decorated w/yellow butterflies & blossoms, Lambeth factory, ca. 1880, 12" d. (ILLUS.)....................................... **$1,500**

Pierced Covered Doulton Potpourri Jar

Potpourri jar, cov., stoneware, a bulbous ovoid body tapering to a wide cylindrical neck, the mottled bluish black ground ap-plied around the shoulder w/pierced blue flower blossoms below an upper band of pierced trefoils, the domed cover w/a knob finial pieced w/small holes separat-ed w/a thin molded scroll band, ca. 1900 (ILLUS.).. **$1,500**

Beaded & Flowerhead Band Salt Dip

Salt dip, stoneware, footed squatty bulbous dish w/silver rim band, the sides in brown, tan & dark blue & molded around the middle w/a band of small flowerheads below beaded shoulder bands, late 19th c. (ILLUS.) **$500**

Doulton Salt with Gilt Circles Design

Salt dip, stoneware, footed wide squatty shape w/a wide flat rim, overall gilt circle decoration, ca. 1884 (ILLUS.) **$400**

Doulton Squatty Footed Salt Dip

Salt dip, stoneware, squatty bulbous dish molded w/stylized cobalt blue & tan leaf devices, raised on three small scroll feet, silver rim band, late 19th c. (ILLUS.) **$500**

Salt Shaker with Diamond Florette Band

Salt shaker w/silver plate rim & top, stoneware, tall urn-form, banded decorated w/a wide center band molded w/florette diamonds in dark blue, shoulder & base bands w/light & dark blue diamonds, buff bands trimmed w/tiny white dots, ca. 1880 (ILLUS.) **$300**

Harrods Stilton Cheese Storage Jar

Storage jar, cov., stoneware, grey cylindrical body w/a brown rim band & inset cover, the side printed in black w/an oval reserve around "Harrods Prize Dairy Stilton Cheese - in Jars," ca. 1910 (ILLUS.) **$250**

Doulton-Lambeth Hunting Ware Tea Set

Miniature Silicon Tankard with Silver Rim

Tankard, miniature, Silicon Ware, footed ovoid black body w/a C-form handle tapering to the silver rim band, the sides molded to resemble stitched leather panels, ca. 1890 (ILLUS.) **$200**

Tea set: large cov. teapot, small cov. teapot, cov. sugar bowl & creamer; Hunting Ware line, dark brown shaded to tan ground decorated w/applied relief-molded English hunting scenes, Doulton-Lambeth marks, ca. 1905, the set (ILLUS., top of page) **$600**

Doulton Marqueterie Ware Teapot

Teapot, cov., Marqueterie Ware, spherical body w/ribs around the lower half, short angled spout, squared handle, small domed cover, Doulton & Rix patent, ca. 1890 (ILLUS.).. **$2,000**

Teapot, cov., stoneware, molded swimming fish decoration around the body, Doulton-Lambeth, ca. 1895 (ILLUS., bottom of page)... **$2,000**

Early Doulton-Lambeth Stoneware Teapot with Swimming Fish Design

Doulton-Lambeth Dragon Design Teapot

Teapot, cov., stoneware, spherical body molded in relief w/a serpentine dragon design, Doulton-Lambeth, ca. 1895 (ILLUS., top of page) **$1,000**

Bird-decorated Faience Tile

Tile, square, faience, a pale cream ground h.p. w/a spread-winged bluebird on a blossom sprig within a brown ring, ca. 1885, 6" w. (ILLUS.) **$350**

Stoneware Mr. Toby Tobacco Jar

Tobacco jar, cov., stoneware, figural Mr. Toby, bulbous cylindrical shape w/molded flaring rim, polychrome decoration, inscribed "The best is not too good," de-

signed by Harry Simeon, ca. 1925, 4 1/2" h. (ILLUS.) **$2,000**

Triple Mr. Toby Stoneware Toby Jug

Toby jug, stoneware, molded around the sides w/three figures of a standing Mr. Toby, dark brown shaded to tan glazing, 1888, 9 1/2" h. (ILLUS.) .... **Rare**

Small Stoneware Dish with Pixie on Rim

Trinket dish (bibelot), stoneware, figural, shallow rounded dish w/a green exterior & cobalt blue interior, mounted on the rim w/the seated figure of a pixie in shades of brown, designed by Harry Simeon, ca. 1925, 4 1/4" d. (ILLUS., previous page) **$2,000**

Doulton Stoneware "Good Luck" Tumbler

Tumbler, stoneware, cylindrical, mottled dark blue & green ground molded at the top w/"Good Luck" above a large molded dark green swastika, ca. 1910 (ILLUS.) **$350**

Doulton Tall Stoneware Tumbler

Tumbler, stoneware, tall slightly tapering cylindrical form, incised w/long stylized

leaves & indigo blue foliage w/dark green trim, impressed marks & dated 1877, 4 5/8" h. (ILLUS.) **$115**

Stoneware Tumbler with Golfing Scenes

Tumbler, stoneware, tall slightly tapering cylindrical form, the tan sides applied w/white relief golfing scenes, a dark brown top band below the silver rim, ca. 1900 (ILLUS.)... **$500**

Flower-decorated Commemorative Tyg

Tyg, stoneware, cylindrical body w/a tan ground & tan brown-lined handles & brown rim, the sides incised & painted w/large pale blue & brown daisy-like flowers & cobalt blue leaves flanked by brown bands, made for the Royal Canoe Club, 1895, 6" h. (ILLUS.) **$1,200**

Doulton Chine Ware Umbrella Stand

Umbrella stand, Chine Ware, cylindrical body w/a short waisted neck below the wide rolled rim, the main body decorated overall w/large pale blue florals on a darker blue ground, ca. 1890, 14" h. (ILLUS.) **$1,000**

Ribbed Doulton Marqueterie Vase

Vase, Marqueterie Ware, footed ribbed ovoid body tapering to a cylindrical neck w/a molded blue band flanked by small gold scroll handles, blue & white body band & gold & blue ground, Lambeth factory, ca. 1895 (ILLUS.) **$800**

Doulton Faience Vase with Irises

Vase, faience, footed ovoid body tapering to a short trumpet neck, the tan foot below the dark cobalt blue body decorated w/large yellow irises & long green leaves, the neck decorated w/brick red blossoms on a tan ground, ca. 1880 (ILLUS.) **$1,200**

Doulton Stoneware Bird with Nest Vase

Vase, stoneware, bulbous ovoid body tapering to a short rolled neck, mottled dark blue ground decorated w/a scene of a blue bird perched on a leafy branch besides its neck, a white full moon in the background, ca. 1925 (ILLUS.) **$850**

Doulton Pate-sur-Pate Vase with Otter

Vase, 6" h., stoneware, small foot below a large bulbous ovoid body tapering to a wide short rolled neck, wide body band in shades of blue decorated in pate-sur-pate w/an otter, brown rim & base bands, designed by W. Edward Dunn, 1883, 6" h. (ILLUS.) **$1,200**

1920s Bird-decorated Stoneware Vase

Vase, 9" h., stoneware, waisted cylindrical shape, the lower body w/a streaky blue & brown glaze, the upper body tube-line decorated w/a wide white band featuring a large brown & white bird perched on a brown branch w/green leaves, designed by Harry Simeon, ca. 1925 (ILLUS.) **$1,300**

Fine Stoneware Vase with Diamond Design

Vase, 7 1/2" h., stoneware, footed ovoid urn-form w/flaring neck & squared shoulder handles, a base band w/incised blue pointed leaves, the neck decorated w/a band of stylized blue blossoms, the body decorated w/a repeating design of large incised dark blue crosses enclosing large dark blue diamonds centered by a molded florette, tan ground, designed by Rosina Harris, ca. 1885 (ILLUS.).................... **$1,000**

Chiné Ware Vase with Blue Flowers

Vase, 10 3/4" h., Chiné Ware, tall baluster-shaped, the flaring banded foot in brown, green & white, the tall ovoid body decorated around the base w/a band of tall pointed mauve leaves, the textured cream ground incised & painted w/large pale blue blossoms on scrolling green & blue leafy stems, the slender trumpet neck decorated w/dark green bands flanking a wide cream band, ca. 1890 (ILLUS.)........... **$500**

Doulton Lambeth Vase with Panels

Vase, 11" h., 7" d., wide baluster-form w/a
  wide neck & flaring molded rim, a dark mottled blue ground decorated w/large buff
  oval scenes of birds in marsh grass & small
  ovals w/grasses & leaves in buff, date mark
  for 1884, artist-initialed (ILLUS.) **$478**

Moon Flask Vase with Wild Roses

Vase, 14" h., faience, moon flask-shaped,
  the flattened round sides in shaded dark
  green h.p. w/a large cluster of white wild
  roses w/greenish yellow leaves all issuing from a small brick red circle, raised on
  pointed flaring brick red feet, ca. 1880
  (ILLUS.) **$1,500**
Vase, 16" h., stoneware, footed very slen-
  der ovoid body tapering to a flaring rim,
  Art Nouveau style, the base band w/blue
  & brown spearpoints below a large band
  of tube-lined round flowerheads in grey &
  blue against a speckled blue ground &
  w/green spearpoints issuing from the top
  of each flower, designed by Eliza
  Simmance, ca. 1905 (ILLUS., top next
  column) **$2,000**

Slender Tall Art Nouveau Floral Vase

Tall Hannah Barlow Livestock Vase

Vase, 18 1/4" h., stoneware, very tall baluster-form body w/a tall trumpet neck, the
  wide body band incised w/a scene of cattle & horses & flanked by bands of pointed brown & blue scrolls & blossoms, mottled glossy dark green & blue ground,
  decorated by Hannah Barlow w/flowers
  probably by Florence Roberts, signed
  (ILLUS.) **$1,955**

Advertising Whiskey Flask with Ship

Whiskey flask, stoneware, wide bulbous body tapering to a short cylindrical neck, dark brown shaded to tan ground, applied on the side with a large black sailing ship representing the Galley of Lorne, flanked above & below by molded white banners reading "Special - Highland Whisky" (sic), made for Greenlees, ca. 1885, 5 3/4" h. (ILLUS.) **$400**

Series Wares

Bowl, Desert Scene Series, shallow rounded shape w/the flaring rim pulled into four tiny tabs, scene of an Arab on a camel, ca.1925.. **$**

Charger, Shakespeare Plays Series, scene from "A Midsummer Night's Dream," 12 5/8" d. **$65**

Pitcher, 9 1/4" h., Shakespeare Characters Series, standing portrait of Sir John Falstaff, tall waisted cylindrical form w/high arched spout, printed around the bottom border "A Tapster is a Good Trade," early 20th c. **$150**

Plate, 10 1/2" d., Shakespeare Characters Series, blue transfer w/center portrait of Shakespeare, border w/twelve characters from his plays **$75**

Rare Royal Doulton Gnomes Series Teapot

Teapot, cov., Gnomes Series, color scene of strange gnomes amid mushrooms, introduced in 1927 (ILLUS.)...................... **$2,000**

Old Mother Hubbard Teapot from Nursery Rhymes Series

Teapot, cov., Nursery Rhymes Series, scene of Old Mother Hubbard, designed by William Savage Cooper, introduced in 1903 (ILLUS.).. **$650**

Teapot, cov., Shakespeare Character Series, color scene of a young woman standing alone in a landscape, introduced in 1912 (ILLUS., bottom of page) **$600**

A Royal Doulton Teapot from the Shakespeare Series

Sir Roger de Coverley Series Teapot

Teapot, cov., Sir Roger de Coverley Series, scene of Sir Roger riding a white horse, introduced in 1911 (ILLUS.) **$600**

Historic England Series Tray

Tray, Historic England Series, rectangular w/ruffled dished sides & rounded corners, a color scene of Kenilworth Castle, ca. 1940 (ILLUS.)........................... **$150**
Vase, 9" h., Welsh Ladies Series, Welsh Ladies decoration... **$225**

Blue Children - Babes in Wood Series

Blue Children Oblong Dish with Woman & Child Holding Cloak Scene

Dish, low-sided oblong diamond-shape w/a patterned border band, the center w/a scene of a woman w/a child holding her cloak, ca. 1900 (ILLUS.)......................... **$1,500**

Girl & Boy at Tree Blue Children Plaque

Plaque, oval, scene of a girl & boy peeping into a tree hole, ca. 1900 (ILLUS.).......... **$1,500**

Girl & Basket Blue Children Oval Plaque

Plaque, oval, scene of a little girl carrying a basket, ca. 1900 (ILLUS.) **$1,500**

Girls & Umbrella Blue Children Plaque

Plaque, oval, scene of two girls sheltering under an umbrella, ca. 1900 (ILLUS.)..... **$1,500**

Baluster-shaped Blue Children Vase

Vase, 8 3/4" h., tall slender baluster shape w/a trumpet neck flanked by gold S-scroll handles, scene of a girl & boy peeping into a tree hole, ca. 1895 (ILLUS.) **$1,000**

Tall Blue Children & Tinkerbell Vase

Vase, 16 1/2" h., flat-bottomed ovoid lower body tapering to a tall slender trumpet neck, scene of three girls watching Tinkerbell, ca. 1900 (ILLUS.) **$1,200**

Pair of Blue Children Hexagonal Vases

Vases, upright hexagonal shape, one decorated w/a scene of children playing hide & seek, the other w/a scene of a girl gathering flowers in a basket, ca. 1915, pr. (ILLUS.) **$1,000**

Coaching Days Series

This series was first introduced in 1905 and produced until 1945. Then production resumed in 1948 and continued until 1967. Each piece features one of several early English coaching scenes in color based on the artwork of Victor Venner.

Coaching Days Series Deep Bowl

Bowl, deep rounded sides w/a wide flat rim, scene of a stopped coach w/a groom holding the lead horse (ILLUS.) **$300**
Bowl, round domed foot supporting the widely flaring melon-lobed bowl w/a wide flat mouth, a scene of horses trudging through snow pulling a loaded coach (ILLUS., next page) **$850**

Astor Shape Coaching Days Celery Tray

Coaching Days Footed, Lobed Bowl

Celery tray, Astor shape, long oval shape w/slightly fluted ends, decorated w/a scene of men boarding a coach while a groom holds the nervous horses (ILLUS., top of page) **$350**

Coaching Days Series Cracker Jar

Cracker jar w/silver plate rim, cover & bail handle, deeply waisted cylindrical

body, scene of a stopped coach w/a man in a grey coat standing beside it (ILLUS.) **$600**

Coaching Days Handled Octagonal Dish

Dish, octagonal flaring sides w/small pierced rim handles, rear view scene of a stopped coach w/two men at the side, one man looking down from the top & dead game hanging from the back (ILLUS.) **$250**

Stopped Coach & Man Square Dish

Dish, square w/low flaring sides & rounded corners, scene of a stopped coach w/a man wearing a grey coat standing nearby (ILLUS.).. **$100-200**

Coaching Days Series Table Lamp

Lamp, table model, gently swelled cylindrical body tapering slightly to a flat rim, a scene of men boarding a coach, fitted w/a brass base band & electric lamp fittings (ILLUS.) **$1,000**

Coaching Days Series Oatmeal Bowl

Oatmeal bowl, rounded shape w/scalloped rim, scene of a stopped coach w/a man in a grey coat standing nearby (ILLUS.) **$300**

Coaching Days Westcott Shape Pitcher

Pitcher, jug-type, Westcott shape, slightly swelled cylindrical body w/a narrow flaring rim, pointed loop long handle, decorated w/a scene of a coach passing through an open gate (ILLUS.) **$350**

Coaching Days Rocket Shape Pitcher

Pitcher, Rocket shape, cylindrical w/a flaring base & long angular handle, scene of people waving goodbye to a departing coach (ILLUS.) **$350**

Coach at Gate Coaching Days Plate

Plate, round w/flanged rim, scene of a large coach pulling through an open gate (ILLUS.).. **$200**

Plate with Stopped Coach Scene

Plate, round w/flanged rim, scene of a stopped coach w/a man walking beside it (ILLUS.).. **$200**

Vase, waisted cylindrical body flanked by long loop handles, scene of a coach moving through an open gate **$300**

Wash bowl & pitcher set, Royal Mail set, early English coaching scenes around the sides of each, four in polychrome, early 20th c., bowl 11 7/8" d., pitcher 7 3/8" h., pr. **$225**

Dickens Ware Series

Artful Dodger Dickens Ware Lennox Bowl

Bowl, Lennox shape, round foot below the wide cylindrical body w/a molded rim band, color scene of the Artful Dodger, Charles Noke, 1912 (ILLUS.) **$1,000**

Dickens Ware Deep Mr. Pickwick Bowl

Bowl, small foot & deep cylindrical sides, color scene of Mr. Pickwick, Charles Noke, 1931 (ILLUS.) **$300**

Octagon Mr. Pickwick Candy Dish

Candy dish, octagon form w/tab rim handles, color scene of Mr. Pickwick, Charles Noke, 1912 (ILLUS.) .... **$200-$300**

Tony Weller Dickens Ware Charger

Charger, round, color scene of Tony Weller, early 20th c., 13 1/2" d. (ILLUS.) .... **$200-$300**

Dickens Ware 1931 Cup & Saucer Set

Cup & saucer, color scenes of Little Nell & Sairey Gamp, Charles Noke, 1931, the set (ILLUS.) **$200**

Dickens Ware Captain Cuttle Oval Dish

Dish, oval, Leeds shape, low flaring & lightly ruffled sides, color scene of Captain Cuttle, Charles Noke, 1931 (ILLUS.) **$450**

Dickens Ware Square Alfred Jingle Dish

Dish, shallow squared shape w/serpentine sides & fluted rounded corners, color scene of Alfred Jingle, Charles Noke, 1931 (ILLUS.)... **$300**

Dickens Ware Footed Alfred Jingle Dish

Dish on pedestal foot, shallow squared shape, color scene of Alfred Jingle, Charles Noke, 1912 (ILLUS.)..................... **$500**

Dickens Ware Bill Sykes Loving Cup

Loving cup, three-handled waisted cylindrical shape, color scene of Bill Sykes, Charles Noke, 1912 (ILLUS.)..................... **$400**

Oatmeal dish, round, color scene of Tony Weller, Charles Noke, darker colors variation, 1931 (ILLUS., top next column)........ **$100**

Pitcher, Friar shape jug-type, footed swelled square body w/an arched rim spout & pointed angled handle, color scene of Trotty Veck, Charles Noke, 1912 (ILLUS., middle next column)............ **$300**

Tony Weller Oatmeal Dish

Dickens Ware Friar Jug with Trotty Veck

Dickens Ware Poor Jo & Fat Boy Pitcher

Pitcher, jug-type, cylindrical body w/rim spout & brown angled handle w/White Hart sign, relief-molded w/a scene of Poor Jo & Fat Boy, No. D5864, Charles Noke, 1937 (ILLUS.) **$600**

Dickens Ware Long Captain Cuttle Sandwich Tray

Plate, round w/flanged rim, color scene of Sairey Gamp, Charles Noke, 1912 .... **$200**

1931 Dickens Ware Tony Weller Plate

Plate, round w/flanged rim, color scene of Tony Weller, Charles Noke, 1931 (ILLUS.)... **$200**

Artful Dodger Porridge Bowl

Porridge bowl, round w/lightly scalloped rim, color scene of the Artful Dodger, Charles Noke, 1912 (ILLUS.) **$300**

Sandwich tray, long narrow waisted sides w/incurved ends & rounded ruffled corners, color scene of Captain Cuttle, Charles Noke, 1931 (ILLUS., top of page) **$250**

Barnaby Rudge Dickens Ware Tea Caddy

Tea caddy, cov., tapering cylindrical body w/an angled green shoulder & small cylindrical neck, color scene of Barnaby Rudge, Charles Noke, 1912 (ILLUS.) **$350**

Dickens Ware Tony Weller Teapot

Teapot, cov., Joan shape, color scene of Tony Weller, Charles Noke, 1912 (ILLUS.) **$500**

Long Dickens Ware Tray with Captain Cuttle & Mr. Toots

Tray, long rectangular form w/low serpentine sides & flaring incurved ends w/notched corners, low-relief scene of Captain Cuttle & Mr. Toots, No. D5833, Charles Noke, 1937 (ILLUS., top of page) **$350**

Dickens Ware Mr. Micawber Vase

Handled Dickens Ware Sairey Gamp Vase

Dickens Ware Vase with Sam Weller

Vase, cylindrical w/a narrow shoulder & flattened mouth, color scene of Mr. Micawber, Charles Noke, 1912 (ILLUS.) **$200**

Vase, footed tapering waisted cylindrical body w/long loop handles up from the base, color scene of Sairey Gamp, Charles Noke, 1912 (ILLUS., top next column) **$500**

Vase, scalloped arched foot & ovoid body w/a narrow flared rim, color scene of Sam Weller, Charles Noke, 1912 (ILLUS., bottom next column).. **$250**

Dickens Ware Alfred Jingle Vase

Vase, waisted cylindrical shape w/long loop handles, color scene of Alfred Jingle, Charles Noke, 1912 (ILLUS.) **$350**

Head Rack Plates
Plate, 10" d., rack-type, Old Jarvey **$75**
Plate, 10 1/2" d., rack-type, The Mayor **$75**
Plate, 10 1/2" d., rack-type, The Squire **$75**

Barlow Family Doulton Wares

Hannah Barlow Beaker with Child & Sheep

Beaker (tall tumbler), stoneware, slightly tapering cylindrical body, the wide center band incised w/a scene of a child w/sheep, decorated by Hannah Barlow, ca. 1880, 5 1/2" h. (ILLUS.) **$750**

Foliate-decorated Florence Barlow Bowl

Bowl, 5 1/4" h., stoneware, footed squatty bulbous shaped w/a wide flat rim, the banded sides carved w/foliate decoration, decorated by Florence Barlow, ca. 1875 (ILLUS.) **$500**

Barlow-Simmance Horses Cache Pot

Cache pot, stoneware, bulbous ovoid form w/a wide, short cylindrical neck, the sides incised w/panels of horses framed by bold cobalt blue scrolling legs, tan neck, decorated by Hannah Barlow & Eliza Simmance, ca. 1885 (ILLUS.) **$2,000**

Hannah Barlow Ewer with Goats & Child

Ewer, stoneware, footed bulbous ovoid body w/a tapering shoulder to the cylindrical neck w/flaring rim w/pinched spout & high arched handle, the wide body band incised w/a scene of goats & a child, decorated by Hannah Barlow, 1881, 11" h. (ILLUS.) **$2,400**

Pair of Hannah Barlow Horses Ewers

Ewers, stoneware, footed ovoid body tapering to a tall cylindrical neck w/pinched rim spout & high arched C-scroll handle, the body incised w/a scene of horses below a foliate shoulder band, decorated by Hannah Barlow, ca. 1905, pr. (ILLUS.) ... **$3,000**

Hannah Barlow Fox Hunting Scene Jug

Jug, stoneware, footed ovoid body tapering to a cylindrical slightly flaring neck w/pinched rim spout, strap handle, incised w/a large scene of a huntsman, his horse & a fox, decorated by Hannah Barlow, ca. 1880 (ILLUS.) **$2,000**

Early Hannah Barlow Tankard Pitcher

Pitcher, stoneware, tankard-style, tall gently tapering sides w/a molded base & rim bands & small rim spout, the sides incised w/a continuous scene of cattle on a tan ground, decorated by Hannah Barlow, ca. 1875 (ILLUS.) **$2,500**

Stoneware Salt Shaker by Hannah Barlow

Salt shaker w/silver domed lid, stoneware, footed baluster-form body, dark blue & brown spearpoint base & neck bands, the wide body band incised w/a scene of deer in dark blue, decorated by Hannah Barlow, ca. 1875 (ILLUS.) **$500**

Hannah Barlow Tyg with Donkeys

Tyg, stoneware, wide cylindrical body w/a silver rim band & long flattened loop handles, incised w/a continuous scene of donkeys, decorated by Hannah Barlow, ca. 1880, 6 3/4" h. (ILLUS.) **$2,500**

Hannah Barlow Sheep Scene Vase

Vase, stoneware, footed ovoid body tapering to a trumpet neck, the wide body band incised w/a scene of sheep, decorative base & neck bands, decorated by Hannah Barlow, ca. 1880 (ILLUS.) **$1,800**

Fine Florence Barlow Wild Turkey Vase

Vase, stoneware, tall gently tapering cylindrical body w/a low rolled rim, decorated w/a pate-sur-pate scene of wild turkeys, decorated by Florence Barlow, ca. 1885 (ILLUS., previous page) **$3,000**

Pair of Florence Barlow Bird Vases

Vases, 12 3/4" h., stoneware, footed wide baluster-form body w/a wide trumpet neck, the main body decorated w/a continuous pate-sur-pate design of birds, decorated by Florence Barlow, ca. 1885 (ILLUS.)... **$2,500**

Tinworth Doulton Pieces

Tinworth Stoneware Banded Beaker

Beaker, stoneware, funnel foot tapering to a gently flaring cylindrical bowl w/a silver rim band, the foot incised w/blue, green & brown lappet leaves below the wide dark blue central band flanked by white dotted bands & decorated w/continuous light blue scroll bands w/leaves & molded florettes, the dark brown rim band incised w/a band of vertical green leaves, ca. 1880 (ILLUS.)... **$800**

Ewer, stoneware, footed tall ovoid body w/a tall gently flaring neck w/rim spout & large C-form handle, the base band incised w/vertical pale blue lappets alternating w/beaded bands on a dark blue ground below a white beaded band, the wide brown central band incised w/a continuous scrolling band of pale green leaves & applied blue florettes, an upper thin white beaded band below the round shoulder incised w/alternating dark green spearpoints & pale blue petals, the brown neck applied w/blue florettes, ca. 1880 (ILLUS., top next column).. **$3,000**

Tall Ornate Tinworth Ewer

Merry Musicians Bell Ringer Figure

Figure, stoneware, young man wearing a hat & seated on a tall pedestal playing hand bells, part of the Merry Musicians series, brown glaze, ca. 1895, 5" h. (ILLUS.) **$2,500**

Rare Tinworth Mouse "Playgoers" Menu Holder

Menu holder, stoneware, figural, a group of mice seated around a puppet show, titled "Playgoers," in shades of pale blue & brown, 1886, 5 1/4" h. (ILLUS.).............. **$6,500**

Fine Pair of Tinworth Religious Terra Cotta Panels

Figural Mouse Musicians Menu Holder

Menu holder, stoneware, figural, two white mouse musicians on a brown & blue molded round base, titled "Harp and Concertina," ca. 1884, 4" h. (ILLUS.) **$3,000**

Panels, terra cotta, tall rectangular forms w/religious scenes, one depicting "Christ on the Cross," the other "Descent from the Cross," 1902, 14" h., framed, pr. (ILLUS., top of page) **$5,000**

Ornately Decorated Tinworth Vase

Vase, stoneware, large ovoid body w/a wide short cylindrical neck, applied & incised overall w/ornate scrolling & leaf designs in dark blue, brick red, brown & blue, ca. 1880 (ILLUS.)... **$3,500**

Dresden

Dresden-type porcelain evolved from wares made at the nearby Meissen Porcelain Works early in the 18th century. "Dresden" and "Meissen" are often used interchangeably for later wares. "Dresden" has become a generic name for the kind of porcelains produced in Dresden and certain other areas of Germany, but perhaps should be confined to the wares made in the city of Dresden.

Compote, large reticulated basket raised on tree-form stem w/applied cherubs, footed base, all-over floral decoration, w/pastel colors on white, made by Carl Thieme Factory, ca. 1901, 19" h. **$728**

Figure group, modeled as standing man & lady flower sellers in 18th c. costume w/a young boy seated in front, all centered by a tall flower-applied covered urn, on a molded oblong base, Thieme factory mark, late 19th c., 9" h. .... **$650-$750**

Plates, 10 7/8" d., each divided into four panels divided by gilt & floral bands & border, alternating designs of colorful

Tinworth Chinè Ware Vase with Putti

Vase, Chinè Ware, a thin foot below the very wide disk-form lower body tapering to cylindrical sides w/the wide flat mouth flanked by the white figures of putti w/a white leafy swag draped between them, the dark blue ground w/brown decoration (ILLUS.)... **$2,500**

flowers & romantic figures in 18th costume, marked "Dresden, Germany," early 20th c., set of 12................................ **$550-$650**

Ornate Dresden, Germany Teapot

Teapot, cov., wide tapering bulbous ribbed lower body tapering to a tall swirled & gently flaring neck w/arched rim, ornate conforming cover w/fancy gold scroll finial, tall molded serpentine spout, very ornate C-scroll handle, decorated w/bands of green trimmed in gold around the top & base, a large cluster of green & white lily-of-the-valley on the sides, Dresden, Germany, ca. 1900 (ILLUS.) **$125**

Dresden Vase with Tiger Scene

Vase, 10 5/8" h., flat-bottomed ovoid body tapering to a slender neck w/upright rounded rim flanked by high ornate pierced scroll gold handles, the body painted w/a realistic landscape showing a tiger descending a rocky ledge among tall grasses within a pale yelllow border, the reverse decorated w/a gilt butterfly & foliage flanked by ducks in flight, cobalt blue neck w/gold trim, gilt castle mark, Germany, early 20th c. (ILLUS.) **$1,680**

Very Ornate Decorated Dresden Vase

Vase, cov., 24 3/8" h., a ringed pedestal base supporting a large bulbous ovoid body tapering to a short flared neck w/a domed cover w/pointed gold finial, cobalt blue ground w/ornate delicate gold trim, the front centered by a large oval reserve h.p. w/two scantily clad putti seated on a classical plinth within a rocky garden landscape, the back decorated w/a loose floral bouquet, jeweled gilt trellis border, blue crowned "RK" & Dresden mark of Richard Klemm (ILLUS.) **$6,000**

East Liverpool, Ohio & Related Potteries

The city of East Liverpool, Ohio has long been a major center of American pottery production. By the late 19th century numerous pottery firms were operating in or near this city. Some of the best known firms include Hall China, Homer Laughlin and Harker Potteries. The following offers a sampling of the wares of some of the less well known potteries.

Brunt, Bloor, Martin & Company

Brunt, Bloor, Martin & Company was one of several partnerships that included William Brunt, Jr. This partnership is believed to cover the period of 1875-1882.

Mug, cylindrical w/molded base, all-white, 3 1/2" h. (ILLUS. front row, second from right, with grouping of Brunt, Bloor, Martin pieces, top next page)...................... **$18-$24**
Mug, Moss Rose patt., 3 3/4" h. (ILLUS. front row, far right, with grouping of Brunt, Bloor, Martin pieces, top next page) ..... **$35-$45**
Pitcher, 8 3/4" h., Moss Rose patt. (ILLUS. back row, left, with grouping of Brunt, Bloor, Martin pieces, top next page) ..... **$30-$40**
Soap dish, cover & insert, Gold Band decoration, 6 1/2" l. (ILLUS. front row, far left, with grouping of Brunt, Bloor, Martin pieces, top next page).......................... **$30-$40**

Large Grouping of Pieces by Brunt, Bloor, Martin & Company

Toothbrush vase, footed baluster-form w/drain holes in the bottom, Gold Band decoration, 6 1/4" h. (ILLUS. back row, center, with grouping of Brunt, Bloor, Martin pieces, top of page)................... **$18-$24**

Tumbler, cylindrical, Gold Band decoration, 4 3/4" h. (ILLUS. front row, second from left, with grouping of Brunt, Bloor, Martin pieces, top of page).............................. **$20-$30**

Wash pitcher, Gold Band decoration, 11 3/4" h. (ILLUS. back row, right, with grouping of Brunt, Bloor, Martin pieces, top of page)... **$50-$65**

Brunt (William Jr.) & Company

The William Brunt Jr. & Company pottery operated under several company names and with several partnerships from about 1856 until 1911. In 1877, William Brunt Jr. began manufacturing white ironstone.

Cup & saucer, Moss Rose patt., 1877-1878, saucer 6" d., cup 3 1/8" h., the set (ILLUS. front row, far left, with other William Brunt pieces, bottom of page) .... **$12-$18**

Mug, Oriental Bird patt., 1892-1911, 4 1/2" h. (ILLUS. front row second from left with grouping of William Brunt pieces, bottom of page).................................... **$18-$24**

Pitcher, 6" h., Bird patt., 1877-78 (ILLUS. front row, second from right with grouping of William Brunt pieces, bottom of page) .... **$30-$40**

Pitcher, 7" h., Bird on Nest patt., black on white, 1877-78 (ILLUS. front row, far right, with grouping of William Brunt pieces, bottom of page) .... **$50-$60**

Teapot, cov., Blue Flowers patt., 1877-78, 9 1/4" h. (ILLUS. back row, right, with grouping of William Brunt pieces, bottom of page).. **$45-$60**

Teapot, cov., footed squatty bulbous body, Oriental Bird patt., 1892-1911, 8 3/4" l. (ILLUS. front row, third from right, with grouping of William Brunt pieces, bottom of page).. **$45-$60**

Teapot, cov., Pink Blossoms patt., 1877-1878, 9" h. (ILLUS. back row, left, with grouping of William Brunt pieces, bottom of page).. **$45-$60**

Large Grouping of William Brunt Jr. & Company Early Ironstone Wares

Grouping of Burford Brothers Pieces

Teapot, cov., square shape, Moss Rose patt., Faux mark, 1877-78, 8" h. (ILLUS. back row, center, with grouping of William Brunt pieces, bottom previous page) .... **$45-$60**

Toothbrush vase, Flying Heron patt., 1877-1878, 5 1/2" h. (ILLUS. front row, third from left, with grouping of William Brunt pieces, bottom of previous page) .... **$18-$24**

Burford Brothers

Burford Brothers operated from 1881 until 1904 and was known for excellent decorations and superior wares.

Bowl, 6 3/8" d., footed, overall dark blue sponging, 1881-1904 (ILLUS. front row, center, with other Burford Brothers pieces, top of page) .... **$20-$25**

Soap dish, cover & insert, overall dark blue sponging, 6 1/4" l. (ILLUS. front row, left, with grouping of Burford Brothers pieces, top of page).............................. **$70-$85**

Soup tureen, cov., Cable shape, decorated w/a brown transfer-printed design of leafy daisies framing small round vi-

gnettes of a house in the woods, 1881-1904, 14" l. (ILLUS. back row, left, with grouping of Burford Brothers pieces, top of page)... **$85-$100**

Wash bowl & pitcher set, overall dark blue sponging, 1881, bowl 14" d., pitcher 12" h., the set (ILLUS. far right with grouping of Burford Brothers pieces, top of page).. **$200-$300**

Cartwright Brothers Company

The Cartwright Brothers Company operated from 1887 until 1927 making dinner and hotel wares.

Pitcher, 6 1/2" h., cream-colored ground, overall embossed design of leafy branches decorated in deep red & small blue birds, 1887-96 (ILLUS. left with Cartwright Brothers teapot, bottom of page) .... **$60-$75**

Teapot, cov., squatty bulbous body w/molded scrolls & a fancy C-scroll handle, decorated w/pink & blue flowers, 1887-1900, 10" l. (ILLUS. right with Cartwright Brothers pitcher, bottom of page) .... **$60-$80**

Cartwright Brothers Pitcher and Teapot

Pieces Produced by Various William Flentke Partnerships

Flentke (William) Partnerships

William Flentke partnered with George and Samuel Morley, James Godwin and David Col-clough operating as Morley, Godwin & Flenke from 1855 to 1878. Godwin & Flentke then oper-ated from 1878 to 1882. Finally, William Flentke operated his own pottery from 1882 until 1886.

Condiment jar, cover w/notched rim, loop scroll handle, all-white, William Flentke, 1882-86, 3 1/2" h. (ILLUS. front row, left, with other Flentke pieces, top of page)... **$35-$45**

Teapot, cov., Cable shape, Moss Rose patt., William Flentke, 1882-86, 9" h. (ILLUS. back row, left, with other Flentke pieces, top of page) .... **$85-$100**

Tureen, cov., all-white, Morley, Godwin & Flentke, 1855-78, 10 1/2" l. (ILLUS. front row, right, with other Flentke pieces, top of page) .... **$45-$60**

Wash bowl & pitcher set, unusual brown transfer Classical vignettes, Godwin & Flentke, 1878-82, bowl 14 1/2" d., pitcher 12" h., the set (ILLUS. back row, right, with other Flentke pieces, top of page) .... **$85-$100**

Goodwin Bros. & Goodwin Pottery Company

Goodwin Brothers and The Goodwin Pottery Company operated from 1885 until 1913. John Goodwin had worked briefly for the Bennett Pot-tery and later for Benjamin Harker, Sr. at his pot-tery.

Pitcher, 7" h., decorated w/black transfer-printed vignettes, a scene of a Swiss cha-let, lake & church on the back & a horse-shoe, violets & scenes of a sailing ship & a Dutch windmill on the front, 1885-98 (ILLUS. left with pitcher & bowl set, bot-tom of page) .... **$20-$25**

Wash bowl & pitcher set, decorated w/light blue transfer-printed Oriental-inspired vi-gnettes including a vase, scroll & flowers, the top of the angled handle molded w/the Cross of St. George, 1885-98, bowl 14" d., pitcher 10 3/4" h., the set (ILLUS. right with Goodwin pitcher, bottom of page) .... **$80-$100**

A Small Pitcher and a Pitcher & Bowl Set by Goodwin Bros.

A Grouping of Early Homer Laughlin Pieces

Homer Laughlin China Company

Homer Laughlin China Company has operated continuously since 1877. The Wells family purchased the interest of the Aaron family only recently. While Homer Laughlin has made a wide variety of wares over the years, many people identify with their very popular Fiesta line of brightly colored wares first offered in the 1930s and reintroduced in new colors in recent years.

Soup tureen, cover, undertray & ladle, Victor shape, decorated w/delicate printed blue & yellow flowers, late 19th c., 14 1/2" l., the set (ILLUS. center with other Homer Laughlin pieces, top of page) ... **$90-$110**

Teapot, cov., Victor shape, Blue Moss Rose patt., 1877-1900, 8 3/4" h. (ILLUS. left with other Homer Laughlin pieces, top of page) .... **$85-$110**

Urn, Victor shape, decorated w/a wide pink body band & large white roses on the front & a spray of white flowers on the back, h.p. violets on the base; note: only two Homer Laughlin urns are known and this shape was not in the Homer Laughlin

catalog; this piece is missing the cover, which could match the lid of the illustrated teapot or have a medallion finial, 7 3/4" h. (ILLUS. right with other Homer Loughlin pieces, top of page) .... **$150-$200**

Knowles, Taylor & Knowles (KTK)

Knowles, Taylor & Knowles (KTK) operated from 1870 until 1929. In the 1880s they produced their scarce and highly sought Lotus Ware. Later they focused on producing semi-porcelain and hotel china. At one time, KTK was one of the largest potteries in the U.S.

Cracker jar, cov., Lotus shape w/wide molded & swirled ribs, decorated w/a shaded green ground & pink flower clusters, 1900-20, 7 1/2" h. (ILLUS. back row, second from right, with other KTK pieces, bottom of page) .... **$40-$50**

Cuspidor, lady's, hand-held, ovoid body w/wide flaring neck & side handle, all-white, 1890-1907, 4 1/4" h. (ILLUS. front row, third from left, with other KTK pieces, bottom of page) .... **$20-$30**

Large Grouping of Knowles, Taylor & Knowles Pieces

Dish set: child's, one 1 3/4" h. cup decorated w/the head of a small dog, a 4 7/8" d. plate w/a scene of a monk & three 3 1/2" d. plates w/various scenes, 1905-29, the set (ILLUS. front row, second from left, with other KTK pieces, bottom previous page) .... **$30-$35**

Match holder & striker, conical shape, all-white, 1890-1910, 2 1/2" h. (ILLUS. front row, third from right, with other KTK pieces, bottom previous page) .... **$20-$30**

Pitcher, 5 3/4" h., Cable shape, blue transfer-printed landscape scene, 1885 (ILLUS. front row, far right, with other KTK pieces, bottom previous page) .... **$20-$25**

Pitcher, 7 1/2" h., embossed body decorated w/pink & blue flowers, 1890-1910 (ILLUS. back row, far left with other KTK pieces, bottom previous page).... **$30-$40**

Relish dish, long pointed almond shape, cream ground decorated w/large pink wild roses & green leaves & ferns, 12 3/4" l. (ILLUS. back row, second from left, with other KTK pieces, bottom previous page) .... **$30-$40**

Syrup (molasses) jug w/hinged metal cover, decorated w/a dark blue ground & pink blossoms w/green leaves, 1885, 8 1/8" h. (ILLUS. back row, far right, other KTK pieces, bottom previous page).. **$40-$60**

Teapot with metal cover, spherical body, decorated w/h.p. pansies, 1885, 9 1/4" l. (ILLUS. front row, second from right, with other KTK pieces, bottom previous page) **$45-$60**

Toothbrush vase, molded basketweave base band & a square neck, brown floral transfer decoration, 1880-90, 4 3/4" h. (ILLUS. front row, far left, with other KTK pieces, bottom previous page) .... **$18-$24**

Morley & Company

George Morley worked for several East Liverpool potteries before partnering with William

Flentke and James Goodwin. He operated under the Morley & Company name in Wellsville and East Liverpool. Collectors are probably most familiar with their Majolica ware. Morley's activities covered the years from 1878 to 1900. Pieces that have an East Liverpool backstamp will have an "EL" in the description while pieces made at Wellsville with a backstamp including "Wsvl" in the description. All pieces listed below were made between 1879 and 1884.

Candy dish, figural, a design of cupped hands in white w/colored sprigs at the wrist, 6 3/4" l. (ILLUS. top row, far right, with large grouping of Morley pieces, bottom of page) .... **$30-$40**

Candy dish, majolica, molded leaf form w/dark yellow, brown & green glaze, 7 1/4" l. (ILLUS. front row, front left, with grouping of Morley pieces, bottom of page).. **$35-$45**

Candy dish, majolica, molded wide pointed leaf-form, mottled dark brown, green & yellow glaze, Wellsville mark, 7 1/2" l. (ILLUS. front row, right front, with other Morley pieces, bottom of page)............ **$60-$75**

Compote, open, 5 1/8" h., 8 1/2" d., majolica, molded wide leaf shape glazed in blue & yellow, Wellsville mark (ILLUS. top row, second from left, with large grouping of Morley pieces, bottom of page).. **$70-$80**

Compote, open, 5 1/2" h., 10 1/2" w., majolica, large rounded shell shape w/a mottled dark blue, green & yellow glaze, some damage, East Liverpool mark (ILLUS. back row, second from right, with large grouping of Morley pieces, bottom of page) .... **$20-$25**

Pitcher, 5 1/2" h., majolica, cylindrical w/brown ground molded w/a leafy stem & blossom, Wellsville mark (ILLUS. front row, second from left, with grouping of Morley pieces, bottom of page)......... **$180-$190**

Large Grouping of Morley & Company Majolica and Other Wares

Pitcher, 6 1/2" h., figural, Gurgle fish design, white w/gold trim (ILLUS. back row, third from right, with large grouping of Morley pieces, bottom previous page) .... **$100-$125**

Pitcher, 6 3/4" h., majolica, figural Gurgle fish design in mottled browns & greens, East Liverpool mark (ILLUS. back row, third from left, with large grouping of Morley pieces, bottom previous page) .... **$180-$210**

Pitcher, 7" h., cylindrical molded tree trunk green body molded w/a branch of flowers & leaves, missing cover, Wellsville mark (ILLUS. back row, fourth from left, with large grouping of Morley pieces, bottom previous page) .... **$75-$90**

Pitcher, 7 1/2" h., majolica, figural, model of an owl w/green & grey feathers, unmarked (ILLUS. front row, far right, with other Morley pieces, bottom previous page) .... **$45-$60**

Pitcher, 8 1/8" h., majolica, figural, model of an owl w/yellow & brown feather design (ILLUS. front row, second from right, with other Morley pieces, bottom previous page) .... **$120-$140**

Pitcher, 8 1/2" h., majolica, figural, Gurgle fish style, bluish grey, pink, yellow & white glaze, East Liverpool mark (ILLUS. front row, third from left, with grouping of Morley pieces, bottom previous page) .... **$85-$100**

Pitcher, 8 1/2" h., majolica, figural, Gurgle fish style, dark grey, pink, yellow & white glaze, Wellsville mark (ILLUS. front row, third from right, with other Morley pieces, bottom previous page) .... **$85-$100**

Plate, 8 3/4" d., majolica, the center molded w/a square white napkin, the leaf & basketweave edges in deep red & green, Wellsville mark (ILLUS. front row, center front, with other Morley pieces, bottom previous page) .... **$60-$75**

Syrup (molasses) pitcher with hinged metal lid, cylindrical w/angled handle, white w/embossed leafy branch, 6 1/8" h. (ILLUS. back row, far left, with large grouping of Morley pieces, bottom previous page) .... **$35-$45**

Tumbler, cylindrical w/molded base, molded brown exterior w/green leaves, pale green interior, East Liverpool mark, factory damage, 4 1/2" h. (ILLUS. front row, far left, with grouping of Morley pieces, bottom previous page) .... **$45-$60**

Mountford and Company

Mountford and Company operated from 1891 to 1897 and made "White Granite" pottery ware and decorated ware.

Pitcher, 5 1/2" h., Moss Rose patt. (ILLUS. left with other Mountford pieces, bottom of page) .... **$35-$45**

Pitcher, 8" h., molded vertical fluted & scrolls w/delicate printed florals (ILLUS. right with other Mountford pieces, bottom of page) .... **$50-$60**

Saucer, Moss Rose patt., 6" d. (ILLUS. center with other Mountford pieces, bottom of page) .... **$8-$10**

Small Grouping of Early Mountford and Company Pieces

Grouping of Decorative National China Company Pieces

National China Company

National China Company operated from 1899 until 1911 and then moved its operation to Salineville, Ohio, where it operated until 1929. All pieces listed here were manufactured at the East Liverpool plant.

Cracker jar, cov., cylindrical w/a fancy molded base decorated in beige w/gold scrolls & a flared, scalloped rim w/further gold scrolls, gold downturned loop sides handles, the front transfer-printed w/a large bouquet of violets, high domed cover w/further decoration & violets, 8 1/2" h. (ILLUS. top row, left, with other National China pieces, top of page) .... **$45-$70**

Cracker jar, cov., cylindrical w/molded scrolls around the base & around the flaring rim, downturned loop side handles, large transfer-printed yellow rose & leaves on the front, the domed cover w/a deep red rose, 8 1/2" h. (ILLUS. top row, right, with other National China pieces, top of page) .... **$45-$70**

Cracker jar, cov., cylindrical w/molded scrolls & pink trim around the base, gilt scrolls around the flaring rim, downturned loop side handles, printed w/a sprig of blue flowers on the front, high domed cover w/pink border & small floral sprigs, 8 1/2" h. (ILLUS. top row, center, with other National China pieces, top of page) ... **$45-$70**

Jardiniere, scroll-molded & scalloped oblong low pedestal base, large deep oblong bowl w/the flaring rim molded w/large scrolls trimmed in gold & dark blue, fancy gold loop end handles, the large front reserve transfer-printed w/a large cluster of pink roses & green leaves, 11" l. (ILLUS. bottom center with other National China pieces, top of page) .... **$50-$60**

Potter's Co-Operative Company

Potter's Co-Operative Company operated from 1882 until 1925 with several partnerships that also did business under the Standard Co-Operative Pottery Company and Dresden Pottery Company names. Unless otherwise identified, the pieces listed here bear the Potter's Co-Operative mark.

Large Grouping of Potter's Co-Operative Company Pieces

Chocolate pot, cov., tapering ovoid body w/wide molded panels decorated w/long burgundy blossom sprigs, rim spout, high domed cover, Dresden Pottery mark, 1890-1900, 9 1/2" h. (ILLUS. back row, second from left, with other Potter's Co-Operative pieces, bottom previous page) .... **$75-$85**

Cracker jar, cov., tapering ovoid body in dark cobalt blue w/a scalloped white top band, low domed cobalt blue cover, 1915, 7 1/2" h. (ILLUS. back row, far right, with other Potter's Co-Operative pieces, bottom previous page) .... **$45-$60**

Cracker jar, cov., wide swelled cylindrical body w/small S-scroll shoulder handles, domed cover w/fanned handle, decorated w/large transfer-printed pink roses & gold trim, Dresden Pottery mark, ca. 1915, 7 1/2" h. (ILLUS. front row, far left, with other Potter's Co-Operative pieces, bottom previous page) .... **$50-$70**

Mustache cup & saucer, personalized w/the name of the original owner, 1890-1900, saucer 6 1/2" d., cup 3 1/4" h., the set (ILLUS. front row, center, with other Potter's Co-Operative pieces, bottom previous page) .... **$45-$60**

Pitcher, 8 1/4" h., baluster-form body w/a fluted shoulder & high arched spout, transfer-printed w/a large burgundy rose, Standard Co-Operative Pottery mark, 1882-85 (ILLUS. front row, second from left, with other Potter's Co-Operative pieces, bottom previous page) .... **$40-$50**

Teapot, cov., Cable shape, transfer-printed w/a light brown wheat sprig & blossom design, 1882-85, 9" h. (ILLUS. front row, second from right, with other Potter's Co-Operative pieces, bottom previous page) .... **$50-$60**

Teapot, cov., Cable shape, transfer-printed w/a spray of pink & green flowers, Standard Co-Operative Pottery Co. mark, 1882-85, 9 1/4" h. (ILLUS. back row, second from right, with other Potter's Co-Operative pieces, bottom previous page) .. **$40-$50**

Teapot, cov., Moss Rose patt., 1882-95, 9 3/8" h. (ILLUS. back row, far left, with other Potter's Co-Operative pieces, bottom previous page) .... **$65-$75**

Teapot, cov., short squatty paneled body, light brown transfer-printed design of wheat sprigs & blossoms, 1882-85, 6 3/4" h. (ILLUS. front row, far right, with other Potter's Co-Operative pieces, bottom previous page) .... **$50-$60**

Sebring China Company

The Sebring China Company began production in 1887 and operated in East Liverpool and East Palestine as well as founding the town of Sebring, Ohio in 1899. The Sebring brothers' several potteries in the new town were consolidated with the Limoges China Company until the Sebring line operations ended in 1948. Pieces listed here were made in East Liverpool.

Cracker jar, cov., squatty bulbous lower body tapering to cylindrical sides w/looped side handles, high domed cover w/an ornate scroll finial, embossed shell panels & scrolls transfer-printed w/pink flowers & green leaves, green & gold trim, 1890-1905, 8" h. (ILLUS. left with two other Sebring pieces, bottom of page) .... **$50-$65**

Rose bowl, scalloped gold-trimmed foot & nearly spherical body w/a closed rim trimmed w/gold, transfer-printed w/clusters of pink & yellow flower & gilt trim, 1890-1905, 4 3/4" h. (ILLUS. center with other Sebring China pieces, bottom of page) .... **$35-$45**

Wash pitcher, wide bulbous ovoid body tapering to a high arched shell-molded rim, transfer-printed in dark brown w/a scene of a bird among garden flowers, a smaller transfer on the back, 1900, 11 3/4" h. (ILLUS. right with other Sebring China pieces, bottom of page).... **$65-$85**

Three Pieces Produced by The Sebring China Company

Grouping of Union Potteries Company Pieces

Union Potteries Company

The Union Potteries Company operated from 1894 to 1905. The firm was organized by East Liverpool Pottery workers and was called the Union Co-Operative Pottery Company until sometime in 1900.

Plate, 8 7/8" d., scroll-molded & paneled border in pale blue, the center finely h.p. w/a colorful oriole perched near its nest on flowering branches (ILLUS. far left with grouping of Union Potteries pieces, top of page) .... **$45-$60**

Plate, 9" d., wide border w/delicate molded scrolls trimmed in dark blue, a dark blue Dutch windmill landscape in the center (ILLUS. far right with other Union Potteries pieces, top of page) .... **$18-$24**

Plate, 11 3/4" w., square w/a raised rim & small loop corner handles, transfer-printed w/sprigs of pink & white daisies, used as an underplate for a teapot (ILLUS. third from left with other Union Potteries pieces, top of page)............................... **$15-$20**

Shaving mug, footed bulbous ovoid body tapering to a flaring scalloped rim, fancy angled handle, transfer-printed w/a green lily pad design, marked w/"Sigsbee" backstamp, 3 1/2" h. (ILLUS. second from left with other Union Potteries pieces, top of page) .... **$25-$30**

Teapot, cov., footed flaring squared body w/ squared cover w/loop finial, angular handle, decorated w/transfer-printed pink & white daisy sprigs, matches square plate shown, 9 1/2" l. (ILLUS. second from right with other Union Potteries pieces, top of page)... **$45-$60**

Wallace & Chetwynd

Wallace and Chetwynd began operation in 1882 after purchasing the former Harker "Wedgwood" pottery in 1881. The Chetwynd of this firm was a moldmaker and his brother had been a moldmaker for Harker until his untimely death. Pieces can be found in identical shapes with one of several Harker backstamps or a Wallace & Chetwynd backstamp. The tall pitcher and the Moss Rose bread plate illustrated here are examples of wares that can carry either mark. This pottery ceased operations in 1901. Wallace & Chetwynd were known for their excellent decorations.

Grouping of Decorative Wallace & Chetwynd Pieces

Wallace & Chetwynd Wash Bowl & Pitcher Set

Bread plate, oval w/open end handles, molded around the wide border "Give Us This Day Our Daily Bread," Moss Rose patt. in the center, 13" l. (ILLUS. center front with other Wallace & Chetwynd pieces, bottom previous page) .... **$45-$60**

Teapot, cov., footed tapering cylindrical paneled body, angular handle, Moss Rose patt., 8 3/4" h. (ILLUS. back row, far right, with other Wallace & Chetwynd pieces, bottom previous page) .... **$60-$80**

Teapot, cov., footed tapering lobed body, angled handle, gold band decoration, 9" h. (ILLUS. back row, far left, with other Wallace & Chetwynd pieces, bottom previous page)......................... **$50-$70**

Wash bowl & pitcher set, each piece decorated w/brown transfer-printed reserves w/pastoral scenes, bowl 14 1/2" d., pitcher 11 1/2" h., the set (ILLUS., top of page) **$80-$100**

Water pitcher, footed tapering body w/molded neck band, decorated w/a long leafy grey stem w/stippled pink blossoms, 12" h. (ILLUS. back row, second

from left, with other Wallace & Chetwynd pieces, bottom previous page)............. **$50-$65**

Water pitcher, footed tapering body w/molded neck band, decorated w/a long leafy branch w/h.p. red currents, 12" h. (ILLUS. back row, second from right, with other Wallace & Chetwynd pieces, bottom previous page)............. **$60-$75**

Wheeling Pottery Company

The Wheeling Pottery Company operated from 1879 until 1910. The name of the firm was then changed to the Wheeling Sanitary Manufacturing Company, which continued operating until at least 1923.

Pitcher, 11" h., fancy bulbous ovoid body tapering to a high arched & scalloped rim & large gold C-scroll handle, the front h.p. w/a scene of a kneeling nymph on a rock looking down into her reflection, against a dark blue ground & framed w/very ornate gold leafy scrolls & latticework, minor damage (ILLUS. left, bottom of page) .... **$75-$85**

Two Decorative Pieces from The Wheeling Pottery Company

Tureen, cov., oval low pedestal base on low squatty oval body w/angular end handles, high domed cover w/matching handle, each part h.p. w/a wide pale blue band highlighted w/large pink flower clusters w/green leaves, 11 7/8" l. (ILLUS. right with Wheeling Pottery tall pitcher, bottom previous page) .... **$35-$45**

Fiesta (Homer Laughlin China Co.-HLC)

Fiesta dinnerware was made by the Homer Laughlin China Company of Newell, West Virginia, from the 1930s until the early 1970s. The brilliant colors of this inexpensive pottery have attracted numerous collectors. On Feb. 28, 1986, Laughlin reintroduced the popular Fiesta line with minor changes in the shapes of a few pieces and a contemporary color range. The effect of this new production on the Fiesta collecting market is yet to be determined.

For additional information on Fiesta see Warman's Fiesta Identification & Price Guide by Glen Victorey (Krause Publications, 2007).

Fiesta Mark

Cobalt Fiesta Ashtray

Ashtray cobalt blue (ILLUS.)..................... **$50-$60**
Ashtray grey .... **$80-$90**
Ashtray medium green .... **$200-$230**
Ashtray yellow .... **$35-$45**
Bowl, cream soup forest green............... **$50-$70**
Bowl, cream soup ivory .... **$50-$70**
Bowl, cream soup red.. **$**
Bowl, dessert, 6" d. chartreuse .... **$35-$50**
Bowl, dessert, 6" d. light green............... **$35-$50**
Bowl, dessert, 6" d. medium green (ILLUS., top next column)................................ **$700-$800**
Bowl, dessert, 6" d. rose .... **$35-$50**
Bowl, dessert, 6" d. turquoise................. **$35-$50**
Bowl, fruit, 11 3/4" d. cobalt blue .... **$300-$350**
Bowl, fruit, 11 3/4" d. ivory.................. **$300-$350**
Bowl, fruit, 11 3/4" d. light green .... **$300-$350**
Bowl, fruit, 11 3/4" d. yellow .... **$300-$350**
Bowl, individual fruit, 4 3/4" d. chartreuse .... **$25-$35**
Bowl, individual fruit, 4 3/4" d. forest green.. **$25-$35**

Rare Medium Green Fiesta Dessert Bowl

Bowl, individual fruit, 4 3/4" d. grey .... **$25-$35**
Bowl, individual fruit, 4 3/4" d., medium green... **$650-$700**
Bowl, individual fruit, 4 3/4" d. red .... **$25-$35**
Bowl, individual fruit, 5 1/2" d. turquoise .... **$25-$40**
Bowl, individual fruit, 5 1/2" d. grey .... **$25-$40**
Bowl, individual fruit, 5 1/2" d. light green .... **$25-$40**
Bowl, individual fruit, 5 1/2" d. red .... **$25-$40**

Rose Individual Fruit Bowl

Bowl, individual fruit, 5 1/2" d. rose (ILLUS.)... **$25-$40**
Bowl, individual salad, 7 1/2" d. medium green... **$100-$150**
Bowl, individual salad, 7 1/2" d. turquoise .... **$100-$150**
Bowl, individual salad, 7 1/2" d. yellow .... **$100-$150**
Bowl, nappy, 8 1/2" d. chartreuse........... **$40-$65**
Bowl, nappy, 8 1/2" d. cobalt blue .... **$40-$65**
Bowl, nappy, 8 1/2" d. forest green .... **$40-$65**
Bowl, nappy, 8 1/2" d. grey..................... **$40-$65**
Bowl, nappy, 8 1/2" d. medium green.. **$150-$175**
Bowl, nappy, 9 1/2" d. cobalt blue .... **$55-$70**
Bowl, nappy, 9 1/2" d. forest green .... **$55-$70**
Bowl, nappy, 9 1/2" d. grey..................... **$55-$70**
Bowl, nappy, 9 1/2" d. ivory .... **$55-$70**
Bowl, nappy, 9 1/2" d. light green............ **$55-$70**
Bowl, nappy, 9 1/2" d. turquoise............. **$55-$70**
Bowl, nappy, 9 1/2" d. yellow.................. **$55-$70**

Bowl, salad, large, footed, 11 3/8" d., co-
balt blue.. $550-$625
Bowl, salad, large, footed, 11 3/8" d., light
green .... $550-$625
Bowl, salad, large, footed, 11 3/8" d., red
.... $550-$625
Bowl, salad, large, footed, 11 3/8" d., tur-
quoise... $550-$625
Bowl, salad, large, footed, 11 3/8" d., yel-
low .... $550-$625
Cake plate, 10 3/8" d. cobalt blue ..... $950-$1,050
Cake plate, 10" d. red.............................. $1,500+
Cake plate, 10" d. ivory .... $850-$900
Cake plate, 10" d. light green .... $900-$950
Calendar plate, 10" d., 1954 ivory .... $40-$50
Calendar plate, 10" d., 1955 ivory .... $40-$50
Calendar plate, 10" d., 1955 light green .. $40-$50
Calendar plate, 10" d., 1955 yellow .... $40-$50
Candleholders, bulb-type, pr. cobalt blue.... $120
Candleholders, bulb-type, pr. ivory $120
Candleholders, bulb-type, pr. red................ $120

Turquoise Bulb-type Candleholders

Candleholders, bulb-type, pr. turquoise
(ILLUS.).. $90-$125
Candleholders, bulb-type, pr. yellow .... $90-$125
Candleholders, tripod-type, pr. cobalt
blue .... $650-$700
Candleholders, tripod-type, pr. ivory .. $600-$650
Candleholders, tripod-type, pr. light green
.... $475-$525
Candleholders, tripod-type, pr. red .... $675-$725
Candleholders, tripod-type, pr. turquoise
.... $675-$725
Candleholders, tripod-type, pr. yellow
.... $400-$425
Carafe, cov. cobalt blue .... $225-$325
Carafe, cov. ivory.................................. $225-$325
Carafe, cov. light green (ILLUS., top next
column) .... $225-$325
Carafe, cov. red .... $225-$325
Carafe, cov. turquoise............................... $250
Carafe, cov. yellow $250
Casserole, cov., two-handled, 9 3/4" d.
chartreuse, ... $300-$325
Casserole, cov., two-handled, 9 3/4" d.
cobalt blue.. $250-$275
Casserole, cov., two-handled, 9 3/4" d.
forest green .... $300-$325
Casserole, cov., two-handled, 9 3/4" d.
grey .... $300-$325
Casserole, cov., two-handled, 9 3/4" d.
ivory.. $250-$300
Casserole, cov., two-handled, 9 3/4" d.
light green .... $150-$175
Casserole, cov., two-handled, 9 3/4" d.
medium green .... $1,600-$1,700

Fiesta Green Covered Carafe

Casserole, cov., two-handled, 9 3/4" d.
red... $250-$300
Casserole, cov., two-handled, 9 3/4" d.
rose .... $300-$325
Casserole, cov., two-handled, 9 3/4" d.
turquoise .... $160-$180
Casserole, cov., two-handled, 9 3/4" d.
yellow $150
Coffeepot, cov. chartreuse.................. $325-$350
Coffeepot, cov. cobalt blue .... $250-$300
Coffeepot, cov. forest green .... $325-$350
Coffeepot, cov. grey............................ $675-$725
Coffeepot, cov. ivory $230
Coffeepot, cov. light green.................. $225-$250
Coffeepot, cov. red .... $275-$325
Coffeepot, cov. rose............................ $375-$425
Coffeepot, cov. turquoise $180
Coffeepot, cov. yellow......................... $200-$250
Coffeepot, cov., demitasse, stick handle
cobalt blue.. $600-$625
Coffeepot, cov., demitasse, stick handle
ivory .... $625-$650
Coffeepot, cov., demitasse, stick handle
light green .... $675-$725

Red Fiesta Demitasse Coffeepot

Coffeepot, cov., demitasse, stick handle
red (ILLUS.) .... $700-$725

Coffeepot, cov., demitasse, stick handle
turquoise .... $700-$725
Coffeepot, cov., demitasse, stick handle
yellow $400
Compote, 12" d., low, footed cobalt blue
.... $200-$225
Compote, 12" d., low, footed ivory ...... $200-$225
Compote, 12" d., low, footed light green
.... $150-$175
Compote, 12" d., low, footed red .... $700-$725
Compote, 12" d., low, footed turquoise
.... $700-$725
Compote, 12" d., low, footed yellow ... $400-$425
Compote, sweetmeat, high stand cobalt
blue .... $75-$100
Compote, sweetmeat, high stand light
green .... $75-$110
Compote, sweetmeat, high stand tur-
quoise $95
Creamer forest green .... $25-$40
Creamer red $25
Creamer yellow .... $25-$40
Creamer & cov. sugar bowl, individual
size, on figure-8 tray, yellow on cobalt
tray, the set .... $700-$750
Creamer, ring-handled, chartreuse .... $25-$40
Creamer, ring-handled, cobalt blue $25
Creamer, ring-handled, grey .... $25-$40
Creamer, ring-handled, light green......... $25-$40
Creamer, ring-handled, medium green
.... $125-$150
Creamer, stick handle cobalt blue .... $60-$65
Creamer, stick handle light green............ $35-$45
Creamer, stick handle turquoise......... $100-$125
Creamer, stick handle yellow .... $35-$45
Cup & saucer, demitasse, stick handle
chartreuse .... $500-$550
Cup & saucer, demitasse, stick handle
forest green .... $400-$450
Cup & saucer, demitasse, stick handle
ivory... $95
Cup & saucer, demitasse, stick handle
red .... $100-$125
Cup & saucer, demitasse, stick handle
rose .... $400-$450
Cup & saucer, ring handle chartreuse .... $30-$45
Cup & saucer, ring handle grey .... $30-$45
Cup & saucer, ring handle light green .... $30-$45
Cup & saucer, ring handle medium green $70
Cup & saucer, ring handle rose .... $30-$45
Egg cup chartreuse.............................. $125-$175
Egg cup forest green .... $125-$175
Egg cup grey.. $500-$550
Egg cup light green................................. $70-$80
Egg cup rose.. $400-$450
Fork (Kitchen Kraft) cobalt blue................... $150
Fork (Kitchen Kraft) red............................... $150
Fork (Kitchen Kraft) yellow $150
French casserole, cov., stick handle co-
balt blue .... $3,550-$3,650
French casserole, cov., stick handle ivory
.... $525-$575
French casserole, cov., stick handle light
green .... $575-$625
French casserole, cov., stick handle yel-
low.. $275-$325
Gravy boat chartreuse .... $70-$80
Gravy boat grey .... $70-$80
Gravy boat light green .... $45-$65

Gravy boat rose....................................... $70-$80

Yellow Fiesta Gravy Boat

Gravy boat yellow (ILLUS.) .... $45-$65
Marmalade jar, cov. cobalt blue.................. $365
Marmalade jar, cov. ivory............................ $365
Marmalade jar, cov. light green .... $300-$400
Mixing bowl, nest-type, size No. 1, 5" d.
cobalt blue... $275
Mixing bowl, nest-type, size No. 1, 5" d.
light green .... $250-$325
Mixing bowl, nest-type, size No. 1, 5" d.
turquoise .... $250-$325
Mixing bowl, nest-type, size No. 2, 6" d.
cobalt blue... $125
Mixing bowl, nest-type, size No. 2, 6" d.
light green .... $110-$160
Mixing bowl, nest-type, size No. 2, 6" d.
yellow .... $110-$160
Mixing bowl, nest-type, size No. 3, 7" d.
cobalt blue....................................... $135-$170
Mixing bowl, nest-type, size No. 4, 8" d.
cobalt blue....................................... $200-$225
Mixing bowl, nest-type, size No. 4, 8" d.
light green .... $100-$120
Mixing bowl, nest-type, size No. 4, 8" d.
turquoise .... $150-$175
Mixing bowl, nest-type, size No. 5, 9" d.
cobalt blue....................................... $225-$270
Mixing bowl, nest-type, size No. 5, 9" d.
light green .... $225-$270
Mixing bowl, nest-type, size No. 5, 9" d.
turquoise .... $225-$270
Mixing bowl, nest-type, size No. 5, 9" d.
yellow .... $225-$270
Mixing bowl, nest-type, size No. 6, 10" d.
ivory .... $300-$375
Mixing bowl, nest-type, size No. 6, 10" d.
light green .... $300-$375
Mixing bowl, nest-type, size No. 7,
11 1/2" d. cobalt blue........................ $550-$650
Mixing bowl, nest-type, size No. 7,
11 1/2" d. light green .... $550-$650
Mixing bowl, nest-type, size No. 7,
11 1/2" d. turquoise .... $550-$650
Mug, chartreuse .... $80-$90
Mug, cobalt blue....................................... $80-$90
Mug, forest green .... $75-$85
Mug, grey .... $70-$80
Mug, ivory... $65-$75
Mug, light green .... $55-$65
Mug, medium green .... $115-$125
Mug red .... $70-$80
Mug, rose .... $75-$85
Mug, turquoise .... $40-$50
Mug, yellow .... $40-$50

Mustard jar, cov. ivory........................... $300-$375
Mustard jar, cov. red .... $300-$375
Mustard jar, cov. yellow .... $300-$375
Onion soup bowl, cov. cobalt blue ...... $700-$750
Onion soup bowl, cov. ivory............... $700-$750
Onion soup bowl, cov. light green....... $700-$750
Onion soup bowl, cov. medium green $700-$750
Onion soup bowl, cov. red .... $700-$750

Rare Fiesta Onion Soup Bowl

Onion soup bowl, cov. turquoise (ILLUS.)
.... $8,000
Onion soup bowl, cov. yellow .... $700-$750
Pie server (Kitchen Kraft) cobalt blue $150
Pie server (Kitchen Kraft) light green........... $150
Pie server (Kitchen Kraft) yellow................. $150
Pitcher, ice, globular, 2 qt. ivory .... $125-$150
Pitcher, ice, globular, 2 qt. red........... $125-$150

Chartreuse Fiesta 2 Pint Jug Pitcher

Pitcher, jug-type, 2 pt. chartreuse (ILLUS.)
.... $125-$150
Pitcher, jug-type, 2 pt. cobalt blue....... $100-$125
Pitcher, jug-type, 2 pt. grey .... $125-$150
Pitcher, jug-type, 2 pt. ivory................. $100-$125
Pitcher, jug-type, 2 pt. light green .... $75-$85
Pitcher, jug-type, 2 pt. rose .... $125-$150
Pitcher, jug-type, 2 pt. turquoise .... $75-$85
Pitcher, jug-type, 2 pt. yellow .... $75-$85
Pitcher, juice, disc-type, 30 oz. grey....... $3,000+
Pitcher, juice, disc-type, 30 oz. red .... $600-$700
Pitcher, juice, disc-type, 30 oz. turquoise
.... $10,000+
Pitcher, juice, disc-type, 30 oz. yellow.... $40-$50
Pitcher, water, disc-type chartreuse ... $250-$300
Pitcher, water, disc-type forest green . $250-$300
Pitcher, water, disc-type light green.... $100-$125
Pitcher, water, disc-type rose .... $275-$375
Pitcher, water, disc-type yellow .... $110-$140
Plate, 10" d. chartreuse .... $40-$50
Plate, 10" d., cobalt blue.......................... $40-$50
Plate, 10" d. forest green .... $40-$50

Plate, 10" d., forest green .... $40-$50
Plate, 10" d. grey .... $40-$50
Plate, 10" d., light green .... $40-$50
Plate, 10" d. medium green .... $150-$200
Plate, 10" d., medium green .... $150-$200
Plate, 10" d., red .... $40-$50
Plate, 10" d. rose .... $40-$50
Plate, 10" d. turquoise .... $40-$50
Plate, 10" d., turquoise .... $40-$50
Plate, 6" d. chartreuse .... $5-$10
Plate, 6" d. forest green .... $5-$10
Plate, 6" d. grey .... $5-$10
Plate, 6" d. medium green .... $25-$35
Plate, 6" d. rose .... $5-$10
Plate, 7" d. chartreuse .... $8-$12
Plate, 7" d. forest green .... $8-$12
Plate, 7" d. grey .... $8-$12
Plate, 7" d. medium green .... $50-$60
Plate, 7" d. rose .... $8-$12
Plate, 9" d. chartreuse .... $15-$25
Plate, 9" d. forest green .... $15-$25
Plate, 9" d. light green .... $15-$25

Fiesta 9" Medium Green Plate

Plate, 9" d. medium green (ILLUS.).......... $70-$80
Plate, 9" d. red $15
Plate, 9" d. rose .... $15-$25
Plate, 9" d. yellow .... $15-$25
Plate, chop, 13" d. chartreuse............... $80-$100
Plate, chop, 13" d. cobalt blue $45
Plate, chop, 13" d. forest green .... $80-$100
Plate, chop, 13" d. grey........................... $80-$100
Plate, chop, 13" d. light green.................. $40-$60
Plate, chop, 13" d. medium green........ $600-$700
Plate, chop, 13" d. rose........................... $80-$100
Plate, chop, 13" d. yellow........................ $40-$60
Plate, chop, 15" d. cobalt blue $90
Plate, chop, 15" d. forest green .... $150-$175
Plate, chop, 15" d. grey......................... $150-$175
Plate, chop, 15" d. light green.............. $150-$175
Plate, chop, 15" d. red .... $80-$110
Plate, chop, 15" d. rose.......................... $150-$175
Plate, grill, 10 1/2" d. chartreuse............. $70-$80
Plate, grill, 10 1/2" d. cobalt blue $40
Plate, grill, 10 1/2" d. forest green .... $70-$80
Plate, grill, 10 1/2" d. light green............. $35-$50
Plate, grill, 10 1/2" d. turquoise....................... $35
Plate, grill, 10 1/2" d. yellow............................ $35
Plate, grill, 12" d. cobalt blue .... $50-$70

Plate, grill, 12" d. ivory .... $50-$70
Plate, grill, 12" d. red .... $50-$70
Plate, grill, 12" d. yellow.......................... $50-$70
Platter, 12" oval chartreuse..................... $45-$65
Platter, 12" oval grey.............................. $45-$65
Platter, 12" oval light green..................... $45-$65
Platter, 12" oval medium green .... $200-$225
Platter, 12" oval red $50
Platter, 12" oval yellow............................ $45-$65
Relish tray w/five inserts cobalt blue $355
Relish tray w/five inserts light green... $300-$375
Relish tray w/five inserts multicolored $300-$375
Salt & pepper shakers, pr. chartreuse .... $25-$45

Cobalt Blue Fiesta Salt & Peppers

Salt & pepper shakers, pr. cobalt blue
(ILLUS.)... $25
Salt & pepper shakers, pr. forest green .. $25-$45
Salt & pepper shakers, pr. grey .... $25-$45
Salt & pepper shakers, pr. light green..... $25-$45
Salt & pepper shakers, pr. medium green
.... $225-$250
Salt & pepper shakers, pr. red $25
Salt & pepper shakers, pr. rose .... $25-$45
Salt & pepper shakers, pr. yellow .... $25-$45
Soup plate, rimmed, 8 3/8" d., chartreuse
.... $40-$65
Soup plate, rimmed, 8 3/8" d. cobalt blue
.... $40-$65
Soup plate, rimmed, 8 3/8" d. forest green
.... $40-$65
Soup plate, rimmed, 8 3/8" d. medium
green... $125-$150
Soup plate, rimmed, 8 3/8" d. red $50
Soup plate, rimmed, 8 3/8" d. rose .... $40-$65
Soup plate, rimmed, 8 3/8" d. yellow ...... $40-$65
Spoon (Kitchen Kraft) light green........ $125-$140
Spoon (Kitchen Kraft) red .... $140-$150
Sugar bowl, cov. chartreuse .... $60-$70
Sugar bowl, cov. forest green .... $60-$70
Sugar bowl, cov. grey .... $60-$70
Sugar bowl, cov. light green .... $45-$60
Sugar bowl, cov. red................................ $60-$70
Sugar bowl, cov. rose .... $60-$70
Syrup pitcher w/original lid, cobalt blue
.... $350-$450
Syrup pitcher w/original lid, ivory .... $350-$450
Syrup pitcher w/original lid, light green
.... $350-$450
Syrup pitcher w/original lid, red .... $350-$450
Syrup pitcher w/original lid, yellow..... $350-$450
Teapot, cov., large size (8 cup), cobalt
blue .... $300-$400
Teapot, cov., large size (8 cup), light green
.... $300-$400
Teapot, cov., large size (8 cup), red ... $300-$400

Teapot, cov., medium size (6 cup), forest
green.. $250-$300
Teapot, cov., medium size (6 cup), grey
.... $425-$475
Teapot, cov., medium size (6 cup), light
green.. $1,600-$1,700

Rare Fiesta Medium Green Teapot

Teapot, cov., medium size (6 cup), medi-
um green (ILLUS.) .... $1,600-$1,700
Teapot, cov., medium size (6 cup), yellow
.... $150-$175
Tumbler, juice, 5 oz. chartreuse .... $550-$600
Tumbler, juice, 5 oz. cobalt blue............. $45-$60
Tumbler, juice, 5 oz. grey .... $225-$275
Tumbler, juice, 5 oz. forest green, ... $400-$500
Tumbler, juice, 5 oz. ivory....................... $45-$60
Tumbler, juice, 5 oz. red.......................... $45-$60
Tumbler, juice, 5 oz. turquoise .... $45-$60
Tumbler, water, 10 oz. cobalt blue................. $80
Tumbler, water, 10 oz. ivory .... $70-$90
Tumbler, water, 10 oz. turquoise .... $70-$90
Utility tray, 10 1/2" l. cobalt blue $45
Utility tray, 10 1/2" l. light green.............. $40-$55
Utility tray, 10 1/2" l. red $45
Utility tray, 10 1/2" l., yellow .... $40-$55
Vase, 10" h. cobalt blue $1,050
Vase, 10" h. ivory........................... $1,000-$1,300
Vase, 10" h. turquoise.................... $1,000-$1,300
Vase, 10" h. yellow .... $1,000-$1,300
Vase, 12" h. ivory........................... $1,100-$1,500
Vase, 12" h. red .... $1,850-$2,000
Vase, 12" h. turquoise.................... $1,500-$1,600
Vase, 8" h. cobalt blue $650
Vase, 8" h. red $650
Vase, 8" h. yellow .... $650-$800
Vase, bud, 6 1/2" h. light green .... $100-$150
Vase, bud, 6 1/2" h. red.............................. $100
Vase, bud, 6 1/2" h. yellow.................. $100-$150

Florence Ceramics

Some of the finest figurines and artwares were produced between 1940 and 1962 by the Florence Ceramics Company of Pasadena, California. Florence Ward began working with ceramics following the death of her son, Jack, in 1939.

Mrs. Ward had not worked with clay before her involvement with classes at the Pasadena Hobby School. After study and firsthand experience, she began production in her garage, using a kiln located outside the garage to conform with city regulations. *The years 1942-44 were considered her "garage" period.*

In 1944 Florence Ceramics moved to a small plant in Pasadena, employing fifty-four employees and receiving orders of $250,000 per year. In 1948 it was again necessary to move to a larger facility in the area with the most up-to-date equipment. The number of employees increased to more than 100. Within five years Florence Ceramics was considered one of the finest producers of semi-porcelain figurines and artwares.

Florence created a wide range of items including figurines, lamps, picture frames, planters and models of animals and birds. It was her extensive line of women in beautiful gowns and gentlemen in fine clothes that gave her the most pleasure and was the foundation of her business. Two of her most popular lines of figurines were inspired by the famous 1860 Godey's Lady's Book and by famous artists from the Old Master group. In the mid-1950s two bird lines were produced for several years. One of the bird lines was designed by Don Winton and the other was a line of contemporary sculpted bird and animal figures designed by the well-known sculptor Betty Davenport Ford.

There were several unsuccessful contemporary artware lines produced for a short time. The Driftware line consisted of modern freeform bowls and accessories. The Floraline is a rococo line with overglazed decoration. The Gourmet Pottery, a division of Florence Ceramics Company, produced accessory serving pieces under the name of Scandia and Sierra.

Florence products were manufactured in the traditional porcelain process with a second firing at a higher temperature after the glaze had been applied. Many pieces had overglaze paint decoration and clay ruffles, roses and lace dipped in slip prior to the third firing.

Florence "Angel," Downcast Eyes

Rare Birthday Girl Figure

Florence Marks

Figures

"Amber," brown hair, pink ruffled long dress & large bonnet, right arm bent & holding a pink parasol at right shoulder, left arm extended w/fingers touching her dress, articulated fingers, 9 1/4" h..... **$425-$475**

"Angel," downcast eyes, yellow hair, arms bent across upper body, part of angel's wings showing, white robe w/gold trimmed rope sash, cuffs & collar, gold & brown ribbon sticker, 7" h. (ILLUS., top next column).. **$50-$75**

"Annabel," Godey lady, standing w/right arm bent & carrying a basket of flowers, left arm in outward position, long full jacket w/gold trim, large hat, articulated fingers, 8 " h. .... **$400-$450**

"Ballet," 7" h. .... **$225-$250**

"Birthday Girl," standing w/her arms bent & hands close together, wearing a long flaring aqua gown, 9 3/4" h. (ILLUS.)...... **$750-$825**

"Bride," porcelain veil, 8 1/2" h. ..... **$1,000-$1,250**

"Butch," boy w/hands in pockets, 5" h. .... **$100-$125**

"Camille," woman standing & wearing white dress trimmed in gold, shawl over both arms made entirely of hand-dipped lace, brown hair, white triangular hat w/applied pink rose, ribbon tied to right side of neck, two hands, 8 1/2" h. ...... **$300-$50**

"Caroline," brocade fabric dress, 15" h. .... **$3,500-$4,500**

"Charles," man standing & wearing 18th c. attire w/a long cape, 8" h................. **$150-$175**

"Charmaine," woman holding a parasol, wearing ruffled long dress, large hat w/flowers, w/articulated hands, 8 1/2" h. .... **$250-$350**

"The Christening" Figure Group

"Christening (The)," woman w/dress trimmed in lace at neck, sleeves & front of dress holding an infant in a long white christening dress, articulated fingers, 10" h. (ILLUS.) .... **$2,000-$2,500**

"Clarissa," woman in full-sleeved jacket & long swirled & pleated skirt, bonnet & holding a muff in right hand, left hand on her shoulder, articulated hand, 7 3/4" h.
.... **$175-$200**

"Colleen," woman standing w/head slightly turned to left, right hand behind back & left arm to the front w/articulated hand, long wind-blown dress w/white collar, bonnet w/ribbon tied under chin, 8" h. .... **$150-$200**

Florence Figure of "Darleen"

"Darleen," standing w/head tilted, brown hair w/curls & roses at neck, long dress w/white underskirt, white lace trim on

bodice & extending to bottom of dress, right arm bent & holding an open parasol at right shoulder, left arm at waist, articulated fingers, 8 1/4" h. (ILLUS.) .... **$600-$650**

"Denise," off-the-shoulder white dress w/gold trim extending down the dress front, violet overskirt, brown hair w/roses, both arms bent at waist w/right hand holding a closed fan, articulated fingers, 10" h. .... **$500-$650**

"Edward," man in late Victorian costume sitting in an armchair, holding his bowler hat on one knee, 7" h. .... **$200-$250**

Rare Variation of "Elizabeth"

"Elizabeth," woman in 18th c. costume w/a wide flaring aqua gown w/half-sleeves & a lace-trimmed bodice, long curls down her neck, seated on a white settee, rare white settee variation, 7" w., 8 1/4" h. (ILLUS.) .... **$1,200-$1,400**

Rare "Georgia" in Brocade Gown

"Georgia," woman standing wearing a long wide real brocade fabric gown, her hands lifting sides of gown at the front, 12" h. (ILLUS.)...................................... **$1,500-$2,000**

"Jeannette," Godey lady, rose colored full-skirted dress w/peplum, white collar, flower at neck, left hand holding hat w/bow, right hand holding parasol, 7 3/4" h.... **$125-$150**

"Joyce," woman wearing full off-the-shoulder gown w/shoulder ruffles, a wide-brimmed picture hat, arms away at the front, 8 1/2" h..................................... **$325-$350**

"Lady Diana" with Plain Cuffs

"Lady Diana," woman stepping forward w/her arms away from her body, wearing flowers in her piled hair & a low-cut narrow lilac gown w/a flaring lacy collar, tight waist & over gown pulled into a bustle, the half-length sleeves w/plain cuffs, 10" h. (ILLUS.) .... **$500-$575**

Rare "Little Princess" Figure

"Little Princess," girl standing in a long-sleeved very wide 17th c. farthingale gown, her hair in long curls, arms outstretched to edges of gown, 8 1/2" h. (ILLUS.) . **$1,000-$1,250**

"Marc Antony," Roman warrior wearing helmet, breastplate, white short garment & long flowing cape, one sandaled leg resting on a rectangular block on a square base, 13" h. .... **$750-$1,000**

Florence "Marilyn" Figure

"Marilyn," woman standing wearing 18th-c. moss green gown w/half-length sleeves w/lace cuffs & large balloon gathers at the waist above the long flaring gown, carrying a basket over one arm, 8 1/2" h. (ILLUS.).. **$350-$400**

"Melanie," Godey lady, wearing a close-fitting bonnet & long-sleeved long coat over a wide dress, arms at her sides, 7 1/2" h. .... **$100-$125**

"Our Lady of Grace," Madonna figure wearing long cloak w/gathered arms over long gown, on rounded domed base, 10 3/4" h... **$175-$200**

"Peter," man standing wearing Victorian frock coat over lacy cravat, one leg to side & leaning on a scroll pedestal w/a hand holding his top hat, 9 1/4" h...... **$225-$250**

"Reggie," boy standing wearing Victorian outfit, Eton jacket & vest & long pants, scrolls at the side bottom, 7" h. .... **$225-$250**

"Sally," woman wearing Victorian outfit, high rounded bonnet tied w/bow, simple ruffled collar & long-sleeved coat over wide swirled & ruffled gown, both hands at sides, 6 3/4" h. .... **$125-$150**

"Story Hour," seated mother & girl, woman reading book held in left hand, wearing rose dress w/lace at neck, roses in her hair, & girl w/blonde hair w/right arm on bench, wearing ruffled lace short-sleeved white dress w/blue & pink trim, no little boy, 8" l., 6 3/4" h. .... **$800-$850**

"Tess," woman standing wearing long dress w/lace ruffle at neckline, large picture hat, arms away w/one hand holding edge of skirt up over shoe, 7 1/4" h. .... **$250-$300**

"Victor," man w/head tilted wearing a Victorian outfit, holding top hat in right hand, frock coat over long pants, swirling long cape, 9 1/4" h. .... **$175-$225**

"Wynkin," boy toddler wearing long blue pajamas & holding a teddy bear, 5 1/2" h. .... **$150-$200**

Other Items

Bust, "American Lady," heavy lace trim, 7 3/4" h. .... **$350-$400**

Bust, "Modern Girl," 9 1/2" h. .... **$100-$125**

Flower holder, "Beth," woman standing in a dirndl-style dress & holding up one corner of her long apron, holder at the back, 7 1/2" h. .... **$50-$75**

Flower holder, "Chinese Child/Girl," bamboo-form holder at side, 7" h. .... **$100-$125**

Flower holder, "Molly," standing girl wearing long gown w/short ruffled sleeves at shoulder, standing beside a large cylinder vase embossed w/leafy boughs, 6 1/2" h. .... **$35-$40**

Head vase, "Fern," girl wearing wide lightly ruffled hat & dress w/small ruffled collar & wide ruffles at the shoulders, 7" h. .... **$125-$150**

TV lamp, "Dear Ruth," 9" h. .... **$800-$1,000**

Flow Blue

Flow Blue ironstone and semi-porcelain was manufactured mainly in England during the second half of the 19th century. The early ironstone was produced by many of the well known English potters and was either transfer-printed or hand-painted (brush stroke). The bulk of the ware was exported to the United States or Canada.

The "flow" or running quality of the cobalt blue designs was the result of introducing certain chemicals into the kiln during the final firing. Some patterns are so "flown" that it is difficult to ascertain the design. The transfers were of several types: Asian, Scenic, Marble or Floral.

The earliest Flow Blue ironstone patterns were produced during the period between about 1840 and 1860. After the Civil War Flow Blue went out of style for some years but was again manufactured and exported to the United States beginning about the 1880s and continuing through the turn of the century. These later Flow Blue designs are on a semi-porcelain body rather than heavier ironstone and the designs are mainly florals. Also see Antique Trader Pottery & Porcelain Ceramics Price Guide, 5th Edition.

ADAMS (Wood & Son, ca. 1907)
Vegetable dish, open, oval, 7 x 12" **$65**

ALDINE (W.H. Grindley & Company, ca. 1891)
Plate, dinner, 10" d. **$75**
Vegetable dish, cov., footed, 12" l. from handle to handle, 8" h. **$225**

ALHAMBRA (Alfred Meakin, Ltd., ca. 1891)

Alhambra Dinner Plate

Plate, dinner, 10" d. (ILLUS.) **$65**

AMERILLIA (Podmore Walker & Co., ca. 1834-1859)
Plate, 7 1/2" d. **$60**
Plate, 8 1/2" d. **$70**
Plate, 10 1/2" d. **$125**
Platter, 16" **$350**
Teapot, cov., ribbed oval body style, Podmore, Walker & Co., England, ca. 1834-59 (ILLUS., bottom of page) **$650**

Amerillia Flow Blue Teapot

AMOY (Davenport, ca. 1844)

Large 16" Amoy Platter

Platter, 16" l. (ILLUS.) $450

ANEMONE (Cumberlidge, Humphreys & Hele, ca. 1889-93)

Anemone Covered Biscuit Jar

Biscuit jar, cov., 6 1/2" h. (ILLUS.) $175

ANEMONE (Minton & Co., ca. 1860)

Plate, 8 1/2" d. $75
Plate, 9 1/2" d. $85
Platter, 14", oval $250
Razor box, cov., 3 x 8" $295

Anemone Covered Vegetable Bowl

Vegetable bowl, cov., footed (ILLUS.) $325

ARABESQUE (T.J. and J. Mayer, ca. 1845)

Creamer $325
Creamer, Classic Gothic style, 6" h. $325
Plate, 7 1/2" d. $65
Soup plate w/flanged rim, 10" d. $175
Sugar bowl, cov., Classic Gothic style $350
Teapot, cov., Classic Gothic style $800

Arabesque Pattern Teapot with Long Octagon Body Shape

Teapot, cov., Long Octagon body shape, ca. 1845 (ILLUS.) $650

ARCADIA (Arthur J. Wilkinson, ca. 1907)

Tea cup & saucer, cup, 3 1/4" d., 2 1/4" h., saucer, 5 1/2" d. $75

ARGYLE (Myott, Son & Co., ca. 1898)

Teapot, cov., 6" h. $300

ARGYLE (W.H. Grindley & Co., ca. 1896)

Butter, cover & drainer $300
Butter dish, cover & drainer $350
Butter pat, 3 1/2" d. $60
Cup & saucer, handled $95
Demitasse cup & saucer, cup 3" d. x 3 1/2" h., saucer 4 1/2" d. $165
Gravy boat $195
Ladle, sauce $700
Oyster bowl, 6" d. x 3" h. $195
Pitcher, 1 1/2 pt. $425
Pitcher, 1 pt. $375
Plate, 7" d. $55
Plate, 8" d. $60
Plate, 9" d. $75
Plate, 10" d. $95
Platter, 14" l. $275

Argyle Platter

Platter, 16" l. (ILLUS.) $350
Platter, 18" l. $450

Arvista Flow Blue Salad Set

Sauce dish $50
Sauce tureen, cover & undertray, 3 pcs...... $495
Soup plate w/flanged rim, 9" d....................... $90
Vegetable bowl, open, medium..................... $185
Vegetable bowl, open, small $165

ARVISTA (Wiltshaw & Robinson, 1906)
Salad set: master bowl w/brass rim &
    matching fork & spoon w/brass fittings,
    pr. (ILLUS., top of page)............................ $450

ASTER & GRAPESHOT (Joseph Clementson, ca. 1840) - Brush-stroke

Aster & Grapeshot 11" Pitcher

Pitcher, 11" h. (ILLUS.).................................. $550

ASTRAL (W.H. Grindley & Co., ca. 1891)
Cake plate, w/tab handles, 9 x 9 1/2"............. $150
Compote, w/pedestal, 9 1/2" d., 4 1/2" h. $175
Egg cup, 3 3/4" h. $125
Platter, 16" l.. $250

ATHENS (Charles Meigh, ca. 1840)

Athens Flow Blue Waste Bowl

Waste bowl (ILLUS.) $225

BIRDS AND BLOOM (George Jones & Sons, ca. 1885)

Birds and Bloom Cache Pot

Cache pot, 7" h. (ILLUS.).............................. $325

BLUE BELL (William Ridgway & Co., ca. 1834-1854)
Dessert tray, leaf shape, one open handle, impressed "Opaque Granite China," 12" l. $350
Vegetable dish, cov., 10 1/4 x 12", 6" h. $350

BLUE DIAMOND (Wheeling and La Belle Potteries, American, ca. 1896)
Charger, 13" d. $350
Creamer & cov. sugar, creamer 4" h., sugar 4 1/2" h., pr. $425

Blue Diamond Iced Beverage Jug

Lemonade/iced beverage jug, cov., pewter lid, 9" h. (ILLUS.) $850

BRIAR (Burgess & Leigh, ca. 1891-1919)

Briar Basin to Pitcher & Bowl Set

Basin, from pitcher & bowl set, 16" d. (ILLUS.) $225

BROOKLYN (Johnson Bros., ca. 1900)
Plate, 7" d. $55

BROOKLYN (Skinner & Walker, ca. 1870)
Plate, 8" d. $60

BUCCLEUCH (maker unknown, ca. 1845)
Fruit compote, reticulated $475
Tea set: 9" h. cov. teapot, 6" h. cov. sugar, 5 1/2" h. creamer; the set.......................... $900

BURGEE (maker unknown, ca. 1860)
Soup tureen on pedestal, cov., 14" w., 13" h. $550

CAMPION (W.H. Grindley & Co., ca. 1891)
Toothbrush vase, 6" h. $175

CANDIA (Cauldon Ltd., ca. 1910) (This pattern looks like "Roseville" by John Maddock)
Syrup, cov., w/pewter lid, 6 1/2" h................. $250

CANNISTER (maker unknown, marked "Germany," ca. 1891) - Miscellaneous (These cannisters, spice jars & kitchen items were made for export. They arrived without the name of the intended contents i.e. "Tea" or "Sugar." Machines were used to print the name after arrival. They were also in different shapes & languages.)

Long Box for Pickled Herring

Box for pickled herring, very unusual, 6 x 14", 6" h. (ILLUS.) $250

Hanging Salt Box

Salt box, hanging type, 5 x 7", 8 1/2" h. (ILLUS.) $145

CANTON (James Edwards, ca. 1845)
Chamber pot, cov., 9" d., 7" h. $250

CANTON (John Maddock, ca. 1850)
Cup & saucer, handleless $175

CASHMERE (Francis Morley, ca. 1850)
Coffeepot, cov., octagonal, 9 1/2" h............ $1,200
Creamer, 5" $795

Cashmere Gothic Shape Creamer

Creamer, Gothic shape (ILLUS.).................... $795
Creamer, Primary shape, 6" $595

Handleless Cup & Saucer

Cup & saucer, handleless (ILLUS.) $250
Mug, 3 1/2" h. $600
Pitcher, 2 qt. $1,500
Plate, 7 1/2" d. $100
Plate, 8 1/4" w., paneled, set of 13 (one
   w/spider crack, one w/flake)...................... $935
Plate, 9 1/2" d. $125
Plate, 10 1/2" d. $175
Plates, 10 1/4" d., paneled, set of 4 .... $715
Platter, 13 3/4 x 17", scalloped edge $450
Sauce tureen, 3 pcs....................................... $995

Cashmere Soup Plate

Soup plate, 10" d. (ILLUS.)........................... $225
Soup plate w/flanged rim, 10 3/4" w., scalloped edges, set of 7............................... $1,375

Cashmere Flow Blue Sugar Bowl

Sugar, cov., Gothic shape (ILLUS.) $850
Syrup pitcher, side handle, wide squatty
   base w/sharply tapering paneled sides,
   rare & unusual, 4 1/2" h. $1,800
Teapot, cov., Broad Shoulder body
   shape, ca. 1850, each $950
Teapot, cov., Classic Gothic body
   shape, ca. 1850, each $950
Teapot, cov., Split Panel Primary body
   shape, ca. 1850, each (ILLUS. of two
   size variations, top of next page) $1,200

Split Primary Body Shape Cashmere Teapots

Teapot, cov., Straight Line Primary shape, ca. 1850...................................... **$1,200**
Wash pitcher & bowl, the set..................... **$3,500**

F. Morley Cashmere Waste Bowl

Waste bowl (ILLUS.)...................................... **$450**

CELTIC (W.H. Grindley & Co., ca. 1897)

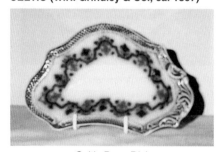

Celtic Bone Dish

Bone dish, crescent shape, 7" w. (ILLUS.)...... **$65**
Creamer, 6 1/2" h. **$175**
Platter, 18" l... **$300**

CHEN-SI (John Maddock, ca. 1842-1855)
Plate, 9" d., twelve-sided (ILLUS., top next column) **$125**
Relish, mitten, 8" w. **$200**

Chen-Si Twelve-sided Plate

CHEN-SI (John Meir, ca. 1835)

Chen-Si Primary Shaper Creamer

Creamer, Primary shape, 5" h. (ILLUS.) **$350**

Chen-Si Flow Blue Teapot by Meir

Teapot, cov., Eight Sided Primary Belted
body shape (ILLUS.) $650

CHUSAN (J. Clementson, ca. 1840)
Creamer, 6" h. $250
Plate, 7 1/2" d. $75
Plate, 9 1/2" d. $95
Platter, 13" l. $300
Platter, 14" l. $350

Clementson Chusan Pattern Flow Blue Teapot

Teapot, cov., Long Hexagon body shape
(ILLUS.) $650
Vegetable bowl, open, 8" l. $200

CHUSAN (Podmore, Walker & Co., ca. 1834-1859)
Vegetable dish, cov. $450

CLOVER (W.H. Grindley & Co., ca. 1910)
Platter, 16" l. $250

COBURG (John Edwards, ca. 1860)
Cup & saucer, handleless $150
Plate, 8 1/2" d. $85
Plate, 10 1/2" d. $125
Platter, 16" $300
Teapot, cov. $650
Vegetable bowl, open, 10" l. $250

CONWAY (New Wharf Pottery & Co., ca. 1891)

Conway Pattern Butter Dish

Butter dish, cov. (ILLUS.) $650

Conway Pattern 8 1/2" Pitcher

Pitcher, 8 1/2" h. (ILLUS.) $650

CONWAY (Wood & Son, ca. 1895)

Wood & Son Conway Cup & Saucer

Cup & saucer the set (ILLUS.) $95

Corea Meat Well Platter

COREA (Wedgwood & Co., ca. 1900)
Meat well platter & cover, 8 1/2 x 11 1/2"
w/cover (ILLUS., top of page) $450

COUNTESS (W.H. Grindley & Co., ca. 1891)
Creamer, 4 1/2" h. $125
Sugar, cov., 5" h. $150
Teapot, cov., 6 1/2" h. $375

CRUMLIN (Myott, Son & Co., ca. 1900)
Creamer, 4 1/2" h. $125
Pitcher, 8" h. $275
Plate, 10" d., w/scalloped rim $85

CYPRUS (Wm. Davenport, ca. 1850)
Platter, 16" l. $350

DAINTY (John Maddock & Son, ca. 1896)
Platter, 12" l. $150

DELHI (Unknown maker, ca. 1860)
Pitcher & bowl set, child's, the set (ILLUS.,
next column) $850

DELHI (Unknown, pattern looks exactly like "Lahore" by Corn)
Pitcher & bowl set, child's size, 2 pcs. $850

DEVON (Alfred Meakin, ca. 1907)
Dinner service: thirteen 9 3/4" d. dinner plates, twelve 7 1/2" d. soup plates, twelve bread & butter plates, eleven dessert plates, twelve dessert bowls, seventeen saucers-underplates, eight coffee cups & four saucers, eight teacups & four saucers, one gravy boat, open sugar bowl, creamer, 8 1/2" d. vegetable dish, small oval relish dish, two open oval vegetable dishes, one two-handled cov. vegetable tureen, oval chop platter & matching 16" l. roasted meats platter & cov. butter dish, the set (ILLUS., bottom of page) **$3,220**

Delhi Child's Bowl & Pitcher Set

DOROTHY (Johnson Bros., ca. 1900)
Bone dish $40
Butter pat, 3 1/2" d. $35
Pitcher, 6 1/2" h. $125
Plate, 8" d. $40
Plate, 9" d. $50
Vegetable bowl, cov. $150

DUDLEY (Ford & Sons, ca. 1890)
Platter, 16" l. $275

Meakin Devon Pattern Flow Blue Dinner Service

DUNDEE (Ridgways, ca. 1910)
Bone dish $45

EBOR (Ridgways, ca. 1910)

Ebor 10" Dinner Plate

Plate, 10" d. (ILLUS.)....................................... $75

FAIRY VILLAS I (William Adams & Sons, ca. 1891)
Butter dish, cov. $325
Creamer, 4 1/2" h. $195
Teapot, cov., , 6 1/2" h. $650

FERN AND TULIP (Unknown, probably 1840s)
Plate, 9" d. $125

FLENSBURG (James Edwards, ca. 1865)

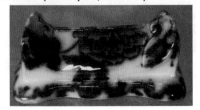

Edwards Flensburg Pattern Pitcher

Pitcher, 6 1/2" h. (ILLUS.) $350

FLORAL (Davenport, ca. 1840)

Early Davenport Floral Knife Rest

Knife rest (ILLUS.)... $550

FLORAL (Laughlin Art China Co., American, ca. 1900)

Three-handled Floral Tyg

Tyg, three-handled (ILLUS.).......................... $250

FLORAL - Roses (Unknown maker, ca. 1860)

Ornate Flow Blue Master Waste Jar

Master waste jar, cov., bulbous ovoid body
w/a molded & scalloped flaring rim, ornate C-scroll handles & low domed cover
w/C-scroll handle, long swags of roses
down the sides (ILLUS.)............................. $450

FLORAL (Unknown maker, ca. 1860)
Teapot, cov., flaring foot, bulbous tapering
body w/flaring rim, domed cover w/floral
finial, serpentine spout & C-scroll handle,
bands of flowers around the base, rim &
cover (ILLUS., next page) $395

Early Unknown Floral Teapot

Floral Vase by an Unknown Maker

Large Floral Pattern Umbrella Stand

Umbrella stand, bulbous base w/wide cylindrical banded body & flared rim, gold trim, 24" h. (ILLUS.) **$650**

Vase, bulbous ovoid base tapering sharply to a tri-lobed flaring rim, large roses (ILLUS., top next column) **$125**

FLORIDA (W.H. Grindley & Co., ca. 1891)

Bone dish, crescent shape, 8" l. **$75**
Cup & saucer, handled **$95**
Plate, 8 1/2" d. **$55**
Plate, 9" d. **$65**
Plate, 10" d. **$85**
Platter, 18" l. (ILLUS., middle next column)
.... **$350**
Soup plate w/flanged rim, 8" d. **$85**
Vegetable bowl, open, small **$145**

Grindley Florida 18" Platter

FLOWERS (maker unknown, ca. 1898)

Rare Flowers Child's Pitcher & Bowl Set

Pitcher & bowl set, child's, the set (ILLUS.)
.... **$2,500**

Early Forget Me Not Child's Sauce Tureen Set

FORGET ME NOT (Unknown maker, ca. 1860)
Sauce tureen, cover, ladle & undertray,
  child's size, 4 pcs. (ILLUS., top of page).... $350

GEISHA (Ford & Sons, ca. 1893)
Plate, 9 1/4" d. $65

GINGHAM FLOWERS (Brushstroke, ca. 1845)
Cup & saucer, handleless $175
Plate, 7 1/2" d. $95

Gingham Flowers Plate

Plate, 9 1/2" d. (ILLUS.).................................. $125
Platter, 14" l. $350

GIRONDE (W.H. Grindley & Co., ca. 1891)
Soup bowl, 9" w. (ILLUS., top next column) $65
Bone dish, crescent shape, 7" l. $75
Creamer, 5" h. $225
Gravy boat w/underplate $225
Platter, 12" l. $175
Platter, 18" l. $350

GRAPE & BLUEBELL (Brushstroke, ca. 1850)
Plate, 8" d. $90
Soup plate w/flanged rim, 10 1/2" $125

GRAPE & BLUEBELL w/Cherry Border (Unknown, ca. 1850, brush-stroke painted)
Platter, 16" l. $400

Gironde Pattern Soup Bowl

GRENADA (Henry Alcock & Co., ca. 1891)
Pitcher, 7" h. $225

Grenada 10" Plate

Plate, 10" d. (ILLUS.) $75

Rare Hong Kong Reticulated Compote & Undertray

HADDON (W. H. Grindley & Co., ca. 1891)

Haddon Flow Blue Pitcher

Harley Toothbrush Vase

Pitcher (ILLUS.) $350

HARLEY (W.H. Grindley & Co., ca. 1891)
Toothbrush vase, 5 1/2" h. (ILLUS., top
    next column) $165
Wash set: pitcher, bowl, cov. slop jar, cov.
    chamber pot, cov. soap dish, shaving
    mug, water pitcher, toothbrush vase; the
    set $1,900

HINDOSTAN (Wood & Brownfield, ca. 1845)
Platter with well & tree, 20" l. $650

HONG KONG (Charles Meigh, ca. 1845)
Compote & undertray, open, footed, flaring
    reticulated sides, 2 pcs. (ILLUS., top of
    page) $4,500

Hong Kong Handled Cup & Saucer

Cup & saucer, handled, farmer size, cup
    4 1/4" d., 3 1/2" h. (ILLUS.) $195
Cup & saucer, handleless $165

Cuspidor, lady's $850
Gravy boat $300
Pitcher, water.. $950
Plate, 10 1/2" d... $125

Hong Kong 18" Platter

Platter, 18" l. (ILLUS.) $675

Meigh Hong Kong Sauce Tureen Set

Sauce tureen, cover, ladle & undertray, 4
pcs. (ILLUS.) $950

Hong Kong Soup Plate

Soup plate w/flanged rim, 10 1/2" d.
(ILLUS.) $150

Fine Hong Kong Flow Blue Soup Tureen

Soup tureen, cover & ladle, the set (ILLUS.) .. $975
Sugar bowl, cov. $450

Rare Hong Kong Syrup Pitcher

Syrup pitcher w/hinged pewter lid
(ILLUS.)... $750
Teapot, cov. $1,095

*Meigh Hong Kong Pattern Teapot in the Long
Octagon Shape*

Teapot, cov., Long Octagon body shape
(ILLUS.)... $850

Hong Kong Teapot in Vertical Panel Gothic Shape

Teapot, cov., Vertical Panel Gothic body
    shape (ILLUS.).. **$750**

Fluted Hong Kong Pattern Teapot by Meigh

Teapot, cov., Twelve Panel Fluted body
    shape (ILLUS.).. **$950**

Hong Kong Flow Blue Teapot by Meigh

Teapot, cov., Ridged Square body shape
    (ILLUS.)... **$750**
Waste bowl **$275**

INDIAN TREE (Unknown, probably English, probably early-Victorian, ca. 1845)

Indian Tree Plate

Plate, 8" d. (ILLUS.) **$40**

JARDINIERE (Villeroy & Boch, German, ca. 1880)

Jardiniere Demitasse Cup & Saucer

Demitasse cup & saucer, 2 1/2" h. x 3" d.
    cup, 5" d. saucer (ILLUS.)......................... **$125**

JOSEPHINE (Ridgways, ca. 1910)
Platter, 19" l. **$575**

KREMLIN (Samuel Alcock & Co., ca. 1843)

Kremlin Pattern Flow Blue Mug

La Belle Flow Blue Celery Dish

Mug (ILLUS., previous page) **$350**

KREMLING (See Kremlin)

LA BELLE (Wheeling Pottery Co., American, ca. 1893-1900)

La Belle Biscuit Jar/Tea Caddy

Biscuit jar/tea caddy, cov., 6" d., 7 1/2" h.
(ILLUS.)... **$450**
Bowl, handled **$225**
Bowl, large, helmet-shaped **$375**

Fancy La Belle Serving Bowl

Bowl, serving, fancy rounded shell-shape
w/fluted & scroll-molded sides trimmed in
gold (ILLUS.)... **$195**
Cake plate **$225**
Celery dish, long narrow oval shape
w/scroll-molded ends, trimmed in gold
(ILLUS., top of page).................................. **$195**
Charger, 13" d.. **$350**
Chocolate pot, cov., 7 1/2" h......................... **$875**
Cracker jar, cov., 7 1/2" h. **$550**
Creamer, 4" h... **$250**
Creamer & cov. sugar bowl, sugar 5" h.,
creamer 4" h., pr. (ILLUS. left & right
w/tray, bottom of page) **$500**

La Belle Sugar Bowl, Creamer & Tray

La Belle Vegetable Bowl

Cup & saucer, handled................................. $125
Demitasse cup & saucer, 2 1/2" h. $175

Plate, 10" d.. $135

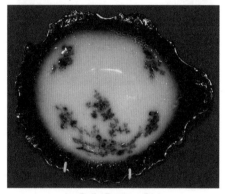

La Belle Dessert Dish

Dessert dish, fancy (ILLUS.) $125
Gravy/sauce boat, two-handled $375
Mug, chocolate $400

LaBelle Ring-handled Dish

Ring-handled dish, 11" l., 10 1/2" w. (ILLUS.) .. $325
Soup plate, 8" d. $125
Tea set: cov. teapot, cov. sugar, creamer, 3
  pcs. $2,500
Tray, rectangular, 8 x 10 1/2" (ILLUS. rear
  w/sugar bowl & creamer, previous page)... $250
Vegetable bowl, cov., round (ILLUS., top of
  page).. $300
Vegetable bowl, open, 7 1/2" d. $175

**LEAF & BERRY (Unknown, ca. 1860s,
brush-stroke painted)**

Leaf & Berry Relish Mitten

Relish mitten, marked w/impressed "Real
Ironstone," a mark that G.L. Ashworth &
Bros. impressed on their pieces ca.
1862, 8 1/2" w. (ILLUS.)............................. $225

La Belle Pitcher

Pitcher, portrait-type, lip repair (ILLUS.) $770
Pitcher, 6 1/2" h. $375
Pitcher, 7 1/2" h. $450
Plate, 8" d... $100

Early Linton Flow Blue Squatty Teapot

LINTON (Thomas Godwin, ca. 1848)
Teapot, cov., footed squatty round shape
w/scroll-molded spout & C-scroll handle
(ILLUS., top of page)................................. **$350**

LOIS (New Wharf Pottery & Co., ca. 1891)

Lois Soup Bowl

Soup bowl, flanged edge, 10" d. (ILLUS.) **$75**

LONSDALE (Ford & Sons, ca. 1898)
Plate, 10 1/2" d... **$95**

LONSDALE (Ridgways, ca. 1910)
Demitasse cup & saucer, 2 1/2" h. **$125**

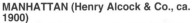

Lonsdale Platter by Ridgways

Platter, 14 x 17" (ILLUS.) **$350**
Vegetable dish, cov., 12" l., 6" h. **$250**

LUCERNE (New Wharf Pottery & Co., ca. 1891)
Bowl, 9" d.. **$90**
Cup & saucer **$65**
Plate, 9" d... **$55**
Vegetable bowl, cov. **$150**
Vegetable dish, cov. **$140**

LUGANO (Ridgways, ca. 1890)
Creamer, 4 1/2" h.. **$195**
Gravy boat **$150**

LUNÉVILLE BLUE (Keller & Guerin, French, ca. 1891)
Tom & Jerry punch bowl, footed, 16" d. ... **$1,400**

MADRAS (Doulton & Co., ca. 1900)
Plate, 6 1/2" d.. **$45**
Soup plate, flanged rim, 8 1/2" d. **$75**
Tea set: teapot, cov. sugar & creamer; the
set **$750**
Vegetable bowl, cov. **$250**

MALTESE (Cotton & Barlow, ca. 1850)
Platter, 14" l. **$350**

MANDARIN (John Maddock, ca. 1850)
Pitcher, 6" h. **$225**

MANHATTAN (Henry Alcock & Co., ca. 1900)

Manhattan Pattern Cup & Saucer

Cup & saucer, the set (ILLUS.) **$65**

MANHATTAN (Johnson Bros., ca. 1895)
Creamer $185
Sugar, cov. $185
Wash basin $150

MANILLA (Podmore, Walker & Co., ca. 1834-1859)

Manilla Flow Blue Gravy Boat
Gravy boat (ILLUS.)... $225

Manilla Mitten-shaped Relish Dish
Relish dish, mitten-shaped (ILLUS.) $250

MARBLE (Warwick China Co., American, ca. 1893)
Ferner, 8" d. $275
Syrup pitcher, 6" h. $325

MARECHAL NEIL (W.H. Grindley & Co., ca. 1895)
Oyster bowl, 5 1/2" d., 3" h. $175
Plate, 10" d. $75
Platter, 14" l. $200

Marechal Neil Flow Blue Teapot

Teapot, cov., deeply waisted & lobed un-
named body shape (ILLUS.) $450
Vegetable dish, cov. $250
Vegetable dish, individual size, 5 1/2"............. $90

MARIE (W. H. Grindley & Co., ca. 1891)

Marie Pattern Soup Tureen
Soup tureen, cov., round, 13" d. (ILLUS.) $350

**MARQUIS, THE (Also See Marquis II)
(W. H. Grindley & Co., ca. 1906)**

Tea Cup & Saucer in The Marquis Pattern
Tea cup & saucer (ILLUS.) $65

MATLOCK (F. Winkle & Co., ca. 1890)

Matlock Covered Vegetable Dish
Vegetable dish, cov., 7 x 11 1/2", 5 1/2" h.
(ILLUS.).. $150

Melbourne Flow Blue Four-Piece Sauce Tureen

MELBOURNE (W.H. Grindley & Co., ca. 1891)

Melbourne Demitasse Cup & Saucer

Demitasse cup & saucer, the set (ILLUS.) ... **$110**
Saucer tureen, cover, ladle & undertray,
    4 pcs. (ILLUS., top of page) **$450**

MINTON'S JAPAN (Minton & Co., ca. 1846)
Rim soup bowl, flanged edge, 10" d. **$100**

MORNING GLORY (Unknown, ca. 1850s, brush-stroke, gaudy)
Sugar, cov., cock's comb handles **$600**

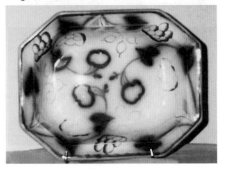

Morning Glory Vegetable Dish

Vegetable dish, open, 7 x 8 1/2" (ILLUS.)..... **$200**

MORNING GLORY (Unknown, ca. 1860)
Foot bath, footed oblong shape w/looped
    end handles, 20" l. (ILLUS., bottom of
    page) **$2,600**

Rare Morning Glory Foot Bath

NANKIN (Wm. Davenport, ca. 1850)
Cup & saucer, handleless $150
Plate, 10 1/2" d. $125
Teapot, cov. $750
Vegetable bowl, cov. $450
Vegetable bowl, open, rectangular, 8" l......... $250

NEOPOLITAN (Johnson Bros., ca. 1900)

Neopolitan Platter

Platter, 16" l. (ILLUS.) $225
Soup tureen, cov. $250

NON PAREIL (Burgess & Leigh - Middleport Potteries, ca. 1891)

Non Pareil Pattern Covered Vegetable

Vegetable dish, cov., oval (ILLUS.)............... $325

NORMANDY (Johnson Bros., ca. 1900)
Bowl, berry, 5" d.. $45
Butter pat, 3 1/2" d....................................... $55
Cup & saucer, handled................................. $95
Gravy boat $175
Plate, 7" d... $55
Plate, 8" d... $60
Plate, 9" d... $65

Normandy Soup Plate

Soup plate w/flanged rim, 10" d. (ILLUS.) $95
Vegetable dish, open, tab handles, 9 1/2" l. .. $175

OLYMPIA (Johnson Bros., ca. 1890)

Olympia Pitcher

Pitcher, 7" h. (ILLUS.)................................... $150

OLYMPIA (W. H. Grindley & Co., ca. 1894)

Olympia Covered Soup Tureen

Soup tureen, cov., round (ILLUS.) $300

OREGON (T.J. and J. Mayer, ca. 1845)
Creamer, pumpkin shape............................. $350
Creamer, classic Gothic, 5" h. $350

Oregon Flow Blue Cup Plate

Cup plate, 4" d. (ILLUS.)................................ $150

Fine Oregon Flow Blue Vegetable Dish

Cup & saucer, handleless cup, the set.......... **$175**

Oregon Flow Blue 6" h Pitcher

Pitcher, 6" h. (ILLUS.) **$450**
Plate, 7 1/2" d. **$95**
Plate, 9 1/2" d. **$110**
Plate, 10 1/2" d. **$125**
Platter, 12" l. **$350**
Platter, 14" l. **$400**
Platter, 16" d. **$475**
Platter, 18" d. **$550**

Flow Blue Oregon Relish Dish

Relish dish, oblong fluted shape (ILLUS.)..... **$195**
Sugar bowl, cov., Primary shape.................. **$350**
Sugar bowl, cov., pumpkin shape **$450**
Teapot, cov. **$750**
Teapot, cov., Classic Gothic body shape
(ILLUS., top next column) **$650**

Early Mayer Oregon Pattern Teapot

Teapot, cov., pumpkin shape......................... **$750**
Vegetable dish, cov., footed oblong shape
w/ruffled rim & loop end handles, rose
bud finial (ILLUS., top of page) **$650**

Rare Oregon Wash Bowl & Pitcher Set

Wash bowl & pitcher set, bowl 13 1/2" d.,
pitcher 13" h., the set (ILLUS.)................ **$2,500**

Waste bowl $250

ORIENTAL (Unknown maker, ca. 1860)

Early Oriental Pattern Decorated Mug

Mug, cylindrical w/angled handle, gold &
polychrome trim (ILLUS.) $325

OSAKA (James Kent, Old Foley Pottery, ca. 1905)
Biscuit barrel $150

OSBORNE (Ridgways, ca. 1905)

Osborne Flow Blue Vegetable Dish

Vegetable dish, cov., oval (ILLUS.).............. $195

OSBORNE (unknown maker, late 19th c.)

Rare Persian Pattern Cheese Dome

Cheese dome & underplate, 13" h., the set
(ILLUS.).. $3,500

OXFORD (Johnson Bros., ca. 1900)

Johnson Bros. Oxford Gravy Boat & Tray

Gravy boat & undertray, 2 pcs. (ILLUS.)...... $145
Mustard jar, cov., 4 1/2" h. $275
Plate, 9" d... $65

PATAGONIA (Brown-Westhead, Moore & Co., registry mark September 12, 1878)

Patagonia Dinner Plate

Plate, dinner, 10 1/4" d. (ILLUS.) $125

PEKIN (Arthur J. Wilkinson, ca. 1909) (Royal Staffordshire)
Tea cup & saucer $65

PELEW (Edward Challinor, ca. 1840)
Pitcher, water, 9" h. $900
Plate, 7 1/2" d.. $110
Plate, 10 1/2" d.. $150
Punch cup $200
Relish dish $275
Soup plate, 10 1/2" d. $175
Teapot, classic Gothic style $650
Teapot, cov., pumpkin shape........................ $650
Teapot, cov., Long Decagon body shape
(ILLUS., top next page).......................... $1,400

Pelew Pattern Teapot in Long Decagon Body Shape

Two Pelew Pattern Teapots in the Grape Octagon Shape

Teapot, cov., Grape Octagon body shape, each (ILLUS. in two size variations, middle of page) **$650**

Vegetable dish, open, rectangular w/cut-corners, 7 5/8" l. **$250**

PINWHEEL (Unknown maker, ca. 1840)

Pinwheel Gaudy Flow Blue Cup & Saucer

Cup & saucer, handleless cup, gaudy decoration, the set (ILLUS.) **$125**

RELIEF-MOLDED JUGS (makers unknown, mid-19th c.)

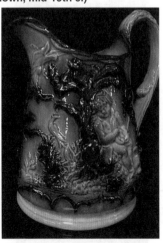

Boy with Nest Relief-molded Jug

Boy with Nest patt., tree & bird trimmed w/copper lustre, 5 1/2" h. (ILLUS., previous page) **$350**

Cherub Resting Against Tree Jug

Cherub Resting Against Tree patt., copper lustre trim, 5 1/2" h. (ILLUS.) **$350**

Molded Foresters' Arms Jug

Foresters' Arms patt. (ILLUS.) **$450**

Goldenrod Relief-molded Jug

Goldenrod patt., squared body w/beaded edges, copper lustre trim (ILLUS.) **$225**

Flow Blue Molded Pears Pattern Jug

Pears patt., 7 1/2" h. (ILLUS.) **$275**

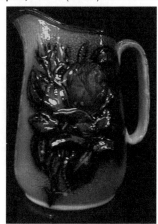

Rose Pattern Relief-molded Jug

Rose patt., copper lustre trim, 7 1/4" h. (ILLUS.) **$295**

Three Cherubs Pattern Jug

Three Cherubs patt., cov., footed, dark
blue around top & base (ILLUS., previous
page) $650
Tulip patt., 7" h. $250
Tulip patt., 8" h. $250

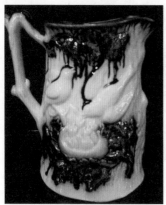

Two Birds with Chicks in Nest Jug

Two Birds with Chicks in Nest patt.,
6 1/2" h. (ILLUS.) $350

RICHMOND (Alfred Meakin, ca. 1891)
Bone dish $75

ROSE (W. H. Grindley & Co., ca. 1893)
Bone dish $65
Plate, 7" d. $45
Plate, 9" d. $55
Platter, 16" l. (ILLUS., top next column)......... $275
Rim soup, flanged edge, 9" d. $65

ROYAL (F. Winkle & Co., ca. 1900)
Soup tureen, cover & underplate $350

Rose Pattern Platter

SCINDE (J. & G. Alcock, ca. 1840)

Scinde Flow Blue Octagonal Pitcher

Pitcher, footed, octagonal, angled handle
(ILLUS.)... $295
Platter, 14" l. (ILLUS., bottom of page) $450

Scinde Pattern 14" l. Platter

Scinde Flow Blue 18" Platter

Platter, 18" l. (ILLUS., top of page) **$450**

Scinde Flow Blue Potato Bowl

Potato bowl, round (ILLUS.)......................... **$395**

Scinde Gothic-shaped Sugar Bowl

Sugar bowl, cov., Full Panel Gothic style
(ILLUS.).. **$450**

SCROLL (Wm. Davenport, ca. 1830)

Scroll Meat Well & Tree Platter

Platter, 22" l., w/meat well (ILLUS.) **$650**

SHANGHAE (Jacob Furnival & Co., ca. 1860)

9" Shanghae Plate

Plate, 9" d., 14-sided (ILLUS.)........................ **$150**
Platter, 18" l. **$350**
Relish dish **$265**
Teapot, cov. **$750**

Grindley Shanghai Open Compote

SHANGHAI (W. H. Grindley & Co., ca. 1898)

Butter pat $55
Charger, 11" d.. $300
Compote, open, shallow bowl on pedestal
    base (ILLUS., top of page)........................ $325
Compote, w/pedestal $325
Pitcher, 8" h. $325
Plate, 10" d. $100
Platter, 14" d. $225

Vegetable dish, cov., oval $250

SHAPOO (Thomas Hughes, ca. 1860)

Early Shapoo Octagonal Sugar Bowl

Sugar bowl, cov., footed octagonal shape
    (ILLUS.)... $350

Shanghai Four-Piece Sauce Tureen

Sauce tureen, cover, ladle & underplate,
    4 pcs. (ILLUS.) $450
Soup tureen, cover & undertray, 3 pcs.
    (ILLUS., bottom of page)........................ $1,525

Rare Shanghai Three-Piece Soup Tureen

Shell Flow Blue Pattern 16" Platter

SHELL (Wood & Challinor, ca. 1840; E. Challinor, ca. 1860)
Platter, 16" l. (ILLUS., top of page) $450

SIMLA (Elsmore & Forster, ca. 1860)
Platter, 14" l. $250

SINGA (Cork, Edge & Malkin, ca. 1865)

Singa Loving Cup

Loving cup/tyg, two-handled, 5" h., 4 3/4" d., 8 1/4" w. from handle to handle (ILLUS.) $350

SOBRAON (Unknown, probably English, ca.1850)
Creamer, pumpkin-shaped (ILLUS., top next column) $395
Platter, 15" l. $350
Platter, 20" l. $550
Waste bowl $325

SUTHERLAND (Doulton & Co., ca. 1905)
Gravy boat, cov. $150

SUTTON (Ridgways, ca. 1900)
Plate, 10" d. $65

Sobraon Pumpkin-shaped Creamer

TEUTONIC (Brown-Westhead, Moore & Co. - Cauldon, ca. 1868)

Teutonic Platter

Platter, 20" l. (ILLUS.) $350

Adams Tonquin Pattern Mitten-shaped Relish Dish

TONQUIN (Wm. Adams & Son, ca. 1845)
Relish dish, mitten-shaped (ILLUS., top of
page) $225

TOURAINE (Henry Alcock & Co., ca. 1898)
Bone dish $95
Butter dish, cov. $275
Cake plate, w/tab handles, 9 1/2" d. $175
Creamer $250
Creamer & cov. sugar bowl, pr. $495

Touraine Cup & Saucer

Cup & saucer, handled (ILLUS.) $95
Gravy boat $200
Milk jug, 6" h. $450
Pitcher, milk, large $750
Plate, 7" d. $50
Plate, 8" d. $60
Plate, 8 3/4" d. $60
Plate, 9" d. $60
Plate, luncheon, 9" d. $60
Plate, 10" d. $95
Platter, 15" oval $250
Soup plate, 7 1/2" d. $85
Sugar bowl, cov. $250
Teapot, cov., fluted urn-form unnamed body
    shape (ILLUS., bottom of page) $750
Teapot, cov. $750
Vegetable bowl, cov. $275
Vegetable bowl, individual size, 5 1/2" w. $125
Vegetable bowl, open, 9" l., oval $120

Alcock Touraine Pattern Flow Blue Teapot

Very Rare Troy Soup Tureen Set

Touraine Waste Bowl

Waste bowl (ILLUS.)..................................... **$175**

TROY (Charles Meigh, ca. 1840)
Soup tureen, cover, ladle & undertray,
the set (ILLUS., top of page).................. **$3,750**

TURKEY (Unknown maker, ca. 1900)

Flow Blue Turkey Platter by Unknown Maker

Platter, 20" l., gold trim (ILLUS.) **$425**

VIRGINIA (John Maddock & Sons, ca. 1891)
Butter pat **$50**

Virginia Pitcher

Pitcher, water, 9" h. (ILLUS.) **$375**

Virginia Platter

Platter, 16" l. (ILLUS.) **$275**
Vegetable dish, cov..................................... **$225**

Waverly Covered Soup Tureen

WAGON WHEEL (unknown maker, brush-stroke, ca. 1860)

Early Flow Blue Wagon Wheel Mug

Mug (ILLUS.) $125

WALDORF (New Wharf Pottery & Co., ca. 1892)

Waldorf Pattern 10" d. Plate

Plate, 10" d. (ILLUS.)....................................... $95

WARWICK PANSY (Warwick China Co., American, ca. 1900)
Cake plate, w/tab handles, 10 1/2" l. $200
Candy dish, flutes (scalloped), 5" d.............. $125
Celery dish, 4 x 9" oblong $225
Chocolate pot, cov., 8" h.............................. $850
Cup, chocolate $300
Dresser tray $210
Pitcher, 7" h. $275
Syrup pitcher w/undertray, 8" h.................. $375

WARWICK (Podmore, Walker & Co., ca. 1850)
Jardiniere $525

WAVERLY (John Maddock & Son, ca. 1891)
Butter pat $50
Plate, 8" d... $55
Platter, 16" l. $295
Soup tureen, cov. (ILLUS., top of page)........ $350
Vegetable bowl, open $120

WAVERLY (W.H. Grindley & Co., ca. 1891)

Grindley Waverly 14" Platter

Platter, 14" l. (ILLUS.) $250

WILLOW (Keeling & Co., ca. 1886)
Teapot, cov., oval tankard shape (ILLUS., top of next page) $450

Keeling & Co. Willow Pattern Teapot

YORK (Cauldon, Ltd., ca. 1905)
Tea cup & saucer $65
Waste bowl, 5" d. $125

Franciscan Ware

A product of Gladding, McBean & Company of Glendale and Los Angeles, California, Franciscan Ware was one of a number of lines produced by that firm over its long history. Introduced in 1934 as a pottery dinnerware, Franciscan Ware was produced in many patterns including "Desert Rose," introduced in 1941 and reportedly the most popular dinnerware pattern ever made in this country. Beginning in 1942 some vitrified china patterns were also produced under the Franciscan name.

After a merger in 1963 the company name was changed to Interpace Corporation and in 1979 Josiah Wedgwood & Sons purchased the Gladding, McBean & Company plant from Interpace. American production ceased in 1984.

Franciscan Mark

Ashtray, Apple patt., 4 1/2 x 9" oval $95
Ashtray, Apple patt., 4 3/4" sq. $150
Ashtray, Desert Rose patt., 4 3/4 x 9" oval $85
Ashtray, Desert Rose patt., square $125
Ashtray, El Patio tableware, coral satin glaze $8
Ashtray, individual, Apple patt., apple-shaped, 4" w., 4 1/2" l. $28
Ashtray, individual, California Poppy patt. $65
Ashtray, individual, Desert Rose patt., 3 1/2" d. $22
Ashtray, individual, Ivy patt., leaf-shaped, 4 1/2" l. $32
Ashtray, individual, Wildflower patt., Mariposa Lily shape, 3 1/2" d. $95
Baker, half-apple-shaped, Apple patt., 4 3/4" w., 5 1/4" l., 1 3/4" h. $225
Baking dish, Apple patt., 1 qt. $275

Baking dish, Cafe Royal patt., 8 3/4 x 9 1/2", 1 qt. $160
Baking dish, Desert Rose patt., 1 qt. $208
Baking dish, October patt., 1 qt. $100
Baking dish, Apple patt., 1 1/2 qt. $350
Baking dish, Desert Rose patt., 9 x 14", 2 1/4" h., 1 1/12 qt. $225
Baking dish, Meadow Rose patt., 9 x 14", 1 1/2 qt. $145
Bank, figural pig, Desert Rose patt. $160
Bell, Desert Rose patt., Danbury Mint, 4 1/4" h. $65
Bell, Cafe Royal patt., 3 3/4" d., 6" h. $65
Bell, dinner, Franciscan $95
Bowl, bouillon soup, cov., 4 1/2" d., Desert Rose patt. $275
Bowl, fruit, 4 1/2" d., California Poppy patt. $33
Bowl, fruit, 5 1/4" d., Apple patt., ca. 1940 ...... $11
Bowl, fruit, 5 1/4" d., Desert Rose patt. $12
Bowl, fruit, 5 1/2" d., Ivy patt. $15
Bowl, fruit, 5 1/2" d., Wildflower patt. $95
Bowl, soup, footed, 5 1/2", Apple patt. $32
Bowl, soup, footed, 5 1/2" d., Desert Rose patt. $32
Bowl, soup, footed, 5 1/2" d., Ivy patt. $36
Bowl, cereal, 6" d., Desert Rose patt. $18
Bowl, cereal or soup, 6" d., Apple patt., ca. 1940 .... $16
Bowl, cereal or soup, 6" d., Fresh Fruit patt. $18
Bowl, cereal or soup, 6" d., Ivy patt. $25
Bowl, cereal or soup, 6" d., Meadow Rose patt. $12
Bowl, cereal or soup, 6" d., Wildflower patt. .. $125
Bowl, 7" d., Picnic patt. $8
Bowl, cereal, 7" d., October patt. $18
Bowl, salad, 10" d., Apple patt. $95
Bowl, salad, 10" d., Desert Rose patt. $95
Bowl, salad, 10" d., Wildflower patt. $450
Bowl, salad, 11" d., Daisy patt. $45
Bowl, salad, 11 1/4" d., Ivy patt., green rim band $145
Bowl, fruit, Arden patt. $12
Box, cov., Desert Rose patt., heart-shaped, 4 1/2" l., 2 1/2" h. $175
Box, cov., Desert Rose patt., egg-shaped, 1 1/2 x 4 3/4" .... $350+
Box, cov., Apple patt., round, 4 3/4" d., 1 1/2" h. .... $245+
Box, cov., Twilight Rose patt., heart-shaped .. $225
Butter dish, cov., Apple patt. $40

Westwood Coffee & Tea Service

Butter dish, cov., California Poppy patt......... $175
Butter dish, cov., Desert Rose patt. $45
Butter dish, cov., Ivy patt................................. $75
Butter dish, cov., October patt. $55
Butter dish, cov., Twilight Rose patt............. $125
Candleholders, Apple patt., pr. $95
Candleholders, Desert Rose patt., pr.............. $75
Candleholders, Starburst patt., pr. $225
Casserole, cov., Apple patt., 1 1/2 qt.............. $90
Casserole, cov., Apple patt., in metal holder
.... $1,500
Casserole, cov., Apple patt., individual size,
    handled, 4" d., 3 1/4" h................................. $60
Casserole, cov., Desert Rose patt., 1 1/2
    qt., 4 3/4" h. $95
Casserole, cov., Desert Rose patt., 2 1/2 qt.
.... $245
Casserole, cov., Wildflower patt., 1 1/2 qt.
.... $850
Celery dish, Apple patt., 7 3/4 x 15 1/2" $28
Cigarette box, cov., Apple patt.,
    3 1/2 x 4 1/2, 2" h. $140
Cigarette box, cov., Desert Rose patt.,
    3 1/2 x 4 1/2", 2" h....................................... $150
Coaster, Apple patt., 3 3/4" d. $53
Coffee server, El Patio tableware, red/or-
    ange glossy glaze (ILLUS., top next col-
    umn).. $40
Coffee server, El Patio tableware, tur-
    quoise glossy glaze $40

El Patio Coffee Server

Coffee & tea service: cov. coffeepot, cov.
    teapot, round serving plate, creamer &
    cov. sugar; Fine China, Westwood patt.,
    the set (ILLUS., top of page)..................... $165
Coffeepot, cov., 10" h., Daisy patt. $65
Coffeepot, cov., Apple patt., ... $100
Coffeepot, cov., demitasse, Coronado Ta-
    ble Ware, coral satin glaze (ILLUS. rear,
    w/demitasse pieces, bottom of page) $95

Coronado Demitasse Pieces

Coffeepot, cov., Desert Rose patt., 7 1/2" h. $140

Coffeepot, cov., Ivy patt., green rim band, 7 1/2" h. $235

Coffeepot, individual, cov., Desert Rose patt. $425

Compote, open, Apple patt., 8" d., 4" h. $75

Compote, open, Desert Rose patt., 8" d., 4" h. $65

Compote, open, Meadow Rose patt., 8" d., 4" h. $85

Condiment set: oil & vinegar cruets w/original stoppers, cov. mustard jar & three-part tray; Starburst patt., the set $275

Cookie jar, cov., Apple patt. $245

Cookie jar, cov., Desert Rose patt. $200

Creamer, Apple patt. $21

Creamer, Bountiful patt. $35

Creamer, Desert Rose patt., 4 1/4" h. $28

Creamer, individual, Desert Rose patt., 3 1/2" h. $65

Creamer, Ivy patt., 4" h. $30

Creamer, October patt. $24

Creamer & cov. sugar bowl, Apple patt., pr. $55

Creamer & cov. sugar bowl, Daisy patt., pr. $45

Creamer & cov. sugar bowl, Desert Rose patt., pr. $55

Creamer & cov. sugar bowl, El Patio tableware, Mexican blue glossy glaze, pr. $35

Creamer & cov. sugar bowl, individual, Apple patt., pr. $53

Creamer & cov. sugar bowl, Ivy patt., pr. $90

Creamer & cov. sugar bowl, Meadow Rose patt., pr. $45

Creamer & cov. sugar bowl, October patt., pr. $45

Creamer & open sugar bowl, individual, Desert Rose patt., pr. $140

Creamer & open sugar bowl, individual, El Patio Nuevo patt., orange, pr. $50

Creamer & open sugar bowl, Tiempo patt., lime green, pr. $25

Cup & saucer, Apple patt. $9

Cup & saucer, Apple patt., jumbo size $78

Cup & saucer, Arden patt. $15

Cup & saucer, California Poppy patt. $35

Cup & saucer, Coronado Table Ware, coral satin glaze $10

Cup & saucer, demitasse, Apple patt. $55

Cup & saucer, demitasse, Coronado, various colors, each set (ILLUS. of variety of colors w/demitasse coffeepot, bottom previous page) $22-28

Cup & saucer, demitasse, Desert Rose patt. $42

Cup & saucer, demitasse, El Patio tableware, golden glow glossy glaze $18

Cup & saucer, demitasse, El Patio tableware, Mexican blue glossy glaze $20

Cup & saucer, demitasse, El Patio tableware, turquoise glossy glaze...................... $18

Cup & saucer, Desert Rose patt., jumbo size $60

Cup & saucer, Desert Rose patt., tall $55

Cup & saucer, El Patio tableware, glossy yellow glaze.. $6

Cup & saucer, Ivy patt. $22

Cup & saucer, October patt............................. $16

Cup & saucer, Starburst patt. $16

Cup & saucer, tea, Desert Rose patt. $5

Cup & saucer, Twilight Rose patt. $26

Dinner service: 6 each dinner plates, soup plates, berry bowls, cups & saucers, 3 salad plates, one each open sugar bowl, creamer, oval platter & vegetable bowl; Coronado patt., matte coral, the set $135

Dish, Desert Rose patt., heart-shaped, 5 3/4" l. $95

Eggcup, Apple patt., double $32

Eggcup, Desert Rose patt., 2 3/4" d., 3 3/4" h. $36

Eggcup, Meadow Rose patt., 2 3/4 d., 3 3/4" h. $36

Eggcup, Twilight Rose patt., 2 3/4" d., 3 3/4" h. $350

Ginger jar, cov., Apple patt. $395

Ginger jar, cov., Desert Rose patt. $295

Goblet, footed, Desert Rose patt., 6 1/2" h. ... $225

Goblet, Meadow Rose patt., 6 1/2" h. $85

Goblet, Picnic patt., 6 1/2" h. $20

Gravy boat, Arden patt. $65

Gravy boat, California Poppy patt. $95

Gravy boat, Desert Rose patt. $45

Gravy boat, Tiempo patt., lime green $20

Gravy boat w/attached undertray, Apple patt. $42

Gravy boat w/attached undertray, Desert Rose patt. $42

Gravy boat w/attached undertray, Ivy patt. $62

Hurricane lamp, Desert Rose patt. $325

Jam jar, cov., Apple patt., redesigned style ... $275

Jam jar, cov., Desert Rose patt. $95

Microwave dish, oblong, Desert Rose patt., 1 1/2 qt. $275

Mixing bowl, Apple patt., 6" d. $75

Mixing bowl, Apple patt., 7 1/2" d. $95

Mixing bowl, Apple patt., 9" d. $125

Mixing bowl, Desert Rose patt., 6" d. $75

Mixing bowl, Desert Rose patt., 7 1/2" d. $95

Mixing bowl, Desert Rose patt., 9" d. $125

Mixing bowl set, Apple patt., 3 pcs. $350

Mixing bowl set, Desert Rose patt., 3 pcs. ... $350

Mug, Apple patt., 10 oz. $120

Mug, Apple patt., 17 oz., rare $110

Mug, Apple patt., 7 oz. $28

Mug, Cafe Royal patt., 7 oz............................. $16

Mug, Desert Rose patt., 10 oz. $125

Mug, Desert Rose patt., 12 oz. $65

Mug, Desert Rose patt., 7 oz. $18

Mug, Meadow Rose patt. $25

Napkin ring, Desert Rose patt. $45

Pepper mill, Duet patt.................................... $75

Pepper mill, Starburst patt.............................. $165

Pickle dish, Desert Rose patt., 4 1/2 x 11"...... $42

Pickle/relish boat, Desert Rose patt., interior decoration, 4 1/2 x 11" $350

Pitcher, water, Coronado Table Ware, burgundy glaze $75

Pitcher, 4" h., Desert Rose patt. $395

Pitcher, milk, 6 1/4" h., Apple patt., 1 qt. $90

Pitcher, milk, 6 1/2" h., Desert Rose patt., 1 qt. $85

Pitcher, milk, 8 1/2" h., Daisy patt.................... $50

Pitcher, water, 8 3/4" h., Apple patt., 2 qt. $125

Pitcher, water, 8 3/4" h., Desert Rose patt., 2 1/2 qt. $95

Various El Patio Plates & Tumblers

Pitcher w/ice lip, El Patio tableware, golden glow glossy glaze, 2 1/2 qt. $65

Pitcher w/ice lip, El Patio tableware, turquoise glossy glaze, 2 1/2 qt. $85

Plate, bread & butter, Arden patt. $6

Plate, dinner, Arden patt. $15

Plate, luncheon, 9 1/2" d., Coronado Table Ware, coral satin glaze................................ $10

Plate, luncheon, Arden patt. $12

Plate, salad, Arden patt. $8

Plate, bread & butter, 6 1/4" d., California Poppy patt. $15

Plate, bread & butter, 6 1/4" d., Ivy patt........... $10

Plate, bread & butter, 6 1/2" d., Apple patt. $6

Plate, bread & butter, 6 1/2" d., Desert Rose patt. $6

Plate, bread & butter, 6 1/2" d., El Patio, apple green (ILLUS. w/various El Patio plates & tumblers, top of page) $6

Plate, bread & butter, 6 1/2" d., October patt. $8

Plate, bread & butter, 6 1/2" d., Wildflower patt. $45

Plate, coupe dessert, 7 1/4" d., Meadow Rose patt. $29

Plate, coupe dessert, 7 1/2" d., Apple patt. $65

Plate, coupe dessert, 7 1/2" d., Desert Rose patt. $65

Plate, dessert, 7 1/2" d., El Patio, Mexican blue (ILLUS. w/various El Patio plates & tumblers, top of page) $12

Plate, salad, 8" d., California Poppy patt. $45

Plate, snack, 8" sq., Apple patt...................... $145

Plate, snack, 8" sq., Desert Rose patt. $125

Plate, side salad, 4 1/2 x 8", Apple patt., crescent-shaped.. $38

Plate, side salad, 4 1/2 x 8", Desert Rose patt., crescent-shaped................................ $35

Plate, side salad, 4 1/2 x 8", Ivy patt., crescent-shaped $49

Plate, side salad, 4 1/2 x 8, Meadow Rose patt., crescent-shaped................................ $29

Plate, salad, 8 1/2" d., Apple patt. $16

Plate, salad, 8 1/2" d., Desert Rose patt. $13

Plate, salad, 8 1/2" d., El Patio, bright yellow (ILLUS. w/various El Patio plates & tumblers, top of page) $14

Plate, salad, 8 1/2" d., Ivy patt......................... $28

Plate, salad, 8 1/2" d., Meadow Rose patt. $15

Plate, salad, 8 1/2" d., October patt. $16

Plate, salad, 8 1/2" d., Picnic patt...................... $8

Plate, salad, 8 1/2" d., Wildflower patt............. $95

Plate, child's, 7 x 9" oval, divided, Desert Rose patt., ... $125

Plate, child's, 7 1/4 x 9", divided, Apple patt. .. $145

Plate, luncheon, 9 1/4" d., Ivy patt................... $28

Plate, luncheon, 8 1/2" d., El Patio, coral satin (ILLUS. w/various El Patio plates & tumblers, top of page) $14

Plate, luncheon, 9 1/2" d., Apple patt. $19

Plate, luncheon, 9 1/2" d., Coronado Table Ware, glossy coral glaze............................ $10

Coronado Table Ware Luncheon Plate

Plate, luncheon, 9 1/2" d., Coronado Table Ware, matt ivory glaze (ILLUS.).................... $8

Plate, luncheon, 9 1/2" d., Desert Rose patt. $22

Plate, luncheon, 9 1/2" d., Wildflower patt...... $125

Plate, small dinner, 9 1/2" d., El Patio, maroon (ILLUS. w/various El Patio plates & tumblers, top of page) $14

Plate, dinner, 10 1/4" d., Ivy patt. $32

Plate, coupe, party w/cup well, 10 1/2" d., Desert Rose patt. $160

Plate, dinner, 10 1/2" d., Apple patt................. $15

Plate, dinner, 10 1/2" d., California Poppy patt. $32

Plate, dinner, 10 1/2" d., Coronado Table Ware, coral satin glaze $10

Plate, dinner, 10 1/2" d., Coronado Table
Ware, ivory matte glaze $16

Desert Rose Dinner Plate

Plate, dinner, 10 1/2" d., Desert Rose patt.
(ILLUS.).. $23
Plate, dinner, 10 1/2" d., Meadow Rose
patt. $26
Plate, dinner, 10 1/2" d., October patt. $28
Plate, dinner, 10 1/2" d., Picnic patt. $10
Plate, dinner, 10 1/2" d., Wildflower patt. $65
Plate, large dinner, 10 1/2" d., grey (ILLUS.
w/various El Patio plates & tumblers, top
of previous page) $26
Plate, coupe, steak,11" l., Apple patt............. $125
Plate, coupe, steak, 11" l., Desert Rose
patt. $125
Plate, grill, 11" d., Apple patt. $95
Plate, grill or buffet, 11" d., Desert Rose
patt. $75
Plate, chop, 11 1/2" d., Desert Rose patt. $52
Plate, chop, 12" d., Apple patt. $65
Plate, chop, 12" d., California Poppy patt...... $125
Plate, chop, 12" d., Wildflower patt................. $325
Plate, T.V. w/cup well, 8 x 13 1/2", Ivy patt. ... $125
Plate, chop, 14" d., Apple patt. $95
Plate, chop, 14" d., Desert Rose patt. $125
Plate, chop, 14" d., Ivy patt............................ $155
Plate, chop, 14" d., Wildflower patt................. $350
Plate, chop, 14" d., Willow tableware (1937-
40).. $145
Plate, T.V. w/cup well, 14" l., Desert Rose
patt. $125
Plate, T.V. w/cup well, 8 1/4 x 14", Starburst
patt. $75
Platter, 13" l., California Poppy patt. $150
Platter, 11" l., oval, Arden patt. $45
Platter, 11 1/4" l., Ivy patt. $65
Platter, 8 1/2 x 12" oval, Cafe Royal patt. $32
Platter, 12 3/4" l., Apple patt. $38
Platter, 12 3/4" l., Desert Rose patt. $38
Platter, 13" l., oval, Ivy patt. $67
Platter, 14" l., Apple patt. $55
Platter, 14" l., Desert Rose patt. $65
Platter, 14" l., Meadow Rose patt.................... $36
Platter, 14" l., October patt.............................. $65
Platter, 14" l. oval, Wildflower patt. $425
Platter, 15" l., Starburst patt. $75
Platter, 19" l., oval, Apple patt........................ $225
Platter, 19" l., oval, Ivy patt., green rim band .. $300

Platter, 19" l., turkey-size, Desert Rose
patt., ... $225
Platter, 19" l., turkey-size, Meadow Rose
patt. $195
Relish dish, Ivy patt., 4 1/2 x 10 1/2".............. $65
Relish dish, three-part, Apple patt.,
11 3/4" l.. $70
Relish dish, three-part, oval, Desert Rose
patt., 12" l. $67
Relish/pickle dish, Wildflower patt., interior
design, 4 1/4 x 12" oval............................. $245
Salt & pepper shakers, Apple patt.,
2 1/4" h., pr... $23
Salt & pepper shakers, Apple patt.,
6 1/4" h., pr... $95
Salt & pepper shakers, Arden patt., pr. $18
Salt & pepper shakers, California Poppy
patt., 2 3/4" h., pr.. $55
Salt & pepper shakers, Desert Rose patt.,
6 1/4" h., pr... $55
Salt & pepper shakers, figural rose bud,
Desert Rose patt., pr.................................. $22
Salt & pepper shakers, Ivy patt., 2 3/4" h.,
pr.. $45
Salt & pepper shakers, Meadow Rose
patt., 6 1/4" h., pr.. $35
Salt & pepper shakers, October patt., pr......... $35
Salt & pepper shakers, Strawberry Time
patt., 3" h., pr.. $45
Salt shaker & pepper mill, Daisy patt., pr. $95
Salt shaker & pepper mill, Desert Rose
patt., 6" h., pr.. $225
Salt shaker & pepper mill, Meadow Rose
patt., 6" h., pr.. $145
Serving bowl, Cafe Royal patt., aka Long &
Narrow, 7 3/4 x 15 1/2", 2 1/4" h. $225
Serving bowl, Desert Rose patt., aka Long
& Narrow, 7 3/4 x 15 1/2", 2 1/4 " h. $350
Sherbet, Apple patt., footed, 4" d., 2 1/2" h. $24
Sherbet, Coronado Table Ware, ivory matte
glaze $12
Sherbet, Desert Rose patt., footed, 4" d.,
2 1/2" h... $24
Sherbet, Ivy patt., footed, 4" d., 2 1/2" h. $32
Soup bowl, footed, Desert Rose patt. $28
Soup bowl, rimmed, Desert Rose patt. $35
Soup plate w/flanged rim, Apple patt.,
8 1/2" d... $28
Soup plate w/flanged rim, Arden patt. $15
Soup plate w/flanged rim, Ivy patt.,
8 1/2" d... $45
Soup tureen, cov., Desert Rose patt. $525
Sugar bowl, cov., Apple patt., 3" h. $25
Sugar bowl, cov., Bountiful patt....................... $45
Sugar bowl, cov., Coronado Table Ware,
glossy coral glaze $14
Sugar bowl, cov., Desert Rose patt................. $38
Sugar bowl, cov., Ivy patt. $35
Sugar bowl, cov., October patt. $25
Sugar bowl, cov., Strawberry Time patt. $30
Sugar bowl, open, individual size, Desert
Rose patt.. $75
Syrup pitcher, Apple patt., 1 pt, 6 1/4" h. $82
Syrup pitcher, Desert Rose patt., 1 pt.,
6 1/2" h. $85
Syrup pitcher, Starburst patt., 5 3/4" h. $65
Tea canister, cov., Desert Rose patt. $225
Tea set: cov. teapot, creamer & sugar bowl;
Coronado Table Ware, white, the set $85

Tea tile, Apple patt., 6" sq. $45
Teapot, cov., Apple patt., 6 3/4" h. $125
Teapot, cov., Arden patt. $95
Teapot, cov., Desert Rose patt., 6 1/2" h. $95

Franciscan Ware Desert Rose Teapot

Teapot, cov., Desert Rose patt., ca. 1960
(ILLUS.).. $100
Teapot, cov., individual size, Desert Rose
patt., 6 1/4" h. $295
Teapot, cov., Ivy patt., green rim band,
5 1/2" h. $225
Thimble, Desert Rose patt., 1" h. $55
Tidbit tray, two-tier, center handle, Ivy patt. .. $145
Tidbit tray, two-tier, Desert Rose patt. $95
Tile, Desert Rose patt., 6" sq. $45
Toast cover, Desert Rose patt., 5 1/2" d.,
3" h. $145
Trivet, Apple patt., 6" d. $245
Trivet, Desert Rose patt., 6" d. $145
Tumbler, Apple patt., 10 oz., 5 1/4" h. $38
Tumbler, Apple patt., juice, 6 oz., 3 1/4" h. $30
Tumbler, California Poppy patt., water, 10
oz., 5 1/4" h. $125
Tumbler, Desert Rose patt., 10 oz.,
5 1/4" h. $38
Tumbler, Desert Rose patt., juice, 6 oz.,
3 1/4" h. $35
Tumbler, El Patio tableware, apple green
(ILLUS. w/various El Patio plates & tum-
blers, top of page 281) $28
Tumbler, El Patio tableware, coral glaze $28
Tumbler, El Patio tableware, flame orange
(ILLUS. w/various El Patio plates & tum-
blers, top of page 281) $28
Tumbler, El Patio tableware, glacial blue
glossy glaze (ILLUS. w/various El Patio
plates & tumblers, top of page 281) $28
Tumbler, El Patio tableware, golden glow
(ILLUS. w/various El Patio plates & tum-
blers, top of page 281) $28
Tumbler, El Patio tableware, Mexican blue
glossy glaze $28
Tumbler, El Patio tableware, redwood
glossy glaze $28
Tumbler, Ivy patt., 10 oz., 5" h. $55
Tumbler, Wildflower patt., water, 10 oz.,
5 1/2" h. $250
Tureen, cov., flat-bottomed, Desert Rose
patt., 8" d., 5" h. $425
Tureen, cov., footed, Apple patt., 8 3/4" d.,
5 3/4" h. $450
Vase, bud, 6" h., Desert Rose patt. $95
Vase, bud, 6" h., Meadow Rose patt. $65
Vegetable bowl, divided, Apple patt.,
7 x 10 3/4" $42

Vegetable bowl, divided, Desert Rose patt.,
7 x 10 3/4"... $55
Vegetable bowl, divided, Ivy patt.,
8 x 12 1/4" $95
Vegetable bowl, open, oval, Arden patt.,
large... $45
Vegetable bowl, open, oval, Daisy patt.,
6 3/4 x 13 3/4", 2 1/4" h................................ $38
Vegetable bowl, open, oval, Desert Rose
patt., 9" l. $35
Vegetable bowl, open, round, Apple patt.,
7 3/4" d.. $35
Vegetable bowl, open, round, Apple patt.,
8 1/4" d.. $45
Vegetable bowl, open, round, Apple patt.,
9" d... $50
Vegetable bowl, open, round, California
Poppy patt., 9" d... $125
Vegetable bowl, open, round, Desert Rose
patt., 8" d.. $24
Vegetable bowl, open, round, Ivy patt.,
7 1/4" d.. $45
Vegetable bowl, open, round, Ivy patt.,
8 1/4" d.. $47
Vegetable bowl, open, round, Wildflower
patt., 9" d.. $225

Frankoma

John Frank started his pottery company in 1933 in Norman, Oklahoma. However, when he moved the business to Sapula, Oklahoma, in 1938 he felt he was home. Still, Mr. Frank could not know the horrendous storms and trials that would follow him.

Just after his move, on Nov. 11, 1938, a fire destroyed the entire operation, which included the pot and leopard mark he had created in 1935. Then, in 1942, the war effort needed men and materials, so Frankoma could not survive. However, in 1943, John and Grace Lee Frank bought the plant as junk salvage and began again. The time in Norman had produced some of the finest art ware that John would ever create and most of the items were marked either "Frank Potteries," "Frank Pottery," or to a lesser degree, the "pot and leopard" mark. Today these marks are avidly and enthusiastically sought by collectors.

Another elusive mark wanted by collectors shows "Firsts Kiln Sapulpa 6-7-38." The mark was used for one day only and denotes the first firing in Sapulpa. It has been estimated that perhaps 50 to 75 pieces were fired on that day.

The clay Frankoma used is helpful to collectors in determining when an item was made. Creamy beige clay know as "Ada" clay was in use until 1953. Then a red brick shale was found in Sapulpa and used until about 1985 when, by the addition of an additive, the clay became a reddish pink. Rutile glazes were used early in Frankoma's history. Glazes with rutile have caused more confusion among collectors than any other glazes. For example, a Prairie Green piece shows a lot of green and it also has some brown. The same is true for the Desert Gold glaze; the piece shows a sandy-beige glaze with some amount of brown. Generally speaking, Prairie Green, Desert Gold, White Sand and Woodland Moss will be the most puzzling to collectors. In 1970 the government closed the rutile mines in America, and Frankoma had to buy it from Australia. It was not the same, and the results were different. Values are higher for the glazes with rutile. Also, the pre-Australian Woodland Moss glaze is more desirable than that created after 1970.

In 1973 John Frank died and his daughter, Joniece Frank, who was a ceramic designer at the pottery, became president of the company. In 1983 another fire destroyed everything Frankoma had worked so hard to create. They rebuilt but in 1990, after the IRS shut the doors for nonpayment, Joniece, true to the Frank legacy, filed for Chapter 11 (instead of bankruptcy) so she could reopen and continue the work she loved. In 1991 Richard Bernstein purchased the pottery and the name was changed to Frankoma Industries.

The company was sold again in 2006. The new buyers are concentrating mostly on dinnerware, none of which is like the old Frankoma. The company has a "Collectors Series," "Souvenir & State Items," and "Heartwarming Trivets." None of these is anything like what Frankoma originally created. The company is doing some Frankoma miniatures such as a dolphin on a wave, a fish, a wolf, a bear, etc. These, too, do not resemble Frankoma miniatures. All their glazes are new.

Frankoma Mark

Ashtray, oval shape w/a cocker spaniel sleeping on the top of one side, Prairie Green, 1942-49 .... **$195**

Frankoma Creative Ceramics Award

Award, Creative Ceramics, originally made for the San Antonio, Texas State Fair, a prize trophy given at art shows for the most original pottery items, Desert Gold medallion w/a person's profile & "Frankoma Pottery Award - Creative Ceramics" around the rim, Prairie Green vase, marked "Frankoma USA" & a piece of red unfired clay, late 1960s - early 1960s, 7" h. (ILLUS.) **$150**

Baker, cov., Wagon Wheel patt., Model No. 94w, Prairie Green, 3 qt. **$75**

Baker, Westwind patt., Model No. 6vs, Peach Glow glaze, 1 1/2 qt. **$38**

Bell, Joniece Frank wedding commemorative, 1-11-62, White Sand, unmarked, 1 3/4" h. **$67**

Bolo tie holder, in the shape of an arrowhead, original strap, White Sand **$65**

Bookends, Bucking Bronco, Model No. 423, Prairie Green glaze, 5 1/2" h., pr. (ILLUS., bottom of page) **$560**

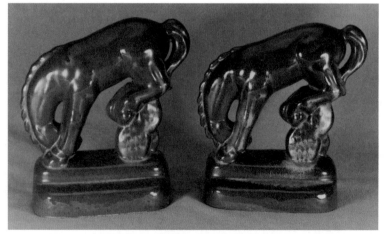

Frankoma Bucking Bronco Bookends

Ocelot Bookends

Bookends, model of a sea horse, Model No. 426, Prairie Green, 1934-38, 5" h., pr. **$2,000**

Frankoma Leopard Bookend

Bookends, model of leopard, Pompeian Bronze glaze, Model No. 431, 9" l., 5 1/2" h., pr. (ILLUS. of one) **$1,800**

Bookends, seated figure, Ivory glaze, Model No. 425, pot & leopard mark, 1934-38, 5 3/4" h., pr. **$1,400**

Bookends, Walking Ocelot on a two-tiered oblong base, black high glaze, Model No. 424, signed on reverse of tiered base "Taylor" denoting designer Joseph Taylor, pot & leopard mark on bottom, 7" l., 3" h., pr. (ILLUS., top of page) **$1,900**

Bottle-vase, V-1, 1969, limited edition, 4,000 created, small black foot w/Prairie Green body, 15" h. **$145**

Bottle-vase, V-7, limited edition, 3,500 created, Desert Gold glaze, body w/coffee glazed stopper & base, signed by Jo-niece Frank, 13" h. **$120**

Frankoma Advertising Bowl

Bowl, 5 3/4" d., shallow form, advertising "Oklahoma Gas Company - Golden Anniversary," 1956, Desert Gold, marked "Frankoma" (ILLUS.) **$186**

Bowl, 6 1/4" d., 3 1/2" h., deep round shape w/three full-figure Tiki gods around the sides, incised "Club Trade Winds, Tulsa, Okla. 6," Prairie Green, Sapulpa clay, early 1960s (ILLUS., bottom of page) **$195**

Unusual Frankoma Tiki God Bowl

Bowl, 11" l., divided, Lazybones patt., Brown Satin glaze, Model No. 4qd $25

Brooch, four-leaf clover-shape, Desert Gold glaze, w/original card, 1 1/4" h. $52

Candleholder, miniature, Aladdin lamp w/finger hold, Prairie Green, marked "Frankoma No. 305," 2 1/4" h. $155

Special Order Frankoma Carafe

Carafe & cover, footed bulbous body tapering to a short cylindrical neck, domed cover w/rounded tab handle, made from the No. 93 pitcher mold created in 1940 & discontinued in 1964, made for an organization, below the five-point colored star is the name "Ted Witt," reverse incised w/a sailboat on water & the dates 1946-47, Turquoise glaze, marked "Frankoma," 6 1/2" h. (ILLUS.) $90

Catalog, 1953, unnumbered sixteen pages, dated July 1, 1953, two versions for color cover, one w/photograph of Donna Frank or one w/photograph of Grace Lee Frank, each $55

Frankoma Fish Tray

Christmas card, figural fish tray, Woodland Moss glaze, marked, "1960 the Franks, Frankoma Christmas Frankoma," 4" l. (ILLUS.) $95

Christmas card, in the form of a creamer, Lazybones dinnerware patt., blue glaze, Ada clay, incised "Xmas - The Franks - 1953," 3" l., 2 1/4" h. (ILLUS., top next column) $95

1953 Frank Family Christmas Card

Christmas card, in the form of a creamer, Model No. 560, incised into Ada clay "Xmas - The Franks - 1948," Prairie Green glaze, rare, 2 1/4" h. $125

Christmas card, "Statue of Liberty Torch," White Sand glaze, created by Grace Lee Frank Smith for her & Dr. A. Milton Smith's friends, 1986, 3 1/2" l. $90

Christmas card tray, cork bark treatment, front marked "The Franks - Christmas 1958," the reverse marked "Frankoma," Desert Gold, 3 3/4" l., 1 1/4" h. $80

Christmas plate, marked "God's Chosen Family," 1987, White Sand, 8 1/2" d. $30

Christmas plate, marked "Good Will Toward Men," 1965, first edition, White Sand, 8 1/2" d. $250

Bronze Green Cigarette Box

Cigarette box, cov., rectangular, cover w/single raised & hard-to-find curved leaf handle, Bronze Green glaze, Ada clay, marked "Frankoma," 4 x 6 3/4", 3 1/2" h. (ILLUS.) $175

Dealer sign, plain wood frame w/milky white Plexiglas, two pencil-thin green borders, one inside the other & a tan artist's palette-type shape inside the green borders, marked "Frankoma Pottery Sold Here!," scarce, 12" sq. $155

Earrings, clip-on type, rectangular, Mayan-Aztec patt., pink, pr. $30

Figure group, a group of deer, Model No. 109, Bronze Green, pot & leopard mark, 9" l., 8 1/4" h. $2,500

Figure of Fan Dancer, seated, No. 113, Ivory glaze, Ada clay, 14" l., 9" h. $1,100

Figure of farmer boy, wearing dark blue overalls, light blue short-sleeved shirt, black scarf tied around neck, yellow hair & ivory wide-brim hat w/only brim showing from front, black shoes, bisque arms, hands, face & neck, marked "Frankoma 702," 6 3/4" h... **$150**

Figure of gardener girl, holding pale green apron to form a basket in front of her, light blue dress w/short puffed sleeves & scooped neckline, long yellow hair w/dark blue bow on top, bisque face, neck, arms & hands, marked "Frankoma 701," 5 3/4" h... **$160**

Frankoma Indian Chief Figure

Figure of Indian Chief, No. 142, Desert Gold glaze, Ada clay, 7" h. (ILLUS.) **$190**

Flower holder, figural, model of a miniature duck, Ada clay, 1942, Prairie Green, marked "Frankoma," rare, 3 1/2" h. **$325**

Rare Frankoma Miniature Flower Holder

Flower holder, model of a miniature hobby horse, Ada clay, 1942, Prairie Green, marked "Frankoma," rare, 3 1/2" h. (ILLUS.) .. **$340**

Jar, cov., rose form, black rim base & lid, Ivory body, #32, 1934-38, pot & leopard mark, 4 1/2" h. **$275**

Rare Early Model of Pekinese

Model of a Pekinese dog, standing on hind legs, designed by Joseph Taylor, 1934-38, glossy black glaze, marked "Frankoma," 7 1/2" h. (ILLUS.) **$590**

Model of fish, miniature, Turquoise, Ada clay, marked "Frankoma," 2 1/2" **$380**

Advertising Mortar & Pestle

Mortar & pestle, advertising "Schreibers Drug Store," White Sand, marked "Frankoma," 3 1/4" (ILLUS.)....................... **$145**

Mug, 1968, (Republican) elephant, white........ **$95**

Mug, 1970, (Republican) elephant.................. **$70**

Mug, 1971, (Republican) elephant.................. **$65**

Mug, 1973, (Republican) elephant.................. **$42**

Mug, 1974, Nixon/Ford elephant.................. **$565**

Frankoma Ornament

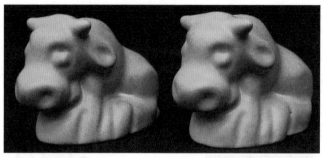

Unusual Frankoma Bull Head Salt & Pepper Shakers

Ornament, "The ABCs of life," gift w/purchase from Tulsa shopping mall, 1987, white background w/sketch of three children, 3 1/2" d. (ILLUS., previous page)........ **$69**

Pin, in the form of an Indian pot, Prairie Green, 1" h. **$40**

Pin, model of a bowling pin, red circle w/applied white bowling pin & applied black bowling ball, 1 1/4" d. **$45**

Pitcher, Mayan-Aztec patt., Nodel No. 7d, Desert Gold, 2 qt. **$55**

Pitcher, Wagon Wheel patt., Model No. 94d, Prairie Green glaze, Ada clay, 2 qt. **$85**

Plate, 8 1/2" d., Bicentennial Series, Limited Edition No. 1, "Provocations," eleven signers of the Declaration of Independence, White Sand glaze, 1972, misspelling of United States as "Staits"........... **$228**

Plate, 7" d., Wildlife Series, Limited Edition No. 1, Bobwhite quail, Prairie Green glaze, 1,000 produced................................ **$170**

Plate, 7 1/2" d., Easter 1972, "Jesus Is Not Here...He Is Risen," scene of Jesus' tomb **$32**

Political chip, John Frank's profile on front surrounded by the words, "Honest, Fair, Capable," & at bottom "Elect John Frank Representative 1962," obverse w/outline of Oklahoma state w/"One Frank" inside it, around it "Oklahomans deserve outstanding leadership" & "For statesmanship vote Republican," unglazed red brick color, 1 3/4" d., 1/8" h. **$38**

Political mug, Nixon-Ford, 1974, Coffee glaze, fewer than 500 made, very rare....... **$285**

Postcard, color photograph of Joniece Frank sitting w/various Frankoma products used to show the current Frankoma glazes, 5 1/2 x 6 1/2"..................................... **$20**

Salt & pepper shakers, figural, in the form of a bull head, Ada clay, matte yellow glaze, 1 3/4" h., pr. (ILLUS., top of page)... **$165**

Salt & pepper shakers, model of a Dutch shoe, Desert Gold glaze, Model No. 915h, ca. 1957-60, 4" l., pr.......................... **$75**

Salt & pepper shakers, model of an elephant, Desert Gold glaze, No. 160h, produced in 1942 only, Ada clay, 3" h., pr....... **$210**

Sign, advertising "Pottery Show - Calif. 1987," Prairie Green, 9" l. (ILLUS., bottom of page)... **$115**

Sign, advertising the "Pottery Show- Calif. 1987," w/a tepee on each end & advertising in the center, Desert Gold, 9" l. **$125**

Frankoma Dealer Teepee Sign

Sign, dealer teepee, Prairie Green, 1940s, marked "Frankoma," 6 1/2" h. (ILLUS.)...... **$725**

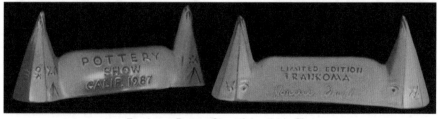

Frankoma Pottery Show Advertising Sign

John Frank Tournament Stein

Stein, footed, advertising-type, for John Frank Memorial Charity Gold Tournament, Blue, 150 created, 1973 (ILLUS.)....... **$30**

Frankoma Wagon Wheel Pattern Teapot

Teapot, cov., Wagon Wheel patt., Desert Gold glaze, Sapulpa, Oklahoma, ca. 1942 (ILLUS.)... **$25**
Teapot, cov., Wagon Wheel patt., Model No. 94j, Desert Gold glaze, Ada clay, 2 cup **$69**
Trivet, decorated w/an eagle sitting on a branch, the large wings filling most of the trivet, Model No. 2tr, Desert Gold, 1966-67, 6" sq. **$69**

Frankoma Eagle Trivet

Trivet, Eagle sitting on branch, large wings fill up most of the trivet, Peach Glow glaze, Model No. 2tr, 6" sq. (ILLUS.) **$76**
Tumbler, juice, Plainsman patt., Model No. 51c, Autumn Yellow glaze, 6 oz................. **$15**

Miniature Frankoma Spherical Vase

Vase, 2 3/4" h., miniature, spherical ringed shape, Desert Gold, Ada clay, marked "Frankoma 500" (ILLUS.) **$190**
Vase, 3 1/2" h., round foot rising to bulbous body w/short neck & rolled lip, unusual high gloss deep blue, marked "Frank Potteries" **$680**
Vase, 4" h., small foot rising to a flat, narrow body w/tab handle on each side, Ivory glaze, marked "Frankoma"........................ **$120**
Vase, 4" h., small foot rising to a flat, narrow body w/tab handle on each side, Ivory glaze, pot & leopard mark **$225**
Vase, 6" h., square-shaped w/relief-molded flying goose, relief-molded reed decoration on reverse, No. 60B **$65**
Vase, 7" h., Art Deco-style w/round foot w/panel on each side at base, rising to a plain, flat body w/stepped small elongated handles, Jade Green glaze, Model No. 41, pot & leopard mark **$218**

Frankoma Stovepipe Vase

Vase, 8 3/4" h., stovepipe, Prairie Green w/silver overlay, 1940s, marked "Frankoma" (ILLUS., previous page) **$645**

Vase, 9" h., round stepped ring base rising to handle on each side, Ivory, #78, pot & leopard mark **$235**

Wall masks, bust of Oriental man, No. 134 & Oriental woman, No. 133, Jade Green glaze, pot & leopard mark, Ada clay, man 5 1/2" h., woman 4 3/4" h., pr.................... **$610**

Frankoma Peter Pan Head Wall Pocket

Wall plaque, figural, modeled as the head of Peter Pan, designed by Joseph Taylor, made 1936-38 & 1972-75, Ada clay, Prairie Green, 6" h. (ILLUS.) **$148**

Wall plaque, miniature, African-American head, black glossy glaze, ca. 1940, very rare, 3 1/4" h. **$185**

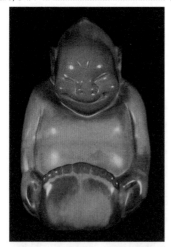

Frankoma Billiken Wall Pocket

Wall pocket, figural, Billiken, Prairie Green, Ada clay, marked "Tulsa Court, No. 47, R.O.J.," 7" h. (ILLUS.) **$178**

Wall vase, figural, model of a Billiken, Ada clay, incised on the bottom "Tulsa Court - No. 47 R.O.J.," Praire Green, ca. 1951-55, 7" h. **$145**

Fulper Pottery

The Fulper Pottery was founded in Flemington, New Jersey, in 1805 and operated until 1935, although operations were curtailed in 1929 when its main plant was destroyed by fire. The name was changed in 1929 to Stangl Pottery, which continued in operation until July 1978, when Pfaltzgraff, a division of Susquehanna Broadcasting Company of York, Pennsylvania, purchased the assets of the Stangl Pottery, including the name.

Fulper Marks

Fulper Galleon Bookends

Bookends, modeled as a galleon under sail on scrolling waves, thick rectangular base, cafe au lait glaze, oval racetrack mark, 6 1/2" h., pr. (ILLUS.) **$288**

Bookends, modeled as a thick open book resting atop a thick closed book, heavy mottled green & tan glaze, vertical black stamp mark, 5" h., pr. (ILLUS., top next page) **$394**

Wide & Low Fulper Flambé Bowl

Bowl, 10 3/4" d., 2 1/2" h., low wide flat-bottomed form w/incurved sides, Chinese Blue Flambé glaze, impressed vertical mark, typical burst glaze bubbles, small grinding chips, some crystalline effect (ILLUS.).. **$184**

Fulper Book-shaped Bookends

Fulper Box with Colorful Cover

Box, cov., wide rounded black base w/a wide overhanging cover sharply pointed in the center & decorated overall w/colorful flowers & leaves, vertical Fulper mark & monogram of Martin Stangl, 7" d., 4" h. (ILLUS.).. **$345**

Tall Paneled Fulper Candlesticks

Candlesticks, a round ringed foot tapering to a tall faceted stem below the tulip-form candle sockets, the top in creamy ivory dripping down & melding into shades of dark brown & light pastel blue w/a pastel blue foot, base impressed w/vertical mark within oval racetrack, 10" h., pr. (ILLUS.) **$300**

Figural Effigy-type Center Bowl

Center bowl, Effigy-type, a wide flat-bottomed shallow bowl w/incurved sides raised on three crouching figures resting on a molded thick disc base, multi-toned brown & blue crystalline glaze, stamped mark, 10 1/2" d., 7" h. (ILLUS.) **$360**

Fine Fulper Drippy Glazed Lamp Base

Fulper Lemonade Set with a Drip Glaze

Lamp base, footed tall ovoid body w/a molded mouth, crystalline Mirrored Black glaze dripped over cream on vertical ribbing, cast hole in bottom, unmarked, 13 3/8" h. (ILLUS., previous page) **$546**

Fulper Lamp Base with Flambé Glaze

Lamp base, 7" h., wide bulbous ovoid body w/the wide shoulder centered by a short flaring neck, Ivory Flambé glaze over a mustard yellow matte glaze, cast hole in the bottom, unmarked (ILLUS.) **$403**

Lemonade set: a tall tapering cylindrical tankard pitcher & four tapering cylindrical 3 1/2" h. mugs; all covered in a multi-toned glossy grey & blue drip glaze, all marked, pitcher 10" h., the set (ILLUS., top of page) **$330**

Perfume lamp, figural, a lady w/her arms away from her body wearing a widely flaring scalloped pink dress & matching pantaloons, marked w/shape number 331, 13 1/2" h. (ILLUS., top next column) **$1,150**

Charming Fulper Figural Perfume Lamp

Figural Fulper Powder Box

Powder box, cov., figural, a cylindrical base & a low domed cover centered by the half-length figure of a woman, impressed vertical race track mark & impressed Martin Stangl monogram, ca. 1920s, 7 1/4" h. (ILLUS., previous page) **$345**

Squatty Chinese Blue Flambé Vase

Vase, 4 1/2" h., footed wide squatty rounded body w/an angled shoulder to the short, wide cylindrical neck, deep Chinese Blue Flambé glaze w/patches of small blue crystals, vertical racetrack ink-stamp mark (ILLUS.) **$138**

Nearly Spherical Fulper Vase

Vase, 5 1/2" h., flat-based nearly spherical shape w/an inward-rolled rim, overall mottled drippy green & brown matt glaze, vertical ink stamp mark (ILLUS.) **$288**

Squatty Bulbous Fulper Vase

Vase, 5 5/8" h., 9" d., wide squatty bulbous form tapering sharply to a small rolled neck, Butterscotch Flambé glaze in

green shaded to light yellow, Shape No. 657, vertical ink stamp mark, some very minor grinding chips on base (ILLUS.) **$518**

Ringed Fulper Vase with Cucumber Glaze

Vase, 6" h., tapering cylindrical form composed of four wide rings, flat mouth flanked by looped vine-stype handles, Cucumber Crystalline glaze, vertical racetrack ink stamp mark (ILLUS.) **$345**

Very Bulbous Footed Fulper Vase

Vase, 6 1/4" h., footed nearly spherical slightly squatty body topped by a wide short cylindrical neck flanked by three small loop shoulder handles, overall dark purple Wisteria glaze, Shape No. 564, raised oval vertical mark, uncrazed (ILLUS.) **$345**

Fulper Spherical Vase with Marbleized Glaze

Vase, 6 3/8" h., bulbous nearly spherical body tapering to small squared handles flanking the small mouth, swirled & marbleized dark blue & purple glazes, vertical inkstamp mark (ILLUS., previous page) $374

Wide Bulbous Fulper Pottery Vase

Vase, 6 1/2" h., 8 1/2" d., wide flat-based bulbous ovoid body tapering to a wide closed mouth flanked by squared handles, light streaky blue glaze merging w/a brownish-tan below w/highlights of mottled brown on the handles, marked w/vertical rectangular black mark (ILLUS.) $420

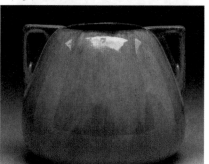

Footed Squatty Fulper Vase

Vase, 7" h., footed squatty bulbous body tapering to a widely flaring neck, dark blue flambé glaze accented w/brown & green, raised oval racetrack mark, small chip off foot (ILLUS.) $403

Vase, 8 1/4" h., ovoid body w/a wide rounded shoulder centered by a small closed mouth, covered in a blue, brown & tan glossy streaky glaze w/green crystalline highlights, marked "Prang" (ILLUS., top next column) $480

Fulper Vase with Streaky Glossy Glaze

Large Vase with Chinese Blue Flambé Glaze

Vase, 9" h., small round foot supporting a very wide ovoid body w/a wide shoulder centered by a short tapering neck flanked by low loop handles, Chinese Blue Flambé glaze, raised vertical mark (ILLUS.) $805

Vase, 9" h., tall ovoid body w/a wide cylindrical neck w/a closed rim flanked by angled loop handles, Ashes of Roses glaze, vertical racetrack mark, very minor grinding chips at base, Shape 659 .... $345

Vase, 10" h., footed squatty bulbous body tapering to a wide banded cylindrical neck w/a flaring rim, green & cobalt blue drippy glazes over a dark blue matte glaze, vertical inkstamp mark, some burst glaze bubbles $374

Unusual Fulper Vaz-Bowl

Vaz-bowl, wide shallow rounded lobed dish w/four of the lobes pulled up into tapering strap handles that are joined above the center of the dish, mottled green matte glaze, vertical inkstamp mark & label from the Pan Pacific International Exposition, San Francisco, 1915, 6 1/2" d. (ILLUS.) **$863**

Fulper Acorn-shaped Wall Pocket

Wall pocket, acorn-shaped, serpentine molded band around the shoulder, mottled matte brown glaze, rectangular inkmark, 7" h. (ILLUS.) **$518**

Green & Yellow Fulper Phoenix Wall Pocket

Wall pocket, figural, model of a long-tailed phoenix in greens, yellow, black & grey, vertical inkstamp mark, Shape 375, small glaze nick on tail feather, 9 1/2" h. (ILLUS.) **$259**

Colorful Fulper Phoenix Wall Pocket

Wall pocket, figural, model of a long-tailed phoenix in yellow, red, blue & black, vertical inkstamp mark, Shape 369, 9" h. (ILLUS.) **$219**

Gallé Pottery

Fine pottery was made by Emile Gallé, the multitalented French designer and artisan who is also famous for his glass and furniture. The pottery is relatively scarce.

Gallé Pottery Mark

Unusual Gallé Fish-handled Basket

Basket, the flaring body composed of ribbed feather-like panels resting on large knobs w/tiny ball feet, the high arched handle formed by two facing fish w/their tails curving up to the top, glazed in steaky glazes in shades of red, green, orange & blue, accent w/overall gold spatter, signed "Emile Gallé - Nancy Déposé," professionally repaired handle, ca. 1890, 8 1/2" h. (ILLUS., previous page) **$1,410**

Ewer, a squatty bulbous body centered by a tall slender stick neck, a long flat handle from near the top of the neck to the shoulder, a crimson glazed decorated w/gold-trimmed dark blackish green foliage & a praying mantis, white blossoms around the neck, accented w/gold spatter, signed in black enamel w/the Cross of Lorraine & "E & G déposé - E. Gallé Nancy," ca. 1890, 9 3/4" h. **$1,880**

Unusual Gallé Decorated Pitcher

Gallé Pottery Ewer with Praying Mantis

Ewer, footed wide squatty bulbous low body centered by a tall flaring & swelled neck w/a pinched spout & long angled handle from top to shoulder, a mottled glossy purple glaze decorated w/sponged gold & enameled w/a large & gangly praying mantis about to land on white spider mums on leafy stems below, all outlined in gold, base stamped in black "E+G déposé - E. Gallé" & a possibly obscured "Nancy," footring w/a few flat chips, 7 1/4" h. (ILLUS.) **$1,725**

Pitcher, 7 1/2" h., footed squatty bulbous body tapering to a cylindrical section & widely flaring cupped rim, applied strap handle, the upper half w/a thick drippy light blue glaze w/gold trim above a mottled brown lower half, enameled w/a large flying insect above long leaved plant, stamped in the glaze "Emile Galle Nancy Déposé" & the E & G monogram, short hairline in bottom, ca. 1890 (ILLUS., top next column) **$3,760**

Squatty Gallé Vase with Village Scene

Vase, 7 1/8" h., footed wide squatty bulbous body centered by a tall upright gently flaring & deeply crimped neck, overall flowing pink & blue glaze, the base h.p. w/a scene of a quiet inlet village painted in sepia tones, various seashells painted around the neck & shoulder, base signed "E. Gallé Fayencerie Nancy," crazed inside & out (ILLUS.)................................. **$1,093**

Vase, 7 1/2" h., a footed bulbous lower body w/deeply pinched-in sides, tapering to a wide cylindrical upper body, glazed in mottled shades of dark mustard brown & black, enameled w/naturalistic flowers & two polychrome butterflies, small low curved side handles trimmed in blue, stamped w/the Cross of Lorraine & "Emilé Gallé - Nancy Déposé" (ILLUS., next page) **$2,350**

Bulbous Pinched Floral-decorated Vase

Gaudy Dutch

This name is applied to English earthenware with designs copied from Oriental patterns. Production began in the 18th century. These copies flooded into this country in the early 19th century. The incorporation of the word "Dutch" derives from the fact that it was the Dutch who first brought the Oriental wares into Europe. The ware was not, as often erroneously reported, made specifically for the Pennsylvania Dutch.

Cup & saucer, handleless, Single Rose patt., orange, green, yellow & blue, early 19th c. (minor enamel flaking on cup) **$550**
Cup & saucer, handleless, War Bonnet patt., orange, green, blue & yellow, early 19th c. (harline & minor stain in cup) **$495**

Gaudy Welsh

This is a name for wares made in England for the American market about 1830 to 1860, with some examples dating much later. Decorated with Imari-style flower patterns, often highlighted with copper lustre, it should not be confused with Gaudy Dutch wares, the colors of which differ somewhat.

Cups & saucers, handleless, paneled rim, Urn patt., pink, orange, green cobalt blue & lustre trim, 19th c., set of 6 (some minor staining) **$715**
Plates, 8 1/2" d., paneled rim, Urn patt., pink, orange, green cobalt blue & lustre trim, 19th c., set of 6 (three w/light staining) **$715**

Geisha Girl Wares

Geisha Girl Porcelain features scenes of Japanese women in colorful kimonos along with the flora and architecture of turn-of-the-century Japan. Although bearing an Oriental motif, the wares were produced for Western use in dinnerware and household accessory forms favored during the late 1800s through the early 1940s. There was minimal production during the Occupied Japan period. Less ornate wares were distributed through gift shops and catalogs during the 1960s-70s; some of these are believed to have been manufactured in Hong Kong. Beware overly ornate items with fake Nippon marks that are in current production today, imported from China. More than a hundred porcelain manufacturers and decorating houses were involved with production of these wares during their heyday.

Prices cited here are for excellent to mint condition items. Enamel wear, flaking, hairlines or missing parts all serve to lower the value of an item. Prices in your area may vary.

More than 275 Geisha Girl Porcelain patterns and pattern variations have been cataloged; others are still coming to light.

The most common patterns include:

Bamboo Tree

Battledore

Child Reaching for Butterfly

Fan series

Garden Bench series

Geisha in Sampan series

Meeting series

Parasol series

Pointing series

The rarest patterns include:

... And They're Off

Bellflower

Bicycle Race

Capricious

Elegance in Motion

Fishing series

Foreign Garden

In Flight

Steamboat

The most popular patterns include:

Boat Festival

Butterfly Dancers

By Land and By Sea

Cloud series

Courtesan Processional

Dragonboat

Small Sounds of Summer

So Big

Temple A

A complete listing of patterns and their descriptions can be found in The Collector's Encyclopedia of Geisha Girl Porcelain. Additional patterns discovered since publication of the book are documented in The Geisha Girl Porcelain Newsletter.

References: Litts, E., Collector's Encyclopedia of Geisha Girl Porcelain, Collector Books, 1988; Geisha Girl Porcelain Newsletter, P.O. Box 3394, Morris Plains, NJ 07950.

Bouillon cup, cover & saucer, Garden Bench J patt., multicolored, marked w/"TN" in Wreath & "Hand Painted Japan," the set $40

Bowl, 5 3/8" d., 1 1/4" h., Gardening patt., red w/gold buds, promotional item for a coffee company, bottom stamped "Fort Dearborn Brand" $18

Bowl, 7 1/4" d., 2 1/4" h., Cherry Blossom patt., three designs in a reserve w/blossom background, red trim $28

Geisha Girl Torii Pattern Bowl

Bowl, 7 1/2" d., 2" h., Torii patt., round w/gently scalloped rim, three border vignettes & central temple by lake scene, unusual combination of stenciled central design w/blue lustre frame & h.p. sides, gilded leaves on border stenciled, red & black highlights, marked in gold w/word "Sphinx" (ILLUS.) $42

Bread dish, Bird Cage patt., red borders & highlights in the design, signed w/Japanese characters, 7 1/4 x 12 1/2" $32

Celery dish, Writing B patt., oblong w/scalloped edge, red trim & yellowish green w/gold buds, 5 1/2 x 11 1/2" $35

Chocolate pot, cov., Parasol F patt., cobalt blue border w/gold lacing, unusual spout, 8 1/2" h. (ILLUS.) $125

Chocolate pot, cov., Parasol F patt., tall tapering body w/rim spout & fancy loop handle, domed cover w/loop finial, red & gold borders framing a stenciled garden scene split between two medallions w/h.p. mums in the background, 7 3/4" h. $35

Chocolate pot, cov., Writing A patt., tall tapering body w/rim spout & unusual S-scroll handle, domed cover w/loop finial, cobalt blue & red borders, well executed, Japan mark, 10" h. $80

Fancy Geisha Girl Writing A Chocolate Pot

Chocolate pot, cov., Writing A patt., tall tapering lobed body w/rim spout & domed cover w/loop finial, unusual long double-loop handle, red background, decorated w/two reserves, one scenic, the other Meeting F patt., colorful stylized butterfly & flowers border, heavy gilt trim, 9 1/2" h. (ILLUS.) $95

Cracker jar, cov., six-lobed shape, lobe designs alternate between diaper of lotus, cherry blossoms & phoenix & Ukiyo-e patt., bent Y-form forked handle, three-footed, in shades of bluish green & red, 5" d., 6 1/2" h. $70

Geisha Parasol F Chocolate Pot

Geisha Girl Small Sounds of Summer Cracker Jar

Cracker jar, cov., Small Sounds of Summer patt., barrel-shaped body on three tiny feet, shot, wide neck & low domed cover w/pointed disk finial, red w/ornate gold & colored background, 8" h. (ILLUS., previous page) **$85**

Creamer, Rokkasen patt., red background, heart-shaped reserve, signed w/Japanese characters, 4 3/8" w........................... **$20**

Cup & saucer, bouillon w/lid, Pointing D patt., black border, signed in Japanese "Tashiro"...................................... **$45**

Demitasse cup & saucer, Parasol C patt., cobalt blue & red borders, marked "G.R.P. Hand Painted Shofu Nippon," the set **$15**

Geisha Girl Demitasse Pot

Demitasse pot, cov., Ikebana in Rickshaw patt., ovoid lightly ribbed body w/serpentine pink w/gold spout & C-scroll handle, ribbed domed cover w/knob finial, rare border color combination of teal blue w/gold, 6" h. (ILLUS.) **$95**

Dish, Court Lady patt., scalloped & lobed shape w/one lobe smaller to form handle, cobalt blue & red borders, pattern in one reserve w/a large gold peacock in another reserve, diapered lozenge background, 5 3/8" d., 1 1/2" h. **$20**

Dish, Fan A patt., square w/eight-lobed bowl, bluish green border w/gold striping, 7" w. **$25**

Geisha Girl Dish in Temple A Pattern

Dish, Temple A patt., shallow oblong shape w/looped & forked brown twig handle on rim, multicolored center scene, brown border band, signed "Kutani," 4 3/4 x 5 7/8", 2 1/2" h. (ILLUS.) **$24**

Eggcup, Garden Bench D patt., red border & red highlights in design, unusually short, marked "Made in Japan," 1 7/8" h...... **$10**

Eggcup, Geisha with Sack patt., odd conical shape, bluish green & red trim, floral border, 2 1/8" h. **$12**

Hatpin holder, Parasol E & Pointing R patterns, Parasol E patt. in a red cherry blossom reserve, Pointing R. patt. in a green cherry blossom reserve, light apple green & red borders, on a background of variously colored cherry blossoms, 4" h....... **$45**

Hatpin holder, Temple B patt., wide base & short stem, red borders & trim, signed "Kutani," 3 3/8" w., 4" h. **$40**

Very Rare Geisha Girl Jardiniere

Jardiniere & pedestal, miniature, Cloud B patt., red borders & red trim, pedestal 3 3/4" h., jardiniere 2 1/8" h., the set, extremely rare, (ILLUS.) .... **No price available**

Lemonade set: 7 1/2" h. pitcher & five 2 3/4" h. mugs; Bellflower patt., dark brown borders & trim, signed in Japanese honoring the artist whose print inspired the decoration, the set..................... **$110**

Mint dish, Seamstress patt., maroon border, black handle, marked "Japan," 3 1/2 x 6 1/2", 3" h.. **$15**

Napkin ring, Rivers Edge patt., semi-circular shape, pine green borders & black trim, marked "T" in Cherry Blossom - "Japan".. **$40**

Temple A Geisha Girl Perfume Bottle

Perfume bottle & stopper, Temple A patt., bulbous body tapering to a short flared neck, large ball stopper, multicolored design w/black trim, marked "Royal Kaga - Nippon," 4 1/2" h. (ILLUS.)........................ **$125**

Pitcher, child's, jug-type, Parasol Modern patt., red borders & trim, Japan mark, 3 1/4" w. **$12**

Unusual Green Geisha Girl Nippon Plate

Plate, 9 3/4" d., a green sponged background decorated in color w/five squared panels, each w/a different pattern, deep center, marked w/Japanese characters & "Nippon" (ILLUS.) **$75**

Plate, 9 1/2" d., Lantern Dance patt., brick red borders & red trim, signed "Kutani" **$38**

Powder jar, cov., Parasol B patt., red borders & trim, 4" d. **$22**

Relish dish, Courtesan Processional patt., double-handled, cobalt blue border w/large gold buds, dark brown trim, gold trim, 6 x 8" **$40**

Sake set: 6" h. pitcher & 1 1/2" h. cups; Child Reaching for Butterfly patt. w/red borders & trim, pitcher w/bird whistle, each cup w/a geisha girl lithophane in the bottom, ca. 1960s, the set **$35**

Salad set: 10 3/4" d. master bowl & six 6" d. individual bowls; Geisha in Peony patt., red borders & trim, the set........................ **$125**

Salt dish, pedestal base, Temple A patt., teal blue borders & dark brown trim, marked "Noritake - Made in Japan," 2 1/8" d., 1 1/2" h... **$25**

Temple B Nippon Geisha Girl Salt Dish

Salt dish, round w/pedestal base, Temple B patt., multicolored decoration w/heavy gilt trim, marked "Royal Kaga Nippon," 3" d., 1 1/2" h. (ILLUS.) **$45**

Two Geisha Girl Fan A Sauce Dishes

Sauce dish, Fan A patt., refined, detailed & unusual underglaze blue, signed in Japanese, 2 5/8" d., 1" h. (ILLUS. of two)........... **$30**

Geisha Girl Triple Border Serving Tray

Serving tray, Geisha in Sampan J patt., round w/scalloped edges & small open handles, three border bands in cobalt blue, red & multicolored flowers, Double "T" in Oval mark, 10 1/4" d. (ILLUS.)............ **$65**

Geisha Girl Shaving Mug

Shaving mug, Lesson/Parasol A patt., molded base w/cylindrical sides & gently flared rim, ring handle, cobalt blue & gold borders, red trim, 3 1/2" h. (ILLUS.)............ **$45**

Snack set: plate w/depression & matching teacup, Pointing G patt., red borders & red trim, plate 7 1/2" d., cup 2" h., the set **$35**

Unusual Geisha Girl Spoon Tray

Spoon tray, Parasol H patt., almond-shaped form w/gold loop end handles, red & brown trim, "M" in Wreath - "Hand Painted Nippon" mark, 4 x 10" (ILLUS.) **$55**

Stickpin holder, Child Reaching for Butterfly patt., bluish green border & red trim, rare shape, poorly executed, Made in Japan mark, 3 1/4" h....................................... **$45**

Geisha Girl Nippon Syrup Jug

Syrup jug, cov., Rivers Edge patt., cylindrical w/large rim spout & long angled handle, slightly domed cover w/loop handle, red & pine green trim & black accents, marked "TN - Nippon," 4 1/2" h. (ILLUS.)..... **$45**

Geisha Parasol B Pattern Tea Caddy

Tea caddy, cov., Parasol B patt., cobalt blue, scalloped border w/gold, missing interior lid, 4" h. (ILLUS.)............................. **$28**

Geisha Girl Duck Watching Child's Teapot

Teapot, cov., child's, Duck Watching patt., pine green borders & black trim, 4" h. (ILLUS.) **$25**

Garden Bench C Individual Teapot

Teapot, cov., individual size, Garden Bench C patt., spherical lobed body w/domed lobed cover, cobalt blue borders & trim & red spout, Japan mark, 4 1/2" h. (ILLUS.) **$25**

Toothbrush holder, Cricket Cage patt., cylindrical, cobalt blue borders & red trim, 4" h... **$22**

Vase, miniature, 3 3/8" h., Geisha on Parade patt., bluish green borders & red trim **$32**

Vase, 5" h., Pointing S patt., cobalt blue borders, red trim & gold lacing on bottom band & shoulder, a background of peonies & a temple complex w/large lanterns & prayer ribbons... **$18**

Vase, 6 1/8" h., 2 1/4" d., Parasol D patt., cylindrical body tapering to a tall cylindrical neck, red trim, unusual shape, later production, signed w/Japanese characters **$30**

Gonder

Lawton Gonder founded Gonder Ceramic Arts in Zanesville, Ohio, in 1941 and it continued in operation until 1957.

The firm produced a higher priced and better quality of commercial art potteries than many firms of the time and employed Jamie Matchet and Chester Kirk, both of whom were outstanding ceramic designers. Several special glazes were developed during the company's history and Gonder even duplicated some museum pieces of Chinese ceramic. In 1955 the firm converted to the production of tile due to increased foreign competition. By 1957 its years of finest production were over.

Increase price ranges as indicated for the following glaze colors: red flambé - 50 percent, antique gold crackle - 70 percent, turquoise Chinese crackle - 40 percent, white Chinese crackle - 30 percent.

Gonder   E-1
GONDER
U.S.A.

Gonder Marks

Ashtray, boomerang shape, Mold No. 223, 6 1/4 x 10 1/2" l. .... **$15-$35**

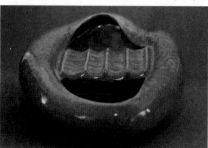

Center Rest Cigar Ashtray

Ashtray, Center Rest Cigar, marked "Gonder Original 219" in script, Red Flambé glaze, 2 1/4 x 7 1/2" (ILLUS.) ... **$50-$75**

Ashtray, form of a bird, Mold No. 224, 8 7/8" l. .... **$35-$50**

Ashtray, form of a fish, Mold No. 113, 4 x 9" l. .... **$75-$100**

Ashtray, round, pie crust rim, Mold No. 807, 9" d. .... **$10-$30**

Ashtray, "S" Swirl, Mold No. 626, 6 1/2 x 9 1/8" l. .... **$20-$30**

Ashtray, Sovereign Fluted Rectangular, Mold No. 807, 1 7/8 x 3 1/4" l. .... **$20-$30**

Ashtray, Sovereign Fluted Round, Mold No. 808, 2 3/4" d. .... **$20-$30**

Ashtray, spiked fish, Mold No. 224, 4 x 7 3/8" l. .... **$40-$60**

Ashtray, square, Mold No. 1800A, 10 11/16" sq. .... **$60-$75**

Ashtray, square w/rounded corners, Mold No. 814, 8" sq. .... **$20-$40**

Ashtray, oblong w/model of Trojan horse head on rim, Mold No. 548, gunmetal glaze, 6 x 6 1/2" .... **$20-$40**

Ashtray, square, Mold No. 805, 9 1/4" w. . **$20-$40**

Ashtray, square, Mold No. 586 .... **$20-$30**

Ashtrays, Mold No. 808, set of 3, each .... **$20-$30**

Bank, figural Sheriff, 8" h. .... **$300-$350**

Base, for Chinese Imperial dragon handle vase No. 535, footed, 4 5/8 x 5 13/16", 2 1/16" h. .... **$55-$80**

Base for ginger jar, Mold No. 530-B ...... **$75-$100**

Basket, shell shape w/overhead handle, Mold No. 674, 7 x 8" .... **$25-$50**

Basket, Mold No. L-19, 9 x 13" .... **$30-$45**

Bell, figural "Sovereign Bonnet Lady," Mold No. 800, 3 1/2" h. .... **$50-$75**

Beverage set: 8" h. pitcher & six 5" h. mugs; LaGonda patt., Mold No. 917 & 909, the set .... **$50-$75**

Bookend, model of horse, Mold No. 582, 10" h. .... **$50-$65**

Bookends, in the form of horses, Mold No. 211, 10" h., pr. .... **$125-$150**

Bowl, 4 3/8" d., fruit, La Gonda, Mold No. 905 .... **$15-$20**

Bowl, 5 11/16" d., 1 3/8" h., w/small leaves, Mold No. B-17 .... **$30-$50**

Bowl, 6 7/8 x 11 7/8", 2 1/2" h., S-shaped, Mold No. 592 .... **$30-$45**

Bowl, 8" d., 2 3/8" h., Mold No. 715 .... **$10-$20**

Bowl, 8" d., 2 7/8" h., fluted, Mold No. 629 or H-29 .... **$10-$15**

Butter warmer, cover & candleholder base, Mold No. 996, 2 1/2 x 4 1/2", 3 pcs. .... **$25-$40**

Candleholder, cubic, Mold No. 726, 3 x 3", 2 1/4" h., pr. .... **$30-$40**

Candleholder, fluted, Mold No. 314, 414, E-14, 4 5/8" w., 1 7/8" h. .... **$5-$10**

Candleholder, Mold No. 518, Triangle, 12 1/2" w. x 10 1/4" l. .... **$150-$175**

Candleholder, Mold No. 520/C, Freeform, 4 1/4" w. x 5 1/2" l., 1 13/16" h. .... **$20-$35**

Candleholders, La Gonda, Mold No. 915, 2 x 2, 2 1/8" h., pr. .... **$15-$20**

Candleholders, Mold No. 521/C, Shell, 6 1/4" l., 3 3/4" h., pr. .... **$25-$35**

Candleholders, model of dolphin, Mold No. 561, 2 1/4 x 5", pr. .... **$40-$60**

Casserole, cov., handled lid, La Gonda, Mold No. 953, 5 1/4 x 8 1/4", 4" h. .... **$15-$25**

Casserole, cov., handled lid, La Gonda, Mold No. 954, 6 1/2 x 10 1/8", 5 1/4" h. **$25-$35**

Chop plate, oblong, Mold No. 912, 8 7/8 x 12 1/4" .... **$100-$125**

Cigarette box, cov., Mold. No. 806, 3 1/2 x 4 3/8", 2 5/8" h. .... **$80-$95**

Console bowl, fluted, w/flowers, Mold No. J-71, 5 1/8 x 12 3/4", 4 3/4" h. .... **$40-$60**

Console bowl, Mold No. 520, 8 7/8 w x 11 1/4" l, 2 5/8" h. .... **$50-$75**

Console bowl, oblong shell-molded w/pointed ends & starfish molded at the sides, speckled brown on yellow glaze, Mold No. 500 .... **$150-$175**

Console bowl, lobed incurved sides, Mold E-12, 2 1/2 x 7" .... **$5-$15**

Console bowl, crescent moon shape, Mold J-55, 5 x 12" .... **$30-$45**

Console bowl, rectangular base, body w/relief-molded center fan shape flanked by cornucopia forms, Mold K-14, 7 1/2 x 12 1/2" .... **$150-$200**

Console bowl, seashell design, Mold No. 505, 7 1/4 x 17 1/2" .... **$75-$90**

Console set: 14" l. bowl & pr. of 5" h. candleholders; shell shape, Mold Nos. 505 & 552, the set .... **$115-$130**

Console set: 16" l. bowl & pr. of candleholders; "Banana Boat" bowl, Mold Nos. 565 & 567, the set .... **$100-$130**

Cookie jar, cov., bulbous shape w/sleeping dog finial, Mold No. 924, 8 1/2" h. .... **$40-$60**

Cookie jar, cov., Pirate, Mold No. 951, 10 1/2" or 12" h. .... **$900-$1,200**

Cookie jar, cov., "Ye Olde Oaken Bucket," brown w/tan & yellow glaze, marked "Gonder Original 974" in script, only two known to exist, 7" h. .... **RARE**

Cookie jar, cov., Sheriff, Mold No. 950, green glaze, 12" h. .... **$800-$1,000**

Cornucopia-vase, flattened form, square base, Mold 305 E-5, 3 3/8 x 7", 7 3/8" h. . **$15-$30**

Cornucopia-vase, ribbed, Mold No. 360, 7" h. .... **$20-$35**

Cornucopia-vase, leaves at base, Mold No. 691, 7 1/2" h. .... **$60-$85**

Cornucopia-vase, held by figural hand, oval base, Mold No. 675, 7 1/2 x 8" .... **$75-$100**

Cornucopia-vase, shell form, Mold No. H-84, 8" h. .... **$25-$40**

Cornucopia-vase, square base, Mold No. H-14, 9" h. .... **$15-$25**

Cornucopia-vase, uneven double swirl design, Mold No. H-48, 4 x 9 3/4" .... **$50-$60**

Cornucopia-vase, on flat square base, Mold No. J-66, 10" l. .... **$20-$35**

Cream soup dish, handled, La Gonda, Mold No. 908, 5 1/2 x 5 3/4", 3 3/8" h. .. **$25-$35**

Creamer, La Gonda, Mold No. 907, 7" w., 4" h. .... **$20-$30**

Creamer, Mold No. P-33, 3 1/2" h. .... **$5-$10**

Custard, cov., handled, La Gonda, Mold No. 952, 3 1/4" h. .... **$15-$25**

Dish, oak leaf design, Mold No. 591, 13" l. .... **$30-$50**

Ewer, bulbous base tapering to a tall slanted top w/pointed spout & integral handle, Mold 410, Chinese Turquoise Crackle glaze .... **$25-$40**

Gonder Mold No. E-60 Fluted Ewer

Ewer, fluted, Mold No. E-60, brown w/yellow mottling, 6" h. (ILLUS.) .... **$5-$15**

Ewer, Mold No. H-73, 8" h. .... **$15-$25**

Carafe-shaped Ewer

Ewer, w/stopper, carafe-shaped, gunmetal glaze, Mold No. 994, 8" (ILLUS.) .... **$35-$50**

Ewer, scrolled handle, Mold No. H-606 & 606, 9" h. .... **$50-$75**

Ewer, Mold No. J-25, 8 x 11" .... **$50-$75**

Ewer, shell-shaped w/starfish on base, Mold No. 508, 14" h. .... **$40-$60**

Figure group, pair of chair bearers w/chair, Mold No. 765, 12 1/2" h. .... **$150-$175**

Figure of bearded Oriental man, Mold No. 775, 8 5/8" h. .... **$50-$60**

Figure of Chinese peasant, standing figure, Mold No. 545, 8" h. .... **$15-$30**

Figure of coolie, kneeling & bending forward, Mold No. 547, 5" h. .... **$15-$30**

Figure of Madonna, standing, Mold No. 549, 9 1/4" h. .... **$50-$75**

Figure of Oriental male, Mold No. 773, 11" h. .... **$40-$60**

Figure of Oriental mandarin, Mold No. 755, 8 3/4" h. .... **$50-$75**

Figure of Oriental woman, holding ginger jar, Mold No. 573, 4 7/8" h. .... **$40-$60**

Figure of Oriental woman, w/right hand to head, Mold No. 776, 9" h. .... **$60-$80**

Figure of turbaned woman w/baskets, Mold No. 762, 14 1/2" h. .... **$125-$150**

Flower frog, three-tier flower, Mold No. 250, 5 7/8" w., 2 5/8" h. .... **$75-$100**

Ginger jar, cov., square, 10" h. .... **$100-$150**

Ginger jar, cov., decorated w/Oriental dragon on pedestal base, Mold No. 533, 11" h., 3 pcs. .... **$150-$200**

Lamp, Aladdin oil style, no number .... **$75-$100**

Lamp, bullet-shaped, Mold No. 2228, 11" h. .... **$75-$100**

Lamp, Driftwood, Mold No. 2017, 30" h. .... **$40-$60**

Lamp, ewer form, Mold No. 4046, 11" h. .... **$35-$55**

Lamp, figural, young woman, Mold No. 587, 4 1/4" sq., 9 3/16" h. .... **$125-$150**

Lamp, Geometric Planes, Mold No. 4037, 9" w., 10" h. .... **$60-$80**

Lamp, Horse Head TV or Console, Mold No. 1901, 14 3/8" h. .... **$30-$50**

Lamp, Keystone, Mold No. 4085, 9 1/4" w., 12 3/4" h. .... **$40-$60**

Lamp, Mill TV, Mold No. 1905, 12" w., 8 1/4" h. .... **$40-$60**

Lamp, Mold No. 522, Scarla Sunfish, 10" l., 9" h. .... **$150-$175**

Lamp, no number, "LG," 8 1/2" h., 6 3/8" w. .... **$75-$100**

Lamp, Scroll, Mold No. 2255, 9 1/4" w., 12 3/4" h. .... **$40-$60**

Lamp, Swirl, Mold No. 3060, 7 3/4" w., 5 1/2" h. .... **$40-$60**

Lamp, Tall Bottle, Mold No. 5506, 17 1/2" h. .... **$125-$150**

Lamp, Vine & Leaves, Mold No. 3031, 9 1/2" h. .... **$40-$60**

Lamp, model of Foo dog, 8" h. .... **$125-$150**

Lamp, cookie jar shape, Mold No. P-24, 8 1/2" h. .... **$20-$40**

Lamp, driftwood design, 12" h. .... **$25-$50**

Lamp, model of two horse heads, 12" h. .... **$40-$50**

Lamp base, Dogwood Globe, Catalog #5507, no mark, Italian Pink Crackle glaze, scarce, 15 1/4" h. .... **$175-$200**

Figure Eight Swirl Lamp Base

Lamp base, Figure Eight Swirl, no mark, Gunmetal Black glaze, 15 5/8" h. (ILLUS.) .... **$75-$100**
Lamp base, Lyre style, no mark, Wine Brown glaze, 15" h. .... **$100-$125**

Gonder Wine Brown Lamp Base

Lamp base, Rectangular Flower Center, no mark, Wine Brown glaze, 4 1/8 x 6 1/8", 11" h. (ILLUS.) .... **$25-$40**
Lamps, Double Link, Mold No. 4039, 24 1/2" h., pr. .... **$45-$65**
Lazy Susan, medium, Mold No. 8, 11 1/2" d. .... **$80-$110**
Model of cat, seated "Imperial Cat," Mold No. 521, 12" h. .... **$200-$250**
Model of elephant, Mold No. 207, 11 1/2" l., 8 7/8" h. .... **$75-$100**

Model of frog, standing, pistachio w/black trim glaze, experimental, no mold number or mark, rare, 10 1/2" h. .... **RARE**
Model of gamecock, w/flowers, Mold No. 525, hard to find, 7 1/8" w., 10 3/4" h. **$150-$175**
Model of head of Chinese coolie, Mold No. 541, 11 1/2" w., 11" h. .... **$300-$400**
Model of head of racing horse, Mold 874, 9 1/4" h. .... **$165-$185**
Model of horse head, Mold No. 872, 15" l, 7" h. .... **$150-$175**
Model of panther, large, reclining, marked "Gonder Original 210" in script, Royal Purple glaze, 6 1/2 x 18 1/2" .... **$200-$250**
Model of panther, large, walking, no mark, Pistachio glaze, Mold #206, 4 1/8 x 18 1/2" .... **$100-$150**
Model of panther, recumbent, Mold No. 217, 12" l. .... **$30-$50**
Model of panther, recumbent, Mold No. 217, 15" l. .... **$75-$100**
Model of penguin, Mold No. A-9, very hard to fine, 3 1/4" w., 4 7/8" h. .... **$60-$80**
Model of racing horse head, Mold No. 576, 13 1/2" l., 5 3/4" h. .... **$150-$175**
Model of two running deer, Mold No. 690, 9 1/4" l., 6" h. .... **$75-$100**
Models of geese, one looking down & one w/neck stretched upward, Mold Nos. B-14 & B-15, 3 1/2 & 5 1/2" h., pr. .... **$25-$40**
Mug, swirled wood finish, Mold No. 902, 5" h. .... **$15-$30**
Pedestal base, Mold No. 533-B, 6" d. ...... **$25-$50**
Pitcher, lizard handle, slotted, Mold No. J-54, 8 1/2" l., 10 5/8" h. .... **$100-$125**
Pitcher, pistol grip, Mold No. 102, 9 1/8" h. .... **$125-$150**
Pitcher, 6 1/2" h., squatty bulbous base, cylindrical neck w/flared rim, zigzag handle, Mold No. E-73 & E-373 .... **$25-$35**
Pitcher, 7" h., ruffled lip, Mold No. 1206 ... **$25-$50**
Pitcher, 8 1/8" h., La Gonda patt., Mold No. 917 .... **$40-$50**
Pitcher, 9" h., plain lip, Mold 1205 .... **$50-$75**
Pitcher, 10" h., Mold No. 682 .... **$50-$75**
Pitcher, 12 1/2" h., water, two-handled, tan glaze decorated w/black figures, Mold No. 104 .... **VERY RARE**
Planter, African Violet two-piece w/flared top, Mold No. 792, 5 1/4" sq., 5 1/8" h. . **$20-$40**
Planter, basket shape w/overhead handle, Mold H-39, 7 x 8" .... **$10-$20**
Planter, cov., rectangular w/ridges & leaves, Mold No. 1004, 5 1/2 x 9 1/2", 4 1/2" h. .... **$35-$50**
Planter, double-footed, Mold No. 711, 5 x 8 5/8", 2 7/8" h. .... **$15-$25**
Planter, "End of Day," footed flared rectangle, Mold No. 779/20, 4 3/4 x 10", 3 1/2" h. .... **$40-$50**
Planter, figure of Bali girl carrying basket on head, very hard to find, 14 1/2" h. ..... **$100-$150**
Planter, figure of Bali woman w/gourds, no bikini top, Mold No. 763, rare, 9 1/8" w., 12 3/8" h. .... **$250-$350**
Planters, figures of Gay '90s man & woman baskets, no number, man 3 1/4" h., woman, 14" h., each .... **$150-$175**
Vase, 9 1/4" h., fan shape, Mold No. H-601 .... **$35-$50**

Grueby

Some fine art pottery was produced by the Grueby Faience and Tile Company, established in Boston in 1891. Choice pieces were created with molded designs on a semi-porcelain body. The ware is marked and often bears the initials of the decorators. The pottery closed in 1907.

GRUEBY
Grueby Pottery Mark

Bowl, 7 1/2" d., 1 1/4" h., wide flattened form w/low incurved sides, bluish green glossy glaze **$161**

Grueby Wide Bowl-Vase

Bowl-vase, 6" d., 5" h., very wide flat mouth above swelled tapering sides, overall blue matte glaze, impressed mark (ILLUS.)........ **$575**

Grueby Blue Scarab Paperweight

Paperweight, model of a scarab beetle, oval, matte blue glaze, impressed circular mark, some small glaze chips at base, 3 7/8" l. (ILLUS.).. **$196**

Grueby Scarab with Oatmeal Glaze

Paperweight, model of a scarab beetle, oval, matte oatmeal glaze, impressed

circular mark, glaze peppering, 3 7/8" l. (ILLUS.) **$345**

Small Bulbous Grueby Vase

Vase, 5" h., wide ovoid body tapering to a short molded neck, the sides incised w/wide, tall pointed leaves, thick green matte glaze, Grueby sticker on bottom & impresed initials (ILLUS.)........................ **$1,495**

Short Squatty Grueby Vase

Vase, 5 1/2" d., wide squatty bulbous body molded w/a repeating design of wide rounded overlapping leaves, a wide shoulder to the wide, short rolled neck, dark green matte glaze, signed "W.P.," restored rim chips (ILLUS.) **$960**

Ovoid Matte Brown Grueby Vase

Vase, 6 1/8" h., wide ovoid body w/a short rolled neck, thick medium brown matte glaze, impressed mark, glaze pucker near base (ILLUS., previous page) **$1,150**

Fine Leaf-Molded Grueby Vase

Vase, 6 5/8" h., footed bulbous ovoid body tapering to a molded mouth, the sides molded w/full-length tapering pointed leaves, fine matte green glaze, modeled by Wilhelmina Post, few minor high point nicks, impressed company mark & artist logo (ILLUS.)... **$3,565**

Grueby Matte Blue Vase

Vase, 6 3/4" h., footed simple ovoid body tapering to a flat mouth, textured matte blue glaze, impressed Grueby mark (ILLUS.) **$690**

Vase, 7 3/4" h., squatty bulbous base w/an angled shoulder to the tall gently flaring neck, tooled floral designs, dark matte green glaze, impressed tulip mark (ILLUS., top next column)...................................... **$1,610**

Grueby Vase with Molded Florals

Grueby Vase with Tall Molded Leaves

Vase, 9" h., tall slender gently tapering cylindrical body molded w/full-length pointed leaves alternating w/flower buds around the slightly flaring & scalloped rim, thick suspended green matte glaze, by Annie Lingley, impressed mark, minor grinding to foot chip, minor chip repair at rim (ILLUS.).. **$2,880**

Grueby Vase with Typical Green Glaze

Vase, 9 1/2" h., footed squatty bulbous lower body tapering to a wide cylindrical neck w/a molded rim, dark green matte glaze (ILLUS.) **$1,265**

Simple Grueby Vase with Unusual Glaze

Leaf & Flower-Molded Fine Grueby Vase

Vase, 9 3/4" h., wide ovoid lower body molded w/arched overlapping leaves issuing slender stems & flowers to the wide angled shoulder tapering to a short cylindrical neck, fine green matte glaze, designed by Lillian Newman, paper company label w/"1623" & paper "tulip" label & symbol (ILLUS.) **$3,450**

Vase, 10 3/4" h., thin footring under swelled cylindrical body w/a curved shoulder to the low molded mouth, unusual mottled oatmeal glaze, reglazed factory glaze skip, marked (ILLUS., top next column) **$978**

Vase, 12 1/2" h., swelled cylindrical body tapering to a short flared neck, matte green glaze w/a number of pinhead burst bubbles, area of thin glaze on side (ILLUS., middle next column) **$1,265**

Tall Grueby Matte Green Vase

Tall Swelled Cylindrical Grueby Vase

Vase, 12 1/2" h., tall swelled cylindrical body tapering to a short flaring neck, fine slightly streaked matte green glaze, some pinhead-sized burst bubbles, area of thin glaze on the side, impressed round mark (ILLUS., previous page) **$2,760**

Rare Grueby "Kendrick" Vase

Vase, 12 5/8" h., "Kendrick" design, tall ovoid body below a wide squatty incurved neck, the sides & neck deeply carved w/wide pointed veined leaves, rich green glaze, dark brown interior glaze, unmarked but remnant of original paper label, neatly drilled hole in bottom, small filled-in base chip, along w/original quality oil font (ILLUS.) **$10,449**

Hadley Pottery

Mary Alice Hale was born in Terre Haute, Indiana in 1911. Her father owned Vigo American clay Company and she spent many childhood hours marking clay figures. In 1930 she married George Hadley and the couple moved briefly to New York City. In 1936 Hadley accepted a teaching job and the couple permanently relocated to Louisville, Kentucky. While Mr. Hadley taught, Mary spent her days painting watercolors and oils.

During the summer months the couple enjoyed boating on the Ohio River. Unable to find dishes she liked for the boat, Mary Hadley created her own beautiful yet functional pieces. Friends raved about her creations and she was soon overwhelmed with requests for her unique dishes.

In 1940 Mary Hadley turned all her talents to making pottery. The business grew so fast that in 1994 the couple purchased an 1840s building, a former factory and wool mill. Mr. Hadley left his teaching career to design pottery making equipment, tend kilns and handle business affairs while his wife created pattern, hired artists and was the firm's salesperson. Mary Alice Hadley

continued working until her death from cancer in 1965. Mr. Hadley sold the company in 1979.

Still located in the Butchertown neighborhood of Louisville, the building and pottery making process has changed little over the years. Eighteen patterns, including eight developed by Mary Hadley, continue to be made in a variety of dinnerware and ornamental pieces featuring their distinctive handpainted blue on grey color. Her Country design is the most popular. Visitors can shop for seconds at the showroom, admire her original artwork and take a free factory tour.

Although most pieces illustrated here are of fairly recent production, some of the designs are classics, such as the Bouquet and Farm patterns. Newer patterns include Frog, Turtle, Lighthouse, Palm Tree, Lob Cabin and Fishing, among others.

Hadley Pottery Bunny Rabbit Cereal Bowl

Bowl, cereal, Bunny Rabbit patt. (ILLUS.) **$10**

Hadley Turtle Pattern Soup Bowl

Bowl, soup, Turtle patt. (ILLUS.) **$10**
Cachepot, tapering cylindrical form, Rearing Stallion patt. (ILLUS., next page) **$15**
Coaster, "A Very Merry Christmas" patt. (ILLUS., next page) **$8**
Coaster, "Happy Father's Day" patt. (ILLUS., next page) **$9**

Hadley Pottery Large Duck Planter

Hadley Rearing Stallion Cachepot

Hadley Happy Father's Day Coaster

Merry Christmas Pattern Coaster

Hadley Rearing Stallion Flaring Mug

Mug, flaring rim, Rearing Stallion patt. (ILLUS.) **$13**

Hadley Sailboat Pattern Pencil Cup

Pencil cup, cylindrical, Sailboat patt. (ILLUS.) **$10**
Planter, figural duck, large size (ILLUS., top
of previous page) **$35**

Hadley Fishing on the Bank Dinner Plate

Plate, dinner, Fishing on the Bank patt.
(ILLUS.) .... **$10-$18**

Hadley Turtle Pattern Dinner Plate

Plate, dinner, Turtle patt. (ILLUS.)............. **$10-$15**

Hadley Pottery Farm Cow Trivet

Trivet, Farm Cow patt. (ILLUS.)..................... **$15**

Hall China

Founded in 1903 in East Liverpool, Ohio, this still-operating company at first produced mostly utilitarian wares. It was in 1911 that Robert T. Hall, son of the company founder, developed a special single-fire, lead-free glaze that proved to be strong, hard and nonporous. In the 1920s the firm became well known for its extensive line of teapots (still a major product), and in 1932 it introduced kitchenwares, followed by dinnerwares in 1936 and refrigerator wares in 1938.

The imaginative designs and wide range of glaze colors and decal decorations have led to the growing appeal of Hall wares with collectors, especially people who like Art Deco and Art Moderne design. One of the firm's most famous patterns was the "Autumn Leaf" line, produced as premiums for the Jewel Tea Company. For listings of this ware see "Jewel Tea Autumn Leaf."

Helpful books on Hall include The Collector's Guide to Hall China by Margaret & Kenn Whitmyer, and Superior Quality Hall China - A Guide for Collectors by Harvey Duke (An ELO Book, 1977).

Hall Marks

Ashtray, triangular, deep, No. 683, tur-
quoise **$15**
Ashtray w/match holder, closed sides, No.
618 1/2, cobalt **$20**
Baker, French Fluted shape, Blue Bouquet
patt. **$25**
Baker, French Fluted shape, Silhouette
patt. **$30**

Baker, French Fluted shape, Yellow Rose patt. **$25**

Five Band Batter Bowl

Batter bowl, Five Band shape, Chinese Red (ILLUS.) **$95**

Batter jug, Sundial shape, Blue Garden patt. **$250**

Bean pot, cov., New England #4 shape, Fantasy patt. **$200**

Bean pot, cov., New England shape, No. 2 & No. 4, each .... **$120-$140**

Bean pot, cov., New England shape, No. 4, Blue Blossom patt. **$225**

Bean pot, cov., New England shape, No. 4, Crocus patt. **$325**

Bean pot, cov., New England shape, No. 4, Shaggy Tulip patt. **$275**

Bean pot, cov., New England shape, No. 4, Wild Poppy patt. **$250**

Bean pot, cov., New England shape, No. 488 patt. **$275**

Bean pot, cov., one handle, orange **$55**

Pert Shape Bean Pot

Bean pot, cov., Sani-Grid (Pert) shape, Chinese Red (ILLUS.) **$100**

Bean pot, cov., tab-handled, Sani-Grid (Pert) shape, Rose Parade patt. **$115**

Bowl, 6" d., Medallion shape, Silhouette patt. **$23**

Bowl, 6" d., Radiance shape, No. 4, Crocus patt. **$25**

Bowl, 6" d., Radiance shape, Yellow Rose patt. **$20**

Bowl, 6" d., Thick Rim shape, Blue Blossom patt. **$40**

Bowl, 7" d., Medallion shape, Silhouette patt. **$25**

Bowl, 7" d., Radiance shape, Crocus patt. **$40**

Bowl, 7 1/2" d., straight-sided, Rose White patt. **$18**

Bowl, 8 1/2" d.,Thick Rim shape, Tulip patt. **$30**

Bowl, 8 3/4" d., Five Band shape, Cactus patt. **$45**

Bowl, 9" d., Radiance shape, Crocus patt. **$45**

Bowl, 9" d., salad, Rose Parade patt. **$44**

Bowl, 9" d., salad, Serenade patt. **$20**

Bowl, 9" d., salad, Silhouette patt. **$25**

Bowl, 10" d., Medallion #6 shape, Chinese Red **$45**

Bowl, 10" d., Medallion shape **$45**

Bowls, Radiance shape, Red Poppy patt., set of 3 .... **$75**

Butter dish, cov., Crocus patt., Zephyr shape, 1 lb. **$1,200**

Cake plate, Primrose patt. **$20**

Canister, cov., Radiance shape, Chinese Red **$200**

Canisters, cov., Medallion shape, Warm Yellow, set of 4 .... **$500**

Casserole with Chrome Base

Casserole, cov., Art Deco w/chrome reticulated handled base (ILLUS.) **$55**

Casserole, cov., Five Band shape, Flamingo patt. **$75**

Casserole cov., GE Refrigeratorware **$20**

Casserole, cov., Medallion shape, Silhouette patt. **$50**

Casserole, cov., Radiance shape, Blue Bouquet patt. **$60**

Casserole, cov., Radiance shape, Crocus patt. **$65**

Casserole, cov., Ribbed line, russet **$45**

Casserole, cov., round, No. 76, Wild Poppy patt., 10 1/2" d. **$75**

Casserole, cov., Sundial shape, No. 4, Chinese Red **$55**

Casserole, cov., tab-handled, Rose Parade patt. **$42**

Casserole, cov., tab-handled, Rose White patt. **$35**

Casserole with Inverted Pie Dish Lid

Grouping of Hall Pieces with a Cookie Jar & Several Teapots

Casserole w/inverted pie dish lid, Radiance shape, No. 488, 6 1/2" d., 4" h. (ILLUS., previous page) $60

Coffeepot, cov., Tricolator, Ritz shape, Chinese Red $135

Coffeepot, cov., Waverly shape, Minuet patt. $65

Cookie jar, cov., Five Band shape, Blue Blossom patt. $330

Cookie jar, cov., Five Band shape, Chinese Red $125

Meadow Flower Cookie Jar

Cookie jar, cov., Five Band shape, Meadow Flower patt. (ILLUS.) $325

Cookie jar, cov., Flareware, Gold Lace design $75

Cookie jar, cov., Flareware (ILLUS., top next column) $65

Cookie jar, cov., Grape design, yellow, gold band $60

Cookie jar, cov., model of a owl, all-white, 12" h. (ILLUS. back row, left, with grouping of Hall teapots, top of page) .... $50-$60

Cookie jar, cov., Owl, brown glaze $120

Cookie jar, cov., Red Poppy patt. $500

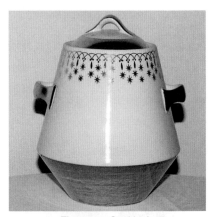

Flareware Cookie Jar

Cookie jar, cov., Saf-Handle (Sundial) shape, Chinese Red $200

Cookie jar, cov., Sundial shape, Blue Blossom patt. $400

Cookie jar, cov., Sundial shape, Chinese Red $235

Cookie jar, cov., Zeisel, Gold Dot design $95

Creamer, Art Deco, Crocus patt. $25

Creamer, Medallion shape, Silhouette patt. $18

Creamer, Modern, Red Poppy patt. $35

Creamer in Autumn Leaf Pattern

Creamer, Radiance shape, Autumn Leaf patt. (ILLUS., previous page) $45

Creamer, individual, Sundial shape, Chinese Red, 2 oz. $65

Creamer, Sundial shape, Chinese Red, 4 oz. $45

Creamer & cov. sugar bowl, Blue Bouquet patt., pr. $70

Custard, straight-sided, Rose Parade patt...... $32

Custard cup, Medallion line, lettuce green...... $12

Custard cup, Radiance shape, Serenade patt. $20

Custard cup, straight-sided, Rose White patt. $25

Custard cup, Thick Rim shape, Meadow Flower patt. $35

Radiance Shape Drip Jar

Drip jar, cov., Radiance shape, Chinese Red (ILLUS.) $60

Drip jar, cov., Thick Rim shape, Royal Rose patt. $25

Drip jar, open, No. 1188, Mums patt................ $35

Gravy boat, Red Poppy patt. $125

Gravy boat, Springtime patt............................ $35

Humidor with Walnut Lid

Humidor, cov., Indian Decal, walnut lid (ILLUS.) $55

Leftover, cov., loop handle, Blue Blossom patt. $150

Leftover, cov., loop handle, Chinese Red $95

Leftover, cov., rectangular, Blue Bouquet patt. $100

Leftover, cov., square, Crocus patt................ $125

Zephyr Shape Leftover

Leftover, cov., Zephyr shape, Chinese Red (ILLUS.)... $110

Fantasy Leftover

Leftover, cov., Zephyr shape, Fantasy patt. (ILLUS.).. $225

Mixing bowl, Thick Rim shape, Royal Rose patt., 8 1/2" d... $30

Mug, beverage, Silhouette patt. $60

Mug, flagon shape, Monk patt......................... $45

Hall Commemorative Mug

Mug, Irish coffee, footed, commemorative, "Hall China Convention 2000" (ILLUS.) $40

Mug, Irish coffee, footed, commemorative United States Bicentennial "Era of Space" Series $35

Mug, Tom & Jerry, Red Dot patt. $15

Pie plate, Orange Poppy patt. $45

Pitcher, ball shape, No. 1, Chinese Red (ILLUS. left with ball shape pitcher No. 3, top next page) $75

Chinese Red Ball Shape Pitchers No. 1 & No. 3

Pitcher, ball shape, No. 3, Chinese Red (ILLUS. right with ball shape pitcher No. 1, top of page) $60

Pitchers, Sani-Grid (Pert) shape, Chinese Red, three sizes (ILLUS. of three, bottom of page) .... $35-$55

Plate, salad, 8 1/4" d., No. 488 patt. $15

Plate, dinner, 9" d., Silhouette patt. $15

Plate, dinner, 10" d., Wildfire patt. $20

Platter, 11 1/4" l., oval, Springtime patt. $20

Platter, 13 1/4" l., oval, Mums patt. $50

Pretzel jar, cov., Crocus patt. $225

Pretzel jar, cov., Pastel Morning Glory patt. .. $125

Punch set: punch bowl & 10 punch cups; Old Crow, punch bowl reads "May YOU always - have an eagle in your pocket ...a turkey on your table - and Old Crow in your glass," the set $175

Salt & pepper shakers, canister style, red, pr. $90

Salt & pepper shakers, Five Band shape, Blue Blossom patt., pr. $75

Salt & pepper shakers, handled, range-type, Blue Blossom patt., pr. $80

Salt & pepper shakers, handled, Royal Rose patt., pr. $34

Salt & pepper shakers, Medallion line, lettuce green, pr. $65

Salt & pepper shakers, Novelty Radiance shape, Orange Poppy patt., pr. $95

Salt & pepper shakers, Radiance shape, canister-style, Chinese Red, pr. $120

Salt & pepper shakers, Rose White patt., holes form letters "S" & "P," pr. $35

Pert Salt & Pepper Shakers

Salt & pepper shakers, Sani-Grid (Pert) shape, Chinese Red, pr. (ILLUS.) $35

Salt & pepper shakers, Sani-Grid (Pert) shape, Rose Parade patt., pr. $35

Salt & pepper shakers, Teardrop shape, Blue Bouquet patt., pr. $35

Soup tureen, cov., Clover style, Crocus patt. $350

Soup tureen, Thick Rim shape, Blue Bouquet patt. $300

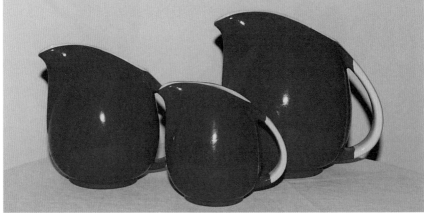

Pert Pitchers in Various Sizes

Hall Automobile Shape Teapot

Stack set, Medallion line, lettuce green $95
Stack set, Radiance shape, Carrot patt. $125
Sugar bowl, cov., Art Deco, Crocus patt. $35
Sugar bowl, cov., Medallion line, Silhouette
    patt. $35
Sugar bowl, cov., Modern, Red Poppy patt. $40
Syrup pitcher, cov., Five Band shape, Blue
    Blossom patt. $165
Tea tile, octagonal, art-glaze blue & white $65
Tea tile, round, Chinese Red $50

Hall Adele Shape Teapot

Teapot, cov., Adele shape, Art Deco style,
    Olive Green (ILLUS.).................................. $200
Teapot, cov., Airflow shape, Chinese Red $130
Teapot, cov., Airflow shape, Cobalt Blue
    w/gold trim, 6-cup... $85
Teapot, cov., Aladdin shape, Canary Yellow
    w/gold trim, w/infuser $65
Teapot, cov., Aladdin shape, Cobalt Blue
    w/gold trim, 6-cup....................................... $125
Teapot, cov., Aladdin shape, Crocus patt. .. $1,950
Teapot, cov., Aladdin shape, oval opening,
    w/infuser, Cobalt Blue w/gold trim.............. $110
Teapot, cov., Aladdin shape, round open-
    ing, Cadet Blue w/gold trim $75

Aladdin Shape Teapot with Serenade Pattern

Teapot, cov., Aladdin shape, w/infuser, Ser-
    enade patt. (ILLUS.)................................... $350
Teapot, cov., Albany shape, Emerald Green
    w/"Gold Special" decoration........................ $60
Teapot, cov., Albany shape, Mahogany
    w/gold trim, 6-cup... $75
Teapot, cov., Automobile shape, Chinese
    Red (ILLUS., top of page) $650
Teapot, cov., Automobile shape, Turquoise
    w/platinum trim... $750
Teapot, cov., Baltimore shape, Ivory Gold
    Label line... $100
Teapot, cov., Basket shape, Cadet Blue
    w/platinum decoration $150

Basket Shape Chinese Red Teapot

Teapot, cov., Basket shape, Chinese Red
    (ILLUS.).. $250
Teapot, cov., Basket shape, Warm Yellow $150
Teapot, cov., Basketball shape, Cobalt Blue
    .... $600
Teapot, cov., Basketball shape, Emerald
    Green w/gold decoration............................ $650

Bellevue Shape Orange Poppy Teapot

Teapot, cov., Bellevue shape, Orange Pop-
    py patt. (ILLUS.)...................................... $1,800

Birch Shape Victorian Line Teapot

Teapot, cov., Birch shape, Victorian line, Blue w/gold decoration (ILLUS.) **$175**

Birdcage Teapot with "Gold Special" Decoration

Teapot, cov., Birdcage shape, Canary Yellow w/"Gold Special" decoration (ILLUS.) .. **$450**

Special Birdcage Autumn Leaf Hall Teapot

Teapot, cov., Birdcage shape, Jewel Tea Autumn Leaf patt., specially produced for the Autumn Leaf Club in 1995 (ILLUS.) **$150**
Teapot, cov., Birdcage shape, Maroon **$350**
Teapot, cov., Birdcage shape, Maroon w/"Gold Special" decoration, 6-cup **$400**
Teapot, cov., Boston shape, Canary Yellow, 2-cup **$45**
Teapot, cov., Boston shape, Chinese Red..... **$150**
Teapot, cov., Boston shape, Cobalt Blue w/gold Trailing Aster design, 6-cup **$150**
Teapot, cov., Boston shape, Crocus patt. **$225**
Teapot, cov., Bowknot shape, Victorian line, Pink **$50**

Hall Bowling Ball Teapot

Teapot, cov., Bowling Ball shape, Turquoise (ILLUS.) **$500**
Teapot, cov., Casual Living Zeisel design **$120**

Hall Forest Green & Gold Centennial Teapot

Teapot, cov., Centennial shape, Forest Green w/gold decoration (ILLUS.) **$125**
Teapot, cov., Cleveland shape, Turquoise w/gold decoration.. **$75**
Teapot, cov., Cleveland shape, Warm Yellow... **$75**
Teapot, cov., Connie shape, Victorian line, Green, 6-cup **$65**
Teapot, cov., Cozy Hot Pot, Ivory w/embossed copper-colored metal cover, Forman Family Products, 6-cup **$40**
Teapot, cov., Cube shape, Emerald Green ... **$100**

Hall Cube Teapot in Green

Hall Cameo Rose Pattern Teapot on E-Shape Dinnerware Body

Teapot, cov., Cube shape, short squared body w/overall green glaze, marked "The Cube" w/listing of design & patent numbers, licensed by Cube Teapots, Ltd., Leicester, England, ca. 1930s, East Liverpool, Ohio (ILLUS., previous page) **$50**
Teapot, cov., Cube shape, Turquoise, 2-cup .. **$140**

Hall Reissued Donut Shape Teapot

Teapot, cov., Donut shape, Autumn Leaf patt., 1993 reissue (ILLUS.) **$150**
Teapot, cov., Donut shape, Chinese Red **$500**

Rare Orange Poppy Pattern Donut Shape Teapot

Teapot, cov., Donut shape, Orange Poppy patt. (ILLUS.) **$450**

Commemorative Hall Donut Teapot

Teapot, cov., Donut shape, part of a limited edition produced for the East Liverpool High School Alumni Assoc., No. 2 of 16, 1997 (ILLUS.) **$100**
Teapot, cov., E-Shape Dinnerware, Cameo Rose patt. (ILLUS., top of page) **$75**
Teapot, cov., figural head of Ronald Reagon, cream glaze, 9 7/8" h. (ILLUS. back row, right, with other Hall teapots & a cookie jar, top of page 312) .... **$125-$150**
Teapot, cov., Flare-Ware line, Gold Lace design **$60**

Football Commemorative Teapot

Teapot, cov., Football shape, commemorative, "Hall 2000 Haul, East Liverpool, Ohio" Ivory (ILLUS.) **$125**

Teapot, cov., Hook Cover shape, cream ground w/gold Star decoration, Gold Label Series, 6-cup, 9 1/2" l. (ILLUS. front row, left, with other Hall teapots & a cookie jar, top of page 312) .... $60-$75

Teapot, cov., Philadelphia shape, aqua blue w/black Frontier Fireplace decal decoration, 6 3/4" h. (ILLUS. front row, right, with other Hall teapots & a cookie jar, top of page 312) .... $100-$120

Teapot, cov., Sani-Grid (Pert) shape, Chinese Red & white, 3-cup .... $35-$45

Teapot, cov. special Hall 100th Anniversary model, cobalt blue w/gold leaf band around the shoulder centered by the name "Hall," issued in 2003, 6-cup, 8" h. (ILLUS. back row, center, with other Hall teapots & a cookie jar, top of page 312) .... $75-$100

Teapot, cov., Star shape, Cobalt Blue $145

Teapot, cov., Star shape, Cobalt Blue w/Standard Gold decoration $125

Teapot, cov., Streamline shape, Chinese Red... $150

Streamline Teapot with Fantasy Pattern

Teapot, cov., Streamline shape, Fantasy patt. (ILLUS.).. $400

Teapot, cov., Streamline shape, Meadow Flower patt. $850

Teapot, cov., Streamline shape, Orange Poppy patt. $350

Teapot, cov., Sundial shape, Ivory w/gold decoration $95

Teapot, cov., Surfside shape, Cadet Blue...... $175

Teapot, cov., Surfside shape, Canary Yellow.. $185

Teapot, cov., Surfside shape, Emerald Green w/gold decoration, 6-cup................ $200

Teapot, cov., T-Ball Bacharach shape, Black w/gold label on base, 6-cup............. $195

Teapot, cov., Tea-for-Four shape, Stock Green $125

Tea-for-Two Teapot in Pink & Gold

Teapot, cov., Tea-for-Two shape, Pink w/gold decoration $150

Teapot, cov., Tea-for-Two shape, Stock Brown w/gold decoration........................... $100

Teapot, cov., Thorley series, Apple shape, Black w/gold decoration.............................. $95

Teapot, cov., Thorley series, Grape shape, Ivory w/Special Gold & rhinestone decoration $295

Teapot, cov., Thorley series, Starlight shape, Pink w/gold & rhinestone decoration $125

Teapot, cov., Thorley series, Windcrest shape, Lemon Yellow w/gold decoration $95

Teapot, cov., Tip-Pot Twinspout shape, Forman Family, Inc., Emerald Green........... $95

Teapot, cov., Victorian "Plume" shape, Pink $50

Teapot, cov., Windshield shape, Gamebird patt. $250

Teapot, cov., Windshield shape, Ivory Gold Label line... $50

Teapot, cov., Windshield shape, Turquoise w/gold decoration....................................... $68

Twin-Tea set: cov. teapot, cov. hot water pot & matching divided tray; art glaze green... $125

Twin-Tea set: cov. teapot, cov. hot water pot & matching divided tray; Pansy patt. $225

Vase, Edgewater, No. 630, cobalt blue $25

Vase, bud, Trumpet, No. 631, Chinese Red $35

Vase, bud, No. 631 1/2, maroon $15

Vase, bud, No. 641, canary yellow.................. $10

Blue Garden Water Bottle

Water bottle, cov., refrigerator ware line, Zephyr shape, Blue Garden patt. (ILLUS.) $650

Water bottle, cov., refrigerator ware line, Zephyr shape, Chinese Red (ILLUS., next page) $350

Water server, cov., Montgomery Ward refrigerator ware, Delphinium blue $55

Water server, Plaza shape, Chinese Red $135

Zephyr Shape Water Bottle

Water server w/cork stopper, Hotpoint refrigerator ware, Dresden blue....................... **$85**
Water server w/hinged cover, Westing-
house refrigerator ware, Hercules shape,
cobalt blue.. **$110**

Hampshire Pottery

Hampshire Pottery was made in Keene, New Hampshire, where several potteries operated as far back as the late 18th century. The pottery now known as Hampshire Pottery was established by J.S. Taft shortly after 1870. Various types of wares, including Art Pottery, were produced through the years. Taft's brother-in-law, Cadmon Robertson, joined the firm in 1904 and was responsible for developing more than 900 glaze formulas while in charge of all manufacturing. His death in 1914 created problems for the firm, and Taft sold out to George Morton in 1916. Closed during part of World War I, the pottery was later reopened by Morton for a short time and manufactured white hotel china. From 1919 to 1921, mosaic floor tiles became the main production. All production ceased in 1923.

J.S.T.&CO.
KEENE. N.H.

Hampshire
HAMPSHIF   pottery

Hampshire Marks

Small Leaf-molded Hampshire Bowl

Bowl, 2 3/4" h., bulbous form molded overall w/overlapping leaves w/a blue & green
semi-matte glaze, marked, Shape No. 24
(ILLUS.)... **$683**

Small Paneled Green Hampshire Vase

Vase, 4 1/4" h., wide ovoid body w/a wide
round shoulder centered by a short
molded neck, large lightly molded
arched panels around the sides, crystalline matte green glaze, marked "Hampshire Pottery 640 - 110" & impressed M
in a circle (ILLUS.)..................................... **$432**

Fine Mottled Blue & Green Hampshire Vase

Vase, 5 1/4" h., squatty bulbous body w/a
wide shoulder centered by a wide gently
flaring short cylindrical neck, mottled blue
& green matte glaze, designed by Cadmon Robertson & marked w/his mono-
gram, Shape No. 118 (ILLUS.) **$690**
Vase, 7 1/2" h., gently swelled cylindrical
body w/an inward-rolled flat mouth,
green crystalline matte glaze, marked
(ILLUS., next page)..................................... **$460**

Hampshire Green Crystalline Vase

Fine Tall Matte Green Hampshire Vase

Vase, 14" h., very tall slender ovoid body tapering to a tall slender neck w/a widely flaring ruffled rim, overall nice green matte glaze, impressed mark (ILLUS.).... **$1,320**

Harker Pottery

Harker Pottery was in business for more than 100 years (1840-1972) in the East Liverpool area of eastern Ohio. One of the oldest potteries in Ohio, it advertised itself as one of the oldest in America. The pottery produced numerous lines that are favorites of collectors.

Some of their most popular lines were intended for oven to table use and were marked with BAKERITE, COLUMBIA BAKERITE, HOTOVEN, OVEN-WARE, Bungalow Ware, Cameo Ware, White Rose Carv-Kraft (for Montgomery Ward) and Harkerware Stone China / Stone Ware brand names.

Harker also made Reproduction Rockingham, Royal Gadroon, Pate sur Pate, Windsong, and many souvenir items and a line designed by Russel Wright that have gained popularity with collectors.

Like many pottery manufacturers, Harker reused popular decal patterns on several ware shapes. Harker was marketed under more than 200 backstamps in its history.

Harker Marks

BakeRite, HotOven

Anti-Q
A decal decoration featuring large yellow and orange roses and blue bachelor's buttons.

Bowl, 6 1/2" d., footed............................... $18-$25
Cookie jar, cov., Modern Age shape w/lifesaver finial on cover, unmarked, 7 7/8" l.
.... $20-$25
Cookie jar, cov., round, 7 7/8" h. .... $40-$50
Dish, cov., square, 5 5/8" w. .... $35-$45
Pitcher, 6 1/2" h., Gargoyle shape........... $35-$45
Pitcher, 7 1/4" h., Bulbous Jug shape....... $40-$50
Pitcher, 7 1/4" h., Gargoyle shape........... $40-$50
Pitcher, cov., 9 1/8" h., Modern Age shape, lifesaver finial on the cover .... $30-$50
Range set: 4 3/4" h., Lard (Drips) jar, 4 1/2" h. salt & pepper shakers; Skyscraper shape, the set .... $40-$50
Utility plate, Virginia shape, decorated w/four decals, 12" w. .... $20-$25
Utility plate, Virginia shape, decorated w/two decals, 12" w............................. $20-$25

Autumn Ivy
Decal design of green and brown leaves w / reddish orange flowers.

Bowl, 6 3/8" d., footed............................... $18-$24
Bowl, 7 1/8" d., footed.............................. $25-$30
Cookie jar, cov., 7 7/8" h. .... $30-$40
Custard cup, 2 5/8" h. .... $4-$8
Pitcher, 6" h., Gargoyle shape................. $35-$40
Teapot, cov., Gargoyle shape, 7" h.......... $40-$50
Vase, 5 1/4" h., florist-type, Melrose shape
.... $40-$50

Birds & Flowers
A decal decoration with flying barn swallows and large grey & orange flowers.

Bowl, 7 1/8 x 9 1/4", Melrose shape .... $18-$24
Creamer, Gem shape, 3" h. .... $30-$35
Creamer, Melrose shape, 5 1/4" l. .... $18-$24
Gravy boat, Melrose shape, 8 1/8" l .... $30-$35
Pie baker, 9 3/4" d. .... $15-$20
Pie baker, 9" d. .... $15-$20
Platter, 11 1/2" l., oval, Embossed Edge shape .... $15-$20
Sugar bowl, open, Gem shape, 3" h. .... $30-$35
Vegetable dish, cov., Melrose shape, 11" l.
.... $35-$45

Countryside
An English thatched roof cottage scene, blue & green decal.

Batter jug, thick-walled pitcher-style, no cover, 5 1/2" h. .... **$70-$80**
Bean pot, cov, 2 1/2" h............................. **$8-$10**
Bowl, 5 1/2" d., Embossed Edge shape.... **$35-$40**
Casserole, cov., 8 1/2" w. .... **$50-$60**
Casserole, cov., unmarked, 7 1/2" w. .... **$40-$50**
Creamer, Gem shape, 3" h. .... **$30-$40**
Cup & saucer, Embossed Edge shape, saucer 6" d., cup 2 1/2" h. .... **$60-$65**
Custard cup, 2" h...................................... **$5-$10**
Dish, cov., Paneled shape, 6 1/2" w., 4 1/2" h... **$40-$50**
Dish, cov., square, 5 1/2" w........................ **$50-$60**
Lifter, 2 1/2 x 9".. **$25-$30**
Lifter, 2 7/8 x 9 1/4" .... **$25-$30**
Pitcher, 7 1/4" h., Bulbous Jug shape...... **$65-$75**
Plate, 6" d... **$10-$15**
Plate, 6 3/8" d., Embossed Edge shape.... **$18-$20**
Plate, 9" d.. **$15-$20**
Plate, 9" d., Embossed Edge shape.......... **$35-$45**
Platter, 11 1/4" l., Nouvelle shape............. **$35-$45**
Platter, 16" l., well-and-tree type.......... **$300-$350**
Range set: 4 3/4" h. Lard (Drips) jar, 4 1/2" h.. salt & pepper shakers; Skyscraper shape, the set........................... **$50-$60**
Scoop, 6" l.. **$40-$50**
Spoon, 8 1/4" l... **$20-$25**
Teapot, cov., bump handle, 8 3/4" l...... **$100-$120**
Utility plate, Virginia shape, 12" w. .... **$50-$60**

Daffodils
Found in two decal color variations: pink & yellow flowers or blue & yellow flowers.

Pitcher, 7" h., Gargoyle shape, blue & yellow flowers .... **$35-$40**
Pitcher, 7" h., Gargoyle shape, pink & yellow flowers .... **$35-$40**
Relish dish, pink & yellow flowers, 11 7/8" l. .... **$25-$30**
Teapot, cov., Gargolye shape, blue & yellow flowers .... **$40-$50**
Vegetable dish, cov., Melrose shape, squared form, pink & yellow flowers, 8 3/4" w. .... **$30-$35**

Modern Age/Modern Tulip
Teapot, cov. .... **$30-$40**

Petit Point Pattern
Bowl, mixing, 10" d., 5 1/2" h. .... **$25-$40**
Coffeepot, cov., Zephyr shape, no brewer basket .... **$30-$50**
Pitcher, cov. jug-type, Hi-rise style, GC shape .... **$40-$50**
Pitcher, jug-type, Square Body................ **$40-$50**
Salad spoon .... **$12-$15**
Salt & pepper shakers, D-Ware shape, pr. .... **$20-$25**

Red Apple I & Red Apple II Patterns
Bowl, 6 1/2" d., Red Apple I patt., Zephyr shape .... **$15-$20**
Bowl, Red Apple I patt., Zephyr shape **$10**
Grease/drips jar, cov., Red Apple II patt., D-Ware shape................................... **$20-$25**
Grease/drips jar, cov., Red Apple II patt., Skyscraper shape .... **$20-$25**
Rolling pin, Red Apple I patt., 14 3/4" l. ... **$70-$90**
Rolling pin, Red Apple II patt., 14 3/4" l. .... **$70-$90**
Salt & pepper shakers, Red Apple II patt., D-Ware shape, pr................................ **$25-$30**

Other Patterns
Butter dish, cov., Monterey patt. .... **$35-$45**
Custard cup, black polka dots on a white body, 2 1/2" h...................................... **$12-$15**
Lifter, cake or pie, Blue Deco Dahlia patt., 9" l. .... **$25-$35**
Teapot, cov., bump handle, black polka dots on a white body, 9" l. .... **$50-$60**
Teapot, cov., Calico Tulip patt., Modern Age shape .... **$45-$60**

Cameoware
Utility plate, Dainty Flower patt., Virginia shape, blue, 12" w. **$25**

Children's Ware
Breakfast set: 6 3/4" d. light green dish picturing horses, colts, lambs & rabbits & a 3" h. matching mug, the set .... **$30-$40**
Breakfast set: 6 3/4" d. teal dish picturing horses, colts, lambs & rabbits & a 3" h. matching mug, the set........................... **$30-$40**
Plate, ABC, color-printed center scene of Sunbonnet Sue titled "I Love You," 6 1/8" d. (ILLUS. center with two other ABC plates, bottom of page)................. **$50-$75**

Group of Three Early Harker ABC Plates

Plate, ABC, color-printed center scene titled "Baby Bunting & Bunch while crossing a log were stared at boldly by an ugly green frog," 6 1/8" d. (ILLUS. left with two other ABC plates, bottom previous page) ...... **$50-$75**

Plate, ABC, color-printed center scene titled "Dolly's Sail," shows two girls, a dog, doll & toy sailboat, 6" d. (ILLUS. right with two other ABC plates, bottom previous page) .... **$50-$75**

Decaled Ware

Countryside (Thatched Roof English Cottage)

Countryside Pattern Plates & Teapot

Plate, 8" sq. (ILLUS. first of three behind teapot) .... **$10-$15**

Plate, 8 7/8" sq. (ILLUS. second of three behind teapot) .... **$15-$20**

Plate, 9 3/4" sq. (ILLUS. third of three behind teapot) .... **$25-$30**

Teapot, cov., Bump Handle style, 8 3/4" l., 5 1/2" h. (ILLUS. front with three plates) .... **$90-$110**

Crayon Apple (pink & orange with green leaves & a few black leaves, black trim)

Cake plate, Concentric Rings shape, 10 7/8" d. .... **$18-$25**

Casserole, cov., vent hole in cover, 8 1/2" w. .... **$25-$35**

Custard, G.C. shape (General Clay with vertical ribs), 2" h. .... **$5-$8**

Lard/drippings jar, cov., Skyscraper shape, 4 1/2" h. .... **$20-$25**

Plate, 10" d. .... **$25-$35**

Stack dish, cov., paneled shape, 6 7/8" w., 2 7/8" h. .... **$25-$35**

Utility plate, Virginia shape, tab handles, 12 1/8" w. .... **$20-$25**

English Ivy

Ashtray, Modern Age shape, 4 7/8" d. ...... **$25-$35**

Bowl & cover with lifesaver finial, 6" d., 5 3/4" h. .... **$40-$45**

Creamer, Gem shape, 3" h. .... **$8-$12**

Creamer & cover with lifesaver finial, Modern Age shape, 5" h. .... **$25-$30**

Creamer with flat lid, Ohio shape, 3 3/4" h. .... **$30-$40**

Fork, Modern Age shape, w/splayed tines for holding spaghetti, 8 3/4" l. .... **$25-$30**

Lifter, Modern Age shape, narrow blade, 8 1/2" l. .... **$18-$25**

Shortening knife/spoon, Modern Age shape, 8 5/8" l. .... **$20-$25**

Spoon, Modern Age shape, 8 1/2" l. .... **$18-$24**

Sugar bowl, open, Gem shape, 3" h. .... **$8-$12**

English Ivy (red poinsettia with grey leaves)

Bowl set, three-piece, 4", 5" & 6" w., the set .... **$30-$40**

Bowl with flat cover, 5 1/8" w., 3 3/4" h., Modern Age shape .... **$20-$30**

Casserole, cov., 7 1/2" w., 4 1/2" h. .... **$18-$25**

Spoon, 8 5/8" l. .... **$15-$20**

Honeymoon Cottage (red roof on yellow cottage, multicolored flowers along narrowing sidewalk leading to cottage, red trim)

Bean pot, 2 1/2" h. .... **$10-$12**

Dish, cov., paneled shape, 6 1/2" h. .... **$20-$25**

Eggcup, 4 1/8" h. .... **$15-$20**

Pie baker, either 8 3/4" or 9 3/4" d., each . **$20-$30**

Salt & pepper shakers, Skyscraper shape, 4 1/2" h., each .... **$15-$20**

Trivet (tea tile), 6 3/8" w. .... **$35-$40**

Ivy Pattern

Harker Ivy Pattern Pieces

Harker Mallow Pattern Pieces

Grease jar, cov., D'Ware shape (ILLUS. left with other Ivy pieces, bottom previous page)... **$20-$30**

Pie baker (ILLUS. second from right with other Ivy pattern pieces, bottom previous page)... **$12-$20**

Pitcher, jug-type, round (ILLUS. right with other Ivy pieces, bottom previous page) .... **$30-$40**

Plate, 10" d., dinner, plain round (ILLUS. second from left other Ivy pieces, bottom previous page) .... **$5-$10**

Spoon, serving (ILLUS. center with other Ivy pieces, bottom previous page) .... **$15-$20**

Jewel Weed (large red & blue flowers with large yellow centers)
Bean pot, 2 1/2" h. .... **$5-$8**
Bowl, oval, 8 3/8" or 9 1/2" l., each .... **$15-$20**
Canister, cov., 6 3/8" w., 5 1/2" h. .... **$35-$40**
Casserole, cov., Sun-Glow (lobed) shape, 7 7/8" w. .... **$45-$60**
Cookie jar, cov., 6 3/8" w., 8 1/2" h........... **$60-$75**
Custard, 3 3/8" w., 2" h. .... **$5-$8**
Jug, cov., 7 3/4" h., straight-sided w/flat cover .... **$45-$60**
Pie baker, large decals, 9 1/8" d. .... **$15-$20**
Pie baker, small decals, 9 1/4" d............... **$20-$25**
Plate, 8 3/4" sq. .... **$10-$15**
Stack dish set, cov., three-piece, 6 1/2" w., 6 1/2" h., the set .... **$40-$50**

Lisa (large single flower in either red, blue or burgundy with different color side flowers)
Bowl, 8 1/8" d., tab handles, red, blue or burgundy .... **$12--$15**
Jug, Gargoyle Handle, yellow glaze w/blue flowers, 4 1/2" h. .... **$25-$35**
Jug, Gargoyle Handle, burgundy, 6 1/2" h. .... **$35-$50**
Jug, Gargoyle Handle, red or blue, 6 1/2" h. .... **$20-$25**
Jug, Gargoyle Handle, yellow glaze w/blue flowers, 7 3/4" h. .... **$45-$55**

Mallow Pattern
Coffeepot, cov., GC shape .... **$45-$65**
Creamer, cov., paneled Ohio jug shape (ILLUS. top right with other Mallow pieces, top of page) .... **$35-$45**
Custard cup (ILLUS. top left with other Mallow pieces, top of page) .... **$8-$12**
Mixing bowl, 9" d. (ILLUS. bottom right with other Mallow pattern pieces, top of page) .... **$25-$30**
Mixing bowl, 9" d., w/rim spout (ILLUS. bottom left other Mallow pattern pieces, top of page)... **$25-$35**

Older White Ware (1879 to 1930)

Three Old Harker Shape Jugs

Jug, Harker shape, decorated w/Dutch children scene w/blue trim, 9" h. (ILLUS. center with two other Harker shape jugs)... **$90-$110**
Jug, Harker shape, h.p. yellow & burgundy pansies, 9" h. (ILLUS. right with two other Harker shape jugs).............................. **$90-$110**

Three Harker Savoy Shape Teapots

Jug, Harker shape, transfer-printed red, pink, yellow & white old roses, 9 1/4" h. (ILLUS. left with two other Harker shape jugs, previous page)............................. **$60-$75**

Republic Ice Water Pitcher & Mug

Jug, Republic shape, heavy wire bail handle & ice retainer spout, Winter scene in brown & white, name printed in gold on front "G.A. Doren, M.D.," 9 7/8" h. (ILLUS. back with matching shaving mug) ...... **$225-$275**

Shaving mug, Iolanthe shape, Winter scene in brown & white, 3 5/8" h. (ILLUS. front with handled Republic jug).......... **$90-$110**

Teapot, cov., Savoy shape, Bird of Paradise patt. w/pink & blue flowers, black trim, 7 7/8" w. (ILLUS. left with two other Savoy teapots, top of page)...................... **$50-$70**

Teapot, cov., Savoy shape, blue blush w/large white & small blue flowers, 7 7/8" w. (ILLUS. center with two other Savoy teapots, top of page) .... **$70-$80**

Teapot, cov., Savoy shape, blue & red Oriental flowers, 7 7/8" w. (ILLUS. right with two other Savoy teapots, top of page) .. **$50-$70**

Moss Rose Vegetable Dish & Undertray

Underplate, square, Elodie (Gargoyle) shape, hand-colored Moss Rose patt., 8 x 9 1/2" (ILLUS. back with Moss Rose vegetable dish)...................................... **$15-$25**

Vegetable dish, cov., Elodie (Gargoyle) shape, hand-colored Moss Rose patt., 5 1/4 x 11 5/8" (ILLUS. front with Moss Rose underplate) .... **$35-$50**

Papyrus (two red flowers on green stems plus black leaves, platinum trim)

Bowl, rectangular, 9" l. .... **$20-$30**

Creamer, Gem shape, 3 1/8" h. .... **$12-$15**

Jug, Gargoyle Handle, 4 3/4" h. .... **$30-$35**

Jug, Gargoyle Handle, 7 3/4" h. .... **$40-$50**

Sugar bowl, Gem shape, 3 1/8" h. .... **$12-$15**

Rolling Pins - 14 1/2" l.

Anti-Q patt. (ILLUS. top with three other rolling pins, top next page)................. **$90-$125**

Blue Roses patt., (ILLUS. bottom with three other rolling pins, top next page) .... **$90-$125**

Godey (Colonial Couple) (ILLUS. second from bottom with three other rolling pins, top next page) .... **$90-$125**

Pink Cyclamen (ILLUS. second from top with three other rolling pins, top next page)... **$90-$125**

Group of Four Harker Rolling Pins

Early Harker Wares (1890-1930)

Blue Transfers

Early Harker Manila Pitcher with Bluebirds

Pitcher, 8" h., cold water size, Manila shape decorated w/bluebirds (ILLUS.)......... **$175-$200**

Plate, 9" d., Waverly shape, decorated w/a scene of turkeys perched on a limb (ILLUS. top left with other turkey plate & platter, bottom of page).. **$40-$75**

Plate, 10" d., Dixie shape, decorated w/a pair of turkeys on the ground (ILLUS. top right with other turkey plate & platter, bottom of page).. **$40-$75**

Platter, 15" l., Dixie shape, decorated w/a pair of turkeys walking (ILLUS. front with two turkey plates, bottom of page)...... **$90-$125**

Christmas Ware

Christmas Ware Baby Feeding Dish

Baby feeding dish, Santa in his sleigh color decal inside, 7" d. (ILLUS.) .... **$45-$60**

Two Turkey-decorated Plates and a Platter

Harker Flow Blue Dutch Scene Berry Bowls & Cake Plate

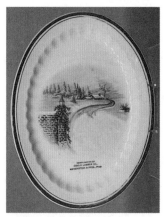

Harker Christmas Ware Platter

Platter, 10 1/2" l., oval, Thumbprint shape, color decal winter landscape w/advertising (ILLUS.) .... **$30-$40**

Flow Blue

Berry bowl, 6" d., individual size, decorated w/a Dutch scene, each (ILLUS. at top & front center with Dutch scene large berry bowl & cake plate, top of page)............. **$20-$30**

Berry bowl, 9" d., master size, decorated w/a Dutch scene, unmarked (ILLUS. front left with other Dutch scene berry bowls & cake plate, top of page)........... **$35-$50**

Bowl, 5" d., deep "36" style decorated w/a scene of a man & dog cart; note: 36 bowls were packed in a barrel w/straw for shipment (ILLUS. left with dog cart gravy boat, bottom of page)........................... **$30-$40**

Cake plate, Dixie shape, decorated w/a Dutch canal scene, 10" d. (ILLUS. top left with Dutch scene chop plate & turkey platter, top next page) .... **$30-$50**

Cake plate, Dixie shape, decorated w/a Dutch scene, 10" d. (ILLUS. front right with Dutch scene berry bowls, top of page).. **$30-$50**

Chop plate, scalloped rim, decorated w/a Dutch windmill scene & printed advertising, 9" d. (ILLUS. top right with Dutch scene cake plate & turkey platter, top next page) .... **$30-$40**

Gravy boat, Paris shape, decorated w/a scene of a man & dog cart, 7 1/4" l. (ILLUS. right with 36 bowl with dog cart scene, bottom of page)... **$40-$50**

Harker Flow Blue Dog Cart Bowl & Gravy Boat

Harker Flow Blue Cake Plate, Chop Plate & Platter

Two Harker Flow Blue Paris Shape Pitchers

Pitcher, 7" h., jug-form, Paris shape, decorated w/a Dutch windmill scene (ILLUS. left with larger Paris pitcher, middle of page) .... **$40-$60**

Pitcher, 9" h., jug-form, Paris shape, decorated w/a Dutch canal scene (ILLUS. right with smaller Paris shape pitcher, middle of page) .... **$45-$75**

Platter, 20" l., oval, Dixie shape, decorated w/a scene of a male turkey (ILLUS. front with Dutch scene cake plate & chop plate, top of page) .... **$500-$650**

Tea Leaf Pattern
Plates, 8" d., gold trim, each (ILLUS. of two, back with other Tea Leaf pieces, bottom of page) .... **$12-$20**

Grouping of Harker Tea Leaf Pattern Pieces

Harker Chesterton Collection

Teapot, cov., Elodie shape (a.k.a. Gargoyle after 1930) tapering squared body, gold trim, 7" h. (ILLUS. front right with other Tea Leaf pieces, bottom previous page) .... **$90-$100**

Vegetable dish, cov., oval, Atlanta shape, gold trim, 11 1/2" l. (ILLUS. front left with other Tea Leaf pieces, bottom previous page).. **$50-$75**

Gadroon and Royal Gadroon

This shape, with its distinctive scalloped edge, was extremely popular and was produced in several glaze colors, with the classic Chesterton grey and Corinthian green (which commands slightly higher prices) presenting an especially elegant table setting. Pate sur pate, though frequently used, is only one of several marks found on this ware. The Royal Gadroon shape was also decorated with numerous colorful decals, including Bridal Rose, Shadow Rose, Royal Rose, Wild Rose, Currier & Ives, Godey, Game Birds, Morning Glories, Violets and White Thistle (silk screened on yellow and pink glazed ware).

Gadroon

Bowl, cereal/soup, lug handles (ILLUS. middle right with Chesterton collection, top of page).. **$3-$5**

Cake set: 10" lug-handled cake plate, six dessert plates & lifter; 8 pcs................ **$25-$35**

Creamer (ILLUS. front right with Chesterton collection, top of page)............................ **$4-$8**

Cup & saucer (ILLUS. middle left with Chesterton collection, top of page) .... **$7-$10**

Gravy boat (ILLUS. middle row, center with Chesterton collection, top of page) .... **$5-$8**

Plate, 7" sq., salad (ILLUS. rear right with Chesterton collection, top of page) .... **$3-$5**

Plate, 9" d., dinner (ILLUS. left rear with Chesterton collection, top of page) .... **$4-$6**

Platter, 13" l., oval...................................... **$10-$12**

Spoon, serving... **$8-$12**

Sugar bowl, cov. (ILLUS. front left with Chesterton collection, top of page) .... **$5-$8**

Vegetable dish, cover w/lug handles........ **$10-$15**

Reproduction Rockingham

Harker Reproduction Rockingham was made in the early 1960s. This line included hound-han-

dled pitchers (the only pieces actually made in the mid-19th century), hound-handled mugs, Jolly Roger jugs*, Daniel Boone jugs*, ashtrays, Armed Forces logo plates and ashtrays, soap dishes, candleholders (for rhw hound-handled mugs), tobacco leaf candy dish/ashtrays, Rebecca at the Well teapots, tidbit trays, Give Us This Day Our Daily Bread plates, octagonal trivets, a 7 1/2" h. bald eagle figure, 6" l. skillet spoon holders (unmarked), Jolly Roger pipes (extremely rare), and even a rolling pin (only one found to date). Colors included brown, gold (honey brown), and bottle green and a light creamy brown trivets and soap dishes have also turned up. Because some pieces have a date of "1840" and are not marked as reproductions, some confusion has resulted, but modern pieces should not confuse anyone familiar with mid-19th century wares and their glazes.

*(Harker called them "jugs" but they were really mugs.)

Ashtray (candy dish), model of a leaf, brown .... **$12-$18**

Ashtray (candy dish), model of a leaf, honey brown or bottle green, each .... **$20-$30**

Bread tray, bottle green........................... **$30-$40**

Bread tray, honey brown (gold) .... **$20-$25**

Jug (mug), figural Daniel Boone head, bottle green .... **$30-$40**

Jug (mug), figural Jolly Roger head, honey brown .... **$20-$30**

Jug (mug), figural Daniel Boone head, brown .... **$18-$24**

Jug (mug), figural Daniel Boone head, honey brown .... **$18-$24**

Jug (mug), figural Jolly Roger head, bottle green.. **$25-$35**

Mug, figural hound handle, honey brown .... **$20-$30**

Mug, figural hound handle, bottle green .... **$25-$35**

Pitcher, jug-type w/figural hound handle, bottle green .... **$65-$80**

Pitcher, jug-type w/figural hound handle, honey brown .... **$50-$60**

Plate, relief-molded American eagle (Great Seal of the U.S.), honey brown or bottle green, each .... **$18-$24**

Russel Wright

White Clover, an intaglio and very modernistic design, was manufactured from 1953 to 1958. This line was made in Meadow Green, Coral Sand, Golden Spice and Charcoal. Clock faces were also made in these colors for General Electric™ clock works.

Clock face, original works, any color .... **$50-$60**
Cup & saucer .... **$6-$10**
Plate, 10" d., any color .... **$12-$15**

Stone China

This heavy ware, with its solid pink, blue, white or yellow glazes over a gray body, was manufacturered in the 1960s and 1970s. The glaze was mixed with tiny metallic chips, which many collectors call "Oatmeal." Later Harker created hand-decorated designs using the intaglio process to create several designs such as Seafare, Peacock Alley, MacIntosh and Acorns, to name a few.

Values listed here are for pieces in any of the four solid colors.

Bowl, oval .... **$5-$10**
Bowl, oval, divided .... **$10-$15**
Carafe .... **$30-$40**
Casserole, w/flat cover .... **$30-$35**
Plate, 10" d. .... **$4-$6**
Platter, 13" oval .... **$8-$12**
Sugar bowl, cov. .... **$5-$10**

Harris Strong Designs

Harris Strong (1920-2006) is so identified with the decorative tiles produced by his company during the 1950s and 1960s that even unsigned tiles of that era are often attributed to him although the style may be markedly different.

Born in Wisconsin, Strong studied ceramics and chemical engineerings at North Carolina State University. In 1947, after working for Kelby Originals, a Brooklyn pottery, Strong and co-worker Robert Krasner founded Potters of Wall Street. Their new firm specialized in ceramic lamps, ashtrays and other decorative pieces, including tiles.

The tiles for which Strong became famous were actually a secondary focus of his, created primarily to test glazes. However, their novelty, whether used as individual accent pieces or grouped together to form a tile "painting," caught on with the public. Buoyed by this success Strong opened his own firm in the Bronx in the early 1950s.

Strong's tile scenes, framed or mounted on burnished wood backings, proved popular with architects, interior decorators and consumers seeking contemporary wall art at affordable prices. Themes included portraits, abstracts and exotic locales as well as medieval and other period depictions. Strong's tile plaques are noted for their vibrant color combinations, the three-dimensionality of the figures and scenes and an attention to detail. Color and form are filtered through the precise parameters of ceramic tile as well as through Strong's own visual sense that encompasses both the primitive and the contemporary.

The sheer size of many Harris Strong plaques made them especially well suited to corporate, hotel and restaurant decor where they made arresting focal points in the interior. In essence, Strong created the early 1950s market for tile-based decorative wall hangings, adapting his designs for nearly every location: ship's lounges, office building facades, elevator interiors and even bowling alleys. One particularly challenging commissioin was the massive "Cathedral Wall" divider created for New York's Waldorf-Astoria Hotel which spanned the entire interior of the hotel's Marco Polo Club.

Attribution of Harris works has often been haphazard since paper labels were used on the back of his plaques rather than a permanent signature. In the absence of a label, one reliable indicator of a Strong plaque is the heart-shaped hooks used for hanging.

Harris G. Strong, Inc. relocated to Maine in 1970 and eventually phased out tile production, focusing instead on paintings, collages and other types of wall decor. For the company's 40th anniversary in 1992 a series of commemorative tiles were produced. The company ceased all production in 1999.

In looking back on his career, Mr. Strong noted "Nobody ever handled tiles the way we did because we regarded them as a piece of pottery; A lot of us worked together to achieve our goal. What I provided, I hope, was the continuing thread that went through all the years --- of quality, workmanship and good design. If I did that then that's enough."

Advisor for this category, Donald-Brian Johnson, is an author and lecturer specializing in Mid-Twentieth century design. Photos are by his frequent collaborator, Leslie Pina.

Ashtray, rectangular, #C-35, a reclining man w/a bird in black on turquoise, 5 3/4" l. (ILLUS. front with larger ashtray, below) .... **$50-$75**

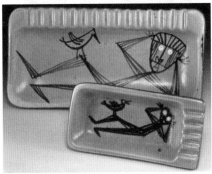

Two Harris Strong Rectangular Ashtrays with a Man and Bird

Ashtray, rectangular, #C-35, a reclining man w/a bird in black on turquoise, 9" l. (ILLUS. back with smaller ashtray) ..... **$75-$100**
Bowl, dark brown rim, light brown body, early, 6" d. .... **$50-$75**
Clock, three robed figures, on walnut, 30" w., 16" h. .... **$325-$350**

Dish, triangular, #B-80, stylized birdcage design within a dark grey border, 8 1/8" l. (ILLUS. right with larger dish, second photo in this column) .... **$100-$125**

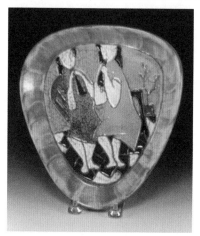

Harris Strong Dish with Musicians

Dish, triangular, #B-75, stylized female musicians, 9 1/2" l. (ILLUS.) .... **$175-$200**

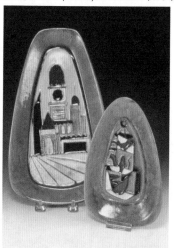

Two Harris Strong Triangular Dishes

Dish, triangular, #B-77, red-domed building on a yellow ground within a green border, 11 3/4" l. (ILLUS. left with smaller dish) .... **$125-$150**

Lamp, table model, decorated w/an incised abstract design on black, 23 3/4" h. .. **$175-$200**

Mirror, wall-type, diamond-shaped, centered in four tiles, wooden frame, 12 1/2" sq. .... **$75-$100**

Plate, 10" l., No. B-76A, ram decoration .... **$175-$200**

Shadowbox, the central tile depicting dancing stick figures, 12 1/4" square (ILLUS., top next column) .... **$175-$200**

Shadowbox with Dancing Stick Figures

Strong Native Dancers Framed Tile

Tile, #A-43, a stylized design of native dancers wearing ceremonial masks in browns on a black ground, linen mat & white oak frame, 10 3/4" sq. (ILLUS.) .... **$150-$175**

Tile, decorated w/autumn trees, framed, 10 3/4" sq. .... **$150-$175**

Tile, decorated w/a single reindeer, framed, 11 1/2" sq. .... **$150-$175**

A Sheep & Ram Tile by Harris Strong

Tile, design of a ram figure in dark blue on a light blue ground, framed, 11" sq. (ILLUS. right with sheep tile) .... **$150-$175**

Tile, design of a sheep figure in dark blue on a light blue ground, framed, 11" sq. (ILLUS. left with ram tile) .... **$150-$175**

Tile, design of multicolored swimming fish on a white ground, framed, 10 3/4" sq. .... **$150-$175**

Tile, #E-18, design of stylized penguins, framed, 10 3/4" sq. .... **$150-$175**

Waller-design "Harlequin" Plaque

Tiles plaque, rectangular, Harlequin," P-15,half-length stylized portrait, a Marvin aller design,9" w.,14" (ILLUS.) .... **$800-$900**
Tiles, puffins depicted on two 6 x 6" tiles .. **$50-$75**
Tray, No. B-78 B, decorated w/a reclining woman, 17" l. .... **$200-$225**

Haviland

Haviland porcelain was originated by Americans in Limoges, France, shortly before the mid-19th century and continues in production. Some Haviland was made by Theodore Haviland in the United States during the last World War. Numerous other factories also made china in Limoges. Also see LIMOGES.

H&C°   **Haviland & C°**   **Limoges.**

Haviland Marks

Ashtray, rectangular, white w/gold Embassy eagle, 3 x 5" **$45**
Baker, oblong open bowl shape, unglazed bottom, Schleiger 33, Blank 19 .... **$75**
Basket, mixed floral decoration w/blue trim, Blank No. 1130, 5 x 7 1/2" **$154**
Beaner, open, oval, Schleiger 876, 3 1/2 x 5" **$45**
Bonbon plate, w/three dividers, h.p., H & Co, 9 1/2" d. **$195**
Bone dish, Schleiger 72, decorated w/roses & green flowers **$30**
Bone dishes, No. 146 patt., Blank No. 133, set of 4 .... **$100**
Bouillon cup & saucer, Drop Rose patt., Schleiger 55C, pale pink **$125**
Bouillon cup & saucer, Ranson blank, Schleiger 42A, flared shape decorated w/pink roses **$50**
Bouillon cups & saucers, No. 72 patt., Blank No. 22, ten sets **$550**
Bouillon w/saucer, cov., Marseilles blank, decorated w/blue flowers, H & Co **$75**
Bowl, 9 1/2" d., soup, cobalt & gold w/floral center, Theodore Haviland **$125**
Bowl, 10" d., 3" h., salad, Schleiger 19, Silver Anniversary **$225**

Bowl, 8 3/8 x 10 3/8", 3 1/2" h., Christmas Rose patt., Blank No. 418 .... **$425**
Broth bowl & underplate, No. 448, 2 pcs....... **$95**
Butter dish, cov., No. 133 patt. **$145**
Butter dish, cov., No. 271A patt., Blank No. 213 .... **$145**
Butter pat, Schleiger 271A, decorated w/blue flowers & pink roses, 3" **$25**
Cake plate, square, CFH/GDM, decorated w/spray of yellow wildflowers, 9" sq. **$85**
Cake plate, handled, 87C patt., Blank No. 2, 10 1/2" d. **$145**
Cake plate, handled, No. 1 Ranson blank, patt. No. 228, 10 3/4" d. **$125**
Cake plate, handled, No. 72 patt., Blank No. 22 .... **$175**
Cake plate, handled, Ranson blank No. 1 ..... **$125**
Candleholders, Swirl patt., decorated w/dainty roses, pr. **$150**
Candlesticks, Marseille blank, h.p. floral decoration, 6 3/4" h., pr. **$325**
Celery tray, Schleiger 150, Harrison Rose, decorated w/small pink roses, 12" l. **$125**
Celery tray, Baltimore Rose patt., Blank No. 207, 5 5/8 x 12" **$275**
Celery tray, Blank No. 305, titled "Her Majesty," 13" l. **$145**
Cereal, Schleiger 57A, Ranson blank, decorated w/pink roses & blue scrolls, 6 x 2" **$32**
Cheese dish w/underplate, CFH/GDM, straight sides, high dome w/flat top, small hole in top near handle, decorated w/blue flowers & gold trim **$250**
Chocolate cup & saucer, No. 72A............... **$55**
Chocolate pot, Autumn Leaf patt., 9" h. **$275**
Chocolate pot, cov., scallop & scroll mold w/floral decoration & gold trim, marked "Haviland Limoges, France," 9" h................ **$275**
Chocolate set: cov. pot & eight cups & saucers; decorated w/pink & blue flowers w/green stems, Blank No. 1, the set **$750**
Chocolate set: cov. pot & eight cups & saucers; Schleiger 235B, decorated w/pink & green flowers & gold trim **$850**
Chocolate set: tall tapering pot & six tall cups & saucers; Albany patt., white w/narrow floral rim bands & gold trim, late 19th - early 20th c., the set (ILLUS., top next page) .... **$450-$650**
Coffee set: cov. coffeepot, creamer, sugar bowl & twelve cups & saucers; Ranson blank No. 1, the set **$975**
Coffeepot, cov., demitasse, Osier, Blank No. 211, impressed "Haviland & Co. - Limoges - France" & English mark **$195**
Coffeepot, cov., Old Wedding Ring patt., white w/gold trim, Old H & Co **$225**
Coffeepot, cov., Paradise, blue edge w/decoration of birds, Theodore Haviland, 8" h. **$195**
Coffeepot, cov., Schleiger 98, Cloverleaf, 9" h. **$450**
Coffeepot, cov., Sylvia patt., 1950s.............. **$225**
Comport, divided, shell-shaped, white w/green trim, full-bodied red lobster at center, non-factory decor of red, green & black.. **$450**
Comport, pedestal on three feet w/ornate gold shell design, top w/reticulated edge, peach & gold design around base & top, 9" d. (ILLUS., next page)........................... **$595**

Haviland Albany Pattern Chocolate Set

Footed Comport with Reticulated Rim

Comport, round, English, shaped like regular pedestal comport without pedestal, Schleiger 56 variation, decorated w/lavender flowers, 9" d. $125

Comport, Meadow Visitors patt., smooth blank, 5 1/8" h., 9 7/8" d. $225

Cracker jar, cov., floral decoration, cobalt, gold & blue bells, 1900 & decorator's marks $650

Cracker jar, cov., Marseille blank $495

Cream soup w/underplate, Schleiger 31, Ranson blank, decorated w/pink roses, 5" d. bowl, 2 pcs. $65

Creamer, Schleiger 146, commonly known as Apple Blossom, Theodore Haviland, 4" $70

Creamer, Moss Rose patt., gold trim, 5 1/2" h. $60

Creamer & open sugar, dessert, Cloverleaf patt., Schleiger 98, pr. $165

Creamer & open sugar, Ranson blank, Drop Rose patt., w/very ornate gold trim, pr. $750

Creamer & sugar, Schleiger 223A, Blank 1, decorated w/pink flowers, pr. $125

Creamer & sugar bowl, Montméry patt., ca. 1953, pr. $125

Cup & saucer, coffee, Schleiger 39D, decorated w/pink roses & gold trim $55

Cup & saucer, demitasse, Arcadia, bird patt. $45

Cup & saucer, tea, Schleiger 19, white w/gold trim $45

Cup & saucer, breakfast, Moss Rose patt. w/gold trim $65

Cup & saucer, demitasse, Papillon Butterfly patt., floral by Pallandre $75

Cup & saucer, Moss Rose patt., "Haviland & Co. - Limoges - France" $45

Cup & saucer, Rosalinde patt., American $45

Meadow Visitors Cup & Saucer

Cups & saucers, Papillon butterfly handles w/Meadow Visitors decoration, six sets (ILLUS. of one set) $900

Cuspidor, smooth blank, bands of roses decorating rim & body, 6 1/2" h. $350

Cuspidor, Moss Rose patt., smooth blank, 8" d., 3 1/4" h. $450

Dessert set: 8 1/2 x 15" tray & four 7 1/4" dishes; Osier Blank No. 637, fruit & floral decoration, the set $325

Dessert set: 9 x 15" oblong tray w/twelve 7" square matching plates; centers decorated w/Meadow Visitors patt. & bordered in rich cobalt blue w/gold trim, commissioned for Mrs. Wm. A. Wilson, 13 pcs. .. $2,500

Haviland Dinnerware in Blank No. 5

Haviland Dinner Service in the Albany Pattern

Dinner service: service for eight w/five-piece place settings & additional bowls, pitcher, gravy boat & other pieces; mostly Blank No. 5 w/delicate pink floral decoration, late 19th - early 20th c., 54 pcs. (ILLUS. of part, previous page) **$2,500**

Dinner service: twelve 8-piece place settings w/additional open & cov. vegetable dishes & oval platter; Albany patt., white w/narrow floral rim bands & gold trim, late 19th - early 20th c., the set (ILLUS., top of page) **$2,700**

Haviland Scenic Dish

Dish, shell-shaped, incurved rim opposite pointed rim, h.p. scene of artist's waterside studio, decorated by Theodore Davis, front initialed "D," back w/presidential seal & artist's signature, part of Hayes presidential service, 8 x 9 1/2" (ILLUS.) **$2,250**

Dresser tray, h.p. floral decoration, 1892 mark **$125**

Eggcup, footed, No. 69 patt. on blank No. 1 .... **$65**

Eggcups, footed, No. 72 patt., Blank No. 22, pr. **$150**

Fish set: 23" l. platter & six 9" d. plates; each w/different fish scene, dark orange & gold borders, Blank No. 1009, 7 pcs.... **$1,250**

Fish set: 22" l. oval platter & twelve 8 1/2" d. plates; each piece w/a different fish in the center, the border in two shades of green design w/gold trim, h.p. scenes by L. Martin, mark of Theodore Haviland, 13 pcs. (ILLUS. of plate, top next column)... **$2,750**

Plate from Fish Set

Fish set: 23 1/4" l. platter & twelve 7 3/8" plates; Empress Eugenie patt., No. 453, Blank No. 7, 13 pcs. **$3,500**

Gravy boat, No. 761 .... **$95**

Gravy boat w/attached underplate, No. 98 patt., Blank No. 24 .... **$145**

Gravy boat w/attached underplate, Schleiger 46, Ranson blank, decorated w/pink & blue flowers **$125**

Haviland Hair Receiver

Hair receiver, cov., squatty round body on three gold feet, h.p. overall w/small flowers in blues & greens w/gold trim, mark of Charles Field Haviland (ILLUS.) **$225**

Honey dish, 4" d., bowl-form, Schleiger 33, decorated w/white flowers, pink shading **$25**

Ice cream set: tray & 6 individual plates; Old Pansy patt. on Torse blank, 7 pcs. **$550**

Pitcher, 9" h., lemonade-type, Schleiger 1026B variation, Blank 117, decorated w/lavender flowers & brushed gold trim, Theodore Haviland $250

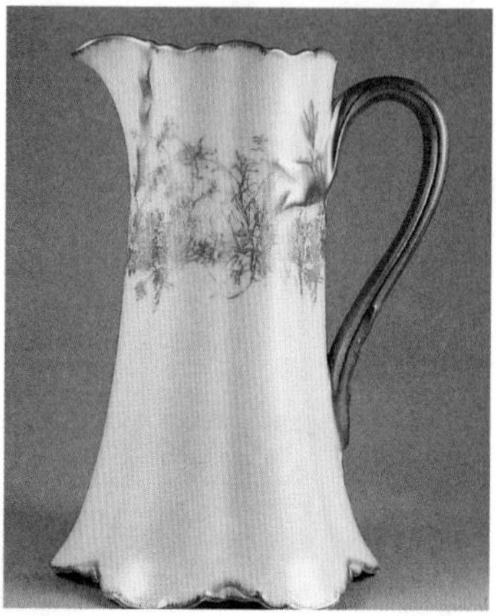

Gold-decorated Lemonade Pitcher

Pitcher, 9" h., tankard-shaped lemonade-type, Ranson blank, delicate floral band around the upper body trimmed in gold, gold handle & trim bands, factory-decorated, Haviland & Co. mark (ILLUS.).......... $250

Pitcher, 9 1/2" h., No. 279 patt., Blank No. 643 .... $225

Place setting: dinner, salad, bread & butter plates, cup & saucer; w/scalloped double gold edge, Schleiger 91A.......................... $135

Plate, dinner, No. 72.. $40

Plate, dinner, No. 9 patt., set of 10................ $300

Plate, dinner, Rosalinde patt., American $32

Plate, Partridge in a Pear Tree from 12 Days of Christmas series, 1970 .... $75

Plate, ice cream, 5" l., leaf-shaped w/handle, cobalt & gold... $95

Paisley Pattern Plate

Plate, bread & butter, 6 1/2" d., Paisley patt., smooth blanks w/gold edge, brownish red ground w/flowers in yellow, bright blue, green & white border design w/yellow flowers & bright blue leaves, turquoise scroll trim, Haviland & Co. mark (ILLUS.)... $28

Plate, bread & butter, 6 1/2" d., Schleiger 340, decorated w/pink roses & blue scrolls... $30

Plate, coupe salad, 7 1/2" d., Baltimore Rose patt, Blank No. 207, set of 8 .... $650

Plate, 8 1/2" d., cobalt & gold Pallandre patt. $175

Plate with Draped Pink Roses

Plate, luncheon, 8 1/2" d., smooth edge, design on border of draped pink roses, Schleiger 152, Theodore Haviland (ILLUS.)..... $30

Plate, 7 1/2 x 8 1/2", heart-shaped, Baltimore Rose patt. $275

Plate, 9 1/2" d., scalloped edge, cobalt & gold w/floral center.................................... $225

Plate, dinner, 9 1/2" d., Dammouse antique rose w/gold medallion & flowers $195

Plate, dinner, 9 1/2" d., Feu de Four, Poppy & Seeds $125

Plate, dinner, 9 1/2" d., Schleiger 19, Silver Anniversary $35

Plate, dinner, 9 1/2" d., Schleiger 29-K, decorated w/pink flowers & gold trim $40

Plate, 9 3/4" d., portrait of woman in forest scene, artist-signed, Blank No. 116 .... $225

Plate, dinner, 10" d., Schleiger 150, known as Harrison Rose, decorated w/small pink & yellow roses $32

Plate, 10 1/2" d., service, Blank 20, white w/gold trim... $45

Plate, chop, 11 1/4" d., 33A patt., Blank No. 19 .... $125

Plate, chop, 12" d., Schleiger 233, The Norma, decorated w/small pink & yellow flowers.. $95

Plates, luncheon, 8 3/8" d., Club Ware, Meadow Visitors patt. & various fruits, set of 8 .... $525

Platter, 16" l., rectangular, Marseilles, Schleiger 9 .... $145

Platter, 12 1/4 x 18" oval, Moss Rose patt. w/blue trim, smooth blank $175

Platter, 14 x 20", Ranson blank No. 1 .... $275

Pudding set, Schleiger 24, white w/gold trim, complete w/unglazed insert & undertray.. $475

Punch bowl, Baltimore Rose patt. $2,000

Double-spouted Sauceboat & Tray

Punch cup, tapering scalloped pedestal foot supporting wide shallow cup bowl, decorated w/flowers in shades of green w/some pink flowers & green leaves, variation of Schleiger No. 249B on Blank 17, Haviland & Co. mark, 4" h. $85

Ramekins & underplates, Ranson Blank No. 1, set of 12 .... $540

Relish, oval, Schleiger 570, two-tone green flowers, gold edge, 8" l. $65

Salad plate, bean-shaped, variation of Schleiger 1190, decorated w/orange flowers & gold trim, 4 1/2 x 9" $95

Salt, CFH/GDM, h.p. flowers, 1 1/2 x 3/4" $45

Salt, Schleiger 31, decorated w/pink roses & gold trim, 2 x 1" $65

Sauce tureen w/attached underplate, cov., No. 146 patt., Blank No. 133, 7" d. underplate, bowl 5 1/4" d. $175

Sauce tureen w/attached undertray, cov., oval, Schleiger 619, green design w/gold trim, Theodore Haviland $175

Sauceboat & undertray, footed double-spouted boat-shaped sauceboat w/looped side handles w/molded rope trim, matching dished undertray, heavy gold trim on white, old Haviland & Co. mark, 2 pcs. (ILLUS., top of page) $150

Serving bowl, Schleiger 235B, 12" d., 2" h. .. $195

Serving dish, quatrefoil form, Multifloral patt., Old H & Co, 9" sq., 2" h. (ILLUS., top next column).. $125

Serving dish, scalloped rectangular form w/a scalloped foot ring below the flaring side w/low open side handles, decorated w/pale yellowish green to dark green poppies & pale pink shadows, gold trim,

variation of Schleiger No. 665, Haviland & Co. mark, 8 x 10" (ILLUS., bottom of page).. $225

Multifloral Serving Dish

Serving plate, blue & burgundy Art Deco decoration, black ground, "Haviland & Co. - Limoges - France," 10 1/2" d. $95

Sipper dishes, Meadow Visitors patt., smooth blank, 4 3/4" d., set of 8................ $176

Sorbet, footed, w/gold embossed trim, Schleiger 276 .... $75

Soup bowls, No. 271A patt., Blank No. 213, set of 8 .... $280

Soup plate w/flanged rim, No. 761 .... $45

Soup tureen, cov., pink Drop Rose patt., on Blank No. 22 .... $895

Soup tureen, round, Ranson blank, Schleiger 29M, decorated w/tiny blue flowers... $350

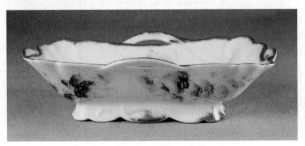

Haviland Serving Dish with Poppies

Haviland Covered Sugar Bowl

Sugar bowl, cov., large cylindrical form w/small loop side handles & inset flat cover w/arched handle, white ground decorated w/sprays of pink daisies touched w/yellow & greyish brown leaves, variation of Schleiger No. 1311, 1 lb. size, Charles Field Haviland, marked "CFH/GDM" (ILLUS.).................................... **$75**

Tea caddy, cov., Ranson blank..................... **$325**

Tea set: cov. teapot, creamer & sugar bowl; floral & leaf mold w/gold trim, 3 pcs. **$495**

Tea set: small cov. teapot, creamer & sugar bowl, six cups & saucers; No. 19 patt., 15 pcs... **$700**

Tea & toast set: scalloped plate & cup; Marseilles blank, decorated w/pink roses, H & Co.. **$175**

Tea & toast tray & cup, No. 482 patt., Blank No. 208, pr... **$175**

Tea tray, round, Schleiger 29A, decorated w/pink flowers, unglazed bottom, 16" d...... **$275**

Teacup & saucer, cup w/tapering cylindrical bowl & figural butterfly handle, h.p. grey band design on rim & border, Haviland & Co. (ILLUS., next column)............... **$125**

Teapot, cov., 4-cup, CFG/GDM, white w/gold, ribbon handle................................. **$250**

Teapot, cov., Henri II blank w/gold & silver decoration **$350**

Butterfly-handled Cup and Saucer

Teapot, cov., wide squatty bulbous tapering sides w/a flat rim, low domed cover w/arched finial, upright serpentine spout & C-scroll handle, white w/gold trim & thin yellow leaf tip bands around the rim & cover, double Haviland mark, ca. 1900 (ILLUS., bottom of page)........................... **$195**

Toothbrush box, cov., Moss Rose patt. w/gold trim, smooth blank, ca. 1860s-70s, 8" l. **$225**

Vases, 15" h., Terra Cotta, brown w/white water lily & large green leaves in relief, Haviland & Co., pr..................................... **$3,500**

Vegetable dish, oval, Schleiger 142A, decorated w/pink daisy-like flowers, blue fences & scrolls, gold trim, Theodore Haviland, 8 x 10"... **$85**

Vegetable dish, cov., Marseille patt., Blank No. 9, 9 1/2" l. **$145**

Vegetable dish, cov., decorated w/small orange roses, Blank No. 24, 10" d. **$165**

Wash pitcher, Moss Rose patt. w/gold trim, smooth blank, 12" h. **$350**

Waste bowl, Schleiger 233A, The Norma, decorated w/tiny pink & yellow flowers & gold daubs, 5 x 3" **$47**

Squatty Haviland Porcelain Teapot

Very Rare Arms of North Carolina Serving Dish

Historical & Commemorative Wares

Numerous potteries, especially in England and the United States, made various porcelain and earthenware pieces to commemorate people, places and events. Scarce English historical wares with American views command highest prices. Objects are listed here alphabetically by title of the view.

Most pieces listed here will date between about 1820 and 1850. The maker's name is noted at the end of the entry.

Arms of North Carolina serving dish, flowers & vines border, spoked wheels equidistant around border, oval w/flanged rim, dark blue, minor edge wear, Mayer, 9 3/4 x 12 3/4", 2 3/4" h. (ILLUS., top of page) **$5,115**

Large Group of Historical Staffordshire Pieces

Bank of the United States, Philadelphia plate, spread-winged eagles, flowers & scrolls border, dark blue, Stubbs, 10 1/8" d. (ILLUS. back row, far right, with grouping of other historical pieces) **$431**

Bramber Church, Sussex tureen w/cover & Luscombe, Devonshire undertray, fruit & florals border, dark blue, R. Hall's Select Views series, flakes on tray, damage on cover, tureen 8 1/4" l., 5 3/4" h., the set (ILLUS. front, left & right, with large grouping of historical pieces, previous column) **$316**

Capitol, Washington (The) plate, vine border, dark blue, rim firing imperfections, 10" d., Stevenson (ILLUS. back row, center, with grouping of historical pieces, previous column).. **$316**

[teapot image]

Castle Howard Staffordshire Teapot

Castle Howard, Scotland teapot, cov., fruit & floral borders, dark blue, J. Hall & Sons, 6 1/4" h. (ILLUS.) **$382**

Harvard College soup plate, acorn & oak leaves border, dark blue, 10" d., Stevenson & Williams (faint knife scratches) **$345**

Hospital, Boston plate, vine border, dark blue, 9" d., faint knife scratches, Stevenson & Williams (ILLUS. back row, left, with grouping of historical pieces, previous column) **$431**

Jedburgh Abbey, Roxburghshire platter, floral border, dark blue, Adams, light stains, 13 1/4 x 17"..................................... **$460**

Regent Street, London Dark Blue Staffordshire Fruit Basket

Library, Philadelphia plate, flowers in medallions border, medium blue, Beauties of America series by Ridgway, light crazing on bottom, 8 1/4" d. **$374**

Octagon Church, Boston soup plate, flowers within medallions border, dark blue, 9 3/4" d. (Ridgway) **$403**

Regent Street, London fruit basket, oval w/reticulated sides & loop end handles, dark blue, William Adams & Sons, 11 1/4" d., 4 3/8" h. (ILLUS., top of page) .. **$529**

Sancho Panza & The Dutchess Platter

Sancho Panza and The Dutchess, floral border, Don Quixote series, dark blue, 14 3/4 x 18 1/2",   old hairline w/stains, Clews (ILLUS.)) **$489**

Hull

In 1905 Addis E. Hull purchased the Acme Pottery Company in Crooksville, Ohio. In 1917 the A.E. Hull Pottery Company began to make a line of art pottery for florists and gift shops. The company also made novelties, kitchenware and stoneware.

Hull's Little Red Riding Hood kitchenware was manufactured between 1943 and 1957 and is a favorite of collectors, as are the beautiful matte glaze vases it produced.

In 1950 the factory was destroyed by a flood and fire, but by 1952 it was back in production. Hull added its newer glossy glazed pottery plus pieces sold in flower shops under the names Regal and Floraline. Hull's brown dinnerware lines achieved great popularity and were the main lines being produced prior to the plant's closing in 1986.

References on Hull Pottery include: Hull, The Heavenly Pottery, 7th Edition, 2001 and Hull, The Heavenly Pottery Shirt Pocket Price Guide, 4th Edition, 1999, by Joan Hull. Also The Dinnerwares Lines by Barbara Loveless Click-Burke (Collector Books 1993) and Robert's Ultimate Encyclopedia of

Hull Pottery by Brenda Roberts (Walsworth Publishing Co., 1992). -- Joan Hull, Advisor.

Hull Marks

Rare Red Riding Hood Feeding Dish

Baby feeding dish, divided, Little Red Riding Hood patt. (ILLUS.) **$1,400**

Basket, hanging-type, Woodland Matte patt., No. W31-5 1/2", 5 1/2" h. **$145**

Basket, Tulip (Sueno) patt., No. 102-33-6", 6" h. **$350**

Basket, Open Rose (Camellia) patt., hanging-type, No. 132-7" **$250**

Basket, Orchid patt., No. 305, 7" h. **$600**

Tokay Pattern Basket

Poppy Pattern Basket, Ewer & Two Vases

Basket, Tokay patt., No. 6, overhead branch
handle, white ground, 8" h. (ILLUS., previ-
ous page) **$95**

Basket, Blossom Flite patt., low-bowl, No.
T9, 10" l. **$135**

Basket, Bow-Knot patt., pink & blue, B12-
10 1/2", 10 1/2" h. **$750**

Basket, Magnolia Matte patt., No. 10,
10 1/2" h. **$325**

Basket, Open Rose (Camellia) patt.,
No.140-10 1/2", 10 1/2" h. **$1,300**

Basket, Tokay patt., round "moon" form,
No. 11, 10 1/2" h. **$125**

Basket, Tuscany patt., round "moon" form,
No. 11, 10 1/2" h. **$125**

Basket, Water Lily patt., tan & brown, No.
L-14-10 1/2" **$350**

Basket, Bow-Knot patt., No. B-29, 12" h.
.... **$2,000**

Basket, Wild Flower Number Series patt.,
No. 66, 10 1/2" h. **$2,000**

Basket, Poppy patt., No. 601, 12" h. (ILLUS.
back with three Poppy vases, top of page)
.... **$1,300**

Basket, Tropicana patt., No. 55, 12 3/4" h. **$750**

Basket, hanging-type, teardrop-shaped,
Capri patt., No. C57, 14 1/2" h. **$85**

Basket, Ebb Tide patt., model of a large
shell w/long fish handle, No. E-11,
16 1/2" l. **$300**

Batter pitcher, Little Red Riding Hood
patt., 6 1/2" h. **$500**

Bell, Sun-Glow patt., No. 87, closed or open
handle, dark yellow or dark pink ground,
6 1/2" h., each (ILLUS. of two, top next
column) .... **$100-$200**

Bonbon dish, Butterfly patt., No. B4, 6" d.
.... **$40**

Bowl, 10 1/2" d., lobed fruit-style, Butterfly
patt., No. B16 .... **$150**

Bowl, footed fruit-type w/turned-up sides,
Serenade patt., No. S15, 11 1/2" l. **$110**

Candleholders, Open Rose (Camelia)
patt., models of doves, No. 117-6 1/2",
6 1/2" h., pr... **$325**

Two Sun-Glow Pattern Bells

Candleholders, Magnolia Matte patt., upright ovoid socket on an oval base
w/small open legs from the bottom to the
base, No. 27-4", 4" h., pr........................... **$100**

Candleholders, Orchid patt., No. 315,
4" h., pr.. **$225**

Candleholders, Water Lily patt., No. L-22-
4", 4" h., pr. **$125**

Candleholders, Iris (Narcissus) patt., No.
411, 5" h., pr.. **$175**

Canister, cov., Little Red Riding Hood patt.,
"Sugar," "Coffee," or "Salt," each **$750**

Sun Glow Pattern Casserole

Casserole, cov., Sun-Glow patt., No. 51-7 1/2", 7 1/2" d. (ILLUS., previous page)...... **$50**

Coffee server, cov., instant coffee-type, Parchment & Pine patt., No. S-15, 8" h...... **$150**

Console bowl, Bow-Knot patt., pink & blue, No. B-16-13 1/2", 13 1/2" l. **$325**

Console bowl, Iris (Narcissus) patt., No. 409-12", 12" l... **$250**

Console bowl, Orchid patt., No. 314-13", 13" l. **$375**

Console bowl, Tokay patt., No. 14, 15 3/4" l. **$165**

Console bowl, Tuscany patt., No. 14, 15 3/4" l. **$165**

Console bowl, Water Lily patt., No. L-21-13 1/2", 13 1/2" l. **$175**

Console bowl, Wildflower patt., No. W-21 - 12", 12" l... **$175**

Console bowl, 13 1/2" h., Bow-Knot patt., No. 15-13 1/2" **$1,300**

Two Gingerbread Man Cookie Jars

Cookie jar, cov., figural Ginger Bread Man, No. 123, grey Flint Ridge line, 1980s, 12" h. (ILLUS. right with sand colored cookie jar)... **$150**

Cookie jar, cov., figural Ginger Bread Man, No. 223, sand Flint Ridge line, 1980s, 12" h. (ILLUS. left with grey cookie jar)...... **$500**

Little Red Riding Hood Cookie Jar

Cookie jar, cov., Little Red Riding Hood patt., many design variations, each (ILLUS.)................................... **$400-$1,000**

Cornucopia-vase, Woodland Gloss patt., No. W2-5 1/2", 5 1/2" h. **$40**

Cornucopia-vase, Woodland Matte patt., No. W2-5 1/2", 5 1/2" h. **$95**

Cornucopia-vase, Woodland patt., Post 1950, No. W2-5 1/2", 5 1/2" h. **$85**

Cornucopia-vase, Water Lily Matte patt., L-7, 6 1/2" h. **$95**

Cornucopia-vase, Ebb Tide patt., figural mermaid on the rim, No. E3, 7 1/2" h........ **$225**

Cornucopia-vase, Dogwood patt., No. 511, 11 1/2" h. **$275**

Cornucopia-vase, double, Magnolia Matte patt., No. 6, 12" h. **$165**

Cornucopia-vase, Parchment & Pine patt., No. S-6, 12" **$100**

Dish, leaf-shaped, Capri patt., No. C63, 14" l. **$85**

Ewer, Magnolia patt., No. 14-4 3/4", 4 3/4" h. **$75**

Ewer, Woodland patt., No. W6-6 1/2", 6 1/2" h. **$125**

Ewer, Water Lily Matte patt., No. L-3, 5 1/2" h. **$95**

Ewer, Rosella patt., No. R-9, 6 1/2" h. ...... **$50-$75**

Ewer, Wildflower Matte patt., No. W-11, 8 1/2" h. **$145**

Ewer, Capri patt., molded pine cone on the side, No. C87, 12" h. **$100**

Ewer, Poppy patt., No. 610, 13" h. (ILLUS. front row, left, with Poppy basket & two vases, top of previous page)..................... **$850**

Ewer, Tulip (Sueno) patt., footed tall baluster-form body w/wide arched rim spout & ornate forked & scrolled handle, No. 109-33, 13" h. **$400**

Ewer, Tropicana patt., No. T56, 13 1/2" h. **$750**

Ewer, Wild Flower Number Series, No. 55, 13 1/2" h.. **$1,200**

Ewer, Ebb Tide patt., No. E-10, figural fish handle, 14" h. **$250**

Flower dish, Butterfly patt., No. B7, 6 3/4 x 9 3/4" **$50**

Grease jar, cov., Sun-Glow patt., No. 53, 5 1/4" h. **$45**

Jardiniere, Iris (Narcissus) patt., No. 413, 5 1/2" h. **$145**

Jardiniere, Open Rose (Camellia) patt., molded rams' head handles, No. 114, 8 1/2" d.. **$175**

Jardiniere, Dogwood patt., No. 514, 4" h. **$110**

Jardiniere, Woodland Gloss patt., No. W7-5 1/2", 5 1/2" h. **$65**

Jardiniere, Woodland Matte patt., No. W7-5 1/2", 5 1/2" h. **$140**

Jardiniere, Woodland patt., Post 1950, No. W7-5 1/2", 5 1/2" h. **$125**

Jardiniere, Bow-Knot patt., blue or pink trim, No. B-18-5 3/4", 5 3/4" h. **$350**

Jardiniere, Orchid patt., No. 310, 9 1/2" d., 6" h.. **$450**

Jardiniere, Calla Lily patt., No. 591, 7" h. **$300**

Jardiniere, Water Lily Matte patt., No. L-24, 8 1/2" h. **$350**

Scarce Hull Tulip Pattern Lamp

Lamp, Tulip (Suena), patt., No. 107-33-61/2", 6 1/2" h. (ILLUS.) .... **$400-$600**

Lavabo & base, Butterfly patt., Nos. B24 & B25, overall 16" h., 2 pcs. **$200**

Match box, hanging-type, Little Red Riding Hood patt., house-shaped, 5 1/2" h. **$900**

Mug, Serenade patt., No. S22, 8 oz., 5 1/2" h. **$55**

Pitcher, 5" h., Iris (Narcissus) patt., No. 401-5" **$100**

Pitcher, 5 1/2" h., Bow-Knot patt., No. B-1..... **$195**

Pitcher, milk, 8" h., Little Red Riding Hood patt. **$425**

Pitcher, 8 1/4" h., Ebb Tide patt., No. E-4-8 1/4" **$150**

Pitcher, 8 1/2" h., Blossom Flite patt., No. T3 .... **$125**

Pitcher, 11 1/2" h., Dogwood (Wild Rose) patt., No. 506-11 1/2" **$350**

Pitcher, 13 1/2" h., Open Rose (Camelia) patt., No. 106 .... **$600**

Planter, model of swan, Capri patt., No. C21, 3" h. **$25**

Planter, model of swan, Capri patt., No. C23, 8 1/2" h. **$35**

Salt box, hanging-type, Utility ware, all-white semi-porcelain, upright rectangular shape, No. 111, 6" h. **$150**

Spice jar, cov. Little Red Riding Hood patt. .. **$850**

Tea set: cov. teapot No.110, open sugar bowl No.112 & creamer No. 111; Open Rose (Camellia) patt., teapot 8 1/2" h. the set **$550**

Tea set: cov. teapot No. 16, creamer No. 17 & cov. sugar No. 18; Tokay patt., the set... **$250**

Tea set: cov. teapot No. 16, creamer No. 17 & cov. sugar No. 18; Tuscany patt., the set .. **$250**

Tea set: cov. teapot No. 23, open sugar bowl No.25 & creamer No. 24, teapot 6 1/2" h., Magnolia patt., the set **$400**

Tea set: cov. teapot No. 72 8" h., cov. sugar bowl No. 74 4 3/4" h. & creamer No. 73 4 3/4" h.; Wild Flower Number Series, the set **$1,500**

Tea set: cov. teapot No. L-18, 6" h., cov. sugar bowl No. L-20 5" h. & creamer L-19 5" h.; Water Lily patt., teapot 6" h., 3 pcs..... **$375**

Tea set: cov. teapot No. T14 8" h., creamer No. T15 & cov. sugar bowl No. T16; Blossom Flite patt., the set................................ **$200**

Tea set: cov. teapot No. S-11, cov. sugar bowl No. S-13 & creamer No. S-12; Parchment and Pine patt., teapot 6" h., 3 pcs........ **$250**

Urn, Capri patt., footed, molded lion head on top sides, No. C50, 9" h. **$45**

Vase, 4" h., Tulip (Sueno) patt., No. 100-33 .... **$95**

Vase, 4 3/4" h., Poppy patt., No. 605 .... **$175**

Vase, 5" h., Rosella patt., No. R-2.................... **$35**

Vase, 5" h., Serenade patt., hat-shaped, No. S4 .... **$55**

Vase, 5 1/2" h., Wildflower Matte patt., No. W1-5 1/2" **$55**

Vase, 5 1/2" h., Wildflower Number Series patt., No. 52 .... **$155**

Vase, 6" h., Calla Lily (Jack-in-the-Pulpit) patt., No. 502-33 .... **$110**

Vase, 6" h., Orchid patt., No. 303.................. **$145**

Vase, 6" h., Thistle patt., No. 51 .... **$150**

Vase, 6" h., Thistle patt., No. 52 .... **$150**

Vase, 6" h., Thistle patt., No. 53 .... **$150**

Vase, 6" h., Thistle patt., No. 54 .... **$150**

Vase, 6 1/2" h., Bow-Knot patt., No. B6-6 1/2" **$215**

Vase, 6 1/2" h., Dogwood (Wild Rose) patt., ovoid body suspended within a rectangular framework w/an oval foot, No. 502-6 1/2" **$225**

Vase, 6 1/2" h., Open Rose (Camelia) patt., No. 120 .... **$135**

Vase, 6 1/2" h., Poppy patt., No. 606 .... **$200**

Vase, 6 1/2" h., Poppy patt., No. 612 (ILLUS. front row center with Poppy pattern basket, ewer & vase, top of page 339) .... **$75-$100**

Vase, 6 1/2" h., Tulip (Sueno) patt., No. 100-33 .... **$125**

Vase, 6 1/2" h., Wildflower Matte patt., No. W-4 .... **$80**

Vase, 6 1/2" h., Woodland Gloss patt., No. W4 .... **$45**

Vase, 6 1/2" h., Woodland Matte patt., No. W4 .... **$125**

Vase, 6 1/2" h., Woodland patt., Post 1950, No. W4 .... **$100**

Group of Four Hull Pagoda Vases

Vase, 7 1/2" h., Pagoda patt., No. P3 (ILLUS. front row, left, with other Pagoda vases, previous page) .... **$30-$50**

Vase, 7 1/2" h., Wildflower Matte patt., No. W-6.. **$90**

Vase, 8" h., Tulip (Sueno) patt., No. 100-33 .. **$225**

Group of Bow-Knot Vases & Wall Pockets

Vase, 8 1/2" h., Bow-Knot patt., No. B-8-8 1/2" (ILLUS. front row, left, with tall Bow-Knot vase & wall pockets)......... **$250-$350**

Vase, 8 1/2" h., Iris (Narcissus) patt., No. 404-8 1/2".. **$150**

Vase, 8 1/2" h., No. 605 (ILLUS. front row, right, with Poppy basket, ewer & vase, top of page 339)............................... **$100-$125**

Open Rose Hand & Fan Vase

Vase, 8 1/2" h., Open Rose (Camellia) patt., No. 126, hand & fan design (ILLUS.) **$325**

Vase, 8 1/2" h., Orchid patt., No. 304............. **$195**

Vase, 8 1/2" h., Rosella patt., No. R-15........... **$75**

Vase, 8 1/2" h., Tropicana patt., No. T53 ...... **$550**

Vase, 8 1/2" h., Water Lily patt., No. L-8 (ILLUS. front row, left, with other Water Lily vases, top next column)............. **$175-$225**

Vase, 8 1/2" h., Water Lily patt., No. L-A (ILLUS. back row with other Water Lily vases, top next column) .... **$200-$225**

Group of Three Hull Water Lily Vases

Vase, 8 1/2" h., Wildflower Number Series, No. 67 .... **$325**

Vase, 8 3/4" h., Sun-Glow patt., molded stork-like bird on the side, No. 85 .... **$50**

Vase, 9" h., Tulip (Sueno) patt., No. 100-33... **$245**

Vase, 9 1/4" h., Ebb Tide, figural angel fish base, No. E-6 .... **$150**

Vase, 9 1/2" h., Water Lily Matte patt., No. L-11.. **$225**

Vase, 9 1/2" h., Wildflower Matte patt., No. W-13.. **$165**

Vase, 10" h., Calla Lily (Jack-in-the-Pulpit) patt., No. 510-33 .... **$145**

Vase, 10" h., Orchid patt., No. 307................. **$325**

Vase, 10" h., Pagoda patt., No. P4 (ILLUS. front row, right, with other Pagoda vases, previous page) .... **$40-$50**

Vase, 10" h., Parchment & Pine patt., No. S-4 .... **$75**

Vase, 10" h., Tulip (Sueno) patt., No. 100-33 .. **$350**

Vase, 10 1/2" h., Bow-Knot patt., No. B-10 (ILLUS. back row with other Bow-Knot vase & wall pockets, previous column) .... **$500-$600**

Vase, 10 1/2" h., Butterfly patt., No. B14-10 1/2".. **$100**

Vase, 10 1/2" h., Serenade, No. S11 .... **$95**

Vase, 10 1/2" h., Wildflower Matte patt., No. W-15.. **$175**

Vase, 10 1/2" h., Wildflower Number Series patt., No. 77 .... **$350**

Tall Ebb Tide Shell-shaped Vase

Vase, 11" h., Ebb Tide patt., upright spiral shell w/figural fish foot, No. E-7, brown ground (ILLUS.) .... **$125-$175**

Vase, 12" h., Open Rose (Camellia) patt.,
No. 124.. **$400**

Vase, 12" h., Pagoda patt., No. P5 (ILLUS.
back row, left, with other Pagoda vases,
page 341)... **$45-$55**

Vase, 12" h., Poppy patt., No. 612 .... **$450**

Vase, 12 1/2" h., Magnolia Matte patt., No.
17-12 1/2", wing-form handles **$300**

Vase, 12 1/2" h., Water Lily patt., No. L-16
(ILLUS. front row, right, with other Water
Lily vases, previous page).......................... **$395**

Vase, 13" h., Calla Lily (Jack-in-the-Pulpit)
patt., No. 560-33 .... **$350**

Vase, 15" h., Pagoda patt., No. P6 (ILLUS.
back row, right, with other Pagoda vases,
page 341)... **$50-$60**

Vase, floor-type, 15" h., Magnolia Matte
patt., No. 20-15" **$500**

Vase, floor-type, 15" h., Wildflower Matte
patt., No. W-20... **$500**

Wall pocket, Bow-Knot patt., model of a
bulbous pitcher, B-26-6", 6" h. (ILLUS.
front row, right, with Bow-Knot vases &
other wall pocket, previous page) **$265**

Wall pocket, Sun Glow patt., model of an
iron, No. 83, 6" h. **$65**

Wall pocket, Rosella patt., No. R-10,
6 1/2" h.. **$85**

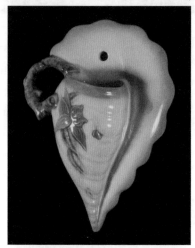

Woodland Gloss Shell Wall Pocket

Wall pocket, Woodland Gloss patt., conch
shell shape, No. W13-7 1/2", 7 1/2" l.
(ILLUS.) **$95**

Wall pocket, Woodland Matte patt., conch
shell shape, No. W13-7 12", 7 1/2" l. **$195**

Wall pocket, Woodland patt., Post 1950,
conch shell shape, No. W13-7 12",
7 1/2" l.. **$145**

Wall pocket, Bow-Knot patt., model of a
whisk broom, No. B27-8", 8" h. (ILLUS.
front row, center, with Bow-Knot pattern
vases & other wall pocket, previous
page).. **$250-$300**

Wall pocket, Poppy patt., cornucopia-
shaped w/asymmetrical handles, No.
609, 9" l.. **$450**

Window box, Parchment & Pine patt., No.
S-5, 10 1/2" l. **$95**

Window box, Woodland Gloss patt., No.
W19-10 1/2", 10 1/2" l. **$95**

Window box, Woodland Matte patt., No.
W19-10 1/2", 10 1/2" l. **$145**

Hull Early Utility & Artware:
Stoneware & Semi-Porcelain

Canisters, cov., "Sugar" or "Coffee," cylindrical w/mottled dark green glaze,
6 1/2" h., each **$100**

Flowerpot & saucer, tapering cylindrical
pot in dark green matte glaze w/streaked
pink, blue, green & tan, 5" h., 2pcs. **$75**

Jardiniere, stepped & ringed tapering cylindrical form w/molded florette bands, drippy dark & light green glaze, No. 536, 8" h.
.... **$100**

Stein, Alpine patt., scenic band around the
center, shaded dark brown to tan glaze,
No. 492, 6 1/2" h. **$45**

Vase, 7" h., flat-bottomed bulbous body tapering to a wide flared neck, green neck
band above a tan body, matte glaze, No.
40, 7" h... **$95**

Imari

*This is a multicolor ware that originated in
Japan, was copied by the Chinese, and imitated
by English and European potteries. It was decorated in overglaze enamel and underglaze-blue.
Made in Hizen Province and Arita, much of it
was exported through the port of Imari in Japan.
Imari often has brocade patterns.*

Colorful Imari Brush Pot

Brush pot, simple wide cylindrical form, a
blue striped base band below the main
body h.p. w/bright red & dark blue stylized blossoms, an upper rim band
w/undulated blue band w/deep red half-
round panels, inside spider crack does
not show through, 19th c., 4" d., 6" h.
(ILLUS.) **$201**

Gilt-Bronze Mounted Imari Jardiniere

Jardiniere, large bulbous ovoid pot w/short flaring rim, mounted on a gilt-bronze base w/four animal head & paw feet & a pierced leaf tip gilt-bronze rim band joined to the base by ornate scrolling handles, late 19th c., 22" d., 16 1/2" h. (ILLUS.)... **$2,750**

Ironstone

The first successful ironstone was patented in 1813 by C.J. Mason in England. The body contains iron slag incorporated with the clay. Other potters imitated Mason's ware, and today much hard, thick ware is lumped under the term ironstone. Earlier it was called by various names, including graniteware. Both plain white and decorated wares were made throughout the 19th century. Tea Leaf Lustre ironstone was made by several firms.

General

Baker, Boote's 1851 shape, all-white, T. & R. Boote, 7" l. **$75**
Baker, Prairie Flowers shape, all-white, Powell & Bishop, 8" l. **$60**

Batter pitcher-milk jug, cylindrical body w/various handles, all-white, often American-made in various sizes.................... **$25-$50**
Bread plate, "Give Us This Day Our Daily Bread" all-white, John Moses, Trenton, New Jersey, 13" l. .... **$125-$150**
Butter dish, cover & insert, Berlin Swirl shape, all-white, Mayer & Elliot .... **$190-$220**
Cake plate, Cherry Scroll shape, all-white, T. & R. Boote, 11 1/2" d. .... **$75-$85**
Cake stand, scalloped apron & fluted pedestal, all-white, marked "J.F.," 11" d.. **$390-$425**

Atlantic Shape Ironstone Chamber Pot

Chamber pot, cov., Atlantic shape, all-white, T. & R. Boote (ILLUS.)........... **$125-$150**
Chamber pot, cov., Canada shape, all-white, J. Clementson, ca. 1877 .... **$90-$110**
Cheese dome with stand, embossed lattice & fern design on dome & stand, ring finial on dome, all-white, 12" d., 13 1/2" h....................................... **$950-$1,000**
Chestnut bowl, Pierced Scroll shape, elaborate pedestaled bowl & tray w/cut openwork design, all-white, John Alcock, ca. 1840s .... **$550-$600**
Compote, open, Alternate Panels shape, all-white (ILLUS., bottom of page) **$225**

Alternate Panels White Ironstone Compote

President Shape All-White Oval Compote

Compote, open, oval, President shape, all-white, John Edwards (ILLUS.)........... **$350-$400**

Compote, open, Classic Gothic shape, all-white, Red Cliff copy, ca. 1960s, 10" d. **$65**

Compote, open, Scalloped Ribs shape, plain pedestal, all-white, John Moses, Trenton, New Jersey, ca. 1880s, 10" d. .... **$90-$120**

Compote, open, Bow Knot shape, all-white, J. & G. Meakin, 12 1/2" d. .... **$275-$300**

Cup & saucer, child's, handleless cup, Ceres shape, all-white, Elsmore & Forster, the set .... **$50-$75**

Cup & saucer, handleless cup, Laurel shape, all-white, Wedgwood & Co. .... **$50-$60**

Cup & saucer, Sydenham shape, all-white, T. & R. Boote, the set........................ **$100-$125**

Ironstone Hen-on-Next Covered Dish

Dish, figural Hen-on-Nest with Chicks, all-white (ILLUS.) **$225**

Eggcup, Ceres shape, all-white, Elsmore & Forster, very rare (ILLUS., top next column)... **$250-$300**

Footbath, Columbia shape, all-white, J. Clementson, 18" l. .... **$1,000-$1,100**

Gravy boat, Bordered Hyacinth shape, all-white, W. Baker & Co. **$65**

Gravy boat, Eagle shape, all-white, Davenport, ca. 1850s (ILLUS., middle next column).. **$110**

Gravy boat, Full Ribbed shape, all-white, J. W. Pankhurst.. **$110**

Rare Ceres Shape Ironstone Eggcup

Eagle White Ironstone Gravy Boat

Rare Paneled Grape Jam Server

Jam server, cov., Paneled Grape shape, all-white, by J.F., rare (ILLUS.) .... **$110-$140**

Master waste jar, cov., Cable & Bar shape, all-white, Knowles, Taylor & Knowles, East Liverpool, Ohio, ca. 1880.......... **$230-$250**

Classic Gothic Octagon Master Waste Jar

Master waste jar, cov., Classic Gothic Octagon shape, all-white, Jacob Furnival (ILLUS.)... **$950-$1,050**
Mug, Baltic shape, all-white, J. Meir & Son.... **$110**
Mug, child's, Sydenham shape, all-white, rare.. **$120**

Chinese Shape Ironstone Mug

Mug, Chinese shape, all-white, Anthony Shaw, ca. 1858 (ILLUS.).............................. **$90**

Corn & Oats Ironstone Mug

Mug, Corn & Oats shape, all-white, Davenport (ILLUS.)... **$90-$110**
Mug, Dolphin shape, all-white, John Edwards.. **$75**
Mug, Plain shape, all-white, Burgess & Goddard & many other makers, ca. 1880-90... **$15-$25**

Potomac White Ironstone Mug

Mug, Potomac shape, all-white, Wm. Baker & Co., 1862 (ILLUS.)......................... **$100-$125**
Pitcher, 11" h., Fig/Union shape, all-white, Davenport .... **$240-$260**
Pitcher, 12" h., Corn & Oats shape, all-white, J. Wedgwood.......................... **$190-$210**
Pitcher, 12" h., DeSoto shape, all-white, Thomas Hughes............................... **$220-$240**
Plate, 10" d., Eagle Diamond Thumbprint, all-white, Gelson Bros., ca. 1869 .... **$60**
Plate, 10" d., Mississippi shape, all-white, E. Pierson **$40**
Platter, 12" l., oval, Niagara shape, all-white, E. Walley .... **$35-$45**
Platter, 17" l., oval, Flora shape, all-white, John Alcock, ca. 1855.............................. **$110**
Platter, 20 1/2" l., well & tree-style, Wheat shape, all-white................................ **$250-$275**
Punch bowl, 12-Fluted Panels shape, all-white, F. Morley, 10" d. .... **$300-$325**
Punch-toddy bowl, cov., Hyacinth shape, all-white, H. Burgess, 12" d.............. **$225-$245**
Relish dish, Leaf & Crossed Ribbon shape, all-white, Livesley & Powell......................... **$45**

Pond Lily Pad Relish Dish

Relish dish, Pond Lily Pad shape, all-white, James Edwards (ILLUS.) .... **$115-$130**
Sauce tureen, cover & undertray, Citron shape, oval w/foliage at handles, pointed bud finial, all-white, the set......................... **$170**
Soap box, cover & insert, Grape Octagon shape, all-white, Livesley & Powell, ca. 1850 .... **$170-$190**

Soap box, cover & insert, Moss Rose
shape, rose bud finial, embossed foliage
& cable, all-white, J. & G. Meakin, the set
.... **$130-$150**

East Liverpool Ironstone Soap Slab

Soap slab, rectangular w/molded scroll
edges, all-white, marked "ELO" [East Liv-
erpool, Ohio] (ILLUS.) .... **$20-$30**
Soup plate, flanged rim, Columbia shape,
all-white, J. Meir & Son., ca. 1855,
9 1/4" d... **$50**
Soup plate, flanged rim, Paneled Grape
shape, all-white, Jacob Furnival, 10" d. **$45**

DeSoto Three-Piece Soup Tureen

Soup tureen, cover & undertray, DeSoto
shape, all-white, 3 pcs. (ILLUS.) .... **$900-$950**

Gothic Octagon 3-Piece Soup Tureen

Soup tureen, cover & undertray, Gothic
Octagon shape, all-white, Wedgwood &
Co., 3 pcs. (ILLUS.) **$900**
Soup tureen, cover, undertray & ladle,
Blackberry shape, all-white, Red Cliff
copy, ca. 1960s, the set .... **$125-$150**

*Classic Gothic Octagon White Ironstone
Soup Tureen Set*

Soup tureen, cover, undertray & ladle,
Classic Gothic Octagon shape, all-white,
Sameul Alcock & Co., ca. 1847, the set
(ILLUS.)... **$1,200**
Sugar bowl, cov., Atlantic shape, all-white,
T. & R. Boote, ca. 1850..................... **$125-$150**
Sugar bowl, cov., Cable & Bar shape, all-
white, Dale & Davis, Trenton, New
Jersey, ca. 1870................................... **$30-$40**

Four Square Wheat Sugar Bowl

Sugar bowl, cov., Four Square Wheat
shape, all-white, unmarked (ILLUS.)............ **$80**
Sugar bowl, cov., Framed Leaf shape, all-
white, J.W. Pankhurst .... **$130-$150**
Sugar bowl, cov., Lily of the Valley with
Thumbprint shape, all-white, Jacob Fur-
nival.. **$110-$125**

Olympic Shape Sugar Bowl

Sugar bowl, cov., Olympic shape, all-white, Elsmore & Forster, 1864 (ILLUS.)............... **$90**

Scalloped Decagon Sugar Bowl

Sugar bowl, cov., Scalloped Decagon/Cambridge shape, all-white, Wedgwood & Co. (ILLUS.) **$100**

Hyacinth Shape Syllabub Cup

Syllabub cup, Hyacinth shape, all-white, Wedgwood & Co., ca. 1865 (ILLUS.)........... **$45**

Gothic Octagon Covered Syrup Pitcher

Syrup pitcher w/hinged pewter lid, Gothic Octagon shape w/Greybeard under spout, all-white, T. J. & J. Mayer, 5" h. (ILLUS.).. **$225-$300**

Tea set: child's, cov. teapot, cov. sugar bowl, creamer & six cups & saucers; Paneled Grape shape, all-white, the set .... **$750-$800**

Alternate Panels Ironstone Teapot

Teapot, cov., all-white, Alternate Panels shape, unknown potter, England, mid-19th c. (ILLUS.)................................. **$125-$150**

Teapot, cov., all-white, Inverted Diamond shape, by T. J. & J. Mayer, England, ca. 1840s (ILLUS., next page) .... **$250-$300**

Inverted Diamond Ironstone Teapot

Red Cliff Sydenham Shape White Teapot

Teapot, cov., all-white Sydenham shape,
copy of Victorian ironstone original design, produced by Hall China for Red
Cliff, ca. 1960s (ILLUS.).............................. **$95**

Ironstone Loop & Dot Shape Teapot

Teapot, cov., all-white, Loop & Dot shape,
by E. & C. Challinor, England, ca. 1865
(ILLUS.)... **$190-$210**

Red Cliff Grape Leaf Pattern Teapot

Teapot, cov., all-white tall paneled & taper-
ing body w/domed cover, molded Grape
Leaf patt., produced by Hall China for
Red Cliff, ca. 1960s (ILLUS.) **$150**

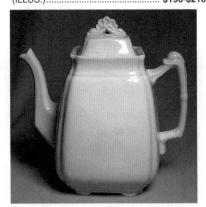

Plain Seashore White Ironstone Teapot

Teapot, cov., all-white, Plain Seashore
shape, molded dolphin on handle & finial,
by W. & E. Corn, ca. 1885 (ILLUS.) .. **$125-$150**

Blue-trimmed Tulip Shape Teapot

Teapot, cov., all-white, Tulip shape,
trimmed in blue, by Elsmore & Forster,
England, ca. 1855 (ILLUS.)............... **$290-$320**

Berlin Swirl White Ironstone Vegetable Tureen

Toothbrush vase & underplate, Centennial shape, all-white, W. & E. Corn, ca. 1876 .... **$170-$190**

Vegetable tureen, cov., Berlin Swirl shape, all-white, T. J. & J. Mayer (ILLUS., top of page) **$190**

Vegetable tureen, cov., Late Rectangular shape, all-white, Johnson Bros., 10" l. ... **$75-$85**

Sydenham Shape Vegetable Tureen

Vegetable tureen, cov., Sydenham shape, all-white, T. & R. Boote, 1853 (ILLUS.) .... **$190-$240**

Divided Gothic Shape White Ironstone Wash Bowl & Pitcher Set

Wash bowl & pitcher set, Divided Gothic shape, all-white, John Alcock, ca. 1848, the set (ILLUS.) .... **$400-$450**

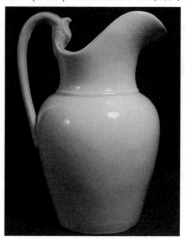

Dolphin-handled Wine Pitcher

Wine pitcher, jug-form, Dolphin-handled shape, all-white, unmarked, ca. 1850s (ILLUS.) .... **$110-$130**

Tea Leaf Ironstone

Tea Leaf Brocade Butter Dish

Butter dish, cover & insert. Brocade patt., Alfred Meakin, flanks inside base, chip on insert (ILLUS.) **$110**

Cable Covered Butter with Insert

Butter dish, cover & insert, Cable shape,
Anthony Shaw (ILLUS.)................................ **$60**

Meakin Butter Dish

Butter dish, cover & insert, Chelsea patt.,
Alfred Meakin, the set (minor flaws)
(ILLUS.)... **$60**
Butter dish, cover & insert, Chelsea
shape, H. Burgess, 3 pcs. **$200**
Butter dish, cover & insert, Simple Square
shape, J. Wedgwood, 3 pcs. **$70**
Cake plate, Brocade shape, Alfred Meakin.... **$120**
Cake plate, by Edge Malkin **$110**
Cake plate, Cable shape, Anthony Shaw **$50**

Tea Leaf Micratex Cake Plate

Cake plate,   Empress patt., Micratex by
Adams, ca. 1960s (ILLUS.) **$160**
Cake plate, Favorite shape, Grindley, minor
glaze wear... **$190**

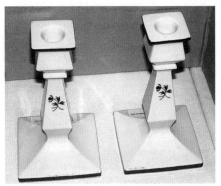

Red Cliff Tea Leaf Candlesticks

Candlesticks, square, Red Cliff, ca. 1970,
pr. (ILLUS.) **$360**
Chamber pot, cov., Cable shape, Anthony
Shaw **$175**

Lily of the Valley Tea Leaf Chamber Pot

Chamber pot, cov., Lily of the Valley shape,
Anthony Shaw (ILLUS.) **$175**
Chamber pot, cov., Peerless/Feather
shape, J. Edwards **$300**

Mayer King Charles Open Chamber Pot

Chamber pot, open, King Charles patt.,
Mayer (ILLUS.).. **$100**

Favorite Shape Tea Leaf Coffeepot

Coffeepot, cov., Favorite shape, Grindley (ILLUS.)... **$170**
Coffeepot, cov., Fig Cousin shape, pink lustre, slight repair, Davenport **$150**

Corn Woodland Pattern Coffeepot

Coffeepot, cov., Woodland patt., W. & E. Corn, minor flaws (ILLUS.)........................... **$60**

Shaw Round Tea Leaf Compote

Compote, open, round top, pedestal base, Anthony Shaw (ILLUS.).............................. **$175**
Compote, open, square w/rounded corners, pedestal base, H. Burgess **$185**

Meakin Square Footed Compote

Compote, open, squared form, pedestal base, Alfred Meakin (ILLUS.).................... **$265**

Adams Empress Cream Soup Bowl

Cream soup bowl, two-handled, Empress shape, Micratex by Adams, ca. 1960s (ILLUS.).. **$35**
Creamer, Blanket Stitch shape, gold Tea Leaf, Alcock **$170**
Creamer, Cable shape, T. Furnival, 5" h........ **$140**

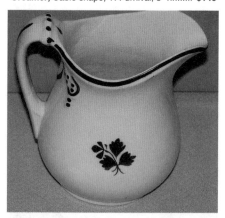

Furnival Cable Tea Leaf Creamer

Creamer, Cable shape, T. Furnival (ILLUS.) **$90**
Creamer, Chelsea shape, Alfred Meakin **$100**
Creamer, Chinese shape, Anthony Shaw **$410**
Creamer, Favorite shape, Grindley............... **$310**
Creamer, Lion's Head shape, Mellor Taylor, 5 1/4" h... **$220**

Wheat in Meadow Lustre Band Creamer & Sugar Bowl

Creamer, Wheat in Meadow shape, lustre band trim (ILLUS. with sugar bowl, top of page) $300

Maidenhair Fern Tea Leaf Creamer

Creamer, Maidenhair Fern patt., T. Wilkinson (ILLUS.) $150

Creamer & cov. sugar bowl, child's, slant-sided shape, Mellor Taylor, pr. $100

Cup plate, Rondeau shape, Davenport $30

Eggcup, Empress shape, Microtex by Adams, ca. 1960s $90

Eggcup, T. Mayer $110

Gravy boat, Basketweave shape, Anthony Shaw $160

Gravy boat, Beaded Band shape, H. Burgess $80

Gravy boat, Bullet shape, small size, Anthony Shaw $130

Gravy boat, Cable shape, T. Furnival............ $70

Gravy boat, Scroll shape, Meakin $110

Gravy boat, Victory/Dolphin shape, Edwards $130

Gravy boat & underplate, Simple Square shape, J. Wedgwood, 2 pcs. $160

Gravy boat & undertray, Chelsea shape, Alfred Meakin, 2 pcs. $180

Empress Micratex Gravy Boat & Tray

Gravy boat with attached undertray, Empress patt., Micratex by Adams, ca. 1960 (ILLUS.) $80

Ladle, sauce tureen-size, Anthony Shaw $400

Ladle, sauce tureen-size, some crazing (ILLUS., bottom of page)........................... $200

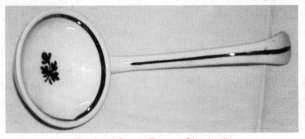

Tea Leaf Sauce Tureen Size Ladle

Fleur-de-Lis Chain Tea Leaf Platter

Ladle, soup-size, gold lustre Tea Leaf, Powell & Bishop **$150**

Rare Ginger Jar Master Waste Jar

Master waste jar, cov., Ginger Jar shape, Elsmore & Forster (ILLUS.) **$1,300**
Mush bowl, Plain shape, Alfred Meakin, 5 1/2" d., 2 1/4" h. **$140**
Mustache cup & saucer, Edge Malkin, professional rim repair **$500**
Nappies, rounded w/paneled sides, T. Mayer, set of 6 (ILLUS., top next column) **$30**
Pitcher, water, Cable shape, Anthony Shaw, rare **$1,200**

Set of Paneled Mayer Nappies

Pitcher, water-size, Chinese shape, minor discoloration, Anthony Shaw **$150**
Pitcher, 8" h., Blanket Stitch shape, Alcock **$140**
Pitcher, 8" h., Square Ridged shape, Wedgwood **$50**
Platter, oval, Fleur-de-Lis Chain patt., Wedgwood & Co., large (ILLUS., top of page) **$50**
Platter, 18" l., Square Ridged II shape, Mellor, Taylor, mild discoloration **$50**
Punch bowl, Cable shape, Anthony Shaw **$400**

Shaw Chinese Shape Tea Leaf Relish Dish

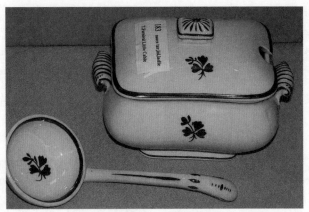

Rare Little Scroll Tea Leaf Sauce Tureen & Ladle

Relish dish, mitten-shaped, Chinese shape, Anthony Shaw (ILLUS., bottom previous page) **$220**

Relish dish, mitten-shaped, Lily of the Valley shape, slight discoloration, Anthony Shaw.... **$200**

Relish dish, rectangular w/rounded ends, T. Mayer **$65**

Sauce tureen, cover & ladle, Little Scroll shape, T. Furnival, 3 pcs. (ILLUS., top of page) **$800**

Pagoda Shape Tea Leaf Sauce Tureen

Sauce tureen, cover & undertray, Pagoda shape, H. Burgess, the set (ILLUS.) **$170**

Sauce tureen, cover, undertray & ladle, Delphi patt., T. Elsmore & Son, 4 pcs. (ILLUS., bottom of page)........................... **$450**

Adams Empress Salt & Pepper Shakers

Salt & pepper shakers, Empress patt., Micratex by Adams, ca. 1960s, pr. (ILLUS.) .. **$130**

Delphi Pattern Four-Piece Sauce Tureen Set

Favorite Pattern Tea Leaf Teapot

Teapot, cov., Favorite patt., Grindley (ILLUS.) .. **$120**

Ginger Jar Pattern Tea Leaf Sugar Bowl

Teapot, cov., Ginger Jar patt., unmarked,
repair to spout (ILLUS.)............................... **$60**

Teapot, cov., Scroll shape, Alfred Meakin **$160**
Toothbrush vase, cylindrical w/molded
handles near pedestal base, drain holes,
no underplate, possibly by Shaw **$850**
Toothbrush vase, Fishook shape, Alfread
Meakin **$110**
Toothbrush vase, Scalloped shape, waist-
ed cylindrical form, Alfred Meakin **$90**
Toothbrush vase & underplate, cylindrical
tapering shape, mild discoloration, An-
thony Shaw, 2 pcs..................................... **$155**
Vegetable dish, cov., Brocade shape, Al-
fred   Meakin,   moderate   crazing,
6 1/4 x 9 1/2".. **$60**

Shaw Bullet Tea Leaf Vegetable Dish

Vegetable dish, cov., Bullet patt., A. Shaw,
minor flaws (ILLUS.) **$65**
Vegetable dish, cov., Cable patt., Anthony
Shaw, 11" l... **$120**
Vegetable dish, cov., Daisy Chain shape,
Wilkinson, 6 x 8 1/4".................................... **$70**
Vegetable dish, cov., Lion's Head shape,
Mellor Taylor **$50**
Vegetable dish, cov., oval, Edge Malkin
(ILLUS., bottom of page).......................... **$325**

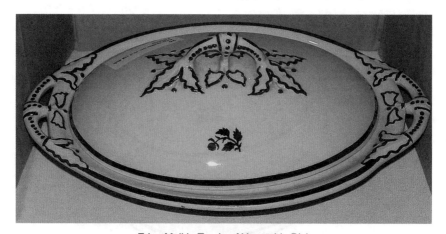

Edge Malkin Tea Leaf Vegetable Dish

Lily of the Valley Wash Bowl & Pitcher

Wash bowl & pitcher, Lily of the Valley shape, Anthony Shaw, the set (ILLUS.) **$525**

Wash bowl & pitcher set, Cable shape, Anthony Shaw, the set **$225**

Chrysanthemum Wash Bowl & Pitcher

Wash bowl & pitcher set, Chrysanthemum patt., H. Burgess, the set (ILLUS.) **$575**

Wash pitcher, Acanthus shape, lustre wear, tight hairline, Johnson Bros. **$525**

Wash pitcher, Hexagon shape, minor flaws, Anthony Shaw **$275**

Wash pitcher, Square Ridged shape, J. Wedgwood **$95**

Waste bowl, Lily of the Valley shape, Anthony Shaw **$130**

Waste bowl, Square Ridged shape, J. Wedgwood **$35**

Tea Leaf Variants

Cake plate, New York shape, lustre band trim w/cobalt blue plumes, Clementson (ILLUS., bottom of page) **$325**

Cake plate, Prairie Flower shape, lustre band trim, slight discoloration, Powell & Bishop **$275**

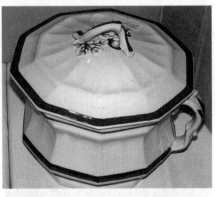

Grape Octagon Lustre Band Chamber Pot

Chamber pot, cov., Grape Octagon shape, lustre band trim, E. Walley, minor flaws (ILLUS.) **$150**

Chamber pot, cov., Pre-Tea Leaf patt., Niagara shape, E. Walley **$1,050**

New York Shape Cake Plate with Lustre Band & Blue Plumes

Pinwheel Grape Octagon Coffeepot

Coffeepot, cov., Pinwheel patt., Grape Octagon shape, E. Walley, slight crazing on cover (ILLUS.) **$230**

Teaberry Chinese Shape Coffeepot

Coffeepot, cov., Teaberry patt., Chinese shape, minor flaws, J. Clementson (ILLUS.) .. **$300**

Tobacco Leaf Fanfare Coffeepot

Coffeepot, cov., Tobacco Leaf patt., Fanfare shape, Elsmore & Forster, minor flaws (ILLUS.) **$400**
Coffeepot, cov., Wheat in Meadow shape, lustre band trim, Powell & Bishop **$325**
Creamer, Teaberry patt., Crystal shape, minor flaws, Clementson **$190**
Creamer, Wrapped Sydenham shape, lustre bands & pinstripes, Edward Walley **$260**
Cup & saucer, handleless, Pre-Tea Leaf patt., Niagara shape, E. Walley **$90**
Gravy boat, Oak Leaf patt., Mayer **$180**
Gravy boat, Scallops patt., Sydenham shape, E. Walley **$250**
Mug, Gothic shape, paneled sides, lustre band, Livesley & Powell **$100**

Laurel Wreath Lustre-trimmed Pitcher

Pitcher, 7 3/4" h., Laurel Wreath patt., lustre trim, Elsmore & Forster, minor flaws (ILLUS.) **$325**
Pitcher, 8" h., milk, Golden Scroll shape, gold lustre trim, Powell & Bishop **$70**

Ceres Green & Lustre Place Setting

Place setting: dinner plate, dessert plate & handleless cup & saucer; Ceres shape, green & copper lustre trim, the set (ILLUS.) .... **$30-$50**

Cinquefoil Wheat Shape Tea Set

Columbia Shape Lustre Band Sugar Bowl

Sugar bowl, cov., Columbia shape, copper
lustre bands, Livesley & Powell (ILLUS.) **$65**

Morning Glory Portland Sugar Bowl

Sugar bowl, cov., Morning Glory patt., Portland shape, Elsmore & Forster, minor
flaw (ILLUS.) **$55**

Sugar bowl, cov., Morning Glory patt.,
Richelieu shape, unmarked slight glaze
wear **$80**

Sugar bowl, cov., Quartered Rose shape,
copper lustre bands & cobalt blue
plumes, minor flaws, J. Furnival **$180**

Sugar bowl, cov., Wheat in Meadow shape,
lustre band trim **$70**

Syrup pitcher w/hinged metal lid, Moss
Rose patt., George Scott **$325**

Tea set: cov. teapot, cov. sugar bowl &
creamer: Cinquefoil patt., Wheat shape,
J. Furnival, some damages & repair, the
set (ILLUS., top of page) **$250**

Teapot, cov., Moss Rose patt. **$100**

New York Lustre Band Teapot

Teapot, cov., New York shape, lustre band
trim, Clementson, professional repair to
finial (ILLUS.) **$60**

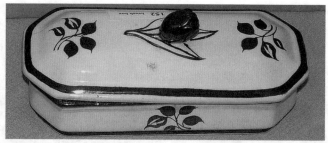

Rare Tobacco Leaf Fanfare Toothbrush Box

Pinwheel Grape Octagon Teapot

Teapot, cov., Pinwheel patt., Grape Octagon shape, finial chip (ILLUS.) **$80**

Teapot, cov., Quartered Rose shape, copper lustre bands & cobalt blue plumes, possibly J. Furnival..................................... **$225**

Teaberry - Ring O' Hearts Teapot

Teapot, cov., Teaberry patt., Ring O' Hearts shape, J. Furnival (ILLUS.) **$650**

Toothbrush box, cov., Lily of the Valley shape, lustre band trim, flake on finial, Anthony Shaw **$250**

Toothbrush box, cov., Tobacco Leaf patt., Fanfare shape, Elsmore & Forster, slight damage (ILLUS., top of page).................... **$675**

Rare Teaberry Heavy Square Toothbrush Vase

Toothbrush vase, Teaberry patt., Heavy Square shape, Clementson Bros., slight flaws (ILLUS.) **$1,350**

Vegetable dish, cov., Quartered Rose shape, copper lustre bands & trim & cobalt blue plumes, slight flaws **$250**

Vegetable dish, cov., Reverse Teaberry patt., Portland shape, Elsmore & Forster (ILLUS., top next page)............................ **$380**

Grape Octagon Wash Bowl & Pitcher

Reverse Teaberry Portland Vegetable Dish

Wash bowl & pitcher set, Grape Octagon
shape, lustre band trim, unmarked, the
set (ILLUS., previous page) **$225**

Moss Rose Wash Bowl & Pitcher Set

Wash bowl & pitcher set, Moss Rose patt.,
Alfred Meakin, the set (ILLUS.) **$350**
Waste bowl, Gothic shape, Chelsea Grape
patt., minor flaws... **$35**
Waste bowl, Morning Glory patt., Portland
shape, Elsmore & Forster **$120**

Jewel Tea Autumn Leaf

*Though not antique, this ware has a devoted
following. The Hall China Company of East Liverpool, Ohio, made the first pieces of Autumn Leaf
pattern ware to be given as premiums by the
Jewel Tea Company in 1933. The premiums were
an immediate success and thousands of new cus-
tomers, all eager to acquire a piece of the durable
Autumn Leaf pattern, began purchasing Jewel
Tea products. Though the pattern was eventually
used to decorate linens, glassware and tinware,
we focus on the ceramics items here. Note: A few
pieces with this pattern have been released by
Hall China in recent years.*

Autumn Leaf Bean Pot

Bean pot, one-handled, 2 1/4 qt. (ILLUS.) **$950**
Bowl, cereal, 6 1/2" d. **$12**
Bowl, flat soup, 8 1/2" d. **$20**
Bowl, salad, 9" d. **$30**

Jewel Tea Butter Dish

Butter dish, cov., square top w/straight
finial, 1/4 lb. (ILLUS.) **$1,400**

Butter Dish with Butterfly Handle

Hall Jewel Tea Autumn Leaf Aladdin Teapot

Butter dish, cov., w/butterfly-type handle
(ILLUS., previous page) **$1,800**

Drip-type Coffee maker

Coffee maker, cov., all china, drip-type
(ILLUS.) **$325**

Autumn Leaf Electric Percolator

Coffeepot, cov., electric, percolator (ILLUS.) .. **$300**
Cup & saucer **$14**
French baker, swirled soufflé-style, 2 pt.
.... **$120-$130**
Gravy boat & undertray, the set.................... **$50**
Mixing bowl, 7" d., part of set........................ **$20**
Pickle dish (gravy undertray) **$25**
Pie baker, 10" **$35**
Plate, dinner, 10" d... **$14**
Salt & pepper shakers, bell-shaped, small,
pr.. **$35**
Salt & pepper shakers, regular size, bell-
shaped, pr. **$500**
Teapot, cov., Aladdin shape (ILLUS., top of
page)... **$75**
Teapot, cov., Newport shape w/gold trim,
1978 version **$200**

Newport Autumn Leaf Teapot

Teapot, cov., Newport shape w/gold trim
(ILLUS.).. **$250**
Vegetable bowl, 10 1/2" oval **$30**

Jugtown Pottery

This pottery was established by Jacques and Juliana Busbee in Jugtown, North Carolina, in the early 1920s in an attempt to revive the skills of the diminishing North Carolina potter's art as Prohibition ended the need for locally crafted stoneware whiskey jugs. During the early years, Juliana Busbee opened a shop in Greenwich Village in New York City to promote the North Carolina wares that her husband, Jacques, was designing and a local youth, Ben Owen, was producing under his direction. Owen continued to work with Busbee from 1922 until Busbee's death

in 1947 at which time Juliana took over management of the pottery for the next decade until her illness (or mental fatigue) caused the pottery to be
closed in 1958. At that time, Owen opened his own
pottery a few miles away, marking his wares "Ben
Owen - Master Potter." The pottery begun by the
Busbees was reopened in 1960, under new management, and still operates today using the identical impressed mark of the early Jugtown pottery
the Busbees managed from 1922 until 1958.

Jugtown Pottery Mark

Fine Chinese Blue Jugtown Vase

Vase, 9 1/2" h., footed wide bulbous lower
body tapering to a cylindrical neck w/wide
flat mouth, small loop shoulder handles,
grey clay body covered in a Chinese Blue
& red glaze w/crystalline highlights, im-
pressed mark (ILLUS.) **$1,440**

Lenox

*The Ceramic Art Company was established at
Trenton, New Jersey, in 1889 by Jonathan Coxon
and Walter Scott Lenox. In addition to true porcelain, it also made a Belleek-type ware. Renamed
Lenox Company in 1906, it is still in operation
today.*

Lenox China Mark

Game plates, 9" d., ivory ground, h.p. in the
center w/a vignette w/a different game
bird perched or in flight, narrow gilt border band, artist-signed, green printed
marks, ca. 1925, set of 12 (ILLUS. flanking the equestrian fox hunt plate, bottom
of page) **$5,040**
Plate, 10 1/2" d., the center painted w/a de-
tailed scene of three mounted fox hunters
in a woodland landscape, wide gold acid-
etched border band of scrollwork & a thin
double blue line rim bands, artist-signed,
printed green marks, ca. 1925 (ILLUS.
center front with Lenox game plates, bot-
tom of page) **$1,800**

Set of Game Plates and Foxhunt Scene Plate

Beautiful Pheasant-decorated Lenox Plates

Plates, 10 1/2" d., each finely h.p. w/a different species of pheasant in their natural habitat, wide gold rim band w/a rinceau scroll within seeded bands, green printed marks, artist-signed, ca. 125, set of 12 (ILLUS. of part, top of page).................... **$4,560**

Fine Decorated Lenox Service Plates

Service plates, round w/slightly scalloped rim, an ivory center decorated in the middle w/a small flower-filled urn within a floral ring, the wide border decorated w/pale blue panels centered by floral urns & separated by narrow floral bars, base marked "Made Expressly for Ovington Bros. New York - 1445/A.326," 10 1/2" d., set of 10 (ILLUS.)................... **$1,200**

Tea set: 6" h. cov. teapot, 3 3/4" h. cov. sugar bowl & 4" h. creamer; each of bulbous ovoid form wrapped around the body w/slender scrolls & starburst designs in sterling silver, each w/the green laurel leaf mark, the set (ILLUS., top next column) **$288**

Lenox Silver-Overlaid Tea Set

Limoges

Limoges is the generic name for hard paste porcelain that was produced in one of the Limoges factories in the Limoges region of France during the 19th and 20th centuries. There are more than 400 different factory identification marks, the Haviland factory marks being some of the most familiar. Dinnerware was commonly decorated by the transfer method and then exported to the United States.

Decorative pieces were hand painted by a factory artist or were imported to the United States as blank pieces of porcelain. At the turn of the 20th century, thousands of undecorated Limoges blanks poured into the United States, where any of the more than 25,000 American porcelain painters decorated them. Today hand-painted decorative pieces are considered fine art. Limoges is not to be confused with American Limoges. (The series on collecting Limoges by Debby DeBay, Living With Limoges, Antique Limoges at Home and Collecting Limoges Boxes to Vases and Antique Trader Limoges Price Guide 2007 are excellent reference books.)

Rare Limoges Ashtray-Matchbox Holder

Ashtray-matchbox holder, squared dished base w/a cigarette indentation at each corner, a vertical holder for a matchbox in the center, h.p. w/violets on a cream ground, underglaze Tresseman & Vogt Mark 7, rare (ILLUS.)...................... **$350**

Limoges Large Rose-Decorated Basket

Basket, long rectangular form w/deeply scalloped sides, gold border band & arched flower-molded gold handle across the center, the interior h.p. at one end w/large red roses & green leaves on a dark green shaded to pale yellow ground, artist-signed "Segur," underglaze green factory mark of Jean Pouyat, 5 x 9" (ILLUS.)... **$550**

Gold-trimmed Limoges Basket

Basket, round w/flattened & scalloped gold rim & arched center gold handle, the interior h.p. w/pink & red roses & green leaves on a pink to blue ground, artist-signed "Pierre," underglaze Limoges, France Mark 2 & overglaze Blakeman & Henderson decorating mark, 6" d., 2 1/2" h. (ILLUS.) **$350**

Beverage set: 11" h. tankard pitcher & five ovoid handled mugs; each piece h.p. w/clusters of small purple grapes on slen-

der leafy vines against a yellow shaded to pale blue ground, Tressemann & Vogt, the set **$489**

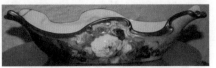

Long Scalloped Limoges Bonbon Dish

Bonbon dish, long oval shaped w/deeply scalloped & scrolled sides, h.p. w/colorful flowers & leaves on a shaded green & yellow ground, artist-signed "Duval," underglaze green factory mark of Jean Pouyat, Mark 5, 5 x 9" (ILLUS.) **$550**

White Poodle Limoges Box from 1970s

Box, cov., figural, a standing white poodle w/a pink ribbon on one ear, on an oval box base w/metal hinge & bands, marked "Peint Main - Limoges France - DE," ca. 1970 (ILLUS.).. **$300**

1970s Figural Poodle Limoges Box

Box, cov., figural, a standing white poodle wearing red caps & red sweater, on an oval box base w/metal hinge & bands, marked "Peint Main - Limoges France," ca. 1970 (ILLUS., previous page) **$300**

White Bust of Boy Based on Houdon

Bust of a young boy, all-white, mounted on a grey socle base, after a model by C. Houdon, green mark for Porcelain de Paris, France, ca. 1920s, 15" h. (ILLUS.) **$1,500**

White Bust of Girl Based on Houdon

Bust of a young girl, all-white, mounted on a grey socle base, after a model by C. Houdon, green mark for Porcelain de Paris, France, ca. 1920s, 15" h. (ILLUS.) **$1,500**

Fine Limoges Bisque Marie Antoinette Bust

Bust of Marie Antoinette, bisque, on a cobalt blue & gilt-banded socle, red printed mark of De Pierre Fiche, ca. 1875, 24" h. (ILLUS.)... **$2,875**

Limoges Charger with Fighting Stags

Charger, large rounded shape w/an ornate scroll-molded gold border, h.p. w/a scene of two battling brown stags against a shaded ground w/leaves in shades of yellow, green & lavender, 13" d. (ILLUS.) .. **$201**

Limoges Porcelain Coffee Set

Coffee set: 9 1/2" h. cov. coffeepot, creamer, cov. sugar & five cups & saucers; each of tapering cylindrical form in pale blue shaded to white, trimmed w/gold bands, mark of Londé Limoges, the set (ILLUS. of part) **$150**

Lovely Hand-painted Limoges Fish Set

Fish set: long narrow oval open-handled 10 x 24" platter, twelve 9 1/2" d. plates & an 8 1/4" l. sauceboat & undertray; each piece w/a gently scalloped rim, the tray h.p. w/a large game fish in browns & greens swimming among lavender water plants against a pale blue ground, each plate & sauceboat h.p. w a different game fish w/similar water plants, greem mark of Latrille Freres, Limoges, France, ca. 1899-1913 & also red HC Limoges, France mark, the set (ILLUS.).... **$1,898**

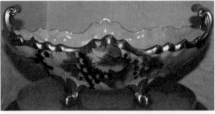

Boat-shaped Fruit Bowl Decorated with Grapes

Fruit bowl, oblong boat-shaped w/high inward-scrolled gold end handles, raised on four gold feet, the exterior h.p. w/purple grapes & green leaves, heavy gold border band, amateur artist-signed, underglaze factory mark for Elite - L - France, ca. 1900, 8 x 12 1/2" (ILLUS.).......................... **$550**

Game set: a 17 3/4" l. oval platter decorated w/a pair of ducks & twelve 9 1/8" d. plates, each w/a different pair of game birds, cobalt blue borders w/ornate gilt scrolls, artist-signed, early 20th c., the set (ILLUS., second from bottom of page).... **$2,115**

Game set: an oval 14 x 18 1/2" platter w/an ornate scalloped & scroll-molded gold border & paneled sides, twelve 9 1/2" d. plates & two 6" d. sauce dishes; each large piece h.p. w/pairs of realistic game birds on a shaded ground, sauce dishes each h.p. w/pheasants, artist-signed, red mark of Lazeyras, Rosenfeld & Lehman, Limoges, early 20th c., the set (ILLUS., bottom of page)..................................... **$2,588**

Jardiniere, on original base, lion head handles, h.p. roses & detail, underglaze factory mark in green "D&Co." (R. Delinières), 12 x 14" **$4,500**

Very Fine Limoges Game Set

Outstanding Hand-painted Limoges Game Set

Limoges Painting of Couple in Garden

Painting on porcelain, rectangular, scene of a romantic couple in 18th c. attire in a garden, he kissing her hand, by an unknown artist, new ornate gold framed, underglaze factory green mark for Tresseman & Vogt, early 20th c., one of a pair, 11 x 14", each (ILLUS. of one)............... **$1,500**

Limoges Tankard Pitcher with Grapes

Pitcher, 14 1/2" h., tankard-type, tall cylindrical form w/a scalloped rim & arched spout, long dragon-form handle, h.p. w/green grapes on a shaded rust to pale yellow & blue ground, Thomas importer mark, Jean Pouyat, Limoges - J.P.L. (ILLUS.)............... **$518**

Two Limoges Tall Tankard Pitchers

Pitcher, 14 1/2" h., tankard-type, a gold & brown ringed base below the slightly tapering cylindrical body w/a reddish brown D-form handle, h.p. w/a friar seated at a tavern table, artist-signed (ILLUS. left with tall grape-decorated pitcher)............... **$518**

Pitcher, 15 1/2" h., tankard-type, a footed tapering cylindrical body molded w/a band of grapevines at the base & w/a long leafy branch handle, a high arched rim spout, the sides h.p. w/large clusters of purple & yellow grapes among leafy vines on a shaded pale cream ground, Tressemann & Vogt (ILLUS. right with tankard pitcher with friar portrait)............... **$259**

Rose-decorated Limoges Planter

Planter, round w/upright waisted sides & a slightly scalloped rim, raised on four gold scroll feet, decorated w/large deep red & pink roses & green leaves on a dark ground, underglaze green Tresseman & Vogt Mark 7, 8" d., 5 1/2" h. (ILLUS.)......... **$850**

Fine & Complete Grape-decorated Limoges Punch Set

Limoges Punch Set with Red Poppies

Punch set: footed punch bowl, 7 footed cups & an undertray; each h.p. w/red poppies & green leaves on a shaded ground, dark rust bases, small chip on one cup, mark of Tressemann & Vogt, (T.V. Limoges), bowl 13 1/2" d., the set (ILLUS.)..................................... **$978**

Punch set: large bowl & base, ten punch cups & a large round tray; the 14" d., 6 1/4" h.deep flaring rounded bowl w/a heavy gold scroll-molded rim above h.p. sides decorated w/purple grape clusters amid yellow, green & orange leaves, gold foot resting on the matching base w/large scroll-molded scroll feet, round handled cups each h.p. a berry sprig & on a gold foot, the 18" d. wide tray w/a shallow gold rim also h.p. in the center w/a grapevine design, marks of Tressemann & Vogt, ca. 1900, the set (ILLUS., top of page) **$1,725**

Limoges Punch Set with Gold Grapes

Punch set: punch bowl, base & ten champagne-style stems; the footed bowl w/deep rounded & flaring sides h.p. around the sides w/large gold leafy grapevines on stems against a pale blue shaded to white ground, on a matching base w/large gold paw feet, the saucer-shaped matching stems w/a wide shallow round bowl on a simple stem, mark of Tressemann & Vogt, Limoges, late 19th - early 20th c., bowl 16" d., 7" h., base 3 1/2" h., stems each 3 1/2" h., some rubbing to gold, the set (ILLUS.) **$1,035**

Pretty Limoges Sauceboat & Undertray

Sauceboat & undertray, footed boat-shaped vessel w/scroll-molded rim & wide arched spout, ornate looped gold handle, h.p. w/white roses on a shaded pink, blue & green ground, matching decor on undertray, underglaze Elite factory Mark 5, 5" l., 6" h., 2 pcs. (ILLUS.)............. **$275**

Tea set: one-cup cov. teapot, open sugar, creamer & oblong tray; each piece painted w/colorful roses, a gold wave scroll band around the teapot & creamer neck, gold loop handles & teapot finial, marks of Gérard, Dufraisseix & Abbot, Limoges, France, ca. 1900-41, the set (ILLUS., top next page) **$900**

GDA Limoges Tea Set on Tray

Six-cup Limoges Teapot From Set

Tea set: six-cup cov. footed spherical teapot w/a low scalloped rim, domed cover w/loop finial, serpentine spout & C-scroll handle, h.p. w/lovely shaded red & pink roses & green leaves, gold trim, matching four-cup teapot, cov. sugar, creamer, cups & saucers & an 18" l. double-handled tray, France, late 19th c., the set (ILLUS. of six-cup teapot) .... **$1,400-$2,000**

Tall Teapot from Three-Piece Set

Tea set: tall cov. teapot, cov. sugar & creamer; teapot w/wide rounded bottom & tall tapering sides, each piece in white w/heavy gold trim on spout, handles, rims & finials, green factory mark "France P.M. deM - Limoges," decorator mark of "Coronet France - Borgfeldt," ca. 1908-14, the set (ILLUS. of teapot) **$350**

Teapot, cov., bulbous tapering ovoid body w/long serpentine spout, high C-form handle & low domed cover w/loop finial, white w/simple trim, mark of Tressemann & Vogt, Limoges, ca. 1900 (ILLUS., top next column) **$200**

Tressemann & Vogt Limoges Teapot

Ornately Decorated Limoges Teapot

Teapot, cov., bulbous tapering ribbed body w/wide domed cover w/fancy loop finial, gold serpentine spout & C-scroll handle, star mark of the Coiffe factory & Flambeau China mark of decorating firm, also a Haviland & Co. mark, France, early 20th c. (ILLUS.) **$100**

Pretty Tressemann & Vogt Teapot

Teapot, cov., squatty bulbous footed body w/domed cover w/double-loop gold finial, serpentine spout, gold C-form handle, h.p. w/swags of roses, factory mark of Tressemann & Vogt, Limoges, France, ca. 1892-1907, 4" h. (ILLUS.) **$400**

Vase, 13 1/4" h., portrait-type, tall tapering ovoid body w/a small widely flaring trumpet neck, a large gold-banded oval reserve h.p. w/a large bust portriat of a lovely young woman w/long brown hair w/a red blossom in the hair & wearing a low-cut pink gown, against a white ground w/a fancy delicate gold lattice design, dark brown neck & base band bordered in gold, decorated in the Stouffer studio, base drilled, Jean Pouyet mark
.... **$2,990**

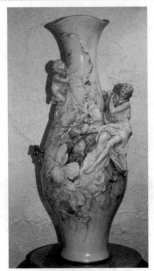

Very Rare "Blown-Out" Limoges Vase

Vase, 23 1/2" h., tall slender baluster shape w/"blown-out" figures of a cherub & a lady on the sides & further h.p. colorful roses, underglaze green marked "CFH/GDM - France" (Charles F. Haviland), very rare blank, ca. 1891-1900 (ILLUS.) **$7,000**

Fine Pair of Limoges Vases

Vases, 15 1/2" h., in the Louis XVI taste, a round pedestal foot on four paw feet supporting a baluster-form body w/a flaring neck, figural Grecian helmet handles at the shoulder, deep gold ground w/one side decorated w/a square reserve enclosing a dockside scene w/figures & a sailing vessel, each reverse decorated w/colorful military trophies, ca. 1900, pr. (ILLUS.)... **$1,610**

Liverpool

Liverpool is most often used as a generic term for fine earthenware products, usually of creamware or pearlware, produced at numerous potteries in this English city during the late 18th and early 19th centuries. Many examples, especially pitchers, were decorated with transfer-printed patriotic designs aimed specifically at the American buying public.

Pitcher, 6 1/4" h., pearlware, bulbous ovoid body w/a wide short cylindrical neck w/rim spout, applied strap handle, black transfer-printed designs, the front w/an American eagle w/a ribbon in its beak inscribed "E. Pluribus Unum," w/fifteen stars above its head; the reverse w/a vignette of an embracing couple, beneath the spout is a fleet of sailing ships, the rim decorated w/blossoms, black enamel striping on the rim, shoulder & handle edges, early 19th c. (minor imperfections) **$999**

Liverpool Jug with Poem & Sailing Ship

Pitcher, 8 1/8" h., jug-form, black transfer-printed design, the front w/the inscription "O Liberty thou Goddes!," a poem in an oval, bordered by a wreath of olive leaves surrounded by an entwined ribbon containing the names of fifteen states, the back w/a stern view of a sailing ship, a spread-winged American eagle below the spout, imperfections (ILLUS.) **$999**

Fine American Memorial Liverpool Pitcher

Pitcher, 10 1/8" h., jug-form, creamware, black transfer-printed designs trimmed in polychrome, one side printed "Success to America - Whole Militia is Better Than Standing Armies...," the back depicting a large oval memorial reserve titled "The Memory of Washington and the Pro-scribed Patriots of America," in addition a spread-winged American eagle w/shield below the spout w/the full Jefferson quote "Peace, Commerce, and honest Friend-ship with all Nations - Entangling Alliances with none - Jefferson Anno Domini 1802," a winged figure blowing a trumpet under the handle, ca. 1802, repaired (ILLUS.) ... **$3,055**

Rare Polychromed Liverpool Pitcher

Pitcher, 12" h., creamware, jug-form, one side transfer-printed & polychrome-enameled w/a scene of the ship "The America," the other side w/another print-ed & colored scene of the "Death of Wolfe," name of owner printed in black within a feathered wreath under the spout above an oval reserve w/an allegorial fig-ure of Hope, early 19th c., imperfections (ILLUS.) **$5,283**

Longwy

This faience factory was established in 1798 in the town of Longwy, France and is noted for its enameled pottery, which resembles cloisonné. Utilitarian wares were the first production here, but by the 1870s an Oriental-style art pottery that imitated cloisonné was created through the use of heavy enamels in relief. By 1912, a modern Art Deco style became part of Longwy's production; these wares, together with the Oriental-style pieces, have made this art pottery popular with collectors today. As interest in Art Deco has soared in recent years, values of Longwy's mod-ern-style wares have risen sharply.

Longwy Mark

Large Footed Longwy Bowl with Flowers

Bowl, 10" w., 4" h., widely flaring deep bowl w/a 12-paneled rim, raised on three gold peg feet, the interior decorated w/a de-sign of stylized pink & white blossoms al-ternating w/large dark turquoise blue & gold leaves against a cream ground, dark turquoise blue exterior, stamped mark (ILLUS.)... **$600**

Bold Longwy Art Deco Charger

Longwy Console Set with Vases & Center Bowl

Charger, round, a black border band surrounding a stylized Art Deco landscape w/three nudes in black or white among fruiting exotic trees in shades of dark blue, grey & brown, marked, minor line & glaze flakes, minor crazing, 15" d. (ILLUS., previous page) **$900**

Console set: a pair of 4 1/2" h. vases & 9 1/2" d. center bowl; each squatty bulbous vase tapering sharply to a trumpet neck, decorated w/long white panels centered by a black stylized flowerhead w/small black panels up the neck, the center bowl w/a wide cylindrical pedestal base in white decorated w/a band of black repeating scrolls supporting the wide cupped white bowl decorated w/a repeating design of black lines, scrolls & half-round rings, all w/stamped mark, the set (ILLUS., top of page) **$1,440**

Colorful Longwy Octagonal Vase

Cylindrical Primavera Bird & Plant Vase

Vase, 4 3/4"h., Primavera, footed wide cylindrical form w/a flat rim, decorated w/a wide body band in blue highlighted by dark blue stylized birds, plants & scattered dots, stamped & impressed marks (ILLUS.) **$300**

Vase, 5" h., footed wide ovoid octagonal shape w/a wide flat rim, decorated w/a repeating design of full-length stripes of graduated dark pink & green blossoms & stems on an ivory crackled ground, dark pink rim & foot trim, stamped mark (ILLUS., top next column) **$300**

Longwy Bottle-form Vase

Vase, 9" h., bottle-form, a round foot supporting the spherical body below a tall gently tapering ringed neck w/a flaring rim, dark turquoise ground decorated overall w/stylized pink & white blossoms & scrolling dark green leaves, a band of white & dark blue trefoils arund the rim, impressed mark (ILLUS.) **$1,020**

Very Tall Slender Longwy Vases

Vases, 14 1/4" h., very tall & slender ovoid octagonal body tapering to a tiny neck w/molded rim, decorated w/alternating narrow panels of turquoise blue w/yellow pinstripes & panels of stylized deep rose, brown & green bellflowers on zig-zag deep rose stems on a cream ground accented w/dark blue dots, stamped mark, pr. (ILLUS.).. **$2,160**

Doughnut-shaped Longwy Wine Flask

Wine flask, footed, doughnut-shaped w/open center, tapering to a cylindrical neck w/a pointed rim spout, arched turquoise blue ropetwist handle, decorated w/ornate exotic birds & flowers in bright shades of pink, blue, green, purple, yellow & brown, stamped on base "Longwy

- 1115 - 16 - D486," 6 1/2" w., 11 1/2" h. (ILLUS.).. **$259**

Lotus Ware - Knowles, Taylor & Knowles (KT&K)

Knowles, Taylor & Knowles made Lotus Ware (bone china) for a very short time. Reference books differ on the starting date but it ranges between 1889 and 1892. There is agreement that production of the ware ceased sometime in 1896. KT&K tried to make Lotus Ware again in 1904 but it proved too costly and was soon abandoned. Many pieces of this ware were hand-painted and hand-decorated. Lotus rivaled some of the finest European decorated bone china in quality and refinement of decoration and artwork. KT&K employed skilled artists, whose work is highly prized to this day by knowledgeable collectors. All photos courtesy of Nancy Wetzel, East Liverpool, Ohio.

Creamer, Davenport design, yellow & orange blush w/h.p. pink flowers, 2 5/8" h. .... **$70-$80**

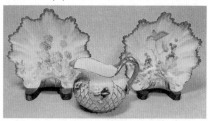

Valenciennces Creamer & Two Shell-shaped Trays

Creamer, Valenciennes design w/fishnet trim, green blush & h.p. multicolored pansies, 3" h. (ILLUS. center with two shell-shaped trays) .... **$175-$250**

Lotus Ware Tiberian Ewer & Vase

Ewer, Tiberian design, white body w/applied Celadon green flowers & leaves, 6 7/8" h. (ILLUS. left with Parmian vase) .... **$900-$1,200**

Luxor Jar and Orleans Rose Jar

Jar, cov., Luxor design, white body w/fili-greed sides & cover, h.p. pink & white flowers, 7" h. (ILLUS. left with Orleans rose jar, top of page)..................... **$900-$1,000**

Nappy (round bowl), white body w/scalloped rim, 5 1/4" w., 2 1/2" h. .... **$40-$60**

Rose jar, cov., Orleans design, white body w/extensive filigree on body & cover, hand-decorated w/red, blue & gold accents, 7 1/8" h. (ILLUS. right with Luxor jar, top of page).......................... **$1,200-$1,500**

Saucer, Lotus design, surface embossing w/pink & cream blush, 5 7/8" w. .... **$25-$40**

Sugar bowl, cov., Davenport design, yellow & orange blush w/h.p. pink flowers, 4" h. .... **$75-$90**

Tray, shell-shaped, yellow blush w/h.p. blackberries, 5 1/8" w. (ILLUS. left with creamer & other shell-shaped tray, previous page) .... **$175-$250**

Tray, shell-shaped, yellow blush w/h.p. gooseberries, 5 1/8" w. (ILLUS. right with creamer & other shell-shaped tray, previous page) .... **$175-$250**

Vase, 8" h., Tuscan design, white body w/filigree ribbing around bottom, beaded rim & beaded star design around mid-vase & ball feet... **$400-$700**

Vase, 8 3/4" h., Lily design, white body w/applied stems & leaves................. **$500-$760**

Vase, 9 1/2" h., 5 1/4" w., Celadon green body w/applied white flowers & leaves (ILLUS. right with Tiberian ewer, previous page) .... **$900-$1,200**

Majolica

Majolica, a tin-enameled glazed pottery, has been produced for centuries. It originally took its name from the island of Majorca, a source of figurine (potter's clay). Subsequently it was widely produced in England, Europe and the United States. Etruscan majolica, now avidly sought, was made by Griffen, Smith & Hill, Phoenixville, Pa., in the last quarter of the 19th century. Most majolica advertised today is 19th or 20th century. Once scorned by most collectors, interest in this colorful ware so popular during the Victorian era has now revived and prices have risen dramatically in the past few years. ALSO SEE OYSTER PLATES

Etruscan

Rare Etruscan Begonia Leaf Basket

Basket, Begonia Leaf patt., wicker-form forked overhead handle, wicker strap border band, 11 1/2" l. (ILLUS.) **$1,120**

Large Grouping of Varied Shell & Seaweed Pieces

Grouping of Etruscan Shell & Seaweed Pieces

Etruscan Pitchers, Syrup Pitchers and Other Pieces

Bowl, 7 1/2" d., Shell & Seaweed patt., great color (ILLUS. front row, far left with Shell & Seaweed cake stand, pitcher and other pieces, bottom previous page)......... **$392**

Bowl, 8" d., Shell & Seaweed patt., minor glaze nick (ILLUS. front row right with other Shell & Seaweed pieces, top of page).. **$224**

Cake stand, Shell & Seaweed patt., good color, 9 1/4" d.,5" h. (ILLUS. top row, far right with Shell & Seaweed pitcher and other pieces, bottom of previous page) **$1,120**

Creamer, Corn patt. (ILLUS. front row, fourth from left with Etruscan pitchers and syrup pitchers, second from top of page).. **$67**

Creamer, Shell & Seaweed patt., 3" h. (ILLUS. front row left with other Shell & Seaweed pieces, top of page).................................... **$134**

Creamer, Shell & Seaweed patt., minor rim nick, 3 1/4" h. (ILLUS. front row center with other Shell & Seaweed pieces, top of page).. **$101**

Creamer & cov. sugar bowl, Shell & Seaweed patt., large size, rim repair on creamer (ILLUS. center row left & right with other Shell & Seaweed pieces, top of page).. **$280**

Cup & saucer, Shell & Seaweed patt., large size, minor rim repair on cup, w/extra saucer (ILLUS. middle row, right with Shell & Seaweed cake stand, pitcher & other pieces, bottom of previous page)...... **$196**

Etruscan Shell & Seaweed Dessert Service

Dessert service: a footed compote, two creamers, a waste bowl, three shell-shaped dishes in two designs, three cake plates & six dessert plates; Shell & Seaweed patt., ca. 1880, compote 9 1/4" d., the set (ILLUS., bottom previous page) .. **$1,320**

Mug, footed ovoid shape, Lily patt. (ILLUS. front row third from left with Etruscan pitchers and syrup pitchers, second from top previous page) **$179**

Mustache cup & saucer, Shell & Seaweed patt., rim nicks on saucer (ILLUS. middle row, center with Shell & Seaweed cake stand, pitcher and other pieces, bottom of page 375) **$179**

Pitcher, 5" h., Sunflower patt., cream ground (ILLUS. center row, middle with Etruscan pitchers and syrup pitchers, middle previous page) **$336**

Pitcher, 5" h., Sunflower patt., cream ground, rim nicks (ILLUS. center row, far right with Etruscan pitchers and syrup pitchers, middle previous page) **$196**

Pitcher, 5" h., Wild Rose patt. w/butterfly spout (ILLUS. front row, third from right with Etruscan pitchers and syrup pitchers, middle previous page) **$168**

Pitcher, 5 1/4" h., Sunflower patt., greenish grey ground, minor rim nicks (ILLUS. front row, second from left with Etruscan pitchers and syrup pitchers, middle previous page) **$280**

Pitcher, 6" h., Hawthorn patt. (ILLUS. front row, far left with Etruscan pitchers and syrup pitchers, middle previous page) **$196**

Pitcher, 7" h., Fern patt., hairline (ILLUS. front row, second from right with other Etruscan pitchers and syrup pitchers, middle previous page) **$336**

Pitcher, 7" h., Fern patt., nicks (ILLUS. front row, far right with other Etruscan pitchers and syrup pitchers, middle previous page) **$196**

Pitcher, 9" h., Wild Rose patt., butterfly spout (ILLUS. center row, far left with Etruscan pitchers and syrup pitchers, middle previous page) **$252**

Plate, 7" d., Shell & Seaweed patt. **$134**

Plate, 8" d., Shell & Seaweed patt. (ILLUS. back row, left with Shell & Seaweed cake stand   and other pieces, bottom page 375) **$123**

Platter, 13 1/2" oval, Shell & Seaweed patt., Albino Ware (ILLUS. front row, right with other platters, bottom of page) **$179**

Platter, 13 1/2" oval, Shell & Seaweed patt., lavender center, great color (ILLUS. back row, left with other platters, bottom of page) **$896**

Platter, 13 1/2" oval, Shell & Seaweed patt., lavender center, very minor rim nicks on back, great color (ILLUS. back row, right with other platters, bottom of page) **$672**

Platter, 13 1/2" oval, Shell & Seaweed patt., yellow center, very minor rim nicks on back, great color (ILLUS. front row, left with other platters, bottom of page) **$448**

Spittoon, Shell & Seaweed patt., Albino Ware, colored trim, 6 1/4" h. (ILLUS. front row, right with Shell & Seaweed cake stand   and other pieces, bottom page 375) **$392**

Spooner, Shell & Seaweed patt., shell rim handles (ILLUS. center row middle with other Shell & Seaweed pieces, top previous page) **$202**

Syrup pitcher w/hinged metal lid, Bamboo patt. (ILLUS. center row, second from left with Etruscan pitchers and syrup pitchers, middle previous page) **$336**

Syrup pitcher w/hinged metal lid, Sunflower patt., cobalt blue ground (ILLUS. back row, right with Etruscan pitchers and syrup pitchers, middle previous page) **$392**

Syrup pitcher w/hinged metal lid, Sunflower patt., pink ground (ILLUS. back row, center with Etruscan pitchers and syrup pitchers, middle previous page) **$392**

Syrup pitcher w/hinged metal lid, Sunflower patt., pink ground, nice color, hairline (ILLUS. back row, left with Etruscan pitchers and syrup pitchers, middle previous page) **$420**

Group of Etruscan Shell & Seaweed Platters

Tea set: cov. teapot, cov. sugar bowl, creamer & spooner; cov., Shell & Seaweed patt., straight spout teapot, sugar cover & handle repaired, wear on creamer & spooner rims, the set (ILLUS. far left with other Shell & Seaweed pieces, top of page 376) **$560**

Tea set: cov. teapot, cov. sugar bowl, creamer & spooner; cov., Shell & Seaweed patt., crooked spout teapot, hairline in creamer, the set (ILLUS. far right with other Shell & Seaweed pieces, top of page 376) **$728**

Teapot, cov., Shell & Seaweed patt., straight spout, good color, hairline (ILLUS. back row middle with other Shell & Seaweed pieces, top of page 376) **$364**

Scarce Etruscan Vase and Wall Pocket

Vase, 5" h., Oak Leaf, Acorn & Basketweave patt., yellow ground, scarce, hairline (ILLUS. left with Etruscan wall pocket) **$700**

Wall pocket, Basketweave & Twig patt., yellow & brown, base chip, rare, 6 1/4" w., 6 1/4" h. (ILLUS. right with Etruscan vase)... **$252**

General

Large George Jones Shell-shaped Bowl

Bowl, 11" w., 7 1/2" h., the small rounded foot molded as coral & seaweed in white, green, yellow & brown supporting the very large shell-shaped bowl w/a cobalt blue exterior & pale blue interior, George Jones, minor professional repair (ILLUS.) **$1,540**

Elephant-shaped Majolica Box

Box, cov., figural, modeled as a walking elephant w/a mahout seated at his neck, a scroll-molded & blanketed howdah forms the cover, possibly Sarreguemines, France, ca. 1880, 11" h. (ILLUS.) **$1,560**

Unusual Majolica Elephant Centerpiece

Centerpiece, figural, modeled as a walking elephant wearing a pink-trimmed pale blue & deep red blanket & supporting a large tall shell-shaped howdah, England, ca. 1870, 15 1/2" h. (ILLUS.)..... **$4,200**

Centerpiece, figural, modeled as two large mermaids supporting a massive seashell between their backs, raised on an oblong shell-formed base, designed by Minton for international exhibitions, 40" w., 24" h. (ILLUS., top next page).............. **$16,500**

Rare Minton Exhibition Figural Centerpiece

Fine Minton Figural Centerpiece

Centerpiece, Rabbits Under Cabbage patt., designed w/the top bowl in the form of a large bluish green cabbage leaf raised on the backs of small white & black rabbits sitting among green foliage, Minton, date code for 1870, 9 1/2" w., 4 1/2" h. (ILLUS.).................. **$10,450**

Ornate Sarreguemines Centerpiece

Centerpiece, the large wide flaring oval bowl molded & pierced w/an entwined guilloche band suspending floral garlands above stiff leaftips, supported on figural adorned mermaids linked by cornucopias & leafy scrolls, the base raised on four scroll feet, Sarreguemines, France, ca. 1880, 23" d. (ILLUS.) **$6,000**

Cheese keeper, cov., Argenta Primrose patt., by Wedgwood, 9 1/2" h. (ILLUS., top next column).. **$440**

Wedgwood Argenta Primrose Cheese Keeper

Very Rare Beehive Cheese Keeper

Cheese keeper, cov., Beehive & Blackberry patt., modeled as a large straw beehive w/a vine loop top handle & blackberry vines wrapping around the sides, the base a square platform w/cut-corners raised on vine legs, Minton, England, ca. 1880s, hairline in base, very rare, 13" h. (ILLUS.)... **$35,200**

Fine Pair of Wedgwood Primrose Compotes

Holdcroft Blackberry Cheese Keeper

Cheese keeper, cov., Blackberry patt., by Holdcroft, professional rim repairs, 9 1/2" h. (ILLUS.) **$1,100**

Fine Victorian Storks & Leaves Compote

Compote, open, 9 1/4" h., 10 1/2" d., the wide shallow dished top composed of large overlapping green leaves raised on a tall green stem framed by three standing storks w/their heads bent down touching their breasts & glazed in mottled yellow to dark brown, on a mottled brown & bluish green tripartite base, unmarked (ILLUS.)..................................... **$518**

Compotes, 12 1/4" d., a round flaring foot tapering to a ringed pedestal supporting the wide brown basketweave bowl bordered around the rim w/a band of white primrose blossoms & leaftips, by Wedg-

wood, date code for 1872, pr. (ILLUS., top of page)... **$2,629**

Majolica Dish with Realistic Animals

Dish, trompe l'oeil style, round, the top molded & applied w/three realistic frogs, two lizards & a snake on a bed of mossy frit, Portugal, ca. 1880, 13" d. (ILLUS.) ... **$1,320**

Butterfly & Iris G. Jones Dresser Tray

Dresser tray, oval, Butterfly & Iris patt., the flowers molded in high-relief, by George Jones, 11" l. (ILLUS.)............................. **$3,300**

Fine Wedgwood Fish Platter

Fish platter, oblong w/slightly serpentine rim, molded in the center w/a large grey fish on a bed of green ferns & leaves, by Wedgwood, 25 1/2" l. (ILLUS., previous page) **$2,750**

Rare Holdcroft Fish Platter

Fish platter, oval w/pointed ends, molded in the center w/a large dark grey & brown fish against a pale blue ground trimmed w/cattails, supported on four cattail feet, by Holdcroft, 26" l. (ILLUS.) **$2,750**

Minton Covered Game Dish

Game dish, cov., the oval tapering bastketweave base trimmed w/green oak leaves, the domed cover molded in high-relief w/realistic dead game, w/the liner, by Minton, date code for 1870, chip to wing of bird, 14" l. (ILLUS.) **$2,200**

Majolica Tree Trunk Garden Seat

Garden seat, cylindrical, molded as a real-istic tree stump in brown w/ivy climbing around the sides, an applied woodpecker & two smaller birds on the sides, draped from the top w/a turquoise blue cloth w/dark blue border bands & large blue

tassels, probably Thomas Forester, England, ca. 1880, 21 5/8" h. (ILLUS.) ... **$2,640**

Majolica Garden Seat in Chinese Taste

Garden seat, hexagonal shape w/short cut-out feet, modeled in the Chinese taste, each panel edged by key & stave faux bois patterns, molded in relief w/flower-ing bamboo flanked by bamboo canes, probably by Joseph Holdcroft, England, ca. 1880, 18 7/8" h. (ILLUS.) ... **$3,360**

Fine G. Jones Floral Garden Seat

Garden seat, the wide squatty round taper-ing top centered by a cluster of three openwork white flowers forming a han-dle, the sides of the top in cobalt blue molded w/large notched green leaves al-ternating w/pendent white & yellow lily-like blossoms, three wide flattened & ta-pering legs decorated w/white & yellow petals on a cobalt blue ground, each end-ing in a tight scroll & raised on a tripartite foot, George Jones, repairs to legs & base, 18 1/2" h. (ILLUS.) **$3,300**

Majolica Jardiniere & Undertray

Jardiniere & undertray, tapering square form molded on each side w/lily-of-the-valley & white bellflowers against a cobalt blue ground, matching blue undertray, by George Jones, England, ca. 1860, 8 3/4" h. (ILLUS.) **$1,320**

Rare Holdcroft Paté Box Set

Paté box, cover & undertray, the deep oval box molded w/a band of upright green leaves on a cobalt blue ground, the cobalt blue domed cover molded in high relief w/a red lobster & seaweed, the matching undertray in cobalt blue trimmed w/green seaweed, Holdcroft, 7 1/2"l., the set (ILLUS.) **$3,850**

Unusual Figural Ostrich Pedestals

Pedestals, figural, a full-figure standing ostrich w/brown & white plumage in front of

a tall flared top naturalistic pedestal w/green, blue & pink glazing, impressed numbers on base but no company name, late 19th c., top 13" d., 32 1/2" h., pr. (ILLUS.) **$2,400**

Rare G. Jones Water Lily & Iris Pitcher

Pitcher, 8" h., Water Lily & Iris patt., the sides molded in high-relief w/water lilies, iris & green leaves on a lavender ground, yellow base & rim band, brown vine-wrapped handle, George Jones, professional rim repair (ILLUS.) **$4,950**

Copeland Egyptian Lotus Pitcher

Pitcher, 8 1/2" h., Egyptian Lotus patt., the four sides each molded w/a tall pointed arch enclosing a large pink lotus blossoms & green leaves, a square flared neck w/a palmette at each corner, fancy scroll handle, Copeland (ILLUS.) **$3,025**

French Majolica Plaque Decorated with Putti

Plaque, oblong, molded in high-relief w/a scene of three putti frolicking in a forest, one holding lovebirds, the other two crowning each other w/wreaths of roses, marked w/monogram of the painter Thomas Sergent, France, ca. 1870, 30" l. (ILLUS.) **$1,195**

Butterfly Plate & Stork in Rushes Wall Plaque

Plate, 9 1/2" w., Butterfly patt., a large rounded green leaf molded in relief w/a large spread-winged butterfly, some surface wear, Minton (ILLUS. front with French Stork in Rushes wall plaque) **$605**

Wedgwood Ocean Crate Sardine Box

Sardine box, cov., square shape, the square flat domed cover molded to resemble a dark blue crate tied w/a yellow rope & w/brown bands, floating on the ocean wave-molded matching base, Wedgwood, professional repair to corner of tray (ILLUS.) **$1,540**

Minton Sardine Box

Sardine box, cov., squared domed cover molded in relief w/grey sardines on green leaves on a cobalt blue ground, the cobalt blue box attached to the cobalt blue undertray w/green leaf band border, Minton, date code for 1884 (ILLUS.) **$1,980**

Sardine box, cov., the oblong boat-shaped base w/alternating black & blue stripes around the sides & titled "Sardinia," a large rectangular brown plank cover w/rope & anchor finial, clusters of fish at the top of each end, impressed mark of Josiah Wedgwood, ca. 1878, slight glaze chip to rim, 9 3/4" l. (ILLUS., top next column) **$881**

Wedgwood Majolica Sardine Box

Minton Mussel Shell-shaped Tureen

Seafood tureen, cov., modeled as a large mussel shell in grey w/a coral & seaweed handle, raised on green seaweed feet, Minton, 8 1/2" l. (ILLUS.) **$990**

George Jones Triple Shell Server

Server, designed as three pink shell dishes centered by a high looped green & brown dolphin handle & raised on a green shell base, George Jones, professional repair to one shell, 15" w. (ILLUS.) **$1,320**

Decorative G. Jones Strawberry Server

Strawberry server, modeled as a large green & blue lily pad style base molded w/vining strawberry blossoms, one edge attached w/two white & yellow lily blossoms forming dishes raised on a twig handle, George Jones, professional repair to one lily flower (ILLUS.) **$1,760**

Majolica Shell & Seaweed Tea Set

Tea set: cov. teapot, cov. sugar bowl & creamer; Shell & Seaweed patt., in mottled shades of grey, pink & brown w/green sea plants, late 19th c., some roughness to creamer rim, teapot 5 1/2" h., the set (ILLUS.) **$374**

New Minton Majolica Mushroom Teapot

Monkey on Coconut Figural Teapot

Teapot, cov., Monkey & Coconut patt., modeled as a large cobalt blue coconut w/green leaves & a dark grey figure of a monkey seated at the top end above the brown branch handle, brown branch spout, small cover w/figural pink bud & green leaves, J. Roth, England, late 19th c., 10" l., 7 1/4" h. (ILLUS.)...................... **$3,696**

Teapot, cov., Mushroom patt., designed by Gordon Brooks, produced by Minton, limited edition of 1,000, introduced in 2002 (ILLUS., top next column) **$750**

Teapot, cov., Spikey Fish patt., the body modeled as a large grey & green bulbous fish raised on green waves, a large branch of brown seaweed w/a shell thumbrest forming the handle, angled brown straight spout emerging from the mouth, the small cover w/an arched spiky fin handle, Mintons, third quarter 19th c., extremely rare, professional repair to spout, base rim & rim of cover, 9 1/2" l., 7" h. (ILLUS.) **$29,120**

Rare Mintons Majolica Teapot

Teapot, cov., oblong sad iron-shaped body w/a short spout, high arched fixed handle, the cobalt blue body molded w/a band decorated w/alternating grey mouse & pink blossom, the top of the handle molded w/the figure of a curled up white cat looking down at a grey mouse & carrot forming the finial of the flat cover, Mintons, England, possibly designed by Christopher Dresser, Model No. 622, date letter for 1876, 7 1/2" h. (ILLUS.) **$47,000**

Extremely Rare Figural Spikey Fish Mintons Teapot

Leafy Tray with Figural Monkey Handle

Tray, oblong shallow form w/a yellow border surrounding large molded leaves & blossoms, one end molded in full-relief w/a monkey seated on a tree branch, attributed to George Jones, 10" l., 5" h. (ILLUS.) .. **$550**

Detailed Palissy Ware Majolica Tray

Tray, 13 3/4" l., oval, Palissy Ware, the center molded in high-relief w/a realistic fish on a bed of leaves & water, the thick border molded w/realistic seaweed & sea creatures on a dark blue ground (ILLUS.) **$3,025**

Tall Flower-encrusted Majolica Vase

Vase, 34 1/4" h., footed slender ovoid body tapering to a very slender tall neck, decorated overall in the Barbotine style w/a large & tall green stem w/pink marguerite daisies & hanging floral garlands, attributed to Capo-di-Monte, Italy, ca. 1900 (ILLUS.)..................................... **$1,920**

"Catch of the Day" Fish Wall Plaque

Wall plaque, figural, "Catch of the Day" design composed of a cluster of three realistic hanging fish, 9 1/2" l. (ILLUS.) **$550**

Wall plaque, pierced to hang, oval w/wide deep molded border w/cattails on a yellow round, the center molded w/a scene of a stork standing in water among reeds, France, late 19th c., 13 1/2" l. (ILLUS. back with Minton Butterfly plate, on page 383)...... **$385**

McCoy

Collectors are now seeking the art wares of two McCoy potteries. One was founded in Roseville, Ohio, in the late 19th century as the J.W. McCoy Pottery, subsequently becoming Brush-McCoy Pottery Co., later Brush Pottery. The other was also founded in Roseville in 1910 as Nelson McCoy Sanitary Stoneware Co., later becoming Nelson McCoy Pottery. In 1967 the pottery was sold to D.T. Chase of the Mount Clemens Pottery Co., who sold his interest to the Lancaster Colony Corp. in 1974. The pottery shop closed in 1985. Cookie jars are especially collectible today.

A helpful reference book is The Collector's Encyclopedia of McCoy Pottery, by the Huxfords (Collector Books), and McCoy Cookie Jars From the First to the Latest, by Harold Nichols (Nichols Publishing, 1987).

McCoy Mark

Bank, figural seaman w/sack over shoulder, white, blue & black, 5 3/4" h. (ILLUS., next page) .... **$115-$130**

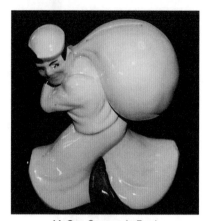

McCoy Seaman's Bank

Bookends, decorated w/swallows, ca. 1956, 5 1/2 x 6" .... **$200-$250**

Astronaut Cookie Jar

Cookie jar, Astronaut, 1963, good gold trim (ILLUS.).. **$500-$800**

Christmas Tree Cookie Jar

Cookie jar, Christmas Tree, ca. 1959 (ILLUS.) .... **$1,000+**
Cookie jar, Hobby Horse, ca. 1948 ...... **$100-$150**

Koala Bear Cookie Jar

Cookie jar, Koala Bear, ca. 1983 (ILLUS.) .... **$125-$150**
Cookie jar, Teepee, 1956-59 .... **$403**
Figurine, head of witch, ca. early 1940s, 3" h... **$400-$600**
Iced tea server, El Rancho Bar-B-Que line, ca. 1960, 11 1/2" h. .... **$250-$300**
Jardiniere, Loy-Nel-Art line, wide bulbous shape w/a wide molded flat rim, painted w/large orange tulips & green leaves on a shaded dark brown ground, unmarked, ca. 1905, 6 1/2" h. **$173**

McCoy Quilted Pattern Jardiniere

Jardiniere, Quilted patt., glossy glaze, deep aqua, marked, 1954, 10 1/2" d., 7 1/2" h. (ILLUS.).. **$144**
Jardiniere, fish decoration, ca. 1958, 7 1/2" h... **$350-$400**
Jardiniere & pedestal base, Leaves & Berries design, ca. 1930s, overall 21" h., 2 pcs. (ILLUS., next page) .... **$250-$350**
Model of cat, ca. 1940s, 3" h. .... **$300-$400**

Leaves & Berries Jardiniere & Pedestal

Oil jar, bulbous ovoid body w/slightly flaring rim, angled shoulder handles, red sponged glaze, 18" h. .... **$300-$400**
Pitcher, embossed w/parading ducks, ca. 1930s, 4 pt. .... **$90-$125**
Pitcher, 10" h., Butterfly line................. **$150-$225**

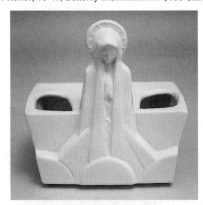

Rare Madonna Planter

Planter, figural, Madonna, white, ca. 1960s, rare, 6" h. (ILLUS.) .... **$200-$250**
Planter, model of Cope monkey head, 5 1/2" h. .... **$100-$200**
Planter, model of fish, green, ca. 1955, 7 x 12" (ILLUS., top next column) .... **$1,000-$1,200**
Planter, model of pomegranate, ca. 1953, 5 x 6 1/2" .... **$125-$150**
Planter, model of snowman, ca. 1940s, 4 x 6" .... **$70-$90**

Rare Fish Planter

Planter, model of "stretch" dachshund, 8 1/4" l. .... **$150-$175**
Planting dish, rectangular, front w/five relief-molded Scottie dog heads, white, brown & green, ca. 1949, 8" l. .... **$50-$60**
Platter, 14" l., Butterfly line, ca. 1940s .. **$250-$600**
Spoon rest, Butterfly line, ca. 1953, 4 x 7 1/2" .... **$90-$125**

McCoy Pottery Shaded Brown Teapot

Teapot, cov., spherical body w/molded rings around the bottom, short spout, squared handle, low domed cover w/pointed loop finial, shaded brown glaze, ca. 1948 (ILLUS.) **$25**

McCoy Strawberry Country Teapot

Teapot, cov., Strawberry Country patt., heavy cylindrical white body w/short spout & C-form handle, printed w/a cluster of strawberries, blossoms & leaves, flat green cover w/knob finial, 1970s (ILLUS.) **$25**

McCoy Fireplace TV Lamp

TV lamp, model of fireplace, ca. 1950s, 6 x 9" (ILLUS.)...................................... **$75-$100**

Vase, 6" h., footed, heart-shape w/embossed roses, ca. 1940s .... **$60-$80**

Vase, 8" h., footed bulbous base w/trumpet-form neck & scrolled handles, embossed peacock decoration, ca. 1948 .... **$40-$60**

McCoy Magnolia Vase

Vase, 8 1/4" h., figural magnolia, pink, white, brown & green, ca. 1953 (ILLUS.)
.... **$250-$300**

Vase, 8 1/2" h., figural wide lily-form, white, brown & green, ca. 1956 .... **$100-$125**

Vase, 14" h., Antique Curio line, ca. 1962
.... **$75-$100**

Wall pocket, figural, clown, white w/red & black trim, ca. 1940s, 8" l. (ILLUS., top next column)..................................... **$100-$150**

Wall pocket, model of apple, ca. early 1950s, 6 x 7" .... **$200-$225**

McCoy Clown Wall Pocket

Wall pocket, model of bird bath, late 1940s, 5 x 6 1/2" .... **$90-$110**

Meissen

The secret of true hard paste porcelain, known long before to the Chinese, was "discovered" accidentally in Meissen, Germany by J.F. Bottger, an alchemist working with E.W. Tschirnhausen. The first European true porcelain was made in the Meissen Porcelain Works, organized about 1709. Meissen marks have been widely copied by other factories. Some pieces listed here are recent.

Meissen Mark

Pretty Meissen Pate-Sur-Pate Box

Box, cov., pate-sur-pate, low squatty rounded shape w/gilt-metal hinged fittings, the cover decorated w/a central roundel of a putto tossing flowers on a peach ground, within a band of alternating dark & light blue lappets enriched w/pate-sur-pate flowers & foliage trimmed w/gold, all on a pale celadon ground w/further flowers, the interior decorated w/a flower spray, blue Crossed Swords mark, late 19th - early 20th c., 6 1/4" d. (ILLUS.) **$4,800**

Two-tiered Meissen Centerpiece

Centerpiece, a domed round gadrooned base tapering to a knopped stem supporting a two-tiered top w/each dished section w/reticulated edges & h.p. in blue w/three cartouches w/blue highlights & flowers, the top center mounted w/a figure of a standing woman holding up her apron full of flowers, overall blue trim, blue crossed swords mark on base, probably late 19th c., base dish 9" d., overall 16" h. (ILLUS.) **$450**

Tall Ornate Figural Meissen Clock

Clock, figural, in the Rococo taste, the tall case molded as a cartouche applied w/flowering garlands enclosing the clock w/a white porcelain dial w/Roman numerals, held by the large figure of the seated

goddess, Diana, raised on a tall waisted rocaille pedesal molded w/a winged head of Father Time above a small putto petting Diana's dog, the center h.p. w/a color vignette of a romantic couple in a wooded landscape, scrolled feet, the sides & back trimmed w/scattered gilt flowers, retailed by Tiffany & Co., New York City, mid- to late 19th c., 15 1/2" h. (ILLUS.) **$6,573**

Meissen Satyr & Putti Figure Group

Figure group, a large seated satyr on a carpeted mound taking grapes from a putto on his left shoulder, another putto pulling his vine, a third playing his pipes & the last tying on a sandel, a goat climbs up the side to eat vegetables from the satyr's lap, on a gilt-trimmed round scrolled base, blue Crossed Swords mark, late 19th - early 20th c., 14 1/2" h. (ILLUS.)... **$2,880**

Elaborate Meissen Figure Group

Two Beautiful Late Victorian Meissen Figure Groups

Figure group, a wide round scroll-footed base in white & pale blue trimmed in gold, supporting a tall central rockwork mound in brown trimmed w/applied "coleslaw" plants, mounted around the lower sides w/two figures of young men & two figures of young women in 18th c. costume, also w/a lamb & gamebirds, at the very top the seated figure of a man in 18th c. costume playing a lute w/a music book at his feet, delicate floral & stripe decoration on the costumes, blue Crossed Swords mark w/dot, illegible mark of the decorator, restorations, late 18th c., 17 1/2" h. (ILLUS., previous page)... **$3,055**

Figure group, composed of a seated mother in 18th c. costume reaching out to her young daughter standing before her, a tea table set w/cups & saucers beside her, on an oblong scroll-molded base in white w/gilt trim, the figures w/detailed colorful costumes, some minor losses, blue Crossed Swords mark, 19th c., 8 1/2" h. **$3,173**

Figure group, depicting an elegant lady in 18th c. dress standing over a cherub reading an open book, they surrounded below by ladies in waiting & two little girls, ovoid naturalistic base, late 19th - early 20th c., 12" h. (ILLUS.)........................... **$6,463**

Figure group, titled "Amor in Noten," the round platform base edged w/a gilt repeating ring design, modeled w/a seated classical woman in a chair beside a young maiden seated on a stool, a naughty Cupid having his wings clipped by the woman, finely decorated in color, blue Crossed Swords mark, late 19th c., 13 1/2" d. (ILLUS. left with other figure group, top of page)................................. **$9,560**

Figure group, titled "Amors Fesselung," the round platform base edged w/a gilt repeating ring design, modeled w/a seated classical woman in a chair beside a young maiden seated on a stool, the woman untethering Cupid, the maiden feeding billing doves, a wreath, bow & quiver at their feet, finely decorated in color, blue Crossed Swords mark, late 19th c., 13 1/2" d. (ILLUS. right with other figure group, top of page)..................... **$10,755**

Figure Group of Zephyr & Flora

Fine Meissen Group with Ladies & Cherub

Figure group, Zephyr & Flora, the standing Flora half nude wearing a pale blue drapery trimmed w/a floral garland standing beside winged Zephyr draped only in a golden brown wrap, square gilt-trimmed base, blue Crossed Swords mark, late 19th c., 11 1/2" h. (ILLUS.)...................... **$2,400**

Meissen Allegorial Putto Figure

Figure of a putto, allegorial, the chubby child w/a staff & flowers wrapped in a long swirled pink drape, probably representing Spring, applied sunflower to the sides, on a domed gold base, underglaze-blue Crossed Swords mark, minor flaws, late 20th c., 14 1/2" h. (ILLUS.)..... **$2,233**

19th C. Meissen Figure of Despina

Figure of Despina, a partially nude standing classical woman leaning back to check the sandal on her foot resting on a large rock, raised on an oval waisted plinth base incised w/a thin wave band over a band w/cattails, tridents & small dolphins, underglaze-blue Crossed Swords mark, late 19th c., 18" h. (ILLUS.)............................. **$5,170**

Pair of Meissen Cherub Figures

Figures, one a seated female cherub wearing a mob cap & apron, seated on a brickwork platform using a coffee grinder w/a tall coffeepot beside her, an oblong scroll-molded base, the second a seated male cherub seated w/a bowl preparing porridge, seated on a brickwork base w/an oblong scroll-molded base, overall gilt trim on both, underglaze-blue Crossed Swords mark, late 19th c., 5 1/4" h., pr. (ILLUS.).................... **$2,115**

Oval Meissen Plaque Decorated with Venus & Putti

Plaque, oval w/molded gilt scroll border band, the center finely painted in the manner of Boucher w/Venus attended by two nymphs & two putti resting in clouds, stringing garlands of flowers, a basket at their right & two further putti above, blue Crossed Swords mark, late 19th c., 21" l. (ILLUS.).. **$10,200**

Lovely Meissen Plate with Center Scene

Plate, 9" d., a small h.p. round central scene in color showing a half-nude Classical male holding a wreath above the head of a half-nude woman, a narrow reticulated outer border band enclosing a wide cobalt blue ground ornately decorated w/delicate gold, blue Crossed-Swords mark, titled "Le Printemps - Watteau," ca. 1900 (ILLUS., previous page) **$1,691**

Meissen Cup & Saucer with City View

Teacup & saucer, the cup w/a cobalt blue ground painted on the side w/a large oblong reserve w/a color scene of a church in Dresden, bordered in gold scrolls, the matching cup w/three oblong reserves painted w/colorful floral bouquets outlined w/gold scrolls, scene titled "Kathol Kirche zu Dresden," blue Crossed-Swords mark, ca. 1850 (ILLUS.) **$1,076**

Teapot, cov., bulbous tapering body w/a foliage-molded wishbone handle & bird's-head spout, the body w/a yellow background painted on each side w/a black-outlined cartouche containing a waterway landscape scene of merchants at various pursuits by barrels, sacks & figures on horseback & boating, low domed cover w/pale red figural strawberry finial flanked by cartouches, further gold, puce & iron-red trim on the spout & handle, blue Crossed-Swords mark & impressed number, ca. 1740, 3 5/8" h. **$4,183**

Urns, each w/a round gadrooned & fluted pedestal base in gold, cobalt blue & white supporting a tall ovoid body w/a wide band of gold flutes around the lower section below the cobalt blue upper body w/a thin white shoulder band below the flaring cobalt blue neck w/a rolled & gadrooned gold & white rim flanked by ornate double-looping white snake handles from the rim to gilt molded leaf clusters at the shoulders, underglaze-blue Crossed Swords marks, mid-19th c., 19 1/2" h., pr. (ILLUS., top next column) **$3,290**

Vase, 6 1/8" h., in the Neo-rococo taste, a square foot below the fluted socle supporting a squatty bulbous body tapering to a short, wide neck w/heavy gilt scrolls

Cobalt, Gold & White Meissen Urns

Small Meissen Vase with Putti Scenes

around the rim, the front of the body decorated w/a scene after Boucher showing a sleeping putto being tickled by another w/a stalk of wheat, the reverse w/a scene of putti drawing, both within flower-encrusted borders, socle & base trimmed in gold, blue Crossed Swords mark, late 19th - early 20th c. (ILLUS.) **$1,020**

Vase, cov., 29 1/2" h., ringed pedestal base below the wide inverted pear-shaped body w/a domed cover topped by a tall finial composed of applied colorful flowers, the body painted w/small vignette of figures in a garden near ruins, the reverse decorated w/a reserve of flowers, all surrounded by large applied flower blossoms & fruits scrolling around the sides & forming vine handles, the lower pedestal base mounted w/the figure of a small nymph holding a basket of flowers, a putto above on the opposite side, blue Crossed Swords mark, late 19th c. (ILLUS., next page) **$15,600**

Elaborate Floral-decorated Meissen Vase

Ornate Meissen Allegorical Vases

Vases, 13 1/4" h., in the neo-Rococo taste, one w/an ornate pedestal base applied w/a leafy tree w/fruit & a fish, the other w/the pedestal base decorated w/icicles, each w/a bulbous inverted pear-shaped body molded w/scrolls & applied decorations, each w/an applied figure seated on the shoulder, one w/a putto representing Summer & the other w/a putto representing Winter, each h.p. w/a small reserve featuring lovers in 18th c. attire, the Summer vase w/a tall slender neck w/ruffled rim & applied summer motifs, the Winter vase w/a matching neck issuing large orange flames, blue Crossed Swords mark, late 19th c., pr. (ILLUS.) **$8,365**

Mettlach

Ceramics with the name Mettlach were produced by Villeroy & Boch and other potteries in the Mettlach area of Germany. Villeroy and Boch's finest years of production are thought to be from about 1890 to 1910. Also see STEINS.

Mettlach Mark

Small Mettlach Candy or Cracker Basket

Candy or cracker basket with silver plate rim, cover & bail handle, No. 1204, the wide short cylindrical body etched repeating scroll & leaf design in grey, white, brown & blue, wear on metal fitting, 5" d., 3 1/4" h. (ILLUS.) **$201**

Mettlach Cameo Plaque with Angel

Plaque, Cameo-style, round slightly dished form centered by a white relief figure of a large crouched angel w/white doves, the central background in cream over blue, No. 2970, 10 1/2" d. (ILLUS.) **$353**
Plaque, No. 1044-1066, PUG decoration of a rustic water pump, some gold wear, artist-signed, 17" d. **$362**

Two Mettlach Allegorical Plaques for Spring & Fall

Pair of Mettlach Plaques with Drinking Cavaliers

Plaque, No. 2898, etched allegorial scene of a young maiden standing amid flowering shrubs & trees, representing Spring, 17 1/2" d. (ILLUS. left with plaque No. 2899, top of page) **$2,174**

Plaque, No. 2899, etched allegorial scene of a young maiden standing carrying a sheaf of wheat amid wide fields of grain, representing Fall, 17 1/2" d. (ILLUS. right with plaque No. 2898, top of page) **$2,174**

Plaques, No. 3161 & No. 3162, each etched w/colorful scenes of seated cavaliers drinking w/white inscribed banners at the bottom, 17" d., pr. (ILLUS., second from top of page) **$1,725**

Fine Mettlach Punch Bowl Set

Punch bowl, cover & undertray, No. 2806, Cameo & etched decoration, a large rectangular blue panel enclosing white relief classical figural, on a green ground trimmed w/bands of stylized pink & yellow blossoms yellow leaves, artist-signed, 9.4 liters, the set (ILLUS.) **$1,208**

White Relief Mettlach Punch Bowl Set

Punch bowl, cover & underplate, No. 2341, the footed spherical body w/a low neck & low domed cover w/large ring handle, figure caryatid handles at the sides, on a nearly flat undertray, the brown sides molded in white relief scene of a drunken man below an inscribed banner, 10 liter, the set (ILLUS.) **$845**

Mettlach Art Deco Tea Set

Tea set: cov. teapot, cov. sugar bowl, creamer & large round tray; simple Art Deco style, tapering octagonal serving pieces w/green-bordered white panels & a band of stylized florets around the rims, the matching tray w/a paneled center & a wide floret border band, No. 3321, some minor professional repairs, ca. 1925, tray 15" d., the set (ILLUS., previous page) **$264**

Mettlach Vase with Nightingales

Two Small Etched Mettlach Vases

Vase, 5" h., No. 1504, small flared foot below a wide cushion band centered by a tall trumpet-form neck, the band molded & etched w/brown buttons, the main body band in dark blue w/stylized leaf-like design below the rim bands w/beaded & leaftip bands in brown & yellow (ILLUS. left with vase No. 2864)................................. **$93**

Vase, 5" h., No. 2864, small flared foot below a wide cushion band centered by a tall trumpet-form neck, the band molded & etched w/blue buttons, the main body in dark blue w/scattered gold dots & thin gold bands (ILLUS. right with vase No. 1504, above) **$217**

Vase, 7 1/2" h., wide ovoid body tapering to a short flaring neck, applied w/two nightingales perched on pine boughs w/a gold moon beyond, on a dark green ground, marked, No. 1514 (ILLUS.) **$288**

Vase, 9" h., No. 1681, footed bulbous ovoid body w/a tall slender ringed cylindrical neck, etched designs w/a wide center band w/large circles framing stylized florette designs, repeating smaller designs around the shoulder & lower body, a small band of rosettes around the neck (ILLUS. right with Mettlach vase No. 1625, previous column)............................. **$169**

Two Etched Mettlach Vases

Vase, 7 1/2" h., No. 1625, footed spherical body tapering to a waisted neck w/a cupped rim, a wide body band etched w/a band of rings enclosing large florettes, lappet bands on shoulder & lower body, dotted design on the neck & bands around the rim (ILLUS. left with Mettlach vase No. 1681)... **$176**

Finely Molded Tall Mettlach Vase

Vase, 11 1/4" h., No. 1409, a low conical foot supporting the large bulbous body w/a tall cylindrical ringed neck flanked by long dragon handles, overall relief-molded repeating leaf & blue & white blossom design w/beaded band trim (ILLUS.) **$380**

Tall Mettlach Vase with Putti Scenes

Vase, 14" h., No. 1537, a footed trumpet-form body w/a wide shoulder centered by a trumpet-form neck, the main body etched w/four oblong panels each enclosing a scene of a classical putti in a different pose, overall decorative bands & arched panels (ILLUS.) **$362**

Fine Mettlach Art Nouveau Vase

Vase, 14 1/2" h., No. 2976, tapering cylindrical body w/a low rolled neck, decorated w/Art Nouveau style tall red blossoms

alternating w/oblong blue panels framing a red heart, rare green color (ILLUS.) **$920**

Minton

The Minton factory in England was established by Thomas Minton in 1793. The factory made earthenware, especially the blue-printed variety, and Thomas Minton is sometimes credited with the invention of the blue "Willow" pattern. For a time majolica and tiles were also important parts of production, but bone china soon became the principal ware. Mintons, Ltd., continues in operation today. Also see OYSTER PLATES.

Minton Marks

Bottle coolers, pate-sure-pate, four gilt-trimmed scroll feet support the squared upright container in ivory white w/ornate gold trim, four pilasters & leafy scroll handles alternate w/chocolate brown reserve decorated w/a white slip pair of putti bordered in gilt, reverse w/reserve decorated w/a putto eating a peach or listening to a shell, gently flared rim band w/pierced repeating loop sections, gilt crowned globe mark & impressed marks, retailer mark for Goode & Co., London, date cypher for 1883, 8" h., pr. (ILLUS., bottom of page) **$71,700**

Rare Mintons Pate-Sur-Pate Cachepot

Extraordinary Pair of Minton Pate-sur-Pate Bottle Coolers

Mintons Dessert Service & Covered Vases

Cachepot, pate-sur-pate, low round foot & deep cylindrical sides w/a flat rim, molded small scroll handles, peacock blue ground, the sides centered by large round reserves w/a chocolate brown field finely painted & hand-tooled in white slip on one side w/a putto symbolizing Ceramic Art, depicted seated on a stool painting a small standing putto, the other side w/another reserve decorated w/a Berainesque urn suspending foliage & flaming torches, both within a scrolling gold border w/gilt trim on the handles & a dotted gold band around the rim, signed by Alboin Birks, cypher date for 1909, 7" h. (ILLUS., previous page) **$19,200**

Centerpiece, allegorial figure-style, the top center mounted w/a tall white molded figure of a classical woman representing Science holding a small globe & caliper, on a turquoise cylindrical ringed pedestal trimmed w/ gilt guillouche bands, centered in a wide concave base w/the rolled rim mounted w/four large raised panels continuing to form strap feet, each in white w/a wide gold border enclosing a delicate trellis design, the turquoise rolled rim also banded in gold, impressed marks, after a model by T. N. Maclean, date cypher for 1876, 20 1/2" h. (ILLUS., top next column) **$4,560**

Fine Mintons Figural Centerpiece

Dessert service: two footed open compotes & nine 10" d. plates; each piece w/a turquoise pierced trellis border flanked by banded gilt ribbons, the center enriched w/ "jeweled" egg-and-dart band, printed crowned globe mark & mark of retailer T. Goode & Co., London & the prince of Wales feather Paris Exhibition of 1878 mark, ca. 1878, the set (ILLUS. back with covered vases, top of page).... **$1,800**

Fine Set of Minton Fish and Game Plates

Fish & game plates, round, six naturalistically h.p. w/various game birds & six h.p. w/various fish, each scene above a large gilt cell-pattern cartouche, the gilt border acid-etched w/fruiting grapevine, each marked w/painted marks & name of the retailer, Tiffany & Co., date letter for 1902, 8 7/8" d., set of 12 (ILLUS., bottom previous page) **$5,040**

Minton Majolica Figural Garden Seat

Garden seat, majolica, figural, modeled as a blackamoor boy seated on a corded & tasseled tufted cushion, wearing a lion pelt, yellow-trimmed green jacket & pale blue tunic, tied at the waist w/a striped sash, above matching boots, supporting a second similar cushion on his inclined head & neck, impressed mark, dated 1883, 19 1/4" h. (ILLUS.) **$16,800**

Rare Minton Figural Majolica Plaque

Plaque, majolica, oval, molded in high-relief w/the head & torso of a Renaissance cavalier holding a torch, within a berried laurel wreath border, bold coloring, unmarked, ca. 1860, 18 1/2" h. (ILLUS.) **$10,200**

Exquisite Mintons Pate-Sur-Pate Rectangular Plaque

Plaque, rectangular, pate-sur-pate, the dark green ground finely painted & hand-tooled in white slip w/six diaphanously draped maidens brewing love potions, one maiden kneels pouring a basket filled w/hearts into the mix while others prod putti w/three-tined forks, a garland above suspends cooking implements & produce, signed by Louis Solon & dated 1879, in a white-washed wooden frame, 8 1/2 x 15 3/4" (ILLUS.)
.... **$38,400**

Extraordinary Group of Minton Dessert Plates with Pate-sur-Pate Medallions

Finely Painted Minton Plaque

Plaque, rectangular, titled "Le Panier Mis-
terieux," finely h.p. w/a scene after
Boucher showing a young shepherd se-
cretly leaving a basket of flowers at the
foot of a young sleeping maiden as her
spaniel looks on, large stone monuments
in a wooden garden in the background,
paper label of retailer Thomas Goode &
Co., London, mid-19th c., in a giltwood
frame, 12 3/4 x 15 3/4" (ILLUS.) **$6,000**

Plates, dessert, 8 7/8" d., a fine radiating
gold-striped border band interrupted by
three pate-sur-pate cameo portrait medallions of classical men & women within
beaded borders & suspended from gold
ribbons, the inner border & cavetto w/fur-
ther flowerheads & gilt beadwork, gilt
crowned globe mark & impressed marks,
No. PA 9390, retailed by Tiffany & Co.,
New York, New York, date cyphers for
1919, set of 12 (ILLUS., top of page)
.... **$11,950**

Very Rare Group of Minton Plates

Plates, dessert & soup, 9 1/2" & 10 1/4" d.,
each center decorated w/a floral wreath,
the turquoise border band enameled in
white w/arabesques, edged by gilt bands,
together w/six similarly enameled soup
plates w/inner gold band, Pattern No. G
5748 & H309, gilt crowned globe mark &
impressed mark, retailed by Tiffany & Co.,
New York, New York, date cyphers for
1902, group of 12 (ILLUS.) **$6,573**

One of Two Early Minton Potpourri Vases

Potpourri vases, cov., Neo-Rococo design, the short pedestal base w/heavy gold scroll feet, the tall trumpet-form body fitted w/a domed cover mounted by a figural putto, cobalt ground, the body painted front & back w/panels showing 18th c. views representing the seasons, framed by heavy gold scrolls & flanked by long ornate gold scroll handles down the sides, the flaring gold-scroll rim supporting the quatrefoil domed cover w/four reticulated rocaille-molded cartouches centering panels painted w/roses, pansies or fruit, ca. 1838, 17 1/2" h., pr. (ILLUS. of one, previous page) **$6,000**

Rare Minton Pate-sur-Pate Tray

Tray, pate-sur-pate, rectangular w/arched & scroll-molded ends trimmed in gold, chocolate brown ground decorated in color-tinted white slip w/the figure of a Grecian maiden resting her hand above a lion-head wall fountain filling a colored jug, a balustrade w/bell-shaped krater vase behind her, a floral landscape beyond, trace of gilt crowned globe mark, signed by Louis Solon, dated 1874, 13 1/8" l. (ILLUS.).............................. **$17,925**

Finely Enameled Minton Turquoise Vase

Vase, 7 7/8" h., pilgrim flask-shaped, gold foot below the flattened turquoise blue rounded body tapering to a small cylindrical neck w/gold rim flanked by gold handles, enameled in color on the front & back w/large roses & fuschia on leafy berried stems, Model No. 1348, ca. 1880 (ILLUS.).. **$2,271**

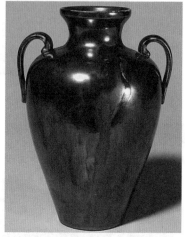

Unusual Minton Astra Ware Vase

Vase, 10" h., Astra Ware, tall ovoid body w/a short trumpet neck & C-scroll shoulder handles, streaky overall metallic glaze, impressed round Astra Ware seal mark (ILLUS.).. **$345**

Large Classical Form Mintons Vase

Vase, 21 1/2" h., classical amphora form w/a small square foot, wide ovoid body & tall trumpet neck flanked by gilt handles to the top of the shoulder, painted overall w/large cascading pink & blush fully blown roses, the neck & foot gilt w/faux fluting, the handles w/acanthus leaves, printed & impressed marks, ca. 1900 (ILLUS.) **$2,880**

Fine Pair of Mintons Pate-sur-Pate Vases

Vases, 7 1/2" h., pate-sur-pate, tapering cylindrical body w/a short shoulder & narrow dotted gold mouth band, the peacock blue ground finely painted & hand-tooled in white slip w/paired mythic arches & putti symbolizing Love & War, the reverse w/corresponding ribbon-tied trophies, signed by Alboin Birks, ca. 1900, pr. (ILLUS.) **$18,000**

Vases, cov., 12 1/4" h., designed after Sevres "Vases de Cote Deparis," a square foot & slender tapering pedestal supporting the classical urn-form body w/a tapering neck w/flanked by leaf-cast loop handles, small domed cover w/pine cone finial, the decoration inspired by the service made for Catherine the Great, each w/a turquoise ground, the pedestal base & neck w/gold fluting, each h.p. on the side en grisaille w/small round portrait medallions above long ribbon-tied floral garlands, impressed marks & date cypher for 1889, pr. (ILLUS. front with dessert service, top of page 397) **$4,800**

Mocha

Mocha decoration is found on basically utilitarian creamware or yellowware articles and is achieved by a simple chemical reaction. A color pigment of brown, blue, green or black is given an acid nature by infusion of tobacco or hops. When this acid nature colorant is applied in blobs to an alkaline ground color, it reacts by spreading in feathery seaweed designs. This type of decoration is usually accompanied by horizontal bands of light color slip. Produced in numerous Staffordshire potteries from the late 18th until the late 19th centuries, its name is derived from the similar markings found on mocha quartz. In addition to the seaweed decoration, mocha wares are also seen with Earthworm and Cat's Eye patterns or a marbleized effect.

Nice Mocha Yellowware Jar

Jar, cov., cylindrical w/molded base band, fitted flat cover w/low button knob, yellowware w/white band around body & cover decorated w/dark green seaweed design, some wear & chip on bottom, 19th c., 7" d., 5" h. (ILLUS.) **$546**

Rare Early Earthworm Mocha Shaker

Pepper pot, footed baluster-form body w/domed top, decorated w/slat blue & burnt orange bands w/the wide middle orange band w/a dotted earthworm design in blue, white & black, 4 1/4" h. (ILLUS.) **$2,530**

Pepper pot, pearlwear, footed baluster form decorated w/brown & gold bands flanking a medial ochre band w/dendritic designs, early 19th c., 4 1/4" h. (very minor chips to top) **$3,290**

Pitcher, 6" h., pearlware, barrel-form w/extruded strap handle w/leaf terminals, banded in black, blue & rust w/five parallel white wavy trailed lines centering the broad ochre band flanked by blue, black & white leaf designs, ca. 1830 (hairlines, glaze wear) **$3,760**

Pitcher, 9 5/8" h., footed tall waisted cylindrical shape w/pinched rim spout, applied extruded strap handle w/foliate terminals, decorated w/a wide light brown band w/brown "seaweed" designs flanked by narrow black bands & a light blue band, a sandblasted capacity mark on the side, England, 1871, 1 gal. (hairline in handle, crazing w/brownish discoloration) **$705**

Monmouth-Western Stoneware & Others

MONMOUTH-WESTERN STONEWARE COM-PANY: *The Western Stoneware Company of Monmouth, Illinois, was formed in April 1906 by the merger of seven existing potteries located in three different states — five in Illinois, one in Missouri and one in Iowa. The fact that the Red Wing Union Stoneware Company was organized just one month earlier is no coincidence. Correspondence between the companies shows that the two remaining Red Wing companies contemplated an offer from the organizers of the new Western Stoneware Company to join them. As we know, the Red Wing companies themselves chose to merge and compete with the new company to the south, rather than join it.*

It is not surprising, then, that the Western Stoneware Company and the Red Wing Union Stoneware Company produced similar product lines (crocks, jugs, churns, water coolers and kitchenwares). The wares also featured similar glazes and decorations (white or "Bristol," blue and white, red and blue sponging) as well as somewhat similar marks and logos (a stenciled maple leaf for Western vs. a red wing for Red Wing; both also used a printed oval mark). Even the companies' advertising catalogs and pamphlets resembled each other.

One of the enduring mysteries, however, is why the Red Wing company, apparently, never made rolling pins even though they were big sellers for Western. One of the most profitable (and prolific) sellers for Western was the "Sleepy Eye" product line. Red Wing may have experimented with a competing line, but it never duplicated the success of the Sleepy Eye pieces.

The Western Stoneware Company continues to operate today in Monmouth, Illinois.

BRUSH-MCCOY POTTERY (Zanesville, Ohio) & BLUE RIBBON BRAND (Buckeye Pottery, Macomb, Illinois, 1882-1941):

The Brush-McCoy Pottery was a successor to the first Brush Pottery that operated in Roseville, Ohio, from 1907 to 1911. It operated a plant in Roseville from 1911 until 1925 and had another plant in nearby Zanesville that produced artwares until it burned in 1918.

This company was succeeded by a second Brush Pottery in Roseville in 1925 that was unrelated to the first Brush firm. It is this pottery, which operated until 1982, that is famous for cookie jars as well as various other useful wares.

Pottery pieces with the trademark "Blue Ribbon Band" were produced by the Buckeye Pottery (NOT related to Buckeye Stoneware) between 1882 and 1941. Not much historical information is available on this firm. Thanks to Gary and Bonnie Tefft, authors of Red Wing Potters and Their Wares, for this information.

Blue Ribbon Pottery Painted Bean Pot

Bean pot, cov., wide bulbous flat-bottomed shape tapering to a short cylindrical neck flanked by small loop handles, inset cover w/disk finial, white ground h.p. under the glaze w/a landscape of a lake, palm trees, birds & a snow-capped peak in the distance, in shades of blue, white & green, Blue Ribbon Brand mark of the Buckeye Pottery, Macomb, Illinois, early 20th c. (ILLUS.)................................. **$150-$200**

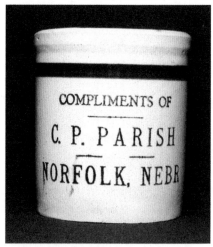

Fine Western Advertising Beater Jar

Beater jar, advertising-type, cylindrical w/molded rim, a dark blue band above printed blue Nebraska advertising, Monmouth-Western Stoneware (ILLUS.).. **$300-$400**

Beater jar, Colonial patt., ribbed cylindrical form printed around the top w/a printed band of blue swags, Monmouth-Western Stoneware, early 20th c. (ILLUS. second from left with various other Colonial pattern pieces, top next page) .... **$325-$375**

Four Various Pieces in the Colonial Pattern

Western Blue-banded Beater Jar

advertising, Monmouth-Western Stoneware (ILLUS., bottom of page)........... **$150-$175**

Bowl, 5" d., Colonial patt., slightly flaring rounded shape w/molded ribs below a printed band of blue swags, Monmouth-Western Stoneware, early 20th c. (ILLUS. second from right with various other Colonial pattern pieces, top of page)......... **$350-$400**

Western Sponged Rolled-rim Bowl

Bowl, 5" d., smooth rounded sides & rolled rim, overall orangish red & blue sponging, Monmouth-Western Stoneware (ILLUS.)
.... **$100-$125**

Bowl, 5" d., smooth sides & wide flat molded rim, overall orangish red & blue sponging, Monmouth-Western Stoneware (ILLUS. right with large sponged bowl, first photo below) .... **$150-$175**

Beater jar, cylindrical w/flaring rim, white-glazed & decorated w/dark blue bands, Monmouth-Western Stoneware (ILLUS.)
.... **$175-$225**

Bowl, advertising-type, wide cylindrical shape, the exterior lightly molded w/a drapery design glazed in dark blue, white-glazed interior w/printed blue Wisconsin

Two Sizes of Western Stoneware Sponged Bowls

Two Views of a Blue Drapery Bowl with Interior Advertising

Two Views of a Blue-banded Western Stoneware Advertising Bowl

Bowl, 7" d., advertising-type, wide short cylindrical shape w/molded rim, white-glazed exterior w/blue bands, interior w/printed blue advertising on the bottom, Monmouth-Western Stoneware (ILLUS. of two views, top of page) .... **$125-$175**

Large Bowl with Blue Blossoms & Scrolls

Bowl, 8" d., deep slightly flaring rounded sides w/molded panels & a smooth upper band printed w/a repeating blue design of a stylized blossom & scrolls, Monmouth-Western Stoneware (ILLUS.) .... **$175-$225**

Deep Blue-banded Western Bowl

Bowl, 9" d., deep rounded sides w/a rolled rim, white-glazed & decorated w/blue bands around the middle, Monmouth-Western Stoneware (ILLUS.) .... **$75-$95**
Bowl, 9" d., smooth sides & wide flat molded rim, overall orangish red & blue sponging, Monmouth-Western Stoneware (ILLUS. left with small sponged bowl, previous page) .... **$100-$125**

Two Sizes of Bowls

Bowls (nappies or pudding pans), each w/a wide flat bottom & shallow bisque-finished sides molded in low-relief w/geometric design, wide flat blue-glazed sawtooth rim band, Monmouth-Western Stoneware, 8" & 10" d., each (ILLUS. with 8" atop the inverted 10") .... **$125-$150**
Butter crock, cov., Colonial patt., deep ribbed cylindrical base w/ribs below a printed band of blue swags, inset cover w/disk finial, Monmouth-Western Stoneware, early 20th c., 2 lb. (ILLUS. far right with various other Colonial pattern pieces, top of previous page) .... **$450-$500**

Western Stoneware 10-lb. Butter Crock

Butter crock, cylindrical w/molded rim, white-glazed & printed w/the blue Western Stoneware maple leaf logo, 10 lb. (ILLUS.) .... **$100-$125**

Blue-trimmed Cookie Jar & Salt Crock

Western 1-lb. Advertising Butter Crock

Butter crock, advertising-type, cylindrical w/molded rim, glazed white & printed overall w/blue advertising for Lambrecht Butter, 1 lb. (ILLUS.) .... **$75-$100**

Western Blue 2-lb. Butter Crock

Butter crock, cov., cylindrical w/molded rim, overall shaded blue decorated on the front w/a printed fancy scroll rectangle enclosing the word "Butter," Monmouth-Western Stoneware, 2 lb. (ILLUS.) ... **$175-$225**

Butter crock, cov., tall cylindrical form w/molded rim & wire bail handle w/wooden grip, pale blue shaded to white, printed on the front w/a blue rectangle enclosing the word "Butter," signed on the bottom "Western Stoneware Co.," 5 lb. (ILLUS., top next column) .... **$225-$275**

Western Tall 5-lb. Butter Crock

Cookie jar, cov., wide cylindrical form w/inset cover, pale blue bands at rim & base, printed in large dark blue Gothic letters "Cookies" flanked by small maple leaves, part of a canister set, Monmouth-Western Stoneware (ILLUS. left with hanging salt crock, top of page)..................... **$350-$400**

Creamer (pitcher), #1 size, Sleepy Eye design, embossed Indian Chief blue & landscape in blue on white, Monmouth-Western Stoneware (ILLUS. right with sugar bowl, top of page) .... **$200-$250**

Brown & White Western Stoneware Crock

Crocks with Stenciled Flowers or Leaves

Crock, cylindrical w/deep molded rim, top half glazed in dark brown, white-glazed bottom half printed w/the blue Western Stoneware maple leaf logo, 1 gal. (ILLUS., previous page) .... **$100-$125**

Crock, cylindrical w/molded rim, white glazed & stenciled in dark blue w/a bouquet of stylized flowers, Monmouth-Western Stoneware, 1 gal. (ILLUS. right with crock decorated with leaves, top of page) .... **$50-$75**

Crock, cylindrical w/molded rim, white glazed & stenciled in dark blue w/a cluster of long stylized leaves, Monmouth-Western Stoneware, 2 gal. (ILLUS. left with floral bouquet-decorated crock, top of page) .... **$50-$75**

Crock, cylindrical w/molded rim, white-glazed w/large blue-stenciled size number above the large Monmouth Pottery (early Western Stoneware) maple leaf logo, 2 gal. (ILLUS., top next column)... **$50-$75**

2-Gallon Monmouth Pottery Crock

Two Early Monmouth Pottery Salt-glazed Crocks

Crock, cylindrical w/molded rim, salt-glazed & stenciled near the rim w/a large "3" in a dotted circle above a cobalt-blue slip-quilled winged design, Monmouth Pottery (early Western), 3 gal. (ILLUS. left with 20-lb. crock) .... **$175-$225**

A Brush-McCoy Pottery Jardiniere & Pitcher

10-Gallon Western Stoneware Crock

Crock, cylindrical w/molded rim flanked by small wire bail handles w/wooden grips, white-glazed w/the blue-printed Western Stoneware maple leaf logo above a blue-printed cluster of tall leaves, Monmouth-Western Stoneware, 10 gal., 17" h. (ILLUS.) **$81**

Crock, short wide cylindrical form w/molded rim, salt-glazed & stenciled in cobalt blue w/a large "3" in a dotted circle, Monmouth Pottery (early Western), rare 20 lb. size (ILLUS. right with 3-gallon crock, bottom previous page) .... **$300-$350**

Custard cup, Colonial patt., deep cylindrical shape w/rounded bottom molded

w/ribs below a printed blue band of swags, Monmouth-Western Stoneware, early 20th c. (ILLUS. far left with other various Colonial pattern pieces, top of page 403) .... **$750-$850**

Jardiniere, cylindrical w/sharply tapering base, molded around the upper body w/a continuous woodland scene, the lower band w/molded overlapping spearpoints, overall glossy green glaze, Brush-McCoy Pottery, Zanesville, Ohio, ca. 1917, 5" h. (ILLUS. right with Brush-McCoy corn pitcher, top of page) .... **$85-$100**

Scarce Sleepy Eye Mug

Mug, Sleepy Eye design, embossed Indian Chief blue & landscape in blue on white, Monmouth-Western Stoneware (ILLUS.)
.... **$300-$400**

Group of Four Various Mugs

Mug, barrel-shaped, dark blue rim shading to white, Monmouth-Western Stoneware, 4 1/2" h. (ILLUS. far right with three other mugs) .... **$50-$75**

Two Blue & White Advertising Mugs

Mug, advertising-type, embossed Bands & Rivets patt., blue & white w/printed blue advertising on the side, Monmouth-Western Stoneware, 4 3/4" h. (ILLUS. left with other advertising mug) .... **$100-$125**

Mug, embossed Bands & Rivets patt., blue & white, Monmouth-Western Stoneware, 4 3/4" h. (ILLUS. second from right with three other mugs, bottom previous page) .... **$50-$75**

Embossed Cattails Blue & White Mug

Mug, embossed Cattails patt., blue & white, Monmouth-Western Stoneware, 4 3/4" h. (ILLUS.) .... **$150-$200**

Mug, advertising-type, blue & white w/embossed panels & a raised oval on the side w/printed blue advertising, Monmouth-Western Stoneware, 5 1/2" h. (ILLUS. right with other advertising mug, top previous column) .... **$125-$150**

Mug, tankard-style w/angled handle, blue & white, Monmouth-Western Stoneware, 5 1/2" h. (ILLUS. far left with three other mugs, bottom previous page) .... **$75-$100**

Mug, tankard-style w/angled handle, white w/dark blue bands near the rim & base, Monmouth-Western Stoneware, 5 1/2" h. (ILLUS. second from left with three other mugs, bottom previous page) .... **$50-$75**

Pitcher, Colonial patt., ovoid ribbed body w/plain neck printed w/a repeating dark blue swag design, D-form handle w/thumbrest, Monmouth-Western Stoneware, early 20th c. (ILLUS. right with other Colonial pattern pieces, bottom of page) .... **$1,000-$1,200**

Pitcher, cylindrical molded yellow ear of corn w/green leaves & squared branch handle, Brush-McCoy Pottery, Zanesville, Ohio, ca. 1917 (ILLUS. left with Brush-McCoy jardiniere, top of previous page) .... **$150-$200**

Pitcher, Sleepy Eye design, embossed Indian Chief blue & landscape in blue on white, blue rim band, Monmouth-Western Stoneware, #4 size (ILLUS. left with #5 pitcher, top next page) .... **$500-$600**

Pitcher, Sleepy Eye design, embossed Indian Chief blue & landscape in blue on white, pale blue rim band, Monmouth-Western Stoneware, #5 size (ILLUS. right with #4 pitcher, top next page) .... **$500-$600**

Pitcher, 6" h., embossed Bands & Rivets patt., blue & white, Monmouth-Western Stoneware (ILLUS. far left with three other Bands & Rivets pitchers, middle next page) .... **$300-$350**

Three Rare Colonial Pattern Pieces

Sleepy Eye #4 & #5 Pitchers

Four Various Sizes of Bands & Rivets Pitchers

Group of Five Cattails Pitchers by Monmouth-Western Stoneware

Pitcher, 6" h., embossed Cattails patt., bulbous shape, blue & white, Monmouth-Western Stoneware (ILLUS. second from left with four other Cattails pitchers, bottom photo this page) .... **$600-$700**

Pitcher, 7" h., embossed Bands & Rivets patt., blue & white, printed blue Nebraska advertising on the side, Monmouth-Western Stoneware (ILLUS. second from right with three other Bands & Rivets pitchers, middle photo on this page) .... **$700-$800**

Pitcher, 7" h., embossed Cattails patt., bulbous shape, blue & white, Monmouth-Western Stoneware (ILLUS. second from right with four other Cattails pitchers, bottom photo this page) .... **$175-$225**

Pitcher, 8" h., embossed Bands & Rivets patt., blue & white, Monmouth-Western Stoneware (ILLUS. second from left with three other Bands & Rivets pitchers, middle of this page) .... **$250-$275**

Pitcher, 8" h., embossed Cattails patt., bulbous shape, blue & white, Monmouth-Western Stoneware (ILLUS. far left with four other Cattails pitchers).............. **$250-$300**

Pitcher, 9 1/4" h., embossed Bands & Rivets patt., blue & white, Monmouth-Western Stoneware (ILLUS. far right with three other Bands & Rivets pitchers, middle this page) .... **$500-$600**

Pitcher, 9" h., embossed Cattails patt., straight-sided shape, blue & white, Monmouth-Western Stoneware (ILLUS. center back with four other Cattails pitchers, third from bottom of page)................ **$225-$250**

Two Bands & Rivets Blue & White Advertising Pitchers

Two Scroll & Leaf Blue & White Advertising Pitchers

Pitcher, 9 1/4" h., embossed Cattails patt., bulbous shape, blue & white, Monmouth-Western Stoneware (ILLUS. far right with four other Cattails pitchers, bottom previous page) .... **$600-$700**

Pitchers, advertising-type, embossed Bands & Rivets patt., side-handle, blue & white w/printed blue advertising, Monmouth-Western Stoneware, each (ILLUS. of two, top of page) **800-900**

Pitchers, advertising-type, embossed Scroll & Leaf patt., shaded blue on white, Monmouth-Western Stoneware, each (ILLUS. of two, second from top of page) .... **$800-$1,000**

Rolling pin, advertising-type, white-glazed body decorated w/rust red bands & printed flour advertising, turned wood handles, Monmouth-Western Stoneware (ILLUS., first before bottom).... **$700-$800**

Rolling pin, advertising-type, white-glazed & decorated w/dark blue end bands & printed Nebraska advertising in the center, turned wood handles, Monmouth-Western Stoneware (ILLUS., bottom of page)... **$800-$1,000**

Rare Rust-decorated Advertising Rolling Pin

Rare Blue-banded Advertising Rolling Pin

Rare Monmouth-Western Colonial Pattern Rolling Pin

Sleepy Eye Sugar Bowl & Creamer

Rolling pin, Colonial patt., cylindrical w/printed blue swag bands at each end, no handles, Monmouth-Western Stoneware, early 20th c. (ILLUS., top of page) .... **$1,000-$1,200**

Salt crock, cov., hanging-type, Colonial patt., deep rounded & ribbed body w/tall arched back tab w/hanging hole, inset cover, decorated around the top w/a printed repeating band of dark blue swags, Monmouth-Western Stoneware, early 20th c. (ILLUS. left with other Colonial pattern pieces, bottom of page 408)........ **$450-$500**

Salt crock, hanging-type, cylindrical w/curved & peaked back tab w/hanging holes, dark blue bands around the top & base, printed on the front w/"Salt" in large Gothic letters flanked by small maple leaves, part of a canister set, Monmouth-Western Stoneware (ILLUS. right with matching cookie jar, top of page 405).. **$225-$250**

Sugar bowl, open, Sleepy Eye design, embossed Indian Chief blue & landscape in blue on white, Monmouth-Western Stoneware (ILLUS. left with #1 pitcher-creamer, second from top of page) .... **$800-$900**

Trivet (hot plate), Sleepy Eye Flour advertising piece, molded design of Chief Sleepy Eye in the center surrounded by a band of teepees & trees in blue on white, Monmouth-Western Stoneware (ILLUS., top next column) .... **$4,000-$4,500**

Tumbler, Colonial patt., ribbed slightly swelled cylindrical form w/the top decorated w/a printed repeating back of blue swags, Monmouth-Western Stoneware, early 20th c. (ILLUS. center with other Colonial pattern pieces, bottom of page 408) .... **$1,000-$1,200**

Vase, Sleepy Eye design, salt-glazed stoneware w/cobalt blue trim, cylindrical w/molded bands at top & base & relief-molded profile bust of Chief Sleepy Eye on the side, early 20th c., Monmouth-Western Stoneware, 9 1/2" h. (ILLUS., bottom next column) **$460**

Very Rare Sleepy Eye Trivet

Early Grey & Blue Sleepy Eye Vase

Moorcroft Pomegranate Small Bowl

Moorcroft

William Moorcroft became a designer for James Macintyre & Co. in 1897 and was put in charge of the art pottery production there. Moorcroft developed a number of popular designs, including Florian Ware, while with Macintyre and continued with that firm until 1913, when it discontinued the production of art pottery.

After leaving Macintyre, Moorcroft set up his own pottery in Burslem, where he continued producing the art wares he had designed earlier, introducing new patterns as well. After Moorcroft's death in 1945, the pottery was operated by his son, Walter.

Moorcroft Marks

Bowl, 5" d., Pomegranate patt., a wide round bulbous bowl raised on a small foot, in shades of dark red, purple, brown & green, signed, impressed mark, minor hairline (ILLUS., top of page) **$840**

Bowl, 5 1/8" h., a flaring pedestal base supporting a wide flaring cylindrical bowl flanked by tall arched looped gilt handles, decorated w/h.p. sprays of roses, tulips & forget-me-nots, printed mark & signed, ca. 1907..................................... **$1,410**

Moorcroft Hibiscus Small Bowl

Bowl, 6" d., footed, Hibiscus patt., dark blue & deep red blossoms & pale green leaves on a dark green ground, impressed marks, initials & paper label (ILLUS.) **$288**

Moorcroft Bowl in Blackberry & Leaf Pattern

Bowl, 7 1/2" d., Blackberry & Leaf patt., footed deep rounded form w/a wide flat rim, in shades of red, brown, blue & green, signed, impressed mark (ILLUS.) ... **$720**

Wide Shallow Moorcroft Bowl

Bowl, 11" d., Pomagranate patt., footed wide flat-bottomed shape w/rounded upright sides, loop side handles, in reddish orange, golden brown & purple on a cobalt blue ground, some crazing on interior (ILLUS.).. **$390**

Large, Shallow Moorcroft Freesia Bowl

Bowl, 12" d., Freesia patt., wide shallow shape, washed blue ground, impressed mark & signed, ca. 1935 (ILLUS., previous page) **$764**

Moorcroft Poppy Pattern Candlesticks

Candlesticks, Poppy patt., flaring round foot tapering to a ringed columnar standard & cupped socket, decorated on the standard & foot w/large orangish poppies against a dark blue ground, impressed mark & signed, ca. 1925, 7 7/8" h., pr. (ILLUS.)... **$1,175**

Early Moorcroft Cracker Jar

Cracker jar, w/silver plate rim, cover & swing bail handle, footed spherical body, white ground h.p. w/a garland of red roses & green leaves, printed mark & signed, ca. 1910, 6 3/8" h. (ILLUS.) **$588**
Lamp base, Orchid patt., a gently swelled cylindrical body in shades of red, white, yellow & green on a dark blue ground,

Tall Moorcroft Orchid Pattern Lamp Base

mounted on a footed bronzed metal base & w/metal top fittings, 15 1/2" h. (ILLUS.) .. **$540**

Early Moorcroft Jug form Pitcher

Pitcher, 5 1/2" h., jug form, footed bulbous ovoid body w/a wide short cylindrical neck & pinched spout, applied strap handle, cream ground w/a central hand h.p. w/stylized deep red florets within an entwined green ribbon design, signed & dated 1912 (ILLUS.).................................... **$235**

Moorcroft Spring Flowers Coffee & Tea Set

Three Colorful Moorcroft Vases

Tea & coffee set: tall cov. coffeepot, footed spherical cov. teapot & two footed ovoid creamers; all decorated in the Spring Flowers patt. in purple, dark pink, white, & green on a pale blue shaded to cobalt blue ground, all signed w/impressed mark, one creamer w/paper label, repaired chips to rim of one creamer, coffeepot 8 1/4" h., the set (ILLUS., bottom previous page) **$660**

Squatty Moorcroft Pansy Vase

Vase, 7 1/4" h., 8" d., Pansy patt., footed very wide squatty bulbous body tapering to a short neck, cobalt blue ground decorated w/large deep purple, white & deep red pansies & pale green leaves, early 20th c. (ILLUS.) **$748**

Vase, 8" h., footed nearly spherical bulbous body tapering to a wide rolled short neck, Anemone patt., large dark purplish blue & dark rose red blossoms & green leaves against a deep green to blue ground, painted by Walter Moorcroft, ca. 1945-49, light overall crazing (ILLUS., top next column) **$432**

Vase, 8 1/4" h., Anemone patt., footed spherical body tapering to a short neck & molded rim, in deep pink, dark purple & maroon & light green on a mottled dark blue & green ground, impressed mark

(ILLUS. right with two other Moorcroft vases, top of page) **$546**

Anemone Pattern Moorcroft Vase

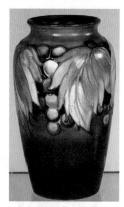

Moorcroft Leaf & Grape Pattern Vase

Vase, 8 1/4" h., Leaf & Grape patt., slightly tapering cylindrical body w/a short rolled neck, the upper half h.p. w/large greenish yellow leaves & dark purple & pink grapes against a dark yellow shading to dark blue ground, satin glaze, impressed mark & signed, ca. 1930 (ILLUS.).............. **$588**

Vase, 10" h., Hibiscus patt., simple swelled cylindrical form w/a short flared neck, dark red & purple & white blossoms on a dark mottled green & blue ground, impressed mark (ILLUS. left with two other Moorcroft vases, top of previous page)...... **$546**

Moorcroft Wisteria & Fruit Vase

Vase, 10" h., Wisteria & Fruit patt., gently swelled cylindrical body w/a short rolled neck, decorated around the upper half w/a wide band of large red, yellow & purple fruits & yellowish green leaves, against a mottled dark blue ground, impressed mark & signed, ca. 1930 (ILLUS.) **$646**

1940s Moorcroft Fruit & Leaf Vase

Vase, 10 1/4" h., Fruit & Leaf patt., gently tapering cylindrical body w/a short rolled neck, large serrated leaf in shades of green, yellow & red suspended from the shoulder & intermixed w/purple & red fruits all on a dark blue ground, impressed mark & signed, ca. 1945 (ILLUS.) **$705**

Vase, 12" h., Big Poppy patt., tall swelled cylindrical body tapering to a short flared neck, shaded red & purple poppy blossoms on tall green leafy stems on a dark blue ground, impressed mark & signed, ca. 1925... **$940**

Vase, 12 1/2" h., Grape & Leaf patt., footed wide compressed lower body tapering sharply to a tall slightly flaring neck, in dark blue, light & dark green & dark blue on a very dark blue ground, impressed mark & paper label (ILLUS. center with two other Moorcroft vases, top previous page) **$633**

Moorcroft Pansy Base on Dark Blue Ground

Vase, 12 1/2" h., Pansy patt., baluster-form w/a short rolled neck, decorated around the top half w/a wide band of large deep rose & purple pansy blossoms against yellowish green leaves & stems, dark blue background, signed & impressed mark, ca. 1925 (ILLUS.) **$470**

Morton Potteries

A total of six potteries were in operation at various times in Morton, Illinois, from 1877 to 1976. All traced their origins from the Morton Brick and Tile Company begun in 1877 by six Rapp brothers who came to America in the early 1870s to escape forced military service under Kaiser Wilhelm I. Sons, nephews and cousins of the founding fathers were responsible for the continuation of the pottery industry in Morton as a result of buyouts or the establishment of new and separate operations. The potteries are listed chronologically by beginning dates.

Morton's natural clay deposits were ideal for the Rapps' venture into pottery production. Local clay was used until it was depleted in 1940. That clay fired out to a golden ecru color. After 1940, clay was imported from South Carolina and Indiana. It fired out snow white. The differences in clay allow one to easily date production at the Morton potteries. Only a few items were marked by any of the potteries. Occasionally, paper labels were used, but most of those have long since disappeared. Glaze is sometimes a determinant. Early glazes were Rockingham brown, green and cobalt blue, or transparent, to produce yellow-ware. In the '20s and '30s colorful drip glazes were used. In the later years solid pastel and Deco colors were in vogue.

Most of Morton's potteries were short-lived, operating for 20 years or less. Their products are elusive. However, Morton Pottery Company was in operation for 54 years, and its products appear regularly in today's secondary market.

Rapp Brothers Brick & Tile Company & Morton Pottery Works (1877-1915) - Morton Earthenware Company (1915-1917)

Churn, mottled brown Rockingham glaze, 4 gal. $250

Rapp Bros. Green-glazed Creamer

Creamer, waisted cylindrical form w/molded bark & flowers under a dark green glaze, 5" h. (ILLUS.) $50

Unusual Pottery GOP Lapel Button

Lapel button, model of an elephant w/embossed "GOP" on side, dark brown glaze, 1 1/8 x 1 3/4" (ILLUS.) $95

Rapp Bros. Turk's Turban Mold

Mold, food, Turk's turban shape, field tile clay w/dark brown glaze, 7" d. (ILLUS.) $80
Mug, cylindrical, w/lightly molded lappet rim band, brown Rockingham glaze, 3 1/4" h., each (ILLUS. left & center, bottom of page) $55
Mug, cylindrical, yellowware, 2 3/4" h. (ILLUS. right with other mugs, bottom of page) $80

Rapp Bros. Sauerkraut Crock

Sauerkraut crock, cover/press, impressed mark, dark brown glaze, 4 gal., rare, 11" h. (ILLUS.) $175
Teapot, cov., acorn-shaped, mottled brown Rockingham glaze, 3 3/4 cup size $90

Three Rapp Brothers Mugs

Cliftwood Art Potteries, Inc. (1920-1940)

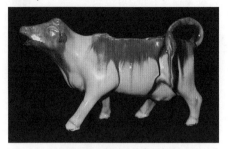

Figural Cow Creamer

Creamer, figural cow, standing, tail forms
handle, chocolate brown drip glaze,
3 3/4 x 6" (ILLUS.)..................................... **$100**

Cliftwood Figure of a Billiken

Figure of a Billiken, seated, dark brown
Rockingham glaze, 10 1/2" h. (ILLUS.)...... **$125**

Cliftwood Art Deco Lamp Base

Lamp base, Art Deco style, spherical body
on four square legs, pinkish orchid drip
glaze, base 4" h. (ILLUS.)........................... **$50**
Model of bison, natural colors of light &
dark brown, 9 1/2" l., 6 1/2" h. (ILLUS.,
bottom of page)... **$200**
Model of elephant, standing, chocolate
brown drip glaze, 7 1/4 x 13 1/2"............... **$125**

Cliftwood Model of a Frog

Model of frog, seated, glass eyes, shaded
green to white glaze, 5" h. (ILLUS.) **$50**

Cliftwood Model of a Bison

Cliftwood Deco Vase with Drip Glaze

Vase, 8" h., Art Deco style, square gently flaring sides w/a widely flared rim, chocolate brown drip glaze (ILLUS.)...................... **$75**

Vase, 18 1/4" h., urn form w/figural snakes swallowing fish handles, No. 132, chocolate brown drip glaze.................................. **$150**

Morton Pottery Company (1922-1976)

Bank, figural, cat, sitting, yellow & white, 8 1/2" h... **$60**

Bank, figural, house, shoe-shaped, yellow w/green roof, 6 1/2" h................................... **$40**

Morton Pottery Teddy Bear Bank

Bank, figural, Teddy bear, seated w/legs outstretched, brown, pink, blue & black on white, 8" h. (ILLUS.)................................ **$50**

Canister set: marked "Coffee," "Flour," "Sugar" & "Tea;" white cylindrical base w/yellow hat-shaped lid w/high button handle, 9" & 10" h., the set (ILLUS., bottom of page)... **$55**

Cookie jar, cov., baby bird in blue & yellow spray over white... **$60**

Cookie jar, cov., basket of fruit, green or brown basket w/colored fruit, No. 3720, each... **$50**

Creamer & sugar bowl, model of chicken & rooster, black & white w/cold-painted red comb, pr... **$55**

Figure of John F. Kennedy, Jr., standing on square base, right hand to head in salute position, gold paint trim, rare version, 7" h. **$125**

Grass grower, bisque, model of a standing pig, 7 1/2" l., 3 3/4" h.................................... **$20**

Head vase, woman w/1920s hairstyle, wide brim hat, white matte glaze **$75**

Head vase, woman w/1940s hairstyle, pill box hat, blue matte glaze............................... **$65**

Head vase, woman w/upswept hairstyle, white w/red lips, bow in hair & heart-shaped locket **$40**

Morton Pottery Jardiniere

Jardiniere, squared form w/swelled sides, low rectangular mouth, tab side handles, small block feet, pink ground w/embossed floral sprig in blue & green, 4 1/2" h. (ILLUS.) **$30**

Morton Pottery Canister Set

Morton Davy Crockett Lamp & Shade

Lamp, table, figural Davy Crockett w/bear
beside tree, original shade (ILLUS.)........... **$200**

Morton Rooster on Rockers Planter

Planter, model of a rooster on rockers, yellow & pink sprayed glaze w/h.p. black &
red trim, 4 1/2" h. (ILLUS.) **$30**

Kitten & Fish Bowl TV Lamp

TV lamp, figural, black kitten seated on
chartreuse stump base reaching for
glass fish bowl, 9" h. (ILLUS.)..................... **$75**
Vase, model of a tree trunk, matte green
glaze, No. 260... **$30**

Christmas Novelties

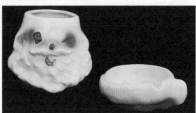

Figural Santa Claus Head Cigarette Box

Cigarette box, cov., figural Santa Claus
head, hat cover becomes ashtray, cold
painted red hat (ILLUS.).............................. **$50**
Lollipop tree, w/holes to insert lollipops,
green bisque, 9 1/4" h. **$60**
Plate, 8", figural Santa Claus face, h.p.
white w/blue eyes, pink cheeks, hat cold
painted red **$50**
Punch set: punch bowl & 8 punch cups; fig-
ural Santa Claus head, white w/pink trim,
green stone eyes, 9 pcs. (ILLUS. of part,
bottom of page)... **$295**

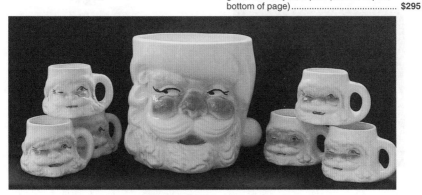

Morton Santa Claus Punch Set

Midwest Potteries, Inc. (1940-1944)

Midwest Leaping Deer Bookends

Bookends, Art Deco style, a stylized leaping deer against an upright disc, round foot, blue glaze, 7 3/4" h., pr. (ILLUS.)......... **$40**

Figure of baseball player, batter, grey uniform, 7 1/4" h... **$300**

Figure of baseball player, umpire, black uniform, 6 1/4" h....................................... **$300**

Model of flamingo, brownish green spray glaze, 10 1/2" h. **$50**

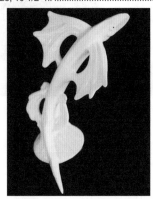

Midwest Potteries Flying Fish

Model of flying fish, stylized form in leaping pose, white glaze, 9 1/4" h. (ILLUS.)...... **$45**

Midwest Potteries Hen & Rooster

Models of hen & rooster, white w/cold painted red & yellow trim, hen 7" h., rooster 8" h., pr. (ILLUS.) **$50**

Pitcher, 4 1/2" h., figural, seated cow, brown & white drip glaze............................. **$30**

Midwest Potteries Owl TV Lamp

TV lamp, model of an owl w/spread wings, sprayed brown on white ground, green eyes, 12" h. (ILLUS.).................................... **$95**

American Art Potteries (1947-1963)

American Art Candlestick

Candlestick, three-light, open doughnut-shaped ring fitted w/three sockets, wide round foot, dark bluish green glaze, No. 140J, 7 1/2" w., 6 1/2" h. (ILLUS.)................ **$35**

French Poodle Table Lamp

Lamp, table, figural, model of a seated French poodle, black ground w/sprayed pink on bands of curls, 15" h. (ILLUS.) **$70**

American Art Bird on Stump Model

Model of bird on stump, white w/gold trim, 7" h. (ILLUS.) **$25**

Chunky Pony Figural Planter

Planter, figural, model of a chunky standing pony, dark streaky mauve & pink spray glaze, sticker on side, No. 49, 5 1/4" l., 4 3/4" h. (ILLUS.) **$15**

Doe and Fawn Figural Planter

Planter, figural, model of a standing doe bending her head down to her reclining fawn, mottled brown glaze, No. 322J, 7 1/4" h. (ILLUS.) **$25**

Vase, 8" h., ewer-form, blue & mauve glaze w/gold trim, No. 209G **$35**

Vase, 10 1/2" h., double cornucopia form, white w/gold trim, No. 208B **$30**

Wall pocket, figural, model of a red apple on a green leaf, No. 127N **$20**

Window sill box, arched diamond design, green & pink spray glaze, No. 32I, 3 1/2 x 4 x 10" **$30**

Mulberry

Mulberry or Flow Mulberry ironstone wares were produced in the Staffordshire district of England in the period between 1840 and 1870 at many of the same factories that produced its close "cousin," Flow Blue china. In fact, some of the early Flow Blue patterns were also decorated with the dark blackish or brownish purple mulberry coloration and feature the same heavy smearing or "flown" effect. Produced on sturdy ironstone bodies, the designs were either transfer-printed or hand-painted (brushstroke) with an Asian, scenic, floral or marble design. Some patterns were also decorated with additional colors over or under the glaze; these are designated in the following listings as "w / polychrome."

Quite a bit of this ware is still to be found and is becoming increasingly sought-after by collectors, although its values lag somewhat behind similar Flow Blue pieces. The standard references to Mulberry wares is Petra Williams' book, Flow Blue China and Mulberry Ware, Similarity and Value Guide and Mulberry Ironstone - Flow Blue's Best Kept Little Secret, by Ellen R. Hill.

ACADIA (maker unknown, ca. 1850)
Creamer, 6" h., Classic Gothic shape **$150**

Acadia Plate

Plate, 8" d. (ILLUS.) **$55**

AMERILLIA (Podmore, Walker & Co., ca. 1850)
Eggcup **$200**

Amerillia Covered Vegetable Dish

Vegetable dish, cov. (ILLUS., previous page) $250

ATHENS (Charles Meigh, ca. 1845)
Creamer, 6", vertical-paneled Gothic shape .. $150
Cup plate $75

Athens Pitcher

Pitcher, 6-paneled, 10" h. (ILLUS.) $350
Punch cup $95
Sugar, cov., vertical-paneled Gothic shape ... $200

ATHENS (Wm. Adams & Son, ca. 1849)
Cup plate $95
Plate, 8 1/2" d. $55
Soup Plate, w/flanged rim, 9" d...................... $75
Sugar, cov., full-paneled Gothic shape $200
Teapot, cov., full-paneled Gothic shape......... $275

AVA (T.J. & J. Mayer, ca. 1850)
Cup & saucer, handleless, w/polychrome $95
Plate, 9 1/2" d., w/polychrome......................... $85
Plate, 10 1/2" d., w/polychrome....................... $95
Platter, 16" l., w/polychrome $250

Ava Sauce Tureen & Undertray

Sauce tureen, cover & undertray, w/polychrome, 3 pcs. (ILLUS.) $350

BEAUTIES OF CHINA (Mellor Venables & Co., ca. 1845)
Cup plate $95
Plate, 7 1/2" d., w/polychrome......................... $65
Platter, 14" l., w/polychrome $225
Sauce tureen, cover, ladle & undertray, long octagon, 4 pcs................................... $500

BOCHARA (James Edwards, ca. 1850)
Creamer, full-paneled Gothic shape, 6" h. $150
Pitcher, 7 1/2" h., full-paneled Gothic shape $195
Plate, 10 1/2" d... $75

Bochara Flow Mulberry Teapot

Teapot, cov., Pedestaled Gothic shape (ILLUS.) $350

BRUNSWICK (Mellor Venables & Co., ca. 1845)
Plate, 7 1/2" d., w/polychrome........................ $65
Platter, 16" l., w/polychrome $275
Relish dish, stubby mitten-shaped, w/polychrome $150
Sugar, cov., Classic Gothic shape, w/polychrome $225

BRYONIA (Paul Utzchneider & Co., ca. 1880)
Cup & saucer, handled................................... $50
Gravy boat $100
Plate, 7 1/2" d... $35

Bryonia Plate

Plate, 9 1/2" d. (ILLUS.) $40

CEYLON (Charles Meigh, ca. 1840)
Plate, 9 1/2" d... $65
Plate, 10 1/2" d., w/polychrome....................... $85
Platter, 14" l., w/polychrome $175
Vegetable bowl, open, small $125

CHUSAN (P. Holdcroft, ca. 1850)
Plate, 9 1/2" d... $80

Chusan Potato Bowl

Potato bowl, 11" d. (ILLUS.)........................... **$175**

CLEOPATRA (F. Morley & Co., ca. 1850)
Basin & ewer, w/polychrome **$600**
Soap box, cover & drainer, 3 pcs................. **$300**
Soup plate, w/flanged rim, 9" d....................... **$75**

COREA (Joseph Clementson, ca. 1850)
Cup & saucer, handleless **$65**
Sugar, cov., long hexagon **$250**
Teapot, cov., long hexagon............................ **$350**

COREAN (Podmore, Walker & Co., ca. 1850)
Cup plate **$100**
Cup & saucer, handled, large.......................... **$85**
Relish, mitten-shaped **$135**
Sauce tureen, cover & undertray, 3 pcs...... **$400**

Corean Covered Sugar

Sugar, cov., oval bulbous style (ILLUS.) **$275**

COTTON PLANT (J. Furnival, ca. 1850)
Creamer, paneled grape shape, w/poly-
    chrome, 6 5/8" h. **$200**
Teapot, cov., cockscomb handle, trimmed
    in polychrome (ILLUS., top next column) .. **$650**

CYPRUS (Wm. Davenport, ca. 1845)
Cup plate **$95**
Gravy boat, unusual handle (ILLUS., mid-
    dle next column).. **$175**
Pitcher, 11" h., 6-sided.................................. **$250**

Cotton Plant Mulberry Teapot

Cyprus Gravy

DORA (E. Challinor, ca. 1850)
Plate, 9 1/2" d.. **$75**

Dora Baltic Shape Teapot

Teapot, cov., Baltic shape (ILLUS.) **$450**

FERN & VINE (maker unknown, ca. 1850)

Fern & Vine Creamer

Creamer, Classic Gothic style, 6" h. (ILLUS.) .. $225
Plate, 7 1/2" d. $55

FLORA (Hulme & Booth, ca. 1850)
Creamer, w/polychrome, grand loop shape,
6" h. $150

FLORA (T. Walker, ca. 1847)
Cup & saucer, handleless $65
Plate, 7 1/2" d. $75
Plate, 9 1/2" d. $85
Sugar, cov., Classic Gothic shape $250

FLOWER VASE (T.J. & J. Mayer, ca. 1850)
Teapot, cov., w/polychrome, Prize Bloom
shape $450-550

FOLIAGE (J. Edwards, ca. 1850)
Gravy boat $150

Foliage Plate

Plate, 8" d. (ILLUS.).. $75

GERANIUM (Podmore, Walker & Co., ca. 1850)

Geranium Plate

Plate, 8" d. (ILLUS.) $65
Waste bowl $135

JARDINIERE (Villeroy & Boch, ca. 1880)
Gravy boat $100
Plate, 7 1/2" d. $35
Plate, 9 1/2" d. $45
Vegetable bowl, open, round $100

JEDDO (Wm. Adams, ca. 1849)
Cup plate $95
Cup & saucer, handleless $85
Relish dish, octagonal $125

Jeddo Sugar Bowl

Sugar, cov., full-paneled Gothic shape
(ILLUS.).. $195
Teapot, cov., Full-Paneled Gothic shape $300

KAN-SU (Thomas Walker, ca. 1847)
Cup & saucer, handleless $65
Plate, 7 1/2" d. $50
Platter, 14" l. $200

Kan-su Covered Vegetable Dish

Vegetable dish, cov., octagonal (ILLUS.)...... **$300**

MARBLE (A. Shaw, ca. 1850)

Marble Creamer

Creamer, 10 panel Gothic shape, 6" h.
(ILLUS.)... **$250**
Invalid feeder, large.. **$500**
Waste bowl **$150**

MARBLE (Mellor Venables, ca. 1845)
Plate, 9 1/2" d.. **$50**
Teapot, cov., child's, Vertical Paneled Goth-
ic shape... **$350**

Marble Pattern Gothic Shape Teapot

Teapot, cov., Vertical Paneled Gothic
shape (ILLUS.).. **$450**

MEDINA (J. Furnival, ca. 1850)
Cup & saucer, handleless **$55**
Gravy boat **$135**
Sugar, cov., cockscomb handle **$300**

NANKIN (Davenport, ca. 1845)

Nankin Pitcher

Pitcher, 8" h., mask spout jug w/poly-
chrome (ILLUS.).. **$350**
Plate, 8 1/2" d., w/polychrome......................... **$75**

NING PO (R. Hall, ca. 1840)
Cup & saucer, handleless **$85**
Plate, 10 1/2" d.. **$95**
Soup plate, w/flanged rim, 10" d..................... **$95**

PARISIAN GROUPS (J. Clementson, ca. 1850)
Plate, 7 1/2" d., w/polychrome......................... **$60**
Plate, 8 1/2" d., w/polychrome......................... **$70**
Sauce dish, w/polychrome **$65**

Parisian Sauce Tureen & Undertray

Sauce tureen, cover & undertray, w/poly-
chrome, 3 pcs. (ILLUS.) **$400**

PELEW (Edward Challinor, ca. 1850)
Cup & saucer, handleless, pedestaled............ **$75**
Plate, 7 1/2" d... **$50**
Plate, 10 1/2" d... **$70**
Punch cup, ring handle **$100**

Pelew Pumpkin-shaped Teapot

Teapot, cov., pumpkin shape (ILLUS.).......... **$450**

PERUVIAN (John Wedge Wood, ca. 1850)

Peruvian Cup & Saucer

Cup & saucer, handleless, "double bulge"
(ILLUS.).. **$65**
Gravy boat **$145**
Teapot, cov., 16-Paneled shape **$400**
Waste bowl, "double bulge" **$150**

PHANTASIA (J. Furnival, ca. 1850)

Phantasia Creamer

Creamer, w/polychrome, cockscomb han-
dle, 6" h. (ILLUS.).................................... **$350**
Cup plate, w/polychrome **$95**
Plate, 9 1/2" d., w/polychrome......................... **$85**
Sugar, cov., w/polychrome, cockscomb
handle **$350**

Teapot, cov., w/polychrome, cockscomb
handle **$550**

RHONE SCENERY (T.J. & J. Mayer, ca. 1850)

Gravy boat **$150**
Plate, 7 1/2" d.. **$35**
Plate, 10 1/2" d... **$55**
Sauce tureen, cover & undertray, 3 pcs...... **$300**
Sugar, cov., full-paneled Gothic shape **$175**

SCINDE (T. Walker, ca. 1847)

Creamer, Classic Gothic shape, 6" h. **$100**
Plate, 9 1/2" d.. **$70**
Soup plate, w/flanged rim, 9" d...................... **$80**
Teapot, cov., Classic Gothic shape **$300**

SHAPOO (T. & R. Boote, ca. 1850)

Plate, 8 1/2" d.. **$75**
Sugar, cov., Primary shape.......................... **$250**
Teapot, cov., Primary shape **$450**
Vegetable dish, cov., flame finial **$300**

TEMPLE (Podmore, Walker & Co., ca. 1850)

Cup plate **$75**

Temple Cup & Saucer

Cup & saucer, handled (ILLUS.) **$75**
Plate, 8 1/2" d.. **$55**
Sugar, cov., Classic Gothic shape **$200**
Teapot, cov., Classic Gothic shape **$300**

VINCENNES (J. Alcock, ca. 1840)

Cup & saucer, handleless, thumbprint **$95**
Plate, 7 1/2" d.. **$60**
Plate, 10 1/2" d... **$80**

Vincennes Punch Cup

Punch cup (ILLUS.)....................................... **$125**

Soup tureen, cover & undertray, 10-sided,
3 pcs... **$850**

Vincennes Compote

Compote, Gothic Cameo shape (ILLUS.)...... **$550**

WASHINGTON VASE (Podmore, Walker & Co., ca. 1850)
Creamer, Classic Gothic shape, 6" h. **$225**
Cup & saucer, handleless **$95**
Plate, 10 1/2" d. **$85**
Soup plate, w/flanged rim, 9" d....................... **$85**
Vegetable bowl, cov. **$300**

WHAMPOA (Mellor Venables & Co., ca. 1845)
Gravy boat **$125**
Plate, 10 1/2" d. **$75**
Sauce tureen, cov., long octagon shape, 2
pcs.. **$250**

WREATH (Thomas Furnival, ca. 1850)

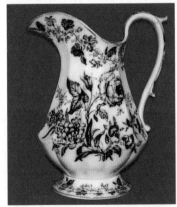

Wreath Ewer

Ewer (ILLUS.).. **$300**
Plate, 9 1/2" d... **$75**

Newcomb College

This pottery was established in the art department of Newcomb College, New Orleans, in 1897.

Each piece was hand-thrown and bore the potter's mark & decorator's monogram on the base. It was always a studio business and never operated as a factory. Its pieces are, therefore, scarce, with the early wares being eagerly sought. The pottery closed in 1940.

Newcomb College Pottery Mark

Newcomb College Bowl with Floral Band

Bowl, 5" d., 2 1/2" h., footed wide squatty bulbous body tapering to a wide flat mouth, molded around the rim w/a band of pink blossoms & green leaves against a blue ground, Newcomb logo, date code & marks of decorator Anna Frances Simpson & potter Joseph Meyer, 1925, tiny chip on base (ILLUS.) **$1,265**
Bowl, 8 3/4" d., footed wide low rounded form w/a flat rim, carved & painted w/a band of jonquil blossoms & leaves against a dark blue ground, by Anna Francis Simpson, marked, No. MJ73 (ILLUS., top next page) **$3,240**

Newcomb Bowl-Vase with Daffodils

Bowl-vase, deep squatty bulbous shaped w/a wide flat mouth & tapering to a flat base, carved & painted around the shoulder w/white daffodil blossoms & pale green leaves against a dark blue ground, by Alma Mason, No. HD7, 7" d., 4 1/2" h. (ILLUS.).. **$2,640**

Unusual Newcomb College Bowl with Jonquils

Newcomb Mug with Glossy Glaze

Mug, tapering cylindrical form w/a C-form handle, decorated around the sides w/tall stems w/leaves & white & yellow blossoms around the top, dark blue base band & handle, marked w/Newcomb insignia, monogram of decorator Sarah Henderson & initials of potter Joseph Meyer, glossy glaze, 1902, crazing, 4 1/4" h. (ILLUS.) **$1,380**

Newcomb College Espanol Style Pitcher

Pitcher, 5" h., Espanol style, cylindrical body flaring at the top w/a pinched spout & applied C-form handle, a wide band of stylized pickets in shades of pale green dark blue & pink around the top, dark blue ground, marked w/shape number 207 (ILLUS.)... **$805**

Small Bulbous Newcomb College Pitcher

Pitcher, 2 1/2" h., squatty bulbous body w/a pinched spout & applied angled handle, decorated w/a repeated design of pale green swirled S-shaped devices on a blue ground, marks of decorator Aurelia Arbo & pottery Joseph Meyer, date code for 1931, tiny bit of roughness at base (ILLUS.) **$460**

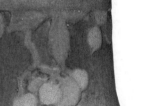

Fine Miniature Newcomb College Vase

Vase, 3 1/2" h., 2 1/4" d., miniature, a swelled base tapering to cylindrical sides w/a flat rim, carved & painted w/a band of leaves & berries suspended from the rim, shades of blue & pink, by Sadie Irvine, Model #64/1 (ILLUS., previous page) **$1,140**

Bulbous Newcomb Vase by J. Meyer

Vase, 3 5/8" h., wide bulbous ovoid shape tapering to a wide flat rim, molded w/a repeating pattern of wide swirled panels alternating pale green & medium blue, Newcomb College logo, shape number & date code for 1931, impressed mark of potter Joseph Meyer (ILLUS.) **$805**

Small Newcomb College Landscape Vase

Vase, 4 1/4" h., gently tapering cylindrical body w/a wide flat mouth, carved & decorated w/a landscape of oak trees w/Spanish moss, in shades of blue, green & cream, Sadie Irvine, No. JR9 (ILLUS.) **$2,880**

Newcomb College Squatty Floral Vase

Vase, 5" h., a wide bulbous squatty body tapering sharply to a small base & to a short tapering neck, carved & painted around the shoulder w/white floral clusters on pale green leaves against a dark blue ground, by Alma Mason, No. HC93 (ILLUS.) **$3,240**

Fine Newcomb College Crocus Vase

Vase, 6" h., gently swelled cylindrical body w/a flat rim, carved & molded w/long-stemmed crocus & tall leaves around the body in pale purple & dark blue on an ivory ground, by Anna Francis Simpson, marked "RO75" (ILLUS.) **$4,200**

Nice Newcomb Moon & Moss Vase

Vase, 8 1/4" h., 3 3/4" d., simple swelled cylindrical form, Moon & Spanish Moss decoration in shades of dark blue, pale blue & yellow, decorated by Anna Frances Simpson, various marks on the bottom, 1919 (ILLUS.)............................ **$6,325**

Rare New College Pottery Vase

Vase, 10" h., 9" d., bulbous baluster-form body w/a wide short flat neck, glazed in moss green & splattered gunmetal, decorated by Elizabeth Rogers & signed on the base, ca. 1900, rare (ILLUS.)............ **$3,450**

Nicodemus

The promise of a job distributing newspapers brought Chester Nicodemus to Cleveland, in 1921 to attend the Cleveland School of Art. Studying sculpture, Chester graduated in 1925 and began teaching at Ohio's Dayton Art Institute. That same year he married his longtime sweetheart, Florine Massett, a costume designer. In 1930, while attending Ohio State University, where he studied under ceramist Arthur Baggs, Chester accepted a position at the Columbus Art School as head of the Sculpture Department. He later became the dean of the Columbus Art School and

president of the Art League. During these early years, Chester was creating mostly portrait heads and fountain figures. During the Depression Chester learned how to do clay casting and began to create smaller pieces that were more affordable to the masses. On a trip through New England in 1939, he carried with him a sampling of his work. He felt encouraged to start his own business after selling all the pieces he carried and receiving orders for many more.

In 1943, due to the war and a subsequent drop in class attendance, Chester left the field of teaching to pursue pottery making full time. His own business, "Ferro-Stone Ceramics," used local clay. Containing a large amount of iron (ferro is the Latin word for "iron"), the Ohio clay had a red color, which imbued a russet brown undertone to the pottery that gave a second dimension to the glaze. It was fired at a very high temperature and rendered stone hard. Known for its durability, it was leak-proof and not easily chipped. Nicodemus Pottery could be purchased at fine showrooms throughout the United States or by knocking on Chester's door and viewing the ceramic pieces in his modest garage salesroom. Keeping stores stocked kept him busy, and in 1973 he decided to retire from the retail business. His home business continued to flourish with new designs.

All created in his studio in Columbus, Ohio, Nicodemus pieces included animals, birds, Christmas cards, medallions, fountains and dinnerware. Colors used were pussy willow, turquoise, dark yellow, mottled green, antique ivory and deep blue. Pieces referred to as "museum quality" are heavily mottled with broken color lines showing more of the red clay body. Most pieces are incised "NICODEMUS" on an unglazed base. Some may also have initials of Nicodemus' students Ellen Jennings or James Thornton. Paper labels bearing the Ferro-Stone name are also found.

Nicodemus was a talented artist who is just beginning to receive proper recognition for his ceramic excellence. His studio was closed in 1990 after a fall that broke his hip. Chester died later that year at the age of 89. As requested by Chester, shortly after his death all Nicodemus molds and glazes were destroyed by his son Darell.

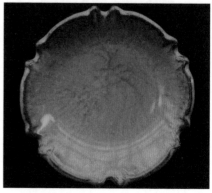

Mottled Green Nicodemus Ashtray

Ashtray, mottled green, incised "Nicodemus," 3 1/2" d. (ILLUS., previous page) **$85**

Nicodemus Promotional Ashtray

Ashtray, round, w/four cigarette rests, advertises "Goucher College Founded 1885," incised "Nicodemus," 4 1/2" d. (ILLUS.) **$126**

Nicodemus Piggy Bank

Bank, in the form of a pig, mottled green, incised "Nicodemus," 3 1/4" h. (ILLUS.) **$590**

Nicodemus Figure of Joseph

Figure of Joseph, No. 4 in a nine-piece nativity set, turquoise, incised "Nicodemus," 7 1/2" h. (ILLUS.) **$428**

Flower holder, figure of girl, dark yellow, "Nicodemus," 6" h. **$397**

Nicodemus Robin

Model of robin, black & red unglazed w/yellow beak, incised "Nicodemus," 3 1/2" h. (ILLUS.)... **$246**

Pitcher, 3 1/2" h., dark yellow, incised "Nicodemus".. **$175**

Nicodemus Mottled Green Pitcher

Pitcher, 3 1/2" h., mottled green, museum-quality glaze, incised "Nicodemus" (ILLUS.) **$380**

Planter, cornucopia, blue, incised "Nicodemus," 10" l. **$310**

Wall pocket, twisted horns, antique ivory, incised "Nicodemus," 9" h. **$860**

Niloak Pottery

This pottery was located in Benton, Arkansas, and featured hand-thrown varicolored swirled clay decoration in objects of classic forms. Designated Mission Ware, this line is the most desirable of Niloak's production, which began early in this century. Less expensive to produce, the cast Hywood Line, finished with either high gloss or semi-matte glazes, was introduced during the Depression of the 1930s. The pottery ceased operation about 1946. Niloak is kaolin spelled backwards.

∩ıᴄᴏᴀʜ

Niloak Pottery Mark

Niloak Mission Ware Jardiniere

Jardiniere, Mission Ware, wide slightly swelled cylindrical form, swirled brown, blue & tan clays, stamped mark, 7" d., 7" h. (ILLUS.) **$411**

Niloak Ovoid Mission Ware Vase

Vase, 6" h., Mission Ware, simple ovoid body tapering to a widely flaring flattened neck, swirled clays in red, taupe, brown tan & blue, impressed mark (ILLUS.) **$138**

Tall Niloak Mission Ware Vase

Vase, 10" h., 5" d., Mission Ware, footed w/bulbous lower body w/sharp shoulder tapering to a tall cylindrical neck, swirled dark teal & brown clays, minute inside rim flecks, stamped mark (ILLUS.) **$294**

Nippon

"Nippon" is a term used to describe a wide range of porcelain wares produced in Japan from the late 19th century until about 1921. It was in 1891 that the United States implemented the McKinley Tariff Act, which required that all wares exported to the United States carry a marking indicating their country of origin. The Japanese chose to use "Nippon," their name for Japan. In 1921 the import laws were revised and the words "Made in" had to be added to the markings. Japan was also required to replace the "Nippon" with the English name "Japan" on all wares sent to the United States.

Many Japanese factories produced Nippon porcelain, much of it hand-painted with ornate floral or landscape decoration and heavy gold decoration, applied beading and slip-trailed designs referred to as "moriage." We indicate the specific marking used on a piece, when known, at the end of each listing. Be aware that a number of Nippon markings have been reproduced and used on new porcelain wares.

Important reference books on Nippon include: The Collector's Encyclopedia of Nippon Porcelain, Series One through Three, by Joan F. Van Patten (Collector Books, Paducah, Kentucky) and The Wonderful World of Nippon Porcelain, 1891-1921 by Kathy Wojciechowski (Schiffer Publishing, Ltd., Atglen, Pennsylvania).

Bowl, 9" d., three gold scroll feet supporting the wide shallow incurved sides flanked by upturned gold loop handles, the upper body in pale yellow h.p. w/a delicate gold floral swag design, the pale yellow interior also h.p. w/a band of ornate gold leafy floral scrolls, green "M" in Wreath mark (ILLUS. front row, far right, with other Nippon bowl, cup & saucer and vases, top of next page) **$70-100**

Bowl, 10 1/2" d., a deep rounded six-lobed form w/a narrow flattened rim h.p. in dark gold w/a tiny floral vine, the interior h.p. w/a wide tropical seaside landscape w/tall palm trees in the foreground, a cottage & mountains in the distance, blue "Maple Leaf" mark (ILLUS. top row, far left, with group of Nippon bowls, cup & saucer and vases, top of next page) **$80**

Bowl, 11" d., a wide shallow shape w/small gold pointed loop rim handles, the interior centered by a wide Arab landscape in pastels w/figures before large squared buildings w/a central dome, a border band composed of three narrow rows each h.p. w/a repeating step-like design in black, tan & brown, green "M" in wreath mark (ILLUS. front row, second from left with group of Nippon vases, middle of next page) **$104**

Group with Nippon Bowls, Cup & Saucer and Vases

Cup & saucer, each w/a pale green ground decorated in white moriage w/a white bird perched on a leafy fruited vine, green "Maple Leaf" mark, the set (ILLUS. bottom row, second from left, with Nippon bowls and vases)... **$230**

Grouping of Nippon Vases and a Bowl

Grouping with a Nippon Humidor, Tray and Vases

Nippon Nut Set & Five Vases

Humidor, cov., bulbous ovoid paneled body w/a domed paneled cover w/bulbous knob, the sides h.p. w/a continuous sunset harbor scene w/sailboats, moriage shoulder band & floral reserve on the knob, blue "Maple Leaf" mark, 6" h. (ILLUS. top row, left, with group of Nippon vases & a tray, bottom previous page).. **$518**

Nippon Humidor with Hunting Scene

Humidor, cov., wide cylindrical body raised on three blocked gold legs, the body h.p. w/a continuous scene of a hunter in a canoe preparing to shoot at a stag on the shore, sunset background, low doned cover w/decorative border band & large domed handled, hairline in the body, early 20th c., 7" h. (ILLUS.) **$86**

Nut set: 7 1/2" d. master bowl & five 3" d. individual dishes; each rounded w/notched corners, the master bowl w/small rim handles, the interior h.p. w/a sheep in the meadow scene w/a large tree & farmhouse on the left side, border band in pale yellow trimmed w/gold vining. scrolls, individual dishes w/matching borders & white interiors, green "M" in Wreath mark, the set (ILLUS. bottom row, right, with five Nippon vases, top of page) **$127**

Plaque, large round form centered w/a pastel Arab landscape w/figures below a group of large buildings & a dome, a double-row border band, one row h.p. w/stylized dog-like animals in white, black & brown & the second row h.p. w/a repeated geometric step design in black, tan, cream & brown, green "M" in Wreath mark, 10" d. (ILLUS. bottom row, second from right with group of Nippon plaques & vases, top of next page)... **$288**

Plaque, large round form decorated w/a desert scene in pastel colors w/Arab on camel beside a tent & grove of palm trees, narrow geometric paneled rim band, green "M" in Wreath mark, 10" d. (ILLUS. top row, far left with group of Nippon plaques & vases, top of next page)............. **$431**

Group of Nippon Vases and Plaques with Desert Scenes

Tray, long shallow swelled boat-form w/flat ends, the interior h.p. w/a sunset lake & forest scene, moriage green & white flowerhead & panel accent bands, blue "Maple Leaf" mark, 6 1/4" l. (ILLUS. bottom row, second from right with Nippon humidor & vases, bottom of page 433) **$173**

Urn, an ornate scroll-footed domed pedestal base w/a small knop supporting a very large urn-form body w/a wide shoulder curving to a small mouth flanked by upright scroll handles, the base & shoulder h.p. in cobalt blue w/gold trim & white reserves h.p. w/pink & red roses, the main body h.p. w/scattered clusters of pink & red roses on a pale yellow shaded to white ground, missing the cover, unmarked, 12" h. (ILLUS. bottom row, far right, with grouping of cobalt blue-trimmed Nippon vases, bottom of page) **$600-900**

Vase, 3 1/2" h., the spherical body raised on three gold peg feet, a small scalloped cobalt blue neck flanked by small pointed loop gold handles, a cobalt band around the base, the main body h.p. w/gold-bordered oblong reserves w/floral sprigs, against a white ground w/gold bands & scattered floral sprigs, Noritake Wheel mark (ILLUS. bottom row, far left with Nippon urn & other cobalt blue-trimmed vases, bottom of page) **$316**

Vase, 5" h., footed bulbous ovoid body tapering to a small neck w/a widely flaring flattened neck flanked by scrolled gold handles w/black moriage trim, the body h.p. w/a continuous lakeside landscape w/a large tree w/orange leaves in the foreground, the shoulder w/a wide band h.p. w/a dark & light green Greek key design accented by three-leaf sprigs, green "M" in Wreath mark (ILLUS. front row, second from left with Nippon humidor, tray & other vases, bottom of page 433) **$230**

Large Group of Cobalt Blue-trimmed Nippon Vases and an Urn

Vase, 5 1/4" h., footed wide ovoid body tapering to a short neck, the body h.p. w/large oval reserves decorated w/stylized mountain landscapes, the cobalt blue ground h.p. w/fancy gold floral & leaf designs & gold bar panels, blue "M" in wreath mark (ILLUS. front row, third from left, with Nippon urn and other cobalt-blue trimmed vases, bottom previous page) $230

Vase, 5 1/2" h., a wide shallow curved bottom raised on three cobalt blue gold-trimmed scroll feet, sharply tapering sides to a widely flaring four-ruffled cobalt blue rim, the swelled shoulder in cobalt blue decorated w/gold flowers & issuing long cobalt blue scroll handles to the lower rim, the main body h.p. w/clusters of purple & white violets & green leaves on a green shaded to white ground, paulowina flower mark (ILLUS. bottom row, third from right with Nippon urn & other cobalt blue-trimmed vases, bottom previous page) $201

Nippon Vase with Lady & Peacock Scene

Vase, 5 3/4" h., bulbous ovoid body tapering to a short flaring neck trimmed in gold & flanked by arched gold shoulder handles, the body centered by a large gold oval reserve painted w/a full-length portrait of an exotic young woman standing in front of a peacock, surrounded by an overall gold lattice & pink rose decoration on the white ground, green Maple Leaf mark, minor gold wear (ILLUS.) $432

Vase, 6" h., a widely flaring square body w/an angled shoulder tapering to a short square neck issuing gold square handles from the rim to the corner of the shoulder, each side h.p. w/a tall rectangular seascape w/sailboats, a dark lavender ground, the base, corners & neck all h.p. w/paneled bands w/geometric designs, green "M" in Wreath mark (ILLUS. top row, right, with Nippon humidor, tray and vases, bottom of page 433)........................ $207

Vase, 6" h., cylindrical waisted shape w/long floral-embossed pale green handles down the sides, green band around neck, the body h.p. w/an autumn landscape w/leafless trees in the foreground & a lane in the distance, blue "M" in Wreath mark (ILLUS. bottom row, second from left with Nippon nut set, top of page 434)... $518

Vase, 7" h., tall waisted diamond-form body w/a wide flattened shoulder centered by a short scalloped neck flanked by small brown shoulder handles, the body h.p. w/a continuous stylized landscape w/tall trees, shrubs & a picket fence in the foreground w/low hills, a path, cottage & trees in the distance, the shoulder decorated w/panels h.p. w/stylized green seated animals on a brown ground & a white shield w/brown cross at each corner, brown & green paneled neck, blue "Maple Leaf" mark (ILLUS. bottom row, far right, with Nippon humidor, tray and other vases, bottom of page 433) $575

Nippon Sharkskin Vase

Vase, 7 1/8" h., "sharkskin" technique, slender slightly tapering cylindrical body w/a narrow shoulder centered by a short neck w/widely flaring mouth, arched & pierced-loop gold shoulder handles, the sides h.p. w/a stylized landscape w/tall trees in the foreground & small houses & a lake in the distance, done in pastel shades of blue, yellow, green, lavender & orange, purple Cherry Blossom mark, tiny glaze nick in the base (ILLUS.) $230

Vase, 7 1/2" h., bulbous ovoid body tapering to a shaped neck, four small Moriage-decorated loop handles around the shoulder, body w/h.p. large pink flowers on green & gold leafy stems, trimmed w/white Moriage unmarked (ILLUS. second from right with three other Nippon vases, top next page)................................. $230

Vase, 7 1/2" h., flaring hexagonal body w/a flattened shoulder centered by a short flaring hexagonal neck, the shoulder, neck & lower half of body in cobalt blue decorated w/ornate gold grapevines, the upper band h.p. w/a continuous lakeside landscape w/a cottage in the distance, green "M" in Wreath mark (ILLUS. bottom row, second from right, with Nippon urn and other cobalt blue-trimmed vases, bottom previous page) $403

Row of Nippon Vases

Vase, 7 1/2" h., footed flaring cylindrical body w/a flattened shoulder & short flaring cupped neck, gold molded ram head shoulder handles joined by gold swags, the body h.p. w/a continous landscape scene w/a path up a hillside to a cottage, green "M" in Wreath mark (ILLUS. front row, second from right with group of Nippon vases & a bowl, middle of page 433) **$144**

Vase, 7 1/2" h., ovoid body tapering to a short neck w/flaring rim flanked by high square loop handles, h.p. landscape scene w/tall trees in foreground & woods & a cottage in the background, green "M" in Wreath mark (ILLUS. far right with three other Nippon vases, top of page)...... **$173**

Vase, 7 1/2" h., ovoid pillow-shape w/short scalloped neck flanked by loop handle, h.p. farmstead in the snow scene, Moriage bands around the shoulder, neck & foot, green "M" in Wreath mark (ILLUS. far left with three other Nippon vases, top of page).......................... **$1,380**

Vase, 8" h., footed hexagonal body w/angled shoulder flanked by upright gold curved handles, the body h.p. w/a continuous landscape scene w/a fence & trees in the foreground & a windmill in the distance, blue "M" in Wreath mark (ILLUS. bottom row, far left with Nippon nut set, top of page 434) **$460**

Vase, 8" h., ovoid body tapering sharply on the upper half to a small mouth flanked by yellow square double-loop handles trimmed w/brown moriage, the body h.p. w/a tall continuous windmill & trees landscape, the neck h.p. w/a wide band w/blue wheel & scroll design below a thin yellow & wavy line band, green "M" in wreath mark (ILLUS. bottom row, far left, with Nippon bowls, cup & saucer and other vases, top of page 433) **$173**

Vase, 8 1/4" h., tall ovoid body tapering to a large incurved neck w/four molded ribs & entwined angular loops trimmed w/white enamel, the body decorated w/a full-length h.p. lakeside landscape w/tall grasses & trees in the distance, the scene overlaid w/white moriage leafy vines, blue "Maple Leaf" mark (ILLUS. front row, far left, with Nippon humidor, tray and other vases, bottom of page 433) **$1,955**

Vase, 8 1/2" h., a round foot supporting a wide bulbous ovoid body tapering to a short trumpet neck, inward-scrolling upright shoulder handles, each side centered by a large oval reserve connected by a wide band & h.p. w/a half-length portrait of a pretty young woman standing holding a large vase full of flowers, trees in the background, the upper & lower background in cobalt-blue ornately decorated gold leafy scrolls, ribbons & "jewels," blue "Maple Leaf" mark (ILLUS. top row, third from left, with Nippon urn and other cobalt blue-trimmed vases, bottom of page 435) **$2,300**

Vase, 8 1/2" h., a tall slightly waisted cylindrical body w/a wide shouler & thin cylindrical neck, h.p. w/a continuous sunset landscape w/tall trees beside a lake, all overlaid w/h.p. gold tall oblong arches & & large gold flowers around the top & bottom, green "M" in Wreath mark (ILLUS. bottom row, far right with other Nippon vases & plaques, top of page 435) **$201**

Vase, 8 1/2" h., a wide ovoid body w/four arched integral open handles from the shoulder to the rim of the small cylindrical neck, the lower body & handles in white w/gold floral swag decorated, the shoulder divided into four large pointed panels each h.p. w/colorful roses & green leaves, green "M" in Wreath mark (ILLUS. top row second from right with other Nippon plaques & vases, top of page 435)............. **$431**

Vase, 8 3/4" h., footed ovoid body w/a wide shoulder to the short trumpet-form neck flanked by high C-scroll handles, body decorated w/a fine lakeside landscape w/birch trees in the foreground w/swans & a cottage in the background, glossy glaze, green "M" in Wreath mark (ILLUS. second from left with three other Nippon vases, top of page) **$518**

Vase, 9" h., a tall baluster-form body w/a cylindrical neck, the body painted w/a continuous design w/large pink roses & green leaves w/a tropical landscape w/palm trees in the background, the neck h.p. w/a wide pale orange band enameled w/dark blue & grey w/triangles w/scallops among scrolling leafy vines, green "M" in Wreath mark (ILLUS. top row, far right, with Nippon bowls, cup & saucer and other vases, top of page 433)... **$230**

Vase, 9" h., a tall ovoid body tapering to a tall slender cylindrical neck w/a cupped rim flanked by large slender square handles from the rim to the shoulder, the body h.p. w/a continuous design of long purple wisteria flowers & green leaves, the shoulder & upper neck h.p. w/paneled bands in pale green & gold w/tiny flower sprigs, green "M" in Wreath mark (ILLUS. bottom row, second from right with Nippon bowls, cup & saucer and other vases, top of page 433) **$403**

Vase, 9" h., squatty bulbous base tapering to a cylindrical body w/a flared neck, h.p. w/a continuous landscape w/a path & flowering tree in the foreground & a cottage & sea in the distance, green "M" in Wreath mark (ILLUS. top row, far right with Nippon nut set, top of page 434) **$230**

Vase, 9" h., the tall slightly tapering cylindrical body raised on three square gold buttress feet, short squared gold buttress handles near the top, the body h.p. w/large white & pink flowers & pale green leaves on a pale yellow ground, the upper body decorated w/h.p. ornate gold swags, the base h.p. w/a scalloped gold band & white "jeweled" stripes, green "M" in Wreath mark (ILLUS. top row, second from right, with Nippon bowls, cup & saucer and other Nippon vases, top of page 433)................................. **$1,093**

Vase, 9 1/2" h., flaring four-footed bottom tapering to a large ovoid four-sided body tapering to a short widely flaring neck heavy squared gold shoulder handles, each side h.p. w/a large reserve h.p. w/a lakeside landscape w/cottage, the background in cobalt blue ornately decorated w/gold grapes & grapevines w/some green leaves, green "M" in Wreath mark (ILLUS. top row, far left, other Nippon urn and other cobalt-blue trimmed vases, bottom of page 435) **$1,035**

Vase, 9 1/2" h., slender ovoid body tapering to a small mouth flanked by pointed loop gold handles, h.p. w/a landscape w/purple wisteria blossoms in the foreground & a path & trees in the distance, green "M" in Wreath mark (ILLUS. top row, second from right with Nippon nut set, top of page 434).. **$345**

Vase, 9 1/2" h., tapestry-type, tall gently tapering cylindrical body w/a flat rim, the upper body decorated w/a wide band of stylized geometric designs in shades of green, blue, rose red & gold & faux jewels, delicate gold beaded swags suspended down the sides, blue Maple Leaf mark (ILLUS., top next column) **$1,150**

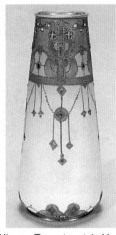

Nippon Tapestry-style Vase

Vase, 10" h., footed swelled cylindrcal body tapering to a narrow flat shoulder & oval short flaring neck w/integral pointed gold handles from rim to the sides, a large central gold-bordered oval reserve h.p. w/a pastoral landscape w/a river & house in a meadow, the background in pale pink h.p. w/a gold lattice covered w/lavender & pink wisteria blossoms & green leaves, green "M" in Wreath mark (ILLUS. top row, far right with other Nippon vases & plaques, top of page 435) **$403**

Vase, 10" h., small four-lobed foot & tall swelled four-lobed body tapering to an incurved four-lobed mouth, decorated in autumn colors w/a landscape of a meadow & trees by a river w/a cottage in the distance, blue "M" in Wreath mark (ILLUS. bottom row, far left with other Nippon plaques & vases, top of page 435)............. **$518**

Vase, 10" h., tall ovoid body raised on three pointed gold legs, tapering to a small flat mouth framed by three squared gold handles w/gold rings, the upper half of the body h.p. with an autumn landscape scene w/trees, hills & a cottage, the lower half in white h.p. w/trailing gold vines w/green leaves & small flowers climbing into the landscape scene, blue "Maple Leaf" mark (ILLUS. top row, second from left with group of Nippon plaques & vases, top of page 435) **$374**

Vase, 10" h., tall ovoid body tapering to a small flat mouth flanked by two pointed gold handles, the main body h.p. w/a large autumn landscape scene w/a forest beside a lake w/a cottage in the distance, green "M" in Wreath mark (ILLUS. bottom row second from left with Nippon plaques & vases, top of page 435) **$288**

Vase, 10 1/4" h., footed ovoid body tapering to a trumpet neck, gold molded C-scroll handles on the shoulder, the body h.p. w/a continuous landscape w/a meadow w/cows in the foreground & a lake & mountains in the distance, gold foot, gold vining bands around the neck & shoulder, green "M" in Wreath mark (ILLUS. top row, far left with Nippon nut set, top of page 434) **$805**

Vase, 10 1/2" h., tall ovoid body w/a low ruffled rim, small gold pointed shoulder handles, the wide central band h.p. w/large pink roses & blossoms & green leaves on a shaded green ground, wide base & shoulder bands h.p. w/groves of pale green trees trimmed w/small blossoms against a dark green ground, green "Maple Leaf" mark (ILLUS. front row, far right with group of Nippon vases & a bowl, middle of page 433) **$374**

Vase, 10 1/2" h., the tall tapering cylindrical body w/four small brown open buttress feet, the curved shoulder & wide flat mouth flanked by squared open handles, the body h.p. w/large shaded purple flowers on tall green leafy stems, blue "Maple Leaf" mark (ILLUS. top row left with group of Nippon vases & a bowl, middle of page 433) **$431**

Vase, 11" h., footed ovoid body tapering to a short trumpet neck flanked by angled gold handles, h.p. w/a large pale lavender poppy blossom on tall leafy stems against a brown shaded to cream ground, green "M" in Wreath mark (ILLUS. top row, right, with other Nippon vases & bowl, middle of page 433) **$460**

Vase, 12" h., footed tall flaring cylindrical body w/an angled shoulder tapering to a wide flat mouth, pointed angled gold handles from shoulder to mid-body, h.p. wide body band w/pink blossoms on green leafy vines against a shaded white ground, shoulder & lower body gold band w/a Greek key design & applied "jewels" beside another paneled & looped pastel band, pale green neck & lower body, "EE" mark (ILLUS. bottom row, far left, with other Nippon vases & a bowl, middle of page 433) **$201**

Vases, 7 1/4" h., footed bulbous ovoid body tapering to a wide tapering & gently swelled neck w/a flat rim, the body h.p. around the sides w/a colorful autumn landscape w/leafy vines in the foreground & a lake & trees in the distance, the neck w/an overall design of stylized flowering vines on a cream ground, gold handles to neck to shoulder & gold rim, green mark, pr. (ILLUS., bottom of page) **$460**

Vases, 10" h., a flaring round foot w/ring supporting the very large bulbous ovoid body tapering to a small, short trumpet neck, each side h.p. w/a large oval reserve connected by a wide band & h.p. w/a sunset lakeside landscape, the upper & lower backgrounds in cobalt blue trimmed w/gold scrolling bands, one w/green "M" in Wreath mark, pr. (ILLUS. top row, second & fourth from left, with Nippon urn and other cobalt blue-trimmed vases, bottom of page 435) **$2,185**

Nippon Blown-Out Lions Wall Plaque

Wall plaque, pierced to hang, round, molded in relief w/a lion & lioness in a rocky landscape, natural coloration, 10 1/2" d. (ILLUS.) **$575**

Nippon Vases Decorated with Autumn Landscapes

Noritake

Noritake china, still in production in Japan, has been exported in large quantities to this country since early in the last century. Although the Noritake Company first registered in 1904, it did not use "Noritake" as part of its backstamp until 1918. Interest in Noritake has escalated as collectors now seek out pieces made between the "Nippon" era and World War II (1921-41). The Azalea pattern is also popular with collectors.

Noritake Mark

Ashtray, decorated w/a horse head design, 3 7/8" w., 4 1/4" h. $60
Ashtray, modeled as a figural black cat, 5" d., 2 3/4" h. $160
Ashtray, center Queen of Clubs decoration, 4" w. $38
Ashtray, figural polar bear, blue ground, 4 1/4" d., 2 1/2" h. $250

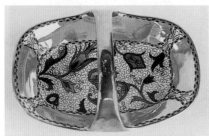

Noritake Basket with Flowers

Basket, oblong w/center handle, gold lustre ground, interior w/center stylized floral decoration & geometric design in each corner & around rim, 7 3/4" l., 3" h. (ILLUS.) $85
Basket-vase, 7 1/2" h. $115
Bonbon, raised gold decoration, 6 1/4" w. $25
Bowl, 6" h., loop handles w/flamingos $95

Noritake Leaf-shaped Bowl with Bird Handle

Bowl, 4 1/2" h., leaf-shaped w/orange iridescent interior, figural blue bird handle at one end (ILLUS.) $250
Bowl, 4 7/8" h., decorated w/two figural owls $475

Rare Noritake Gemini Bowl

Bowl, 6 1/8" h., Gemini patt., a rounded orange bowl w/floral rim band, molded at each side w/an arched lady figure wearing a long flowered gown (ILLUS.) $3,050

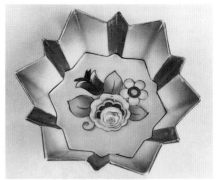

Art Deco Bowl

Bowl, 6 1/2" d., 2" h., fluted sides of alternating light & dark grey panels w/pointed rims, center w/Art Deco floral decoration (ILLUS.) $160
Bowl, 6 1/2" w., geometric shape w/many sharp corners, decorated in green, yellow & silver $100
Bowl, 7" w., square w/incurved sides, three-footed, interior w/relief-molded filbert nuts in brown trimmed w/h.p. autumn leaves $85
Bowl, 7 3/8" w., 3" h., footed, molded on the interior w/nuts & leaves $110
Bowl, cov., 5 1/4 x 7 3/4", 3 1/2" h., figural ducks on the cover $700

Handled Bowl with Art Deco Flowers

Bowl, 8 1/2" d., wide shallow bowl decorated on the interior w/bold stylized Art Deco flowers & leaves in deep red, orange, blue & brown, yellow border band, dark blue loop side handles (ILLUS.) $170
Bowl, 9 3/8" w., 3 1/2" h., hexagonal w/two rim handles, decorated w/birds in trees $150
Bowl, soup, Azalea patt. $30

Noritake Geometric Art Deco Box

Box, cov., square geometric Art Deco design, side panels in tan decorated in black w/stylized flowers & leaves, mottled black & brown corner panels, flat inset square cover w/upright flat rectangular finial, 4 1/2" w., 4 1/2" h. (ILLUS.) $250
Butter dish, cover & drain insert, Azalea patt., 3 pcs. $80

Figural Art Deco Lady Covered Box

Box, cov., slender cylindrical base w/a figural cover designed as an Art Deco lady wearing a flowered dress, legs on the base, 5" h. (ILLUS.) $670

Noritake Oriental Scene Cake Plate

Cake plate, rectangular, open-handled, turquoise border w/oval center Oriental scene on black ground, 10" l. (ILLUS.) $140
Cake set: 14 x 6 1/4" oblong tray w/pierced handles & six 6 1/2" d. serving plates; white w/pale green & gold floral border, 7 pcs. $90
Candy dish, octagonal, Tree in Meadow patt. $60
Celery set: celery tray & 6 individual salt dips, decal & h.p. florals & butterflies decoration, 7 pcs. $90
Celery tray, narrow oblong shape w/figural rams' head handles, decorated w/a stylized floral design, 5 1/2 x 12 3/8", 2 1/2" h. $60
Chocolate set: cov. pot & six cups & saucers; stylized bird decoration, the set......... $400
Cigarette box, cov., the cover decorated w/a sailing ship, 2 3/4 x 3 1/2", 1 1/2" h. $75
Cigarette holder, Art Deco decoration, 2 2/3" w., 3" h. $90
Cracker jar, cov., footed spherical body decorated w/a black band w/white

swords & shields design & center oval yellow medallion w/scene of white sail-boat on lake, white clouds in distance & blue stylized tree in foreground, black & white geometric design bands around rim & cover edge, orange lustre ground, 7" h. $210

Creamer, Tree in Meadow patt. $20

Creamer & cov. sugar bowl, Azalea patt., pr. $75

Creamer & Sugar in Art Deco Style

Creamer & open sugar bowl, Art Deco-style checked decoration in black, blue, brown & white, orange lustre interior basket-shaped sugar bowl w/overhead handle, creamer 3" h., sugar bowl 4 1/2" h., pr. (ILLUS.).. $125

Cup & saucer, Tree in Meadow patt............... $20

Desk set: heart-shaped tray w/pen rack at front & two cov. jars w/floral finials; decal & h.p. florals, 6 1/2" w. $385

Dinner bell, figural Chinaman, 3 1/2" h.......... $250

Rare Large Noritake Lady Dresser Box

Dresser box, cov., figural Art Deco lady w/the cover & box forming her wide gown, her upper body forming the handle, decorated w/a stylized floral design in black, white, orange, red, yellow & purple, largest size, 6 1/4" d., 6 1/2" h. (ILLUS.) $2,450

Dresser box, cov., figural woman on lid, lustre finish, 5" h... $770

Noritake Elegant Lady Figurine

Figure of a lady, tall slender stylized Art Deco lady wearing a long-sleeved blue gown, overall light blue glaze, resting on original round metal base, 10 3/4" h. (ILLUS.) $650

Figurine, advertising Geisha figurine w/"Noritake China" printed on her fan, professional repair to fan, 7 7/8" h. $950

Figurine, maiden carrying a bundle of sticks on her head... $55

Flower holder, model of bird on stump, base pierced w/four flower holes, 4 1/2" h... $95

Hair Receiver in Art Deco Style

Hair receiver, cov., Art Deco style, geometric design on gold lustre ground, 3 1/2" d. (ILLUS.)... $190

Hair receiver, cov., decorated w/an Art Deco design, 3 1/2" d., 3 1/4" h. $85

Honey jar, cov., designed as a figural house w/figural bees on the cover, 2 1/2 x 2 3/4", 3 7/8" h. **$195**

Humidor, cov., cylindrical w/an owl molded in relief, 4 1/4" d., 6 3/4" h. **$650**

Humidor, cov., model of an owl w/head as cover, lustre finish, 7" h. **$770**

Inkwell, model of an owl, Art Deco style, 3 1/2" h. **$260**

Melon-shaped Jam Jar Set

Jam jar, cover & underplate, melon-shaped, pink ground w/grey leaves, handle & leaf-shaped underplate, 5 3/4" l., 4 1/4" h., the set (ILLUS.) **$115**

Rare Noritake Figural Clown Jar

Jar, cov., figural, designed as clown w/the wide cylindrical body in iridescent orange & purple, the wide green ruffled collar cover centered by the upturned head, rare design, hairline crack, 5 1/2" h. (ILLUS.) **$1,250**

Lemon dish, loop center handle, decorated w/a geometric Art Deco design, 5 1/4" d., 2 1/2" h. **$80**

Lemon plate, Azalea patt. **$35**

Mayonnaise set, Azalea patt., 3 pcs. **$70**

Muffineer set: shaker & creamer; each w/a flaring hexagonal foot & angular hexagonal body w/a tapering neck, the shaker w/a domed cover w/holes, the creamer w/an angular handle, each decorated w/long alternating stripes of iridescent orange & bands of red & yellow flowers on white, the set (ILLUS., top next column) **$105**

Noritake Floral Striped Muffineer Set

Napkin ring, decorated w/an Art Deco man, 2 1/4" w., 3 1/8" h. **$55**

Night light, figural woman, 9 1/4" h., 2 pc. . **$4,400**

Nut set: 6" d. bowl shaped like open chestnut & six 2" d. nut dishes; earthtone ground w/h.p. nuts & leaves, the set **$135**

Oil & vinegar bottles w/stoppers, one-piece construction, 5 7/8" w., 3 1/2" h. **$150**

Noritake Footed Perfume Bottle

Perfume bottle & stopper, footed tall ovoid body tapering to a slender neck flanked by gold handles, gold pointed stopper, the creamer body decorated w/an exotic bird on a flowering branch, 1 1/2" d., 6" h. (ILLUS.) **$125**

Salt & pepper shakers, flattened upright round shape, decorated as Flapper ladies' heads w/red tops, 1 3/4" h., pr. $205

Art Deco Noritake Figural Salt & Pepper

Salt & pepper shakers, stylized Art Deco figures, tall slener ovoid shape body wearing a green shawl & long blue & white striped cape, small rounded head forms the top, 4 1/2" h., pr. (ILLUS.) $210

Noritake Taxi Driver Salt & Pepper Shakers

Salt & pepper shakers, stylized figure of a taxi driver in yellow, blue, black, white & brown, 3 2/3" h., pr. (ILLUS.) $165

Salt & pepper shakers, Tree in Meadow patt., pr. $20

Sandwich plate, Art Deco design w/a bird-form center handle, 8" d., 5" h. $195

Shaving mug, landscape scene w/tree, birds & moon decoration $70

Smoke set: cov. cigarette jar & match holder on an oval tray; decorated w/stylized flowers, tray 7" l., jar 2 1/4" h., the set $140

Noritake Double Spoon Holder

Spoon holder, double tray-form, oblong shape w/gold angular center handle, orange lustre interior, exterior decorated w/flowers & butterfly on black ground, 6 1/2" l., 2 1/2" h. (ILLUS.) $90

Spoon holder, plain lustre decoration, 8 2/3" l., 2 3/4" h. $45

Sugar shaker, lavender & gold decoration, blue lustre trim $40

Sweetmeat set, Art Deco lady decoration on the set & the lacquer box, box 11 1/2" w. $875

Syrup & jam set, decorated w/an Art Deco design, 5 3/4" w., 5" h, three pcs. $110

Syrup jug, Azalea patt. $70

Tea set, child's: cov. teapot, cov. sugar bowl, creamer, eight dessert plates & eight cups & saucers; Nursery Rhymes patt., the set $750

Tea set: cov. teapot, cov. sugar, creamer & oblong undertray; each piece w/a squared tapering body w/gold angled handles, each side decorated w/colorful Oriental floral clusters framed by decorated borders, early 20th c., the set (ILLUS., bottom of page) $80-100

Colorful Noritake Tea Set

Part of a Noritake Tea Set

Tea set: cov. teapot & six cov. cups; each in
a low cylindrical shape in white w/vertical
red & black hooked scrolls, low covers in
red w/white scrolls & a black handle, teapot w/overhead swing bamboo handle,
teapot 5" h., the set (ILLUS. of part) **$300**
Tea strainer & underplate, stylized floral
decoration, the set....................................... **$60**

Tea Tile with Art Deco Lady

Tea tile, round, dark iridescent blue ground
centered by a white diamond enclosing
the bust portrait of an exotic Art Deco la-
dy, 5" d. (ILLUS.)....................................... **$260**
Tea tile, round, decorated w/a woman
smelling a flower, 6 1/2" d., 5" h. **$240**

Crinoline Lady Noritake Teapot

Teapot, cov., Crinoline Lady patt., bulbous
slightly tapering body w/C-form handle &

long serpentine spout, domed cover
w/knob finial, Victorian lady in a garden
against a blue background, Noritake mark
"38.016 DS," 5 1/2" l., 3 3/4" h. (ILLUS.) **$175**

Noritake Teapot with Stylized Flowers

Teapot, cov., footed bulbous ovoid body
w/angled green shoulder & domed cover
w/oval loop finial, C-scroll handle & long
serpentine spout, large stylized blossoms
on a slender leafy tree, in shades of blue,
purple, green & brown, Noritake mark
"27.1 DS," 8 1/4" l., 5 3/4" h. (ILLUS.) **$45**

Rare Noritake Lady & Bird Teapot

Teapot, cov., Lady & Bird in Garden patt., tall
footed urn-form body w/long serpentine
spout, tall arched black-trimmed blue handle, domed cover in red w/black urn-shaped
finial, dark blue background w/an Art Deco-
style scene of a crinolined lady holding a
bird in one hand w/a birdcage in front of her,
in shades of yellow, green, black, white,
light blue & orange, Noritake mark "27.1
DS," 6 3/4" l., 6 1/4" h. (ILLUS.) **$645**
Toast rack, figural bird, 5 1/2" w., 3 3/8" h....... **$70**
Tray, pierced handles, decal & h.p. fruit border, lustre center, 11" w. **$80**

Long Floral-decorated Noritake Tray

Tray, rectangular, pierced end handles, floral decoration on white ground, green edge trim w/brown trim on handles, 17 1/2" l. (ILLUS., previous page) **$90**

Rare Trinket Dish with Lady on Rim

Trinket dish, oblong shape w/the figure of a seated young woman at the back rim, 5" l., 4" h. (ILLUS.) **$1,950**
Trinket dish, oblong w/small figural owls on the rim, 5 1/4 x 5 3/4", 4" h. **$475**

Noritake Urn in Radio City Pattern

Urn, cov., Radio City patt. w/alternating red & black & gold stripes, low cover w/scalloped rim & a small figural handle of a man holding an umbrella, 8 3/4" h. (ILLUS.) **$925**

Noritake Landscape Vase with Cockatoo

Vase, 5" h., tall slender trumpet-form vase in light orange decorated w/a tree & cottage scene, standing on a rounded yellow rockwork base w/a white cockatoo beside it (ILLUS.) **$125**
Vase, 7" h., 5 1/2" w., double-tube, figural parrot **$200**

Unusual Noritake Butterfly Vase

Vase, 8" h., footed ovoid body w/squared rim handles, butterfly decoration on shaded & streaked blue & orange ground (ILLUS.)... **$250**
Vase, 8 1/4" h., Indian motif & lustre decoration **$140**
Vase, 8 1/2" h., bulbous body, Tree in Meadow patt. **$90**
Vegetable dish, cov., round, Azalea patt. **$75**

Scenic Noritake Wall Plaque

Wall plaque, pierced to hang, silhouetted Art Deco-style scene of woman in gown w/full ruffled skirt, sitting on couch & holding mirror, white lustre ground, 8 3/4" d. (ILLUS.).. **$840**

Wall pocket, designed as a figural lady molded in relief, 4 1/4" w., 8" h.................... **$860**

Wall pocket, double, conical two-part form w/arched backplate, decorated w/an exotic blue & yellow bird among branches of red & blue stylized blossoms against a cream ground, purple lustre rim band, 8" l. .. **$165**

Wall pocket, trumpet-form, wide upper band decorated w/an autumn sunset scene, lavender lustre rim band & base, 8 1/4" l. **$90**

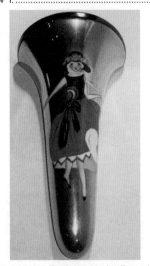

Noritake Wall Pocket with Art Deco Lady

Wall pocket, trumpet-shaped, gold ground decorated w/an Art Deco lady wearing an orange & black dress, 4 1/4" w., 8" h. (ILLUS.) **$650**

Waste bowl, Azalea patt. **$55**

North Dakota School of Mines

All pottery produced at the University of North Dakota School of Mines was made from North Dakota clay. In 1910, the University hired Marg-

aret Kelly Cable to teach pottery making, and she remained at the school until her retirement. Julia Mattson and Margaret Pachl also served as instructors between 1923 and 1970. Designs and glazes varied through the years ranging from the Art Nouveau to modern styles. Pieces were marked "University of North Dakota - Grand Forks, N.D. - Made at School of Mines, N.D." within a circle and also signed by the students until 1963. Since that time, the pieces bear only the students' signatures. Items signed "Huck" are by the artist Flora Huckfield and were made between 1923 and 1949.

North Dakota School of Mines Mark

Pasque Flowers Bowl-Vase by M. Cable

Bowl-vase, wide squatty bottom tapering sharply to a flat mouth, decorated w/a wide band of stylized flowers in lavender, dark blue & pale green against a white ground, UND inkstamp & incised "Pasque Flowers - M. Cable 154," 3 3/8" h. (ILLUS.).. **$575**

Scarce North Dakota Lamp Base

Lamp base, round domed foot below the tall cylindrical body w/a molded rim fitted w/a cap, body & base marked w/ink stamp logo, bottom of vase marked "T-538 - 20," incised initials of Freida Hammers under the cap, h.p. w/large dark blue flowers on a dark shaded to light blue ground, flat chip on bottom of base, ca. 1926, overall 11" h. (ILLUS.) **$1,610**

University of North Dakota Paperweight

Paperweight, round flattened form, molded w/the seal of the University of North Dakota, overall dark blue glaze, back marked w/blue UND inkstamp logo & name of M. Cable, ca. 1930, 3 5/8" d. (ILLUS.)............... **$81**

Covered Wagon Design on Paperweight

Paperweight-dish, round dished form w/an incised center design of oxen pulling a covered wagon, medium brown glaze, blue inkstamp UND logo & incised initials of student finisher (ILLUS.) **$173**

Vase, 4 7/8" h., rounded tapering cylindrical form, decorated w/stylized floral trees in dark blue & green accented w/blue & green bands all on a cream ground, inkstamped UND logo & incised "Huck 226," Flora Huckfield (ILLUS., top next column) **$374**

Vase, 6" h., squatty nearly spherical body w/a closed rim, decorated around the top w/a band of abstract animals in dark & light blue on a bluish white ground, decorated by June Marks, dated 1949 (ILLUS., middle next column).................. **$863**

Banded Floral Vase by Flora Huckfield

Spherical Vase with Abstract Animals

Ringed Vase by the Cable Sisters

Vase, 8 1/8" h., gently swelled cylindrical form w/a narrow shoulder & short rolled neck, molded ring design down the sides glazed in shades of brown & green, UND inkstamp logo & incised "M. Cable - 1934 - 1118 - Huckfield-," Margaret Cable & Flora Cable Huckfield, 1934, very faint crazing (ILLUS.) **$345**

Ohr (George) Pottery

George Ohr, the eccentric potter of Biloxi, Mississippi, worked from about 1883 to 1906. Some think him to be one of the most expert throwers the craft will ever see. The majority of his works were hand-thrown, exceedingly thin-walled items, some of which have a crushed or folded appearance. He considered himself the foremost potter in the world and declined to sell much of his production, instead accumulating a great horde to leave as a legacy to his children. In 1972 this collection was purchased for resale by an antiques dealer.

Ohr Pottery Marks

Small Ohr Bulbous Bowl-Vase

Bowl-vase, footed squatty bulbous body w/a thin ring around the upright neck w/a roughly scalloped rim, multi-toned pinkish brown glaze, impressed marks, cracked & glues, 3 1/2" h. (ILLUS.) **$360**

Cylindrical Brown Ohr Bowl-Vase

Bowl-vase, wide cylindrical shape sharply tapering at the base, an upright ruffled rim w/thin incised bands, multi-toned brown glaze, impressed mark, 2" h. (ILLUS.) **$1,080**

Unusual Ohr Pottery Puzzle Mug

Puzzle mug, waisted cylindrical form w/a large hole on the outside of the rim above two rows of small holes below on each side, angled molded ropetwist handle, multi-toned glossy brown glaze, signed, 3 1/2" h. (ILLUS.) **$1,920**

Small Ohr Vase with Volcanic Glaze

Vase, 3 1/4" h., miniature, wide low flaring round foot below the wide bulbous body tapering to a wide gently flaring rim, volcanic multi-toned brown, red & green matte glaze, impressed mark (ILLUS.) **$1,320**

Vase, 3 3/4" h., miniature, bulbous ovoid body tapering to a short wide cylindrical neck, overall black glossy glaze w/swirling green & white highlights, impressed mark (ILLUS., next page) **$1,440**

Small Black-glazed George Ohr Vase

Old Sleepy Eye

Sleepy Eye, Minnesota, was named after an Indian chief. The Sleepy Eye Milling Co. had stoneware and pottery premiums made at the turn of the century first by the Weir Pottery Company and subsequently by Western Stoneware Co., Monmouth, Illinois. On these items the trademark Indian head was signed beneath "Old Sleepy Eye." The colors were Flemish blue on grey. Later pieces by Western Stoneware to 1937 were not made for Sleepy Eye Milling Co. but for other businesses. They bear the same Indian head but "Old Sleepy Eye" does not appear below. They have a reverse design of teepees and trees and may or may not be marked Western Stoneware on the base. These items are usually found in cobalt blue on cream and are rarer in other colors. In 1952, Western Stoneware made a 22 oz. and 40 oz. stein with a chestnut brown glaze. This mold was redesigned in 1968. From 1968 to 1973 a limited number of 40 oz. steins were produced for the board of directors of Western Stoneware. These were marked and dated and never sold as production items. Beginning with the first convention of the Old Sleepy Eye Club in 1976, Western Stoneware has made a souvenir that each person attending receives. These items are marked with the convention site and date. It should also be noted that there have been some reproduction items made in recent years.

Pitcher, 5 1/4" h., cobalt blue on white, w/small Indian head on handle, Western Stoneware Co., 1906 -37, pint **$176**
Pitcher, 7 3/4" h., cobalt blue on white, w/small Indian head on handle, Western Stoneware Co., 1906-37, half-gallon
.... **$150-$250**
Vase, stoneware, cylindrical, Indian & Cattails patt., Flemish blue on grey, hairline at rim **$235**

Owens

Owens pottery was the product of the J.B. Owens Pottery Company, which operated in Ohio from 1890 to 1929. In 1891 it located in Zanesville and produced art pottery from 1896, introducing "Utopian" wares as its first art pottery. The company switched to tile after 1907. Efforts to rebuild after the factory burned in 1928 failed, and the company closed in 1929.

Owens Pottery Mark

Owens Utopian Humidor with Cigar

Humidor, cov., Utopian line, footed bulbous tapering body w/a wide fitted cover w/mushroom knob, h.p. brown cigar & matches on a dark brown to dark green ground, unmarked, some small chips to cover interior, some surface scratches, 7 1/8" h. (ILLUS.) **$288**

Owens Cyrano Line Jardiniere

Jardiniere, Cyrano line, footed waisted cylindrical body, lacy squeezebag applied filigree band around the middle & beading at rim, glossy mottled dark brown & pale yellow ground, white & brown band, unmarked, small piece of filigree missing, glaze crazing, 7 1/2" h. (ILLUS., previous page) **$230**

Blue Speckled Owens Cyrano Jardiniere

Jardiniere, Cyrano line, footed waisted cylindrical body, lacy squeezebag applied filigree band around the middle & beading at rim, glossy streaky & speckled blue ground, light green & blue band, unmarked, 8 1/8" h. (ILLUS.) **$288**

Owens Etched Delft Line Jardiniere

Jardiniere, Delft line, bulbous ovoid body w/a low wide flaring rim, "Old Holland" scene w/an etched design of a Dutch mother & daughter looking out to sea, in blue, white & brown, unmarked, 8 x 9 1/2" (ILLUS.) **$374**

Fine Owens Henri Deux Jardiniere

Jardiniere, Henri Deux line, four-sided gently arched foot trimmed in gold support, the wide gently waisted cylindrical body w/a gently swelled & scalloped rim, etched design of a seated Art Nouveau maiden in a landscape in black, dark brown & dark blue, gilt trim around bottom, unmarked, 7 1/2" h. (ILLUS.) **$460**

Owens Moss Aztec Umbrella Stand

Umbrella stand, 21 5/8" h., Moss Aztec line, tall cylindrical form w/flared rim, molded "Springtime" landscape design w/semi-nude maidens, Shape No. 530 (ILLUS.) **$575**

Unusual Owens Henri Deux Line Vase

Vase, 11 1/2" h., Henri Deux line, large round & ornately molded black footed pedestal base supporting the wide cylindrical body w/a wide cupped mouth, the sides incised & decorated w/colored clays in greens, tans, gold & brown to form a stylized forest scene w/a maiden, unmarked, several chips at base, some small nicks (ILLUS.) **$375**

Rare Tall Owens Opalesce Vase

Vase, 13" h., Opalesce line, flared foot & gently flaring cylindrical body w/a rounded shoulder to the short rolled neck, gold iridescent ground h.p. w/Art Nouveau style vining deep red blossoms & dark green leaves hanging from the rim (ILLUS.).......... **$978**

Tall Slender Owens Art Vellum Vase

Vase, 13 1/4" h., Art Vellum line, very slender baluster-form body w/a tiny mouth, decorated w/shaded purple grape cluster w/mottled greenish blue leaves & brown vine, on a shaded dark blue to cream to dark blue ground, Owens torch mark & Shape No. 1046, two glaze nicks (ILLUS.) **$690**

Unusual Malachite Beaded Utopian Vase

Vase, 13 3/8" h., Malachite Beaded Utopian Ware, a flaring ringed base tapering to a tall slender cylindrical body w/a bulbed top, a large bold orange blossom w/twig running up the side against a beaded dark green ground (ILLUS.) **$805**

Tall Slender Owens Utopian Vase

Vase, 15" h., Utopian line, very tall slender slightly waisted cylindrical body tapering to a tiny cylindrical neck, h.p. thistle & leaves on a shaded dark brown to green ground, artist-signed, impressed mark, Shape No. 1067, some slight scratches (ILLUS.)... **$288**

Oyster Plates

These special plates were very stylish during the second half of the 19th century. Used to serve fresh oysters on the half-shell, they are most often found made of porcelain or majolica, although other materials were sometimes used. In recent years fine individual pieces and sets have become extremely sought after.

Glass, five-well, wide crescent shape w/central sauce indentation, molded pineapple in each well, Lalique, France, 20th c., 8" w. (ILLUS. second row, center, with other silver plate & glass oyster plates, on page 455) **$220**

Glass, six-well, shell-shaped wells around center sauce well, clear, Cambridge Glass Co., w/original paper label, early 20th c., 10 1/4" d. (ILLUS. bottom row, right, with other silver plate & glass wells, on page 455) **$28**

Glass, six-well, shell-shaped wells around a center sauce well, opaque, Portieux, France, early 20th c., 8 3/4" d. **$55**

Glass, six-well, shell-shaped wells spiraling around a round sauce well, Portieux, France, early 20th c., 8 3/4" d. (ILLUS. bottom row, left, with other silver plate & glass oyster plates, on page 455) **$28**

Glass, six-well, shell-shaped wells around a center sauce well, clear w/beaded border band, early 20th c., 9 1/2" d. (ILLUS. bottom row, center, with other silver plate & glass oyster plates, on page 455) **$28**

French 12-Well Majolica Oyster Plate

Majolica, 12-well, hexagonal, the shaded dark grey to light grey shell-shaped wells against a green ground, center handle, France, 19th c., 12 1/2" w. (ILLUS.)........... **$440**

Five Well Oyster Plate with Pink Wells

Majolica, five-well, crescent-shaped, pink wells on a dark brown ground w/a green coral sprig at the center top, 19th c., 10" w. (ILLUS.)....................................... **$1,100**

Very Rare Fish & Shell Minton Plate

Majolica, five-well, dark blue shell-shaped wells alternating w/green & yellow fish, all on a brown ground, Minton, 10 1/2" d. (ILLUS.).. **$6,050**

Fine Holdcroft, England Oyster Plate

Majolica, four-well, light blue cockleshell wells centered by an oval pink sauce well, accent w/blossom sprigs, Holdcroft, England, minor professional repair on the back, 7 1/2 x 9" (ILLUS.) **$3,025**

Very Rare Minton Oyster Plate

Majolica, four-well, rounded rectangular shape w/pale blue wells on a yellow basketweave ground, brown central sauce dish, Minton, England, 7 1/2 x 9" (ILLUS.) **$4,180**

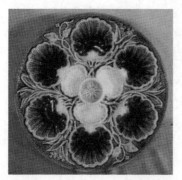

Rare Rostrand, Sweden Oyster Plate

Majolica, six-well, brown cockleshell wells alternating w/green seaweed sprigs, three small inner shell wells centered by a round sauce dish, Rostrand, Sweden, 19th c., 11" d. (ILLUS.) **$3,025**

Majolica, six-well, hexagonal, dark grey shell-shaped wells on a turquoise blue ground w/central sauce dish, Long-champ, France, 8 3/4" w. (ILLUS. bottom with two other French oyster plates, second photo this column) **$285**

Minton Plate with Fish-shaped Wells

Majolica, six-well, molded shaded grey fish wells on a brown ground, centered by a round blue sauce dish, Minton, 11" d. (ILLUS.) **$3,300**

Majolica, six-well, pale pink alternating w/pale yellow wells & brown center sauce dish, brown ground w/green seaweed sprigs, Fielding, England, minor surface wear, late 19th c., 9 1/4" d. (ILLUS. bottom with two other Fielding oyster plates, next page) **$385**

Group of Three French Oyster Plates

Majolica, six-well, shaded green to white shell-shaped wells centered by a white sauce dish, on an emerald green ground, France, late 19th c., 9 1/4" d. (ILLUS. top left with two other French oyster plates) **$121**

Majolica, six-well, tan shell-shaped wells centered on a shaded brown sauce dish, on a green ground, Sarreguemines, France, 9 1/2" d. (ILLUS. top right with two other French oyster plates, above) **$110**

Majolica, six-well, turquoise blue wells & center sauce dish on a brown ground, Fielding, England, late 19th c., 9 1/4" d. (ILLUS. top right with two other Fielding oyster plates, next page) **$385**

Fine Set of German Porcelain Oyster Plates

Three Fielding Majolica Oyster Plates

Majolica, six-well, turquoise blue wells & center sauce dish, on a cream ground w/green seaweed sprigs, Fielding, England, late 19th c., 9 1/4" d. (ILLUS. top left with two other Fielding oyster plates) ... **$440**

Unusual Russian Oyster Plate

Majolica, six-well, unusual stylized maple leaf shape w/fanned & pointed wells & fleur-de-lis shaped handle, glazed in blue, blue & dark yellow, Russian Imperial Eagle mark, 7 x 9" (ILLUS.) **$825**

Porcelain, six-well, shell-shaped wells alternating pale pink & yellow & pale blue, pink central sauce compartment, brown

ground, Germany, late 19th c., 9" d., set of 12 (ILLUS., top of page)...................... **$1,610**

Grouping of Silver Plate & Glass Plates

Silver plate, eight-well, round wells centered by a sauce compartment, Reed & Barton, late 19th - early 20th c., 12 1/2" d. (ILLUS. top row, left, with other silver plate & glass oyster plates) **$193**

Silver plate, six-well, shell-shaped wells & center sauce compartment, from the Palace Hotel, Denver, Colorado, late 19th - early 20th c., 11" d. (ILLUS. top row, right, with other silver plate & glass oyster plates, above) **$358**

Silver plate, three-well, round w/upright center dolphin-shaped handle, Canterbury Silver Plate, early 20th c., 9" d. (ILLUS. top row, center, with other silver plate & glass oyster plates, above) **$110**

Silver plate cast metal, six-well, baking dish w/shell-shaped wells w/hinged covers & round center sauce compartment, shell-shaped handle, marked "Property - Cape Cod Products Co. No. 204," 20th c., 7 1/2" w. (ILLUS. second row, right, with other silver plate & glass oyster plates, above) **$220**

Silver plate cast metal, six-well, shell-shaped wells & central sauce indentation, 8" d. (ILLUS. second row, left, with other silver plate & glass oyster plates) **$110**

Paul Revere Pottery

This pottery was established in Boston, Massachusetts, in 1906, by a group of philanthropists seeking to establish better conditions for underprivileged young girls of the area. Edith Brown served as supervisor of the small "Saturday Evening Girls Club" pottery operation, which was moved, in 1912, to a house close to the Old North Church where Paul Revere's signal lanterns had been placed. The wares were mostly hand decorated in mineral colors, and both sgraffito and molded decorations were employed. Although it became popular, it was never a profitable operation and always depended on financial contributions to operate. After the death of Edith Brown in 1932, the pottery foundered and finally closed in 1942.

Paul Revere Marks

Paul Revere Bowl with Scarabs

Bowl, 4 1/4" d., bulbous ovoid body w/a wide flat mouth, decorated around the top w/a yellow band accented by flying scarabs in light green, streaky pale blue glaze, marked "S.E.G. - 05-1-14," crazing, 1914 (ILLUS.) **$1,093**

Paul Revere Bowl with White Lilies

Bowl, 6" d., squatty bulbous wide form w/a wide closed rim, decorated around the rim w/a band of repeating stylized white lilies against a dark blue ground, SEG mark & initialed by artist, dated "11-14," hairline, chip at rim (ILLUS.) **$780**

Rare Paul Revere Pottery Inkwell

Inkwell, a rectangular box form w/a squared fitted cover on the top opening to an inkwell insert, dark blue ground decorated around the base w/a repeating design of sailing ships in light blue, green & yellow, signed & dated w/the SEB mark, 4" l. (ILLUS.) **$2,400**

Set of 12 Paul Revere - Saturday Evening Girls Luncheon Plates

Paul Revere - Saturday Evening Girls Tea Set

Plates, 8 1/2" d., luncheon, creamy white w/a dark blue border band decorated w/stylized white lotus blossoms, Saturday Evening Girls mark & dated 1910, set of 12 (ILLUS., bottom previous page) **$2,645**

Tea set: cov. bulbous 4 3/4" h. teapot, 4 1/4" h. cylindrical creamer, 4" h. cylindrical cov. sugar bowl & 5 1/4" w. square tea tile; each decorated w/a dark blue glaze w/a border band of stylized white lotus blossoms, all marked w/the Saturday Evening Girls mark & dated 1910, teapot cover cracked, glued chip on inner rim of teapot, the set (ILLUS., top of page) **$1,955**

Peters & Reed

In 1897 John D. Peters and Adam Reed formed a partnership to produce flowerpots in Zanesville, Ohio. Formally incorporated as Peters and Reed in 1901, this type of production was the mainstay until after 1907, when they gradually expanded into the art pottery field. Frank Ferrell, a former designer at the Weller Pottery, developed the "Moss Aztec" line while associated with Peters and Reed, and other art lines followed. Although unmarked, attribution is not difficult once familiar with the various lines. In 1921, Peters and Reed became Zane Pottery, which continued in production until 1941.

Peters & Reed Mark

Tall Blue-Glazed Paul Revere Vase

Vase, 13 1/2" h., tall gently tapering ovoid shape w/a wide low molded rim, overall light matte blue glaze, signed w/SEG mark & dated 1929 (ILLUS.) **$900**

Small Peters & Reed Landsun Vase

Vase, 4 3/4" h., Landsun line, baluster-form body w/a dark blue upper band above the mottled & streaked blackish brown, tan & yellow green lower body, unmarked, some burst glaze bubbles near base (ILLUS.) **$104**

Small Peters & Reed Shadowware Vase

Vase, 5 7/8" h., Shadowware line, flaring foot tapering to tall slender cylindrical body, swirled blue & yellow over a dark blue ground, unmarked (ILLUS.)............... **$127**

Peters & Reed Shadowware Vase

Vase, 6 3/4" h., Shadowware line, baluster-form body w/a short flared neck, streaky dripping dark blues & pale green over a tan background, unmarked, few tiny underglaze inclusions (ILLUS.) **$150**

Vase, 7 1/4" h., Wilse line, gently tapering cylindrical body w/a wide cupped top, overall speckled glossy blue glaze, impressed Zane Ware mark (ILLUS., top next column).. **$69**

Vase, 7 1/2" h., Shadow Ware, footed flaring trumpet-form body below the angled shoulder centered by a short molded neck, drippy streaks of blue, black & yellow down over a caramel ground, unmarked, overall crazing (ILLUS., middle next column).. **$460**

Peters & Reed Wilse Line Blue Vase

Interesting Shadow Ware Vase

Peters & Reed Mottled Landsun Vase

Vase, 7 5/8" h., Landsun Ware, footed gently swelled cylindrical body w/a flaring molded rim, mottled matt green & dark blue on a tan ground, unmarked (ILLUS.) .. **$259**

Banded Landsun Line Vase

Vase, 8" h., Landsun line, flared foot & swelled cylindrical body w/a wide ringed & molded wide flat mouth, overlapping angled streaky blue & brown bands around the sides against the pale green ground, impressed Zane Ware logo (ILLUS.) **$195**

Tall Peters & Reed Marbleized Vase

Vase, 10" h., Marbleized line, flaring base tapering to a trumpet-form body, streaky

bands of black & yellow on the brown ground, glossy glaze, unmarked, overall crazing (ILLUS.) **$127**

Pickard China

Pickard, Inc., making fine decorated china today in Antioch, Illinois, was founded in Chicago in 1894 by Wilder A. Pickard. The company now makes its own blanks but once only decorated those bought from other potteries, primarily from the Havilands and others in Limoges, France.

Pickard Mark

Pitcher, 9" w., cider-type, a very wide squatty body tapering to a golden scalloped rim w/wide spout, wide ruffled gold handle, the sides h.p. w/large pink & red roses & pale green leaves on a dark green shaded to yellow ground, Limoges blank, artist-signed **$575**

Pitcher, 13" h., tankard-type, a sharply tapering cylindrical body w/a high & wide arched rim spout bordered in gold, long C-form gold handle, the sides h.p. w/purple & green grape clusters among green & yellow & orange leaves against a ground shaded from orange to yellow to dark green, artist-signed **$1,495**

Tea set: cov. teapot, cov. sugar bowl, creamer & footed compote; serving pieces w/a wide low squatty bulbous body w/looped gold handles & a gold teapot spout, a creamy lower body below a wide middle band decorated w/colorful stylized flowering vines on a white ground, turquoise blue border bands, marked, early 20th c., the set (ILLUS., bottom of page) **$460**

Lovely Pickard-decorated Porcelain Tea Set

All Gold Pickard-decorated Tea Set

Tea set: cov. teapot, cov. sugar bowl, creamer & six 6" d. plates; each piece decorated overall w/a textured gold glaze, the scalloped plates w/stamped floral borders, each marked, ca. 1930, the set (ILLUS.) **$201**

Pierce (Howard) Porcelains

Born in Chicago, Illinois in 1912, Howard Pierce was destined to become one of the most talented ceramic wildlife creators of his time. He attended the Chicago Art Institute and in 1935 he decided to move to Claremont, California. For about three years Mr. Pierce worked for William Manker. In 1941, he married Ellen Voorhees who was a resident of National City, California. For a few years they lived in Claremont where Howard built their small home and art studio. In 1968, they moved to Joshia, California.

In the beginning, Howard created miniature animal figures, some of which he made for a very short time. He discovered he was allergic to this material so only a few were made. They are high on collectors' lists today.

Howard Pierce was prolific in his output. He was also curious and experimented with a number of different mediums: Wedgwood Jasperware-type body; porcelain bisque animals and plants that he put near or in open areas of vases; Mt. St. Helens ash which is probably the most scarce of any products made by Howard; a lava treatment which he described as "...bubbling up from the bottom...," gold leaf, which is hard to find; a gold treatment that he did for Sears (not being happy with it he stopped production as soon as possible); a "tipping" process that is clearly shown in such pieces as the droopy eared dogs and the ermine.

Near the end of 1992, due to health problems, Howard and Ellen Pierce destroyed all the molds they had created over the years. Still, Mr. Pierce needed to create. So he purchased a smaller kiln and began creating miniature versions of past porcelain wares. He also added a few new items as there seemed to be no way for him to block his creative processes. These smaller pieces were simply stamped "Pierce." Today, many collectors search only for the pieces marked "Pierce," which has created a demand causing the values to rise quickly. Howard Pierce passed away in February, 1994.

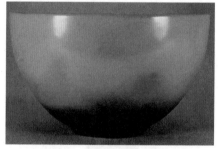

Marks

Bank, model of a turtle, speckled glossy glaze in teal w/black accents, stamped "Howard Pierce," hard to find, 7 3/4" l. **$275**

Howard Pierce Round Bowl

Bowl, 7" d., 4 1/4" h., small round black base flaring gently to a larger rim, sky blue inside, incised "Pierce 1990" & H52 (ILLUS.).. **$75**

Bowl, 7 1/4" d., 4 1/4" h., fluted body flaring to a fluted rim, Manker influence, pale & deep blue w/black accents, incised mark, "Pierce 1983" in script **$205**

Bowl, 7 1/4" d., 4 1/4" h., fluted body flaring to a fluted rim, William Manker influence, pale & deep blue w/black accents, incised "Pierce" & 1983 in script **$125**

Bowl, 13" l., 2" h., freeform, black outside, speckled black & white inside, 1950s (ILLUS., bottom of page)......................... **$100**

Long Freeform Howard Pierce Bowl

Model of an eagle, perched on an arched tree stump base, head looking forward, white body w/brown accents, stamped "Howard Pierce," 7" h. $200

Model of bear, brown, 7" l................................ $91

Model of bird on branch, brown & white polyurethane, signed "Pierce" on base, 4 1/4" h. $1,275

Circus Horse Model by Howard Pierce

Model of circus horse, head down, tail straight, leaping position w/middle of body supported by small, round center base, light blue w/cobalt accents, experimental glaze, 7 1/2" l., 6 1/2" h. (ILLUS.) $285

Howard Pierce Hippopotamus

Model of hippo, standing, short tail, bulbous body, large nose & mouth, small ears & eyes, very distinct features, dark grey bottom, mottled grey top, 1950s, stamp marked "Howard Pierce Porcelain," 9 3/4" l., 3" h. (ILLUS.) $255

Model of monkey totem pole, three monkeys stacked on top of one another, marked "Hear No Evil - See No Evil - Speak No Evil," one-piece in black or brown, Model No. 300P, stamped "Howard Pierce," late 1950s, 15" h. $295

Howard Pierce Mouse

Model of mouse, pink & ivory high glaze, "Howard Pierce Porcelain" stamp, 2" h., 3 1/4" l. (ILLUS.) $390

Model of panther, pacing position, brown glaze, 11 1/2" l., 2 3/4" h. $435

Model of rabbit, pale green w/white, cement, no mark, 5 1/2" h., 10 1/2" l. $542

Howard Pierce Skunk

Model of skunk, black w/blue & white stripes on back, "Howard Pierce Porcelain" stamp, 4 3/4" h. (ILLUS.) $175

Howard Pierce Rough Textured Skunk

Model of skunk, rough textured matte glaze, 6" h. (ILLUS.) $220

Model of turkey, miniature, brown high glaze, "Pierce" stamp, 2" h. $238

Set of Birds on Stumps

Models of birds, blue on black tree stumps, "Howard Pierce Porcelain" stamp & one signed "Pierce" on base, 5" & 4 1/2" h., the set (ILLUS.) $288

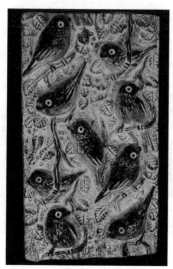

Large Pierce Wall Plaque with Songbirds

Wall plaque, rectangular, molded in relief w/nine songbirds, pale green ground w/darker green birds, unmarked, 8" w., 13" h. (ILLUS.) **$710**

Quimper

This French earthenware pottery has been made in France since the end of the 17th century and is still in production today. Because the colorful decoration on this ware, predominantly of Breton peasant figures, is all hand-painted and each piece is unique, it has become increasingly popular with collectors in recent years. Most pieces offered today date from about the mid-19th century to the present. Modern potteries continue to operate today, with contemporary examples available in gift shops.

The standard reference in this field is Quimper Pottery: A French Folk Art Faience by Sandra V. Bondhus (privately printed, 1981).

Quimper Marks

Bank, figural, model of a pig, decorated on the side w/a seated man w/a pipe in his mouth, bold red daisy on the reverse, HenRiot Quimper mark, 4" h. **$100**

HB Quimper Bookends & Knife Rests

Bookends, figural, Modern Movement, creamy angled base, one mounted w/a peasant lad playing the bagpipes, the other w/a seated little girl, marked "HB Quimper 940v," mint, pr. (ILLUS. center w/Quimper knife rests) **$425**

Bowl, 7 1/2" w., 3" h., deep w/incurved sides & angled corners, decorated w/a peasant lady, leafy sprigs on each interior side, mark of HR Quimper, mint (ILLUS. right with bagpipe wall pocket, bottom of page) **$75**

Butter dish, cov., oval shape w/an attached undertray, yellow background glaze, marked "HenRiot Quimper 71 France," mint, 6" l. **$100**

Butter tub, cov., decorated w/a traditional peasant lady & flower garland, flat cover w/blue round button knob, marked "HB Quimper 25/485," near mint w/tiny glaze wear on inside rim, 6" w. **$35**

Quimper Bowl & Bagpipe-shaped Wall Pocket

HB Quimper Cake Plate

Cake plate, round w/open loop handles, decorated in the center w/a man in the costume of Aurillac, mark of HB Quimper, mint, 12" d. (ILLUS.) **$85**

Candlesticks, each decorated w/a peasant couple & flowers, stamped mark "HB Henriot Quimper f. 130 d 318," 5 3/4" h., pr. **$175**

Chamberstick, round dished back w/center socket & ring handle, decorated w/twin daisy flowers, marked "Henriot Quimper 66," mint, 6 1/2" d. **$75**

Charger in "Broderie Breton" Pattern

Charger, round, "Broderie Breton" patt., the center w/a sea shore scene w/a Breton fisherman holding his net, a little boy w/his toy sailboat standing beside him, marked "HB Quimper ...x," mint, 12 1/2" d. (ILLUS.) **$425**

Charger, round, Modern Movement style decorated w/a fully-rigged sailing ship, titled "Thonniers" (Tuna Fishermen) below the ship among waves & fish, marked "HB Quimper France l...x," small rim chip, 12 1/2" d. **$90**

HB Quimper Charger with Dancing Couple

Charger, round w/gently scalloped rim, the center decorated w/a dancing peasant couple, four flower nosegays around the rim, marked "HB Quimper . o.o," mint, 14" d. (ILLUS.) **$225**

Adolphe Porquier Open Compote

Compote, 8 3/4" h., open, short pedestal base, deep round bowl decorated w/a traditional peasant lady flanked by floral sprigs, mark of Adolphe Porquier, 19th c., near mint w/glaze flecks (ILLUS.) **$150**

Compote, open, 7 x 11 1/2", oblong flaring bowl w/serpentine sides & molded open mistletoe branch handles, decorated on the inside in the "demi-fantasie" style w/a peasant man & woman w/gorse & pink bellflower sprigs, marked "Henriot Quimper 142," mint (ILLUS. of inside top, top next page) **$400**

Creamer, tall bulbous shape, decorated w/traditional peasant man & geometric panels on each side of the handle, mark of HR Quimper, mint, 3" h. **$45**

Dish, doll-sized, overall geometric design, marked "Henriot Quimper France 117," mint, 3" d. **$30**

Henriot Quimper Compote Decorated in the "Demi-fantasie" Style

Rare Henriot Quimper Swan-shaped Eggcup Server

Eggcup, Modern Movement style decorated w/a kneeling lady holding a basket on her back, HenRiot Quimper & C. Maillard mark, 2 1/2" h. **$150**

Eggcup server, figural, the base in the shape of a large swan w/an overall dotted blue & brown design, the back molded w/slx oval indentations for the small swan-shaped eggcups, mark of Henriot Quimper, near mint w/slight glaze flecks on eggcups, swan 12" l., the set (ILLUS., middle of page) **$750**

Eggcups, decorated in the traditional design w/yellow & blue concentric bands & a peasant figure on each w/flowers, marked "Henriot Quimper France 93" & "Henriot Quimper France 124," 3" h., pr....... **$50**

Ewer, tall classical form w/pedestal base, tall ovoid & slender cylindrical neck w/high arched spout continuing into the high arched handle, Decor riche patt. featuring a pair of musicians on the front & a bouquet of Breton wild flowers on the back, HB Quimper France mark, 18" h. (ILLUS., next column) **$375**

Tall Quimper Ewer with Musicians

Fancy HB Quimper Footed Jardiniere

Jardiniere, squatty bulbous oval form raised on lion paw feet, a molded figural satyr head at each end, the lower body decorated w/a scene of a peasant couple seated on the ground, "décor riche" blue acanthus trim above, marked "HB Quimper - 20," mint, 12" l., 8" h. (ILLUS., top of page) **$400**

Knife rest, figural, modeled as a man stretched out on his stomach, Modern Movement colors, HenRiot Quimper & C. Maillard mark, 4" l. **$100**

Knife rest, triangular, decorated on one side w/a peasant lady, flowers on the reverse, marked "HenRiot Quimper France 492," 3 3/4" l. **$30**

Knife rests, Modern Movement, figural, one designed as a reclining peasant man, the other w/a peasant woman reclining on her stomach w/her head in her hands, by the artist C. Maillard, marked by the artist & by Henriot Quimper, mint, pr. (ILLUS. left & right with Quimper bookends, on page 462) **$200**

Quimper Modern Movement Lamp Base

Lamp base, figural, modeled as a standing peasant lady holding a basket on her shoulder, a blue pond in front of her & figural ducks & hens flanking her feet, Modern Movement style, by artist C. Maillard, HenRiot Quimper & CM mark, 9 1/2" h. (ILLUS.) **$375**

Menu card holder, figural, modeled as a bagpipe, decorated w/a peasant lady & flowers, HenRiot Quimper mark, 3 1/2" h. **$200**

Henriot Quimper Fancy Pipe Rack

Pipe rack, modeled as a bagpipe, the half-round bottom molded at the front w/the top of the bagpipe w/a blue ribbon & pierced w/a row of four pipe holes, the upright arched & scalloped back topped by a crown above a scroll reserve forming the crest of Brittany above a peasant man & woman, marked "Henriot Quimper France 75," professional restoration to tiny glaze flekcs on back of crown, 10" l., 7 1/2" h. (ILLUS.) **$350**

Pitcher, 6" h., figural, Modern Movement, modeled as the bust of an elderly peasant man lighting his pipe, by artist Andre Galland, the hat ribbons form the handle, marked "HenRiot Quimper 140 ag," mint **$200**

Pitcher, 7" h., decorated w/a traditional peasant man & flowers, signed on the side near the handle "HenRiot Quimper France 70" **$55**

Quimper Rectangular Planter in the Demi-fantasie Pattern

Double-spouted Odetta Pitcher

Pitcher, 8" h., 9" l., gresware, Odetta style double-spouted squatty bulbous body w/high arched handle joining the spouts, in brown, charcoal & white, linear & triangular designs, marked "HB Quimper Odetta 64.1086" (ILLUS.) $450

Planter, figural, model of a swan, a trefoil cartouche on the breast encloses a seated man playing the flute, marked "HenRiot Quimper France 89," 4" h. $100

Planter, figural, modeled as a tall swan, decorated w/a peasant lady in a medalion on the breast of the swan, mark of HenRiot Quimper, mint, 4" h. $85

Quimper Cradle-form Planter

Planter, model of a cradle, rectangular w/gently canted sides & corner posts, serpentine top edges, decorated w/peasant figures on the front & a flower spray on the back, mark of HR Quimper, mint, 7 1/4" l., 4" h. (ILLUS.) $325

Planter, rectangular w/beveled corners, loop end handles, raised on small tab feet, Demi-fantasie patt. w/a couple seated in a field w/latticework at the corners, the reverse w/blue forget-me-nots & a stylized rose, one handle professionally repaired, HR Quimper mark, 5 x 11" (ILLUS., top of page).................... $225

Plate, doll's, 2 1/4" d., Modern Movement geometric design, marked "HenRiot Quimper France 83" mark............................ $35

Plate, 9" d., dinner, decorated w/a traditional peasant man holding a walking stick, Sujet ordinaire patt., yellow & blue concentric banded border, HenRiot Quimper France mark $45

Very Rare Porquier-Beau Plate

Plate, 9" d., round w/gently scalloped rim, First Period Porquier-Beau w/"scene bretonne" titled "Joyeux compagnons de Faouet," marked "Le Faouet" & blue intersecting PB mark, 19th c. (ILLUS.) $850

Plate, 9" d., round w/scalloped rim, Second Period Porquier-Beau w/"scene bretonne" of a Breton lady & man entitled "Devideuse de Penhars," intersecting PB Quimper mark, mint $450

HB Quimper Oval Platter with Peasant Couple

Platter, 10 x 13" oval, the center decorated w/a scene of a traditional peasant couple, flower garland border, mark of HB Quimper, mint, 19th c. (ILLUS., top of page)... **$200**

Salt dip, figural, modeled as a pair of wooden shoes w/a ring handle, decorated on one shoe w/a peasant lady, a flower sprig on the other shoe, marked "HenRiot Quimper France 596," 4" l. **$35**

Salt & pepper server, figural, open, modeled as a long pair of shoes joined w/a center ring handle, mark of HB Quimper France, mint, 3" l. **$35**

Snuff bottle, heart-shaped, decorated w/a peasant man on one side, a pansy on the reverse, pale blue spongework outer edge, HB Quimper mark, 3" h. **$250**

Snuff bottle, heart-shaped, decorated w/a peasant man, the back w/a two-tone yellow fleur-de-lis, blue sponged outer rim, mark of HB Quimper, mint, 3" h. (ILLUS. left with two other snuff bottles, bottom of page)... **$150**

Snuff bottle, heart-shaped, decorated w/a rooster, the back w/a large flower blossom, unsigned, mint, 19th c., 3" h. (ILLUS. right with two other Quimper snuff bottles, bottom of page) **$300**

Snuff bottle, oval w/a lattice geometric design surrounded by a yellow border on both sides, Porquier, unsigned, near mint w/tiny glaze wear on lip, 19th c., 3" h. (ILLUS. center with two other Quimper snuff bottles, bottom of page) **$325**

Spoon rest, figural, long shallow fish-shaped dish decorated w/a traditional peasant lady, marked "HenRiot Quimper France 238," mint, 4 1/2" l. **$30**

Group of Three Quimper Snuff Bottles

Henriot Quimper Tea Set in the "Croisille" Pattern

Tea set: footed spherical cov. teapot, spherical footed cov. sugar bowl w/scroll loop handles & footed ovoid double-spouted creamer, all in the "croisille" patt., w/"demi-fantasie" peasant figures & intricate latticework & flower sprigs, marked "Henriot Quimper France," mint, the set (ILLUS., top of page)................................... **$350**

Toby pitcher, figural, modeled as a peasant lady decorated in Modern Movement colors, mark of HenRiot France, mint, 3 1/2" h.. **$65**

Trivet, squared shape w/serpentine sides, raised on four peg feet, the top decorated w/a naively painted peasant man, flower sprigs in each corner, marked "HB" only, hairline, 6" w. (ILLUS.) **$100**

Quimper Decor Riche Fan-shaped Vase

Vase, 5" h., 8" l., fan-shaped, Decor riche patt., HB Quimper mark (ILLUS.)............... **$350**

Vase, 7 1/2" h., figural, modeled as a bagpipe, decorated w/a "demi-fantasie" lady, the back w/bold flowers, marked "Henriot Quimper 96 France," mint (ILLUS. center with two wall pockets, bottom of page) **$150**

Quimper Square Footed Trivet

Quimper Bagpipe Vase & Two Wall Pockets

Rare Quimper Pique Fleurs Vase

Vase, 8" h., 9" l., pique-fleurs style, Modern Movement style, figural, a kneeling peasant lady lifting a large round basket-form holder, top pierced w/holes for flowers, HenRiot Quimper & C. Maillard mark (ILLUS.) **$750**

Henriot Quimper Fan-shaped Vase

Vase, 8" h., 10 1/2" w., fan-shaped body raised on molded dolphin feet, in the "Ivoire Corbeille" patt. w/a bust portrait of a Breton lady, the reverse w/flowers & Celtic swirls, marked "Henriot Quimper 72," mint (ILLUS.) **$225**

Vase, 12 1/2" h., footed ovoid body tapering to a slender neck & flattened rim flanked by long handles down the sides, "décor riche" w/Celtic trim, decorated w/Breton musicians, Crest of Quimper on the back, marked "Henriot Quimper 130," mint (ILLUS., top next column) **$450**

Vases, 9" h., ovoid body tapering to a cupped rim, angled open arms from the rim to the mid-body, in the "demi-fantasie" style, h.p. detailed peasant figures w/a large flower bouquet on the back, marked "Henriot Quimper France," mint, pr. (ILLUS., second next column).............. **$300**

Wall pocket, figural, modeled as a bagpipe decorated w/a peasant lady, molded blue bows at the top & bottom, mark of HB Quimper, 9" h. (ILLUS. left with square Quimper bowl, bottom of page 462)............. **$85**

Henriot Quimper "Décor Riche" Vase

Pair of Henriot Quimper Vases

Wall pocket, tapering conical shape, decorated w/a "demi-fantasie" style lady, marked "Henriot Quimper France 96," near mint w/glaze wear near the tip, 10" h. (ILLUS. right with bagpipe vase & other wall pocket, bottom previous page) **$75**

Wall pocket, tapering conical shape, decorated w/a "demi-fantasie" style musician playing the bagpipes, mark of Henriot Quimper, mint, 9" h. (ILLUS. left with bagpipe vase & other wall pocket, bottom previous page) **$75**

Quimper Cone-shaped Wall Pockets

Wall pockets, cone-shaped, decorated in
the Demi-fantasie patt., marked "HenRiot
Quimper France 8," 10 3/4" l., pr. (ILLUS.) .. **$200**

R.S. Prussia & Related Wares

*Ornately decorated china marked "R.S. Prus-
sia" and "R.S. Germany" continues to grow in
popularity. According to the Third Series of Mary
Frank Gaston's Encyclopedia of R.S. Prussia
(Collector Books, Paducah, Kentucky), these
marks were used by the Reinhold Schlegelmilch
porcelain factories located in Suhl in the Ger-
manic regions known as "Prussia" prior to World
War I, and in Tillowitz, Silesia, which became
part of Poland after World War II. Other marks
sought by collectors include "R.S. Suhl," "R.S."
steeple or church marks, and "R.S. Poland."*

*The Suhl factory was founded by Reinhold
Schlegelmilch in 1869 and closed in 1917. The
Tillowitz factory was established in 1895 by
Erhard Schlegelmilch, Reinhold's son. This china
customarily bears the phrase "R.S. Germany" and
"R.S. Tillowitz." The Tillowitz factory closed in
1945, but it was reopened for a few years under
Polish administration.*

*Prices are high and collectors should beware of
the forgeries that sometimes find their way onto
the market. Mold names and numbers are taken
from Mary Frank Gaston's books on R.S. Prussia.*

*The "Prussia" and "R.S. Suhl" marks have
been reproduced, so buy with care. Later copies of
these marks are well done, but quality of porcelain
is inferior to the production in the 1890-1920 era.*

*Collectors are also interested in the porcelain
products made by the Erdmann Schlegelmilch
factory. This factory was founded by three brothers in Suhl in 1861. They named the factory in
honor of their father, Erdmann Schlegelmilch. A
variety of marks incorporating the "E.S." initials
were used. The factory closed circa 1935. The
Erdmann Schlegelmilch factory was an earlier
and entirely separate business from the Reinhold
Schlegelmilch factory. The two were not related to
each other.*

R.S. Prussia & Related Marks

R.S. Germany

Berry set: 9" master bowl & six matching
5 1/2" sauce dishes, Iris mold, decorated
w/large red roses, 7 pcs................... **$600-$900**
Bowl, 10" d., decorated w/wild roses, rasp-
berries & blueberries, glossy glaze ... **$350-$400**
Bowl, large, Lettuce mold, floral decoration.
lustre finish....................................... **$325-$375**

R.S. Germany Cake Plate

Cake plate, double-pierced small gold side
handles, decorated w/a scene of a maid-
en near a cottage at the edge of a dark
forest, 10" d. (ILLUS.) .... **$300-$325**
Creamer, Mold 640, decorated w/roses, gold
trim on ruffled rim & ornate handle......... **$40-$60**
Cup & saucer, demitasse, ornate handle,
eight-footed....................................... **$80-$125**
Mustard jar, cov., calla lily decoration .. **$100-$150**
Plate, 7 1/4" d., poppy decoration............. **$40-$60**
Salad set, 10 1/2" d. lettuce bowl & six 8" d.
matching plates, Mold 12, Iris decoration
on pearl lustre finish, 7 pcs. .... **$350-$450**
Tray, handled, decorated w/large white &
green poppies, 15 1/4" l. .... **$300-$350**

R.S. Prussia

Bell, tall trumpet-form ruffled body w/twig
handle, decorated w/small purple flowers
& green leaves on white ground, un-
marked, 3 1/2" l. .... **$325-$375**
Berry set: master bowl & six sauce dishes,
five-lobed, floral relief rim w/forget-me-
nots & water lilies decoration, artist-
signed, 7 pcs.................................... **$400-$450**

Ribbon & Jewel Melon Eaters Berry Set

Berry set: master bowl & six sauce dishes; Ribbon & Jewel mold (Mold 18) w/Melon Eaters decoration, 7 pcs. (ILLUS.) **$3,000-$4,000**

Bowl, 9 3/4" d., Iris variant mold, rosette center & pale green floral decoration **$200-$400**

Bowl, 10" d., Mold 202, gold beaded rim, double swans center scene in shades of beige & white, unmarked .... **$200-$225**

Bowl, 10 1/4" d., center decoration of pink roses w/pearlized finish, border in shades of lavender & blue w/satin finish, lavish gold trim (unlisted mold).......... **$300-$500**

Bowl, 10 1/2" d., Countess Potocka portrait decoration, heavy gold trim........ **$1,800-$2,200**

Bowl, 10 1/2" d., decorated w/scene of Dice Throwers, red trim .... **$1,200-$1,800**

Bowl, 10 1/2" d., Iris mold, poppy decoration .... **$400-$500**

Bowl, 10 1/2" d., Point & Clover mold (Mold 82), decorated w/pink roses & green leaves w/shadow flowers & a Tiffany finish... **$250-$400**

Bowl, 11" d., 3" h., Sunflower mold, satin finish.. **$350-$550**

Bowl, 11" d., Mold 22, four large jewels, satin finish... **$300-$400**

Bowl, 11" d., 3" h., Fishscale mold, decorated w/white lilies on purple & orange lustre ground, artist-signed .... **$400-$450**

Bowl, 15" d., Icicle mold (Mold 7), Snow Bird decoration, scenic reserves around the rim, very rare .... **$15,000-$18,000**

Butter dish, cover & insert, Mold 51, floral decoration, unmarked .... **$200-$400**

Floral Decorated Cake Plate

Cake plate, open handled, decorated w/pink & white flowers, green leaves, pink & yellow ground, gold trim, 9 3/4" d. (ILLUS.) .... **$250-$350**

Cake plate, open-handled, Fleur-de-Lis mold, Spring Season portrait, 9 3/4" d. .... **$1,400-$1,800**

Cake plate, open handles, Mold 256, satin ground decorated w/flowers in blue, pink & white w/gold trim, 11 1/2" d. .... **$300-$400**

Cake plate, open-handled, Mold 330, decorated w/snapdragons on pastel ground, artist-signed, 11 1/2" d. .... **$300-$400**

Cake plate, open-handled, Fleur-de-Lis mold, decorated w/a castle scene in rust, gold, lavender & yellow, 10 1/4" d. .... **$1,000-$1,350**

Cake plate, open-handled, Medallion mold, center Flora portrait, Tiffany finish w/four cupid medallions, unmarked, 10 1/2" d. .... **$900-$1,000**

Cake plate, Iris mold, yellow poppy decoration, 11" d. .... **$300-$400**

Cake plate, open-handled, Carnation mold (Mold 28), dark pink roses against teal & green w/gold trim, 11" d. .... **$600-$800**

Cake plate, open-handled, Mold 155, hanging basket decoration, 10" d............. **$300-$400**

Cake plate, Hidden Image mold, light blue highlights, 11 1/2" d.......................... **$450-$500**

Cake plate, open-handled, Mold 259, decorated w/pink & yellow roses, pearl button finish, 10" d. .... **$300-$400**

Cake plate, open-handled, modified Fleur-de-Lis mold, floral decoration, beaded, satin finish, artist-signed, 11" d. .... **$300-$400**

Cake plate, open-handled, Mold 343, Winter figural portrait in keyhole medallion, cobalt blue inner border, gold outer border, 12 1/2" d............................... **$3,000-$3,500**

Cake plate, Bow-tie mold, pink & gold .. **$500-$600**

Cake plate, open-handled, Carnation mold, decorated w/multicolored roses .... **$400-$600**

Celery dish, Carnation mold, carnations & pink roses decoration on white shaded to peach ground, iridescent Tiffany finish, 9" l. .... **$400-$600**

Celery dish, Hidden Image mold, colored hair, 5 x 12"...................................... **$400-$450**

Celery dish, Mold 25, oblong, pearlized finish w/Surreal Dogwood blossoms w/gold trim, 6 x 12 1/4" .... **$250-$350**

Lebrun-decorated Chocolate Set

Celery tray, Mold 254, decorated w/green & pink roses, lavish gold tracery, artist-signed, 12" l. .... **$250-$350**

Celery tray, Ribbon & Jewel mold (Mold 18), pink roses & white snowball blossoms within a wide cobalt blue border w/gilt trim, 12" l. .... **$600-$800**

Celery tray, Mold 255, decorated w/Surreal Dogwood decoration, pearlized lustre finish, artist-signed, 12 1/4" l. .... **$350-$400**

Celery tray, open-handled, decorated w/soft pink & white flower center w/lily-of-the-valley, embossed edge of ferns & pastel colors w/gold highlights, 12 1/2" l. .... **$200-$250**

Centerpiece bowl, Carnation mold, decorated w/pink & yellow roses, 15 1/2" d. .... **$3,500-$4,500**

Chocolate cup & saucer, decorated w/castle scene.. **$150-$250**

Chocolate pot, cov., Carnation mold (Mold 526), pink background & pink roses w/gold-trimmed leaves & blossoms & ornate gold handle, 12" h. .... **$1,200-$1,600**

Chocolate pot, cov., Icicle mold (Mold 641), rosebush decoration, 10" h. .... **$400-$500**

Chocolate pot, cov., Hidden Image mold, image on both sides, light green, 9 3/4" h. .... **$1,000-$1,100**

Chocolate pot, cov., peacock & pine trees decoration .... **$650-$750**

Chocolate pot, cov., Swag & Tassel mold, decorated w/scene of sheepherder & swallows....................................... **$900-$1,000**

Chocolate set: cov. pot & four cups & saucers; sunflower decoration, the set.. **$800-$1,200**

Chocolate set: 10" h. cov. chocolate pot & four cups & saucers; Mold 729, pansy decoration w/gold trim, the set .... **$900-$975**

Chocolate set: 10" h. cov. chocolate pot & four cups & saucers; Ribbon and Jewel mold, scene of Dice Throwers decoration on pot & single Melon Eater scene on cups, the set............................... **$4,500-$6,000**

Chocolate set: tankard-style cov. pot & six cups & saucers; Mold 510, laurel chain decoration, the set .... **$1,000-$1,300**

Chocolate set: 10" h. cov. chocolate pot & six cups & saucers; Mold 517, Madame Lebrun portrait decoration, the set (ILLUS. top of page)................................. **$7,500-$8,200**

Coffeepot, cov., Mold 517, raised floral designs as part of border, unmarked .... **$250-$300**

Cracker jar, cov., Mold 540a, beige satin ground w/floral decoration in orchid, yellow & gold, 9 1/2" w. handle to handle, overall 5 1/2" h. .... **$300-$350**

Cracker jar, cov., Mold 634, molded feet, surreal dogwood blossoms decoration on pearlized lustre finish, 8" d., 6 1/2" h. **$250-$300**

Cracker jar, cov., Mold 704, grape leaf decoration, 7" h...................................... **$450-$500**

Cracker jar, cov., decorated w/hanging basket of flowers, satin finish, 6 x 9 1/2" .... **$325-$375**

Cracker jar, cov., Hidden Image mold, image on both sides, green mum decoration .... **$900-$1,000**

Cracker jar, cov., Lebrun portrait decoration, no hat, satin finish .... **$1,500-$2,000**

Creamer & cov. sugar bowl, floral decoration, green highlights, pr................... **$100-$250**

Creamer & cov. sugar bowl, Mold 505, pink & yellow roses, pr. .... **$125-$175**

Creamer & cov. sugar bowl, Ribbon & Jewel mold, single Melon Eater decoration, pr. (ILLUS., top next page).. **$1,500-$1,800**

Creamer & cov. sugar bowl, satin finish, Tiffany trim, pr. .... **$175-$200**

Cup & saucer, decorated w/pink roses, peg feet & scalloped rim, cup 1 3/4" h., saucer 4 1/4" d., pr................................. **$125-$175**

Dessert set: 9 1/2" d. cake plate & six 7" d. individual plates; Carnation mold, decorated w/carnations, pink & white roses, iridescent Tiffany finish on pale green, the set .... **$1,200-$1,400**

Dessert set: pedestal cup & saucer, oversized creamer & sugar bowl, two 9 3/4" d., handled plates, eleven 7 1/4" d. plates, nine cups & saucers; plain mold, decoration w/pink poppies w/tints of aqua, yellow & purple, all pieces are matching, the set...................... **$2,200-$2,500**

Dresser tray, decorated w/mill scene, shaded green ground, 7 x 11".................. **$400-$500**

Dresser tray, Icicle mold, scenic decoration, Man in the Mountain, 7 x 11 1/2"........ **$400-$500**

Ferner, six vertical ribs, scalloped, decorated w/lilies-of-the-valley on shaded pastel ground, artist-signed, 3 7/8 x 8 1/4" . **$300-$400**

Melon Eaters Creamer & Sugar

Hair receiver, cov., Mold 814, Surreal Dogwood decoration .... **$150-$175**

Match holder w/striker, floral decoration
.... **$100-$125**

Model of a lady's slipper, embossed scrolling on instep & heel & embossed feather on one side of slipper, a dotted medallion w/roses & lily-of-the-valley on the other, shaded turquoise blue w/fancy rim trimmed w/gold, 8" l.................... **$250-$300**

Mug, Lily mold, Lebrun portrait decoration (no hat).. **$200-$250**

Mug, rose decoration on pink satin finish
.... **$125-$175**

Mustache cup, Mold 502 .... **$250-$300**

Mustard pot, cov., Mold 509a, decorated w/white flowers, glossy light green ground... **$150-$175**

Mustard pot, cov., Mold 521, pink rose decoration, satin finish .... **$200-$300**

Nut bowl, footed, Point & Clover mold, decorated w/ten roses in shades of salmon, yellow & rose against a pink, green & gold lustre-finished ground, 6 1/2" d. .... **$150-$200**

Nut dish, Carnation mold (Mold 28), floral decoration w/pearlized finish .... **$200-$250**

Pin dish, cov., Hidden Image mold, floral decoration, 2 3/4 x 4 3/4" .... **$350-$450**

white above, gold trim, only one known (ILLUS.).................................... **$13,00-$17,000**

Carnation - Summer Season Pitcher

Pitcher, tankard, 12 1/2" h., Carnation mold (Mold 526), Summer Season decoration, pink border trim (ILLUS.)............. **$7,000-$8,000**

Carnation Mold Pitcher with Roses

Pitcher, tankard, 13" h., Carnation mold (Mold 526), decorated w/clusters of dark pink & creamy white roses w/a shaded

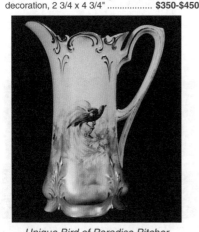

Unique Bird of Paradise Pitcher

Pitcher, tankard, 12 1/4" h., Mold 569, very rare Bird of Paradise decoration w/shaded gold & light green in the lower half, dark green ground & pale green molded blossoms (ILLUS.)....................... **$1,000-$1,200**

Pitcher, cider, 7" h., iris decoration w/green & gold background .... **$250-$300**

Pitcher, tankard, 10" h., Mold 584, decorated w/hanging basket of pink & white roses .... **$700-$750**

R.S. Prussia Tankard Pitchers

Pitcher, tankard, 12" h., Mold 538, decorated w/Melon Eaters scene (ILLUS. left)
.... **$3,500-$4,000**

Pitcher, tankard, 13" h., decorated w/scene of Old Man in Mountain & swans on lake (ILLUS. right w/other tankard pitcher)
.... **$4,000-$4,500**

Pitcher, tankard, 13 1/2" h., Carnation Mold, pink poppy decoration, green ground.. **$1,400-$1,800**

Plaque, decorated w/scene of woman w/dog, 9 1/4 x 13" .... **$2,000-$2,500**

Plate, 7 1/2" d., Carnation mold, decorated w/pink roses, lavender ground, satin finish.. **$400-$500**

Plate, 8 1/2" d., Gibson Girl portrait decoration, maroon bonnet .... **$800-$1,200**

Plate, 8 1/2" d., Mold 263, pink & white roses decoration............................... **$175-$200**

Plate, 8 3/4" d., Mold 278, center decoration of pink poppies on white ground, green border.. **$175-$200**

Mold 91 Rose-decorated Plate

Plate, 8 3/4" d., Mold 91, yellow roses decoration on pink ground, shiny yellow border (ILLUS.)...................................... **$200-$300**

Plate, 9 3/4" d., Icicle mold, swan decoration .... **$800-$900**

Plate, 11" d., Point & Clover mold, Melon Eaters decoration........................... **$900-$1,100**

Plate, dessert, Mold 506, branches of pink roses & green leaves against a shaded bluish green to white ground w/shadow flowers & satin finish .... **$100-$125**

Relish dish, Iris mold (Mold 25), oval w/scalloped sides & end loop handles, Spring Season portrait surrounded by dark border w/iris, 4 1/2 x 9 1/2" . **$1,500-$1,800**

Relish dish, scene of masted ship, 4 1/2 x 9 1/2".................................... **$250-$300**

Relish dish, Mold 82, decorated w/forget-me-nots & multicolored carnations, six jeweled domes.................................. **$125-$175**

Spooner/vase, Mold 502, three-handled, decorated w/delicate roses & gold trim, unsigned, 4 1/4" h. .... **$75-$100**

Syrup pitcher & underplate, Mold 507, white & pink roses on a shaded brown to pale yellow ground, 2 pcs. .... **$200-$250**

Tea set: cov. teapot, creamer & cov. sugar bowl; floral decoration, the set .... **$300-$350**

Tea set: cov. teapot, creamer & cov. sugar bowl; pedestal base, scene of Colonial children, 3 pcs.................................. **$600-$700**

Toothpick holder, ribbed hexagonal shape w/two handles, decorated w/colorful roses
.... **$265-$300**

Toothpick holder, three-handled, decorated w/white daisies on blue ground, gold handles & trim on top .... **$150-$175**

Tray, pierced handles, Mold 82, decorated w/full blossom red & pink roses, gold Royal Vienna mark, 8 x 11 1/8"........ **$250-$300**

Vase, 4" h., salesman's sample, handled, Mold 914, decorated w/large lilies & green foliage, raised beading around shoulder, gold handles, shaded green ground, artist-signed .... **$150-$250**

Vase, 5 1/2" h., cottage & mill scene decoration, cobalt trim .... **$600-$900**

Vase, 6 1/4" h., decorated w/brown & cream shadow flowers .... **$100-$200**

Vase, 8" h., cylindrical body w/incurved angled shoulder handles, decorated w/parrots on white satin ground, unmarked
.... **$2,200-$2,600**

R.S. Prussia Vases with Animals

Vase, 8" h., ovoid body w/wide shoulder tapering to cylindrical neck w/flared rim, decorated w/scene of black swans (ILLUS. left)
.... **$1,200-$1,500**

Vase, 10" h., ovoid body decorated w/scene of two tigers, pastel satin finish (ILLUS. right, previous page) .... **$5,500-$7,000**

Red Wing

Various potteries operated in Red Wing, Minnesota, from 1868, the most successful being the Red Wing Stoneware Co., organized in 1877. Merged with other local potteries through the years, it became known as Red Wing Union Stoneware Co. in 1906, and was one of the largest producers of utilitarian stoneware items in the United States. After a decline in the popularity of stoneware products, an art pottery line was introduced to compensate for the loss. This was reflected in a new name for the company, Red Wing Potteries, Inc., in 1936. Stoneware production ceased entirely in 1947, but vases, planters, cookie jars and dinnerwares of art pottery quality continued in production until 1967, when the pottery ceased operation altogether.

Red Wing Marks

Art Pottery

Red Wing Pottery Cookie Jar

Cookie jar, cov., barrel-shaped w/molded rim & wide cover w/disk finial, molded in relief w/cattails & the word "Cookies" against a stippled ground, dark brown bands at the rim & base w/tan center (ILLUS.) .... **$250-$300**

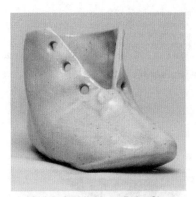

Model of a Miniature Baby Shoe

Model of a baby shoe, miniature, overall white glaze (ILLUS.)......................... **$450-$550**

Miniature Red Wing Spaniel Dog

Model of a dog, miniature, Staffordshire-style seated spaniel, white glaze w/blue eyes, 3" h. (ILLUS.)......................... **$250-$300**

Rare Red Wing Florist-style Vase

Vase, advertising florist-type, cylindrical w/flared base & molded flat rim, white glaze trimmed w/blue bands & blue rectangle enclosing "Alpha Floral Co.," early 20th c. (ILLUS., previous page) .. **$1,000-$1,200**

Dinnerwares & Novelties

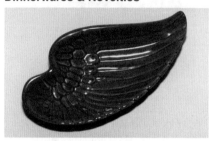

More Common Red Wing Ashtray

Ashtray, earthenware, model of a wing w/a deep red glaze, bottom marked earthenware, "Red Wing Potteries" (ILLUS.)..... **$50-$60**

Rare "Pretty Red Wing" Wing Ashtray

Ashtray, earthenware, "Pretty Red Wing" style, model of a large red-glazed wing embossed w/a bust profile of an Indian maiden (ILLUS.) .... **$400-$450**

Stoneware & Utility Wares

Baking dish, advertising-type, wide flat bottom w/deep sides w/molded graduating bands, overall glossy maroon glaze, dark blue printed advertising on inside bottom (ILLUS. of two views, bottom of page) .... **$375-$425**

Sponged Advertising Baking Dish

Baking dish, advertising-type, wide flat bottom w/deep sides w/molded graduating bands, overall red & blue sponging on white, printed advertising on the inside bottom (ILLUS.)................................. **$375-$425**

Brown & White Advertising Bean Pot

Bean pot, cov., advertising-type, wide bulbous flat-bottomed body tapering to a molded cylindrical wide neck flanked by loop handles, inset cover, dark brown glazed cover & upper body, white lower body printed w/blue Minnesota advertising (ILLUS.)....................................... **$100-$125**

Two Views of a Maroon Baking Dish with Interior Advertising

Two Views of a Blue-glazed Red Wing Advertising 1/2-Pint Bowl

Two Miniature Red Wing Bowls

Red Wing Saffron Ware Ribbed & Banded Bowl

Bowl, nappie-style, Saffron ware, ribbed sides below the wide flat rim decorated w/a white band flanked by thin brown bands (ILLUS.) .... **$250-$300**

Bowl, mixing-type, advertising-type, rounded bottom w/thick flat rim band, blue-glazed exterior, white-glazed interior w/printed blue advertising, 1/2 pt. (ILLUS. of two views, top of page) .... **$400-$500**

Bowl, miniature, 3" d., 1 1/4" h., rounded base w/wide flat rim, overall black sponging on white (ILLUS. right with other miniature bowl, second from top of page) ... **$600-$700**

Bowl, miniature, 3" d., 1 1/4" h., rounded brown base w/wide flat white rim (ILLUS. left with other miniature bowl, second from top of page)............................... **$600-$700**

Bowl, 5" d., deep rounded paneled sides & a wide molded rim, overall red & blue sponging on white (ILLUS.).............. **$550-$650**

Rare Small Ribbed & Sponged Bowl

Bowl, 5" d., wide ribs around the lower body, wide flat rim, overall red & blue sponging (ILLUS.) .... **$375-$425**

Small Blue-banded Saffron Ware Bowl

Bowl, 5" d., Saffron Ware, wide ribs around the lower base, wide flat rim w/two thin blue bands (ILLUS.) .... **$225-$250**

Rare Small Paneled & Sponged Bowl

Rare Small Ribbed & Sponged Bowl

Bowl, 5" d., rounded bowl w/narrow ribs below the thick flat rim, overall red & blue sponging on a tan ground (ILLUS.)... **$375-$425**

Small Blue & White Greek Key Bowl

Bowl, 6" d., embossed Greek Key patt., pale blue on white glaze (ILLUS.)..... **$125-$145**

Rare Deep Cap-style Sponged Bowl

Bowl, 7" d., cap-style, footed deep cylindrical form w/narrow molded bands & molded rim, overall red & blue sponging on white (ILLUS.) .... **$1,000-$1,200**

Saffron Ware Sponged 7" Bowl

Bowl, 7" d., Saffron Ware, deep rounded bowl w/narrow ribbing below the thick flat rim, overall red & blue sponging (ILLUS.)
.... **$100-$125**

Large Ribbed & Blue-banded Bowl

Bowl, 9" d., white-glazed, deep rounded bowl w/narrow molded ribs below the thick flat rim trimmed w/two blue bands (ILLUS.).. **$75-$100**

Blue & Pink-Banded Saffron Bowl

Bowl, 10" d., Saffron ware, deep rounded & ribbed sides w/pink & blue bands below the thick flat rim w/matching bands (ILLUS.) .... **$75-$125**

Large Paneled & Sponged Bowl

Bowl, 11" d., deep rounded paneled sides & a wide molded rim, overall red & blue sponging on white (ILLUS.).............. **$325-$350**

Three All-Blue Red Wing Bowls

Bowls, mixing-type, deep fluted base & wide flat rim, overall dark blue glaze, bottom marked "Red Wing USA," 5", 6" & 7" d., each (ILLUS. of three) .... **$125-$145**

Miniature Commemorative Butter Churn

Butter churn, cov., miniature, advertising-
and commemorative-type, swelled cylindrical body w/a flared rim, eared handles
& original cover w/wooden dasher, white-
glazed w/blue script number above a pair
of printed birch leaves above a printed
oval w/advertising, also marked "Iowa
Chapter Red Wing Collectors Society
2nd Annual Conf. 1994," 4" h. (ILLUS.) **$127**

Two Churns with Leaves Marks

Butter churn, cov., tapering cylindrical
body w/molded rim, eared handles & inset cover, white-glazed w/a large blue
printed size number above a pair of
birch leaves over the oval Red Wing
Union Stoneware fancy "ski" mark, 2 gal.
(ILLUS. left with 4-gallon churn)....... **$550-$600**

Small 2-Gallon Red Wing Butter Churn

Butter churn, cov., tapering cylindrical
body w/molded rim & inset cover, white-
glazed w/a large blue printed size number above a 4" red wing mark & the blue
oval Red Wing Union Stoneware mark, 2
gal. (ILLUS.)..................................... **$475-$525**

Rare 3-Gallon Advertising Butter Churn

Butter churn, advertising-type, tall slightly
tapering cylindrical white-glazed body
w/thick molded rim & eared handles,
printed black "3" above two large birch
leaves, printed rectangle w/Nebraska advertising, 3 gal. (ILLUS.) .... **$4,000-$4,500**

Churn with Fancy Red Wing "Ski" Mark

Butter churn, cov., tapering cylindrical
body w/molded rim & inset cover, white-
glazed w/a large blue printed size number above a 4" red wing mark & the blue
oval Red Wing Union Stoneware fancy
"ski" mark, 3 gal. (ILLUS.)................. **$450-$500**

Butter churn, cov., tapering cylindrical body w/molded rim & inset cover, white-glazed w/a large blue printed size number above a pair of birch leaves over the oval Red Wing Union Stoneware fancy "ski" mark, 4 gal. (ILLUS. right with 2-gallon churn, previous page)................. **$450-$500**

Very Rare Red Wing 4-Gallon Churn

Butter churn, tall slightly tapering cylindrical salt-glazed body w/thick molded rim & eared handles, cobalt blue slip-quilled "4" above a large leaf, impressed Red Wing Stoneware mark on the side, 4 gal. (ILLUS.) .... **$3,000-$3,500**

5-Gallon Red Wing Butter Churn

Butter churn, cov., tapering cylindrical body w/molded rim & inset cover, white-glazed w/a large blue printed size number above a large 6" red wing mark & the blue oval Red Wing Union Stoneware fancy "ski" mark, 5 gal. (ILLUS.)........ **$550-$600**

Large Rare Red Wing Butter Churn

Butter churn, tall slightly tapering cylindrical salt-glazed body w/thick molded rim & eared handles, cobalt blue slip-quilled "6" above a butterfly & flower design, unsigned, 6 gal. (ILLUS.) .... **$2,500-$3,000**

Banded Advertising Butter Crock

Butter crock, cov., advertising-type, cylindrical w/molded rim & inset cover, white glaze w/wide reddish pink bands at the rim & base, printed black rectangle enclosing advertising (ILLUS.) .... **$350-$400**

Butter crock, cov., Gray Line (Sponge Band) style, narrow flaring foot below the cylindrical ribbed body w/a narrow orange sponged band flanked by thin blue bands under the molded rim, inset matching cover, wire bail handle w/turned wooden grip, 3 lb. (ILLUS., next page).. **$550-$600**

Gray Line (Sponge Band) Butter Crock

Rare 10-lb. Banded Advertising Butter Crock

Butter crock, cov., advertising-type, deep cylindrical form w/molded rim, decorated w/pairs of blue bands at the top & bottom,

a large blue printed rectangle w/Chicago advertising in center, 10 lb. (ILLUS.) .... **$2,000-$2,500**

Very Large Red Wing Butter Crock

Butter crock, wide cylindrical body w/molded rim, white-glazed, printed w/a large dark blue rectangle w/"20 lbs." above a 4" red wing mark, 20 lb. (ILLUS.) .... **$1,000-$1,200**

Butter crocks, advertising-type, cylindrical w/molded rim, white-glazed, each w/a printed blue rectangle w/advertising, various sizes, each (ILLUS. of three, bottom of page) .... **$150-$300**

Rare Embossed & Sponged Casserole

Casserole, cov., wide rounded flat-bottomed bowl w/embossed leaves & flowers & a molded rim, low domed cover w/button finial, overall red & blue sponging on white (ILLUS.) .... **$900-$1,000**

Three Sizes of Advertising Butter Crocks

Two Gray Line (Sponge Band) Red Wing Casseroles

Casserole, cov., Gray Line (Sponge Band) type, deep flat-bottomed bowl w/molded ribbing below a narrow orange sponged band flanked by thin blue bands, inset slightly domed cover w/button finial & matching decoration, 4 1/2" d. (ILLUS. left with larger casserole, top of page) ..... **$500-$550**

Casserole, cov., Gray Line (Sponge Band) type, deep flat-bottomed bowl w/molded ribbing below a narrow orange sponged band flanked by thin blue bands, inset slightly domed cover w/button finial & matching decoration, 5 3/4" d. (ILLUS. right with smaller casserole, top of page) .... **$500-$550**

Rare 2-Gallon Molded Pantry Jar Cover

Cover, for pantry jar, slightly domed, white glazed decorated w/double blue stripes & a center ring of embossed petals, 2 gal. (ILLUS.)... **$650-$700**

Red Wing 3-Gallon Water Cooler Cover

Cover, for water cooler, slightly domed, white glaze decorated w/double blue stripes & a center ring of embossed petals, 3 gal. (ILLUS.) .... **$350-$400**

Half-Gallon Advertising Honey Crock

Crock, advertising-type, cylindrical w/molded rim, white glaze printed in black w/an oval enclosing Wisconsin honey advertising, 1/2 gal. (ILLUS.) .... **$200-$250**

1-Gallon Red Wing Advertising Crock

Crock, advertising-type, cylindrical w/molded rim, white glaze printed in blue w/an oval enclosing Nebraska advertising, 1 gal. (ILLUS.)................................. **$1,000-$1,500**

Red Wing 3- & 5-Gallon Crocks

Two Slip-decorated Red Wing Crocks

Crock, cylindrical salt glazed body w/molded rim & eared handles, cobalt blue slip-quilled "3" above a lazy eight & target design, unsigned, 3 gal. (ILLUS. right with 5-gallon crock, top of page).............. **$150-$200**

Crock, cylindrical salt-glazed body w/molded rim & eared handles, cobalt blue slip-quilled "3" above a lazy eight & target design, side stamped "Red Wing Stoneware," 3 gal. (ILLUS. left with 4-gallon crock, second from top of page).. **$900-$1,000**

Crock, cylindrical salt-glazed body w/molded rim & eared handles, cobalt blue slip-quilled "4" above a lazy eight & target design, side stamped "Red Wing Stoneware," 4 gal. (ILLUS. right with 3-gallon crock, second from top of page).. **$900-$1,000**

Crock, cylindrical salt glazed body w/molded rim & eared handles, cobalt blue slip-quilled "5" above a red cage design, unsigned, 5 gal. (ILLUS. left with 3-gallon crock, top of page) .... **$275-$325**

Crock, cylindrical w/molded rim, white glaze printed w/a large blue size number, large red wing logo & the oval mark of the Red Wing Union Stoneware Company, 5 gal. (ILLUS., top next column) .... **$175-$200**

Crock, cylindrical salt-glazed body w/molded rim & eared handles, cobalt blue slip-quilled "6" above a large leaf, side stamped "RWSCo.," 6 gal. (ILLUS., bottom next column)......................... **$1,000-$1,200**

Red Wing Crock with Wing & Oval Marks

Rare Red Wing Decorated 6-Gallon Crock

Group of Rare Red Wing Advertising Fruit Jars

Two Union Stoneware Stone Mason Fruit Jars

Fruit (or canning) jar, cylindrical w/angled shoulder & twist-off metal lid, blue-printed Stone Mason Fruit Jar logo, 1 qt. (ILLUS. left with gallon jar) .... **$275-$300**

Fruit (or canning) jar, cylindrical w/angled shoulder & twist-off metal lid, blue-printed Stone Mason Fruit Jar logo, 1 gal. (ILLUS. right with quart jar) .... **$900-$1,100**

Fruit (or canning) jar, dome-top style, twist-on metal lid, printed blue shield logo of the Red Wing Union Stoneware Company, 1 gal. (ILLUS., next column) .... **$4,500-$5,500**

Fruit (or canning) jar, cov., cylindrical body w/sloping shoulder to a small mouth w/original screw-on zinc lid, Bristol glaze

w/blue printed square printed "Stone Mason Fruit Jar - Union Stoneware Co. - Red Wing, Minn.," also impressed on the bottom "Pat. Jan 24, 1899," ca. 1899, 1 gal., 10 1/2" h. (surface chip on very bottom front edge, overall light blue drip stain from use) **$385**

Very Rare Gallon Red Wing Fruit Jar

Fruit (or canning) jars, advertising-type, cylindrical w/angled shoulder & twist-off metal lids, Stone Mason-type, each w/panels of printed advertising on the front, each (ILLUS. of three, top of page) .... **$2,800-$3,200**

Front & Back of Miniature Red Wing Advertising Jug

Three Miniature Brown & White Advertising Jugs

Jug, advertising-type, short cylindrical white body w/a tapering brown neck & handle, front w/blue-printed advertising, small red wing mark at the back (ILLUS. of front & back, bottom previous page) .... **$550-$650**

white bottom printed in blue w/advertising for the Merchant's Hotel, St. Paul, Minn., 1/8 pt. (ILLUS. left with two other miniature jugs, top of page) .... **$550-$650**

Advertising Beehive Jug with Birch Leaves

Jug, beehive-shaped, advertising-type, white glaze, printed blue birch leaves mark & an oval panel w/Kansas advertising (ILLUS.) .... **$3,500-$4,000**

Jug, miniature, advertising-type, cylindrical w/rounded shoulder & small neck, white glaze printed w/oval mark for the Red Wing Union Stoneware Co. (ILLUS., next column) .... **$600-$700**

Jug, miniature, advertising-type, fancy-type beehive-shaped w/brown top above a

Miniature Red Wing Union Stoneware Jug

Jug, miniature, advertising-type, fancy-type beehive-shaped w/brown top above a white bottom printed in blue w/advertising for J.D. Parker, Lincoln, Nebraska, 1/8 pt. (ILLUS. right with two other miniature jugs, top of page) .... **$1,000-$1,300**

Jug, miniature, advertising-type, fancy-type beehive-shaped w/brown top above a white bottom printed in blue w/advertising for the Victoria Sanatorium, Colfax, Iowa, 1/8 pt. (ILLUS. center with two other miniature jugs, top of page) .... **$1,000-$1,300**

Two Views of Rare Labeled Minnesota Stoneware Miniature Jug

Three Varied Brown & White Red Wing Miniature Souvenir Jugs

Jug, miniature, beehive-shaped, overall dark brown glaze, original yellow paper label for the Minnesota Stoneware Company on the base, 1/8 pt. (ILLUS. of side & bottom, bottom previous page) .... **$1,000-$1,200**

Minnesota-Michigan Miniature Jug

Jug, miniature, fancy-style, white base & brown shoulder, printed in blue "Minnesota - Michigan," 1/8 pt. (ILLUS.) ...... **$275-$325**

Very Rare Miniature Blue-sponged Jug

Jug, miniature, fancy-type, overall dark blue sponging, unsigned, 1/4 pt. (ILLUS.) .... **$2,500-$3,000**

Jug, miniature, souvenir-type, cone-top style, cylindrical white base & brown shoulder, printed in blue "Souvenir of Red Wing" (ILLUS. left with two other brown & white miniature jugs, top of page) .... **$450-$550**

Rare Miniature Convention Souvenir Jug

Jug, miniature, souvenir-type, cylindrical white body w/rounded brown shoulder, printed on the base w/the emblem of the Minnesota State Federation of Labor w/dates of its 1909 convention (ILLUS.) .... **$700-$800**

Jug, miniature, souvenir-type, fancy style, white base & brown shoulder, printed in blue "Souvenir of Red Wing" (ILLUS. right with two other brown & white miniature jugs, top of page) .... **$600-$700**

Jug, miniature, souvenir-type, fancy style, white base & brown shoulder, printed in black "Excelsior Springs, MO - 1903" (ILLUS. left with other fancy style miniature jug, top next page) .... **$375-$425**

Jug, miniature, souvenir-type, fancy style, white base & brown shoulder, printed in blue "Souvenir - Excelsior Springs, Missouri" (ILLUS. right with other fancy style miniature jug, top next page) .... **$350-$400**

Two Fancy Style Miniature Souvenir Jugs

Three Miniature Ovoid Souvenir Jugs

Jug, miniature, souvenir-type, shoulder-type style, cylindrical white base & brown shoulder, printed in blue "Souvenir of Red Wing" (ILLUS. center with two other brown & white miniature jugs, top of previous page)...................................... **$800-$900**

Jug, miniature, souvenir-type, white ovoid body tapering to a brown rim, printed in blue w/the Moose Lodge logo & the dates of its 1930 convention (ILLUS. left with two other miniature souvenir jugs, second from top of page)........................ **$600-$700**

Jug, miniature, souvenir-type, white ovoid body tapering to a brown rim, printed in blue w/"Souvenir of Red Wing" (ILLUS. center with two other ovoid souvenir jugs, second from top of page) .... **$650-$750**

Jug, miniature, souvenir-type, white ovoid body tapering to a brown rim, printed in blue w/Elks Lodge logo & dates of its 1929 convention (ILLUS. right with two other ovoid miniature souvenir jugs, second from top of page)........................ **$600-$700**

Jug, beehive-shaped, overall dark brown glaze, mark on bottom for the Minnesota Stoneware Company, 1/2 gal. (ILLUS., next column).. **$75-$95**

Minnesota Stoneware Brown Jug

Very Rare Decorated Red Wing Jug

Jug, beehive-shaped, salt-glazed & decorated w/a slip-quilled "5" above a large leaf, impressed mark of the Red Wing Stoneware Company on the side, 5 gal. (ILLUS.)...................................... **$7,000-$9,000**

Red Wing 5-Gallon Beehive Jug

Jug, beehive-shaped, white w/blue printed size number & oval mark of the Red Wing Union Stoneware Co. & the 4" red wing, 5 gal. (ILLUS.) .... **$400-$450**

Jug, shoulder-style, cylindrical body w/rounded shoulder & small neck, white glaze, printed blue size number, oval Red Wing Union Stoneware mark & a 4" red wing, 5 gal., 18" h. (ILLUS., top next column) **$173**

Red Wing 5-Gallon Marked Jug

Extremely Rare Sample Master Waste Jar

Master waste jar, cov., miniature, embossed Lily patt., salesman's sample, w/original wire bail handle, 4" h. (ILLUS.) .... **$6,000-$7,000**

Rare Miniature Red Wing Doctor's Bag

Model of a doctor's bag, miniature, overall dark brown glaze (ILLUS.) .... **$800-$1,000**

Four Various Blue-banded Red Wing Pantry Jars

Pantry jar, advertising-type, cylindrical w/molded rim, white glaze w/blue band trim, red wing mark on one side & printed blue rectangle w/South Dakota advertising on the other .... **$1,200-$1,500**

Blue-banded Red Wing Pantry Jar

Pantry jar, cov., advertising-type, cylindrical w/molded rim & ringed domed cover, white glaze w/double blue bands at the top & bottom, printed blue rectangle w/Nebraska advertising, red wing mark (ILLUS.)... **$900-$1,000**

Pantry jar, cov., cylindrical w/molded rim, decorated w/double blue bands & a large red wing mark, 1 lb. (ILLUS. far left with three other pantry jars, top of page).. **$650-$750**

Pantry jar, cov., cylindrical w/molded rim, decorated w/double blue bands & a large red wing mark, 3 lb. (ILLUS. second from right with three other pantry jars, top of page).. **$750-$850**

Pantry jar, cov., cylindrical w/molded rim, decorated w/double blue bands & a large red wing mark, 5 lb. (ILLUS. second from left with three other pantry jars, top of page).. **$650-$750**

Pantry jar, cov., cylindrical w/molded rim, decorated w/double blue bands & a large red wing mark, 1 gal. (ILLUS. far right with three other pantry jars, top of page) .... **$900-$1,000**

Red Wing Brown & White Pipkin

Pipkin, cov., squatty bulbous pitcher-form body tapering to a wide flat mouth w/rim spout, C-form handle, white glaze on top half, brown glaze on lower half, marked "Minnesota Stoneware Co.," 3 pt. (ILLUS.) .... **$200-$250**

Two Rare Red Wing Embossed & Sponged Advertising Pitchers

Three Blue-trimmed Red Wing Cherry Band Pitchers

Pitcher, advertising-type, embossed Cherry Band patt., cylindrical w/overall red & blue sponging, blue rectangle on front w/printed advertising (ILLUS. left with bulbous floral sponged pitcher, bottom previous page) .... **$2,000-$2,250**

Pitcher, advertising-type, embossed florals, bulbous body w/overall red & blue sponging, printed Iowa advertising inside the bottom (ILLUS. right with Cherry Band sponged pitcher, bottom previous page) .... **$2,000-$2,250**

Pitcher, shorter cylindrical hall-boy style w/molded rings, overall blue sponging .... **$700-$800**

Pitcher, tapering cylindrical body w/ringed base, wide rim spout & angled handle, embossed scene of Dutch boy & girl, white glaze w/dark blue overglazing on lower half, Red Wing Union circle mark on base, largest size (ILLUS. at right with three smaller sizes, top of page 492) .... **$2,000-$2,500**

Pitcher, 6" h., embossed Cherry Band patt., advertising-type, white glaze w/blue bands around rim & base & a large blue rectangle w/Nebraska advertising below the spout (ILLUS. center with two other Cherry Band pitchers, top of page 491) .... **$1,000-$1,200**

Pitcher, 6" h., embossed Cherry Band patt., white glaze w/light blue bands around rim & base (ILLUS. center with two other Cherry Band pitchers, top of page) ... **$375-$425**

Pitcher, 7 1/2" h., Gray Line ware, advertising-type, tapering cylindrical body w/molded ribbing below an orange sponged band & blue pinstripes, printed

blue advertising dated 1929 at top, molded rim spout & angled handle (ILLUS. right with other Gray Line pitcher, bottom of page).. **$750-$850**

Pitcher, 7 1/2" h., Gray Line ware, tapering cylindrical body w/molded ribbing below an orange sponged band & blue pinstripes, molded rim spout & angled handle (ILLUS. left with advertising pitcher, bottom of page)................................ **$300-$350**

Red Wing Potteries Pitcher with Irises

Pitcher, 7 3/4" h., tapering cylindrical body w/wide spout & angled handle, molded large cluster of irises & leaves, overall dark brown glaze, Red Wing Potteries, ca. 1940 (ILLUS.)............. **$300-$400**

Two Red Wing Gray Line Pitchers

Three Various Cherry Band Advertising Pitchers

Pitcher, 8 1/4" h., embossed Cherry Band patt., advertising-type, white glaze w/blue bands around rim & base & a large blue oval w/Nebraska advertising below the spout (ILLUS. right with two other Cherry Band pitchers, top of page) .... **$800-$1,000**

Pitcher, 8 1/4" h., embossed Cherry Band patt., white glaze w/light blue bands around rim & base (ILLUS. left with two other Cherry Band pitchers, top previous page)... **$250-$350**

Unique Cherry Band Advertising Pitcher

Pitcher, 9 1/4" h., embossed Cherry Band patt., advertising-type, white glaze w/large blue rectangle w/unique printed image of a two-story store above advertising dated 1914 (ILLUS.) .... **$3,000-$3,500**

Pitcher, 9 1/4" h., embossed Cherry Band patt., advertising-type, white glaze w/blue bands around rim & base & a large blue oval w/Nebraska advertising below the spout (ILLUS. left with two other Cherry Band pitchers, top of page) .... **$1,000-$1,500**

Pitcher, 9 1/4" h., embossed Cherry Band patt., white glaze w/light blue bands around rim & base (ILLUS. right with two

other Cherry Band pitchers, top of previous page)... **$350-$400**

Very Rare Red Wing Sponged Hall Boy

Pitcher, 9 1/4" h., tall cylindrical hall-boy style w/molded rings, overall red & blue sponging (ILLUS.) .... **$3,500-$4,000**

Two Red Wing Blue-sponged Pitchers

Pitcher, 9 1/4" h., tall cylindrical hall-boy style w/molded rings, overall blue sponging (ILLUS. left with shorter blue-sponged pitcher) .... **$600-$800**

Four Red Wing Dutch Boy & Girl Pitchers

Two Red Wing Saffron Ware Advertising Pitchers

Two Red Wing Poultry Drinking Founts

Pitchers, tapering cylindrical body w/ringed base, wide rim spout & angled handle, embossed scene of Dutch boy & girl, white glaze w/dark blue overglazing on lower half, Red Wing Union circle mark on bases, each of three smaller sizes (ILLUS. at left with largest size, top of page) .... **$1,000-$1,200**

Pitchers, 6 1/2" h., advertising-type, Saffron Ware, yellowware, tapering cylindrical body w/molded ribbing below thin white & brown bands below blue-printed advertising, pointed rim spout & angled handle, each (ILLUS. of two, second from top of page) .... **$300-$350**

Poultry drinking fount, bell-style, advertising-type, cylindrical w/domed shoulder & small mouth, white-glazed w/blue rectangular w/advertising "Oak Leaf - Simmons Hardware Co. - Made in U.S.A.," w/original wide underplate, 1 gal. (ILLUS. left with quart fount top, third from top of page) .... **$200-$250**

Red Wing Advertising Poultry Fount

Poultry drinking fount, bell-style, advertising-type, cylindrical w/domed shoulder & small mouth, white-glazed w/printed blue circle w/Iowa advertising, complete w/underplate, 1 gal., 9" h. (ILLUS.).................... **$196**

Poultry drinking fount, Eureka-style, cylindrical, oval Red Wing Union Stoneware mark, 1 gal. (ILLUS. right with 2-gallon fount, bottom of page)....................... **$175-$225**

Poultry drinking fount, Eureka-style, cylindrical, oval Union Stoneware Co. blue mark & Minnesota Stoneware Co. mark on the bottom, 2 gal. (ILLUS. left with 1-gallon fount, bottom of page) .... **$350-$400**

Poultry drinking fount top, bell-style, advertising-type, cylindrical w/domed shoulder & small mouth, white-glazed w/blue rectangular w/wording "Red Wing - Poultry Drinking Fount - and - Buttermilk Feeder," 1 qt., top only (ILLUS. right with complete fount, previous page)......... **$200-$250**

Refrigerator jar, advertising-type, short cylindrical stacking-type w/molded rim, white glaze decorated w/blue band & printed w/advertising for a Nebraska merchant, early 20th c. (ILLUS., top next column)... **$500-$600**

Red Wing Advertising Refrigerator Jar

Short Red Wing Refrigerator Jar

Refrigerator jar, stacking-type, short wide cylindrical form w/molded rim, white glaze printed w/blue bands & "Red Wing Refrigerator Jar," early 20th c. (ILLUS.) .... **$250-$350**

Very Rare Red Wing Stoneware Spittoon

Spittoon, deep cylindrical salt-glazed form w/top opening & oval side drain opening, double-stamped on the side "Red Wing Stoneware Company" (ILLUS.)... **$3,000-$3,500**

Two Red Wing Eureka-style Poultry Drinking Founts

Red Wing Stoneware 3- and 5-Gallon Water Coolers

Water cooler, bulbous barrel-shaped body w/wide cylindrical neck & molded rim, cylindrical base band w/metal spigot, Red Wing Union Stoneware oval mark & red wing below "3 - Water Cooler" in blue, trimmed w/blue bands, wire bail handles w/wooden grips, no cover, 3 gal. (ILLUS. left with 5-gallon water cooler, top of page) .... **$500-$600**

Water cooler, bulbous barrel-shaped body w/wide cylindrical neck & molded rim, cylindrical base band w/metal spigot, Red Wing Union Stoneware oval mark & red wing below "5 - Water Cooler" in blue, trimmed w/blue bands, wire bail handles w/wooden grips, no cover, 5 gal. (ILLUS. right with 3-gallon water cooler, top of page) .... **$350-$450**

Very Rare Red Wing Stoneware Cooler

Water cooler, slightly tapering cylindrical salt-glazed body w/molded rim & eared handle, molded hexagonal spigot hole at bottom front, blue slip-quilled "8" above a stylized daisy, side stamped "Red Wing Stoneware Co.," 8 gal. (ILLUS.) . **$8,000-$10,000**

Redware

Red earthenware pottery was made in the American colonies from the late 1600s. Bowls,

crocks and all types of utilitarian wares were turned out in great abundance to supplement the pewter and handmade treenware. The ready availability of the clay, the same used in making bricks and roof tiles, accounted for the vast production. The lead-glazed redware retained its reddish color, although a variety of colors could be obtained by adding various metals to the glaze. Interesting effects occurred accidentally through unsuspected impurities in the clay or uneven temperatures in the firing kiln, which sometimes resulted in streaks or mottled splotches.

Redware pottery was seldom marked by the maker.

Large Old Redware Bowl

Bowl, 14 1/2" d., 4" h., flat-bottom w/widely flaring angled side, orange ground w/streaking dark brown decoration, probably New England, first half 19th c. (ILLUS.) .. **$345**

Rare Early English Redware Dish

Dish, deep round shape, tan-glazed & incised impressed w/tight scrolls, leaf sprigs & the monogram "BC" at the top & "1764" at the bottom, England, 10 7/8" d. (ILLUS., previous page) **$2,115**

Early Redward Fish Food Mold

Food mold, modeled as a jumping fish w/detailed scales & fins on the interior, brown-daubed glaze, edge chips, 19th c., 10" l. (ILLUS.) **$173**

Rare Early Basket-form Redware Jar

Jar, basket-shaped, ovoid body w/thick molded rim & applied arched handle, running daubs of manganese glaze, glaze flakes, missing cover, attributed to Pennsylvania, 19th c., 7 1/2" h. (ILLUS.) **$2,530**

Jar, bulbous ovoid body tapering to a rolled neck, light green glaze overall on exterior, 19th c., some minor rim roughness, 7" d., 9" h. (ILLUS., top next column) **$1,495**

Jar, bulbous ovoid body tapering to a short neck, lead-glazed w/olive green streaked w/manganese & yellowish orange halos, glaze losses, rim chip, New England, late 18th - early 19th c., 9 1/2" h. (ILLUS., middle next column) **$1,998**

Jar, bulbous ovoid body tapering to a wide flat mouth, eared handles, green glaze w/orange lines resembling surface cracks, 19th c., two small rim chips, some glaze roughness, 5 1/2" d., 6 1/2" h. **$173**

Rare Green-glazed Redware Jar

Early New England Redware Jar

Old Redware Covered Jar

Jar, cov., cylindrical w/tapering shoulder to a cupped mouth w/an inset cover, incised lines around rim & shoulder, lead glaze w/brown splotches, glass loss around rim, probably Connecticut, ca. 1830-60, 11" h. (ILLUS.) **$353**

Early Eastern U.S. Redware Jug

Jug, bulbous ovoid body tapering to a small mouth, applied reeded strap shoulder handle, incised lines around the shoulder, splotches of transparent olive green glaze on neck & shoulder, early United State, early 19th c., chips, glaze wear, 10 3/4" h. (ILLUS.) **$881**

Fine Redware Jug with Green Glaze

Jug, bulbous ovoid body w/a small neck & applied strap handle, light green glaze w/orange highlights, 19th c., 5" d., 6 1/4" h. (ILLUS.) **$1,265**

Pitcher, 7 3/8" h., ovoid body tapering to a coggled neck band & flaring neck w/pinched spout & coggled rim, applied reeded strap handle, lead-glazed w/brown mottling, probably New England, early 19th c. (ILLUS., top next column) **$499**

Pitcher, cov., 8 1/2" h., 7" d., tapering ovoid body w/short flaring rim w/pinch spout, applied strap handle, inset cover w/knob finial, green slip glaze streaked w/dark brown, wavy incised line at the neck, cover w/light brown glaze w/splotchy green & yellow, 19th c. (ILLUS., middle next column) **$4,313**

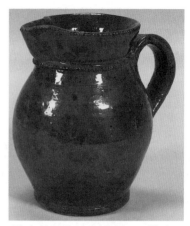

Early New England Redware Pitcher

Very Rare Redware Covered Pitcher

Footed Redware Pot

Pot, footed bulbous ovoid body w/a wide flat molded rim, orange glaze w/small red dots outside & inside, unglaze rim, small rim chip & tight hairline, 19th c., 6 1/2" d., 5 1/4" h. (ILLUS.) **$173**

Vinegar jug, ovoid body w/incised lines around the shoulder & base, applied reeded strap handle, speckled dark brown glaze, early 19th c., 6 1/8" h. (chips, glaze wear) **$176**

Rockingham Wares

The Marquis of Rockingham first established an earthenware pottery in the Yorkshire district of England around 1745, and it was occupied afterwards by various potters. The well-known mottled brown Rockingham glaze was introduced about 1788 by the Brameld Brothers and became immediately popular. It was during the 1820s that the production of true porcelain began at the factory, and it continued to be made until the firm closed in 1842. Since that time the so-called Rockingham glaze has been used by various potters in England and the United States, including some famous wares produced in Bennington, Vermont. Very similar glazes were also used by potteries in other areas of the United States including Ohio and Indiana, but only wares specifically attributed to Bennington should use that name. The following listings will include mainly wares featuring the dark brown mottled glaze produced at various sites here and abroad.

Rockingham Flask Based on a Glass Flask

Figural Woman Rockingham Inkwell

Inkwell, figural, modeled as a woman reclining asleep on an oblong rockwork base, yellowware w/overall mottled dark brown Rockingham glaze, several old edge chips, reportedly made by the Larkin Bros. Company, Newell, West Virginia, ca. 1850-80, 3 7/8" h. (ILLUS.) **$101**

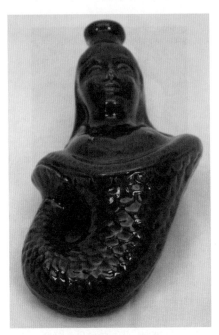

Rockingham Mermaid Flask

Flask, figural Mermaid design, dark brown glaze, ca. 1860, 8" h. (ILLUS.) **$187**

Flask, flattened ovoid shape tapering to a fluted neck & ringed mouth, molded on one side w/the American Eagle & on the other w/a morning glory vine, dark brown Rockingham glaze, No. G11-19, several old glaze chips, ca. 1840-60, pt. (ILLUS., top next column).. **$308**

Unusual Advertising Pig Jug

Jug, advertising-type, figural, model of a walking pig, impressed on the rear "Bieler's Ronny Club," yellowware w/a mottled brown Rockingham glaze, original white porcelain stopper marked "Brookfield Rye Bieler," reportedly from Cincinnati, Ohio, ca. 1880-1900, 9 1/2" l., 5 1/4" h. (ILLUS., previous page) **$1,232**

Model of a dog, seated spaniel facing viewer, on oblong base, yellowware w/an overall dark brown Rockingham glaze, hollow body w/open bottom, probably late 20th c., excellent condition, 4 1/2" h.... **$165**

Model of a dog, seated spaniel facing viewer, on oblong base, yellowware w/an overall dark brown Rockingham glaze, finely detailed fur & facial details, base molded w/acanthus leaf border, edge chips on base, small glaze chip on body, 12 1/2" h. **$345**

Rockingham Model of a Lion

Model of a lion, recumbent animal raised on a deep rectangular base, mottled dark brown glaze, restoration to minor surface roughness along base, ca. 1860, 6 3/4 x 9" (ILLUS.) **$303**

Rogers (John) Groups

Cast plaster and terra cotta figure groups made by John Rogers of New York City in the mid- to late 19th century were highly popular in their day. Many offer charming vignettes of Victorian domestic life or events of historic or literary importance, and those in good condition are prized today.

"Is It So Nominated in The Bond?," a scene from Shakespeare's "The Merchant of Venice," including Antonio Bassanio, Portia & Shylock, some restoration w/a new patina, 12 1/2 x 19 1/2", 23" h. (ILLUS., top next column) **$288**

Shakespeare Scene Rogers Group

"Parting Promise" John Rogers Group

"Parting Promise," the figure of a young man about to start on a journey standing & placing an engagement ring on her finger, molded title on the front of the oval base "Provenance," some surface chipping around base, 22" h. (ILLUS.) **$633**

Rip Van Winkle on Mountain Group

"Rip Van Winkle on The Mountain," figure of Rip holding his rifle & holding back his dog & standing over a mountain gnome w/a keg on his knee, old repaint w/some restoration, 9 x 9 1/2", 21" h. (ILLUS.) **$460**

Rip Van Winkle Returned Rogers Group

"Rip Van Winkle Returned," figure of Rip in ragged clothes standing in the gateway of his ruined old homestead, new patina, some restoration, 8 x 9", 21" h. (ILLUS.).... **$518**

"The Council of War," President Lincoln seated reading a document & flanked by General Grant & Secretary of State Stanton, patent-dated 1868, flaking to the surface & very minor chips, 24 1/2" h. (ILLUS., top next column)...... **$1,955**

"The Council of War," President Lincoln seated reading a document & flanked by General Grant & Secretary of State Stanton, version w/Stanton wiping his glasses over Lincoln's shoulder, patent-dated 1868, some minor chips, 24" h. (ILLUS., middle next column) **$2,645**

"The Council of War" Rogers Group

Rarer Version of "The Council of War"

Rare "The Traveling Magician" Group

"The Traveling Magician," an old man & a small boy seated below a raised stand w/the magician who pulls a rabbit out of a top hat, a young tambourine girl asleep beside the platform, titled on the front, base marked "Patented Nov 27, 1877," some restoration w/new patina, 23" h. (ILLUS., previous page) **$3,565**

Rogers Group of "The Wounded Scout"

"The Wounded Scout," a standing black man in ragged clothes supporting a wounded Union soldier, round base, some chipping & restoration, 8 1/2" d., 22 3/4" h. (ILLUS.) **$690**

Rookwood

Considered America's foremost art pottery, the Rookwood Pottery Company was established in Cincinnati, Ohio, in 1880 by Mrs. Maria Nichols Longworth Storer. To accurately record its development, each piece carried the Rookwood insignia or mark, was dated, and, if individually decorated, was usually signed by the artist. The pottery remained in Cincinnati until 1959, when it was sold to Herschede Hall Clock Company and moved to Starkville, Mississippi, where it continued in operation until 1967.

A private company is now producing a limited variety of pieces using original Rookwood molds.

Rookwood Mark

Rookwood Ashtrays with Moths

Ashtray, production-type, a rectangular dish w/a cigarette notch at each corner, a small upright rectangle at the back rim, the interior molded w/a band of moths, overall yellowish green Matte glaze, Shape No. 1669, 1910, 2 1/2 x 5" (ILLUS.) **$150**

Pair of Large Rook Rookwood Bookends

Bookends, figural, modeled as a large rook perched on an open book, dark brown glossy glaze, Shape No. 2274, 1916, chip to to of flower next to one rook, 6" h., pr. (ILLUS.) **$863**

Ivory Rookwood Galleon Bookends

Bookends, modeled as galleons under full sail, designed by William McDonald, Ivory Mat glass, Shape No. 2695, 1936, 5 1/2" h., pr. (ILLUS.) **$230**

Rookwood Bowl with Large Leaves

Bowl, 8 3/4" d., production ware, a small footring below the deep widely flaring sides w/a flat rim, the interior & exterior sides molded w/a band of large pointed leaves alternating w/small berry clusters,

light blue matte glaze, Shape No. 6430,
1945 (ILLUS.)... **$206**

Large Rookwood Arts & Crafts Bowl

Bowl, 10" d., 5" h., Arts & Crafts style, deep
rounded sides w/a wide closed rim, the
rim incised w/a bold geometric design of
repeating angular curls, dark green matte
glaze, No. 231Z, 1903 (ILLUS.) **$480**

Rookwood Production Bowl & Flower Frog

Bowl & flower frog, production ware, the
rounded bowl w/a flattened undulating
rim molded at one side w/a large stylized
blossom, the flower frog molded &
pierced in the form of water lilies &
leaves, both w/a light blue matte glaze,
1931, bowl 11" w., the set (ILLUS.)............ **$176**

Fine Rookwood Bowl-Vase with Swans

Bowl-vase, footed wide squatty bulbous
shape w/a short, wide neck, Standard
glaze, finely painted w/creamy flying
swans against a shaded brown ground,
ornate pierced & scrolling silver-overlay
designs w/hunting equipment up two
sides & around the neck, 1892, Kataro
Shirayamadani, 12" w. (ILLUS.)............ **$10,200**

Inverted Mushroom Chamberstick

Chamberstick, vegetal form resembling an
inverted large mushroom w/the cap forming the dished base incised w/fine lines &
w/a looped mushroom-shaped ring edge
handle, central stem w/socket resembles
a mushroom stem, mottled Matte green
glaze, Shape No. 331 Z, 1902, Anna Val-
entien, 4 3/8" h. (ILLUS.) **$748**

Bulbous Rookwood Standard Glaze Creamer

Creamer, four peg feet supporting the
squatty bulbous body w/a closed rim,
side spout & scrolled ring handle, Standard glaze, decorated w/golden clover &
green leaves on a shaded green, gold &
brown ground, Shape No. 616, 1897,
Constance Baker (ILLUS.) **$230**

Early Rookwood Dull Finish Creamer

Creamer, low rectangular form w/swelled
sides, a gilt rim spout at one end & an angled gilt handle at the other, the Dull Finish glaze in pale green decorated w/brick
red stylized blossoms on twigs, Shape
No. 43, 1885, Anna Marie Bookprinter,
2" h. (ILLUS.) **$173**

Group with a Rookwood Ewer, Pitcher & Two Vases

Ewer, footed very wide & thin disk-like lower body centered by a very tall slender neck w/a three-lobed incurved rim, a long slender handle from the rim to the shoulder, Standard glaze, decorated w/blue blossoms on leafy stems around the lower body, dark green & tan shaded to dark brown ground, 1894, Sadie Markland, 7" h. (ILLUS. far left with Rookwood pitcher & two vases, top of page)............... **$382**

Unusual Standard Glaze Fernery

Fernery & separate liner, wide flat-bottomed dish w/a shallow swelled round lower body tapering to a low flaring & finely scalloped rim, taller wide cylindrical liner, Standard glaze, the dish decorated on the exterior w/dark orange pansies against a shaded dark brown to green ground, Shape No. 652 C, 1897, Lenore Asbury, 9" d., 2 3/4" h., 2 pcs. (ILLUS.) **$575**

Rookwood Blue Figural Flower Frog

Flower frog, figural, a stylized seated faun on a large turtle, light blue Matte glaze, Shape No. 2336, 1922, some crazing & mild peppering, 6 3/4" h. (ILLUS.)............. **$173**

Square Blue Rookwood Inkwell

Inkwell, cov., footed slightly tapering square form w/beveled corners, square flat cover w/button finial, dark blue Matte glaze, includes original ink cup, Shape No. 2747, 1924, 3 1/2" h. (ILLUS.) **$317**

Standard Glaze Jug with Corn Decoration

Jug w/original stopper, ovoid body tapering to a small molded neck w/handle from rim to shoulder, pointed stopper, Standard glaze, decorated w/ears of golden corn & green leaves suspended from the top against a brown, dark green & brown shaded ground, Shape 512 A, 1899, Lenore Asbury, 10 1/4" h. (ILLUS.) **$1,150**

Rookwood Jug with Chevron Design

Jug w/original stopper, wide squatty bulbous body tapering to a small neck & molded rim, small arched shoulder handle, pointed & paneled stopper, the body incised w/a repeating design of chevrons in a red, green & purple matte glaze, Shape #274Z, 1901, A.M. Valentien, 8" h. (ILLUS.) **$1,440**

Rookwood Silver-Overlaid Sea Green Mug

Mug, gently tapering cylindrical form, shaded green ground decorated w/pale green clover leaves & red blossoms, silver-overlay flower embossed rim band continuing to form the long handle, Sea Green glaze, silver marked by Gorham, Sally E. Coyne, 1905, 5" d., 5 1/2" h. (ILLUS.) **$978**

Mug, slightly tapering cylindrical body w/large C-form handle, Standard glaze, decorated w/a scene of the Cheshire Cat grinning down from a tree branch, sterling silver overlay incised w/a floral & grasses design & a crest depicting a barrel & snake, silver by Gorham, 1892, Harriet W. Wilcox, 4 1/2" d., 5" h. (ILLUS., top next column)... **$3,220**

Rookwood Mug with Cheshire Cat

Small Matte Green Peacock Feather Pitcher

Pitcher, 4 1/4" h., gently flaring cylindrical body w/a tricorner wide mouth, angular side handle, Green Matte glaze, incised w/a tall stylized dark blue peacock feather at each corner, Shape No. 259 E, 1907, Albert Pons (ILLUS.)........................ **$748**

Rookwod Pitcher with Brownies

Pitcher, 6 1/4" h., 5 1/2" d., nearly spherical body tapering to a small neck w/a widely flaring rim w/pinched rim spout & extending into the strap handle, Standard glaze, decorated w/a group of Brownies playing tug-of-war w/an oak, in tones of yellow & green, enveloped by braided sterling silver by Gorham Mfg. Co., 1893, Bruce Horsfall (ILLUS.)..................................... **$2,875**

Pitcher, 7 1/2" h., bulbous base tapering to cylindrical sides w/a flat rim & long pinched rim spout, large D-form handle, Ivory Cameo glaze, a dark reddish brown shading to cream & pale green ground, decorated w/large stylized white blossoms on slender twigs, 1888, Harriet Wilcox (ILLUS. second from right with Rookwood ewer and two vases, top of page 502) **$470**

Early Crab-decorated Rookwood Pitcher

Pitcher, 8 1/4" h., 6 3/4" d., bulbous ovoid body w/a tall cylindrical neck & applied arched handle, in the Japanese style, h.p. w/large brown & red crabs on a speckled sea foam green ground, Albert R. Alentien, 1884 (ILLUS.).................................. **$2,300**

Rare Rookwood Pitcher with Sprite

Pitcher, 10 5/8" h., tankard-type, tapering cylindrical form w/a ringed base, small pinched rim spout & angled handle down the side, Standard glaze, decorated w/a winged sprite riding on the back of an omnious looking winged dragon, blackish

green shaded down to brown ground, Shape No. 564, 1891, Kataro Shirayamadani (ILLUS.)...................................... **$4,255**

Rookwood Misty Landscape Scenic Plaque

Plaque, rectangular, misty landscape w/slender leafy trees on the banks of a small river, Vellum glaze, ogee rosewood frame, 1914, Fred Rothenbusch, plaque 8 3/8 x 10 1/2" (ILLUS.) **$6,325**

Early Limoges-style Rookwood Plate

Plate, 10" d., Limoges-style decoration of a Japanese-style design of white rounded leaves & a blossom on a shaded dark brown ground, 1886, Matt Daley (ILLUS.) .. **$294**

Rookwood Stein with A. Jackson Portrait

Stein w/hinged pottery cover, balusterform body & domed cover, Standard glaze, decorated w/a bust portrait of Andrew Jackson, Shape 820, 1896, Sturgis Laurence, handle break w/old metalband repair, 9 3/4" h. (ILLUS.) **$5,750**

Rookwood Stein with Monkey Figures

Stein w/sterling silver cover, slightly tapering cylindrical body w/thin molded rings near the base, Standard glaze, decorated w/a scene of comical monkeys walking & carrying a bottle & scratching his head, Shape 537C, 1895, Bruce R. Horsfall, 7" h. (ILLUS.) **$6,038**

Rookwood Blue Ship Pattern Teapot

Teapot, cov., Dinnerware line, Blue Ship patt., ten-sided slightly tapering cylindrical body w/a flat shoulder w/inset cover w/knob finial, squared spout & angular handle, Shape M-18, ca. 1920s, 3 3/4" h. (ILLUS.).. **$115**

Rookwood Hi-glaze Vase with Blossoms

Vase, 4 1/2" h., wide bulbous ovoid body w/a wide flat rim, Hi-glaze, decorated around the lower half w/stylized pink & white flowers w/green leaves on brown stems, upper body in white w/a narrow streaky brown rim band, No. 931, 1931, Lorinda Epply (ILLUS.)............................. **$520**

Small Matte Glazed Nasturium Vase

Vase, 4 3/4" h., bulbous base tapering to a wide cylindrical neck, Matte glaze, decorated w/large pink & yellow stylized nasturium blossoms & green leafy stems on a turquoise blue ground, Shape No. 6101, 1939, Sallie Coyne (ILLUS.) **$460**

Vase, 5" h., baluster-form body w/a short flaring trumpet neck, Standard glaze, decorated w/braches of dark blue berries & dark green leaves against a dark green shading to blackish brown ground, 1899, Laura E. Lindeman (ILLUS. far right with Rookwood ewer, pitcher and other large vase, top of page 502) **$411**

Rare Small Dark Iris Glazed Fish Vase

Vase, 5 1/4" h., wide ovoid body tapering to a wide flat mouth, Dark Iris glaze, decorated around the center w/three large swimming green fish in a salmon & white current, the top & bottom bands in shaded dark green, Shape No. 942 D, 1906, E.T. Hurley (ILLUS.)............................... **$10,063**

French Red Glazed Floral Band Vase

Vase, 7" h., bulbous ovoid body w/a wide flat mouth, French Red glaze, a wide band around the shoulder w/deep pink blossoms clusters & green leaves flanked by a white della robbia-style bands all against a very dark grey ground, Shape No. 915 D, 1920, Sara Sax (ILLUS.).. **$6,613**

Rookwood Vase with Stormy Seas Scene

Vase, 7" h., simple ovoid body tapering to a small, short cylindrical neck, Vellum glaze, decorated w/a scene of a storm at sea w/boats in shades of darka blue, grey & cream, No. 900D, 1910, Fred Rothenbusch (ILLUS.)...................................... **$1,440**

Rookwood Brown & Green Matte Vase

Vase, 7" h., bulbous ovoid shape w/a wide flat rim, incised overall w/an organic design under a mottled dark brown & green matte glaze, Shape 915D, 1919, L.N. Lincoln (ILLUS.) **$720**

Vellum Glazed Vase with Flower Band

Vase, 7" h., slightly waisted cylindrical shape, Vellum glaze, a medium blue ground decorated around the base w/a band of pink & white flower clusters & stems on a dark blue ground, No. 1358E, 1925, Lenore Asbury (ILLUS.) **$1,560**

Jewel Porcelain Floral Vase

Vase, 7 1/4" h., 4 1/4" d., slightly tapering cylindrical body w/a wide flat mouth, Jewel Porcelain glaze, decorated w/large stylized peony blossoms in pink, blue & tan on brown leafy stems against a shaded grey ground, blue rim band, 1921, Arthur Conant (ILLUS.) **$5,750**

Exceptional Shirayamadani Iris Glaze vase

Rookwood Vase with Silver Overlay

Vase, 7 1/2" h., cylindrical body swelled at the top below the flat mouth, sterling silver overlay in Art Nouveau looping designs, Standard glaze, decorated w/orange tulips on green stems on a shaded dark green to brown ground, Shape 935N, 1904, Edith Noonan, on a carved squared wooden base (ILLUS.) **$1,955**

Vase, 7 3/4" h., gently tapering cylindrical form w/a short flared rim, Iris glass, decorated w/a continuous forest scene w/tall thin leafy trees & bushes against a blue shaded to pale pink sky, Shape No. 1658 E, Kataro Shirayamadani, 1911 (ILLUS., top next column)................................... **$16,675**

Vellum Glazed Vase with Landscape

Vase, 7 7/8" h., gently swelled cylindrical body w/a narrow flared rim, Vellum glaze, decorated w/a stylized landscape w/a house & barn in a wooded setting in shades of light & dark blue, lavender & green, Shape No. 808, 1923, Fred Rothenbusch (ILLUS.) **$3,910**

Vase, 8" h., simple swelled cylindrical body w/a small rolled neck, Standard glaze, decorated around the shoulder w/green maple leaves & pods against a very dark brown ground shading to reddishs tan, 1900, Leonore Asbury (ILLUS. second from left with Rookwood ewer, pitcher and smaller vase, top of page 502)............ **$441**

Large Standard Glaze Floral Vase

Vase, 13" h., large ovoid body tapering to a low rolled mouth, upturned loop shoulder handles, Standard glaze, decorated w/very large dark yellow & orange Cereus blooms on dark green stems against a shaded dark green ground, Shape No. 581 C, restoriation to one handle, 1894, Albert Valentien (ILLUS.) **$4,945**

Extraordinary Rookwood Vase

Vase, 11 3/4" h., 6 1/2" d., wide ovoid body tapering to a small trumpet neck, Sea Green glaze, decorated in relief w/a panoramic scene of a large sea gull flying above crashing waves at dawn, in tones of blue, pink, green & black, 1899, William P. McDonald (ILLUS.) **$69,000**

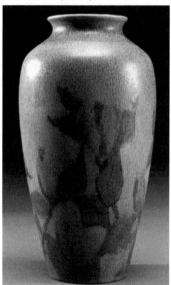

Fine Marine Vellum Rookwood Vase

Vase, 12 3/4" h., 7 1/2" d., ovoid body tapering to a flat mouth, Marine Vellum glaze, decorated w/a scene of ships at sea against a distant city skyline under grey clouds, in tones of cream, blue, green, brown & pink, 1916, Carl Schmidt (ILLUS.)... **$10,925**

Fine Rookwood Turquoise Matte Vase

Vase, 13" h., tall swelled cylindrical body tapering to a short rolled neck, Turquoise Matte glaze, a slightly mottled blue ground decorated around the lower half w/large stylized red flowers on green leafy stems, 1929, Jen Jensen (ILLUS.) **$1,645**

Rare Rookwood Silver-Overlay Vase

Vase, 13 1/4" h., 10 1/2" d., bulbous ovoid body tapering to a short flaring neck, Standard Glaze, shaded dark to light brown ground decorated w/large orange mums & green leaves, decorated w/ornate leafy scroll silver-overlay marked by Gorham, Matthew A. Daly, 1893 (ILLUS.) **$14,950**

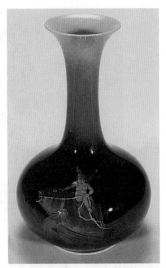

Rare Tall Rookwood Vase with Sprite

Vase, 14 1/2" h., footed wide squatty bulbous lower body tapering to a tall cylindrical neck w/a widely flaring rim, Standard glaze, painted w/a winged sprite riding a large green fish swimming through turbid water, dark blackish green shaded up to tan to gold neck, decorated by Kataro Shirayamadani, Shape No. 537, 1891 (ILLUS.).. **$5,750**

Very Rare Carved Black Iris Glazed Vase

Vase, 13 1/2" h., 6" d., gently swelled baluster-form body, rare Carved Black Iris glaze, decorated in large poppies in burgundy w/green leaves & pods carved in relief on a jet black ground, 1900, Matthew A. Daly (ILLUS.)........................... **$57,500**

Lovely Large Scenic Vellum Vase

Vase, 15" h., gently flared cylindrical body w/a narrow flat shoulder to a low cylindrical rim, Scenic Vellum glaze, decorated w/a misty landscape w/tall trees in the foreground & a wide waterway & meadow in the distance, in shades of dark & light greens, blues, pinks & cream, slight bruise at rim, light overall crazing, Shape No. 1369 B, 1912, Kataro Shirayamadani (ILLUS.).. **$8,050**

Rose Medallion Armorial Plates & a Rose Mandarin Shrimp Dish

Rose Medallion & Rose Canton

The lovely Chinese ware known as Rose Medallion was made through the past century and into the present one. It features alternating panels of people and flowers or insects, with most pieces having four medallions with a central rose or peony medallion. The ware is called Rose Canton if florals and birds or insects fill all the panels. Unless otherwise noted, our listing is for Rose Medallion ware.

Bowl, 9" d., 2 1/4" h., rounded sides w/a scalloped rim, 19th c. **$588**

Plates, 9 5/8" d., armorial Rose Medallion, each decorated w/alternating panels of exotic birds & butterflies & groups of figures, the panel separated by bars w/tiny florals & a butterfly, an orange armorial crest in the center, slight wear, one w/short hairline, the other w/small filled-in rim chips, pr. (ILLUS. back with Rose Mandarin shrimp dish, top of page) **$575**

Plates, 9 3/4" d., Rose Mandarin, each w/the same border w/brilliant blue fretwork, pink flowers & baskets on a dark mustard yellow iridescent ground, each w/a detailed figural center scene, one showing women & children in a courtyard, the other w/a man brandishing a sword at a woman, minor wear, pr. (ILLUS. at right with platter, bottom of page) **$460**

Platter, 14 x 17", oval, the border in the rare kissing carp motif alternating w/blue & green scrolls, the center decorated w/a detailed figural scene w/26 figures including children, courtiers w/large necklaces & a man holding a sceptre, faint orange peel glaze, minor wear to gilt accents (ILLUS. left with two Rose Mandarin plates, bottom of page) **$1,955**

Pair of Rose Mandarin Plates & a Platter

Large Rose Medallion Punch Bowl

Punch bowl, deep rounded sides w/colorful alternating panels of flowers & Oriental figures, late 19th c., 15" d., 6" h. (ILLUS.) **$1,668**

Smaller Rose Medallion Punch Bowl

Punch bowl, rounded deep & flaring shape, decorated inside & out w/large alternating panels of flowers & Oriental figures, second half 19th c., 11 1/2" d., 4 3/4" h. (ILLUS.) **$1,150**

Shrimp dish, Rose Madarin, shallow shell-like form w/a wide pointed gold tab handle at one side, the center decorated w/an interior scene w/various figures including ladies around a table, the border decorated w/small bright flowers, fruit & butterflies, orange peel glaze, minor wear, shallow rim flake, 10 1/8 x 10 1/4" (ILLUS. front with armorial Rose Medallion plates, top previous page) **$805**

Fine Rose Medallion Teapot

Teapot, cov., small round raised foot supporting the deep rounded lower body w/a sharply angled gently angled shoulder centering the low flat mouth fittled w/a high domed cover, ornate C-scroll handle & serpentine spout, the sides & cover decorated w/alternating panels of colorful flowers or Chinese figures, mid-19th c., 8 1/4" h. (ILLUS.) **$1,093**

Large Rose Medallion Floor Vase

Vase, 24" h., floor-type, Rose Medallion, decorated w/large panels w/figures alternating w/floral panels, the tall trumpet neck flanked by gold applied Foo dog & dragon handles, late 19th c. (ILLUS.) **$1,150**

Very Large Rose Medallion Palace Vase

Vase, palace-style, 35 1/2" h., 13 1/2" d., wide cylindrical body w/the rounded shoulder tapering to a large waisted neck w/a widely flaring flattened rim, the neck w/large figural Foo dog & ball handles, each side of the body & neck decorated w/large panels w/scenes of numerous people in buildings, detailed floral background & gold trim, one under rim chip, 19th c. (ILLUS.) **$2,300**

Rosenthal

The Rosenthal porcelain manufactory has been in operation since 1880, when it was established by P. Rosenthal in Selb, Bavaria. Tablewares and figure groups are among its specialties.

Rosenthal Marks

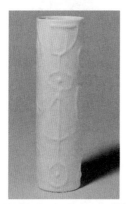

1960s Modernist Rosenthal Vase

Vase, 9 7/8" h., cylindrical, all white molded w/a stylized leaf design, marked "Rosenthal Germany - Cuno Fischer - Studio Line," ca. 1963 (ILLUS.) **$115**

Rosenthal 1930s Silver-Overlay Vase

Vase, cov., 12 1/4" h., temple jar form w/tapering ovoid body w/short cylindrical neck supporting a domed flanged cover w/a knob finial, black ground decorated w/a silver overlay design of a large bird of paradise flying over an intricate flower highlighted in orange & white, marked, ca. 1936 (ILLUS.) **$575**

Roseville

Roseville Pottery Company operated in Zanesville, Ohio, from 1898 to 1954, having been in business for six years prior to that in Muskingum County, Ohio. Art wares similar to those of Owens and Weller Potteries were produced. Items listed here are by patterns or lines.

Roseville Mark

Apple Blossom (1948)
White apple blossoms in relief on blue, green or pink ground; brown tree branch handles.

Blue Apple Blossom Hanging Basket

Basket, hanging-type, bulbous form tapering to a pointed base, narrow shoulder & wide flat neck flanked by tiny branch handles, blue ground, No. 361-5", 8" (ILLUS.) **$173**

Basket, footed, long narrow oval body w/arched sides & arched low overhead branch handle, green ground, No. 310-10", 11 1/2" l., 10" h. (ILLUS. third row, far left, with other Roseville basket, bookends, jardinieres, teapot & vases, top next page) **$242**

Roseville Apple Blossom Console Bowl

Console bowl, long boat-shaped form w/branch end handles, pink ground, No. 331-12", 12" l. (ILLUS.) .... **$75-$150**

Small Pink Apple Blossom Jardiniere

Grouping of Various Roseville Basket, Bookends, Jardinieres, Teapot & Vases

Jardiniere, wide bulbous body w/a molded flat mouth flanked by small twig handles, pink ground, No. 300-4", 4" h. (ILLUS., previous page) **$69**

Planter, footed tall rectangular form w/a cut-out in the lower half framing a tree branch, green to purple, No. 1054-8 1/2", 8 1/2" w., 6 1/2" h. (ILLUS.) .... **$75-$125**

Pink Apple Blossom Trumpet-form Vase

Vase, 10" h., wide flaring foot w/base twig handles, trumpet-form body, pink ground, some crazing, No. 388-10" (ILLUS.)............ **$138**

Artwood (1951)
Stylized molded flowers and woody branches framed within cut-outs within geometrically shaped picture planters and vases. Glossy glaze in mottled shades of dark green, yellow & grey, all with a dark purple band around the base.

Upright Flaring Artwood Vase

Vase, 6" h., flattened upright out-curving sides, stylized flower within cut-out, green to purple, No. 1051-6" (ILLUS.)............ **$75-$125**

Aztec (1915)
Muted earthy tones of beige, grey, brown, teal, olive, azure blue or soft white with slip-trailed geometric decoration in contrasting colors.

Artwood Tall Rectangular Planter

Green Flower-decorated Aztec Vase

Vase, 9" h., squatty bulbous base & tall cylindrical sides below the flattened widely
flaring rim, pale green ground h.p. w/a
thin band of tiny rectangles around the
base & below the rim, long curved stylized dark blue thin stems supporting four-
petal white & yellow blossoms, tight line
at the rim, Shape 21 (ILLUS., previous
page) **$431**

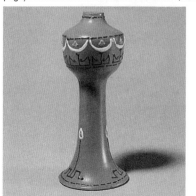

Tall Aztec Lamp-form Vase

Vase. 10 3/4" h., tall lamp-style, a flaring foot
tapering to a tall cylindrical base supporting a bulbous font-form top w/a shoulder
tapering to a small mouth, medium greyish blue decorated around the top
w/squeezebag white swags & tiny yellow
blossoms over a band of thin dark blue angular lines, further lines around the foot issuing thin stems w/white & yellow teardrop blossoms, Shape 5 (ILLUS.) ...... **$350-$400**

Baneda (1933)

*Band of embossed pods, blossoms and leaves
on green or raspberry pink ground.*

Small Roseville Baneda Vase

Vase, 4" h., footed bulbous body w/incurved
flat rim, flat shoulder handles, green
ground, No. 587-4" (ILLUS.) **$403**

Small Squatty Roseville Baneda Vase

Vase, 4" h., footed, wide squatty bulbous
base tapering sharply to small molded
mouth, tiny rim handles, green ground,
No. 603-4" (ILLUS.) **$518**

Roseville Baneda 5" Green Vase

Vase, 5" h., footed, pear-shaped w/small
loop handles near rim, green ground, No.
601-5" (ILLUS.) **$374**

Slender Ovoid Roseville Baneda Vase

Vase, 6" h., footed slender ovoid body w/a wide cylindrical mouth flanked by small C-scroll handles, green ground, No. 588-6" (ILLUS., previous page) **$518**

Squatty 6" Roseville Baneda Vase

Vase, 6" h., footed squatty bulbous body tapering sharply to a small neck flanked by C-scroll handles, green ground, No. 605-6" (ILLUS.) **$690**

Vase, 7" h., footed wide cylindrical body w/wide collared rim, small loop handles from shoulder to rim, green ground, pea-sized repaired base chip, No. 610-7" **$518**

Footed Globular Roseville Baneda Vase

Vase, 8" h., footed, globular w/low flat neck & shoulder handles, green ground, No. 595-8" (ILLUS.) **$1,150**

Bittersweet (1940)
Orange bittersweet pods and green leaves on a grey blending to rose, yellow with terra cotta, rose with green or solid green bark-textured ground; brown branch handles.

Yellow Bittersweet Bowl-Vase

Bowl-vase. 5" d., spherical w/flaring lobed rim & small angled twig shoulder handles, yellow ground, No. 841-5" (ILLUS.) **$115**

Bittersweet Creamer & Sugar Bowl

Creamer & open sugar bowl, No. 871-C & No. 871-S, grey ground, pr. (ILLUS.) **$81**

Bittersweet Double-Bud Vase

Vase, double bud, 6" h., grey ground, No. 873-6" (ILLUS.) **$115**

Blackberry (1933)
Band of relief clusters of blackberries with vines and ivory leaves accented in green and terra cotta on a green textured ground.

Long Blackberry Console Bowl

Console bowl, rectangular w/small handles, No. 228-10", 3 1/2 x 13" (ILLUS., previous page) **$431**

8" Blackberry Spherical Jardiniere

Jardiniere, spherical body w/heavy molded rim & small loop rim handles, No. 623-8", 8" h. (ILLUS.) **$633**

Small Bulbous Blackberry Vase

Vase, 4" h., bulbous body w/a low wide flared neck flanked by small loop handles, No. 567-4" (ILLUS.) .... **$400-$500**

Bulbous Ovoid Blackberry 6" Vase

Vase, 6" h., bulbous ovoid tapering to a flat wide rim, small loop shoulder handles, No. 571-6" (ILLUS.).................................... **$500**

Flaring Roseville Blackberry Vase

Vase, 6" h., rounded lower body w/a wide trumpet-form upper body flanked by two handles at midsection, No. 573-6" (ILLUS.) .... **$550-$650**

Globular Roseville Blackberry Vase

Vase, 6" h., globular w/wide low neck flanked by tiny handles, No. 574-6" (ILLUS.) **$518**

Blackberry Ovoid Vase

Vase, 8 1/4" h., ovoid body tapering to a short wide cylindrical neck flanked by small loop handles, No. 576-8" (ILLUS.).... **$863**

Bleeding Heart (1938)
Pink blossoms and green leaves on shaded blue, green or pink ground.

Bleeding Heart Vase with Large Grouping of Other Roseville Vases

Vase, 8" h., footed w/wide squatty lower body w/a wide shoulder tapering to a tall trumpet-form neck w/flaring paneled rim, angular handles from lower neck to shoulder, blue ground, minor professional repair to rim tip, No. 969-8" (ILLUS. third row, second from left, with large grouping of Roseville vases & bowls, top of page) **$150**

Tall Pink Bleeding Heart Vase

Vase, 10 1/4" h., footed tall slender ovoid body w/a flattened widely flaring paneled neck, a long C-form handle down one side & a short one on the other side, pink ground, No. 973-10" (ILLUS.) .... **$250-$350**

Bushberry (1948)
Berries and leaves on blue, green or russet bark-textured ground; brown or green branch handles.

Console set: footed ovoid basket No. 369-6 1/2" w/angled rim & high pointed branch handle & pair of No. 153-6" cornucopias, the set (ILLUS. front row, center, with Roseville Apple Blossom basket & other bookends, jardineres, teapot & vases, top of page 513) **$345**
Vase, 6" h., footed cylindrical body w/asymmetrical branch handles near rim, russet ground, No. 29-6" (ILLUS. third row, second from left, with Apple Blossom basket & other bookends, jardinieres, teapot & vases, top of page 513) **$138**
Vase, 7" h., footed ovoid body w/closed rim flanked by long pointed handles, russet ground, No. 31-7" (ILLUS. third row, far left, with grouping of Bleeding Heart Roseville vases & other vases & bowls, top of page) **$207**

Carnelian I (1915-27)
Matte smooth glaze with a combination of two colors or two shades of the same color with the darker dripping over the lighter tone. Generally in colors of blue, pink and green.

Blue Carnelian I 7" Bowl

Bowl, 7" d., 2 3/4" h., a low cylindrical foot below the widely flaring rounded bowl w/a closed rim & low scroll handles down the sides, drippy dark blue over pale blue, ink stamped mark, No. 160-7" (ILLUS.) ..... **$75-$100**

Large Blue Carnelian I Bowl

Bowl, 14" d., short pedestal foot below compressed round body w/incurved sides & wide flaring rim, scrolled handles, dark drippy blue over pale blue, No. 168-10" (ILLUS.) .... **$100-$150**

Simple Carnelian I Candleholders

Candleholders, simple round foot & gently flaring socket, green ground, No. 1059-2 1/2", 2 1/2" h., pr.2.5 (ILLUS.) .... **$75-$100**

Carnelian I Simple Style Console Set

Console set: console bowl w/footring & very widely flaring low sides, No. 156-12", & a pair of simple footed candleholders, No.1059-2 1/2" h.; each w/dark drippy moss green over pale green; ink stamped marks, candlesticks 2 1/2" h., bowl 12 1/2" d., the set (ILLUS.) .... **$200-$250**

Drippy Green Carnelian I Console Set

Console set: console bowl of footed shallow oval form w/angled end handles, No. 157-14", & pair of candleholders w/a low flaring round foot supporting a flaring candle socket w/slender scroll handles from the edge of foot; bowl w/a dark drippy moss green over pale green w/matching candleholders, candleholders 3" h., console bowl 16" l., 2 3/4" h., the set (ILLUS.) .... **$150-$200**

Bluish Green Carnelian I Console Set

Console set: console bowl of footed shallow oval form w/angled end handles, No. 157-14", & pair of candleholders w/a low flaring round foot supporting a flaring candle socket w/slender scroll handles from the edge of foot; bowl w/a dark greenish blue drippy band over turquoise blue & the candleholders in turquoise blue, candleholders 3" h., console bowl 16" l., 2 3/4" h., the set (ILLUS.) .... **$200-$300**

Blue Carnelian I Flower Frog

Flower frog, stepped rockwork form, dark blue dripping over pale blue, No. 60-6", 6 1/4" w., 2 1/2" h. (ILLUS.) .... **$100-$150**

Carnelian I Flaring Flower Holder

Flower holder, wide tapering foot supporting a wide flattened half-round container w/a row of small round openings along the top rim, drippy dark blue over pale blue, ink stamp mark, No. 50-4", 6 1/2" w., 4 1/8" h. (ILLUS.) **$81**

Blue & Tan Carnelian I Flower Holder

Flower holder, widely flaring oval foot tapering sharply to a short ringed stem below the wide flat-sided fanned upper container supported by delicate scrolled side legs & pierced across the top w/a row of flower holes, dark blue dripping over tan, blue stamped mark, No. 63-5 1/2", 5 1/2" h. (ILLUS.) **$81**

Shaded Blue Carnelian I 8" Vase

Vase, 8" h., footed ovoid base & tall ringed neck flanked by long stepped angular handles, dark greenish blue dripping over pale blue, No. 312-8" (ILLUS.) **$127**

Carnelian I Shaded Green Vase

Vase, 9" h., footed ovoid body w/collared neck & rolled rim, drippy dark moss green over pale green, No. 314-9" (ILLUS.)......... **$127**

Unusual Green Carnelian I 10" Vase

Vase, 10" h., compressed globular base w/trumpet form neck, ornate angled handles from base to midsection, drippy dark moss green over pale green, No. 323-10" (ILLUS.)... **$100-$150**

Roseville Carnelian I Floor Vase

Vase, 15 1/2" h., floor-type, round foot & tall ovoid body w/a wide flat mouth flanked by low C-form shoulder handles, green & tan, No. 339-15" (ILLUS.) **$500**

Green Fanned Carnelian I Wall Pocket

Wall pocket, widely fanned, pleated & pointed top tapering sharply to a pointed base, ornate long openwork stylized leaf side handles, drippy dark moss green over pale green, ink stamped mark, No. 1247-8", 8" h. (ILLUS.)............................... **$173**

Wall pocket, simple pointed bullet form w/a flaring stepped rim, long low handles down the sides, drippy dark moss green over pale green, ink stamped mark, No. 1248-8", 8" h. (ILLUS., next page)............. **$230**

Carnelian I Bullet-form Wall Pocket

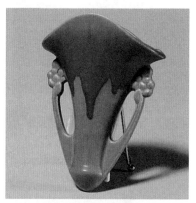

Carnelian I Arched Blue Wall Pocket

Wall pocket, tall fan-shaped body w/a high arched front, long side handles topped by stylized floral clusters, drippy dark blue over light blue, No. 1248-8", 8" h. (ILLUS.) .... **$200-$300**

Carnelian II (1915-31)
Intermingled colors, some with a drip effect, giving a textured surface appearance. Colors similar to Carnelian I.

Carnelian II Bowl with Mottled Glaze

Bowl, 10" d., 3 1/4" h., footed widely flaring flattened sides w/inward-scrolled rim handles, mottled greenish blue over dark blue glaze, No. 154-6" (ILLUS.) .... **$200-$300**

Wide Low Classical Carnelian II Bowl

Bowl, 14" d., short pedestal foot below compressed round body w/incurved sides & wide flaring rim, scrolled handles, mottled dark pink & green glaze, partial small black sticker, similar to shape No. 168-10" (ILLUS.) **$374**

Unusual Carnelian II Flower Holder

Flower holder, wide tapering foot supporting a wide flattened half-round container w/a row of small round opening along the top rim, mottled & streaky dark pink & olive green glaze, ink stamp mark, No. 50-4", 6 1/2" w., 4 1/8" h. (ILLUS.) **$173**

Mottled Green & Pink Carnelian Bud Vase

Vase, bud, 6" h., footed gently flaring cylindrical form w/ornate handles from base to mid-section, mottled & streaky dark olive green over a mottled dark pink ground, No. 341-6" (ILLUS.) **$150**

Bulbous Carnelian II Vase

Vase, 7" h., footed, bulbous base tapering
to wide cylindrical neck w/rolled rim, ornate handles from shoulder to below rim,
mottled rose, grey & green glaze, No.
311-7" (ILLUS.) **$317**

Double-gourd Carnelian II Vase

Vase, 7" h., double-gourd form graduated
body w/a swelled neck w/a widely flaring
rim, angular downswept handles from the
neck to the shoulder, greenish blue over
dark blue mottled drip glaze, No. 310-7"
(ILLUS.) .... **$200-$300**

Carnelian II Ovoid Handled Vase

Vase, 7" h., footed ovoid body tapering to a
short cylindrical neck flanked by angled
scroll handles, overall mottled dark &

light greenish blue, No. 311-7" (ILLUS.)
.... **$175-$250**

Carnelian II Green & Dark Pink Vase

Vase, 7" h., footed widely flaring lower body
w/a wide angled shoulder to a small
rolled neck flanked by low S-scroll shoulder handles, mottled & drippy dark green
glaze over a dark rose pink mottled
ground, No. 331-7" (ILLUS.) .... **$250-$300**

Carnelian II Vase with Fine Glaze

Vase, 7" h., footed widely flaring lower body
w/a wide angled shoulder to a small
rolled neck flanked by low S-scroll shoulder handles, mottled drippy light blue
over mauve glaze, No. 331-7", minor
grinding chips on base (ILLUS.)................ **$546**

Carnelian II Swelled Cylindrical Vase

Vase, 7 1/2" h., footed gently swelled cylindrical body w/a short wide flared neck, dark green mottled & drippy glaze over mottled dark pink, No. 308-7" (ILLUS., previous page) **$316**

Squatty Bulbous Carnelian II Vase

Vase, 8" h., footed wide squatty bulbous body w/a short cylindrical neck flanked by angled handles, mottled rose ground w/olive green to mulberry drip glaze, No. 335-8", repaired handle chip (ILLUS.)........ **$230**

Carnelian II Swelled Cylindrical Vase

Vase, 8 1/4" h., footed gently swelled cylindrical body w/a narrow shoulder to the short, wide cylindrical neck, dark drippy mottled lavender over mottled dark pink, No. 316-8" (ILLUS.)........................... **$350-$400**

Vase, 9" h., footed swelled cylindrical body w/a narrow shoulder to the shoulder cylindrical neck w/a flared rim, drippy medium blue above a mottled lighter blue ground, No. 314-9" (ILLUS., top next column).. **$196**

Vase, 10" h., compressed globular base w/trumpet form neck, ornate angled handles from base to midsection, mottled blue glaze, No. 323-10" (ILLUS., middle next column).................................... **$250-$300**

Carnelian II Drippy Blue 9" Vase

Mottled Blue Carnelian II Vase

Tall Unusual Carnelian II Vase

Vase, 10" h., compressed globular base w/trumpet form neck, ornate angled handles from base to midsection, mottled dark pink & green drippy glaze over a mottled rose & amber glaze, No. 323-10" (ILLUS.).................................... **$345**

Wall pocket, wide arched & fanned top w/panels down the sides, heavy loop side handles from under rim to near base, mottled blue & green glaze, No. 1252-8", 8" l. **$460**

Cherry Blossom (1933)
Sprigs of cherry blossoms, green leaves and twigs with pink fence against a combed blue-green ground or creamy ivory fence against a terra cotta ground shading to dark brown.

Pair of Blue-Green Cherry Blossom Lamps

Lamps, footed spherical vase body w/a short neck flanked by small loop handles, a low domed cap at the top for wiring, blue-green ground, No. 625-8", 9" h., pr. (ILLUS.).. **$1,840**

Clematis (1944)
Clematis blossoms and heart-shaped green leaves against a vertically textured ground, white blossoms on blue, rose-pink blossoms on green and ivory blossoms on golden brown.

Bookends, open book-shaped w/blossom in center, green ground, minor glaze flake on one blossom point, No. 14, pr. (ILLUS. front row, far left, with Roseville Apple Blossom basket & other bookends, jardineres, teapot & vases, top of page 513)... **$150**

Ewer, footed squatty bulbous lower body tapering sharply to a tall forked neck w/a very tall arched spout, long pointed handle from rim to shoulder, shaded pale green ground w/white flowers, No. 17-10", 10 1/2" h. (ILLUS. back row, second from right, with Roseville Bleeding Heart vases & other vases & bowls, top of page 517)... **$305**

Ewer, footed tall ovoid body tapering to a split rim w/a tall duck-bill spout & long pointed handle, body crazed, blue ground, No. 18-15", 15" h. (ILLUS., top next column).. **$173**

Tall Roseville Clematis Ewer

Columbine (1940s)
Columbine blossoms and foliage on shaded ground, yellow blossoms on blue, pink blossoms on pink shaded to green, and blue blossoms on tan shaded to green.

Tan Roseville Columbine Tall Vase

Vase, 14" h., floor-type, slender ovoid body tapering to a flared & shaped rim, pointed angular handles at midsection, flat disk base, tan ground, No. 26-14" (ILLUS.) **$431**

Cosmos (1940)
Embossed blossoms against a wavy horizontal ridged band on a textured ground, ivory band with yellow and orchid blossoms on blue, blue band with white, and orchid blossoms on green or tan.

Short Tapering Bulbous Cosmos Vase

Vase, 4" h., footed bulbous sharply tapering body w/a fluted cylindrical neck flanked by long arched handles to mid-body, tan ground, glazed-over chip on rim, No. 944-4" (ILLUS.) **$81**

Tall Blue Cosmos Vase

Vase, 12 1/2" h., footed ovoid w/large loop handles from sides of short paneled neck to sides of shoulders, blue ground, No. 956-12" (ILLUS.) **$260**

Dahlrose (1924-28)
Band of ivory daisy-like blossoms and green leaves against a mottled tan ground.

Vase, 8" h., small conical foot supporting the bulbous ovoid body w/a wide molded mouth flanked by tiny pointed shoulder handles, No. 365-8" (ILLUS., top next column) **$184**

Roseville Dahlrose 6 x 11" Window Box

Window box, rectangular w/swelled sides, No 375-10", 6 x 11 1/4" (ILLUS.) **$259**

Footed Ovoid Dahlrose Vase

Dealer Signs

Art Deco Design Roseville Dealer Sign

Sign, counter-top type, long rectangular shape w/a geometric Art Deco design, mottled bluish-green matte glaze, small glaze skip at bottom, 9 3/4" l., 4" h. (ILLUS.)....... **$1,725**

Decorated Art (ca. 1900)
Highly decorated Victorian-style line, mainly consisting of jardinieres, vases and umbrella stands. Often decorated with transfer-printed panels of flowers and fruit centered on fancy scroll-molded shapes. Many of these styles were used for the Rozane Royal line.

Roseville Decorated Art Vase

Vase, 10 1/4" h., tall slender waisted shape w/a dark blue ground h.p. w/large red roses & green leaves trimmed w/gold, a Rozane Mongol body shape & marked w/the Mongol raised seal mark, a hairline from the rim, some gold wear (ILLUS., previous page) **$288**

Donatello (1915)
Deeply fluted ivory and green body with wide tan band embossed with cherubs at various pursuits in pastoral settings.

Rare Tall Donatello Vase

Vase, 12 1/2" h., tall waisted cylindrical body w/a wide flat mouth, long serpentine angled handles down the sides, restoration to rim & handles, rare shape (ILLUS.) **$375**

Earlam (1930)
Mottled glaze on various simple shapes. The line includes many crocus or strawberry pots.

Bulbous Earlam Green & Brown Vase

Vase, 4" h., bulbous ovoid body w/a wide flat mouth, small loop shoulder handles, dark green shaded top tan ground, No. 515-4" (ILLUS.) .... **$150-$200**

Early Embossed Pitchers (pre-1916)
High-gloss utility line of pitchers with various embossed scenes.

Landscape Pitcher

Landscape, 7 1/2" h. (ILLUS.) **$95-100**

Early Tulip Pitcher

Tulip, blue blossom, green leaves & stem on a cream shaded to brown ground, 7 1/2" h. (ILLUS.) **$127**

Egypto, Rozane (1905)
Various shapes, many copied from original ancient Egyptian designs. Pieces covered in a soft matte green glaze

Low Squatty Egypto Bowl

Bowl, 8" d., 2 3/4" h., a wide low squatty form w/three loop handles around the rim, nice glaze, tight hairline (ILLUS.) **$115**

Bulbous Ovoid Roseville Egypto Vase

Vase, 5 1/2" h., wide bulbous ovoid body tapering to a wide flat mouth, overall dark green suspended matte glaze, unmarked (ILLUS., previous page) **$300**

Ferella (1931)
Impressed shell design alternating with small cut-outs at top and base; mottled brown or turquoise and red glaze.

Ferella 8" Brown Vase

Vase, 8" h., small foot & large ovoid body w/a wide low flared rim, brown glaze, No. 508-8" (ILLUS.) .... **$600-$800**

Florane I (1920s)
Terra cotta shading to either dark brown or deep olive green on simple shapes, often from the Rosecraft line.

Florane I Shade Brown Handled Vase

Vase, 9 1/2" h., oblong foot supporting a tall slender cylindrical vase flanked by asymmetrical long curved handles, terra cotta shading to dark brown, No. 7-9" (ILLUS.) .... **$125-$150**

Florentine (1924-28)
Bark-textured panels alternating with embossed garlands of cascading fruit and florals; ivory with tan and green, beige with brown and green or brown with beige and green glaze.

Florentine 7" Bulbous Jardiniere

Jardiniere, bulbous footed body w/a wide molded mouth flanked by tiny angled rim handles, beige w/brown & green, No. 602-7", 9 1/2" d., 7" h. (ILLUS.) .... **$200-$250**

Large Florentine Brown Jardiniere

Jardiniere, bulbous footed body w/a wide molded mouth flanked by tiny angled rim handles, brown w/beige & green, No. 602-10", 10" h. (ILLUS.) .... **$250-$350**

Tall Florentine Jardiniere & Pedestal

Jardiniere & pedestal base, beige w/brown & green, No. 602-10", overall 28" h., 2 pcs. (ILLUS.) .... **$900-$1,200**

Florentine 8" Beige Footed Vase

Vase, 8 1/2" h., footed slender ovoid body w/a small flat mouth flanked by small square shoulder handles, beige w/brown & green, No. 231-8" (ILLUS.) .... **$150-$175**

Florentine II (after 1937)
Similar to the ivory Florentine, but with lighter backgrounds, less decoration and without cascades on the dividing panels.

Florentine II 7" Bowl

Bowl, 7" d., 2 3/4" h., a footring below the wide low squatty body w/incurved sides, No. 126-7" (ILLUS.) .... **$75-$125**

Foxglove (1940s)
Sprays of pink and white blossoms embossed against a shaded dark blue, green or pink matte-finish ground.

Blue Foxglove Double Bud Vase

Vase, double bud, 4 1/2" h., gate-form, blue ground, No. 160-4 1/2" (ILLUS.) .... **$125-$175**
Vase, 8" h., footed cylindrical body, angled handles from lower base to rim, green ground, No. 48-8" (ILLUS. second row, far right, with Roseville Bleeding Heart vase & other vases & bowls, page 517) **$184**

Tall Green & Pink Foxglove Vase

Vase, 12 1/2" h., footed tall swelled cylindrical body w/a flat mouth flanked by down-swept loop handles, green shaded to pink, No. 52-12" (ILLUS.) **$316**

Blue Foxglove Pattern Floor Vase

Vase, 18" h., floor-type, two-handled, footed baluster-form w/narrow flared rim, blue ground, No. 56-18" (ILLUS.) **$690**

Freesia (1945)
Trumpet-shaped blossoms and long slender green leaves against wavy impressed lines, white and lavender blossoms on blended green, white and yellow blossoms on shaded blue, or terra cotta and brown.

Pair of Blue Freesia Candlesticks

Candlesticks, disk base, cylindrical w/low handles, blue ground, No. 1161-4 1/2", 4 1/2" h., pr. (ILLUS., previous page) .. **$100-$150**

Terra Cotta 10" Freesia Ewer

Ewer, footed gently swelled ovoid body below the wide stepped rim w/wide spout, pointed angled handles, terra cotta ground, No. 20-10", 10" h. (ILLUS.) .. **$150-$250**

Tall Green Freesia Ewer

Ewer, round ringed foot & tall slender ovoid body w/a high arched & pointed rim spout & pointed arched handle, blue ground, green ground, No. 21-15", 15" h. (ILLUS.) .. **$345**

Large Green Freesia Jardiniere

Jardiniere, footed nearly spherical body w/a very wide flat mouth flanked by tiny rim handles, green ground, No. 669-8", 8" (ILLUS.) **$264**

Freesia Terra Cotta 8 1/4" Vase

Vase, 8 1/4" h., globular base & flaring rim, handles at midsection, terra cotta ground, No. 122-8" (ILLUS.) .... **$225-$250**

Tall Green Freesia Wall Pocket

Wall pocket, waisted long body w/small angled side handles, green ground, No. 1296-8", 8 1/2" h. (ILLUS.) .... **$225-$325**

Fuchsia (1939)

Coral pink fuchsia blossoms and green leaves against a background of blue shading to yellow, green shading to terra cotta, or terra cotta shading to gold.

Fuchsia Squatty Handled Blue Bowl

Bowl, 4" d., footed wide squatty bulbous tapering body w/a wide flat mouth, D-form handles down the sides, blue ground, No. 346-4" (ILLUS.) **$184**

Low Squatty Blue Fuchsia Bowl

Bowl, 5" d., footed wide squatty bulbous body w/incurved rim & small loop shoulder handles, blue ground, No. 348-5" (ILLUS.) .... **$175-$200**

Bulbous Green Fuchsia 6" Bowl

Bowl, 6" d., footed bulbous body w/wide flat rim, loop shoulder handles, green ground, No. 347-6" (ILLUS.) .... **$150-$250**

Fuchsia Mushroom-form Flower Frog

Flower frog, mushroom-shaped w/two handles from rim to round base, blue ground, No. 37, 3 1/4" h. (ILLUS.) **$173**

Small Spherical Fuchsia Jardiniere

Jardiniere, footed spherical body w/short wide neck flanked by small angled handles, blue ground, No. 645-3", 3" h. (ILLUS.).......... **$115**

Vase, 6" h., footed ovoid w/handles rising from shoulder to short cylindrical neck rim, overall crazing, green ground, No. 892-6" .. **$104**

Footed Tapering Ovoid Fuchsia Vase

Vase, 7" h., bulbous ovoid base tapering to flaring rim, large loop handles from shoulder to below rim, brown ground, No. 895-7" (ILLUS.) .... **$225-$275**

Blue Fuchsia 8" Footed Vase

Vase, 8" h., footed bulbous body tapering slightly to a wide gently tapering cylindrical neck w/a rolled rim, long curved handles from just under the rim to the mid-body, blue ground, No. 898-8" (ILLUS.) .... **$350-$400**

Roseville Fuchsia 12" Terra Cotta Vase

Vase, 12" h., cylindrical body w/slightly flared neck, two handles rising from above base to neck, terra cotta ground, No. 903-12" (ILLUS., previous page) .... **$450-$550**

Futura (1928)
Varied line with shapes ranging from Art Deco geometrics to futuristic. Matte glaze is typical although an occasional piece may be high gloss.

Futura Sharply Pointed Hanging Basket

Basket, hanging-type, wide flat ringed rim above wide sloping shoulders, sharply canted sides forming a bottom point, tan & green w/embossed stylized multicolored leaves, No. 344-5", 5" h. (ILLUS.) ...... **$250-$300**

Futura 6" Jardiniere

Jardiniere, squared handles rising from wide sloping shoulders to wide flat mold-ed rim, sharply canted sides, terra cotta ground w/green & orange florals, No. 616-6", 6" h. (ILLUS.) **$288**

Green Futura Jardiniere with Pink Leaves

Jardiniere, angular handles rising from wide sloping shoulders to rim, sharply canted sides, dark greyish green ground

w/pink & lilac leaves, No. 616-9", 9" h. (ILLUS.) .... **$250-$275**

Futura Jardiniere with Colored Leaves

Jardiniere, angular handles rising from wide sloping shoulders to rim, sharply canted sides, tan ground w/multicolored leaves, No. 616-9", 9" h. (ILLUS.) **$345**

Rare Futura Jardiniere & Pedestal Set

Jardiniere & pedestal base, jardiniere w/angular handles rising from wide slop-ing shoulders to rim, sharply canted sides, matching pedestal w/wide flaring ringed foot, green ground w/stylized pink leaves & purple triangular blossoms, No. 616-10", overall 28" h. (ILLUS.) .. **$2,500-$3,500**

Pink Rectangular Roseville Futura Vase

Vase, 4" h., 6 1/2" l., called the "Two-Pole Pink Budvase," rectangular w/pointed ends & upright rim above tapering sides flanked by end stick handles to the flaring paneled foot, pink ground, pinhead piece of clay on base, No. 85-4" (ILLUS., previous page) **$259**

Blue & Apricot Futura Vase

Vase, 6" h., 3 1/2" d., cylindrical body swelling to wider bands at the top & base, long pierced angled handles down the sides, apricot w/blue bands & handles, light crazing, No. 381-6" (ILLUS.) **$259**

Green & Apricot Futura Vase

Vase, 6" h., 3 1/2" d., cylindrical body swelling to wider bands at the top & base, long pierced angled handles down the sides, apricot w/green bands & handles, No. 381-6" (ILLUS.) **$403**

Futura "Telescope" Design Vase

Vase, 7" h., nicknamed the "Telescope" vase, sharply canted base, handles rising from angled shoulder to below rim of long cylindrical stepped neck, greyish-green & tan, No. 382-7" (ILLUS.) ...... **$400-$500**

Spherical Futura Footed Vase

Vase, 7" h., nicknamed "The Bamboo Ball," spherical top w/large pointed dark blue & green leaves curving up the sides, resting on a gently sloped rectangular foot, shaded blue & green blue ground, No. 387-7" (ILLUS.) .... **$750-$1,000**

Futura Ball Bottle Vase

Vase, 8" h., nicknamed "The Ball Bottle" vase, bottle-shaped w/stepped back bands, grey-blue & pink, No. 384-8" (ILLUS., previous page) **$403**

Futura "Spaceship" Design Vase

Vase, 8" h., nicknamed the "Spaceship," cylindrical base expanding to bulbous double-ringed top, four dark blue Art Deco stepped buttress feet, light blue matte ground w/green shoulder design, No. 405-7 1/2" (ILLUS.) .... **$900-$1,100**

Futura Pink Twist 8" Vase

Vase, 8" h., nicknamed the "Pink Twist" vase, square, slightly tapering body twisting toward the rim, pink ground, No. 425-8" (ILLUS.) **$500**

Vase, 8" h., 3 3/4" d., nicknamed "The Pleated Star," star-shaped slender tapering body on stepped circular base, pink & dark greenish grey ground, original black foil sticker, No. 385-8" (ILLUS., top next column) .... **$450-$550**

Vase, 8 1/2" h., spherical body w/a small trumpet neck raised on four slender square short open legs above the asymmetrical rectangular base, white & pale yellow circles around the shoulder on the mottled green ground, No. 404-8" (ILLUS., middle next column) **$1,035**

Futura "Pleated Star" Vase

Spherical Footed Futura Vase

Futura Emerald Urn Vase

Vase, 9" h., nicknamed the "Emerald Urn," angular handles rising from bulbous base to rim, sharply stepped neck shaded dark to light green high gloss glaze, No. 389-9", some uneven places in the glaze, unmarked (ILLUS.)....................................... **$374**

Futura "The Bomb" 12" Vase

Vase, 12" h., nicknamed "The Bomb," wide ovoid body on a footring, the neck composed of tapering bands, smooth sides, turquoise glaze w/gunmetal shading, No. 394-12" (ILLUS.) **$978**

Futura Cylindrical Vase

Vase, 12" h., nicknamed the "Weeping Tulip," slightly tapering tall cylindrical body w/flat flared rim, molded w/a tall thin leafy stem w/a pale yellow tulip blossom, flanked by long tapering buttress handles, No. 437-12" (ILLUS.) .... **$1,200-$1,500**

Wall pocket, sharply tapering sides to pointed base, wide flat mouth flanked by angular rim handles, geometric design in blue, yellow, green & lavender on brown ground, black Roseville sticker, No. 1261-8", 6" w., 8 1/4" h. (ILLUS., top next column) .... **$300-$400**

Colorful Futura Wall Pocket

Gardenia (1940s)
Large white gardenia blossoms and green leaves over a textured impressed band on a shaded green, grey or tan ground.

Ewer, footed tall slender ovoid body w/a very slender neck & tall upright split rim w/wide spout, handle from lower neck to shoulder, grey ground, No. 618-15", 15" h. (ILLUS. back row, second from left, with Roseville Bleeding Heart vase & other vases & bowls, top of page 517)....... **$431**

Imperial II (1924)
Much variation within the line. There is no common characteristic, although many pieces are heavily glazed, and colors tend to run and blend.

Deep Imperial II Bowl

Bowl, 7" d., 4 5/8" h., footed wide & deep form w/gently rounded sides, repeating design of double bars w/rounded tops, tan & brown glaze, tight line from rim, spider cracks in base, No. 202-6" (ILLUS.) **$670**

Large Imperial II Bowl

Bowl, 9" d., 5" h., wide cylindrical form w/a ringed body below a border band of repeating stylized rounded leaves, streaky brown, pale green & pink glaze, No. 206-8", small nick inside rim (ILLUS.) **$978**

Large Oval Imperial II Bowl

Bowl, 8 x 12 1/2", 5" h., oval, footed deep widely flaring sides w/bands around the lower body, streaky blue & ochre crystalline glaze, No. 207-8 x 12" (ILLUS.)........... **$403**

Rare Imperial II Trumpet-form Vase

Vase, 5 3/4" h., wide trumpet-form body, dark maroon dripping over a pale bluish green ground, No. 470-5 1/2", crazing, small rim chip (ILLUS.)........................... **$1,725**

Tall Blue & Yellow Imperial II Vase

Vase, 11" h., tall ovoid body tapering to a short rolled neck, streaky yellow on a dark blue ground, original paper label, minor restoration under base (ILLUS.)....... **$720**

Iris (1938)

White or yellow blossoms and green leaves on rose blending with green, light blue deepening to a darker blue or tan shading to green or brown.

Roseville Iris Basket

Basket w/semicircular overhead handle, rose ground, No. 355-10", 9 1/2" h. (ILLUS.)... **$300-$500**

Small Blue Iris Jardiniere

Jardiniere, two-handled, footed squatty bulbous body w/a wide short cylindrical mouth, blue ground, No. 647-3", 3 1/2" h. (ILLUS.)... **$92**

Tan Iris Pattern Rose Bowl

Rose bowl, tan ground, footed squatty bulbous body tapering to a flat mouth flanked by angular shoulder handles, No. 357-4", 4" h. (ILLUS.).................................. **$104**

Blue Iris Vase

Vase, 6 1/2" h., two handles rising from shoulder of globular base to midsection of wide neck, blue ground, No. 917-6" (ILLUS.)........ **$173**

Iris Tall Footed Vase

Vase, 9 1/4" h., footed tall ovoid body w/a wide flat mouth flanked by pointed & stepped shoulder handles, tan ground, No. 924-9" (ILLUS.) **$219**

Tall Blue Iris Vase

Vase, 15 1/2" h., footed large ovoid body tapering to a paneled & scalloped neck flanked by loop handles, blue ground, No. 929-15" (ILLUS.) **$518**

Blue Iris Handled Wall Pocket

Wall pocket, two handles rising from base to below flaring rim, blue ground, No. 1284-8", 8" h. (ILLUS.)............................... **$432**

Ixia (1930s)

Embossed spray of tiny bell-shaped flowers and slender leaves, white blossoms on pink ground, lavender blossoms on green or yellow ground.

Console bowl, oval base band on oval body w/molded tab end handles & arched & notched rim, pink ground, No. 330-9", 9" l. (ILLUS. second row, far left, with Roseville Bleeding Heart vase & other vases & bowls, top of page 517) **$150**

Tall Cylindrical Yellow Ixia Vase

Vase, 12" h., cylindrical, closed upright shoulder handles, yellow ground, No. 864-12" (ILLUS.) .... **$200-$300**

Jonquil (1931)

White jonquil blossoms and green leaves in relief against textured tan ground, green lining.

Jonquil Basket with Tall Pointed Handle

Basket w/tall pointed overhead handle, bulbous body, No. 324-8", 8" h. (ILLUS.)... **$500**

Small Jonquil Vase

Vase, 3" h., wide, low, squatty, tapering, cylindrical body w/wide flat mouth, inverted D-form loop handles from rim to edge of base, No. 523-3" (ILLUS.) **$173**

Jonquil Vase No. 526-6 1/2"

Vase, 6 1/2" h., bulbous base w/wide, slightly tapering sides to a wide flat mouth, curved handles from rim to mid-section, glaze separation on exterior base, dark spider crack on interior, light crazing, No. 526-6 1/2" (ILLUS.) **$230**

Slender Jonquil Bud Vase

Vase, bud, 7" h., swelled base & a tall slender tapering body w/a widely flaring trumpet mouth, low arched handles from edge of base to part way up the sides, small rough spot at base, crazing, No. 102-7" (ILLUS.) **$230**

Jonquil Vase with Turned-down Handles

Vase, 8" h., ovoid body tapering to short cylindrical neck, turned-down shoulder handles, No. 529-8" (ILLUS.) **$345**

La Rose (1924)
Swags of green leaves and red roses on a creamy ivory ground.

Roseville La Rose Candleholders

Candleholders, straight open handles rising from round flaring base to just below the cupped nozzle, No. 1051-4", 4" h., pr. (ILLUS.) .... **$150-$200**

La Rose 8" Bullet-form Wall Pocket

Wall pocket, wide pointed bullet-form body w/a molded rim & arched handle, No. 1234-8", 8" h. (ILLUS.) .... **$350-$450**

Long Slender La Rose Wall Pocket

Wall pocket, long slender pointed body w/an asymmetrical arched rim & pointed loop handle, No. 1235-11", 11" h. (ILLUS.). **$400-$450**

Laurel (1934)
Laurel branch and berries in low relief with reeded panels at the sides. Glazed in deep yellow, green shading to cream or terra cotta.

Bulbous Laurel Terra Cotta Urn

Urn, bulbous base w/ringed neck, closed shoulder handles, terra cotta ground, No. 250-6 1/4", 6 1/4" h. (ILLUS.) .... **$175-$250**

Tapering Green Laurel Vase

Vase, 6 1/4" h., tapering cylinder w/wide mouth, closed angular handles at shoulder, terra cotta, No. 667-6" (ILLUS.) **$345**

Tapering Terra Cotta Laurel Vase

Vase, 7 1/4" h., tapering cylinder w/pierced angular handles at midsection, terra cotta, No. 671-7 1/4" 9 (ILLUS.)...................... **$345**

Laurel Trumpet-form Terra Cotta Vase

Vase, 8" h.,footed trumpet-form body w/low angled tab handles on the sides, terra cotta, No. 673-8" (ILLUS.)......................... **$184**

Luffa (1934)
Relief-molded ivy leaves and blossoms on shaded brown or green wavy horizontal ridges.

Roseville Luffa 6" Jardiniere

Jardiniere, large squatty bulbous body w/a wide flat rim flanked by tiny squared shoulder handles, brown ground, No. 631-6", 6" (ILLUS.)..................................... **$138**

Luffa Lamp with Jardiniere Base

Lamp, spherical body w/a wide flat mouth flanked by small squared handles, attached copper foot & cap w/electric fitting, green ground, jardiniere conversion, No. 631-7", overall 12" h. (ILLUS.)............. **$288**

Magnolia (1943)
Large white blossoms with rose centers and black stems in relief against a blue, green or tan textured ground.

Basket, footed large snail-shaped body w/a long asymmetrical overhead handle, green ground, minor glaze skip, flakes on base, No. 386-12", 12" h. (ILLUS. second row, second from right, with Roseville Bleeding Heart vase & other vases & bowls, top of page 517)............................. **$230**
Vase, 8" h., footed bulbous ovoid body tapering to a flat mouth flanked by long pointed handles down the sides, tan ground, No. 91-8".. **$138**
Vase, 8" h., footed bulbous ovoid body tapering to a flat mouth, pointed angled shoulder handles, green ground, No. 92-8" (ILLUS. top row, far left, with Roseville Apple Blossom baskets & other baskets, bookends, jardiniere, teapot & vases, top of page 513) .. **$150**

Matt Green (before 1916)
Matte green glaze on smoking set, jardinieres, fern dishes, hanging baskets, planters, some smooth with no pattern, some embossed with leaves or children's faces spaced evenly around the top.

Matt Green Gate-form Double Bud Vase

Vase, double bud, 5" h., 8" w., fluted columns joined by a gate, No. 7, small glaze skp on one foot (ILLUS., previous page)...... **$81**

Ming Tree (1949)
High gloss glaze in mint green, turquoise, or white is decorated with Ming branch; handles are formed from gnarled branches.

Green Ming Tree 13" Basket

Basket w/overhead branch handle, ruffled rim, green ground, No. 509-12", 13" h. (ILLUS.).. **$225-$250**

White Ming Tree Console Set

Console set: oblong boat-form 14" l. bowl w/branch end handles, No. 528-10" & pair of candleholders, No. 551; white ground, 3 pcs. (ILLUS.).................... **$225-$250**

Green Ming Tree Cylindrical Vase

Vase, 6" h., cylindrical w/asymmetrical branch handles at top, green ground, No. 581-6" (ILLUS.) **$58**

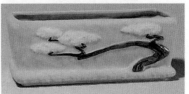

Ming Tree Blue Window Box

Window box, long rectangular shape, blue ground, No. 569-10", 4 1/4 x 11" (ILLUS.) .... **$125-$175**

Montacello (1931)
White stylized trumpet flowers with black accents on a terra cotta band, light terra cotta mottled in blue, or light green mottled and blended with blue backgrounds.

Squat Green 4" Montacello Vase

Vase, 4" h., footed squat rounded lower body w/an angled shoulder tapering sharply to a wide flat mouth, loop handles from neck to shoulder, green ground, No. 555-4" (ILLUS.) **$230**

Terra Cotta 4" Montacello Vase

Vase, 4" h., footed squat rounded lower body w/an angled shoulder tapering sharply to a wide flat mouth, loop handles from neck to shoulder, green ground, terra cotta ground, No. 555-4" (ILLUS.) **$259**

Small Montacello Green Handled Vase

Vase, 5" h., waisted cylindrical body w/two handles at mid-section, green ground, No. 556-5" (ILLUS.)..................................... **$316**

Terra Cotta Montacello 9" Vase

Vase, 9" h., bulbous ovoid w/flat rim, loop handles, terra cotta ground, rim chip repair, No. 564-9" (ILLUS.)............................ **$350**

Green Montacello 9" Vase

Vase, 9" h., bulbous ovoid w/flat rim, loop handles, green ground, No. 564-9" (ILLUS.)........ **$575**

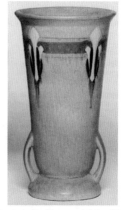

Montacello Trumpet-form Vase

Vase, 10" h., footed trumpet-form w/base handles, blue ground, minor glaze flaws, No. 565-10" (ILLUS.) .... **$500-$550**
Vase, 10" h., footed trumpet-form w/base handles, terra cotta ground, No. 565-10"... **$1,760**

Morning Glory (1935)
Delicately colored blossoms and twining vines in white or green with blue.

Spherical Morning Glory Urn-Vase

Urn-vase, bulbous nearly spherical body tapering to a wide flat mouth, squared shoulder handles, green ground, No. 269-6, 6" h. (ILLUS.) **$575**

Rare Tall Morning Glory Vase

Vase, 14 1/4" h., tapering cylindrical body w/flared rim, angled handles from shoulder to mid-section, green ground, No. 732-14" (ILLUS., previous page) **$920**

Moss (1930s)
Green moss hanging over brown branch with green leaves; backgrounds are pink, ivory or tan shading to blue.

Pair of Short Blue Moss Candleholders

Candleholders, flat disk base, ball-shaped, blue ground, No. 1109-2", 2" h., pr. (ILLUS.) **$115**

Pink & Blue Moss Urn-form Vase

Vase, 8 1/2" h., urn-form, flared foot, bulbous body w/pointed side handles & wide flaring rim, pink shading to blue ground, No. 779-8" (ILLUS.) **$288**

Blue & Tan Moss Vase

Vase, 10 1/2" h., two-handled, footed ovoid body w/flaring neck, blue shading to tan, No. 784-10" (ILLUS.) **$460**

Tall Blue Moss Vase

Vase, 12 1/2" h., footed tall ovoid body w/a small short neck, long low pointed handles down the sides, blue ground, No. 785-12" (ILLUS.) **$460**

Mostique (1915)
Indian designs of stylized flowers and arrowhead leaves, slip decorated on bisque, glazed interiors. Occasional bowl glazed on outside as well.

Large Bulbous Mostique Jardiniere

Jardiniere, wide bulbous body w/a very wide flat rim, geometric designs in dark yellow, brown & blues alternating w/long dark & medium blue vertical leaf-like geometric designs on a light tan ground, No. 740-8", 8" d., 7" h. (ILLUS.) **$210**

Cylindrical Mostique Vase with Swelled Rim

Orian Deep Rose Console Bowl

Vase, 9 3/4" h., cylindrical w/squatty swelled mouth, blue & grey ground, No. 21-10" (ILLUS., previous page)................. **$345**

Cylindrical Mostique Vase with Leaves

Vase, 10" h., cylindrical w/wide closed mouth, dark green incised rings around the base & light green matching rings around the top, decorated w/a dark green square enclosing a square white blossom & suspending a pale green sprig of incised leaves, light tan ground, N0. 15-10" (ILLUS.).. **$345**

Orian (1935)
Characterized by handles formed on blade-like leaves with suggestion of berries at base of handle, high-gloss glaze; blue or tan with darker drip glaze forming delicate band around rim, deep rose exterior & turquoise blue interior or in plain yellow with no over drip.

Console bowl, 8 x 12", square pedestal foot below the very long oval bowl w/fluted ends, deep rose exterior, turquoise blue interior, gold foil sticker, tiny rim & base chips, corner of base cracked, No. 275-12 x 8" (ILLUS., top of page) .... **$70-$100**

Vase, 6" h., flared foot below a cylindrical body w/a spherical top & short cylindrical neck, long & low loop handles down the sides, glossy deep rose w/turquoise lining, slight crazing, No. 733-6" (ILLUS., top next column)... **$207**

Orian Cylindrical Handled Rose Vase

Panel (Rosecraft Panel 1920)
Background colors are dark green or dark brown; decorations embossed within the recessed panels are of natural or stylized floral arrangements or female nudes.

Rare Rosecraft Panel Green Lamp Base

Lamp base, ovoid body on low foot, collared neck w/small squared handles, female nudes, green ground, No. X1, 10" h. (ILLUS.) **$1,840**

Bulbous Rosecraft Panel Vase

Vase, 8" h., wide bulbous body w/a round shoulder to the molded neck, decorated w/vines, leaves & fruit in orange on brown ground, No. 293-8" (ILLUS.)........... **$546**

Tall Dark Green Rosecraft Panel Vase

Vase, 11" h., footed conical form w/long low angular handles from rim down sides, nude in panel, dark green ground, professional restoration to one handle, some glaze bubbling, No. 298-11" (ILLUS.) **$460**

Wall pocket, cylindrical w/rounded end, curved asymmetrical rim, long tan trailing leaves & berries down the front on a dark brown ground, 9" h. (ILLUS., top next column) **$260**

Window box, long narrow deep rectangular shape w/three panels on each long side, swirling flower & leaf design, light green on dark green ground, smal firing line on the interior, 6 x 12" (ILLUS., middle next column) **$316**

Brown Rosecraft Panel Wall Pocket

Rosecraft Panel Floral Window Box

Peony (1942)
Floral arrangement of white or dark yellow blossoms with green leaves on textured, shaded backgrounds in yellow with mixed green and brown, pink with blue, and solid green.

Teapot, cov., pink shading to green ground, No. 3 (ILLUS. third row, far right, with Roseville Bleeding Heart basket & other baskets, bookends, jardinieres & vases, top of page 513)... **$207**

Persian (1916)
Creamware decorated by means of pouncing technique, in bright colors. Water lily and pad most common motif, although a variety of others were also used.

Colorful Small Persian Jardiniere

Jardiniere, small foot below wide rounded bottom & cylindrical sides w/a shoulder band below the wide molded mouth, vining repeated stylized lotus blossom design in yellow, tan, marron & grey w/pale green accent bands, No. 557, 5" h. (ILLUS.).............. **$150**

Pine Cone (1935 & 1953)

Realistic embossed brown pine cones and green pine needles on shaded blue, brown or green ground. (Pink is extremely rare.)

Blue Pine Cone Hanging Basket

Basket, hanging-type, squatty bulbous body tapering toward the base, w/a short wide cylindrical neck flanked by tiny branch hanging handles, blue ground, one hanging hole w/pinhead nick, No. 352-5", 7" d., 5 1/2" h. (ILLUS.).......... **$250-$350**

Green Pine Cone Basket

Basket, w/overhead branch handle, asymmetrical fanned & pleated body, green ground, No. 408-6", 6 1/2" h. (ILLUS.) **$230**

Pine Cone Brown Trumpet-form Basket

Basket, wide flaring foot & trumpet-form body w/an overhead branch handle, brown ground, No. 338-10", 10" h. (ILLUS.)... **$350-$550**

Tall Green Pine Cone Basket

Basket, wide flaring foot & trumpet-form body w/an overhead branch handle, green ground, some glaze crazing, No. 338-10", 10" h. (ILLUS.)............................ **$260**

Bookends, open book-form w/pine sprig from top to base, green ground, minor touch-up on one corner, No. 1, pr. (ILLUS. bottom row, far left, with Roseville Bleeding Heart vase & other vases & bowls, top of page 517) **$316**

Small Brown Pine Cone Bowl

Bowl, 6" l., 2 3/4" h., oval boat-shape w/banded sides & angled twig handle at one end, brown ground, No. 455-6" (ILLUS.) **$259**

Pine Cone Brown Footed Oval Bowl

Bowl, 9" l., 4" h., footed oval low body w/fanned sections at each end & small twig end handles, brown ground, No. 279-9" (ILLUS.) .... **$275-$325**

Bowl, 9" l., 4" h., footed oval low body w/fanned sections at each end & small twig end handles, green ground, No. 279-9" (ILLUS. bottom row, second from left, with Roseville Bleeding Heart vase & other vases & bowls, top of page 517)............ **$259**

Pine Cone Wide Round Bowl

Bowl, 11" d., 4 1/4" h., flat bottom & rounded sides w/wide flat mouth, small twig handles at rim, green ground, No. 276-9", small silver foil sticker (ILLUS.) **$104**

Small Bulbous Pine Cone Bowl-Vase

Bowl-vase, footed squatty bulbous body w/a wide low cylindrical neck, small asymmetrical shoulder branch handles, green ground, No. 400-4" (ILLUS.) **$138**

Small Green Pine Cone Candleholer

Candleholder, flat disc base supporting candle nozzle in the form of a pine cone flanked by needles on one side & branch handle on the other, green ground, partial gold foil label, No. 112-3", 3" h. (ILLUS.) ... **$115**

Brown Pine Cone Candleholders

Candleholders, flat disc base supporting candle nozzle in the form of a pine cone flanked by needles on one side & branch handle on the other, brown ground, No. 112-3", 3" h., pr. (ILLUS.) **$230**

Pair of Triple Pine Cone Candleholders

Candleholders, triple, domed round base w/an open high arched pine needle & branch supporting three graduated cup-form sockets, green ground, No. 1106-5 1/2", 5 1/2" h., pr. (ILLUS.) **$259**

Brown 12" Pine Cone Console Bowl

Console bowl, footed long oval form w/lobed rim w/long pine needle clusters & small end twig handles, brown ground, No. 322-12", 12" l. (ILLUS.) .... **$350-$450**

Large Pine Cone Cornucopia-Vase

Cornucopia-vase, green ground, No. 128-8", 8" h. (ILLUS.) .... **$225-$325**

Brown Pine Cone 10" Ewer

Ewer, footed ovoid body tapering to a split neck w/a high arched spout, branch handle, brown ground, No. 909-10", 10" h. (ILLUS., previous page) .... **$500-$600**

Tall Brown Pine Cone Ewer

Ewer, footed tall swelled cylindrical body w/narrow shoulder to short neck & high arched spout, long branch handle down from the shoulder, brown ground, No. 851-15", 15" h. (ILLUS.)...................................... **$805**

Very Small Blue Pine Cone Jardiniere

Jardiniere, spherical w/two twig handles, blue ground, No. 632-3", 3" h. (ILLUS.) **$230**

Small Blue Pine Cone Jardiniere

Jardiniere, footed wide squatty bulbous body w/a wide flat mouth, small asymmetrical twig handles, blue ground, No. 632-4", 4" h. (ILLUS.).. **$316**

Large Bulbous Pine Cone Jardiniere

Jardiniere, footed bulbous spherical body w/a low wide mouth flanked by small twig handles, green ground, No. 403-10", 10" h. (ILLUS.) **$288**

Jardinieres, footed wide squatty bulbous body w/a wide flat mouth, small asymmetrical twig handles, brown ground, one w/foot flake & minor repair, No. 632-4", 4" h., pr. (ILLUS. third row, second from right, with Roseville Apple Blossom basket & other baskets, bookends, jardinere, teapot & vases, top of page 513) **$184**

Large Ovoid Pine Cone Pitcher

Pitcher, 9 1/2" h., ovoid body tapering to a small neck w/pinched rim, small branch handle, green ground, No. 708-9" (ILLUS.)
.... **$600-$800**

Brown Pine Cone Tumbler

Tumbler, tall cylindrical shape tapering slightly at the base, brown ground, No. 414-5", 5" h. (ILLUS., previous page) **$207**

Green Pine Cone Tall Tumbler

Tumbler, tall cylindrical shape tapering slightly at the base, green ground, No. 414-5", 5" h. (ILLUS.) .... **$175-$250**

Spherical Green Pine Cone Vase

Vase, 6" h., 6 1/2" d., footed spherical body w/closed rim, small branch handle at one side of rim, green ground, soft mold, No. 261-6" (ILLUS.) **$173**

Vase, 6" h., footed bulbous base w/wide cylindrical neck, handles from shoulder to midsection of neck, green ground, No. 839-6" (ILLUS. third row, third from right, with Roseville Apple Blossom basket & other baskets, bookends, jardinieres, teapot & vases, top of page 513) **$184**

Square-footed Bulbous Pine Cone Vase

Vase, 7" h., square foot & large bulous nearly spherical body w/a wide flat neck, small asymmetrical branch handles, brown ground, No. 745-7" (ILLUS.)... **$350-$450**

Brown Pine Cone Waisted Shape Vase

Vase, 7" h., footed waisted cylindrical body tapering to slightly flaring rim, asymmetrical twig handles, brown ground, minor glaze inclusions, No. 840-7" (ILLUS.) **$219**

Brown Pine Cone Vase

Vase, 7" h., footed waisted cylindrical body w/small asymmetrical twig handles, brown ground, No. 841-7" (ILLUS.)............ **$259**

Handled Pine Cone Bud Vase

Vase, 7 1/4" h., bud-type, round foot & slender tall ovoid body w/twig handle down one side, green ground, small base chips professionally repaired, No. 841-7" (ILLUS.)...... **$104**

Vase, 8" h., footed wide pillow-shape w/two notches in wide arched rim, small twig handles, brown ground, No. 845-8" (ILLUS. top row, far right, with Roseville Bleeding Heart vase & other vases & bowls, top of page 517) **$460**

Blue Pine Cone Pillow-shaped Vase

Vase, 8" h., footed wide pillow-shape w/two notches in wide arched rim, small twig handles, blue ground, No. 845-8" (ILLUS.) .. **$500**

Brown Pine Cone Pillow-type Vase

Vase, 8 1/2" h., pillow-type, wide flattened bulbous body w/asymmetrical branch handles, brown ground, gold foil label, No. 114-8" (ILLUS.) **$633**

Vase, 8 1/2" h., horn-shaped w/fanned & pleated rim, pine needles & cone-form handle from base of oval foot to mid-section, brown ground, No. 490-8" (ILLUS., top next column) **$316**

Vase, 10 1/2" h., footed expanding cylinder w/wide flat mouth flanked by small twig handles, blue ground, No. 709-10" (ILLUS., middle next column) .... **$550-$750**

Vase, 10 1/2" h., flaring foot beneath an expanding conical body flanked by long handles from base to mid-section in the form of pine needles & pine cone, brown ground, No. 747-10" (ILLUS., third next column) .... **$500-$550**

Brown Pine Cone Horn-shaped Vase

Fine Blue Pine Cone Footed Vase

Brown Pine Cone 10 1/2" Vase

Vase, 10 1/2" h., flaring foot beneath an expanding conical body flanked by long handles from base to mid-section in the form of pine needles & pine cone, green ground, original paper sticker, minute rim bruise, No. 747-10" (ILLUS. top row, third from left, with Roseville Bleeding Heart vase & other vases & bowls, top of page 517) **$288**

Blue Pine Cone 10 1/2" Vase

Vase, 10 1/2" h., flaring foot beneath an expanding conical body flanked by long handles from base to mid-section in the form of pine needles & pine cone, blue ground, No. 747-10" (ILLUS.) **$660**

Tall Green Pine Cone Vase

Vase, 12 1/2" h., tall tapering corseted form w/asymmetric branch handles, green ground, w/original gold foil sticker, No. 712-12" (ILLUS.) **$374**

Green Pine Cone Wall Shelf

Wall shelf, long pointed shelf supported by a pine sprig, green ground, No. 1-5 x 8", 8 1/4" h. (ILLUS.) **$518**

Long Narrow Pine Cone Window Box

Window box, narrow long rectangular form w/a pine cone sprig along each long side w/a tiny tiny twig handle, green ground, No. 379-9-3-3 1/2" (ILLUS.) **$288**

Poppy (1930s)
Shaded backgrounds of blue or pink with decoration of poppy flower and green leaves.

Vase, 6" h., footed ovoid body w/a short cylindrical neck flanked by C-scroll handles, pink ground, No. 867-6" (ILLUS. second row, second from left with other Roseville Bleeding Heart vases & bowls, top of page 517)... **$173**

Poppy Vase in Green & Pink

Vase, 8" h., footed, wide cylindrical form w/C-form handles, green ground, No. 871-8" (ILLUS.) **$115**

Primrose (1932)
Cluster of single blossoms on tall stems, low pad-like leaves; backgrounds are blue, tan, or pink.

Rose bowl, footed spherical body w/closed rim flanked by small pointed handles, pink ground, No. 284-4", 4" d. (ILLUS. front row, second from right, with Roseville Bleeding Heart vase & other vases & bowls, top of page 517)............... **$104**

Vase, 6 1/2" h., gently flaring cylindrical body tapering to a short neck, long angular side handles, pink ground, No. 760-6" (ILLUS. third row, second from right, with Roseville Bleeding Heart vase & other vases & bowls, top of page 517)............... **$104**

Blue Primrose Pattern Vase

Vase, 6 1/2" h., gently flaring cylindrical body tapering to a short neck, long angular side handles, blue ground, No. 760-6" (ILLUS.) **$138**

Tall Blue Primose Vase

Vase, 14 5/8" h., footed tall ovoid body w/a wide flat mouth, low pointed angled handles at center of sides, blue ground, No. 772-14", silver foil sticker & original retailer sticker (ILLUS.) **$432**

Rosecraft Vintage (1924)

Dark brown backgrounds with band at shoulder formed by repetitive arrangement of leaves, vines, and berries, in colors of beige to orange.

Rosecraft Vintage 8" Shallow Bowl

Bowl, 8" d., 2" h., footed wide shallow form w/narrow angled shoulder band w/pattern, No. 143-8" (ILLUS.) .... **$150-$200**

Rosecraft Vintage Small Vase

Vase, 4" h., barrel-shaped body w/a wide shoulder to a short widely flaring neck flanked by small buttress handles, No. 273-4" (ILLUS.) **$219**

Rosecraft Vintage Wall Pocket

Wall pocket conical w/pointed top & loop side handles, No. 1241-8", 9" h. (ILLUS.) .... **$375-$425**

Rozane (1900)

Dark blended backgrounds; slip decorated underglaze artware.

Unusual Rozane Basket with Clover

Basket, footed long boat-shaped body w/a notched rim & high center handle, h.p clover decoration, Rozane wafer seal, 10" l., 7 1/2" h. (ILLUS.) **$259**

Tall Bulbous Rozane Ewer with Iris

Ewer, bulbous ovoid body tapering sharply to a tall slender cylindrical neck w/a tricorner rim, long C-scroll handle from rim to shoulder, shaded dark brown to green ground decorated w/a large brown & yellow iris, initialed by the artist, glaze bruise on handle, crazing, No. 905, 10 3/4" h. (ILLUS.) **$207**

Rozane Royal Dark Mug with Plums

Mug, Royal Dark, slightly tapering cylindrical sides w/fancy C-scroll handle, dark brown ground decorated w/plums hanging from leafy branches, artist-signed by Hester Pillsbury, crazing, No. 886 (ILLUS.) **$115**

Roseville Rozane Paperweight with Pansies

Paperweight, rectangular w/rounded corners, dark brown & green ground decorated w/dark brown & yellow pansies, artist-signed by Grace Neff, some light scratching, crazing, 3 3/4 x 4", 2 1/2" h. (ILLUS.) ... **$150**

Tankard Pitcher with Terrier Portrait

Pitcher, 14" h., tankard-type, flared foot & tall cylindrical sides w/a pointed rim spout, long D-form side handle, h.p. w/a portrait of a small terrier, artist-signed, Impressed "Rozane 855..." (ILLUS.) **$1,150**

Unusual Rozane Vase with Clover Decor

Vase, 6 7/8" h., Royal Dark type, footed very wide disk-form lower body tapering sharply to a tall slender neck w/a four-lobed flaring rim issuing two long slender handles curving down to the lower body, decorated w/red clover & leaves, impressed "Rozane 843 RPCo. 6" (ILLUS.) **$219**

Rozane Vase with Iris

Vase, 7 3/4" h., bulbous ovoid body tapering to a tall slender neck w/widely flaring rim, h.p. with a large yellow & deep red iris & green leaves on a shaded dark brown to green ground, impressed mark "Rozane 838 5," overall crazing (ILLUS., previous page) **$173**

Rozane Vase with Portrait of Spaniel

Vase, 12 3/4" h., swelled cylindrical body w/a short flaring neck, dark brown ground decorated w/the head of a brown & white spaniel, artwork by Mae Timberlake, overglazed chip on rim, two chips & hairline at base, crazing, No. 812 (ILLUS.) **$500**

Tall Rozane Vase with Horse Portrait

Vase, 14" h., Royal Dark type, sharply tapering ovoid body a short molded neck, nicely decorated w/a portrait of a horse, artist-signed by Arthur Williams, unmarked, several small base chips, a glaze nick or two (ILLUS.) **$1,150**

Vase, 18 1/2" h., Royal Dark type, a slender sharply tapering cylindrical body w/a trumpet neck, h.p. w/orange flowers & a bee, artist-signed, impressed "Rozane 865...," small glaze nick at base, few glaze scratches on rear (ILLUS., top next column) **$690**

Very Tall Slender Rozane Vase

Fine Rozane Vase with Roses

Vase, 20 3/4" h., tall ovoid body tapering to a short trumpet neck, h.p. w/yellow & peach roses & green leaves on a shaded greenish yellow to dark brown ground, artist-signed, crazing (ILLUS.) **$2,990**

Rozane Whiskey Jug with Blackberries

Whiskey jug, Royal Dark type, sharply tapering ovoid body w/a short cylindrical ringed neck w/an arched handle to the shoulder, decorated w/a large cluster of blackberries & leaves, artist-initials, marked w/the Rozane Ware wafer seal, 6 3/4" h. (ILLUS., previous page).............. **$230**

Rozane Pattern (ca. 1941)
Simple traditional and contemporary shapes decorated with softly blended or mottled matte glazes.

Shaded Blue Rozane Pattern Vase

Vase, 6" h., squatty bulbous base tapering to a slightly swelled cylindrical body w/a flat rim, tiny angled handles halfway down the sides, light blue shaded to dark blue mottled glaze, No. 1-6" (ILLUS.) .... **$100-$150**

Rozane Pattern Footed Cylindrical Vase

Vase, 9" h., oblong foot & tall slender cylindrical body flanked by a long & short curved handle from the body to the base, light blue shaded to dark blue, No. 7-9" (ILLUS.)... **$196**

Silhouette (1950)
Recessed area silhouettes nature study or female nudes. Colors are rose, orange, turquoise, tan and white with turquoise.

Vase, 9" h., double, base w/canted sides supporting two square vases w/sloping rims, joined by a stylized branch-form center post, florals, orange shading to green ground, No. 757-9" (ILLUS. second row, far left, with Roseville Apple Blossom basket & other baskets, bookends, jardinieres, teapot & vases, top of page 513)..... **$288**

Snowberry (1946)
Brown branch with small white berries and green leaves embossed over spider-web design in various background colors (blue, green and rose).

Bookends, open book-shaped, shaded blue ground, one w/some professional repair, 1BE, 5 1/4" h., pr. (ILLUS. front row, far right, with Roseville Apple Blossom basket & other baskets, bookends, jardineres, teapot & vases, top of page 513)..... **$150**
Candleholders, squatty w/angular handles at shoulder, shaded rose ground, No. 1CS1-2", 2" h., pr. (ILLUS., bottom of page).. **$69**

Roseville Snowberry Rose Console Set

Console set: 12" l. long low oval bowl w/gently arched sides & upright ends w/small pointed end handles & pair of No. 1CS1- 2" candleholders; shaded rose ground, No. 1BL2-12, 3 pcs. (ILLUS.)......... **$161**
Console set: 12" l. long low oval bowl w/gently arched sides & upright ends w/small pointed end handles & pair of No. 1CS1- 2" candleholders; shaded blue ground, No. 1BL2-12, 3 pcs. (ILLUS. of bowl, bottom row, far right, with Roseville Bleeding Heart vase & other vases & bowls, top of page 517)............... **$259**

Squatty Rose Snowberry Candleholders

Snowberry Green 4" Jardiniere

Jardiniere, two-handled, shaded green ground, No. 1J-4", 4" h. (ILLUS.) **$58**

Tall Rose Snowberry Vase

Vase, 12 1/2" h., conical base tapering to a tall, fanned body w/a flaring stepped rim, pointed handles at the lower body, shaded rose ground, No. 1V2-12" (ILLUS.) **$150**

Sunflower (1930)
Tall stems support yellow sunflowers whose blooms form a repetitive band. Textured background shades from tan to dark green at base.

6" Roseville Sunflower Vase

Vase, 6" h., swelled cylindrical body w/short cylindrical neck flanked by small loop handles, No. 485-6" (ILLUS.) **$547**

Sylvan (1918)
Tree bark textured exterior in shades of grey or sandy tan with incised forest scenes including hunting dogs, foxes and owls, sometimes with a scattering of leaves or acorns; glazed interior.

Sylvan Jardiniere with Hunting Dogs

Jardiniere, wide tapering ovoid form w/a wide flat mouth, light green band of hunting dogs decoration against a light brown tree bark ground, some very small glaze nicks, No. 568, 10" h. (ILLUS.) **$375**

Thorn Apple (1930s)
White trumpet flower with leaves reverses to thorny pod with leaves. Colors are shaded blue, brown and pink.

Pink Thorn Apple 6" Vase

Vase, 6" h., footed bulbous ovoid body w/wide cylindrical neck, small angular shoulder handles, shaded pink ground, No. 811-6" (ILLUS.) **$115**

Tourmaline (1933)
Although the semi-gloss medium blue, highlighted around the rim with lighter high gloss and gold effect seems to be accepted as the stan-

dard Tourmaline glaze, the catalogue definitely shows this and two other types as well. One is a mottled overall turquoise, the other a mottled salmon that appears to be lined in the high gloss but with no overrun to the outside.

Pair Blue Tourmaline Candlesticks

Candlesticks, flared ribbed base, flaring nozzle, mottled blue ground, gold labels, No. 1089-4 1/2", 4 1/2" h., pr. (ILLUS.) **$127**

Turquoise Tourmaline Candlesticks

Candlesticks, flared ribbed base, flaring nozzle, mottled turquoise ground, No. 1089-4 1/2", 4 1/2" h., pr. (ILLUS.).... **$100-$150**

Gold Tourmaline Globular Urn

Urn, footed globular body w/embossed lines around shoulder interrupted w/some vertical bands, mottled gold, No. 238-5", 5 1/2" h. (ILLUS.) **$81**

Tourmaline Pink Pillow-type Vase

Vase, 6" h., rectangular pillow-type w/horizontally ribbed lower half flanked by small scroll handles, mottled pink w/pale blue upper band, gold foil sticker, No. A-65-6" (ILLUS.) **$69**

Tourmaline Blue Pillow-type Vase

Vase, 6" h., rectangular pillow-type w/horizontally ribbed lower half flanked by small scroll handles, mottled blue w/drippy green upper band, No. A-65-6" (ILLUS.) **$92**

Spherical Pink Tourmaline Vase

Vase, 6" h., footed nearly spherical body w/a wide band of narrow rings just below the wide rolled rim, mottled pink, No. 611-6" (ILLUS.) **$81**

Vase, 7 1/2" h., square, tapering slightly towards base, embossed design around rim, mottled blue over tannish grey glaze, foil label on base, No. 612-7" **$184**

Twisted Hexagonal Tourmaline Vase

Vase, 8" h., tall hexagonal twisted paneled shape, medium streaky blue w/ivory & amethyst drips from the rim, No. A-425-8" (ILLUS.) **$230**

Tourmaline Blue Waisted Vase

Vase, 8" h., ringed foot below the waisted cylindrical body w/a band of rings near the rim, mottled white to dark blue matte glaze, No. 613-8" (ILLUS.) **$115**

Vase, 8 1/4" h., footed flating cylindrical body w/a ringed base, tapering pointed tab handles at lower sides, the body molded in low-relief w/narrow ribbed strips joined around the top by a molded leaf band, mottled blue (ILLUS., top next column) **$184**

Vase, 8 1/4" h., flattened loop base handles flanking the footed bulbous lower body tapering to a tall trumpet neck, streaky medium blue w/creamy tan drips from the rim, No. A-332-8" (ILLUS., middle next column) **$127**

Blue Tourmaline Vase with Leaf Band

Streaky Blue Tourmaline Vase

Blue Tourmaline Vase in Scarce Shape

Vase, 9" h., flared foot below buttressed base, trumpet-form body, mottled blue glaze, No. A-429-9" (ILLUS.) **$317**

Square Blue Tourmaline Vase

Vase, 9 1/2" h., footed gently flaring square form w/a narrow molded herringbone band below the flared rim, mottled blue ground, No. 615-9" (ILLUS.) **$260**

Tuscany (1928)

Marble-like finish most often found in a shiny pink, sometimes in matte grey, more rarely in a dull turquoise. Suggestion of leaves and berries, usually at the base of handles, are the only decorations.

Short Tuscany Turquoise Vase

Vase, 4" h., 6 1/2" w., bowl-form, footed widely flaring trumpet-form w/open handles from under rim to the foot, mottled turquoise, No. 67-4" (ILLUS.) **$92**

Velmoss (1935)

Characterized by three horizontal wavy lines around the top from which long, blade-like leaves extend downward. Colors are green, blue, tan and pink.

Rare Velmoss Umbrella Stand

Umbrella stand, tall cylindrical form w/long bold-relief pointed leaves up the sides in shaded green to tan, unmarked, 20 3/8" h. (ILLUS.) **$1,840**

Velmoss - Early (ca. 1916)

This version of Velmoss features an Arts & Crafts design of molded overlapping and repeating simple leaves & buds in shades of green, yellow and brown.

Early Velmoss Leaf Sprig Vase

Vase, 8" h., simple baluster-form body w/a flaring neck, molded around the lower half of the body w/upright five-leaf sprigs, mottled green & brown matte glaze, No. 130-8", unmarked (ILLUS.) **$510**

Early Velmoss Vase in Green & Yellow

Vase, 10" h., gently tapering cylindrical form w/a molded rim, molded w/a repeating design of tall pointed & ribbed dark green leaves overlapping dark yellow leaves, matte glaze, unmarked, rim hairline (ILLUS.) **$330**

Vista (1920s)

Embossed green coconut palm trees & lavender blue pool against grey ground.

Tall Cylindrical Vista Vase

Vase, 12" h., 4 3/4" d., footed, bulbous base tapering to tall wide cylindrical neck w/flat rim, No. 125-12" (ILLUS.)........................... **$978**

Water Lily (1943)

Water lily and pad in various color combinations: tan to brown with yellow lily, blue with white lily, pink to green with pink lily.

Water Lily Shaded Blue Tea Set

Tea set: cov. teapot No. 5, open sugar bowl No. 5-S & creamer No. 5-C; squatty bulbous forms, shaded blue ground, the set (ILLUS.)... **$345**

Blue Water Lily No. 79-9" Vase

Vase, 9" h., footed bulbous ovoid body w/a large trumpet neck flanked by angled handles, blue ground w/white lily, No. 79-9" (ILLUS.)` **$88**

White Rose (1940s)

White roses and green leaves against a vertically combed ground of blended blue, brown shading to green, or pink shading to green.

White Rose Blended Blue Console Bowl

Console bowl, long low oval form w/small loop end handles, blended blue ground, No. 391-10", 10" l. (ILLUS.) **$127**
Console bowl, long low oval form w/small loop end handles, brown shading to green ground, No. 391-10", 10" l. ..... **$100-$125**
Console bowl, footed oblong paneled body w/large pointed end handles, blended blue ground, No. 393-12", 16 1/2" l. (ILLUS. second row, center, with Roseville Apple Blossom basket & other baskets, bookends, jardineres, teapot & vases, top of page 513) **$150**
Vase, 8 1/2" h., small footring below a squatty, bulbous base & tall, wide, cylindrical body w/notched flat rim, long loop handles from rim to edge of base, blended blue ground, No. 985-8" (ILLUS. top row, center, with Roseville Apple Blossom basket & other baskets, bookends, jardineres, teapot & vases, top of page 513).. **$207**

Pair of Pink to Green White Rose Vases

Vases, 6" h., cylindrical w/short collared neck, angular handles at shoulder, pink shading to green ground, No. 979-6", pr. (ILLUS.)... **$207**

Wincraft (1948)

Revived shapes from older lines such as Pine Cone, Bushberry, Cremona, Primrose and others. Vases with animal motifs, contemporary shapes in high gloss of blue, tan, lime and green.

Brown Wincraft Console Set

Console set: No. 268-12" rectangular bowl w/narrow tab end handles & pair of No. 252 candleholders; brown ground, the set (ILLUS., previous page) **$161**

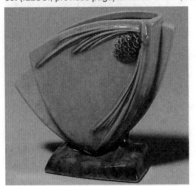

Wincraft Blue Fan-shaped Vase

Vase, 6" h., asymmetrical fan shape, pine cones & needles in relief on glossy shaded light blue to dark blue ground, No. 272-6" (ILLUS.) **$115**

Asymmetrical Blue Wincraft Vase

Vase, 6" h., asymmetrical fan shape, pine cones & needles in relief on shaded blue ground, crazing, No. 272-6" (ILLUS.) **$81**

Wincraft Lily-form Brown Vase

Vase, 8" h., flowing lily form w/asymmetrical side handles, tulip & foliage in relief on glossy brown ground, No. 282-8" (ILLUS.) **$69**

Trumpet-form Wincraft Vase

Vase, 8" h., tall tan trumpet-form vase on a rounded dark brown base w/green pine sprig & small brown branch base handles, brown ground, No. 283-8" (ILLUS.)... **$150**

Tall Flaring Cylindrical Wincraft Vase

Vase, 16" h., thick disk foot below the tall cylindrical body w/a fanned rim, pale yellowish green shaded to brown ground, No. 288-15" (ILLUS.) .... **$350-$450**

Windsor (1931)
Brown or blue mottled glaze, some with leaves, vines and ferns, some with a repetitive band arrangement of small squares and rectangles in yellow and green.

Rare Squatty Windsor Vase with Ferns

Vase, 7" h., wide squatty bulbous body centered by a short wide cylindrical neck flanked by arched handles to the shoulder dark blue above mottled green ferns, small chip on one handle, No. 582-7" (ILLUS., previous page) **$1,725**

Wisteria (1933)

Lavender wisteria blossoms and green vines against a roughly textured brown shading to deep blue ground or brown shading to yellow and green; rarely found in only brown.

Blue Squatty Tapering Wisteria Vase

Vase, 4" h., wide squatty bulbous tapering body w/a wide flat mouth flanked by small pointed rim handles, blue ground, No. 242-4" (ILLUS.) .... **$350-$450**

Shaded Squatty Tapering Wisteria Vase

Vase, 4" h., wide squatty bulbous tapering body w/a wide flat mouth flanked by small pointed rim handles, brown shaded to green & yellow ground, No. 242-4" (ILLUS.) .... **$250-$350**

Squatty Tapering Wisteria 4" Vase

Vase, 4" h., squatty lower body w/small angular handles on the sharply canted upper body, brown shaded to green & yellow ground, No. 629-4" (ILLUS.) **$316**

Tapering Ovoid Wisteria 6" Vase

Vase, 6" h., ovoid body tapering to short cylindrical neck flanked by small loop handles, brown shaded to yellow & green ground, No. 631-6" (ILLUS.) .... **$350-$450**

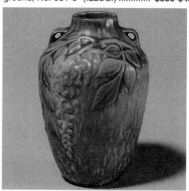

Ovoid Shaded Brown Wisteria Vase

Vase, 6 1/2" h., 4" d., ovoid body w/the shoulder tapering up to a small mouth, small angled shoulder handles, light brown shaded to yellow & green ground, No. 630-6" (ILLUS.) **$460**

Brown Tapering Wisteria Vase

Vase, 8" h., 6 1/2" d., wide, tapering, cylindrical body w/small angled handles flanking the flat rim, brown ground, small gold sticker, No. 633-8" (ILLUS., previous page)......... **$575**

Brown Shaded Tapering Wisteria Vase

Vase, 8" h., 6 1/2" d., wide, tapering, cylindrical body w/small angled handles flanking the flat rim, brown shaded to yellow & green ground, small gold sticker, No. 633-8" (ILLUS.) **$633**

Shaded Brown Flaring Wisteria Vase

Vase, 10 1/4" h., bulbous lower body tapering sharply to a tall trumpet neck, angled handles from center of neck to lower body, brown shaded to yellow & green ground, No. 682-10" (ILLUS.) .... **$500-$1,000**

Zephyr Lily (1946)

Tall lilies and slender leaves adorn swirl-textured backgrounds of Bermuda Blue, Evergreen and Sienna Tan.

Zephyr Lily Terra Cotta Hanging Basket

Basket, hanging-type, terra cotta & green ground, No. 472-5", 7 1/2" h. (ILLUS.)
.... **$150-$200**

Blue Zephyr Lily 8" Basket

Basket, footed flaring rectangular body w/upcurved rim & long asymmetrical handle, blue ground, No. 394-8", 8" h. (ILLUS.) .... **$250-$300**
Basket, footed flaring rectangular body w/upcurved rim & long asymmetrical handle, green & brown ground, No. 394-8", 8" h... **$225-$275**

Zephry Lily Tall Green Basket

Basket, footed flaring rectangular body w/upcurved rim & long asymmetrical handle, green ground, No. 394-8", 8" h. (ILLUS.) **$173**

Zephyr Lily Small Cornucopia-Vase

Cornucopia-vase, green ground, No. 203-6", 6" h. (ILLUS., previous page)....... **$100-$150**

Large Blue Zephyr Lily Cornucopia-Vase

Cornucopia-vase, blue ground, No. 204-8" 8 1/2" h. (ILLUS.) .... **$150-$200**

Zephyr Lily Blue 10" Ewer

Ewer, footed flaring lower body w/angled shoulder tapering to a tall forked neck w/upright tall spout, long low arched handle, blue ground, No. 23-10", 10" h. (ILLUS.) .... **$225-$250**

Tall Terra Cotta Zephyr Lily Ewer

Ewer, footed flaring lower body w/angled shoulder tapering to a tall forked neck w/upright tall spout, long low arched handle, terra cotta ground, No. 23-10", 10 3/8" h. (ILLUS.) **$127**

Zephyr Lily Terra Cotta Flowerpot

Flowerpot, terra cotta ground, water deposits in bottom, no undertray, No. 672-5", 5" h. (ILLUS.) **$81**

Zephyr Lily Flowerpot & Saucer

Flowerpot w/saucer, terra cotta ground, No. 672-5", 5" h. (ILLUS.) .... **$150-$175**

Green Zephyr Lily Small Jardiniere

Jardiniere, squatty bulbous body w/a wide flat mouth flanked by small low loop handles, green ground, No. 671-4", 4" h. (ILLUS.) **$58**

Fine Blue Zephyr Lily Jardiniere Set

Jardiniere & pedestal base, large bulbous jardiniere w/low shoulder handles, No. 671-8" & tall pedestal flaring at the base, shaded blue ground, overall 24 1/2" h. (ILLUS.).. **$1,035**

Blue Zephyr Lily Leaf-shaped Tray

Tray, leaf-shaped, blue ground, No. 477-12", 14 1/2" l. (ILLUS.) .... **$150-$225**

Zephyr Lily Bulbous Urn-Vase

Urn-vase, wide tapering bulbous form w/a wide flat mouth & low handles below the shoulder, terra cotta & green ground, No. 471-6", 6" h. (ILLUS.)........................ **$175-$225**

Zephyr Lily Blue Pillow-type Vase

Vase, 7" h., rectangular footed pillow-type w/base handles & three-opening top, blueground, No. 206-7" (ILLUS.) ...... **$175-$225**

Zephyr Lily Blue Urn-form Vase

Vase, 8 1/2" h., footed urn-form body w/a wide gently flaring neck flanked by curved handles to shoulder, blue, No. 202-8" (ILLUS.) .... **$125-$175**

Zephyr Lily 15 1/2" Tall Floor Vase

Vase, 15 1/2" h., floor-type, terra cotta ground, minor glaze roughness, No. 141-15" (ILLUS., previous page) **$374**

Zephyr Lily Large Blue Floor Vase

Vase, 18" h., floor-type, footed tall swelled cylindrical form w/a short neck & C-form shoulder handles, blue ground, No. 142-18" (ILLUS.) .... **$700-$900**

Green Zephyr Lily Floor Vase

Vase, 18" h., floor-type, footed tall swelled cylindrical form w/a short neck & C-form shoulder handles, green ground, No. 142-18" (ILLUS.) **$633**

Royal Bayreuth

Good china in numerous patterns and designs has been made at the Royal Bayreuth factory in Tettau, Germany since 1794. Listings below are by the company's lines, plus miscellaneous pieces. Interest in this china remains at a peak and prices continue to rise. Pieces listed carry the company's blue mark except where noted otherwise.

Among the important reference books in this field are Royal Bayreuth - A Collectors' Guide and Royal Bayreuth - A Collectors' Guide - Book II by Mary McCaslin (see Special Contributors list).

Royal Bayreuth Mark

Corinthian

Cake plate, classical figures on black ground, 10" d. .... **$100-$175**
Creamer, classical figures on green ground .... **$40-$65**
Creamer & cov. sugar bowl, classical figures on black ground, pr. .... **$100-$125**
Pitcher, milk, classical figures on green ground.. **$75-$100**

Corinthian Pitcher

Pitcher, tankard, 6 7/8" h., 3 3/4" d., orange inside top, classical figures on black satin ground, gold bands w/black & white geometric design around neck & base (ILLUS.) .... **$175-$200**
Planter, classical figures on red ground.. **$120-$140**
Toothpick holder, classical figures on black ground, 2 1/4" h. .... **$225-$250**

Devil & Cards

Ashtray .... **$175-$200**
Ashtray, two cards.............................. **$250-$300**
Ashtray w/match holder .... **$275-$300**
Candleholder, short..................................... **$550**
Candleholder, tall, 6 1/4" h. .... **$4,500-$6,500**
Creamer, figural red devil, 3 1/2" h. ...... **$400-$600**
Creamer, figural devil handle, 3 3/4" h. ... **$300-$400**
Creamer, figural red devil, 4 1/2" h. ...... **$400-$650**
Match holder, hanging-type, 4" w., 5" h. .... **$700-$800**

Mug, 4 3/4" h. .... $450-$600
Mug, w/blue rim .... $500-$650
Pitcher, milk, 5" h. .... $700-$800
Pitcher, water, 7 1/4" h. .... $600-$850
Plate, 6" d. .... $400-$600
Salt dip, master size .... $300-$400
Salt shaker .... $350-$500
Stamp box, cov., 3 1/2" l. .... $700-$900
Sugar bowl, cov. .... $400-$500
Sugar bowl, open, short .... $400-$550

Mother-of-Pearl
Ashtray, Spiky Shell patt. .... $60-$75
Basket, reticulated rim, ornate handle, rose
    decoration, 3 3/4 x 4" oval, 4 1/4" h. . $125-$150
Bowl, 3 1/2" octagonal, white w/green high-
    lights, pearlized finish .... $50-$65
Bowl, 5 1/2" d., grape cluster mold, pearl-
    ized white finish .... $100-$125
Bowl, 6 1/2 x 9", oak leaf-shaped, footed,
    pearlized finish w/gold trim .... $600-$850
Bowl, 10" oval, handled, figural poppy mold,
    apricot satin finish .... $500-$600
Cake plate, decorated w/roses, 10 1/2" d.
    .... $100-$125
Compote, open, 4 1/2" d., 4 1/2" h., reticu-
    lated bowl & base, decorated w/delicate
    roses, pearlized finish .... $100-$150
Compote, open, decorated w/roses, pearl-
    ized finish, small .... $25-$50
Creamer, grape cluster mold, pearlized
    white, 3 3/4" h. .... $125-$175
Creamer, Spiky (Murex) Shell patt., white
    pearlized finish, 4 1/2" h. .... $125-$175
Creamer, boot-shaped, figural Spiky Shell
    patt., 4 3/4" h. .... $200-$250
Creamer & cov. sugar bowl, grape cluster
    mold, pearlized yellow, colorful foliage,
    pr. .... $250-$350
Cup & saucer, demitasse, footed, figural
    Spiky Shell patt., pearlized finish ...... $100-$125
Cup & saucer, demitasse, Oyster & Pearl
    mold .... $200-$350
Dish, cov., Spiky Shell patt., large .... $125-$150
Hatpin holder, figural poppy mold, pearl-
    ized white finish .... $450-$550
Hatpin holder, white pearlized finish .... $125-$175
Humidor, cov., Spiky Shell patt. .... $600-$800
Mustard jar, cov., Spiky Shell patt., white
    pearlized finish, 3 1/2" h. .... $125-$225
Nappy, grape cluster mold, pearlized white
    finish, 6" x 7" .... $125-$175
Nappy, handled, figural poppy mold, pearl-
    ized satin finish. .... $150-$200
Pitcher, milk, boot-shaped, figural Spiky
    Shell patt., pearlized finish, 5 1/2" h.
    .... $250-$350
Sugar bowl, cov., footed, figural Spiky Shell
    patt., pearlized finish, 3 1/2" h. .... $200-$250
Toothpick holder, Spiky Shell patt., pearl-
    ized finish .... $125-$175
Toothpick holder, Spiky Shell patt. .... $110-$120
Wall pocket, figural grape cluster, pearlized
    finish, 9" h. .... $350-$500

Old Ivory
Basket, 3" h., 7 3/4" l. .... $150-$250
Bowl, 4 x 6" .... $150-$250
Pitcher, water, 9" h. .... $600-$800
Toothpick holder .... $350-$450

Rose Tapestry
Basket, rope handle, base & outer rim,
    three color roses, 4 1/4" w., 4" h. ...... $200-$300
Basket, two-color roses, 3" h. .... $200-$300
Basket, two-color roses, 4 1/4" w., 3 3/4" h.
    .... $300-$400
Basket, rope handle, tiny pink roses frame the
    rim, small bouquet of yellow roses on each
    side & yellow roses on the interior, shadow
    green leaves, 2 1/2 x 4 1/4 x 4 1/2" ...... $250-$350
Basket, three-color roses, 4 3/4 x 5 1/4" $300-$400
Basket, two color roses on yellow ground,
    braided decoration around rim .... $300-$400
Bell, pink American Beauty roses, 3" h. $300-$500
Bell, gold loop handle, three-color roses,
    3 1/4" h. .... $300-$400

Rose Tapestry Bowl

Bowl, 10 1/2" d., gently scalloped rim w/four
    shell-molded gilt-trimmed handles, three-
    color roses (ILLUS.) .... $800-$1,100
Bowl, 10 1/2" d., shell- & scroll-molded rim,
    three-color roses .... $800-$1,000
Box, cov., pink & white roses, 2 1/2" sq. $150-$175
Box, cov., two-color roses, 1 1/2 x 2 1/2"
    .... $150-$175
Box, cov., three-color roses, 2 1/2 x 4 1/2",
    1 3/4" h. .... $225-$300
Box, w/domed cover, three-color roses,
    4 1/2" d., 2 3/4" h. .... $350-$400
Box, cov., shell-shaped, 3 x 5 1/2" .... $300-$350
Cake plate, three-color roses, freeform fan-
    cy rim w/gold beading, 9 1/2" w. .... $350-$400
Cake plate, pierced gold handles, three-col-
    or roses, 10 1/2" d. .... $550-$650
Candy dish, three-color roses, 8" oval . $200-$300
Chamberstick, a shaped & flattened base
    centered by a waisted cylindrical short
    standard supporting the dished socket
    w/three rim points, an ornate C-scroll
    handle down the side, three-color roses,
    4 1/4" h. .... $750-$900
Chocolate pot, cov., apricot, white, pink &
    yellow roses, leaf finial, gold trim,
    8 1/2" h. .... $1,400-$1,800
Chocolate set: cov. chocolate pot w/four
    matching cups & saucers, three-color
    roses, 9 pcs. .... $2,600-$3,000
Clock, table-model, three-color roses, up-
    right rectangular case w/a flaring base &
    domed top .... $800-$1,000

Creamer, wide cylindrical body slightly flaring at the base & w/a long buttress spout & gilt angled handle, two-color roses on a rose ground, 3" h.............................. **$200-$300**

Creamer, ovoid body w/flared base & long pinched spout, three-color roses, 3 1/2" h. .... **$150-$200**

Creamer, corset-shaped, three-color roses, 3 3/4" h... **$150-$250**

Creamer, two-color roses, 3 1/2" d., 4" h. **$200-$350**

Creamer, pinched spout, two-color roses **$200-$350**

Creamer & cov. sugar bowl, pink & white roses, pr. .... **$500-$600**

Creamer & cov. sugar bowl, two-color roses, pr. .... **$500-$600**

Cups & saucers, demitasse, three-color roses, 2 sets, each set .... **$100-$150**

Dessert set: large cake plate & six matching small serving plates; three-color roses, 7 pcs................................... **$800-$1,000**

Dish, three-color roses, 2" w., 4 1/2" l, 1 1/2" h.. **$100-$150**

Dish, handled, clover-shaped, decorated w/yellow roses, 5" w. .... **$150-$200**

Dish, leaf-shaped, three-color roses, 5" l. **$200-$250**

Dresser box, cov., kidney-shaped, double pink roses, 2 x 5 1/4"......................... **$300-$350**

Flowerpot & underplate, three-color roses, 3 x 4", 2 pcs. .... **$250-$300**

Hair receiver, cov., footed, two-color roses, 4" d., 2 1/2" h. .... **$300-$350**

Hatpin holder, small red roses at top & base, large yellow roses on body, reticulated base, gold trim, 4 1/2" h. .... **$450-$500**

Hatpin holder, two-color roses, scroll-molded reticulated gilt-trimmed foot below the baluster-form body w/a flaring gilt-trimmed rim, 4 1/2" h........................ **$500-$600**

Humidor, cov., three-color roses, 7" h. . **$650-$700**

Match holder, hanging-type, three-color roses .... **$400-$450**

Match holder, wall hanging-type, a bulbous rounded pouch w/a wide arched backplate w/hanging hole, white & pink roses ..... **$350-$400**

Model of a high-top woman's shoe, pink roses w/a band of green leaves around top, 3 1/2" h...................................... **$500-$600**

Model of a shoe, decorated w/pink roses & original shoe lace .... **$400-$500**

Model of a Victorian woman's high-heeled shoe, three-color roses .... **$400-$500**

Nappy, tri-lobed leaf shape, decorated w/orange roses, 4 1/2" l. .... **$100-$150**

Nappy, open-handled, three-color roses, 5" d.. **$150-$200**

Nut set: master footed bowl & six small footed bowls; decorated w/pink roses, 7 pcs. .... **$1,100-$1,400**

Pitcher, 5" h., wide cylindrical body tapering slightly toward rim, three-color roses, 24 oz. .... **$300-$400**

Pitcher, 5 3/4" h., waisted shape, C-scroll handle angled at bottom, three-color roses .... **$300-$400**

Planter, squatty bulbous base below wide, gently flaring sides w/a ruffled rim, small loop handles near the base, three-color roses, 2 3/4" h................................... **$250-$300**

Plate, 6" d. .... **$150-$200**

Plate, 7" d., three-color roses............... **$200-$250**

Plate, 7 1/2" d., round, w/slightly scalloped rim & four sections of fanned ruffles spaced around the edge, three-color roses .... **$250-$400**

Plate, 10 1/2" d., overall colorful roses w/four gilded scrolls around the rims .... **$200-$300**

Powder box, cov., footed, three-color roses, 4" d., 2 1/2" h.......................... **$300-$400**

Powder jar, cov., footed squatty rounded base w/a squatty domed cover, three-color roses, 3" d., 2 1/2" h. .... **$350-$400**

Relish dish, open-handled, three-color roses, 4 x 8"................................... **$300-$350**

Relish dish, oblong, w/gilt-trimmed scalloped rim, decorated w/large pink roses, 4 3/4" w., 8" l. .... **$350-$400**

Salt dip, ruffled rim, 3" d. .... **$150-$250**

Salt & pepper shakers, three-color roses, pr... **$400-$500**

Salt shaker, pink roses .... **$200-$250**

Sugar bowl, cov., two-handled, one-color rose, 3 1/2" d., 3 1/4" h. .... **$250-$350**

Tray, rectangular, with short rim, three-color roses, 11 1/2 x 8" .... **$450-$600**

Vase, 2 3/4" h., miniature, a thin footring & swelled bottom ring below the gently flaring sides w/a scalloped rim, tiny gold rin handles at the bottom sides, two-color roses (ILLUS. right with other Rose Tapestry vase and Tapestry pin tray, bottom of page)... **$106**

Two Rose Tapestry Vases and a Miscellaneous Tapestry Pin Tray

Vase, 4 1/4" h., footed swelled base tapering to cylindrical sides, two-color roses .... **$250-$350**

Vase, 4 1/2" h., decorated w/American Beauty roses .... **$300-$350**

Vase, 4 1/2" h., ovoid body decorated w/clusters of small red roses at top & base, large yellow roses in center, short neck flaring slightly at rim .... **$200-$250**

Vase, 4 3/4" h., slightly swelled slender cylindrical body w/a short rolled neck, three-color roses in pink, yellow & white .... **$250-$300**

Vase, 5" h., baluster-form body w/a small short neck, large pink roses (ILLUS. center with other Rose Tapestry vase and Tapestry pin tray, bottom previous page)... **$176**

Vase, 6 1/2" h., decorated w/roses & shadow ferns................................ **$350-$450**

Vase, 7" h., bulbous ovoid body tapering to a short tiny flared neck .... **$350-$450**

Wall plaque, pierced to hang, large pink roses .... **$500-$600**

Wall pocket, three-color roses, 5 x 9" .... **$1,000-$1,200**

Sand Babies
Trivet .... **$100-$150**

Snow Babies
Creamer .... **$125-$150**
Pitcher, 3 1/2" h. .... **$100-$150**
Salt shaker .... **$100-$150**
Tea tile .... **$100-$150**
Trivet .... **$100-$150**

Sunbonnet Babies
Ashtray, babies cleaning .... **$200-$250**
Bell, babies fishing .... **$350-$400**
Bell, babies sewing, unmarked .... **$350-$400**
Candlestick, babies ironing, 5" d., 1 3/4" h. .... **$250-$300**
Candlestick, babies washing, 5" d., 1 3/4" h. .... **$250-$300**
Creamer, babies ironing, 3" h. .... **$250-$300**
Creamer & open sugar bowl, babies sewing, pr. .... **$400-$500**
Creamer & open sugar bowl, boat-shaped, babies fishing on sugar, babies cleaning on creamer, pr. .... **$400-$500**
Cup & saucer, babies washing............. **$200-$250**
Dish, diamond-shaped **$200**
Dish, heart-shaped.. **$200**
Mug, babies washing............................. **$300-$350**
Pitcher, milk, 4 1/4" h., babies washing **$250-$300**
Pitcher, milk, babies mending.............. **$325-$400**
Plate, 6" d., babies washing .... **$250-$300**
Tea set, child's .... **$750-$900**
Toothpick holder, babies mending ...... **$450-$550**
Vase, 3" h., babies fishing .... **$200-$250**

Tomato Items
Tomato bowl, berry .... **$25-$50**
Tomato bowls, 5 3/4" d., set of 4 .... **$100-$150**
Tomato box, cov., w/green & brown finial, 3" d.. **$45**
Tomato creamer, cov., large .... **$100-$150**
Tomato creamer, cov., small................... **$50-$75**

Tomato Creamer & Sugar Bowl

Tomato creamer & cov. sugar bowl, creamer 3" d., 3" h., sugar bowl 3 1/2" d., 4" h., pr. (ILLUS.) .... **$75-$100**
Tomato cup & saucer, demitasse.......... **$75-$100**
Tomato mustard jar, cover & figural leaf spoon, 3 pcs................................. **$100-$150**
Tomato pitcher, milk, 4 1/2" h. .... **$200-$250**
Tomato plate, 4 1/4" d., ring-handled, figural lettuce leaf... **$20-$35**
Tomato plate, 5 1/2" d., ring-handled, figural lettuce leaf w/molded yellow flowers .... **$30-$35**
Tomato plate, 7" d., ring-handled, figural lettuce leaf w/molded yellow flowers..... **$30-$45**
Tomato salt & pepper shakers, pr. ...... **$100-$150**
Tomato tea set: cov. teapot, creamer & cov. sugar bowl; 3 pcs. .... **$250-$350**
Tomato teapot, cov., small................... **$250-$350**

Miscellaneous
Ashtray, figural elk............................... **$200-$250**
Ashtray, figural lobster......................... **$100-$150**
Ashtray, figural, oyster & pearl design, 4" l. .... **$200-$300**
Ashtray, figural shell, 4 1/2 x 4 1/2"....... **$50-$75**
Ashtray, mountain goat decoration, 5 1/2" l. .... **$350-$450**
Ashtray, scenic decoration of Dutch woman w/basket, 5 1/2" d. .... **$50-$75**
Ashtray, stork decoration, artist-signed, 4 1/2" l.. **$75-$100**
Ashtray, stork decoration on yellow ground, 3 1/4 x 5", 1 1/4" h............................ **$100-$150**
Basket, miniature, scene w/cows, unmarked... **$50-$75**
Basket, "tapestry," footed, bulbous body w/a ruffled rim & ornate gold-trimmed overhead handle, portrait of woman w/horse, 5" h. .... **$500-$600**
Basket, handled, boy & donkey decoration, artist-signed, 5 3/4" h. .... **$150-$200**
Basket, w/reticulated handles, decorated w/white roses, 7 3/4" l., 3 1/2" h. ...... **$100-$150**
Bell, nursery rhyme decoration w/Jack & the Beanstalk .... **$400-$450**
Bell, nursery rhyme decoration w/Little Bo Peep.. **$300-$400**
Bell, peacock decoration, 2 1/2" d., 3" h. .... **$300-$350**
Bell, scene of musicians, men playing a cello & mandolin .... **$250-$300**
Bell, w/original wooden clapper, decorated w/scene of ocean liner being brought into harbor by tugboats............................ **$250-$300**

Royal Bayreuth Berry Set with Pink Roses

Berry set: 10" d. master bowl & six berry dishes; round w/deep lobed sides decorated in the center w/a cluster of large pink roses & scattered small roses around the sides, very minor flake on one small bowl, the set (ILLUS., top of page) ... **$230**

Royal Bayreuth Musicians Berry Set

Berry set: 9 3/4" d. bowl & five 5" d. sauce dishes; Peasant Musicians decoration, 6 pcs. (ILLUS.) .... **$350-$450**

Berry set: 9 1/2" d. bowl & six 5" d. sauce dishes; portrait decoration, 7 pcs. ..... **$650-$750**

Bowl, 9 1/2" l., 3 3/4" h., raised enameled white roses & foliage on creamy ivory ground, flared, gently ruffled rim, four gold-trimmed reticulated reserves, four short gold feet .... **$250-$350**

Bowl, 5 3/4" d., nursery rhyme scene w/Jack & Jill...................................... **$100-$150**

Bowl, 6" d., figural conch shell .... **$50-$100**

Bowl, 6 7/8" d., 2 1/2" h., footed, shallow slightly scalloped sides, Cavalier Musicians decoration, gold trim on feet ...... **$75-$150**

Bowl, 8" l., 4" h., figural lobster .... **$200-$250**

Bowl, 6 1/4 x 8 1/2", shell-shaped......... **$300-$400**

Bowl, 9 1/2" d., figural poppy **$135**

Bowl, 10" d., decorated w/gold roses.... **$150-$200**

Bowl, 10" d., decorated w/pink roses.... **$125-$150**

Bowl, 5 x 10", footed, handled, figural poppy, apricot satin finish........................ **$600-$700**

Bowl, 10 1/2" d., floral decoration, blown-out mold .... **$250-$300**

Bowl, 10 1/2" d., "tapestry," decorated w/Colonial scene .... **$1,000-$1,200**

Box, cov., four-footed ring base, scenic decoration of Dutch children .... **$125-$150**

Box, cov., shell-shaped, nursery rhyme scene, Little Boy Blue decoration...... **$200-$225**

Royal Bayreuth Box with Arab Scene

Box, cov., square, desert scene decoration on cover, Arabs w/camels on background colors of pink & brown, unmarked, 2 x 2 1/2", 1 3/4" h. (ILLUS.) .... **$50-$75**

Royal Bayreuth Heart-shaped Box

Box, cov., heart-shaped, decorated w/scene of two brown & white cows & trees in pasture, green & yellow background, unmarked, 2 x 3 1/4", 1 1/2" h. (ILLUS.)... **$75-$100**

Box, cov., scene of woman on horse, woman & man w/rake watching, 4 1/4" d., 2 1/4" h... **$150-$200**

Box, cov., figural turtle, 2 3/4 x 5" .... **$800-$900**

Box, cov., shell-shaped, Little Jack Horner decoration, 5 1/2" d.......................... **$200-$250**

Cake plate, decorated w/scene of men fishing .... **$200-$250**

Rare Cake Plate with Polar Bears

Cake plate, decorated w/snowy scene & two polar bears, gold trimmed scalloped border (ILLUS.) .... **$1,500-$2,000**
Candleholder, figural rose .... **$500-$600**

Royal Bayreuth Santa Candleholder

Candleholder, figural, Santa, very rare (ILLUS.) .... **$8,000-$10,000**
Candleholder, penguin decoration .... **$250-$300**
Candlestick, figural bassett hound, brown, 4" h. .... **$400-$500**
Candlestick, decorated w/scene of cows, 4" h. .... **$75-$100**
Candlestick, elks scene, 4" h. .... **$125-$150**
Candlestick, decorated w/frog & bee, 6 1/2" h. .... **$400-$450**
Candlestick, figural clown, red, 4 1/2 x 6 1/2" .... **$500-$600**
Candlestick, w/match holder, figural clown, 7" h. .... **$1,100-$1,300**
Candlestick, oblong dished base w/a standard at one edge flanked by downswept open handles, tulip-form socket w/flattened rim, interior of dished base decorated w/scene of hunter & dogs .... **$250-$300**

Candy dish, figural lobster.................. **$100-$150**
Candy dish w/turned over edge, nursery rhyme scene w/Little Miss Muffet...... **$100-$150**
Celery dish, figural lobster.................. **$100-$150**
Chamberstick, wide, deeply dished, round pinched sides, central cylindrical socket w/flattened rim, S-scroll handle from side of dish to socket, dark brick red ground, decorated w/"Dancing Frogs" & flying insects, rare .... **$1,200-$1,500**

Royal Bayreuth Cheese Dishes

Cheese dishes, miniature, decorated w/scenes of cattle, each (ILLUS. of two) .... **$450-$550**

Royal Bayreuth Chocolate Pot

Chocolate pot, cov., tall tapering cylindrical body w/a rim spout, long gold leaf-scroll handle, inset domed cover w/knob finial, color scene of a boy w/three donkeys, 8 1/2" h. (ILLUS.) **$230**
Chocolate pot, cov., figural poppy, tall pink blossom w/ruffled rim, figural poppy on cover, light green & white leafy footed base & large leaf & stem handle, 8 1/2" h. .... **$1,200-$1,800**
Cracker jar, cov., figural lobster............ **$400-$600**
Cracker jar, cov., figural poppy, 6" h. ... **$600-$900**
Creamer, Arab scene decoration.................... **$95**
Creamer, blue cylindrical body w/flared base & figural brown & grey cat handle, 3 3/4" h... **$300-$350**
Creamer, Brittany Girl decoration **$75**
Creamer, cobalt blue, Babes in Woods decoration, unmarked............................ **$200-$250**
Creamer, crowing rooster & hen decoration, 4 1/4" h... **$100-$150**

Goats in Snow & Sheep in Snow Creamers

Water Buffalo Creamer

Creamer, figural water buffalo, black & white (ILLUS.) .... **$125-$200**

Creamer, figural water buffalo, souvenir of Portland, Oregon .... **$150-$250**

Creamer, figural watermelon .... **$250-$300**

Creamer, flow blue, Babes in Woods decoration .... **$200-$250**

Creamer, "Huntsman," scene of hunter & dogs, small flying bird on flared rim, 4" h. .... **$75-$125**

Creamer, left-handled, scene of two girls under umbrella, 3 1/2" h. .... **$300-$400**

Creamer, miniature, "tapestry" scene of girl & horse .... **$200-$250**

Creamer, pasture scene w/cows & trees, 3 1/4" h. .... **$50-$100**

Creamer, pinched spout, "tapestry," goats decoration, 4" h. .... **$300-$350**

Creamer, scene of girl w/basket, salmon color .... **$500-$700**

Creamer, "tapestry," footed ovoid body tapering to a wide rounded & flaring neck w/a pinched spout & small C-scroll handle, sheep in the meadow decoration, 3 3/4" h. .... **$250-$350**

Creamer, "tapestry," Scottish highland goats scene .... **$250-$300**

Creamer, "tapestry," wide ovoid body w/a flaring foot & a long pinched spout, ornate gilt D-form handle, "The Bathers" landscape scene, 3 1/2" h. .... **$300-$450**

Creamer, w/scene of goats in snow (ILLUS. left w/sheep in snow creamer, top of page) .... **$100-$200**

Creamer, w/scene of sheep in snow (ILLUS. right w/goats in snow creamer, top of page) .... **$100-$200**

Creamer & cov. sugar bowl, figural apple, pr. .... **$250-$350**

Creamer & cov. sugar bowl, figural grape cluster, purple, pr. .... **$150-$250**

Creamer & cov. sugar bowl, figural pansy, lavender, pr. .... **$300-$400**

Creamer & cov. sugar bowl, figural poppy, pr. .... **$300-$350**

Creamer & cov. sugar bowl, figural rooster, pr. .... **$300-$350**

Creamer & cov. sugar bowl, figural strawberry, unmarked, pr. .... **$400-$450**

Creamer & open sugar bowl, each decorated w/a mountain landscape w/a boy & donkey, 3" h., pr. .... **$200-$350**

Creamer & open sugar bowl, figural poppy, pr. .... **$300-$500**

Creamer & open sugar bowl, figural poppy, white satin finish, pr. .... **$300-$500**

Creamer & open sugar bowl, figural rooster, creamer w/multicolored feathers & sugar bowl in black, pr. .... **$800-$1,200**

Creamer & open sugar bowl, figural strawberry, unmarked, pr. .... **$400-$600**

Creamer & open sugar bowl, "tapestry," barrel-shaped, the creamer w/a long pinched spout, creamer w/goose girl scene, sugar w/Alpine village scene, sugar bowl 3 7/8" h., creamer 4 1/4" h., pr. ... **$450-$650**

Cup & saucer, decorated w/hunting scene of man & dog .... **$75-$125**

Cup & saucer, figural rose .... **$150-$200**

Cup & saucer, floral decoration on the inside & outside, gold handle on cup, scalloped standard saucer, ca. 1916 .... **$35-$75**

Cup & saucer, scene of man w/turkeys.. **$75-$125**

Cup & saucer, "tapestry," floral decoration .... **$150-$250**

Cup & saucer, demitasse, Castle scene decoration, artist-signed.................. **$110-$150**

Cup & saucer, demitasse, figural apple .... **$100-$150**

Cup & saucer, demitasse, figural grape cluster .... **$100-$150**

Cup & saucer, demitasse, figural orange .... **$100-$150**

Dish, leaf-shaped, nursery rhyme decoration w/Little Miss Muffet.................. **$100-$150**

Dish, leaf-shaped, "tapestry," scenic Lady & Prince decoration .... **$100-$150**

Royal Bayreuth Dresser Tray

Dresser tray, rectangular, w/gently ruffled rim, decorated w/depiction of Little Boy Blue sleeping in haystack (ILLUS., top of page)... **$400-$550**

Dresser tray, rectangular, "tapestry," Lady & Prince scenic decoration, 7 x 9 1/4" .... **$400-$500**

Boy & Donkeys Dresser Tray

Dresser tray, rectangular w/rounded corners, scene of boy & three donkeys in landscape, 8 x 11" (ILLUS.) **$150-250**

Dresser tray, rectangular w/rounded corners, "tapestry" decoration of a young courting couple wearing early 19th c. attire, 11 1/2" l. .... **$400-$500**

Dresser tray, decorated w/hunting scene .... **$200-$250**

Ewer, scene of hunter w/dog, 4 1/2" h. .... **$150-$200**

Ewer, cobalt blue, Babes in Woods decoration, 6" h. .... **$500-$650**

Flower holder w/frog-style cover, hunt scene decoration, 3 3/4" h. .... **$150-$200**

Gravy boat w/attached liner, decorated w/multicolored floral sprays, gadrooned border, gold trim, cream ground........... **$50-$75**

Gravy boat & underplate, figural poppy, satin finish, 2 pcs............................... **$200-$300**

Hair receiver, cov., decorated w/scene of boy & donkey .... **$100-$150**

Hair receiver, cov., "tapestry," scene of farmer w/turkeys .... **$200-$300**

Royal Bayreuth "Tapestry" Hair Receiver

Hair receiver, cov., "tapestry," small gold scroll feet & low squatty rounded body w/a fitted low cover w/a small ruffled center opening, decorated w/a scene of swans on a lake, 4" d. (ILLUS.) .... **$200-$300**

Hair receiver, cov., three-footed, scene of dog beside hunter shooting ducks .... **$200-$300**

Hair receiver, cov., decorated w/a scene of a Dutch boy & girl, 3 1/4" h. .... **$100-$150**

Hatpin holder, figural owl .... **$600-$850**

Penguin Hatpin Holder

Hatpin holder, model of a penguin, in red, white & grey, signed (ILLUS.) .... **$600-$800**

Royal Bayreuth Vase, Shoe & Sprinkling Can

Model of woman's shoe, old fashioned high-button shoe in silver tapestry design, 5" l., 3 1/2" h. (ILLUS. center w/tapestry vase with lady & sprinkling can, top of page) .... **$2,000-$2,500**

Mug, figural clown .... **$400-$500**

Mug, beer, figural elk .... **$300-$400**

Mug, beer, figural elk, 5 3/4" h.............. **$450-$600**

Mug, decorated w/Cavalier scene, 4 1/2" h. .... **$100-$150**

Mug, candle lady decoration, 5" h. .... **$250-$350**

Mustard jar, cov., figural grape cluster, yellow... **$125-$175**

Mustard jar, cov., figural lobster .... **$150-$250**

Mustard jar, cov., figural rose .... **$400-$500**

Mustard jar, cov., figural shell.............. **$100-$160**

Mustard jar, cov., figural pansy, 3 1/4" h. .... **$300-$600**

Mustard jar, cover & spoon, figural poppy, red, green spoon, 3 pcs. .... **$200-$300**

Nappy, handled, figural poppy .... **$100-$150**

Nut set: large pedestal-based open compote & six matching servers; each decorated w/a colorful pastoral scene w/animals, 7 pcs. .... **$400-$450**

Pin dish, decorated w/Arab scene .... **$75-$100**

Pin tray, "tapestry," a shallow three-lobed & ruffled dish w/a forked loop rim handle w/worn gold, decorated w/the Cavalier Musicians scene, 5" w. (ILLUS. left with two small Rose Tapestry vases, botom of page 566) **$71**

Pin tray, triangular, "tapestry" portrait decoration of woman wearing large purple plumed hat, 5 x 5 x 5" .... **$200-$250**

Pincushion, figural elk head .... **$300-$350**

Pipe holder, figural bassett hound, black .... **$350-$500**

Royal Bayreuth Water Pitcher

Pitcher, water, bulbous body w/scene of fisherman standing in boat against wooded backdrop, flaring neck & spout, applied handle (ILLUS.) .... **$400-$500**

Royal Bayreuth Tapestry Water Pitcher

Pitcher, water, jug-type body w/applied handle, set-in spout, portrait "tapestry" decoration of 18th c. lady in plumed hat (ILLUS.)... **$750-$900**

Royal Bayreuth Miniature Pitchers

Pitcher, 2" h., miniature advertising piece w/scene of "sanatorium grounds" on front, angled handle (ILLUS. left w/miniature Hupo bird pitcher) .... **$150-$250**

Pitcher, 2" h., miniature, w/picture of Hupo bird on front, angled handle (ILLUS. right w/miniature advertising pitcher, above) .... **$250-$350**

Pitcher, 2 1/2" h., scene w/cows........... **$125-$200**

Royal Bayreuth Pitcher & Vase

Pitcher, 3 1/8" h., 2 3/8" w., squared waisted body w/short, wide spout & angled gilt
handle, scene of Arab on horse (ILLUS.
right) .... **$100-$150**

Cavalier Scene Tapering Pitcher

Pitcher, 3 1/4" h., 2" d., decorated w/Cav-
alier scene, two Cavaliers drinking at a
table, grey & cream ground, unmarked
(ILLUS.) .... **$50-$75**
Pitcher, 3 1/2" h., nursery rhyme scene
w/Little Boy Blue............................... **$150-$250**
Pitcher, 3 1/2" h., scenic decoration of Arab
on horse .... **$50-$100**

Pitcher with Musicians Scene

Pitcher, 3 1/2" h., 2 1/4" d., scene of musicians, one playing bass & one w/mando-
lin, unmarked (ILLUS.) .... **$50-$75**

Pitcher, 3 3/4" h., corset-shaped, Colonial
Curtsey scene w/a couple................. **$125-$165**
Pitcher, 4 1/2" h., scene of a skiff w/sail. **$75-$150**
Pitcher, 5" h., Arab w/horse decoration **$100-$125**
Pitcher, 5" h., double handles, scene of
fisherman in boat w/sails .... **$100-$150**
Pitcher, 5" h., figural crow.................... **$150-$200**
Pitcher, 5" h., scene of an Arab on white
horse w/brown horse nearby............. **$100-$150**
Pitcher, 5" h., 5" d., squatty, decorated
w/hunting scene................................. **$75-$125**

Rare Royal Bayreuth Santa Pitcher

Pitcher, 5 1/4" h., figural, Santa Claus,
pack on back serves as handle (ILLUS.)
.... **$3,500-$4,500**
Pitcher, 5 1/4" h., jug-type, narrow handle,
decorated w/picture of jester on cream
ground shading to light green (ILLUS. right
w/hunting stein, bottom of page 574) .. **$450-$550**
Pitcher, 5 1/4" h., pinched spout, "tapestry,"
scene of train on bridge over raging river
.... **$450-$550**
Pitcher, 6" h., decorated w/hunting scene
.... **$100-$175**

Royal Bayreuth Butterfly Pitcher

Pitcher, water, 6 1/2" h., in the form of a
perched butterfly, in shades of green,
deep pink & light blue, handle in the form
of a stem w/leaves (ILLUS.)........ **$5,500-$7,500**
Pitcher, 6 3/4" h., wide ovoid body w/a flaring, lightly scalloped base & a long
pinched spout, "tapestry" finish w/a color
landscape "Don Quixote" scene .... **$450-$600**

Plaque, decorated w/scene of Arab on horse, 9 1/2" d. .... **$100-$150**

Royal Bayreuth "Tapestry" Plaque

Plaque, pierced to hang, "tapestry," round w/a scroll-molded gilt-trimmed border, center portrait of woman leaning on horse, 9 1/2" d. (ILLUS.) .... **$700-$850**

Plate, 5 1/4" d., leaf-shaped, decorated w/small yellow flowers on green ground, green curved handle .... **$25-$50**

Plate, 6" d., decorated w/soccer scene .... **$150-$200**

Plate, 6" d., handled, figural leaf & flower .... **$60-$100**

Plate, 7" d., decorated w/scene of girl walking dog .... **$75-$125**

Plate, 7 1/2" d., nursery rhyme scene w/Little Bo Peep.. **$100-$150**

Plate, 8" d., decorated w/pink & yellow flowers, gold rim, pink ground, blue mark.... **$50-$75**

Plate, 8" d., scene of man hunting .... **$75-$150**

Plate, 8 1/2" d., scene of man fishing...... **$75-$150**

Plate, 8 1/2" d., scene of man hunting .... **$75-$150**

Plate, 9" d., candle girl decoration......... **$125-$185**

Plate, 9" d., Cavalier Musicians scene .... **$225-$275**

Plate, 9" d., figural ear of corn.............. **$450-$500**

Plate, 9" d., scene of man smoking pipe **$150-$200**

Plate, 9 1/2" d., nursery rhyme scene w/Jack & the Beanstalk..................... **$250-$300**

Plate, 9 1/2" d., scroll-molded rim, "tapestry," toasting Cavalier scene .... **$700-$825**

Plate, 9 1/2" d., "tapestry," landscape scene w/deer by a river .... **$250-$300**

Plate, 9 1/2" d., "tapestry," woman w/horse scene .... **$600-$800**

Playing card box, cov., decorated w/a sailing ship scene.................................. **$150-$250**

Powder box, cov., Cavalier Musicians scene .... **$150-$200**

Powder box, cov., round, "tapestry," scenic Lady & Prince decoration................. **$150-$200**

Powder jar, figural pansy, 4 1/4" h. ...... **$450-$600**

Relish dish, open-handled, footed, ruffled edge, cow scene decoration, 8" l. ..... **$125-$175**

Relish dish, figural cucumber, 5 1/4 x 12 1/2".................................. **$100-$250**

Relish dish, figural Murex Shell............ **$150-$250**

Salt & pepper shakers, figural conch shell, unmarked, pr...................................... **$75-$125**

Salt & pepper shakers, figural ear of corn, pr.. **$500-$800**

Salt & pepper shakers, figural grape cluster, purple, pr.................................... **$125-$200**

Salt & pepper shakers, figural poppy, red, pr.. **$250-$400**

Salt & pepper shakers, figural shell, pr. .... **$100-$150**

Salt shaker, figural elk.................................... **$135**

Sprinkling can, miniature size, "tapestry," decoration of woman & pony, 2 3/4" h. (ILLUS. left w/tapestry vase with lady & shoe, top of page 572)...................... **$500-$700**

Stamp box, cov., colorful scene of Dutch children .... **$100-$150**

Stamp box, cov., "tapestry," Cottage by Water Fall scene.............................. **$150-$250**

Stein, w/pewter hinged top, decorated w/scene of stag swimming away from hunting dogs, 6" h. (ILLUS. left w/jester pitcher, bottom of page).................... **$400-$500**

String holder, hanging-type, figural rooster head... **$350-$550**

Sugar bowl, cov., Brittany Girl decoration .... **$50-$125**

Sugar bowl, cov., figural lemon .... **$100-$150**

Sugar bowl, cov., figural pansy, purple .... **$150-$250**

Sugar bowl, cov., figural poppy, red..... **$150-$250**

Royal Bayreuth Stein & Pitcher

Royal Bayreuth Child's Tea Set

Sugar bowl, cov., figural rose .... **$300-$400**
Sugar bowl, cov., figural shell w/lobster handle .... **$125-$225**
Sugar bowl, cov., figural lobster, 3 3/4" h. .... **$75-$150**
Tea set: child's, cov. teapot, cov. sugar, creamer, two plates, & two cups & saucers; ovoid bodies, each piece decorated w/a scene of children playing, the set (ILLUS., top of page) .... **$700-$800**
Tea strainer, figural pansy, 5 3/4" l. ...... **$200-$300**
Tea strainer, figural red poppy, 5 3/4" l. **$200-$300**
Teapot, cov., child's, decorated w/a scene of hunters, 3 3/4" h. .... **$100-$150**
Teapot, cov., child's, boy & donkey decoration, green, unmarked, 4" h. .... **$150-$250**
Teapot, cov., demitasse, decorated w/scene of rooster & hen .... **$200-$300**
Teapot, cov., figural orange, 6 1/2" h. .. **$350-$450**
Teapot, cov., figural poppy, red............ **$300-$350**
Toothpick holder, ball-shaped, w/overhead handle, "tapestry," woman w/horse scene.. **$450-$550**
Toothpick holder, Bird of Paradise decoration .... **$200-$250**
Toothpick holder, decorated w/scene of girl w/two chickens .... **$125-$225**
Toothpick holder, figural bell ringer, 3 1/2" h. .... **$200-$250**
Toothpick holder, figural elk head, 3" h. .... **$225-$250**
Toothpick holder, figural Murex Shell........... **$175**
Toothpick holder, figural poppy, red.... **$250-$350**
Toothpick holder, man hunting turkeys scene.. **$150-$250**
Toothpick holder, rooster & hen decoration, 2 1/2" h. .... **$200-$300**
Toothpick holder, round, one side handle, decorated w/scene of man tending turkeys.. **$200-$300**
Toothpick holder, "tapestry," scene of woman w/pony & trees, 2 2/5" h. ...... **$400-$550**
Toothpick holder, three-handled, floral decoration, 2 1/4" h. .... **$150-$225**
Toothpick holder, three-handled, harvest scene decoration............................. **$150-$200**
Toothpick holder, three-handled, hunt scene decoration, 3" h. .... **$200-$275**
Toothpick holder, three-handled, scene of horse & wagon .... **$125-$200**
Toothpick holder, three-handled, three feet, nursery rhyme decoration w/Little Boy Blue... **$200-$250**

Toothpick holder, two-handled, four-footed, scene of horsemen, unmarked ..... **$75-$150**
Tray, club-shaped, scene of hunter w/dog .... **$100-$175**

Tray with Girl & Geese Scene

Tray, decorated w/scene of girl w/geese, molded rim w/gold trim, 9 x 12 1/4" (ILLUS.) **$350-$500**

Tall Royal Bayreuth Vase with Parrots

Vase, baluster-form body w/decoration of red & blue parrots & pink flowers, trumpet neck, short pedestal on disc foot, side handles w/images of human faces where they attach to body (ILLUS.) .... **$400-$425**

Vase, 3 1/4" h., 1 7/8" d., footed, conical body tapering to a silver rim, small tab handles, decorated w/scene of white & brown cows w/green & brown ground (ILLUS. left with Arab scene pitcher, page 573) .... **$50-$125**

Vase, 3 1/2" h., spherical shape w/small gold rim opening, w/scenic "tapestry" decoration of woman in garden (ILLUS. left w/shoe & sprinkling can, top of page 572) .... **$500-$650**

Ornate Handled Vase with Peacock

Vase, 9 1/2" h., peacock decoration, open-work on neck & at base, ornate scroll handles, lavish gold trim (ILLUS.) ..... **$600-$725**

Small Royal Bayreuth Vases

Vases, 3 1/8" h., 2 5/8" d., squatty bulbous lower body below the tall tapering sides ending in a ringed neck & flanked by loop handles, one w/scene of Dutch boy & girl playing w/brown dog & the other w/scene of Dutch boy & girl playing w/white & brown dog, green mark, pr. (ILLUS.)... **$50-$150**

Wall pocket, figural red poppy, 9 1/2" l.
.... **$600-$700**

Royal Copley

Royal Copley was a trade name used by the Spaulding China Company of Sebring, Ohio, during the 1940s and 1950s for a variety of ceramic figurines, planters and other decorative pieces. Similar Spaulding pieces were also pro-

duced under the trade name "Royal Windsor," or carried the Spaulding China mark.

Dime stores generally featured the Royal Copley line, with Spaulding's other lines available in more upscale outlets.

The Spaulding China Company ended production in 1957, but for the next two years other potteries finished production of its outstanding orders. Today these originally inexpensive wares are developing a dedicated collector following thanks to their whimsically appealing designs.

Advisor for this category is Donald-Brian Johnson, an author and lecturer specializing in Mid-Twentieth Century design.

Figurines

Royal Copley Airedale Figurine

Airedale, seated, brown & white, 6 1/2" h. (ILLUS.)... **$40-$45**

Black Cat, 8" h. .... **$75-$100**

Blackamoor Man & Woman Figures

Blackamoor Man & Blackamoor Woman, kneeling, 8 1/2" h., pr. (ILLUS.)......... **$100-$120**

Cockatoo, rose or green, 8 1/4" h., each
.... **$45-$50**

Cockatoos, 7 1/4" h. .... **$50-$60**

Cocker Spaniel, 6 1/4" h. .... **$35-$40**

Figure of Dancing Lady

Dancing lady, wearing hat & long full-skirted dress, one hand holding her hat in place while wind blows at her dress, four colorations, unmarked, 8" h., each (ILLUS.).. **$135-$150**
Deer & Fawn, 8 1/2" h. .... **$60-$70**
Dog, 6 1/2" h. .... **$30-$35**
Dog, 8" h. .... **$40-$45**
Dog pulling wagon, sitting dog, brown w/black & white spots, wagon imprinted "FLYER" on side, unmarked, 5 1/4" h. . **$35-$50**

Royal Copley Gadwells Drake Figurine

Gadwells drake & duck, Game Bird series, signed "A.D. Priollo" on base, Royal Windsor mark, series consists of Gadwells, Teals & Mallards, Gadwells & Teals are hardest to find, sizes vary, pr. (ILLUS. of drake).............................. **$150-$250**
Hen & Rooster, large, Royal Copley mark, 7" & 8" h., pr. .... **$100-$130**
Hen & Rooster, Royal Windsor mark, 6 1/2" & 7" h., pr. .... **$120-$140**
Hen & Rooster, small, Royal Copley mark, 6" & 6 1/2" h., pr. .... **$90-$100**
Hen & rooster, black & white w/red trim, green base, (rooster is harder to find), 5 1/2" h. & 6" h., pr. .... **$350-$400**

Large Black & White Hen & Rooster

Hen & rooster, black & white w/red trim, green base, 7" h. & 8" h., pr. (ILLUS.)
.... **$200-$225**
Hen & rooster, black & white w/red trim, white base, 7" h. & 8" h., pr. (rooster is harder to find)... **$225**
Hen & rooster, brown breast, Royal Windsor mark, 10" h. & 10 1/2" h., pr. (hens are harder to find) .... **$300-$350**
Hen & rooster, teal breast, Royal Windsor mark, 10" h. & 10 1/4" h., pr. (hens are harder to find).................................... **$350-$400**
Hunt's Swallow, female flying toward ground, male flying upward, four colorations, some are hand-decorated, cobalt pair & females hardest to find, 8" h., pr. (ILLUS. of female, right w/Jay bird, bottom of page)..................................... **$150-$250**
Kingfishers, one on leaf base w/wings extended, the other flying downward, blue, rose or yellow, blue is hardest to find, rose pairs are hard to match, 5" h., pr., each (ILLUS., bottom of page).......... **$100-$150**

Models of Kingfishers

Kitten, brown to brown grey, 8" h., each (colors hard to match) .... **$100-$125**

Models of Black & White Kittens

Kittens, black & white w/red bow at neck, sitting, one looking up & one looking down, one shown on left is harder to find, 8" h., each (ILLUS.)............................... **$75-$85**

Mallard Duck, 7" h. .... **$40-$45**

Oriental Boy & Girl Figurines

Oriental Boy & Oriental Girl, standing, 7 1/2" h., pr. (ILLUS.) .... **$35-$55**

Parrots, 8" h. .... **$35-$45**

Rooster, all-white, 10" h. **$129**

Sea Gulls, 8" h. .... **$35-$55**

Spaniel Pup with Collar Figurine

Spaniel Pup with Collar, 6" h. (ILLUS.)... **$40-$45**

Swallow w/extended wings, cobalt, rose or yellow, blue is hardest, choicest & priciest coloration, 7" h., each........... **$110-$130**

Swallows on Double Stump, 7 1/2" h., pr. .... **$120-$140**

Teddy bear, eyes closed & playing concertina, brown, unmarked, 7 1/2" h. (hard to find in mint condition) .... **$90-$100**

Thrushes, 6 1/2" h. .... **$20-$25**

Titmouse, 8" h. .... **$25-$35**

Wrens, 6 1/4" h. .... **$20-$25**

Planters

Large Kneeling Angel Planter

Angel, large, kneeling, blue robe, 8" h. (ILLUS.).. **$70-$85**

Angel on Star Planter

Angel on Star, white relief figure on creamy yellow ground, 6 3/4" h. (ILLUS.) .... **$30-$40**

Apple and Finch, 6 1/2" h. .... **$50-$60**

Balinese Girl, 8 1/2" h. .... **$50-$60**

Bare Shoulder Lady head vase, 6" h. ...... **$70-$80**

Big Hat Chinese Boy & Girl, 7 1/2" h., pr. .... **$50-$60**

Birdhouse with Bird, 8" h. .... **$150-$175**

Cat & Cello, rare, 7 1/2" h..................... **$150-$175**

Royal Copley Clown Planter
Clown, 8 1/4" h. (ILLUS.) .... **$120-$145**

Doe & Fawn Head Planter
Doe & Fawn Head, rectangular log-form
planter, 5 1/4" h. (ILLUS.) .... **$50-$60**

Dog in Picnic Basket Planter
Dog in Picnic Basket, 7 3/4" h. (ILLUS.) . **$80-$90**

Dog with Raised Paw Planter
Dog with Raised Paw, 7 1/2" h. (ILLUS.). **$70-$80**
Dog with String Bass, rare, 7" h.......... **$175-$200**

Elf and Shoe Planter
Elf and Shoe, 6" h. (ILLUS.) .... **$60-$70**

Fancy Finch on Tree Stump Planter
Fancy Finch on Tree Stump, red, white &
black bird perched on brown leafy branch
beside white planter, 7 1/2" h. (ILLUS.)
.... **$90-$100**

Hummingbird Planter & Pigtail Girl Wall Pocket

Gazelle, 9" h. .... $60-$70

Girl on Wheelbarrow Planter

Girl on Wheelbarrow, 7" h. (ILLUS.) .... $50-$55
Gloved Lady, 6" h. .... $80-$90

Hummingbird on flower, blue or red & white bird, red flower, green leaves form base, blue bird brings higher price, 5 1/4" h. (ILLUS. left, top of page) .... $50-$75
Indian Boy & Drum, 6 1/2" h. .... $50-$60

Kitten and Book Planter

Kitten and Book, 6 1/2" h. (ILLUS.) .... $45-$55

Horse Head with Mane Planter

Horse Head with Flying Mane, 8" h. (ILLUS.) .... $35-$55

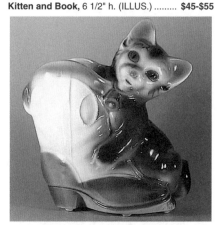

Kitten on Cowboy Boot Planter

Kitten on Cowboy Boot, 7 1/2" h. (ILLUS.) .... $65-$70

Palomino Horse Head Planter

Palomino Horse Head, 6 1/4" h. (ILLUS.) **$50-$60**
Pigtail Girl, 7" h. .... **$50-$55**

Rooster Planter

Rooster on wheelbarrow, 8" h. (ILLUS.)
.... **$100-$125**
Running Horse, design on one side, 6" h. **$35-$55**

Reclining Poodle Planter

Poodle, reclining, white w/black nose &
eyes, 8" l. (ILLUS.) .... **$80-$90**
Ram's Head, also used as bookends, plant-
er **$55**

Siamese Cats Planter

Siamese cats, two, one sitting & one recumbent, white w/black trim, blue eyes, green
or rust woven basket, green is more desir-
able, 8" h., each (ILLUS.).................... **$175-$200**

Ribbed Star Royal Windsor Planter

Ribbed Star, all-white, "Royal Windsor"
sticker, 4 3/4" h. (ILLUS.) .... **$35-$40**

Stuffed Animal Dog Planter

Stuffed Animal Dog, white & brown,
5 1/2" h. (ILLUS.) .... **$70-$80**

Wall pocket, figural, "Pigtail Girl," bust f girl w/ruffled collar & bonnet, grey, deep red, turquoise, pink & deep blue, marked "Royal Copley," deep red & blue are the most desired & therefore harder to find & costlier, 7" h., each (ILLUS. right w/Hummingbird planter, top of page 580) ...... **$75-$125**

Royal Dux

This factory in Bohemia was noted for the figural porcelain wares in the Art Nouveau style it exported around the turn of the 20th century. Other notable figural pieces were produced through the 1930s. The factory was nationalized after World War II.

Royal Dux Marks

Royal Dux Bull & Farmer Group

Royal Dux Arab & Camel Figure Group

Royal Dux Figural Shell & Nymph Piece

Center piece, figural, in the form of a large open conch shell raised on a large coral branches, an Art Nouveau sea nymph seated on one end of the shell, painted in pale shades of green, creamy yellow & brown, applied pink triangle mark, early 20th c., 12" h. (ILLUS.).............................. **$776**

Figure group, a large cream-colored bull being held on a rein by a standing farmer wearing a hat, long-sleeved sheet, pants & boots, on a naturalistic rectangular base, decorated in dark gold, pink triangle mark & impressed number, late 19th - early 20th c., 13" l., 11" h. (ILLUS., top next column).. **$748**

Figure group, an Arab man wearing a hood & flowing robes seated atop a tall walking camel, a half-naked young boy below struggling w/two large bags, decorated in shades of deep red, brown, tan, cream & gold, pink triangle & Made in Czechoslovkia marks on base, 6 x 14", 18" h. (ILLUS., middle next column).................... **$480**

Figure of a bather, the semi-nude young maiden seated on a rockwork base, in naturalistic colors, signed w/the applied

Fine Royal Dux Figure of a Bather

pink triangle mark, early 20th c., 21" h. (ILLUS.)... **$3,335**

Royal Dux Peasant Man & Woman

Figures, peasant man & woman, he standing wearing a wide-brimmed hat, gold shirt & brown pants & holding a bag over one shoulder & a net in the other, on a round naturalistic base w/stump & chain she wearing a short-sleeved blouse & vest & long deep red dress w/one hand holding up her gold apron full of apples & a jug over her arm, on a matching rounded base, pink triangle & impressed triangle marks w/numbers, 20" & 22" h., pr. (ILLUS.) **$720**

Royal Dux Lamp with Horse & Boy

Lamp, figural table model, the oblong base enclosed in a brass frame & mounted w/the model of a large creamy white work horse carrying a removable young farm boy wearing a cap, shirt & rolled up pants, trimmed in dark gold, pink triangle mark & impressed "1602," metal upright at back w/electric fitting & decorated creamy silk shade, early 20th c., figure 12" l., 14" h. (ILLUS.) **$690**

Royal Dux Mirror with Maiden Figure

Mirror, figural table-type, an upright oval beveled edge mirror set along one side w/a curved flower & vine support raised on a tree trunk base, a tall classical maiden standing to the side wearing long deep red robes, squared dished base, pink triangle mark, late 19th - early 20th c., base 16" w., overall 17" h. (ILLUS.) ... **$1,323**

Royal Dux Floral Art Nouveau Vase

Vase, 20 1/2" h., 11 1/2" d., Art Nouveau style, footed wide squatty base section below the tall gently tapering upper body tapering to a wide cupped rim, molded down the sides & around the base section w/realistic leaves & blossoms w/undulating loop handles down the sides, dusted black finish & gold trim, pink triangle & impressed numbers, late 19th - early 20th c. (ILLUS.) **$518**

Pretty Royal Dux Figural Vases

Vases, 11" h., figural, each w/a block-form base supporting a short stone block pedestal topped w/a tall column forming a vase, one mounted in front w/the figure of a standing maiden wearing a tight-fitting robe w/wide sleeves, her hands behind her head; the other mounted w/the figure of a young shepherd w/a cap, animal skin outfit & playing the pipes of Pan, decorated in shades of reddish brown, dark mustard yellow & cream, applied pink triangle marks, facing pair (ILLUS.) **$431**

Pair of Royal Dux Figural Vases

Vases, 12" h., figural, a large cylindrical molded tree trunk form, one applied w/a the figure of a boy playing a lyre & the other w/the figure of dancing girl w/a lamb, cream ground w/heavy gold trim, pink triangle marks & impressed numbers, late 19th - early 20th c., pr. (ILLUS.) **$408**

Royal Vienna

The second factory in Europe to make hard paste porcelain was established in Vienna in 1719 by Claud Innocentius de Paquier. The factory underwent various changes of administration through the years and finally closed in 1865. Since then, however, the porcelain has been reproduced by various factories in Austria and Germany, many of which have also reproduced the early beehive mark. Early pieces, naturally, bring far higher prices than the later ones or the reproductions.

Royal Vienna Mark

Vienna Style Charger with Romantic Scene

Charger, round, h.p. w/a romantic mythological scene of a pretty maiden seated on a garden bench beside a fountain & playfully scolding Cupid who has broken his bow, an orb at her feet, artist-signed, within a pink velvet & giltwood frame, early 20th c., 11" d. (ILLUS.) **$2,400**

Ewer & undertray, the ewer w/ a domed foot & ringed stem supporting the tall ovoid body tapering to a divided mouth w/a high arched & pointed spout, a high arched gold handle from rim to center of side, ruby & gold ground, h.,p. w/a continuous scene of Roman & Renaissance figures gathered before a pyre worshipping, discussing & destroying art, reserved on a gilt ground decorated w/raised gilt grasses, titled under the base in German, within borders of fruiting vine & scrolling leaves, the ruby ground matching round undertray decorated w/ornate acanthus leaf scrolls within blue & gilt borders, blue Beehive mark, artist-signed, late 19th c., overall 17 3/4" h., 2 pr. (ILLUS. center with pair of covered vases, top next page)............................ **$2,880**

Vienna-style Ewer & Undertray and a Pair of Covered Vases

Pretty Royal Vienna Portrait Plate

Vienna Tray with Allegorial Scene

Plate, 9 5/8" d., portrait-type, Art Nouveau taste, the center painted w/a bust profile of a lovely young brunette maiden wearing an off-the-shoulder robe, the wide gently scalloped border in pale green accented with deep maroon reserves decorated overall w/ornate gold scrolls, flowers & spider webs, artist-signed, titled in German on the back, impressed crowned "PF" mark, late 19th - early 20th c. (ILLUS.) **$1,800**

Tray, oval, the center h.p. w/a large rectangular panel showing a classical view allegorical of the Triumph of the Arts & Science, depicted as a gathering of classical figures supporting emblems of knowledge, attended by putti among clouds, supporting white classical portrait roundels, the outer dark green ground ornately decorated w/leafy scrolls & trellis, artist-signed, blue Beehive mark, late 19th c., 16 1/2" l. (ILLUS., top next column) ... **$3,120**

Pretty Royal Vienna Portrait Vase

Vase, 5" h., ovoid body tapering to a slender neck w/a flaring rim, gilt openwork vine-like gold handles from the center neck to shoulder, a large gold oval enclosing a color portrait of a young maiden w/brown hair, background in pale shaded green w/ornate gilt decoration, artist-signed, marked on the base "Germany - Sincerity - 3666," tiny flat nick on the rim (ILLUS., previous page) **$575**

Napoleon & Josephine Vienna Vases

Vases, 7 5/8" h., tall slightly tapering squared body w/a rounded shoulder & short cylindrical neck w/rolled rim, short gold scroll handles from rim to shoulder, ruby ground, each centered by an oval reserve h.p. w/a color bust portrait of Napoleon or Josephine, each within a raised gold border below a trellis & diaper cartouche, the back decorated w/an octagonal turquoise 'jeweled' panel of scrolling leaves above ribbon-tied floral garlands, red Beehive mark, early 20th c., pr. (ILLUS.) **$3,360**

Vases, cov., 13 3/4" h., a stepped molded high square plinth base attached to a slender tapering pedestal supporting a flaring urn-form body w/an angled shoulder & short flaring neck flanked by angular long gold handles, a tapering pointed cover w/pointed gold finial, ruby & gold ground, the body h.p. w/a continuous scene of youths drinking, eating, playing cards & singing reserved on a richly gilt-seeded ground, ornate leaf & scroll decoration on the lower body, neck, cover & plinth base, gilt & blue border bands, blue Beehive mark, titled in German under the base, late 19th c., pr. (ILLUS. left & right with ewer & undertray, top of page 585) **$5,040**

One of Two Very Ornate Vienna Vases

Vases, cov., 45" h., the high octagonal base w/a flaring foot supporting a large bulbous ovoid body on a ringed pedestal, the tapering neck flanked by ornate arched & looping gold dragon handles, the domed cover w/two figures, a man & a woman dressed as Classical warriors, the main body of each painted on each side w/colorful scenes of Achilles, Diana, Hector or Thetis, the body & base in deep maroon trimmed w/elaborate gilt scrolls & leaf designs & bands of white & gold bands, the pedestal base decorated w/four panels showing Classical scenes in color alternating of maroon panels w/elaborate gilt scrolling, late 19th c., blue shield marks, one handle possibly reattached, the other w/minor professional repairs, pr. (ILLUS. of one) **$43,475**

Royal Worcester

This porcelain has been made by the Royal Worcester Porcelain Co. at Worcester, England, from 1862 to the present. Royal Worcester is distinguished from wares made at Worcester between 1751 and 1862, which are referred to only as Worcester by collectors.

Royal Worcester Marks

Basket, a molded wicker ivory exterior, the low round foot tapering to a short body w/a very widely flaring & undulating upright rim band molded w/a design of wicker arches, a high arched handle across the top w/a gilded molded wicker design & ropetwist center section, late 19th c., 7" h. **$259**

Royal Worcester Candelabra & Variety of Other Pieces

Candelabra, figural, designed w/a round rockwork base supporting the figure of a young peasant girl seated in the fork of two tree trunks the continue up to form the leaf-molded candle sockets, h.p. delicate hues of green, brown & roses, late 19th c., 9" h. (ILLUS. top row, second from left with large grouping of various Royal Worcester pieces, top of page) **$345**

Pierced Royal Worcester Charger

Charger, round, in the Persian taste, ivory ground, the center pierced w/a quatrefoil panel decorated in three-tone gold w/scrolling vines & enameled flower blossoms in coral, white & turquoise, a matching pierced border band, puce printed crowned mark, date cypher for 1880, 11 1/4" d. (ILLUS.) **$1,200**

Set of 12 Demitasse Cups & Saucers

Demitasse cups & saucers, cobalt blue ground, each printed & enriched around the rim w/a flowering rinceau vine above a stepped geometric gilt band, the interiors & wells decorated in gilt, puce printed monogram mark, date cyphers for 1903, original box, set of 12 (ILLUS.) **$1,800**

Ewer, a round gold-rimmed low foot supporting a very wide bulbous ovoid ivory body tapering to a gold neck ring below the very high & arched spout, high arched & scrolled gold handle w/tiny beading from the rim to the shoulder, the body h.p. w/a large bouquet of yellow & pink blossoms & green leaves surrounded by smaller floral sprays, late 19th c., 10" h.. **$460**

Pretty Royal Worcester Floral Ewer

Ewer, a small rounded pedestal base supporting the large ovoid body tapering to a tall slender neck w/a long upright & arched spout, ornate scroll & leaf handle, ivory ground decorated around the sides w/a fancy gold floral swag design w/further gold on the neck, handle & base, ca. 1899, 13 1/4" h. (ILLUS.) **$382**

Royal Worcester Ewer with Salamander Handle

Ewer, bulbous lower body tapering to a slender cylindrical neck w/gold-trimmed rim w/small spout, the ivory textured ground h.p. w/colorful leafy floral branches, a large gold coiling salamander handle down the side, signed on base w/the green mark, late 19th c., 11 1/4" h. (ILLUS.) **$575**

Ewer, ringed gold foot below a band of upright gold leaves, the tall swelled ovoid body w/a rounded shoulder to the tall pointed rim spout outlined in gold, gold pointed scroll handle, the ivory sides h.p. w/large pale blue daisy-like flowers on leafy stems, late 19th c., 6" h. **$345**

Ewer, tusk-form, the round base w/a wide molded gold band, the tapering gently curved creamy sides w/a tall cylindrical upright spout, a gold forked antler-form handle, the body h.p. w/orange & gold wildflowers, late 19th c., 7 1/2" h. (ILLUS. bottom row, second from right with variety of other Royal Worcester pieces, top of previous page) **$201**

Ewers, footed wide squatty bulbous body tapering to a ribbed lower gold neck continuing to a slender cylindrical upper neck topped w/a high arched & stepped spout, long vine-form gold handle from neck to shoulder, the body h.p. w/a continuous color forested landscape w/a peacock, late 19th c., 7 1/2" h., pr. (ILLUS. bottom row, second & third from left, top previous page) **$1,610**

Lovely Figure of the Goddess Diana

Figure of Diana, titled "The Bather Surprised," the standing semi-draped goddess w/three-tone metallic robe resting on a tree stump, raised on a canted rectangular gold base, gilt crowned monogram mark, date cypher for 1919, 23 1/8" h. (ILLUS.) **$1,920**

Royal Worcester Water Carrier Figures

Figures, a male & female Middle Eastern water carrier, she standing w/a jar on her shoulder pouring into a large bowl below, he standing w/holding a jar in one hand & pouring into a large bowl below, each decorated in green, tan & gold on an ivory ground, modeled by James Hadley, Shape No. 594, ca. 1891, artist-signed & printed marks, each w/gilt wear, one liner w/rim chip, 17" & 17 3/4" h., pr. (ILLUS., previous page) **$881**

Royal Worcester Harvester Figures

Figures, a standing male & female in peasant costume, she holding a small keg & he holding a scythe, a tree trunk vase behind each, the old ivory ground decorated in shades of gold, tan, green & red, modeled by James Hadley, ca. 1888, printed & impressed marks, 13 3/4" & 14" h., pr. (ILLUS.).. **$999**

Royal Worcester Greenaway-style Figures

Figures, modeled as Kate Greenaway-style young man & maiden each holding a basket, a tree trunk base behind each, decorated in shades of green, blue, brown & gold, Shape No. 880, printed mark, ca. 1890, 9 3/4" h., pr. (ILLUS.) **$588**
Jar, cov., rounded upright cylinder molded in low-relief as a cluster of bamboo & leaves in ivory h.p. around the sides w/scrolling leafy vines w/flowers in green, brown, yellow & green, the flat cover w/a pointed gold twig handle & fur-

ther flowers, gold rim bands, late 19th c., 6" h. (ILLUS. bottom row, far right with grouping of various Royal Worcester pieces, top of page 587) **$431**
Pitcher, 7" h., jug-type, a gold round foot below the wide bulbous body tapering to an upright high stepped spout rim, gold ribbed vine handle, the ivory ground h.p. w/a large colorful cluster of flowers & leaves in shades of deep pink, yellow, green & blue, No. 1094, ca. 1900 .... **$259**

Very Rare Royal Worcester Plate

Plate, 7 7/8" d., the wide reticulated sides w/a honeycomb design in blue trimmed w/gold dots, a narrow outer & inner solid band in pink w/white & turquoise jeweling, the solid center w/a lightly embossed gilt landscape, printed mark, attributed to George Owen, dated 1882 (ILLUS.) **$16,450**
Plates, 10 1/2" d., each h.p. with a detailed landscape w/a castle in the distance, shaped gold rim band, puce printed crowned monogram mark, date cypher for 1930, set of 12 (ILLUS., top next page) ... **$5,400**

Royal Worcester Commemorative Plates

Plates, 10 5/8" d., commemorative, yellow ground ornately decorated w/delicate gilt scrollwork issuing flaming torches, the center h.p. in color w/a tight floral bouquet, the back w/a presentation inscription dated 1927, gilt printed crowned marks, set of 12 (ILLUS.)........................ **$2,400**

Set of Castle Scene Royal Worcester Plates

Lovely Decorated Royal Worcester Plates

Plates, 10 5/8" d., ruby & ivory ground, the wide border decorated w/ornate gilt scrollwork issuing flaming torches, the further ornate gold on the ivory band surrounding the central reserve of a tight bouquet of colorful flowers, puce printed crowned monogram mark, date cypher for 1909 (ILLUS.)...................................... **$1,440**

Tea set: cov. teapot, open sugar bowl, creamer & cup & saucer; each w/a gilt rim & raised gilt dots to a blue glazed honeycomb pierced body, white & turquoise jeweled borders over pink bands, printed & raised marks, attributed to George Owen, dated 1878, teapot 4 1/2" h., the set (ILLUS., bottom of page)................ **$28,200**

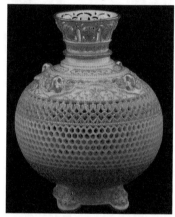

Rare Reticulated Royal Worcester Vase

Vase, 4 3/8" h., a small lobed & flaring gilt-trimmed foot below the spherical reticulated yellow ground body w/a creamy shoulder decorated w/delicate gilt scrolls & four small gilt lug handles, a short flaring ringed & reticulated neck, attributed to George Owen, puce printed crowned monogram mark, ca. 1891 (ILLUS.)........ **$9,600**

Extraordinary Royal Worcester Reticulated Tea Set

Vase, 6 1/2" h., figural, modeled w/a round base mounted w/small seashells & centered by an upright branch of coral supporting a large nautilus shell, painted w/pastel shades of pink, green, tan & gold, late 19th c. (ILLUS. bottom row, far left with various other Royal Worcester pieces, top of page 587)...................... **$400-600**

Unique & Rare Royal Worcester Vase

Vase, 6 5/8" h., footed spherical reticulated body tapering to a slender, ringed reticulated neck w/gold trim & a flaring top, long scrolled serpent handles trimmed in gold from the neck to the shoulders, glazed in pale blue & buff & trimmed w/raised gilt dots, Shape No. 871, attributed to George Owen, ca. 1900, printed mark (ILLUS.)... **$31,725**

Vase, 7 1/2" h., figural, modeled as a large swan w/its wings raised to frame an urn-form vase, h.p. in pastel shades of pink & ivory w/gold highlights, late 19th c. (ILLUS. top row, second from right with grouping of other Royal Worcester pieces, top of page 587) **$546**

Grainger's Worcester Pate-Sur-Pate Vase

Vase, 8 1/2" h., pate-sur-pate, footed tapering ovoid body w/a wide cupped rim, dou-

ble loop vine handles down the neck, blue ground finely h.p. in white slip & hand-tooled w/a blossoming branch of cinquefoil blossoms & leaves, the back w/an insect in flight, Royal China Works mark of Grainger's Worcester, date letter for 1893 (ILLUS.) **$2,400**

Fabulous Royal Worcester Pierced Vase

Vase, 9" h., a low round reticulated foot supporting the large spherical reticulated body tapering to an ornately pierced tall slender trumpet neck, ornate red-stained male mask head handles on the shoulder, gilt decoration w/large pierced medallions on a wide pale blue center band, Shape No. 1552, attributed to George Owen, dated 1894, printed mark (ILLUS.) **$30,500**

Scarce Royal Worcester Sabrina Ware Vase

Vase, 9 3/4" h., Sabrina Ware, tall ovoid body w/a short flared neck, decorated in dark blue & white w/a landscape w/white cranes wading in a marsh w/large trees in the distance, marked "Royal Worcester England - Sabrina Ware - 2472" (ILLUS.) .. **$805**

Royal Worcester Spherical Floral Vase

Vase, 10 3/8" h., a small pedestal foot supporting the large spherical body w/a tall slender waisted neck, ivory ground w/polychrome enamel floral bouquet on the side, bordered in translucent bluish grey, printed mark, ca. 1900, missing cover, gilt rim wear (ILLUS.)........................ **$147**

Vase, 10 1/2" h., footed wide bulbous body topped by a ringed & gently flaring cylindrical neck, the creamy body divided into panels w/molded leaf & leafy scroll stripes, each panel h.p. w/a different wildflower in gold & deep maroon, a molded band at the base & top of the neck, the sides of the neck also decorated w/small panels h.p. w/gold plants, gold band outlines, late 19th c. (ILLUS. top row, far left of Royal Worcester pieces, top of page 587) **$431**

Vase, 11" h., a gold-banded fluted & ringed pedestal base supporting the wide compressed rounded lower body w/a wide shoulder tapering to the tall slender cylindrical neck w/a flared rim, ornate gold scroll handles flank the neck, the ivory body h.p. w/a large bouquet of flowers in shades of yellow, rose red, yellow & blue, late 19th c.. **$604**

Vase, 12" h., a round flaring foot w/a molded lappet band & gold rings, the large bulbous ivory body h.p. w/a cluster of gold fern leaves & tiny blossoms, a pointed arched & pierced band w/a gold starburst finial at the base of the cylindrical ringed neck w/a molded swirled scroll band below the flared rim, ornate arched serpen-

tine stylized dolphin handles enclosing gold leafy scrolls, minor professional repair to rim, late 19th c. (ILLUS. top row, far right with various other Royal Worcester pieces, top of page 587) **$431**

Elaborate Persian Style Tall Vase

Vase, cov., 21 3/4" h., in the Persian taste, ivory ground, a square foot w/angled corners supports the bell-form stem & tall ovoid body tapering to a ringed cylindrical neck w/flaring rim topped by a domed & pierced cover w/a pierced ball-form finial, the front & back of the body w/quatrefoil panels h.p. w/large chrysanthemums in shades red & green trimmed in gold, joined at the sides by rosettes & acanthus leaf panels among delicate elaborate leafy scrolls, the lower body & socle base w/conforming beaded strapwork lappets, iron-red crowned monogram mark, mark of retailer Davis Collamore & Co., New York City, ca. 1880 (ILLUS.).......................... **$4,800**

Vases, 4 1/4" h., spherical finely reticulated body w/blue glazed honeycomb bands flanking a buff-stained band, raised on a lobed flaring foot w/gold trim, the solid shoulder molded w/four lug handles w/gold trim, flaring & ringed cylindrical neck w/gold trim, attributed by George Owen, Shape No. 1257, printed marks, ca. 1891, pr. (ILLUS., top next page).. **$15,250**

Vases, bud, 5" h., a round molded bronzed gold base band below the ivory molded cylindrical bamboo-form body highlighted w/a cluster of bronzed gold long pointed leaves, No. 1049, late 19th c., pr. **$92**

Very Rare Pair of Small Reticulated Royal Worcester Vases

Beautiful Reticulated Royal Worcester Vases

Vases, 6 3/4" h., gently swelled cylindrical reticulated body tapering to a short cylindrical gold neck, a pierced central unique band w/a unique pierced design flanked by finer honeycomb bands in pale blue w/gilt jeweling, upper & lower border bands enameled & jeweled w/a zig-zag design, attributed to George Owen, dated 1892, printed mark, pr. (ILLUS.)....... **$21,150**

Rozart Pottery

George and Rose Rydings were aspiring Kansas City (Missouri) potters who, in the late 1960s, began to produce a line of fine underglaze pottery. An inheritance of vintage American-made artware gave the Rydings inspiration to recreate old ceramic masters' techniques. Some design influence also came from Fred Radford, grandson of well-known Ohio artist Albert Radford (ca. 1890s-1904). Experimenting with Radford's formula for Jasperware and sharing ideas with Fred about glazing techniques and ceramic chemistry led the Rydings to a look reminiscent of the ware made by turn-of-the-century American art pottery masters such as Weller and Rookwood. The result of their work became Rozart, the name of the Rydings' pottery.

Many lines have been created since Rozart's beginning. Twainware, Sylvan, Cameoware, Rozart Royal, Rusticware, Deko, Krakatoa, Koma and Sateen are a few. It is rare to find a piece of Rozart that is not marked in some way. The earliest mark

is "Rozart" at the top of a circle with "Handmade" in the center and "K.C.M.O." (Kansas City, Missouri) at the bottom. Other marks followed over the years, including a seal that was used extensively. Along with artist initials, collectors will find a date code (either two digits representing the year or a month separated by a slash followed by a two-digit year). George signs his pieces "GMR," "GR," or "RG" (with a backwards "R"). Working on Twainware, Jasperware and Cameoware in the early years, George has many wheel-thrown pieces to his credit. Rose, who is very knowledgeable about Native Americans, does scenics and portraits. Her mark is either "RR" or "Rydings." Four of the seven Rydings children have worked in the pottery as well. Anne Rydings White (mark is "Anne" or "AR" or "ARW") designed and executed many original pieces in addition to her work on the original Twainware line. Susan Rydings Ubert (mark is "S" over "R") has specialized in Sylvan pieces and is an accomplished sculptor and mold maker. Susan's daughter Maureen does female figures in the Art Deco style. Becky (mark is "B" over "R"), now a commercial artist, designed lines such as Fleamarket, Nature's Jewels, and Animals. Cindy Rydings Cushing (mark is "C" over "R" or "CRC") developed the very popular Kittypots line. Mark Rydings is the Rozart mold maker.The Rozart Pottery is still active today. Pottery enthusiasts are taking notice of the family history, high quality and reminiscent beauty of Rozart. Its affordability may soon cease as Rozart's popularity and recognition are on the rise.

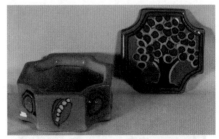

Rozart Box with Lid

Box w/lid, Arts & Crafts style, quatrefoil shape w/image of tree painted on lid and various decorations about sides of box, George Rydings, 6" w. (ILLUS.)................ **$212**

Rozart Letter Holders

Model of duck, on base (ILLUS.) **$82**

Rozart Ewer with Mouse Design

Ewer, sgraffito mouse design, Rose Ry-
dings, 10" h. (ILLUS.) **$255**
Letter holders, rectangular, w/various de-
signs painted on front, limited edition,
4 1/2" h., 6 1/2" l., each (ILLUS. of three,
top of page) **$75**

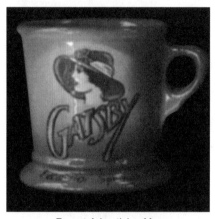

Rozart Advertising Mug

Mug, advertising Gatsby Days Excelsior
Springs, Missouri, May 1998, w/picture of
woman in old-fashioned picture hat on
front, 3 1/2" h. (ILLUS.) **$56**
Mugs, w/various incised Native American
designs, signed "RR," 5" h., each **$120**
Sign, for Rozart Pottery dealer, "Rozart" in
script, no base, first issue, 5 1/2" l. **$275**

Rozart Duck

Rozart Pottery Dealer Sign

Sign, for Rozart Pottery dealer, "Rozart Pottery" in script, w/base, Copperverde
glaze, 5 1/2" l. (ILLUS.) **$125**

Rozart Pillow Shape Vase with Bird

Vase, 7 1/2" h., pillow shape w/bird on branch on front, Cindy Cushing (ILLUS.) ... **$150**

Rozart Indian Portrait Vase

Vase, 14 1/2" h., w/Indian portrait on front, Becky White (ILLUS.) **$290**

Rozart Royal Vase with Eagle

Vase, 15" h., Rozart Royal, w/eagle in landing position on front, Rose Rydings (ILLUS.) **$345**

Satsuma

These decorated wares have been produced in Japan since the end of the 18th century. The early pieces are scarce and high-priced. Later Satsuma wares are plentiful and, with prices rising, are also becoming highly collectible.

Bowl, 7 1/4" d., a wide rounded form w/a lightly scalloped rim, a wide gold decorative rim band, the interior h.p. w/an elaborate scene w/a procession of Buddhist figures through a landscape, colors & heavy gold trim, the exterior w/floral designs, signed, minor chip, ca. 1900........... **$529**

Fine Dragon-trimmed Satsuma Teapot

Teapot, cov., footed squatty spherical body w/a wide shoulder centered by a tall cylindrical neck fitted w/a small domed cover, a long gold dragon wrapped around the base of the neck w/the neck & head forming the spout & the arched tail forming the handle, the creamy background h.p. w/exotic birds among colorful flowering plants in shades of red, blue, white & purple w/heavy gold trim, black & gold chop mark on the base, late 19th - early 20th c., 6 3/4" h. (ILLUS.) **$1,006**

Vase, 6" h., baluster-form body w/a short flared neck, base & shoulder bands w/ornate geometric gold bands, the wide body band decorated w/a scene of dozens of Buddhist saints in gold robes seated in a landscape, signed, ca. 1900 .... **$588**

Fine Satsuma Vase on Bronze Stand

Vase, 9 1/4" h., a flared round foot w/gold geometric bands below the large bulbous ovoid body w/a flat closed rim flanked by gold lion head & ring shoulder handles, the sides h.p. w/large oval panels filled w/Geisha wearing gold-trimmed robes in a landscape w/a lake & trees in the distance, the other side w/an oval panel decorated w/Rakans, signed, raised on an ornate high squared & footed bronze stand, late 19th c. (ILLUS. of vase & stand) **$588**

Boldly Decorated Large Satsuma Vase

Vase, 16 1/4" h., a large ovoid body tapering to a wide trumpet neck, a decorative gold base band, the sides h.p. w/wide deep orange ground decorated w/large h.p. flowering peony trees & butterflies in white, gold, brown & light blue, the shoulders w/a gold molded drapery design, the neck decorated w/a band of large gold Mon emblems below a narrow paneled rim band, ca. 1900 (ILLUS.) **$441**

Fine Satsuma Floor Vase

Vase, 29" h., 10" d., floor-type, tall slightly tapering body w/a slightly bulbed base band w/three cut-outs, the angled shoulder tapering to a cylindrical neck, the neck & shoulder decorated w/diaper panels & stylized florals, the upper body divided into a band of large arched panels each h.p. w/a different flower plant, the lower body decorated w/various geometric designs & floral panels, all in shades of gold, tan, rose red & light blue, 19th c. (ILLUS.) **$390**

Satsuma Vases with Buddhist Saints

Vases, 9 1/2" h., 4 1/2" d., footed ovoid six-sided body w/a short flaring neck, the sides decorated w/groups of Buddhist saints in color w/heavy gold trim, figural elephant shoulder handles, painted chop mark on the base, probably late 19th c., pr. (ILLUS.) **$259**

Schoop (Hedi) Art Creations

Hedi Schoop (1906-1966) was one of the most popular (and most imitated) California ceramic artists of the 1940s and '50s. Born in Switzerland, Schoop spent her early years studying sculpture, fashion design and acting. With her husband, famed movie composer, Frederick Hollander, she fled Nazi Germany in the early 1930s, settling in Hollywood, where his career flourished.

In her new environment, Schoop amused herself by creating plaster dolls, which she then painted and dressed in fashions of the day. A successful showing of the dolls at a Los Angeles department store prompted her to adapt these ideas to a more permanent medium: ceramics. Early slip-cast figures sold well from Schoop's small workshop, and a larger, North Hollywood facility, "Hedi Schoop Art Creations," opened in 1940.

Schoop designed and modeled most of the figurines released by her company, and many came equipped for secondary uses — from flower holders and wall pockets to candlesticks and soap dishes. She was perhaps the most commercially successful California ceramics designer of the postwar period, and certainly the most ubiquitous. If a Schoop figure proved popular with consumers, an entire line of accompanying decor objects, such as planters, bowls, ashtrays and candy dishes, would be built around it. At its busiest in the late 1940s, the studio produced over 30,000 giftware items per year and employed over fifty workers.

Hedi Schoop figurines are largely representational and achieve their visual impart through overall shape and size rather than through minute detailing. The figures are often caught in motion - arms extended, skirts aflutter, heads bowed - but that motion is fluid and unhurried. Rough and incised textures combine with smooth ones; colorful glossy glazes contrast with bisque. Her subjects - ethnic dancers, musicians, peasant boys and girls - are captured at a specific moment in time. A figurine by Hedi Schoop is a captivating still photo.

The broadly drawn features, soft colors, and rippling garments of Schoop's oversize figurines and planters unfortunately made them easy to copy. During the height of her career similar designs were turned out by a variety of other California ceramics firms, usually run by former Schoop employees. The most persistent was one-time Schoop decorator Katherine Schueftan. As "Kim Ward," her imitations resulted in a 1942 court injunction prohibiting "Kim" from copying the Schoop line. Schueftan complied until 1945, when she resurfaced with a new name, "Kaye of Hollywood," but similar Schoop-like figures. No further court action is reported.

Due to look-alike stylings by the numerous Schoop competitors, signature identification is an important means of object verification. While some pieces carried paper labels, most featured stamped or incised signatures, often with the additional words "Hollywood, Cal." or "California."

The Schoop factory was destroyed by fire in 1958. After collaborating for a time with The Cal-

ifornia Cleminsons, popular creators of decorative kitchenwares, Schoop retired from ceramic design, focusing instead on painting - but her glamorous legacy lives on.

Advisor for this category is Donald-Brian Johnson, an author and lecturer specializing in Mid-Twentieth century design. Photos are by his frequent collaborator, Leslie Piña.

By far one of the most talented artists working in California in the 1940s and 1950s was Hedi Schoop. She designed and modeled almost every piece in her line. She began her business in 1940 in Hollywood, California. Barker Brothers department store in Los Angeles discovered Schoop's work which encouraged her to open the small Hollywood studio. Shortly after a move to larger quarters, financed by her mother, Hedi began calling her business Hedi Schoop Art Creations. It would remain under that name throughout Schoop's career which was ended when a fire destroyed the operation in 1958. At that time, Hedi decided to free-lance for other companies (see: Cleminson Clay). Probably one of the most imitated artists of the time, other people began businesses using Schoop's designs and techniques. Hedi Schoop decided to sue in court and the results were settled in Schoop's favor. Among those imitators were Kim Ward, and Ynez and Yona. Hedi Schoop saw forms differently than other artists and, therefore, was able to create with ease and in different media. While Hedi made shapely women with skirts that flared out to create bowls as well as women with arms over their heads holding planters, she also produced charming bulky looking women with thick arms and legs. When TV lamps became popular, Hedi was able to easily add her talents to creating those designs with roosters, tragedy and comedy joined together in an Art Deco fashion, and elegant women in various poses. A variety of marks were used by Schoop including her signature (incised or stamped) which also, on occasion, shows "Hollywood, Cal." or "California," and there was also a sticker used but such pieces are hard to find.

Hedi Schoop
HOLLYWOOD CAL.
HEDI SCHOOP
HOLLYWOOD, CALIF.

Hedi
Schoop

Schoop Marks

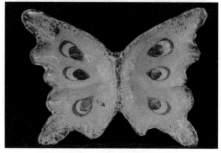

Hedi Schoop Butterfly Ashtray

Ashtray, in the shape of a butterfly w/spread wings, yellow w/gold trim & "eyes" on wings, inkstamp overglaze, 5 1/2" w. (ILLUS., previous page) **$66**

Hedi Schoop Bird-shaped Ashtray

Ashtray, model of a bird, 7 1/2" l., 5 1/4" h. (ILLUS.)... **$50-$75**
Ashtrays, butterfly-shaped, white w/gold decoration, 5 1/2" w., pr. .... **$25-$50**
Candleholder, figural, a mermaid holding a single candle socket in each hand above her head, rare, ca. 1950, 13 1/2" h. **$695**
Candleholder, figure of dancing girl kneeling, 10" h. .... **$75-$100**
Candleholders, pink swirl pattern, 5 1/4" d., 5" h., pr... **$25-$50**

Young Chinese Musicians Console Set

Console set: "Young China Musicians," Chinese boy & Chinese girl w/rectangular planter; planter 11" l., girl 10 1/4" h., boy 10 3/4" h., the set (ILLUS.)................ **$300-$350**
Dish, experimental, kidney-shaped, etched lines on black through yellow glaze... **$150-$175**

Hedi Schoop Dancers

Figural group, cowboy & woman dancing, bisque faces & hands, cowboy wears hat & kerchief, woman wears black top & ruffled yellow full-length skirt, cowboy has one hand around woman's waist, woman holds skirt out w/one hand, incised unglazed mark "Hedi Schoop, California," 11" h. (ILLUS.) **$400**
Figure, Madonna & Child, 7" h............. **$175-$200**
Figure of ballerina, on a thin round base, long skirt flared upward revealing right foot, right arm extended & holding up skirt, left arm extended forward w/head turned to front, bluish grey w/silver overtones, impressed mark "Hedi Schoop," 9 1/4" h.. **$180**

Hedi Schoop Chinese Woman Figure

Figure of Chinese woman, standing on a round black base, white floor-length skirt, black, white & green blouse w/long sleeves flaring at wrists, a white flower in black hair above each ear, right fingers bent to hold a pot w/black cloth handle & in same colors as blouse, right leg bent at knee, woman 9" h., pot 2 1/2" h., 2 pcs. (ILLUS.)... **$215**
Figure of clown, standing w/one leg crossed over the other, one hand to head, other hand to mouth, bucket & mop at his side, 10 1/2" h. **$290**
Figure of girl, "Debutante," standing & holding handmade flowers in both arms, rough textured finish, ca. 1943, 12 1/2" h. ... **$260**
Figure of girl, standing on cobalt blue-glazed round base, legs slightly apart, arms stretched out to sides, hands folded to hold jump rope, rough textured black hair w/pigtails out to sides & held in place w/cobalt blue glossy ties, light blue long sleeved shirt, cobalt blue overblouse w/straps, rough textured cobalt blue short skirt & socks, inkstamp on unglazed bottom, "Hedi Schoop Hollywood, Cal.," 8 1/2" h.. **$240**

Hedi Schoop Flower Holder

Flower holder, figure of woman w/brown hair dressed in pale blue dress w/white textured hem & short puff sleeves, pink rose applied at waist, one hand holds basket on head, other hand holds skirt out to side, creating opening for flowers, inkstamp underglaze "Hedi Schoop, Hollywood, Cal.," 12 3/4" h. (ILLUS.)............... **$227**

Flower holder, figure of woman w/dark brown hair dressed in white dress w/brown & mauve h.p. scalloping & flowers, mauve hat, holds basket in each hand, incised underglaze "Hedi Schoop," 11 1/2" h. **$188**

Hedi Schoop Figural Flower Holder

Flower holder, figure of woman w/long light hair & a wide picture-style hat, dressed in ruffled teal off-the-shoulder long-sleeved full-length dress & teal picture hat w/scalloped rim, hands clasped in front holding

matching basket, all w/applied pink flowers, inkstamp underglaze "Hedi Schoop, Hollywood, Cal.," 11" h. (ILLUS.) **$245**

Flowerpot, floral decoration, 7 3/4" d., 7 1/2" h. .... **$25-$50**

Schoop Jardiniere with Chinese Scene

Jardiniere, cylindrical, incised stylized design of a kneeling Chinese woman w/Ming trees & animals, base & design in gold glaze on a light green body, 7" h. (ILLUS.) **$148**

Lamp, figural, TV-type, Comedy & Tragedy masks on a base w/full Comedy, part Tragedy conjoined, dark green w/gold trim, ca. 1954, 10 3/4" l., 12" h. **$637**

Model of cat lying down, head up, tail wrapped around side, paws tucked under body, brown collar around neck w/two yellow bells & two small brown pots attached, white rough textured body, inkstamp under glaze, "Hedi Schoop Hollywood, Cal.," 6 3/4" l., 6 1/2" h. **$157**

Planter, figure of a girl reading, green glaze, 9" h. .... **$75-$100**

Windswept Lady & Basket Planter

Planter, figure of a windswept lady squatting & holding a basket, 11" h. (ILLUS.) .... **$175-$200**

Planter, "Marguerita," figure of a girl in a black dress w/white planter basket on her head, 12 1/2" h. .... **$75-$100**

Hedi Schoop Fan Shell Planter

Figural Hedi Schoop Tray

Planter, model of a fan shell, 11 1/2" l. (ILLUS., previous page)...................... **$50-$75**
Planter, model of a horse, brown & white glaze, 7 3/8" h. .... **$125-$150**
Planter, model of a horse, rough textured mane & tail, white glossy glazed body w/mint green face accents, saddle, bows in assorted areas & scalloped edging at the base, inkstamp mark "Hedi Schoop," 7 1/2" h. **$126**
Planter, "Tyrolean Girl," 11 1/2" h. .... **$75-$100**
Planters, "My Sister & I," figure of a Dutch boy & Dutch girl carrying baskets, 11" h., pr. .... **$200-$225**
Plaque, African woman, 7 1/2 x 11" ...... **$100-$125**
Plate, grey cat w/blue eyes, 7 1/2" sq. .... **$75-$100**
Plate, white cat in a garden, 7 1/2" sq. ..... **$75-$100**
Server, four-pocket design w/figural duck handle, 11" d. .... **$50-$75**
Server, reversible, "two-faced" lady figure holding a tray overhead, blue, green & black glaze, 13 1/2" h. .... **$75-$100**
Tray, figural, divided w/irregular leaf-shaped raised edges, the rim mounted w/the figure of a cherub on her knees, arms outstretched beside her, head tilted, beige & gold tray interior, beige w/pink-tinged cherub, gold wings, rose on left wrist, belt of roses around her waist w/rose-glazed bowl exterior & rose hair, bottom of tray also in a glossy rose, incised "Hedi Schoop," 11 1/2" l., overall 6" h. (ILLUS., top of page) **$268**
Vase, model of a tulip, pink, 10 1/2" h. ...... **$25-$50**
Vase, 9" h. at highest point, 4 1/2" h., at lowest point, 9" l., seashell-form, footed oval base, fluted edge rising from the low end to the higher end, dark green base w/dark green & gold fading to light green, rim trimmed in gold, transparent textured glossy glaze, marked w/a silver label w/red block letters, "Hedi Schoop Hollywood, Calif." on two lines **$110**

Sèvres & Sèvres-Style

Some of the most desirable porcelain ever produced was made at the Sèvres factory, originally established at Vincennes, France, and transferred, through permission of Madame de Pompadour, to Sèvres as the Royal Manufactory about the middle of the 18th century. King Louis XV took sole responsibility for the works in 1759, when production of hard paste wares began. Between 1850 and 1900, many biscuit and softpaste pieces were made again. Fine early pieces are scarce and high-priced. Many of those available today are late productions. The various Sèvres marks have been copied, and pieces listed as "Sèvres-Style" are similar to actual Sèvres wares but not necessarily from that factory. Three of the many Sèvres marks are illustrated here.

Sèvres marks

Floral-decorated Sèvres Center Bowl

Center bowl, the wide oval bowl w/a bleu-du-roi ground h.p. on the sides w/large oval flower-filled reserves framed by ornate gilt scrolls, the rim mounted w/a narrow gilt-bronze band joined to the high leafy scroll end handles & raised on a gilt-bronze bottom band raised on four pierced scroll legs joined by leafy swags, late 19th c., 16" w., 8" h. (ILLUS.).............. **$690**

Celeste Blue & Gilt-Bronze Centerpiece

Centerpiece, a deep bowl w/a celeste blue ground decorated on the exterior w/a large oval reserve h.p. w/a scene of cherubs in musical & literary pursuits, mounted w/an openwork gilt-bronze rim band joined to large high forked leafy scroll gilt-bronze handles & resting atop a gilt-bronze base w/a short pedestal & paneled foot, late 19th c., 18" w., 14" h. (ILLUS.) **$3,565**

Fine Sèvres-style Coffee Set Decorated with Napoleonic Scenes

Coffee service: cov. coffeepot, cov. sugar bowl, cov. hot milk jug, six 9 3/8" d. plates, twelve teacups & saucers & a large 19 3/4" d. round tray; Sèvres-style, the serving pieces w/slightly tapering cylindrical bodies, each piece h.p. w/a different scene showing the campaigns of Napoleon I, each titled & artist-signed, wide cobalt blue borders w/gilt lotus & leaftip trim, 2nd half 19th c., the set (ILLUS.) **$12,925**

Cup & saucer, a footed round dished saucer holding a footed bulbous ovoid cup w/a flaring rim & a gold scroll handle, each piece w/a dark blue ground w/ornate leafy gold bands, the cup decorated on the front w/a gold round reserve h.p. in color w/a half-length portrait of Napolean in uniform, Sevres-style cypher & letter A, 19th c., overall 3 1/2" h., the set (ILLUS., top next column) **$441**

Sevres-style Napolean Portrait Cup & Saucer

Fine Floral-painted Sèvres Cup & Saucer

Cup & saucer, each piece finely h.p. w/a wide band of colorful garden flowers edged by gilt bands & ivory formed as vitruvian scrolls, cup handle molded as a lotus blossoms, blue-stenciled interlaced "Cs" & incised & w/gilt marks for the years 1821-29, saucer 6" d., the set (ILLUS.) **$2,868**

Fine Sèvres Figure of Catherine the Great

Figure of Catherine II of Russia, bisque, the empress shown seated on a rocky ledge in formal dress, her left hand resting on a crowned orb, her right hand holding a scepter, a branch of laurel, symbolizing her artistic talents, growing up the rock at her left, impressed uppercase lozenge mark & name of artist, dated 1898, 17 3/8" h. (ILLUS., previous page) **$19,200**

Sèvres Bisque Figure of Cupid

Figure of Cupid, the winged bisque figure seated on a rock holding his right index finger to his lips, his left hand on the quiver of arrows, raised on a bleu nouveau cylindrical stand w/four projecting buttress feet, titled & trimmed in gold, impressed company mark, after the model by Eti-

enne-Maurice Falconet, date cyphers for 1889-1890, 12 1/2" h. (ILLUS.) **$1,920**

Very Elaborate Painted Sèvres-Style Garniture Set

Garniture set: pedestal-based bowl & matching cov. vases; each w/a round gilt-bronze base w/rectangular block panels over scroll feet all w/classical details, supporting a gilt round wreath ring & domed pedestal tapering to a rolled gadrooned band in cobalt blue w/ornate gilt decoration, the wide deep rounded bowl in cobalt blue w/each side decorated w/a large oblong panel w/a wide gilt scroll border enclosing a color scene of a romantic couple in 18th c. dress, the rim mounted w/a wide openwork gilt-bronze band decorated w/repeating leafy scrolls flanked by long open gilt-bronze handles topped by figural caryatid heads, the matching vases w/large shield-shaped gold-bordered panels also h.p. w/romantic scenes, matching rim band & handles, the domed & ringed cobalt blue covers w/ornate gilt decoration & a tall pineapple-shaped gilt-bronze finial, reattached rim chip on one cover, marked w/pseudo-Sèvres interlaced "L" marked w/code letter E, late 19thc., vases 28 1/2" h., the set (ILLUS.) **$34,075**

Fine Sèvres-Style Glass Coolers

Glass coolers, Sèvres-Style, a gilt footring supporting the deep rounded bowl w/molded arches just below the flaring serpentine rim w/molded scroll rim handles, the pink ground h.p. w/an oblong reserve decorated w/colorful scenes of lovers in gardens, each within ornate gilt leafy borders, decorated in the style of Francois Boucher, the back of each h.p. w/a reserve filled w/a tight bouquet of fruit & flowers, spurious blue interlaced "Ls" marks, mid- to late 19th c., 7" w., pr. (ILLUS.) **$3,585**

Outstanding Set of Sevres Plates with Butterflies & Floral Bands

Plates, 9 1/4" d., white ground w/the center of each h.p. w/a different colorful butterfly enclosed by double rings of delicate tiny pink rose sprigs, the wide border hand decorated w/a continuous band of blue floral swags alternating w/small pink rose drops, thin leaf & gilt border bands, blue Sevres marks & decorator initials, late 19th c., five w/bottom rim chips, one w/a repair, two w/upper rim chips, set of 18 (ILLUS.)... **$4,370**

Set of Bird & Branch-Painted Sevres Plates

Grouping of Fine Sèvres Plates with Napoleonic Scenes

Plates, 9 1/2" d., each a cobalt blue border decorated w/ornate gilt leaf sprigs & ribbons & an "N" for Napoleon at the upper rim, each h.p. in the center w/a different scene of various military campaigns of Napoleon, each titled & signed on the back, set of six w/one similar Napoleonic plate, the set (ILLUS.) **$2,013**

Plates, 9 1/2" d., white center w/a central gold starburst w/filigree, the wide border band h.p. w/small reserves h.p. w/small colorful birds & insects bordered by flowering leafy branches, a small oval border reserve w/the gilt monogram "LP" above a crown, blue mark in circle & additional wreath & crown "Chateau de Fontainebleau" mark, late 19th c., two w/rim chips, set of 12 (ILLUS., top next column)......... **$1,323**

Rare Reticulated Sèvres Cup & Saucer

Teacup & saucer, handleless cup w/a raised foot, double-walled w/the exterior pierced w/two tiers of quatrefoils within ogival arches, the interior painted w/gilt lines radiating from a central lozenge, a stylized chrysanthemum on each line, the gilt lines extending to issue from scrolls between each lappet of the border of flowers within red-edged ogival lappets, matching saucer w/a matching pierced border band, from a dejeuner chinois set, blue printed Louis Philippe decorating cypher, artist-signed, 1836, the set (ILLUS.).. **$6,600**

Very Ornate Gilt-Bronze Mounted Sèvres-Style Tray

Tray, Sèvres-Style, rectangular slightly dished form w/rounded cortners, h.p. in the center w/a large scene of Narcissus & companion gazing into a reflecting pool in a wooded landsape as Cupid looks on, framed by ornate gilt strapwork on a pale pink ground, mounted around the rim w/an ornate gilt-bronze scrolling band w/large curved & forked scroll end handles, raised on a leaf-cast gilt-bronze base raised on ornate scrolling legs, artist-signed, late 19th - early 20th c., 19 1/2" l. (ILLUS., top of page)............... **$7,170**

Pair of Tall Slender Sèvres Urns

Urns, cov., very tall slender ovoid body raised on a slender flaring knopped pedestal raised on a square cast brass base, the domed cover w/a brass rim, long scrolled brass handles from the rim to mid-body, cobalt blue ground, each h.p. w/a long oval reserve framed by ornate gilt scrolls, one scene shows a man & woman sitting on a bench w/sheep by their side, the other shows a man & woman w/a dog & bird in a cage, both w/back panels decorated w/a landscape scene w/buildings, marked under the base "Sèvres - Handpainted - Made in France," early 20th c., 17 1/2" h., pr. (ILLUS.) **$1,208**

Unusual Sévres Ear of Corn Vase

Vase, 5 3/4" h., Art Nouveau style, "pate nouvelle" type, naturalistically molded as an ear of corn w/two green husk leaves forming loop handles, textured yellow corn kernels showing between the leaves, black-stencilled triangle mark for 1903 (ILLUS.)... **$3,840**

Fine Sèvres Pate-Sur-Pate Vase

Vase, 6 1/8" h., pate-sur-pate, footed bulbous body tapering to a tall slightly flaring cylindrical neck, the mauve ground decorated w/layers of colored paste & centered by a round reserve w/the portrait head of an early Grecian hero suspended from crossed branches within a gilt surround further enclosed within wreaths & flowering vine, the far side undecorated, the mouth delicately gilt w/beading & pendants, the foot w/a cell design band, printed "RF" monogram marks, artist-signed, 1886-92 (ILLUS.) **$6,000**

Sèvres Ovoid Vases with Gold Flowers

Vases, 7 1/4" h., footed bulbous ovoid body tapering to a tall gently flaring stick neck, bright blue ground decorated w/an overall small gold flowerheads, the dark blue rim & foot band trimmed w/gold half-flowerheads within an egg-and-dart band, Second Republic era, iron-red stenciled mark & green stenciled oval, 1868-84, pr. (ILLUS.) **$2,629**

Fine Pair of Sévres "Delhy" Vases

Vases, 8 1/2" h., vase "Delhy" style, bottle-form w/a footed squatty bulbous body tapering to a tall cylindrical neck centered

by a large ring, white ground h.p. w/brightly colored garlands of flowers & paler ferns suspended from a band of gilt lappets flanking the neck ring & around the lower body & foot, printed marks, 1865-67, pr. (ILLUS.) **$4,800**

Fine Sèvres-Style Covered Vases

Vases, cov., Sèvres-style, each of baluster-form, turquoise blue ground, the domed cover, neck & socle w/gilt trailing vine decoration, each w/a large squared reserve on the front w/portraits of Emperor Napoleon I or Empress Josephine after works by David, framed within a gilt beaded cartouche w/leafy scrolls & Napoleonic symbols, cover, stem & squared foot of ormolu, the back of each w/a gilt crowned eagle, spurious Sèvres marks, late 19th c., 16 1/8" h., pr. (ILLUS.) **$4,541**

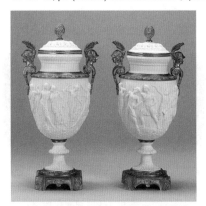

Pair of Sèvres-Style Bisque Vases

Vases, cov., gilt-bronze mounted bisque, Sèvres-style, Louis XVI-Style, each of large urn form, the wide body molded w/a continuous scene of classical figures, gilt-bronse shoulder band w/Minerva head handles, gilt-bronze border on low domed cover fitted w/a gilt-bronze pineapple finial, all raised on a flaring fluted trumpet pedestal resting on a gilt-bronze square base w/patera toes, late 19th c., 16 3/4" h., pr. (ILLUS.) **$4,406**

Shawnee

The Shawnee Pottery Company of Zanesville, Ohio, opened its doors for operation in 1936 and, sadly, closed in 1961. The pottery was inexpensive for its quality and was readily purchased at dime stores as well as department stores. Sears, Roebuck and Co., Butler Bros., Woolworth's and S. Kresge were just a few of the companies that were longtime retailers of this fine pottery.

Shawnee Pottery Company had a wide array of merchandise to offer, from knickknacks to dinnerware, although Shawnee is quite often associated with colorful pig cookie jars and the dazzling "Corn King" line of dinnerware. Planters, miniatures, cookie jars and Corn King pieces are much in demand by today's avid collectors. Factory seconds were purchased by outside decorators and trimmed with gold, decals and unusual hand painting, which makes those pieces extremely desirable in today's market and enhances the value considerably.

Shawnee Pottery has become the most sought-after pottery in today's collectible market.

Reference books available are Mark E. Supnick's book Collecting Shawnee Pottery, The Collector's Guide to Shawnee Pottery by Duane and Janice Vanderbilt or Shawnee Pottery - An Identification & Value Guide by Jim and Bev Mangus.

Shawnee
U.S.A.

Shawnee Mark

Ashtray, figural Indian Arrowhead, marked, 4 1/2"h. .... **$250-$375**

Shawnee Figural Ashtrays

Ashtray, figural kingfisher, parrot, bird, fish, terrier or owl, marked "U.S.A.," dusty rose, turquoise, old ivory, white or burgundy, 3" h., each (ILLUS. of fish, kingfisher & bird).. **$55-$65**

Shawnee Figural Banks

Bank, figural bulldog, 4 1/2" h., unmarked (ILLUS. left)...................................... **$150-$175**
Bank, figural bulldog, unmarked, 4 1/2" h. .... **$150-$175**

Figural Howdy Doody Bank

Bank, figural Howdy Doody riding a pig, marked "Bob Smith U.S.A.," 6 3/4" h. (ILLUS.) .... **$500-$576**
Bank, figural tumbling bear, unmarked, 4 3/4" h. (ILLUS. right, top this column) .... **$150-$175**
Bank, figural tumbling bear, unmarked, 4 3/4" h. .... **$150-$175**
Bank-cookie jar, figural Smiley Pig, chocolate or butterscotch base, marked "Patented: Smiley Shawnee 60 U.S.A.," 10 1/2" h. (ILLUS. left w/Winnie Pig bank-cookie jar, top next page)........ **$350-$375**
Bank-cookie jar, figural Winnie Pig, chocolate or butterscotch base, marked "Patented: Winnie Shawnee 61 U.S.A." 10 1/2" h. (ILLUS. right w/Smiley Pig bank-cookie jar, top next page)........ **$350-$375**
Bookends, figural, full figure of a man at potter's wheel, dark green, embossed on the front "Zanesville, Ohio,"embossed on the back "Crafted by Shawnee Potteries Zanesville, Ohio 1960," 9" h., pr. ..... **$675-$775**

Winnie Pig & Smiley Pig Banks/Cookie Jars

Shawnee Canister with Fruit Decal

Canister, cov., squared shape w/rounded corners, pale blue w/colorful fruit decal, marked "U.S.A.," 7" h. (ILLUS.)............. **$35-$45**

Pyramid-shaped Medallion Finish Clock

Clock, Pyramid shape, copper-clad Medallion finish, w/pink or copper face, marked "951 Kenwood U.S.A.," 7 1/2" h. (ILLUS.)
.... **$95-$125**

Coffeepot, cov., Pennsylvania Dutch patt, marked "U.S.A. 52," 42 oz. .... **$125-$150**

Coffeepot, cov., Sunflower patt, marked "U.S.A.," 42 oz. .... **$125-$150**

Indian Motif Cigarette Box

Cigarette box, cov., embossed Indian arrowhead on lid, rusty brown, marked "Shawnee," 3 1/4 x 4 1/2" (ILLUS.) ... **$475-$525**

Valencia Line Coffeepot

Coffeepot, cov., Valencia line, tangerine glaze, 7 1/2" h. (ILLUS.)...................... **$95-$125**

Cookie jar, cov., figural cottage, marked "U.S.A. 6," 7" h. .... **$650-$800**

Cookie jar, cov., figural Drum Major, gold dtrim, marked "U.S.A. 10," 10" h. ...... **$500-$550**

Cookie jar, cov., figural Drum Major, marked "U.S.A. 10," 10" h. .... **$150-$200**

Cookie jar, cov., figural ear of corn, Corn King line, No. 66, 10 1/2" h. .... **$200-$225**

Cookie jar, cov., figural Puss 'n Boots, long tail, burgundy bow, marked "Patented Puss N Boots U.S.A.," 10 1/2" h. ...... **$100-$125**

Cookie jar, cov., figural Puss 'n Boots, long tail, gold trim & decals, marked "Patented Puss N Boots U.S.A.," 10 1/2" h. ..... **$325-$375**

Cookie jar, cov., figural Sailor Boy, decorated w/decals & gold trim, marked "U.S.A.," 11 1/2" h. .... **$525-$575**

Smiley Pig with Shamrocks Cookie Jar

Cookie jar, cov., figural Smiley Pig, shamrock decoration, marked "U.S.A.," 11 1/4" h. (ILLUS.) .... **$150-$200**

Winnie Pig - Green Collar Cookie Jar

Cookie jar, cov., figural Winnie Pig, w/green collar, marked "Patented Winnie U.S.A.," 11 3/4" h. (ILLUS.) .... **$175-$200**

Pink Elephant Cookie Jar/Ice Bucket

Cookie jar-ice bucket, cov., figural elephant, pink, marked "Shawnee U.S.A. 60" or "Kenwood U.S.A. 60" (ILLUS.)
.... **$95-$100**

Creamer, ball-shaped, non-figural Red Feather circled by blue dots, marked "U.S.A.," 4" h. .... **$175-$250**

Dutch-style Red Feather Creamer

Creamer, ball-type, Dutch style, decorated w/red feather, marked "U.S.A. 12," 4 1/2" h. (ILLUS.) .... **$100-$125**

Creamer, ball-type, Dutch style, decorated w/tulip & blue around neck, marked "U.S.A.," 4 1/4" h. (ILLUS. left w/pitcher, top next page) .... **$175-$200**

Dutch-style Creamer & Pitcher

Smiley Pig with Flower Creamer

Creamer, figural Smiley Pig, decorated w/embossed peach flower, marked "Patented Smiley U.S.A.," 4 1/2" h. (ILLUS.) .... **$55-$75**

White Corn Line Pieces

Creamer, White Corn line, airbrushed & gold trim, marked "U.S.A.," 4 3/4" h. (ILLUS. third from left, front row, with White Corn Line pieces) .... **$95-$125**

Shawnee Lobster Ware Creamer

Creamer, Lobster Ware, satin charcoal grey or Van Dyke brown, figural lobster handle, marked "U.S.A.," 4 1/2" h. (ILLUS.) .... **$75-$85**

Valencia Line Dealer's Display Sign

Grouping of Shawnee Miniature Animals

Grouping of Various Miniature Shawnee Animals

Dealer's display sign, figural Spanish dancers, "Valencia" embossed across base, tangerine glaze, 11 1/4" h. (ILLUS., previous page) .... **$400-$450**

Figurine, miniature, model of 2 3/8" h. tropical fish, 3" h. bunny on haunches, 2 3/4" h. circus horse, 2 1/2" h. seated terrier or 2" h. fish, bright white or old ivory, unmarked, each (ILLUS. left to right, top of page) .... **$15-$25**

Figurine, miniature, model of a 2 3/8" h. bear cub, 2 1/4" h. standing lamb, 2 1/4" h. standing pig, 2 1/8" h. rooster, 1 3/4" h. baby bird or 2 1/2" h. bunny w/ears down, bright white or old ivory, unmarked, each (ILLUS. left to right, second from top of page) .... **$15-$25**

Figurine, model of deer, no mark, 3" h. (ILLUS. far right w/various figurines, bottom of page) .... **$175-$200**

Figurine, model of Pekinese, no mark, 2 1/2" h. (ILLUS. center w/various figurines, bottom of page) .... **$50-$55**

Figurine, model of puppy, no mark, 3" h. (ILLUS. second from left w/various figurines, top of page) .... **$45-$50**

Figurine, model of rabbit, sitting, no mark, 3" h. (ILLUS. second from right w/various figurines, bottom of page) .... **$55-$65**

Figurine, model of squirrel, no mark, 2 1/2" h. (ILLUS. third from right w/various figurines, bottom of page) .... **$45-$50**

Figurine, model of Teddy bear, no mark, 3" h. (ILLUS. third from left w/various figurines, bottom of page) .... **$45-$50**

Figurine, model of tumbling bear, no mark, 3" h. (ILLUS. far left w/various figurines, bottom of page) .... **$65-$75**

Flower frog, figural dolphin, swan or seahorse w/low base, colors of old ivory, turquoise or flax blue, unmarked, 3 3/4" h., each .... **$30-$45**

Lamp base, figural Clown on drum, cold-painted, unmarked, 7 3/4" h. .... **$35-$50**

Lamp base, figural Deer, unmarked, 7 1/2" h. .... **$20-$35**

Lamp base, figural Elephant on ball, cold-painted, unmarked, 7 1/2" h. .... **$35-$50**

Shawnee Figural Puppy Table Lamp

Lamp base, figural Puppy, brown on cream base, unmarked, 4 3/4" h. (ILLUS.) .... **$65-$75**

Various Shawnee Figurines

Smiley Pig Pitcher with Flowers

Pitcher, 7 3/4" h., figural Smiley Pig, pink &
blue flower decoration, marked "Patent-
ed Smiley U.S.A." (ILLUS.) .... **$75-$85**
Pitcher, 8" h., White Corn line, airbrushed &
gold trim, marked "U.S.A." (ILLUS. back
row, left w/White Corn pieces, page 609)
.... **$195-$250**

Tandem Bicycle Planter

Planter, model of a bicycle built for two
w/man & woman riders dressed in Gay
Nineties style, gold trim, marked "Shaw-
nee U.S.A. 735," 6" h. (ILLUS.) .... **$75-$100**

Fox & Bag Planter

Planter, model of a fox & bag, marked
"U.S.A.," 4 1/2" h. (ILLUS.) .... **$50-$65**

Shawnee Pink Angel Fish Planter

Planter, model of an angel fish, marked
"U.S.A.," found in yellow, flax blue, old
ivory & pink, 8 1/2" h. (ILLUS.).............. **$55-$65**
Plate, Lobsterware, stylized lobster claw
shape, charcoal glaze, marked "Ken-
wood 912 U.S.A.," 11 1/2" l. .... **$95-$125**
Range set: tall flattened & tapering salt &
pepper shakers & flattened, domed sugar bowl/grease jar; Sahara line, Medallion copper-clad finish w/blue or pink
base on sugar bowl, sugar marked "Kenwood U.S.A. 997," sugar 3 1/2" h., shakers 5 1/2" h., the set (ILLUS., bottom of
page)... **$65-$75**

Sahara Line Copper-clad Range set

Yellow & Blue Shawnee Elephant Teapots

Fruit & Basket Sugar or Grease Jar

Sugar bowl-grease jar, cov., Fruit & Basket patt., w/gold trim, marked "Shawnee U.S.A. 81," 5 1/2" h. (ILLUS.)............ **$125-$175**

Sugar bowl-grease jar, open, Pennsylvania Dutch patt., w/h.p. heart & tulip design, marked "U.S.A.," 2 3/4" h. .... **$95-$125**

Sugar bowl-grease jar, cov., White Corn line, airbrushed & gold trim, marked "U.S.A." (ILLUS. front row, far left, w/White Corn pieces, page 609) .... **$95-$125**

Sugar shaker, White Corn line, airbrushed & gold trim, marked "U.S.A.," 5 1/4" h. (ILLUS. front row, second from left, w/White Corn pieces, page 609) .... **$350-$375**

Sugar shaker, White Corn line, single hole, airbrushed & gold trim, marked "U.S.A.," 5 1/4" h.. **$275-$375**

Sugar shaker, White Corn line, single hole, marked "U.S.A.," 5 1/4" h. .... **$65-$95**

Shawnee Figural Cottage Teapot

Teapot, cov., figural Cottage, marked "U.S.A. 7," 5 1/2" h. (ILLUS.) .... **$375-$450**

Teapot, cov., figural Elephant patt., green, bright blue or yellow glaze, marked "U.S.A.," 6 1/2" h., each (ILLUS., top of page).. **$165-$225**

Shawnee Figural Elephant Teapot

Teapot, cov., figural Elephant w/burgundy, green & brown h.p. on white ground, marked "U.S.A.," 6 1/2" h. (ILLUS.) .. **$225-$275**

Teapot, cov., figural Granny Ann, in peach w/blue trim or purple w/blue trim, marked "Patented Granny Ann U.S.A.," either... **$65-$75**

Two Versions of the Tom the Piper's Sons Teapot

Two Granny Ann Teapots with Gold & Floral Decals

Teapot, cov., figural Granny Ann, lavender apron w/gold trim & floral decals or peach apron w/blue & red trim w/gold trim & floral decals, marked "Patented Granny Ann U.S.A.," each (ILLUS. of both designs)... **$250-$275**

Rare Version of Tom the Piper's Son Teapot

Teapot, cov., figural Tom the Piper's Son, airbrushed matte reddish orange & greenish yellow w/gold trim, marked "Tom the Piper's Son Patented U.S.A. 44" (ILLUS.)..................................... **$325-$375**

Teapot, cov., figural Tom the Piper's Son, white body w/h.p. trim or airbrushed in blues & reds, marked "Tom the Piper's Son patented U.S.A. 44," 7" h., each (ILLUS. of both designs, top of page). **$65-$75**

Teapot, cov., figural Tom the Piper's Son, white body w/h.p. trim w/patches & gold trim, marked "Tom the Piper's Son patented U.S.A. 44," 7" h. .... **$225-$250**

Teapot, White Corn line, airbrushed & gold trim, marked "U.S.A.," 30 oz. (ILLUS. back row, right w/White Corn pieces, page 609)... **$250-$275**

Shawnee Mini Vase with Spinning Wheel

Vase, miniature, 2 1/2" h., embossed spinning wheel, found in burgundy, green & cobalt blue, marked "U.S.A." (ILLUS.)..... **$125-$150**

Shawnee Miniature Vase with Stagecoach

Vase, miniature, 2 1/2" h., embossed stagecoach scene, found in burgundy, green & cobalt blue, marked "U.S.A." (ILLUS.). **$125-$150**

Shelley China

Members of the Shelley family were in the pottery business in England as early as the 18th century. In 1872 Joseph Shelley formed a partnership with James Wileman of Wileman & Co. who operated the Foley China Works. The Wileman & Co. name was used for the firm for the next fifty years, and between 1890 and 1910 the words "The Foley" appeared above conjoined "WC" initials.

Beginning in 1910 the Shelley family name in a shield appeared on wares, although the firm's official name was still Wileman & Co. The company's name was finally changed to Shelley in 1925 and then Shelley China Ltd. after 1965. The firm changed hands in the 1960s and became part of the Doulton Group in 1971.

At first only average quality earthenwares were produced, but in the late 1890s new shapes and better quality decorations were used.

Bone china was introduced at Shelley before World War I, and these fine dinnerwares became very popular in the United States and are increasingly popular today with collectors. Thin "eggshell china" teawares, miniatures and souvenir items were widely marketed during the 1920s and 1930s and are sought-after today.

Shelley Mark

Rare Blocks Pattern Shelley Bowl-Vase

Bowl-vase, 7" h., Art Deco style, wide low rounded lower body below sharply tapering cylindrical sides, Blocks patt., decorated in shades of blue (ILLUS.) **$750**

Art Deco Crocus Pattern Cup & Saucer

Cup & saucer, Crocus patt., Eve Shape, #11971, Art Deco style, ca. 1930, the set (ILLUS.)... **$225-$275**

Early Wileman Art Nouveau Jardiniere

Jardiniere, Art Nouveau style, rounded foot tapering to a slender pedestal flanked by slender S-curve legs supporting a wide squatty bulbous bowl w/a widely flaring rim, in shades of brown, blue, white & green, No. 3567, Wileman & Co., ca. 1900 (ILLUS.) .... **$300-$400**

Fluted Shape Floral Dessert Set

Luncheon set (trio): cup & saucer & dessert plate; Fluted shape, Rose, Pansy, Forget-me-not patt., 3 pcs. (ILLUS.) ..... **$75-$90**

Archway of Roses Dessert Set

Luncheon set (trio): cup & saucer & dessert plate, Queen Anne Shape, Archway of Roses patt., ca. 1928, 3 pcs. (ILLUS.)
.... **$150-$200**

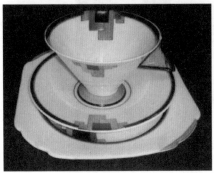

Art Deco Blocks Pattern Luncheon Set

Luncheon set (trio): cup & saucer & dessert plate; Vogue shape, Blocks patt., #11785, 3 pcs. (ILLUS.)..................... **$250-$300**

Horn of Flowers Pattern Luncheon Set

Luncheon set (trio): cup & saucer & dessert plate; Vogue shape, Horn of Flowers patt., 3 pcs. (ILLUS.)........................ **$225-$250**

Marguerite Pattern Pin Dish

Pin dish, round w/widely flaring fluted sides, Marguerite patt., 4 3/4" d. (ILLUS.) .... **$45-$50**
Tea set: cov. teapot, open sugar bowl, creamer, cup & saucer, rimmed soup plate & sandwich plate; Dainty Blue patt., the set (ILLUS., bottom of page)....... **$775-$800**

Shelley Dainty Blue Tea Set

Rare Art Deco Diamonds Pattern Tea Set

Rare Art Deco Blue Lines & Bands Shelley Tea Set

Tea set, cov. teapot, open sugar bowl, creamer & six cups & saucers; Diamonds patt., Mode shape, very rare Art Deco design, the set (ILLUS., top of page) **$4,000**

Tea set: cups & saucers, open sugar, creamer, cake plate & more; Art Deco style, Blue Lines & Bands patt., 21 pcs. (ILLUS. of part, second from top of page) **$3,000**

Teapot, cov., Dainty Big Floral Shape, Capper's Strawberry patt. No. 2396, from the Seconds group, 1959 (ILLUS.) .... **$200-$300**

Shelley Thistle Teapot in Dainty Shape

Teapot, cov., Dainty Shape, Thistle patt. No. 13829, from the Best Ware group, 1955 (ILLUS.).................................... **$200-$300**

Shelley Capper's Strawberry Teapot in Dainty Big Floral Shape

Shelley Poppies Teapot, Cup & Saucer in Princess Shape

Teapot, cov., New York Shape, Saltcoats Crested design, 1890-1905, overall 5 3/4" l., 4" h. .... **$70-$100**

Teapot, cov., Princess Shape, Poppies, orange patt. No. 12227, Floral style, from the Best Ware group, 1933, teapot only (ILLUS. w/matching cup & saucer, top of page).. **$350-$550**

Teapot, cov., Queen Anne Shape, Blue Iris patt. No. 11561, Floral style, from the Best Ware group, 1919, various sizes, each (ILLUS. of various sizes, bottom of page).. **$300-$400**

Rare & Unusual Oriental Shape Teapot

Teapot, cov., Oriental Shape, Intarsio decoration, Wileman & Co., patt. No. 3081, short production period, 1899 (ILLUS.) .... **$1,200-$1,500**

Fine Wileman Shell Shape Teapot

Teapot, cov., Shell Shape, Wileman & Co., patt. No. 5137, introduced in 1891 (ILLUS.) .... **$500-$600**

Blue Iris Teapots of Various Sizes in Queen Anne Shape by Shelley

Modern Pastello Vase with Cottage

Vase, footed swelled cylindrical body tapering to a tiny flared neck, Pastello Ware,
decorated w/a country landscape w/a
cottage w/smoke rising from the chim-
ney, modern (ILLUS.).................................. **$450**

Shelley Crested Ware Small Vase

Vase, 4 3/4" h., simple baluster form
w/short flat mouth, Crested Ware, white
ground w/the color coat-of-arms of a
town in England (ILLUS.) .... **$25-$30**
Vase, 7 1/2" h., footed wide gently flaring
sides w/a flattened shoulder to the short
widely flaring neck, Crane patt., burnt orange ground w/blue & green crane &
black shoulder band (ILLUS., top next
column) .... **$225-$250**
Vases, 6 3/4" h., Art Deco style, tapering
ovoid body w/a short widely flaring
neck, Jazz Circles patt., black ground,
pr. **$300**

Shelley Crane Pattern Vase

Slipware

*This term refers to ceramics, primarily red-
ware, decorated by the application of slip (semi-
liquid paste made of clay). Such wares were made
for decades in England and Germany and elsewhere on the Continent, and in the Pennsylvania
Dutch country and elsewhere in the United
States. Today, contemporary copies of early Slipware items are featured in numerous decorator
magazines and offered for sale in gift catalogs.*

Slipware Bowl with Lines & Initials

Bowl, 11 1/4" d., 3 1/2" h., deep flat flaring
sides w/a smooth rim, decorated around
the interior rim w/a thin wavy line & a
swagged line in yellow slip, initial "M" in
the bottom, 19th c. (ILLUS.)...................... **$480**

Fine Early Slipware Loaf Dish

Loaf dish, oval dished form decorated w/two long lines trimmed w/dashes & wavy short banners at each end, scattered stylized leaf sprigs, all in yellow slip on the reddish ground, coggled rim, minor edge flaws, 19th c., 11 3/4 x 16", 3" h. (ILLUS., previous page) **$1,093**

Slipware Loaf Dish with Diamond Lattice

Loaf dish, rectangular w/rounded corners & a coggled rim, overall wavy diamond lattice decoration in yellow slip, edge flakes, possibly late, 10 1/2 x 13" (ILLUS.) **$144**

Pie plate, round w/coggled rim, a group of three elongated S-scrolls w/feathered ends in the center, edge flakes, 9" d. (ILLUS. top with 8" pie plate, below) **$173**

Two Yellow Slipware Pie Plates

Pie plate, round w/coggled rim, a long band across the center composed of four triple-line sections, a side band at each side w/three short wavy lines at each end, 19th c., 8" d. (ILLUS. bottom with 9" pie plate) **$345**

Early Pie Plate with Bar & Scroll Designs

Pie plate, round w/coggled rim, a long yellow slip bar across the center w/forked ends, four slip S-scroll devices w/crossbars, some wear, minor edge flakes, 19th c., 10 1/4" d. (ILLUS.) **$259**

Extremely Rare Inscribed Slip Plate

Plate, 12 1/4" d., circular redware w/a coggled rim, yellow slip trail inscription reading "Norwalk feb'y the 13 1854," attributed to the Smith Pottery, Norwalk, Connecticut, 1854, minor rim chips, slip repairs (ILLUS.) **$19,975**

Spatterware

This ceramic ware takes its name from the "spattered" decoration, in various colors, generally used to trim pieces handpainted with rustic center designs of flowers, birds, houses, etc. Popular in the early 19th century, most was imported from England.

Related wares, called "stick spatter," had freehand designs applied with pieces of cut sponge attached to sticks, hence the name. Examples date from the 19th and early 20th century and were produced in England, Europe and America.

Some early spatter-decorated wares were marked by the manufacturers, but not many. Twentieth century reproductions are also sometimes marked, including those produced by Boleslaw Cybis.

Bowl, Leeds-type, 7 1/4" d., 3 1/2" h., Peafowl patt. in five colors w/spatter trees around the border, two rim hairline, flakes on table rim **$1,840**

Creamer, footed bulbous body w/a high arched spout & high leaf-scroll handle, brown spatter rim band w/a large dot under the spout, both sides decorated w/a green tree design, rim hairline, 4 1/4" h. (ILLUS. top row, second from right, with grouping of spatterware cups & saucers, plates, teapot & sugar bowl, top of next page) **$345**

Creamer, paneled shaped, molded shell under fan, Rainbow patt. w/dark blue & deep red stripes, stains, hairline & minor flakes, 4 5/8" h. **$345**

Creamer, Peafowl patt., red spatter background, the bird in blue, pale yellow & green, minor edge flakes & light stain, 4" h. ... **$230**

Creamer, Rainbow patt. w/red & blue stripes, stains, hairlines, minor rim flakes, 3 1/2" h. **$488**

Grouping of Spatterware Cups & Saucers, Creamer, Teapot & More

Spatter Grouping with Cups & Saucers, a Pitcher & a Sugar Bowl

Cup, handleless, miniature, Rainbow patt. in green & deep plum, 1 5/8" h............ **$400-800**

Cup plate, Beehive patt., a narrow dark purple spatter border, glued repairs, 4 1/8" d. (ILLUS. front row, second from right, with grouping of spatterware pitcher, sugar bowl & cups & saucers, second from top of page)....................................... **$316**

Cup plates, Peafowl patt., paneled sides w/blue spatter border, peafowl in red, yellow & green, impressed "Stoneware PW & Co.," one w/stains, 4" d., pr. (ILLUS. of one, top row second from left, with grouping of spatterware creamer, teapot, sugar bowl & cups & saucers, top of page)......... **$173**

Cup & saucer, handleless, Acorn patt. in yellow & green, red spatter border, light stains, the set.. **$1,725**

Cup & saucer, handleless, Cockscomb patt., a wide yellow spatter border, the flower in red & green, the set (ILLUS. front row, far right, with grouping of spatterware pitcher, sugar bowl & cups & saucers, second from top of page)......... **$1,610**

Cup & saucer, handleless cup, blue Adams Rose patt., blue spatter background, centered by the rose design in dark blue,

impressed mark fo W. Adams & Sons, small glaze misfire, tight hairline in cup, the set (ILLUS. bottom row, second from right, with grouping of spatterware creamer, teapot, sugar bowl & cups & saucers, top of page) **$115**

Cup & saucer, handleless cup, Dove patt., narrow purple spatter border bands, the dove in yellow, blue & green, cup professionally repaired, the set (ILLUS. top row, far right, with grouping of spatterware creamer, teapot, sugar bowl & cups & saucers, top of page) **$1,006**

Cup & saucer, handleless cup, Thistle patt., the border w/alternating bands of black & green spatter, the central thistle in red & green, the set (ILLUS. top row, far left, with grouping of spatterware creamer, teapot, sugar bowl & cups & saucers, top of page)... **$5,635**

Cup & saucer, handleless cup, Tulip patt., the border w/alternating panels of purple & yellow spatter, the large tulip in yellow, white & dark blue w/green leaves, hairlines, the set (ILLUS. back row, left, with grouping of spatterware pitcher, sugar bowl & cups & saucers, second from top of page)... **$2,530**

Large Grouping of Spatter Cups & Saucers, Plates & Other Pieces

Cup & saucer, handleless, Four Petal Flower patt. in blue & red, red spatter background, cup w/minor roughness, the set (ILLUS. bottom row, second from right, with large grouping of spatter pieces, top of page) **$288**

Cup & saucer, handleless, Primrose patt., a wide red spatter border, the flower in purple & yellow w/green leaves, the set (ILLUS. front row, far left, with grouping of spatterware pitcher, sugar bowl & cups & saucers, second from top previous page) **$776**

Cup & saucer, handleless, Thistle patt. in red & green, rainbow spatter borders in red & mustard yellow, saucer w/filled-in flake, the set **$1,150**

Cup & saucer, handlelesss cup, Holly Berry patt., wide red spatter border above a delicate vining design of holly berries & leaves in red & green, sauce w/glued break, the set (ILLUS. bottom row, second from left with grouping of spatterware creamer, teapot, sugar bowl & cups & saucers, top previous page) **$81**

Cup & saucer, miniature, handleless cup, Thistle patt., red & green spatter stripes, the thistle in red & green, light stains in cup, the set... **$1,265**

Cups & saucers, handleless, Peafowl patt. in blue, yellow & red, green spatter ground, one cup w/ flake, one saucer w/flake & hairline, set of 2 (ILLUS. top row, far left & right, with large grouping of spatter pieces, top of page)....................... **$575**

Pitcher, 8" h., tapering paneled sides w/a high arched spout & long angular handle, Adams Rose patt., dark blue spatter background, the flower in red & green, light staining, small edge flakes (ILLUS. front row, second from left, with grouping of spatterware pitcher, sugar bowl & cups & saucers, previous page) **$460**

Plate, 8" d., Peafowl patt. in blue, yellow & red, green spatter border **$518**

Plate, 8" d., Peafowl patt. in red, yellow & green, blue spatter ground, impressed mark "Pearl Stone Ware - PW & Co." (ILLUS. bottom row, far right, with large grouping of spatter pieces, top of page) .. **$173**

Plate, 8 1/4" d., Thistle patt. in red & green, wide blue spatter border, faintly molded feather-edge, spider crack **$172**

Plate, 8 3/8" d., Schoolhouse patt. in red, green spatter tree **$2,645**

Plate, 8 1/2" d., Peafowl patt. in blue, yellow & green, paneled red spatter border, faint wear **$200**

Plate, 8 1/2" w., Peafowl patt., paneled sides in red spatter, the peafowl in blue, green & red, impressed Adams mark, lightly discolored on the bottom **$374**

Plate, 9 1/8" d., paneled sides, Dahlia patt., a wide dark purple spatter border, the center w/a large six-petal flower in dark blue & red (ILLUS. bottom row, far left, with grouping of spatterware creamer, teapot, sugar bowl & cups & saucers, top previous page) **$546**

Plate, 9 1/2" d., Bull's-eye patt., the border in light red & green spatter **$748**

Plate, 9 1/2" d., Schoolhouse patt. in red, green & black, red spatter border, repaired rim flakes (ILLUS. bottom row, far left, with large group of various spatter pieces, top of page) **$489**

Plate, 9 5/8" d., Pomegranate patt. in red, green, blue & yellow, blue spatter border .. **$288**

Plates, 8 1/2" w., paneled sides, Peafowl & Clover patt., a narrow dark red spatter border band, the large peafowl in green, blue & red, impressed Adams mark, small rim flakes, hairline & overglaze flaked (ILLUS. of one, bottom row far right with grouping of spatterware creamer, teapot, sugar bowl & cups & saucers, top previous page) **$633**

Saucer, Schoolhouse patt. in red, red spatter border, 5 3/4" d. **$546**

Saucer, Six-point Star patt. in red, yellow & green, blue spatter border, 5 3/4" d. (ILLUS. top row, second from left, with grouping of various spatter pieces, top of page) **$518**

Saucer, Thistle patt. in red & green, rainbow spatter border in yellow & blue, glued chip......... **$1,150**

Sugar bowl, cov., footed paneled baluster-form w/tab side handles & a domed cover w/pointed finial, decorated w/full-length alternating stripes of red & green spatter, closely mismatched cover, minor base rim stains, cover w/stains & repairs, 7 1/4" h. (ILLUS. back row, right, with grouping of spatterware pitcher, sugar bowl & cups & saucers, page 620)............ **$575**

Sugar bowl, cov., Peafowl patt., bulbous body w/a tapering shoulder to a wide flat rim & low domed cover, dark brown spatter border bands, small peafowl in dark blue, yellow & red, stains, rim flake & hairline, 5" h. (ILLUS. bottom row, third from left, with grouping of spatterware creamer, teapot, sugar bowl & cups & saucers, page 620) **$230**

Sugar bowl, cov., Tulip patt. in red, white, blue & green, dark red spatter borders, rim flakes on cover, base w/spider crack in glaze........ **$288**

Sugar bowl, no cover, footed ovoid body, Parrot patt. in green, red & yellow, red spatter border, mismatched lid not shown, slight staining, roughness & chipped lid, 4 1/2" h. (ILLUS. top row, third from left, with grouping of various spatter pieces, page 621).......................... **$690**

Teapot, cov., Peafowl patt. in blue, yellow & green, red spatter borders, few rim flakes on teapot, 7" h. **$460**

Teapot, cov., Thumbprint patt., footed wide squatty paneled lower body w/sharply tapering paneled sides, domed cover w/pointed finial, serpentine spout & pointed loop handle, a dark blue spatter ground decorated w/black scattered thumbprints, light overal stains, repaired spout & cover, 7 1/2" h. (ILLUS. top row, third from left, with grouping of spatterware creamer, teapot, sugar bowl & cups & saucers, page 620) **$690**

Teapot, cov., wide ovoid body tapering to a flat rim & low domed cover, serpentine spout & C-scroll handle, Rainbow patt. in red & green spatter, repaired spout & cover, 7" h. (ILLUS. bottom row, third from left, with group of various spatter pieces, page 621)..................................... **$633**

Toddy plate, Tulip patt., paneled border in light blue spatter, red, white & blue tulip w/green leaves, slight wear w/stains, 5" w. **$489**

Toddy plate, Peafowl patt. in in blue, green & red, banded purple, red & blue spatter border, small repaired rim flake, 5 1/4" d. (ILLUS. top row, second from right, with group of various spatter pieces, page 621)... **$805**

Toddy plate, Schoolhouse patt. in red, black, brown & green, blue spatter border, repaired rim flakes, 5 3/4" d. (ILLUS. bottom row, second from left, with group of other spatter pieces, page 621) **$633**

Stick Spatter

Rare Stick Spatter Rabbits Charger

Charger, round w/flanged rin, Rabbits patt., large central transfer-printed scene of rabbits playing tennis, framed by brushed & stick spatter flowers & leaves in red, dark blue, green & yellow, minor glaze flakes, late 19th - early 20th c., 12 1/2" d. (ILLUS.)... **$805**

Spongeware

Spongeware's designs were spattered, sponged or daubed on in colors, sometimes with a piece of cloth. Blue on white was the most common type, but mottled tans, browns and greens on yellowware were also popular. Spongeware generally has an overall pattern with a coarser look than Spatterware, to which it is loosely related. These wares were extensively produced in England and America well into the 20th century.

1 1/2 Qt. Batter Pitcher

Batter pitcher, no cover, dark blue sponging, printed on the front "1 1/2 Qt." (ILLUS.) **$625**

Batter pitcher, no cover, dark blue sponging, printed on the front "1 Qt." (ILLUS., next page) **$625**

Butter crock, cov., dark blue sponging around an oval reserve printed "Butter," 6" d., 5" h. (ILLUS., next page) **$250**

Fine 1 Qt. Batter Pitcher

Nice Spongeware Covered Butter Crock

Spongeware Lid-less Butter Crock

Butter crock, no cover, blue sponging, printed on the front in black "Butter," 6" d., 5" h. (ILLUS.) **$150**

Canister, cov., footed cylindrical shape w/a domed cover w/knob finial, dark blue large sponging around a zigzag oval reserve printed in fancy script "Coffee," 6" h. (ILLUS., top next column) **$1,000**

Rare Covered Coffee Canister

Fine Spongeware Advertising Canister

Canister, open, advertising-type, heavy dark blue sponging around a reserve printed in dark blue fancy lettering "Old Honesty Coffee," 6" h. (ILLUS.) **$1,000**

Banded Spongeware Hallboy Pitcher

Pitcher, 6" h., Hallboy-type, blue sponged bands around the rim & base, a wide dark blue body band flanked by pinstripe bands, angular handle (ILLUS.)................. **$250**

Nice Ovoid Blue Spongeware Pitcher

Pitcher, 8 1/4" h., slender ovoid body w/a pinched rim spout & pointed arched handle, overall dark blue patterned sponging (ILLUS.).. **$358**

Cylindrical Blue Spongeware Pitcher

Pitcher, 8 3/4" h., slightly tapering cylindrical body w/rim sout & C-form applied handle, overall dark blue sponging, a few tight hairlines (ILLUS.)............................... **$275**

Fine Pine Cone Spongeware Pitcher

Pitcher, 9 1/2" h., embossed Pine Cone patt., cylindrical w/D-form handle, heavy overall dark blue sponging, Burley-Winter Pottery Company (ILLUS.).................... **$800**

Rare Banded Spongeware Umbrella Stand

Umbrella stand, cylindrical, decorated w/narrow blue sponged bands around the rim & base, each flanked by two wide blue bands, two wide blue sponged bands around the middle flanked by two dark blue bands, 21" h. (ILLUS.) **$2,000**

Blue Spongeware Vegetable Dish

Vegetable dish, shallow rectangular shape w/rounded corners, overall dark blue sponging, wear, minor clay separation at rim, 9 3/4" l. (ILLUS.) **$121**

Unusual Old Fulper Water Filter

Water filter, wide cylindrical body w/a stepped domed cover, heavy dark blue sponging w/two thin bands near the top, a rectangular white panel printed "No. 7," a large shield-form mark on the lower front reading "Improved Natural Stone Germ Proof Filter - Fulper Pottery Co.,

Flemington, N.J. Est. 1805," crack at rim & chip on cover, 12 1/2" h. (ILLUS.)........... **$230**

Staffordshire Figures

Small figures and groups made of pottery were produced by the majority of the Staffordshire, England potters in the 19th century and were used as mantel decorations or "chimney ornaments," as they were sometimes called. Pairs of dogs were favorites and were turned out by the carload, and 19th-century pieces are still available. Well-painted reproductions also abound, and collectors are urged to exercise caution before investing.

Fine Pair of Staffordshire Cat Figures

Cats, seated facing viewer, on a flaring rect-angular blue pillow w/gilt trim, each white w/sponged black & yellow spots, a yellow neck ribbons & painted facial features, 19th c., 7 1/2" h., pr. (ILLUS.) **$431**

Early Staffordshire Pug Dog Figure

Dog, lead glazed creamware model of a re-cumbent Pug dog, modeled atop a deep rectangular base, overall translucent mottled brown glaze, 18 c., 3 1/2" l. (ILLUS.)... **$1,528**

Dogs, lead-glaze pearlware seated Pug-like dogs each sitted on a square pillow, dogs decorated w/yellow, tan & dark brown spots on a cream ground, the pillows w/green & brown trim, ca. 1800, 3 3/8" h., pr. (ILLUS., bottom of page).... **$2,350**

Nice Old English Staffordshire Dogs

Dogs, Spaniels in a seated pose w/head facing the viewer, white w/a rust-red spotted curly coat, h.p. head details & painted collar & chain, England, late 19th c., 10" h., pr. (ILLUS.) **$570**

Pair of Staffordshire Spaniels & Figure of The Lion Slayer

Dogs, Spaniels in a seated pose w/head facing the viewer, white w/yellow eyes & gilt chains & fur trim, England, late 19th c., gilt wear, one w/scuff mark, 14 5/8" h., pr. (ILLUS. flanking figure of The Lion Slayer).. **$431**

Rare Early Staffordshire Dogs on Pillows

Rare Early Staffordshire Equestrian Figures

Equestrian figures, each overglaze enamel decorated & modeled as military officers in parade garb, mounted atop stepped oval bases, each on a prancing brown steed, early 19th c., one w/restoration to one of the horse's feet, reins, stirrup straps, both ears, the other restored to all of the horse's feet, an ear, part of the reins & stirrup straps, chip to base & plume on hat, parts of stirrups missing on each, 9 3/4" h., pr. (ILLUS., top of page)............ **$5,875**

Figure group, modeled as the English Royal Coat of Arms decorated in polychrome overglaze enamels, impressed mark "Walton" within a raised scroll on the back, ca. 1820, 6" h. **$4,406**

Figure group of Joan & Darby, seated middle aged couple sharing an evening drink, colorful enameled trim, 19th c., 5 5/8" h. (ILLUS. second from left, bottom, with grouping of Staffordshire figures, bottom of page)................................... **$86**

Figure group of Little Red Riding Hood, seated w/her basket, the small wolf seated to her side, crazing, minor wear, hairline, 19th c., 9" h. (ILLUS. far left with grouping of Staffordshire figures, bottom of page).. **$230**

Figure group of Mother Goose, Mother Goose wearing a tall hat & seated astride a flying white goose, brown-dabbed green & yellow base, hairline, repairs, 19th c., 7 1/4" h. (ILLUS. second from left, top, with grouping of Staffordshire figures, bottom of page)............................ **$288**

Scarce Mismarked B. Franklin Figure

Figure of Benjamin Franklin, standing w/a document in one hand & his hat under his other arm, all white except for decorated waistcoat, facial features & black trim, on a plinth base incorrectly labeled "Washington," mid-19th c, 15" h. (ILLUS.) **$1,035**

Grouping of Varied Staffordshire Figures

Figure of man holding cat, standing wearing striped breeches, blue waistcoat & tan coat, holding a calico cat, 7 3/4" h. (ILLUS. third from right with group of Staffordshire figures, bottom previous page) **$230**

Figure of naughty barmaid, standing wearing a long white dress w/h.p. flowerheads & a bonnet, holding a bottle, rear view shows she's not wearing undergarments, 19th c., 8 1/8" h. (ILLUS. second from right with grouping of Staffordshire figures, bottom previous page) **$345**

Figure of Temperance man, double-sided, one side shows a well-dressed man holding coin purse & labeled "Water," reverse shows a man dressed in rages holding a bottle & labeled "Gin," mid-19th c., 8 3/8" h. (ILLUS. far right with grouping of Staffordshire figures, bottom previous page) **$259**

Figure of The Lion Slayer, a Scotsman w/a claymore standing & holding a lion by it back paw, minor wear, mid-19th c., 16 1/8" h. (ILLUS. center with large Spaniels, page 763) **$403**

Hound, standing slender animal w/head down, white w/large black spots, on an oblong green grass & tree stump base, early 19th c., 6 3/4" l. **$1,410**

Unusual Cottage Pastille Burner

Pastille burner, modeled as a two-part cottage w/two sheep under a open pillar in front, trimmed in blue, black, yellow, green & orange, chimney w/a hold for the smoke, some loss to paint, small chip on base w/small crack, 9" w., 8" h. (ILLUS.) ... **$489**

Staffordshire Transfer Wares

The process of transfer-printing designs on earthenwares developed in England in the late 18th century, and by the mid-19th century most common ceramic wares were decorated in this manner, most often with romantic European or Oriental landscape scenes, animals or flowers. The earliest such wares were printed in dark blue, but a little later light blue, pink, purple, red, black, green and brown were used. A majority of these wares were produced at various English potteries right up until the turn of the 20th century, but French and other European firms also made similar pieces and all are quite collectible. The best reference on this area is Petra Williams' book Staffordshire Romantic Transfer Patterns -

Cup Plates and Early Victorian China (Fountain House East, 1978).

Unusual Small Blue Clews Bowl

Bowl, 7 1/2" d., 1 1/2" h., dark blue, marked "The Valentine - From Wilkies Designs," by Clews, rare form (ILLUS.) **$288**

Early Handled Dark Blue Bowl

Bowl, 10" d., 4 3/4" h., a footed deep round form w/molded shell-form rim handles, dark blue & white, the interior printed w/a central romantic landscape w/two fishermen in the foreground & a tower & forest in the background framed by a wide parrot & flower border, the exterior printed w/a scene of a shepherd among Gothic ruins, edge wear, ca. 1820s (ILLUS.) **$633**

Cup plate, Moral Maxim patt., red, two border reserves, minor edge wear, 4 1/8" d. (ILLUS. top row, left, with other cup plates & toddy plate, top next page) **$121**

Cup plate, Moses & the Ten Commandments patt., red, floral & shell border, 4" d. (ILLUS. top row, right, with other cup plates & toddy plate, top next page) ... **$176**

Cup plate, Prunus Wreath patt., medium dark blue, impressed mark for Rogers, 4" d. (ILLUS. bottom row, right, with other cup plates & toddy plate, top next page) ... **$165**

Pair of "The Valentine - From Wilkies Designs" by Clews

Grouping of Staffordshire Cup Plates & a Toddy Plate

Plates, 9" d., dark blue, marked "The Valentine - From Wilkies Designs," by Clews, pr. (ILLUS., previous page) **$345**

Dark Blue Italian Scenes Platter

Platter, 16 1/2 x 21", oval, titled on back "Italian Scenes, Turin," dark blue landscape w/town in the distance across a lake, figures in the foreground framed by tall arching leafy trees, ca. 1830, hairline, small firing imperfection (ILLUS.) **$575**

Platter, 12 1/4 x 15 1/2", Wild Rose patt., center landscape scene w/a bridge w/men in small boats, a house in the distance, impressed anchor mark, Middlesborough Pottery, medium to dark blue, knife scratches, ca. 1830 .... **$201**

Platter, 12 1/2 x 15 7/8", Wild Rose Roma patt., wild rose border & center landscape scene w/a bridge, men in a boat & a cottage in the distance, medium blue, areas of wear, stains mainly on the back, ca. 1830.. **$230**

Early Jedburgh Abbey Oval Platter

Platter, 12 3/4 x 17", oval, wide tulip & zinnia borders, central landscape titled "Jedburgh Abbey, Roxburghshire," dark &

medium blue, by Adams, ca. 1830, glued flake, small chips (ILLUS.) **$230**

Unusual Brown & Green Scenic Platter

Platter, 6 1/2 x 19 3/4" oval, gently scalloped rim, large central landscape scene w/a large mansion in a pastoral wooded landscape, wide border band w/four large scroll-bordered floral sections alternating w/small oblong bird-decorated panels, printed in green & brown, England, ca. 1840, some light stain (ILLUS.).................. **$690**

Rare Dark Blue Seashells Platter

Platter, 20 1/2" l., oval, dark blue, Seashells patt., Longport, ca. 1830 (ILLUS.)........... **$1,955**

Large Oval Well-and-Tree Platter

Platter, 16 x 20 3/4" oval, well-and-tree style, the interior decorated w/a large exotic Far Eastern landscape w/large castle & temple ruins, the wide naturalistic border band w/leafy trees & flowers, deep blue on white, impressed mark of Rogers & Son or J. & G. Rogers, England, ca. 1830 (ILLUS.)... **$1,438**

Large Blue Platter with Landscape

Platter, 16 3/4 x 21", oval w/angled corners, a large central rural landscape w/a castle bridge w/moat, figures & cattle, scrolled floral bordeer w/fleur-de-lis, impressed Clews mark, dark blue, minor knife scratches (ILLUS.) **$633**

Teapot, cov., footed deep oblong body w/a rim band & flaring collar & wide arched spout, serpentine spout & fancy scroll handle, highd domed cover w/pointed knob finial, Seashell patt., dark blue, hairlines, flakes & stains, ca. 1830, 7 1/4" h. ... **$374**

Toddy plate, the center w/a multi-colored landscape w/a thatched roof cottage at the foot of a hill topped by castle ruins, sepia butterfly design border, 4 3/4" d. (ILLUS. bottom row, left, with other cup plates, top of page 628) **$88**

Stangl Pottery

Johann Martin Stangl, who first came to work for the Fulper Pottery in 1910 as a ceramic chemist and plant superintendent, acquired a financial interest and became president of the company in 1926. The name of the firm was changed to Stangl Pottery in 1929 and at that time much of the production was devoted to a high grade dinnerware to enable the company to survive the Depression years. One of the earliest solid-color

dinnerware patterns was its Colonial line, introduced in 1926. In the 1930s it was joined by the Americana pattern. After 1942 these early patterns were followed by a wide range of hand-decorated patterns featuring flowers and fruits, with a few decorated with animals or human figures.

Around 1940 a very limited edition of porcelain birds, patterned after the illustrations in John James Audubon's "Birds of America," was issued. Stangl subsequently began production of less expensive ceramic birds, which proved to be popular during the war years 1940-46. Each bird was handpainted and well marked with impressed, painted or stamped numerals indicating the species and the size.

All operations ceased at the Trenton, New Jersey, plant in 1978.

Two reference books collectors will find helpful are The Collectors Handbook of Stangl Pottery by Norma Rehl (The Democrat Press, 1979), and Stangl Pottery by Harvey Duke (Wallace-Homestead, 1994).

Stangl Mark

Birds

Pair of Large Stangl Cockatoos

Cockatoos, large, colorful decoration, No. 3584, 11 3/8" h., pr. (ILLUS.) **$460**

Steins

Anheuser Busch, Bud Man, ceramic, solid head-type, by Ceramarte, 1/2 liter (ILLUS. left with two other Anheuser Busch steins, top next page).. **$367**

Anheuser Busch, Budweiser 100 Years, ceramic, footed tapering gold cylinder w/molded company eagle logo & wording in red, white & blue, by Ceramarte, 1976, 1/2 liter (ILLUS. center with two other Anheuser Busch steins, top next page)... **$140**

Anheuser Busch, The Brew House Clock Tower, figural, ceramic, by Ceramarte, 1/2 liter (ILLUS. right with two other Anheuser Busch steins, top next page)........................ **$288**

Three Anheuser Busch Steins by Ceramarte

Decorative Capo-di-Monte Stein

Capo-di-Monte, porcelain, footed cylindrical body w/high-relief draped & nude children, hinged porcelain cover w/kneeling child finial, winged female head handle, late 19th - early 20th c., 1 liter (ILLUS.) **$483**

Fine Porcelain Barmaid Character Stein

Character, "Barmaid," porcelain, finely detailed w/her arms behind her head, shades of brown & tan, by Schierholz, small repaired chip on interior top edge, 1/2 liter (ILLUS.)............................ **$2,029**

Rare Man Holding Cat Stein

Character, "Man Holding Cat," pottery, by Diesinger, No. 765, small flake on hat, 1/2 liter (ILLUS.)................................ **$1,378**

Goebel Porcelain Monk Stein

Character, "Monk," porcelain, original pewter lid, impressed "Monschau" on front, full-bee mark of Goebel, Germany, ca. 1950, 1/2 liter (ILLUS.)................................ **$357**

Monkey & Skull Character Steins

Character, "Monkey," porcelain, inlaid lid, by E. Bohne & Sohne, hairline on top of handle attachment repaired, 1/2 liter (ILLUS. right with Skull stein) **$1,416**

Rare Gentleman Rabbit Stein

Character, "Rabbit," porcelain, wearing green hat & coat, monocle in one eye, by Schierholz, 1/2 liter (ILLUS.) **$2,657**

Character, "Skull on Book," porcelain, inlaid lid, by E. Bohne & Sohne, 1/2 liter (ILLUS. left with Monkey stein, top previous column) **$604**

Faience, bulbous base tapering to cylindrical sides & a domed cover w/a pewter hinge, high-fired cobalt blue h.p. decoration, 18th c., chipping on edges, top rim hairlines, 1 liter, 10 3/4" h. (ILLUS. left with two other faience steins, bottom of page) **$460**

Faience, cylindrical, high-fired polychrome castle & foliate decoration, domed pewter lid dated 1816, higline on side, 1 liter, 10" h. (ILLUS. center with other two faience steins, bottom of page) **$725**

Faience, cylindrical, high-fired polychrome double-headed eagle crest on a pale blue ground, pewter footring & domed cover, hairline in side, pewter repaired, Austria, 18th c., 1 liter, 9 1/2" h. (ILLUS. right with two other faience steins, bottom of page) **$604**

Pottery Munich Child Stein

Character, "Munich Child," pottery, pottery-inlaid lid, marked by Lichtinger, Munchen, 1 liter (ILLUS.) **$497**

Three Early Decorated Faience Steins

Mettlach Etched Steins No. 2403, 2583 & 3170

Mettlach Courting of Siegfried Stein

Mettlach, No. 2402, etched, the courting of Siegfried, inlaid lid, 1/2 liter (ILLUS.).......... **$907**

Mettlach, No. 2403, etched color scene of Wartburg Castle, inlaid lid, 1/2 liter (ILLUS. center with Mettlach steins 2583 & 3170, top of page).. **$604**

Fine Mettlach Cameo Hunting Scene Stein

Mettlach, No. 2530, cameo-style, pale & dark green bands separated by thin brown bands, the wide dark green center band decorated in white relief w/a boar hunting scene, a narrow pale green base band decorated in white relief w/a repeated design of running rabbits & foxes, inlaid lid, 1 liter (ILLUS.)................................ **$736**

Mettlach, No. 2583, etched color Egyptian figural panel, inlaid lid, 1/2 liter (ILLUS. left with Mettlach steins No. 2403 & 3170, top of page).. **$966**

Cavalier Drinking Mettlach Stein

Mettlach, No. 2640, etched color scene of a cavalier drinking at a tavern table, inlaid lid, 1/2 liter (ILLUS.) **$501**

Student Counting Mice Mettlach Stein

Mettlach, No. 2662, large etched scene of a drunken student counting white mice, inlaid lid, 1/2 liter (ILLUS., previous page) **$2,174**

Art Nouveau Mettlach PUG Stein

Mettlach, No. 2685-179, PUG (painted under glaze), Art Nouveau h.p. design of radishes on a dark greenish blue ground, signed by Richard Riemerschmid, flat Art Nouveau pewter lid, 1/2 liter (ILLUS.) **$725**

Mettlach Etched Art Nouveau Stein

Mettlach, No. 2801, etched Art Nouveau design of stylized gold wheat centered by a small red heart, dark blue background, inlaid lid, 2.15 liter (ILLUS.) **$834**

Mettlach, No. 3024 II, cameo-type, footed ovoid light green body tapering to a cylindrical neck w/applied tan band & spout, the front w/a white cameo relief of a Cavalier, inlaid pewter lid, 1.8 liter (ILLUS., top next column)... **$431**

Mettlach, No. 3170, etched band design of stylized figures walking on a winter night, artist-signed by Ludwig Hohlwein, inlaid lid, firing discoloration on handle, 1/2 liter (ILLUS. right with Mettlach steins No. 2403 & 2583, top previous page) **$725**

Mettlach No. 3024 II Cameo Stein

Cheese Maker Occupational Stein

Occupational, cheese maker, porcelain, wide colorful band showing two scenes of the occupation, lithophane in the bottom, domed pewter lid, 1/2 liter (ILLUS.) **$242**

German Post Coach Driver Stein

Occupational, post coach driver, porcelain, wide colorful scene of a German post coach, domed pewter lid, 1/2 liter (ILLUS.).. **$483**

Rare Stoneware Regimental Stein

Regimental, stoneware, short bulbous ovoid shape, decorated w/three photographic scenes of telegraphers at work, domed pewter lid decorated w/the Munich Child in relief, Munich, 190709, minor wear, 1/2 liter, 6 1/4" h. (ILLUS.)....... **$2,536**

German Brewery Advertising Stein

Stoneware, brewery advertising-type, tall gently tapering cylindrical body incised "Mahr's brau - Bamberg" highlighted in cobalt blue, pewter lid w/inlaid porcelain disk h.p. w/a farming scene, scratches on body, lid dented, 1 liter (ILLUS.)................. **$173**

Sarreguemines Stoneware Relief Stein

Stoneware, cylindrical body decorated in color relief w/a scene of a drunken man walking past a lamp post w/a monkey on it, a cat nearby, porcelain-inlaid pewter lid w/a relief-molded deer, No. 2888, Sarreguemines, France, 1 liter (ILLUS.).......... **$966**

Stoneware, cylindrical body, fancy applied relief designs of deer & foliage & engraved florals, domed pewter lid dated 1788, Westerwald, ca. 1790, 1/2 liter, 8 1/2" h. (ILLUS. right with other Westerwald stein, below) **$554**

Two Early Westerwald Stoneware Steins

Stoneware, cylindrical body, hand-engraved scene of a leaping stag among leafy floral vines, dark cobalt blue ground, domed pewter lid dated 1769, Westerwald, ca. 1770, pewter repair at attachment point on lid, 1/2 liter, 8 1/4" h. (ILLUS. left with other Westerwald stein) **$725**

Rare Early Altenburg Stoneware Stein

Stoneware, short slightly tapering cylindrical tan body, thin incised rings below a wide center body w/a hex sign-style cut design w/applied blue beads, a pewter base band & two thin body bands, domed pewter lid, Altenburg, ca. 1650, 6 3/4" h. (ILLUS.).. **$4,830**

Stoneware

Stoneware is essentially a vitreous pottery, impervious to water even in its unglazed state, that has been produced by potteries all over the world for centuries. Utilitarian wares such as crocks, jugs, churns and the like were the most common productions in the numerous potteries that sprang into existence in the United States during the 19th century. These items were often enhanced by the application of a cobalt blue oxide decoration. In addition to the coarse, primarily salt-glazed stonewares, there are other categories of stoneware known by such special names as basalt, jasper and others.

Early Brown Altenburg Stoneware Stein

Stoneware, tall cylindrical brown-glazed body w/thin incised upper & lower bands & two bands decorated w/cobalt blue dots, a wide center band w/cobalt blue stylized florals, pewter base & rim band, domed pewter lid w/hinged replaced, Altenburg, 17th c., 1 liter, 9 1/2" h. (ILLUS.) **$1,328**

Stoneware, tall cylindrical form, transfer-printed & enameled in color w/a shield enclosing the standing Munich Child, German printed inscription for the anniversary of the Munich Octoberfest, 1810-1935, artist P. Neu, domed pewter lid, factory glaze flaw on base, 1 liter (ILLUS. right with other Munich Child stoneware stein, below) **$430**

Batter Pail with Original Handle & Cap

Batter pail w/original wire bail handle & turned wood grip, wide ovoid body tapering to a short cylindrical neck, short angled cylindrical spout w/tin lid, cobalt blue brushed flower below the spout, unsigned by probably New York State, one very minor surface chip at rim, ca. 1860, 9" h. (ILLUS.) **$743**

Two Stoneware Munich Child Steins

Stoneware, tall cylindrical form, transfer-printed & enameled in color w/a side view of the standing Munich Child standing on an orb, "Munchen" printed below, artist Ludwig Hohlwein, domed pewter lid w/repaired strap, ca. 1908, 1 liter (ILLUS. left with other Munich Child stoneware stein) **$966**

Handled Batter Pail with Running Bird

Batter pail w/original wire bail handle w/wooden grip, wide ovoid body tapering to a short cylindrical neck, short angled cylindrical spout, decorated w/a cobalt blue slip-quilled running bird below the number "4" typical of Whites, Utica, New York, some surface roughness to spout, cinnamon clay color, 4 qt., ca. 1865, 9 1/2" h. (ILLUS., previous page)..... **$578**

Extraordinary Decorated Mini Churn

Butter churn, miniature, swelled cylindrical shape w/three pairs of boldly molded rings up the sides, slightly flaring cylindrical neck & eared handles, incised bands between each pair of rings including a crosshatch design, random squiggly lines & at the top, a detailed fish, unmarked, minor surface roughness at rim, ca. 1830, 5 1/2" h. (ILLUS.)............ **$29,150**

Butter churn, swelled cylindrical body w/a flared molded rim, eared handles, dark cobalt blue slip-quilled decoration of a large paddletailed bird perched on a stem w/large leaves & two blossoms, impressed mark of N. A. White & Son, Utica, N.Y., professional restoration to hairline on front, ca. 1870, 5 gal., 16 1/2" h. (ILLUS.).................. **$550**

Flower-decorated Stoneware Churn

Butter churn, tall slightly swelled cylindrical body w/a molded rim & eared handles, original stoneware guide, cobalt blue slip-quilled decoration of a large upright daisy-like flower w/a bud & long leaves below "5," impressed mark of John Burger, Rochester, New York, professional restoration to hairlines, 5 gal., ca. 1865, 18" h. (ILLUS.)... **$2,530**

5 Gallon Butter Churn by White & Son

Butter Churn with Unusual Tree Decor

Butter churn, tall swelled cylindrical body w/a molded rim w/inset cover, eared handles, fancy cobalt blue slip-quilled decoration of a large leafy tree above leafy plants, impressed mark of C.W. Braum, Buffalo, NY, lid probably not original, ca. 1870, 4 gal., 16" h. (ILLUS., previous page) **$4,510**

Harrington Butter Churn with Partridge

Butter churn & cover, tall swelled cylindrical body w/a short flared rim & eared handles, cobalt blue slip-quilled very long banded & dotted partridge perched on a formed flowering branch, impressed mark of T. Harrington, Lyons, NY above a "6," professional restoration to glaze exfoliation around base, ca. 1850, 6 gal., 19 1/2" h. (ILLUS.) **$2,750**

J. & E. Norton Churn with Rare Design

Butter churn & original cover, tall swelled cylindrical body w/a molded rim & eared handles, ornate cobalt blue slip-quilled landscape design w/a reclining stag, a large tree & a house in the woods, impressed mark of J. & E. Norton, Bennington, VT, 9" tight hairline down from the rim, age spider on right side, ca. 1855, 3 gal., 16" h. (ILLUS.) **$8,800**

Scarce Flower-decorated Cake Crock

Cake crock, low wide cylindrical shape w/molded rim & eared handles, cobalt blue slip-quilled double stylized flowers on thin leafy stems, brushed blue dashes above, impressed "Tripe" eleven times & w/name P.F. Finnegan, couple of minor chips, ca. 1860, 17" d., 10" h. (ILLUS.)... **$1,595**

Unusual Early Chicken Waterer

Chicken waterer, beehive shape tapering to a tiny neck & eared handles, a projecting domed at the front w/an arched opening, cobalt blue brushed highlights down the front & on the handles, unsigned, some minor surface chiping, ca. 1860, 1/2 gal., 7 1/2" h. (ILLUS.) **$798**

Rare Early New York Cream Pot

Cream pot, wide ovoid body w/a wide flat rim flanked by upright loop handles, incised & cobalt blue slip-quilled swag & tassel design around the shoulder above the impressed mark of Commeraws Stoneware - N. York, clay separation on interior in the making, some interior wear, ca. 1790, about 1 gal., 7" h. (ILLUS.)...................... **$7,425**

Rare Cowden & Wilcox Cream Pot

Cream pot, wide ovoid body w/a wide molded rim, cobalt blue brushed designs of a C-form man-in-the-moon design below the impressed mark of Cowden & Wilcox, Harrisburg, PA, stack marks on base, ca. 1870, 1 1/2 gal., 8 1/2" h. (ILLUS.).......... **$7,150**

Crock, cylindrical w/molded rim & eared handles, cobalt blue slip-quilled hen pecking at corn, minor stains & chips at rim, impressed mark of Adam Caire, Pokeepsie (sic), New York, 3 gal., ca. 1880, 10" h. (ILLUS., top next column) **$495**

Crock, cylindrical w/molded rim & eared handles, cobalt blue slip-quilled large three leaf cluster enclosing a large "5," impressed mark of John Burger, Rochester, New York, two hairlines down from rim, one by ear & one at back, 5 gal., ca. 1865, 13" h. (ILLUS., middle next column) **$743**

Three Gallon Stoneware Crock with Hen

Crock with Large Three-Leaf Cluster

Stoneware Crock with Large Starburst

Crock, cylindrical w/molded rim & eared handles, cobalt blue slip-quilled large six-point starburst enclosing a blossom, impressed mark of A. O. Whittemore, Havana, New York, large surface chip at rim, tight hairline at back, 5 gal., ca. 1870, 12" h. (ILLUS., previous page) **$2,035**

Bird-decorated Advertising Crock

Crock, cylindrical w/molded rim & eared handles, cobalt blue slip-quilled long-tailed bird perched on a tree stump, impressed advertising "C. O. Barnes & Co. - 317 & 319 North Main Str.- Providence, R.I.," unknown maker, probably from Fort Edward, New York, 1 gal., ca. 1870, 7" h. (ILLUS.)..................... **$2,750**

Very Rare Large Crock with Phoenix

Crock, cylindrical w/molded rim & eared handles, rare cobalt blue slip-quilled decoration of a large spreadwinged phoenix among leafy shrubs, very detailed, impressed mark of N. Clark & Co., Rochester, New York, some hairlines, 6 gal., ca. 1850, 14 1/2" h. (ILLUS.) **$72,600**

Crock, small swelled cylindrical body w/flared lip & applied loop side handles, cobalt blue brushed watch spring designs around the sides, unsigned, decoration attributed to James Morgan, Jr., Cheesequake, New York, tight clay separation line along bottom, 1 pt., ca. 1790, 5 3/4" h. (ILLUS., top next column) **$19,800**

Very Rare Early Handled Pint Crock

Unusual 1860s Political Crock

Crock, wide ovoid body w/a molded rim & eared handles, cobalt blue brushed inscription "J.S. Wadsworth - Governor Of NY State," probably from his campaign in 1862, minor chipping & hairlines, 1 1/2 gal., ca. 1862, 8 1/2" h. (ILLUS.)............. **$2,750**

Rare Early Crock with Incised Bird

Crock, wide ovoid body w/a wide flat rim, eared handles, incised design of a bird perched on a leaf accented in cobalt blue, impressed mark of S. Fayette & Co., Utica, New York, chip at rim, minor surface wear, ca. 1835, 9" h. (ILLUS.).... **$2,860**

Early Stoneware Cuspidor

Cuspidor, short cylindrical form w/concave top centered by a hole, a drainage hole on one side, cobalt blue brushed accents, unsigned, ca. 1840, 7 1/2" d., 3 1/4" h. (ILLUS.) **$198**

Very Rare Stoneware Eagle Decanter

Decanter, figural, modeled as a spread-winged American eagle w/a large American shield on the breast accented w/dark blue & red, impressed on the bottom "M & W - GR," possibly a German maker, probably a commemorative of the 1876 U.S. Centennial, two-piece removable head, very rare, 10 1/2" h. (ILLUS.) **$2,200**

Early Stoneware Flask

Flask, flattened ovoid shape tapering to a small molded   neck, undecorated & unsigned, ca. 1830, 7 1/4" h. (ILLUS.) **$88**

Rare Early New York Decorated Flask

Flask, flattened ovoid shape tapering to a small molded reeded neck, cobalt blue brushed stylized tree design on one side, unsigned by typical of New York City, ca. 1800, 8" h. (ILLUS.) **$1,650**

Rare Early Stoneware Inkwell

Inkwell, short cylindrical form w/impressed scribe lines & pen hole in top rim, impressed mark of M. Tyler, Albany, New York, accented in cobalt blue, couple of surface chips, ca. 1840, 4 3/4" d., 2" h. (ILLUS.).. **$7,070**

Large Inscribed Covered Jar

Jar, cov., wide low pedestal base & ovoid body w/a molded rim flanked by eared handles, a high domed cover w/an acorn finial, the body incised & trimmed in blue w/narrow bands & the inscription "Mrs. Anna Munson - 1885" framed w/a leafy wreath & a large leaf, edge chips, hairline in base, 18 1/4" h. (ILLUS., previous page) **$7,475**

Rare Early Jar with Hand Design

Jar, ovoid w/molded rim & eared handles, cobalt blue brushed design of a large open hand centered by a "2," impressed mark of N. Clark & Co., Lyons, New York, 2 gal., ca. 1830, very minor surface chips, 10 1/2" h. (ILLUS.) **$9,350**

Rare Jug with Human Profile Design

Jug, beehive shape tapering to a small mouth & strap handle, cobalt blue brushed folky human profile, impressed mark of E.W. Farrington & Co., Elmira, New York, 1 gal., ca. 1890, 11" h. (ILLUS.) **$5,500**

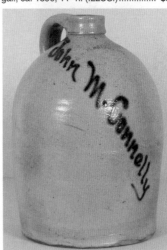

Stoneware Jug with Inscribed Name

Jug, beehive-shape w/small mouth & strap handle, cobalt blue slip-quilled name "John M. Connolly" diagonally down the side, impressed mark of E.W. Farrington, Elmira, New York, 1 gal., ca. 1890, 10" h. (ILLUS.)... **$209**

Rare Stoneware Iowa Advertising Jug

Jug, beehive-shaped w/a small molded mouth & strap handle, a cobalt blue slip-quilled "5" on the shoulder, the body w/a stenciled blue shield enclosing advertising "From Fry's Hotel and Mineral Springs, Colfax, IA.," small rim chip, 16" h. (ILLUS.) **$558**

Remmey-style Flower-decorated Pitcher

Pitcher, 10 1/2" h., wide ovoid body tapering to a wide cylindrical neck w/pinched spout, cobalt blue brushed design of a large tall flower on a leafy stem flanked by leafy branches, feathered design around the neck, in the style of Remmey, two chips at base, unsigned, ca. 1850, 1 1/2 gal. (ILLUS.) **$1,320**

Advertising Preserve Jar with Bird Decor

Preserve jar, cylindrical tapering slightly to a heavy molded mouth flanked by eared handles, cobalt blue slip-quilled decoration of a bird on a scrolled branch, impressed advertising "P. Morton - Crockery - 127 Market St. - Newark, N.J.," design attributed to the factory of Adam Caire, Pokeepsie (sic), NY, rim chip, small hairline near name on front, ca. 1880, 2 gal., 11 1/2" h. (ILLUS.)................. **$413**

Preserve Jar with Rare Rooster Design

Preserve jar, cylindrical tapering to a short flared neck, eared handles, cobalt blue slip-quilled decoration of a large prancing rooster, impressed mark of W. A. MacQuoid & Co. Pottery Works Little - 12st - New York, couple of minor glaze flakes, ca. 1870, 12" h. (ILLUS.) **$11,550**

Preserve Jar with Bird Eating Berries

Preserve jar, gently swelled cylindrical body w/a short flared rim, eared handles, cobalt blue slip-quilled bird perched on a leafy sprig & leaning down to eat berries, impressed mark of W.A. Macquiod & Co., New York, Little Wst 12th St., 1 1/2 gal., professional restoration to hairlines, ca. 1870, 11" h. (ILLUS.) **$1,073**

Stoneware 6 Gallon Water Cooler

Water cooler, slightly swelled cylindrical shape, decorated w/cobalt blue rim & base bands & two double blue bands around the body centering a stenciled crown logo enclosing a "6," w/attached metal spigot & funnel, late 19th - early 20th c., 6 gal., 21" h. (ILLUS.).................... **$147**

Large Early Water Cooler with Designs

Water cooler, tall ovoid body w/a small neck, bung hole at bottom front, incised & blue-washed front shoulder design of ribbed leaves & a pineapple, blue-wash band around bung hole, impressed mark of Goodwin & Webster, Hartford, stone ping on back, mottled glaze discoloration, orignal carved wood stopper, ca. 1810, 4 gal., 19" h. (ILLUS.).................... **$5,500**

Extraordinary Presentation Cooler

Water cooler, wide tapering cylindrical shape w/a small molded neck & strap handle, large extended bung hole on the back, extraordinary cobalt blue slip-quilled presentation decoration w/the name "John Gunn" above a large bird & long leafy stems flanked by large blossoms below large crossed leaves at the top, produced by the Frank B. Norton Factory, Worcester, Massachusets but unsigned, ca. 1870, 2 gal., 13 1/2" h. (ILLUS.)................................. **$25,300**

Teco Pottery

Teco Pottery was actually the line of art pottery introduced by the American Terra Cotta and Ceramic Company of Terra Cotta (Crystal Lake), Illinois, in 1902. Founded by William D. Gates in 1881, American Terra Cotta originally produced only bricks and drain tile. Because of superior facilities for experimentation, including a chemical laboratory, the company was able to develop an art pottery line, favoring a matte green glaze in the earlier years but eventually achieving a wide range of colors including a metallic lustre glaze and a crystalline glaze. Although some hand-thrown pottery was made, Gates favored a molded ware because it was less expensive to produce. By 1923, Teco Pottery was no longer being made, and in 1930 American Terra Cotta and Ceramic Company was sold. A book on the topic is Teco: Art Pottery of the Prairie School, by Sharon S. Darling (Erie Art Museum, 1990).

Teco Mark

Small Leather Brown Teco Vase

Vase, 4 1/4" h., simple ovoid body w/a small
flared neck, golden brown leather glaze,
double-struck mark (ILLUS.) **$518**

Small Teco Green Matte Vase

Vase, 4 1/4" h., simple ovoid body w/a small
flared neck, matte green glaze, double-
struck mark (ILLUS.) **$500**

Vase, 4 5/8" h., 5 3/4" d., very wide squatty
body tapering sharply to a tiny flared
neck, smooth matte green glaze, double-
stamped mark (ILLUS., top next column)
.... **$1,035**

Vase, 5 3/4" h., footed swelled cylindrical
body tapering to a short flared neck,
overall smooth organic green matte
glaze, impressed trademark (ILLUS.,
middle next column) **$575**

Vase, 7 3/4" h., upright gently swelled triangular body w/a wide flattened shoulder &
low molded mouth, matte green glaze
w/charcoaling at one corner, double-
struck mark (ILLUS., bottom next column)
.... **$1,093**

Unusual Squatty Teco Vase

Teco Swelled Cylindrical Vase

Teco Triangular Vase

Tall Teco Squared & Lobed Vase

Rare Mauve-glazed Teco Vase

Vase, 11 1/2" h., tall slender cylindrical shaped w/small square buttress handles down the sides, unusual matte mauve glaze, impressed mark, No. 438 designed by W.D. Gates (ILLUS.).............. **$2,400**

Vase, 15 3/4" h., squatty bulbous base below the slender tall squared four-column sides w/a flared mouth, nicely charcoaled green matte glaze, designed by W.D. Gates & Fritz Albert, two impressed marks on base (ILLUS.)......................... **$2,645**

Tall Rare Teco Pottery Vase

Long Teco Green Wall Pocket

Vase, 13 1/4" h., bulbous double-gourd shape w/four open buttresses extending from the lower body to the mid body, tall slender flaring neck, good matte green glaze, impressed marks, designed by W.B. Mundie (ILLUS.) **$14,800**

Wall pocket, paneled bullet shape tapering w/a spearpoint base, overall dark green matte glaze, designed by Fritz Albert, impressed mark, repaired, 15" l. (ILLUS.) **$480**

Tiffany Pottery

In 1902 Louis C. Tiffany expanded Tiffany Studios to include ceramics, enamels, gold, silver and gemstones. Tiffany pottery was usually molded rather than wheel-thrown, but it was carefully finished by hand. A limited amount was produced until about 1914. It is scarce.

Tiffany Pottery Mark

Rare Tiffany Ear of Corn Vase

Pitcher, 10 1/4" h., modeled as a tall ear of corn w/the cob just showing through the husk at the top, one husk leaf forms the long handle, cream unglazed exterior, olive green-glazed interior, signed (ILLUS.) **$5,019**

Miniature Tiffany Pottery Mushroom Vase

Vase, 3 1/2" h., flaring base & cylindrical sides modled in relief w/mushrooms, unglazed cream-color exterior & green-glazed interior, signed on base, slight discoloration on side of base (ILLUS.)......... **$1,725**

Huge Green Tiffany Pottery Vase

Vase, 15" h., a round foot below the large wide flaring cylindrical body w/a wide angled shoulder centering a wide low mouth, overall mottled green glaze, signed "L.C.T. 7 - Pottery," hairline & possible restoration (ILLUS.) **$1,610**

Tiles

Tiles have been made by potteries in the United States and abroad for many years. Apart from small tea tiles used on tables, there are also decorative tiles for fireplaces, floors and walls. This is where present collector interest lies, especially in the late 19th century American-made art pottery tiles.

American Encaustic Water Mill Tile

American Encaustic Tiling Co., Los Angeles, California, branch, square, lightly embossed water mill scene covered w/a golden greenish brown glossy glaze, marked, some small corner chips & crazing, 6" w. (ILLUS.)..................................... **$150**

Framed Cambridge Art Portrait Tiles

American Encaustic Portrait Tile

American Encaustic Tiling Co., Los Angeles, California, branch, square, molded bust profile portrait of a bearded Renaissance era man wearing a large plumed hat, medium blue glossy glaze, marked, crazing, 6" w. (ILLUS.) **$184**

Interesting American Encaustic Tile

American Encaustic Tiling Co., Los Angeles, California, branch, square, advertising-type, a central molded bust portrait of a classical lady enclosed by a scrolled banner reading "Dedication: A.E. Tile Works - Zanesville, O. - April 19, 1892," shaded dark blue glossy glaze, marked on the back "detimLloCL-TEA - AET Co. Limited," crazing, 4 1/8" w. (ILLUS.) **$150**

Cambridge Art Pottery, Cambridge, Ohio, square, a bust profile portrait of a young Victorian girl wearing a sailor-style cap & a bust profile portrait of a young Victorian boy wearing a hat w/visor, both w/a yellowish green glossy glaze, each marked on the back, facing pair, in new frame, minor edge nicks, some surface nicks, 6 x 12", the pair (ILLUS., top of page) **$432**

Columbia Victorian Lady Portrait Tile

Columbia Tile Company, Anderson, Indiana, square, molded w/a profile bust portrait of a young Victorian lady wearing a large boater-style hat & dress w/a ruffled collar, shaded deep rose glossy glaze, marked, crazing, notch cut in back, 6" w. (ILLUS.) **$173**

Long Delft Tile with Flying White Duck

Colorful Delft Commemorative Tile

de Porceleyne Fles, Delft, Holland, rectangular, a colorful incised & painted interior scene of a pottery shop w/potters at work, in shades of blue, brown, green, white & black, a light blue base band impressed w/the factory logo flanked by the dates 1900 & 1950, probably a special commemorative for the factory, framed, 6 x 8 1/4" (ILLUS.) **$345**

Delft Wartime Commemorative Tile

de Porceleyne Fles, Delft, Holland, rectangular, an vertical landscape incised w/a scene of a woman & child standing & wav-

ing at a large war plane passing overhead, a large rising sun & small village in the distance, glazed in shades of blue, white, yellow, green, orange & brown, rectangular base panel inscribed in Dutch "Voedsel, Vrede, Vryheid" (Food, Peace, Freedom) & the dates April 29 to May 5, 1945, company logo on the back, very minor back edge chips, framed, 6 x 8 1/4" (ILLUS.) **$317**

Delft, Holland, rectangular, a long narrow design w/a large white flying duck above grasses & water, impressed jug mark & Delft name, 4 x 12 1/4" (ILLUS., top of page)... **$518**

Fine Grueby Landscape Tile

Grueby Pottery, Boston, Massachusetts, square, an incised & painted landscape w/two large fir trees in the foreground, in shades of dark & light green, blue & yellow, No. 39, 6" w. (ILLUS.)..................... **$3,600**

Framed Grueby Tulip Tile

Pair of Trent Tiles with Young Victorian Girls

Grueby Pottery, Boston, Massachusetts, square, decorated w/a yellow tulip w/long green leaves on a dark green ground, framed in a contemporary flat handmade frame, tile 6" sq. (ILLUS., previous page) **$1,170**

Longwy Tile with Colorful Bird Scene

Longwy Pottery, Longwy, France, square, a colorful scroll-bordered oblong central scene of bluebirds perched on bamboo stalks above a pond & peonies, narrow scrolled yellow border, outer ground in dark blue decorated w/pink, blue & purple flowers & green leaves, marked, minor chip on back, few flakes to corners, 8" w. (ILLUS.) **$270**

Trent Tile Company, Trenton, New Jersey, rectangular, composed of three tiles forming the figure of a Cavalier holding a flute, shaded dark green & yellow glossy glaze, marked, crazing, several edge & corner chips, older frame, 6 x 18" (ILLUS., next column) **$288**

Trent Tile Company, Trenton, New Jersey, square, one w/a bust profile portrait of a very young Victorian girl w/a ribbon in her hair & wearing a lace-trimmed dress, a second w/a bust profile portrait of a very young Victorian girl wearing a lace-trimmed dress, both w/a shaded blue glossy glaze, newly framed, un-

marked, minor surface nicks, 6 x 12", facing pair (ILLUS., top of page) **$403**

Trent Tile Cavalier Portrait Tiles

Toby Mugs & Jugs

The Toby is a figural jug or mug usually delineating a robust, genial drinking man. The name has been used in England since the mid-18th century. Copies of the English mugs and jugs were made in America.

For listings of related character jugs, see DOULTON & ROYAL DOULTON.

Nice Rockingham-glazed Toby Jug

Rockingham-glazed Toby, seated Mr. Toby w/a high tricorn hat, wearing a jacket, vest & kneebreeches, a grapevine-molded back handle, overall dark brown mottled glaze, unmarked, possibly Bennington, Vermont, 19th c., 6 1/2" h. (ILLUS.)..................... **$210**

Staffordshire Toby, seated man wearing brown tricorn hat, brown jacket, blue vest, tan breeches & brown boots, legs apart seated on a large block, arms away from body, one hand holding tumbler, the other holding a bottle, Prattware-style, late 18th c., minor chips, 11 3/8" h. **$780**

Fine Staffordshire Toby with Pitcher

Staffordshire Toby, seated Mr. Toby wearing a black tricorn hat, orange jacket, tan kneebreeches & holding a deep red pitcher on one knee & a white glass in the other hand, script "3" on the bottom, probably 19th c., 10" h. (ILLUS.)................ **$230**

Van Briggle

The Van Briggle Pottery was established by Artus Van Briggle, who formerly worked for Rookwood Pottery, in Colorado Springs, Colorado, at the turn of the century. He died in 1904, but the pottery was carried on by his widow and others. From 1900 until 1920, the pieces were dated. It remains in production today, specializing in art pottery.

Early Van Briggle Pottery Mark

Van Briggle Low Bowl with Molded Insects

Bowl, 8 1/2" d., a wide flat-bottomed form w/low incurved sides, molded around the rim w/four large stylized moth-like insects, matte green shading to reddish brown glaze, ca. 1920 (ILLUS.) **$264**

Fine Very Early Van Briggle Bowl

Bowl, 9" d., 4 3/4" h., the squatty smooth lower half below an angled tapering upper body molded w/birds in flight, fine green & blue leathery matte glaze, Shape No. 512, 1907 (ILLUS.)......................... **$1,380**

Small Mulberry Van Briggle Bowl-Vase

Bowl-vase, footed wide squatty rounded lower sides below the wide sharply angled shoulder to a wide flat mouth, the shoulder molded w/repeating looping vine-like design, overall mulberry matte glaze, Shape No. 735, early 20th c., 3 3/8" d. (ILLUS.) **$173**

Small Blossom-molded Van Briggle Vase

Vase, 4 1/2" h., short squatty ovoid shaped w/molded stylized blossoms around the flat mouth, matte bluish green glaze, incised marks, ca. 1907-12 (ILLUS.)............ **$780**

Simple Ovoid Van Briggle 5" Vase

Vase, 5" h., simple ovoid body tapering to a wide, flat mouth, overall light matte green glaze, incised mark, ca. 1915 (ILLUS.) **$288**

Vase, 8 1/2" h., 5 1/2" d., bottle-form, bulbous ovoid lower body tapering to a tapering cylindrical neck, mustard yellow & dark blue leathery matte glaze, 1914 (ILLUS., top next column) **$460**

Vase, 10" h., wide bulbous ovoid body w/the round shoulder tapering to a wide flat mouth, the neck & shoulder molded fanned stylized flowers w/the stems down the sides, dark blue shaded to dark maroon matte glaze, an Anna Van Briggle design, late teens or early 1920s (ILLUS., middle next column) **$633**

Early Bottle-form Van Briggle Vase

Large Bulbous Van Briggle Vase

Vernon Kilns

The story of Vernon Kilns Pottery begins with the purchase by Mr. Faye Bennison of the Poxon China Company (Vernon Potteries) in July 1931. The Poxon family had run the pottery for a number of years in Vernon, California, but with the founding of Vernon Kilns, the product lines were greatly expanded.

Many innovative dinnerware lines and patterns were introduced during the 1930s, including designs by such noted American artists as Rockwell Kent and Don Blanding. In the early 1940s items were designed to tie in with Walt Disney's animated features "Fantasia" and "Dumbo." Various commemorative plates, including the popular "Bits" series, were also produced over a long period of time. Vernon Kilns was taken over by Metlox Potteries in 1958 and ceased production in 1960.

Vernon Kilns Mark

"Bits" Series

Plate, 8 1/2" d., Bits of Old New England,
Haying .... **$20-$30**

Plate, 8 1/2" d., Bits of Old New England,
Old Dobin .... **$20-$30**

Plate, 8 1/2" d., Bits of Old New England
Series, The Cove **$30**

Plate, 8 1/2" d., Bits of Old New England
Series, The Whaler .... **$20-$30**

Plate, 8 1/2" d., Bits of Old South, Cypress
Swamp .... **$30-$45**

Plate, 8 1/2" d., Bits of the California Missions Series, San Rafael Archangel **$40**

Plate, 8 1/2" d., Bits of the Old South Series,
Cotton Patch **$40**

Plate, 8 1/2" d., Bits of the Old West Series,
The Fleecing **$40**

Plate, 8 1/2" d., California Missions, San
Rafael Archangel .... **$30-$45**

Plate, chop, 14" d., Bits of the Old South-
west Series, Pueblo **$75**

Dinnerwares

Bowl, chowder, tab handle, Desert Bloom
patt. .... **$12-$15**

Bowl, chowder, tab handle, Native Califor-
nia patt. .... **$12-$15**

Bowl, fruit, Calico patt. .... **$10-$15**

Bowl, fruit, Coastline series, Turnbull de-
sign. .... **$50-$60**

Bowl, soup, Early California patt. .... **$12-$15**

Bowl, salad, 13" d., Organdie patt. .... **$90-$100**

Butter dish, cov., Arcadia patt. .... **$60-$75**

Butter dish, cov., Heavenly Days patt. ..... **$25-$40**

Butter dish, cov., R.F.D.patt. .... **$50-$60**

Candleholders, teacup form w/metal fittings, Tam O'Shanter patt., pr. .... **$100-$125**

Casserole, cov., individual, Gingham patt.,
4" d. .... **$35-$45**

Casserole, cov., individual, Organdie patt.,
4" d. .... **$30-$35**

Casserole, cov., Organdie patt. .... **$50-$65**

Casserole, cov., Tam O'Shanter patt. .... **$50-$70**

Casserole, cov., Tweed patt. .... **$80-$100**

Casserole, cov., Vernon's 1860s patt. ...... **$75-$85**

Coaster, Gingham patt. .... **$25-$30**

Constellation Pattern Coffee Server

Coffee server, spherical w/cylindrical neck
& rim spout, attached plastic handle,
Constellation patt. (ILLUS.) .... **$250-$300**

Coffee server w/stopper, carafe form, Ear-
ly California patt. .... **$45-$60**

Coffee server w/stopper, carafe form, Tam
O'Shanter patt. .... **$60-$70**

Coffeepot, cov., 1860s patt. .... **$75-$95**

*Modern California Creamer & Sugar Bowl in
Orchid*

Creamer, Modern California patt., orchid
color (ILLUS. right with matching sugar
bowl) .... **$15-$20**

Creamer, Native patt. .... **$15-$20**

Cup & saucer, after-dinner size, Native
patt. .... **$20-$30**

Cup & saucer, after-dinner size, Organdie
patt. .... **$25-$30**

Cup & saucer, colossal size, Raffia patt.
.... **$175-$225**

Cup & saucer, jumbo size, Organdie patt.
.... **$40-$50**

Eggcup, Brown Eyed Susan patt. .... **$40-$50**

Eggcup, Early California patt. .... **$20-$25**

Eggcup, Early California patt., turquoise
(ILLUS. with Early California cups & sau-
cers) .... **$20-$25**

Eggcup, Gingham patt. .... **$25-$30**

Eggcup, Mayflower patt. .... **$25-$30**

Vernon Kilns Barkwood Flowerpot

Flowerpot, Barkwood patt., 4" h. (ILLUS.)
.... **$30-$40**

Flowerpot & saucer, Gingham patt., 5" h.,
the set .... **$45-$55**

Organdie Flowerpot & Saucer

Flowerpot & saucer, Organdie patt., 4" h.,
the set (ILLUS.) .... **$50-$60**
Gravy boat, Gingham patt. .... **$20-$25**
Gravy boat, Native California patt. **$35**
Lapel pin, plate-shaped, Bel Air patt.,
2 1/2" w. .... **$25-$35**
Mixing bowls, nesting set, Gingham patt.,
5" to 9" d., five pcs. .... **$175-$200**
Mixing bowls, nesting set, Raffia patt., 5" to
9" d., five pcs. .... **$150-$175**
Muffin cover, Early California patt., red,
cover only .... **$125-$150**
Mug, Barkwood patt., 9 oz. **$25**
Mug, Homespun patt., 9 oz. .... **$40-$50**

Ultra Pattern Mug in Maroon

Mug, Ultra patt., maroon (ILLUS.) .... **$50-$65**
Pepper mill, Homespun patt. .... **$150-$175**
Pitcher, Streamline shape, Tam O'Shanter
patt., 1/4 pt. .... **$40-$50**
Pitcher, jug-form, bulb bottom, Tam
O'Shanter patt., 1 pt. .... **$25-$35**
Pitcher, Modern California patt., jug-type, 1
pt. .... **$25-$40**
Pitcher, Streamline shape, Hawaiian Coral
patt., 1 qt. (ILLUS., top next column) .... **$45-$55**
Pitcher, Streamline shape, Organdie patt.,
1 qt. .... **$45-$65**
Pitcher, Streamline shape, Gingham patt.,
2 qt. .... **$50-$75**

Hawaiian Coral Streamline Pitcher

Pitcher w/ice lip, Early California pat., 2 qt.
.... **$85-$95**
Plate, 7" d., Calico patt. .... **$10-$15**
Plate, 7" d., Coastline patt. .... **$40-$50**
Plate, 7" d., Native patt. .... **$8-$10**
Plate, 7 1/2" d., salad, Tweed patt. .... **$10-$12**

Coastline Series Florida Plate

Plate, 9 1/2" d., Coastline series, Florida
patt., Turnbull design (ILLUS.) .... **$100-$125**

Garden Plate Series Celery Plate

Plate, 9 1/2" d., Garden Plate series, Celery patt., Turnbull design (ILLUS.) .... **$50-$75**
Plate, 9 1/2" d., luncheon, Organdie patt. . **$10-$12**
Plate, 9 1/2" d., Native American series, Going to Town patt., Turnbull design .... **$35-$45**
Plate, 9 1/2" d., Trader Vic patt. .... **$100-$125**
Plate, 10 1/2" d., Casa California Hermosa patt., Turnbull design............................ **$25-$30**
Plate, 10 1/2" d., dinner, Calico patt. **$25**

Vernon Kilns Turnbull Design Plate

Plate, 10 1/2" d., dinner, T631 patt., Turnbull design (ILLUS.)................................ **$25-$30**
Plate, 10 1/2" d., dinner, Winchester '73 (Frontier Days) patt. .... **$75-$85**
Plate, 10 1/2" d., Floral series, Iris patt., Harry Bird design .... **$50-$60**
Plate, 10 1/2" d., Floral series, Petunia patt., Harry Bird design .... **$50-$75**
Plate, chop, 12" d., Brown Eyed Susan patt. .... **$25-$35**
Plate, chop, 12" d., Cottage Window patt., Turnbull design...................................... **$75-$95**
Plate, chop, 12" d., Frontier Days patt. . **$150-$175**
Plate, chop, 12" d., Monterey patt. .... **$25-$35**
Plate, chop, 12" d., Organdie patt. .... **$25-$30**
Plate, chop, 14" d., Gingham patt. .... **$35-$40**
Plate, chop, 14" d., Rio Vista patt............. **$40-$50**
Plate, chop, 17" d., Early California patt.... **$30-$50**
Platter, 12" d., round, Organdie patt. .... **$20-$25**
Platter, 12" l., oval, Tam O'Shanter patt. .. **$15-$25**
Platter, 14" l., oval, Native California patt. **$30-$35**
Platter, 14" l., oval, Organdie patt. .... **$25-$35**
Relish dish, leaf-shaped, four-part, Native California patt. .... **$50-$75**
Relish dish, single leaf shape, Monterey patt., 12" l... **$35-$45**

Large Gingham Pattern Salt & Pepper

Salt & pepper shakers, Gingham patt., large size, pr. (ILLUS.).......................... **$50-$60**
Salt & pepper shakers, Gingham patt., regular size, pr. **$20**
Salt & pepper shakers, Native California patt., pr. **$20**
Salt & pepper shakers, Organdie patt., regular size, pr. .... **$10-$15**
Salt & pepper shakers, Tam O'Shanter patt., large size, pr. .... **$45-$65**

Trumpet Flower Saucer

Saucer, Trumpet Flower patt., Harry Bird design (ILLUS.).................................... **$10-$15**
Spoon rest, Homespun patt. .... **$95-$110**
Spoon rest, Organdie patt. .... **$75-$85**
Sugar bowl, cov., Barkwood patt............. **$10-$15**
Sugar bowl, cov., Modern California patt., orchid color (ILLUS. right with matching creamer, page 804)............................. **$15-$20**

Tweed Pattern Sugar Bowl
Sugar bowl, cov., Tweed patt. (ILLUS.) ... **$30-$35**

Raffia Pattern Syrup Jug

Syrup jug w/metal top & plastic handle,
Raffia patt. (ILLUS.) .... **$50-$75**
Teacup & saucer, colossal size, Homespun
patt., 15" d. saucer, 4 qt. .... **$250-$275**
Teacup & saucer, jumbo size, Homespun
patt. .... **$45-$55**
Teacup & saucer, Ultra patt. .... **$10-$12**
Teacup & saucer, Winchester '73 (Frontier
Days) patt.. **$45-$50**

Vernon Kilns Chinling Pattern Teapot

Teapot, cov., Chinling patt. (ILLUS.) .... **$50-$75**
Teapot, cov., Linda patt........................... **$40-$50**

Vernon Kilns Organdie Pattern Teapot

Teapot, cov., Organdie patt. (ILLUS.) .... **$40-$50**

Santa Barbara Pattern Teapot

Teapot, cov., Santa Barbara patt. (ILLUS.)
.... **$75-$95**
Teapot, cov., Tam O'Shanter patt............. **$45-$55**
Tidbit, two-tier w/wooden handle, Home-
spun patt. .... **$30-$35**
Tumbler, Bel Air patt................................. **$20-$25**

Vernon Kilns Gingham Pattern Tumbler

Tumbler, Gingham patt. (ILLUS.) .... **$20-$25**
Tumbler, Homespun patt................................ **$35**
Tumbler, Tickled Pink patt............................ **$20**
Vegetable bowl, open, divided, Gingham
patt.. **$25-$35**
Vegetable bowl, open, Ultra patt., 9" d. ... **$20-$25**
Vegetable bowl, open, Tam O'Shanter
patt., 9" d.. **$15-$20**

Disney "Fantasia" & Other Items

Bowl, 6" d., chowder, Nutcracker patt............. **$50**
Bowl, 8" d., soup, Flower Ballet patt. **$50**
Bowl, 8" l., No. 134, decorated figural bird .. **$75-$85**
Decanter, Penquin patt. .... **$100-$125**
Figure of Baby Weems, No. 37, 6" h... **$150-$175**
Figure of Sari, May & Veive Hamilton de-
sign, 14 1/2" h. .... **$2,600+**
Plate, 17" d., chop, Fantasia patt. .... **$600+**
Salt & pepper shakers, Hop Low patt., pr.
.... **$50-$75**
Tray, hors d'oeuvre, May & Vieve Hamilton
design, 16" d. .... **$400-$600**
Vase, 4 1/2" h., Pine Cone patt., No. 5, ivory
.... **$95-$125**
Vase, 5" h., Pine Cone patt., No. 2, Tur-
quoise .... **$225-$275**
Vase, 12" h., carved handles, May & Vieve
Hamilton design .... **$1,500+**

Don Blanding Dinnerwares

Creamer, after-dinner size, Hawaiian Flowers patt., blue .... **$40-$50**

Creamer, Lei Lani patt., regular size .... **$35-$45**

Cup & saucer, after-dinner size, Hawaiian Flowers patt... **$75-$95**

Cup & saucer, after-dinner size, Hilo patt. **$50-$75**

Cup & saucer, Coral Reef patt., blue........ **$40-$50**

Cup & saucer, Lei Lani patt. .... **$40-$50**

Plate, 7" d., Honolulu patt........................... **$40-$50**

Plate, chop, 14" d., Hilo patt................. **$150-$200**

Plate, chop, 14" d., Honolulu patt. .... **$150-$200**

Platter, 16 1/2", Lei Lani patt................. **$200-$250**

Salt & pepper shakers, Hawaiian Flowers patt., maroon, pr. .... **$25-$40**

Salt & pepper shakers, Lei Lani patt., pr. **$25-$40**

Sugar bowl, cov., Coral Reef patt., blue... **$85-$95**

Sugar bowl, cov., Hawaiian Flowers patt., blue .... **$75-$85**

Teapot, cov., Hawaiian Flowers patt. ..... **$275-$300**

Tumbler, Hilo patt., #4, 5 1/2" h. .... **$125-$150**

Music Masters

Plates, 8 1/2" d., brown transfer-printed, the complete set of 8............................... **$100-$150**

Rockwell Kent Designs

Bowl, chowder, "Our America" series, coconut tree, blue .... **$60-$70**

Rare Red Moby Dick 11" Salad Bowl

Bowl, 11" d., salad, Moby Dick patt., red (ILLUS.) .... **$325-$375**

Creamer, regular, "Our America" series, houseboaters, brown .... **$75-$90**

Cup & saucer, Moby Dick patt., maroon .. **$45-$50**

Blue Our America Cup & Saucer

Cup & saucer, Our America patt., blue (ILLUS.).. **$50-$65**

Cup & saucer, Salamina patt. .... **$50-$60**

Dinner service: four 9 1/2" d. luncheon plates, four 6 3/4" w. chowder bowls, four 6 1/4" d. bread & butter plates, four cups & saucers, an 8" d. bowl & a 9" d. bowl; Salamina patt., ca. 1935, one chowder bowl repaired, the set (ILLUS. of part, bottom of page)... **$920**

Plate, 6 1/2" d., "Our America" series, steamship, blue.................................... **$45-$50**

Plate, 6 1/2" d., Salamina patt......................... **$40**

Plate, 9 1/2" d., Moby Dick patt., blue ... **$110-$145**

Plate, 10 1/2" d., Salamina patt. .... **$50-$75**

Plate, 17" d., chop, Salamina patt........ **$400-$500**

Sugar bowl, cov., Moby Dick patt............ **$35-$50**

Sugar bowl, cov., Moby Dick patt., blue .... **$85-$105**

States Map Series - 10 1/2" d.

Plate, Connecticut.. **$20**

Plate, Delaware, blue .... **$20-$25**

Plate, Georgia, blue .... **$20-$25**

Plate, Texas, blue .... **$40-$50**

Portion of Rockwell Kent Salamina Pattern Dinner Service

Blue Virginia State Map Plate

Plate, Virginia, blue (ILLUS.) .... $20-$25

States Picture Series - 10 1/2" d.
Plate, Alaska, blue... $25
Plate, Hawaii, multicolored .... $40-$50
Plate, New Jersey, multicolored .... $40-$50
Plate, North Dakota, multicolored.................... $25

Blue Rhode Island States Picture Plate

Plate, Rhode Island, blue (ILLUS.) .... $15-$25
Plate, Vermont, blue................................. $18-$20
Plate, Virginia, maroon .... $18-$20

Blue Wisconsin States Picture Plate

Plate, Wisconsin, blue (ILLUS.)................. $15-$25
Plate, Wyoming, multicolored.................... $40-$50

Miscellaneous Commemoratives

Round Red Connecticut Ashtray

Ashtray, Connecticut, round, red (ILLUS.) **$15-$20**
Ashtray, Vermont...................................... **$15-$20**
Cup & saucer, after-dinner size, Niagara
Falls **$25**

Oklahoma A& M After-dinner Cup & Saucer

Cup & saucer, after-dinner size, Oklahoma
A&M (ILLUS.).. **$20-$30**
Cup & saucer, after-dinner size, Yosemite
National Park .... **$20-$30**
Plate, 8 1/2" d., Memento Plate of factory........ **$75**
Plate, 10 1/2" d., Alaskan Huskey, multicol-
ored.. **$30-$45**
Plate, 10 1/2" d., Beaumont, Texas, Spin-
dletop .... **$70-$85**
Plate, 10 1/2" d., Caracas, Venezuela ...... **$25-$35**

Christmas Tree Pattern Pieces

Plate, 10 1/2" d., Christmas Tree patt.
(ILLUS. w/Christmas Tree teacup &
saucer, previous page) .... **$65-$75**
Plate, 10 1/2" d., General MacArthur, brown
.... **$20**
Plate, 10 1/2" d., Hollywood Stars, blue .... **$70-$80**
Plate, 10 1/2" d., Knott's Berry Farm, Cali-
fornia **$35**
Plate, 10 1/2" d., Notre Dame University,
brown .... **$20-$25**
Plate, 10 1/2" d., Old Man of the Mountain,
New Hampshire..................................... **$20-$25**

Maroon Vernon Kilns Presidents Plate

Plate, 10 1/2" d., The Presidents, maroon
(ILLUS.)... **$20-$30**

1952 Postmasters Convention Plate

Plate, Postmasters Convention, showing
buildings in Boston, border reading "Souvenir of the 48th National Convention of
the National Association of Postmasters
of the United States - Boston, Massachusetts, October 12-16, 1952," multicolor
(ILLUS.)... **$30-$35**
Plate, Statue of Liberty, multicolored......... **$50-$75**

Plates, 8 1/2" d., Cocktail Hour series,
brown transfer, complete set of 8...... **$400-$600**
Teacup & saucer, Christmas Tree (ILLUS.
with Christmas Tree plate, previous pa-
gae)... **$30-$35**

Warwick

More pottery and china collectors have turned their attention to the products of the Warwick China Company that operated in Wheeling, West Virginia from 1887 to 1951. Prime interest seems to be in items manufactured prior to 1911, especially the items marked "IOGA," which were produced from 1903 to December 1910. Many collectors have speculated over the years the exact meaning of the word "IOGA." After much research is has been discovered that this is a Native American word meaning "beautiful." The innovator of the "IOGA" ware was company president Thomas Carr.

Products produced from 1887 until 1911 were made of a semi-porcelain clay, including fine china and earthenware items, IOGA ware as well as Flow Blue china that was made during the mid-1890s. In 1911 Warwick China switched to a vitrified clay and produced heavier restaurant (commercial) ware as well as fine china.

From its founding through 1911, the firm decorated its wares with colorful decals of beautiful women, monks, Native Americans, fraternal order symbols, flowers, birds, pinecones, fishermen, champion bulldogs as well as portraits of notable men or many nationally recognized buildings. There were also some other miscellaneous designs. Warwick China Company was the first company to use photographic transfers as decorations on the IOGA pieces beginning in 1905. These transfers were used on the grey vases and depicted the "Wheeling Girls of the Evening." Many of the decals were based on paintings by artists such as H. Richard Boehm, Richard Beck and Arthur Stambra. Some of the pieces were also individually hand-painted.

As noted, in 1911 the Warwick China Company began production of restaurant ware, banquet ware as well as fine dinnerware. This change of products was brought about by the new company president, Charles Jackson. Warwick continued making these wares until the company closed in 1951.

Should you wish to know more about Warwick china, you should contact the National Association of Warwick China & Pottery Collectors. Information and details on this group is found in the back of this book in Appendix I.

Warwick Mark

Warwick Flower-decorated Cuspidor

Cuspidor, squatty low round body w/a widely flaring rim, white ground decorated w/colorful flower bouquets, ca. 1930s, 7 1/2" d., 5"h. (ILLUS.) **$55**

Warwick Pitcher with Native American

Pitcher, 10" h., 6 1/4" d., tankard-style, style "VP," long handle from rim to base, dark brown shaded to yellow ground printed w/a color Native American portrait, IOGA mark, ca. 1908 (ILLUS.) **$300**

Tall Warwick Tankard Pitcher

Pitcher, 12 3/4" h., 4" d., tankard-style, style, tall slightly tapering cylindrical shape, printed w/a color Native American portrait of Chief Mountain-Black Feet, IOGA mark, ca. 1908 (ILLUS.) **$395**

Warwick "Chicago" Vase with Pretty Lady

Vase, 8" h.,"Chicago" style, footed cylindrical shape w/arched & scalloped rim, semi-porcelain, IOGA mark, dark brown shaded to tan ground w/a color portrait of a pretty young woman, rare matte finish (ILLUS.).. **$250**

Warwick "Hyacinth" Vase with Roses

Vase, 11 1/2" h., 6" d., "Hyacinth" style, tall ovoid body w/a short flaring neck, dark blue shaded ground w/decals of large pink, yellow & red roses, IOGA mark, ca. 1906 (ILLUS.)... **$275**

Tall Verona Vase with Rear View of Nude

Vase, 11 3/4" h., "Verona" style, tall slightly tapering lobed & ribbed design w/small loop handles near the top, dark brown shaded to yellow decorated w/full-length rear view of a nude young lady, a "Wheeling Girl of the Evening," semi-porcelain, IOGA mark, ca. 1906, very rare (ILLUS.)................................... **$1,500**

Verona Vase with Side View of Nude

Vase, 11 3/4" h., "Verona" style, tall slightly tapering lobed & ribbed design w/small loop handles near the top, dark brown shaded to yellow decorated w/full-length side view of a seated nude young lady, a "Wheeling Girl of the Evening," semi-por-

celain, IOGA mark, ca. 1906, very rare (ILLUS.).. **$1,500**

Verona Vase with Half-Nude Lady

Vase, 11 3/4" h., "Verona" style, tall slightly tapering lobed & ribbed design w/small loop handles near the top, dark grey shaded to white decorated w/three-quarters length view of a half-nude young lady w/arms above her head, a "Wheeling Girl of the Evening," semi-porcelain, IOGA mark, ca. 1906, very rare (ILLUS.).......... **$1,500**

Watt Pottery

Founded in 1922, in Crooksville, Ohio, this pottery continued in operation until the factory was destroyed by fire in 1965. Although stoneware crocks and jugs were the first wares produced, by 1935 sturdy kitchen items in yellowware were the mainstay of production. Attractive lines like Kitch-N-Queen (banded) wares and the hand-painted Apple, Cherry and Pennsylvania Dutch (tulip) patterns were popular throughout the country. Today these hand-painted utilitarian wares are "hot" with collectors.

A good reference book for collectors is Watt Pottery, An Identification and Value Guide, by Sue and Dave Morris (Collector Books, 1933).

Watt Pottery Mark

Baker, cov., Apple patt., No. 96, w/advertising, 8 1/2" d., 5 3/4" h. **$50**
Baker, cov., Apple (two-leaf) patt., No. 70 .... **$95**
Baker, open, Apple patt., No. 95...................... **$65**

Baker, Apple patt., rectangular, No. 85, 5 1/4 x 10", 2 1/4" h. (tight hairline down side) **$700**
Baker, cover & warming stand, Apple patt., No. 601, ribbed, 8" d. **$105**
Bean cup, Apple patt., No. 75, 3 1/2" d. **$235**
Bean pot, cov., Apple patt., No. 93, only one known **$3,500**
Bean pot, cov., Apple patt., oversized, No. 502 (minor chip on bottom edge) **$900**
Bowl, Apple patt., No. 95 .... **$55**
Bowl, Apple patt., oversized spaghetti, No. 25 .... **$265**
Bowl, Apple patt., small sized spaghetti, No. 24.. **$75**
Bowl, canoe-shaped, Brown Drip Glaze, No. 88... **$90**
Bowl, canoe-shaped, Brown Drip Glaze, No. 89... **$85**
Bowl, 4" d., Kolor Kraft line, No. 04, w/lip & shoulder, green **$145**
Bowl, 4" d, 2" h., Cherry patt., No. 04 .... **$55**
Bowl, 4 3/4" d., 1 3/4" d., Apple patt., No. 602, ribbed, South Dakota advertising **$50**
Bowl, 5 3/4" d., Apple patt., No. 23 .... **$85**
Bowl, 6" d., Kolor Kraft line, No. 06, w/lip & shoulder, blue **$20**
Bowl, 6" d., 1 3/4" h., cereal or salad, Apple patt., No. 94... **$25**
Bowl, cov., 7 1/2"d., Apple patt., No. 66 .... **$125**
Bowl, cov., 7 1/2"d., Apple patt., w/adver-tising, No. 66 .... **$205**
Bowl, cov., 7 3/4" d., 3" h., Apple patt., No. 600, ribbed, advertising **$60**
Bowl, 8" d., 1 1/2" h., individual sphaghetti, Apple patt., #44, green band on inside **$110**
Bowl, 8" d., 1 1/2" h., individual sphaghetti, Apple patt., #44 RF, green band on out-side.. **$205**
Bowl, cov., 8" d., 3 3/4" h., Apple patt., No. 110 .... **$75**
Bowl, cov., 8 1/2" d., Apple patt., No. 67 .... **$70**
Bowl, 9" d., Kolor Kraft line, No. 09, w/lip & shoulder, yellow **$35**
Bowl, 9 1/2" d., 4" h., salad, Apple patt., No. 73, w/South Dakota advertising **$45**
Bowl, 10 1/2" d., Apple patt., No. 58, rare...... **$600**
Bowl, 13" d., Apple patt., spaghetti, No. 39 ... **$145**

Two-leaf Apple Spaghetti Bowl

Bowl, 13" d., Apple (two-leaf) patt., spa-ghetti, No. 39 (ILLUS.) **$95**
Canister, cov., Apple patt., No. 72, 9 1/2" h. .. **$425**

Canister, cov., "Coffee," Apple patt., No. 82 (minor nick) **$425**
Canister, cov., "Flour," Apple patt., No. 81 (minor hairline in cover) **$425**
Canister, cov., Apple patt., No. 82, three leaves on cover, 7" h., 5" d. **$950**
Casserole, cov., Apple patt., individual, tab handled, No.18, 8" l. **$195**
Casserole, cov., Apple patt., No. 2/48.......... **$255**
Casserole, cov., Apple patt., No. 52, 6 1/2" d. (small repaired chip on cover) **$115**
Casserole, cov., Apple patt., No. 53, w/ad-vertising, 7 1/2" d. **$135**
Casserole, cov., Apple patt., No. 54, 8 1/2" d... **$225**
Casserole, cov., Apple patt., square, No. 84, rare (minor hairline in base, lid does not fit snugly)... **$300**
Casserole, cov., Apple (two-leaf) patt., in-dividual, French handled, No.18, 8" l. **$80**
Casserole, cov., oval, Apple patt., No. 86, glued chip on cover edge, rare, 8" l. **$600**
Casserole, cov., Silhouette, patt., individu-al, tab handled, No.18, 8" l........................... **$75**
Casserole, cover & metal warming stand, Apple patt., No. 3/19, casserole 8 1/2" d., 5 1/4" h.. **$195**
Casserole, cover & metal warming stand, Apple (two leaf) patt., No. 3/19, casserole 8 1/2" d., 5 1/4" h. **$75**
Casserole warmer, electric, Apple patt., cut-away base rim, No. 133, 7" d., 2" h..... **$1,400**
Casserole warmer, electric, round w/flat base, Apple patt., No. 133, rare **$2,800**
Cheese crock, cov., Apple patt., No. 80, two-leaf cover... **$725**
Chip-n-dip set, Apple patt., No. 119 & 120 bowls, the set **$185**

Very Rare Watt Apple Coffee Server

Coffee server, cov., Apple patt., No. 115, rare (ILLUS.) **$4,000**
Cookie jar, cone-top, Apple patt., No. 91, 10 3/4" h. (minor crow's-foot in cover) **$750**
Cookie jar, cov., Apple patt., eared han-dles, No. 503, 8 1/4" h., 8 1/4" d. **$450**

Autumn Foliage Creamer & Pitchers

Cookie jar, cov., Apple patt., No. 21, 7 1/2" h. (minor hairline in cover) **$175**

Cross-Hatch Pansy Cookie Jar

Cookie jar, cov., Cross-Hatch Pansy (Old Pansy) patt., No. 21, 7 1/2" h. (ILLUS.)...... **$375**
Creamer, Apple patt., No. 35, very rare, 5" l., 2 3/4" h.. **$1,700**
Creamer, Apple patt., No. 62, w/advertising .. **$155**
Creamer, Apple (two leaf) patt., No. 62, 4 1/4" h.. **$135**
Creamer, Autumn Foliage patt., No. 62, 4 1/4" h. (ILLUS. right w/Autumn Foliage pitchers, top of page) **$235**
Creamer, Brown Banded, No. 62, 4 1/4" h..... **$525**
Creamer, Brownstone line, No. 62, brown body, green neck, 4 1/4" h. **$265**

Creamer cinnamon drip glaze over brown, No. 62, 4 1/4" h., 4 1/2" d........................... **$350**
Creamer, Dutch Tulip patt., No. 62, 4 1/4" h. .. **$175**

Rare Open Apple No. 62 Creamer

Creamer, Open Apple patt., No. 62, hairline in handle, 4 1/4" h. (ILLUS.)....................... **$825**
Creamer, Rooster patt., No. 62, 4 1/4" h. (ILLUS. left w/pitchers, bottom of page)..... **$200**
Creamer, Starflower (five-petal) patt., No. 62, w/advertising, 4 1/4" h. **$305**
Creamer, Tear Drop patt., No. 62, 4 1/4" h. **$300**
Cruet set, cov., oil & vinegar bottles, Apple patt., No. 126, 7" h., the set **$2,000**

Rooster Pattern Creamer & Pitchers

Cup, Tropicana patt., rare $800
Cup & saucer, Cut-Leaf Pansy (Rio Rose) patt., No. 40, the set.................................... $105
Fondue pot, cov., handled, Apple patt., No. 506, hairline in cover, chip inside rim, 9" l., 3" h... $275
Grease jar, cov., Apple patt., w/Wisconsin advertising, No. 01, 5 1/2" h...................... $375

Rare Apple Grease Jar with Advertising

Grease jar, cov., Apple patt., No. 47, w/advertising, 5" h. (ILLUS.) $700
Ice bucket, cov., Apple patt., No. 59 .... $185
Ice bucket, cov., Butterfly patt., No. 59 (repaired spot on cover) $475
Mixing bowl, Apple patt., 7 1/2" d., 5" h., No. 64... $55
Mixing bowl, Apple patt., No. 06, rimmed, w/advertising, 6" d............................... $70
Mixing bowl, Apple patt., No. 65, 8 1/2" d., 5 3/4" h....................................... $45
Mixing bowl, Apple (two leaf) patt., No. 05, ribbed, 5" d., 2 3/4" h................................. $45
Mixing bowl, Apple (two-leaf) patt., No. 04, ribbed, 4 1/4" d., 2" h................................. $75
Mixing bowl, Apple (two-leaf) patt., No. 05, ribbed, 5" d., 2 3/4" h................................. $75
Mixing bowl, Apple (two-leaf) patt., No. 64, 7 1/2" d., 5" h.................................. $30
Mixing bowl, Apple (two-leaf) patt., No. 65, 8 1/2" d., 5 3/4" h.............................. $50
Mixing bowl, Apple (w/only stem) patt., No. 09, ribbed, w/South Dakota advertising, rare, 9" d., 5" h. $350
Mixing bowl, Butterfly patt., No. 05, 5" d., 2 3/4" h.. $775
Mixing bowl, Cherry patt., No. 04, ribbed, 4 1/4" d., 2" h................................. $105
Mixing bowl, Double Apple patt., No. 05, ribbed, 5" d., 2 3/4" h.............................. $75
Mixing bowl, Double Apple patt., No. 06, ribbed, 6" d., 3 1/2" h.............................. $105
Mixing bowl, Double Apple patt., No. 07, ribbed, 7" d., 4" h.............................. $115
Mixing bowl, Dutch Tulip patt., No. 05, ribbed, w/advertising, 5" d., 2 3/4" h.......... $185
Mixing bowl, Dutch Tulip patt., No. 05, rimmed, 5" d., 2 3/4" h.............................. $115

Mixing bowl, Old Pansy patt., No. 05, ribbed, banded, 5" d., 2 3/4" h. $60
Mixing bowl, Open Apple patt., No. 05, ribbed, 5" d., 2 3/4" h, ... $165
Mixing bowl, Raised Pansy patt., No. 05, ribbed, 5" d., 2 3/4" h. $85
Mixing bowl, Reduced Decoration Apple patt., No. 63, deep sides, 6 1/2" d., 4" h. $70
Mixing bowl, Reduced Decoration Apple patt., No. 64, deep sides, 7 1/2" d., 5" h. $75
Mixing bowl, Rooster patt., No. 05, rimmed, 5" d.. $55
Mixing bowl, Starflower patt., No. 05, rimmed, 5" d $35
Mixing bowl, Tear Drop patt., No. 05, ribbed, 5" d., 2 3/4" h. $40
Mixing bowl, White Daisy patt., No. 05, ribbed, 5" d., 2 3/4" h. $165
Mixing bowl, Apple patt., No. 04, ribbed, 4 1/4" d., 2" h. $40
Mixing bowl, Cross-Hatch Pansy (Old Pansy) patt., No. 05, ribbed, 5" d., 2 3/4" h..... $145
Mixing bowl, Apple patt., ribbed, No. 06, w/Minnesota advertising, 6" d., 3 1/2" h....... $30
Mixing bowl, Cross-Hatch Pansy (Old Pansy) patt., No. 6, ribbed, 6" d., 3 1/2" h....... $100
Mixing bowl, Cross-Hatch Pansy (Old Pansy) patt., No. 07, ribbed, 7" d., 4" h....... $90
Mixing bowl, Apple (two-leaf) patt., No. 08, ribbed, 8" d., 4 1/2" h. $75
Mixing bowl, Cross-Hatch Pansy (Old Pansy) patt., No. 08, ribbed, 8" d., 4 1/2" h....... $75
Mixing bowl, Apple patt., No. 09, ribbed, w/North Dakota advertising, 9" d., 5" h. $45
Mixing bowl, Cross-Hatch Pansy (Old Pansy) patt., No. 09, ribbed, 9" d., 5" h. $85
Mixing bowls, Apple (two-leaf) patt., No. 63, 6 1/2" d., 4" h. $25
Mug, Apple patt., cylindrical, No. 61, rare, 3 3/4" d., 3" h. $1,700
Mug, Apple patt., No.501, barrel-shaped, 4 1/2" h.. $300
Mug, Apple patt., No. 701, cylindrical, 3 3/4" h.. $650
Mug, Apple patt., waisted cylindrical form, No. 121, 3 3/4" h................................... $115

Starflower (Five Petal) No. 61 Mug

Mug, Starflower (five-petal) patt., cylindrical, No. 61, 3 3/4" d., 3" h. (ILLUS.).......... $225
Pie plate, 1993 WCA Commemorative $450
Pitcher, 4 1/2" h., olive green over brown drip glaze, No. 62....................................... $225

Three Sizes of Watt Tulip Pattern Pitchers

Pitcher, 5 1/2" h., Apple patt., No. 15 .... **$50**
Pitcher, 5 1/2" h., Apple patt., No. 15, sample-type w/wording "This is a sample imprint for this size space," rare **$375**
Pitcher, 5 1/2" h., Apple patt., No. 15, w/advertising in black print (hairline in handle) .. **$100**
Pitcher, 5 1/2" h., Apple patt., No. 15, w/advertising in red print **$115**
Pitcher, 5 1/2" h., Apple (two leaf) patt., No. 15 .... **$140**
Pitcher, 5 1/2" h., Cherry patt., No. 15 .... **$175**
Pitcher, 5 1/2" h., Cherry patt., No. 15., w/advertising **$155**
Pitcher, 5 1/2" h., Double Apple patt., No. 15 .... **$305**
Pitcher, 5 1/2" h., Dutch Tulip patt., reduced design w/some leaves omitted, rare, No. 15 .... **$425**
Pitcher, 5 1/2" h., Old Pansy patt., No. 15 ..... **$195**
Pitcher, 5 1/2" h., olive green over brown drip glaze, No. 15 .... **$85**
Pitcher, 5 1/2" h., Rooster patt., No. 15 (ILLUS. center w/Rooster creamer & pitcher, bottom of page 816) **$175**

Starflower Four-Petal No. 15 Pitcher

Pitcher, 5 1/2" h., Starflower (four-petal) patt., No. 15 (ILLUS.) **$85**
Pitcher, 5 1/2" h., Starflower (four-petal) patt., No. 15, w/Minnesota advertising **$50**
Pitcher, 5 1/2" h., Tear Drop patt., No. 15 .... **$40**
Pitcher, 5 1/2" h., Tulip patt., No. 15 (ILLUS. center with other Tulip pitcher & creamer, top of page) **$475**
Pitcher, 5 1/2" h., Yellow Swirl patt., No. 15 .... **$60**

Pitcher, 6 1/2" h., Apple patt., No. 16 .... **$155**
Pitcher, 6 1/2" h., Apple patt., No. 16, w/ Ohio advertising **$125**
Pitcher, 6 1/2" h., Apple (two leaf) patt., No. 16 .... **$140**
Pitcher, 6 1/2" h., Autumn Foliage patt., No. 16 (ILLUS. left w/Autumn Foliage creamer, top of page 816) **$65**
Pitcher, 6 1/2" h., Brownstone line, No. 16, brown body, green neck **$105**
Pitcher, 6 1/2" h., Butterfly patt., No. 16, very rare (repair to top edge) **$375**
Pitcher, 6 1/2" h., Cherry patt., No. 16 .... **$85**
Pitcher, 6 1/2" h., Dutch Tulip patt., No. 16 ... **$235**
Pitcher, 6 1/2" h., Rooster patt., No. 16 (ILLUS. right w/Rooster creamer & pitcher, bottom of page 816) **$195**
Pitcher, 6 1/2" h., Starflower (five-petal) patt., No. 16 .... **$70**
Pitcher, 6 1/2" h ., Tear Drop patt., No. 16 .... **$105**
Pitcher, 6 1/2" h., Tulip patt., No. 16 (ILLUS. left with other Tulip pitcher & creamer, top of page) **$115**
Pitcher, 8" h., 8 1/2" d., Apple patt., w/ice lip, bulbous body, No. 17 .... **$170**
Pitcher, 8" h., Apple patt., No. 17 .... **$350**
Pitcher, 8" h., Quilted Morning Glory patt., w/ice lip, No. 17 (repair by spout) **$235**
Pitcher, 8" h., 8 1/2" d., refrigerator-type, square-shaped, Apple (two-leaf) patt., No. 69 (minor rough spot on lip) **$205**
Plate, dinner, Apple patt., No. 29 .... **$300**
Plate, dinner, Apple patt., No. 29, w/advertising **$350**

Rare Apple Divided Dinner Plate

Plate, 10 1/2" d., dinner, divided, Apple patt., two-color leaves, signed on the back by Betty Baughman, mint (ILLUS., previous page) **$3,700**

Platter, 12" d., Apple patt., No. 49 .... **$205**

Platter, 15" d., Apple patt., No. 31 .... **$95**

Platter, 15" d., Bull's-eye Pansy patt., No. 31 .... **$50**

Platter, 15" d., Cross-Hatch Pansy (Old Pansy) patt., No. 31 .... **$135**

Refrigerator set, cov., two-part stack-type, No. 02, very rare **$4,600**

Salt & pepper shakers, Apple patt., barrel-shaped, No. 45 & No. 46, 4" h., the set...... **$700**

Salt & pepper shakers, Apple patt., hour-glass shape, No. 117 & No. 118, raised "S" & "P", 4 1/2" h., pr.............................. **$245**

Apple Hourglass Salt & Pepper Shakers

Salt & pepper shakers, Apple patt., hour-glass shape, w/advertising, No. 117 & No. 118, pr. (ILLUS.) **$175**

Salt shaker, Dutch Tulip patt., barrel-shaped, No. 45, rare, 4" h. **$525**

Salt shaker, Cherry patt., barrel-shaped, No. 45, 4" h. **$45**

Snack bowl, "Chips," 7" d., 2 3/4" h................. **$95**

Snack bowl, "Corn," 6 1/2" d., 2 1/2" h. **$105**

Snack bowl, "Pretzels," 8 1/2" d., 3 1/2" h. **$110**

Sugar bowl, cov., Apple patt., No. 98, w/advertising, 4 1/2" h. **$225**

Sugar bowl, cov., Brown Banded, No. 98, 4 1/2" h.. **$200**

Sugar bowl, open, two-handled, Star Flower (five-petal patt., No. 35, rare **$525**

Teapot, cov., Apple patt., No. 112, rare, 6" h. (rought spout) **$1,800**

Teapot, cov., Apple patt., No. 505, 5" h. **$4,700**

Tumbler, round-sided, Starflower (five-petal) patt., No. 56, 4 1/2" h. **$110**

Tumbler, slant-sided, Starflower (five-petal) patt., No. 56, 4 1/2" h. **$200**

Wedgwood

Reference here is to the famous pottery established by Josiah Wedgwood in 1759 in England. Numerous types of wares have been produced through the years to the present.

WEDGWOOD

Early Wedgwood Mark

Basalt

Bust of the Duke of Edinburgh, mounted on a waisted round socle, impressed title & mark, dated 1953, 9" h. **$353**

Wedgwood Basalt Bust of Venus

Bust of Venus, posed w/her head tilted down, mounted atop a waisted round socle, impressed mark, 19th c., 9 1/4" h. (ILLUS.)... **$705**

Black Basalt Candlesticks

Candlesticks, a wide round foot w/an arabesque floral border tapering to a cylindrical columnar shaft molded in relief w/classical figures, round cupped socket, first half 20th c., 9 3/4" h. (ILLUS.)............. **$235**

Candlesticks, each w/a very tall slender fluted columnar standard w/the socket having a pierced rim, raised on a square plinth base w/foliate trim, impressed mark, early 19th c., 12 1/2" h., pr. (one socket rim restored, footrim chips)............. **$646**

Fine Wedgwood Basalt Ewer

Ewer, Classical urn-form body on a square foot & ringed & reeded pedestal, the body w/a fluted lower body & narrow molded band below large molded grapevine swags, the angled shoulder w/a cylindrical neck & high arched spout w/the figure of a crouching satyr reaching around the base of the spout to grasp the horns of a goat mask below the spout, the loop handle issuing from the shoulders of the satyr, 19th c., 15 1/2" h. (ILLUS.)................... $863

Wedgwood Basalt Figure of Nude Male

Figure of a nude male, standing w/legs crossed & playing a flute, leaning against a tall tree trunk w/his cloak pinned at one shoulder & draping down around the stump, 19th c., 17 1/4" h. (ILLUS.)............. $920

Figure of Cupid, shown seated on a rock atop w raised round base, impressed mark & title, late 19th c., 8" h. $411

Incense burner, a squatty bulbous round bowl molded w/foliate festoons, raised on three figural dolphin legs atop w/molded round base, pierced insert & flat cover, 19th c., 4 1/8" h. (restoration to dolphin tails, shallow flakes on cover) $823

Potpourri, cov., wide gently flaring cylindrical base w/upturned loop rim handles, low domed cover pierced w/overall holes centered by a knop handle, impressed mark, 19th c., 9" d. $940

Tea set: cov. teapot, cov. sugar bowl & creamer; footed squatty bulbous bodies w/angular handles & low domed covers, each piece decorated in color w/floral sprays on the black ground, covers w/figural sybil finials, early 20th c., impressed marks, teapot 5 1/4" h., the set $353

Urn, a wide round low foot supporting the wide campana-form crater bowl w/a flaring rim flanked by high upright looped handles, the sides decorated w/polychrome floral sprays, top fitted w/a pierced grid, impressed mark, mid-19th c., 10 1/4" w. $1,998

Vase, 14" h., footed tall ovoid body tapering to a tall slender cylindrical ringed neck w/a flattened rim, upright arched lion head & mask shoulder handles, molded w/a central relief frieze depicting Hercules in the Garden of the Hesperides within foliate borders, impressed mark, dated 1868 (haldes w/chips & restored terminals) $1,293

Caneware

Honey pot, cov., designed as a beehive dish w/cover set on a four-legged bench, impressed mark, early 19th c., 6 3/4" h. (cover restored)....................................... $1,293

Pie dish, cov., a low shallow oval pie crust form base w/a low slightly domed latticework cover w/a grape leaf handle, ca. 1800, impressed mark, 7 3/4" l. (slight rim chip) $588

Jasper Ware

Unusual Jasper Basketweave Bowl

Bowl, cov., 5 1/4" h., a flaring short foot supporting the bulbous wide tapering bowl w/a fitted domed cover w/a lily blossom finial, the sides w/carved alternating black & white stripes w/yellow basketweave design, the cover reversible w/a flower finial on one side & a candle socket on the other, marked on the bottom, two small chips to pod finial (ILLUS.)................................ $3,968

Grouping of Wedgwood Jasper Objects Including a Bowl, Tray & Other Pieces

Bowl, cov., 6" h., tall cylindrical base sharply tapered at the bottom, flat rim fitted w/a high domed cover w/a knop finial, the base sides applied w/white relief classical scenes within foliate frames, radiating acathus leaves on the cover, dark blue ground, late 18th - early 19th c. (ILLUS. front row, second from left, with tea tray, custard cup & other pieces, top of page) **$1,116**

Cheese dish & cover, round base w/flanged rim trimmed w/applied white relief running oak leaf border, the wide domed cover w/a continuous band of white relief classical figures, white relief oak leaf band on the top centered by a low loop handle, black ground, impressed mark, ca. 1900, 11" d. **$1,116**

Cracker jar, cov., cylindrical dark yellow body w/applied black fruiting grapevine festoons around the sides between lion masks & rings, silver plate rim, cover & bail swing handle, impressed mark, ca. 1930, worn plating, 5 1/4" h. (ILLUS. center with two pitchers, bottom of page) **$764**

Custard cup, cov., cylindrical solid white cup w/a twisted handle & latticework surface, pierced lattice cover, impressed mark, late 18th c., 2 1/2" h. (ILLUS. front row, second from right with covered bowl, tray & other pieces, top of page)............. **$1,175**

Dish, round, engine-turned striping radiating from central applied white relief scene of "The Infant Academy" & white an acanthus & stiff leaf border, blue ground, impressed mark, late 18th c., rim repair, firing line to center relief, 8" d. (ILLUS. front row, far right, with covered bowl, tray & other pieces, top of page) **$176**

Dish, deep, round, white relief engine-turned striping surrounding a central cameo depicting "The Infant Academy," acanthus & stiff leaf border, lilac ground, impressed mark, late 18th c., firing lines in the relief, 8 1/4" d. (ILLUS. front row, far left, with covered bowl, tray & other pieces, top of page) **$1,293**

Earrings, teardrop-shaped, each w/applied white relief classical figures centering borders of stiff leaves & beaded festoons, dark blue ground, late 18th - early 19th c., 1 1/4" l, pr. (very slight nick to relief)....... **$1,175**

Medallion, oval, applied white classical relief two classical women standing under a swag, on a solid blue ground, mounted in a cut-steel beaded frame attributed to Matthew Boulton, impressed mark, late 18th c., overall size 1 3/4 x 2 5/8" **$1,410**

Jasper Ware Cracker Jar & Two Pitchers

Jasper Ware Plaque with Judgment of Hercules Scene

Medallion, pyrometer-type, oval, white jasper ground decorated w/a blue wash on the impressed bead border surrounding "By J. Wedgwood F.R.S.," No. 79 on the back, late 18th c., 1 1/2 x 2" (back edge chips).. **$1,116**

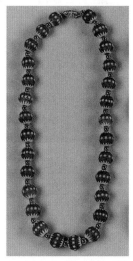

Wedgwood Jasper Ware Bead Necklace

Necklace, consisting of 28 round beads, each w/applied white relief stiff leaf borders & banded star centers, dark blue ground, 19th c., restrung, 18" l. (ILLUS.).. **$1,998**

Pitcher, 5 1/2" h., jug-form, the ovoid body decorated w/applied white relief classical figures between vertical bands & foliate borders, crimson ground, impressed mark, ca. 1920, relief loss (ILLUS. left with cracker jar & other pitcher, bottom previous page) **$646**

Pitcher, 8" h., footed bulbous body tapering to a tall cylindrical neck w/a flat rim w/pinched rim spout, applied strap handle, applied white relief band of classical figures between floret banded borders, impressed mark, ca. 1900, slight firing flaw below spout (ILLUS. right with cracker jar & crimson pitcher, bottom previous page) **$1,528**

Plaque, long narrow rectangular shape, applied white relief scene of the Judgment

of Hercules against a light blue ground, impressed mark, 19th c., mounted in an ebonized wood frame, some surface wear, 5 3/4 x 16" (ILLUS., top of page)... **$1,763**

Portrait medallion, double-type, oval, applied white relief bust portraits of Phthias facing Sappho, on a solid blue ground, Wedgwood & Bentley impressed mark, ca. 1779, 2 x 2 3/4" (rim chip) **$441**

Grouping Early Portrait Medallions

Portrait medallion, oval, a light blue ground applied w/a white relief profile bust portrait of Henry Dundas, First Viscount of Melville, impressed name below the bust, impressed mark, ca. 1785, unframed, 3 1/8 x 4" (ILLUS. top left with three other portrait medallions) **$1,998**

Portrait medallion, oval, a raised white relief portrait of the young Queen Charlotte, on a solid blue ground, impressed mark of Wedgwood & Bentley, ca. 1779, mounted in a turned walnut frame, 2 1/2 x 3 1/4" (ILLUS., next page).......... **$1,410**

Portrait medallion, oval, dark blue ground applied w/a white relief profile bust portrait of Benjamin Franklin, unmarked, restored rim chips, unframed, 19th c., 3 1/2 x 4 1/8" (ILLUS. top row, right, with other portrait medallions, above) **$323**

Early Jasper Ware Portrait Medallion

Portrait medallion, oval, dark blue ground applied w/a white relief profile portrait bust of Admiral Keppel, impressed title & mark, slight rim flake to surface, rim flakes on back, ca. 1779, 3 7/8" l. (ILLUS. bottom row, right, with group of portrait medallions, previous page)................................. $529

Portrait medallion, oval, double, applied white relief bust portraits of two facing classical heads, one identified as Chrysippus, on a solid blue ground, impressed mark, ca. 1779, mounted in a brass frame, 2 2 3/4" (surface flake, back edge chips)... $823

Portrait medallion, oval, medium blue ground applied w/a face-on white relief bust portrait of Michael de Ruyter, a Dutch Admiral, impressed title & mark, slight back edge chips, ca. 1785, 2 5/8 x 3 3/8" (ILLUS. bottom row, left, with other portrait medallions, previous page).. $411

Early Jasper Ware Portrait Medallion

Portrait medallion, oval w/a green ground & a white relief bust portrait of Granville-Leveson-Gower, the First Marquis of Stafford, set in a period oval brass frame, ca. 1787, impressed mark, 2 3/4 x 3 3/8" (ILLUS.)............................. $1,293

Portrait medallion of Francisco Albani, oval, applied white relief almost full face bust on a solid blue ground, impressed

mark of Wedgwood & Bentley, ca. 1779, 1 3/4 x 2 1/8"... $323

Pretty Wedgwood Jasper Scent Bottle

Scent bottle w/hallmarked silver screw top, flatted teardrop shaped body in blue jasper centered by a long oval olive green reserve framed by a ring of small white relief blossoms & enclosing a scene of a classical woman seated on a chair w/cupid in her lap, the reverse scene shows a woman walking w/cupid leading the way, w/original fitted case, bottled 3 1/4" l. (ILLUS.)......................... $1,035

Tea bowl & saucer, footed deep rounded bowl w/white relief engine-turned striping & applied relief of putti, lapidary-polished interior, matching saucer w/white relief engine turning w/an acanthus & stiff leaf border, on a green ground, impressed marks, late 18th c., saucer 5 1/8" d., the set (ILLUS. front row, third from left, with cov. bowl, tray & other pieces, page 667) $1,410

Tea tray, oval, applied white narrow acanthus & stiff leaf border band & central sunflower within an oval band, blue ground, impressed mark, late 18th c., 17 1/2" l. (ILLUS. top row with covered bowl, custard cup & other pieces, page 667) $1,528

Wedgwood Crimson Jasper Teapot

Teapot, cov., a squatty bulbous body w/a short angled spout & C-form handle, domed cover w/button finial, crimson ground applied w/white classical figures, ca. 1920, restoration to a figure & to rim chips on cover, 5 1/4" h. (ILLUS.) $940

Tobacco jar, cov., wide tapering cylindrical body w/ a fitted low domed cover w/button finial, the sides decorated in applied white relief w/Egyptian figures & designs, star & zigzag borders, black ground, retailed by W.T. Lamb & Sons, 20th c., 6 1/4" h. (cover restored, slight nicks to jar rim) **$764**

Vase, cov., 10" h., thick square base supporting the classical urn-form body w/a tapering shoulder & domed cover w/acorn finial, engine-turned white striping on the pedestal, lower body, shoulder & cover, the upper body w/a wide panel of white relief classical figures depicting the Dancing Hours, applied leaf sprigs around the square base, on a black ground, impressed mark, dated 1954 .... **$499**

Vase, cov., 12 1/4" h., small round pedestal base support the large urn-form body w/the wide shoulder centered by a rolled rim & fitted w/a low domed cover w/pointed finial, long C-scroll white handles from the shoulder to the base of the body, the body decorated in applied white relief w/a band of zodiac signs at the top above applied floral swags joining oval classical medallions, white lappet designs on the rim & cover, black ground, impressed marks, mid-19th c. (rim chip under edge of cover) **$2,350**

Rosso Antico

Fine Early Rosso Antico Wine Cooler

Wine cooler, barrel-shaped w/scrolled male mask head handles, incised vertical lines to a black slip surface, horizontal engine-turned bands, impressed mark, ca. 1800, shallow chips to handles, 9" h. (ILLUS.)... **$2,585**

Miscellaneous

Boston cup, Fairyland Lustre, a low cylindrical footring supporting the wide rounded bowl, the exterior decorated w/the Leaping Elves patt., yellowish brown upper sides decorated w/fairing w/transparent gold wing frolicking on a green & blue ground w/mushroom, the upper section sprinkled w/printed gold stars; the interior decorated w/the Elves on a Branch patt. w/two small elves perched on a prickly branch w/black bat & bird around the leafy rim, base w/the Portland Vase mark & "ZXXXX," 5 1/4" d. (ILLUS., top next column) **$1,725**

Wedgwood Fairyland Lustre Boston Cup

Miniature Wedgwood Lustre Bowl

Bowl, miniature, 2 1/4" w., Lustre Ware, footed octagonal shape, the exterior w/a mottled orange lustre glaze decorated w/various gold mythological beasts between gold rim & base bands, the dark blue mottled interior decorated w/a stylized spider (ILLUS.) **$260**

Rare Small Fairyland Lustre Bowl

Bowl, 3 1/2" w., 2" h., Fairyland Lustre, thin footring below the octagonal bowl decorated on the exterior w/the paneled Dana patt. featuring scenes of a village, water & mountains, interior decorated w/elves picking insects from a spider web among mushrooms & trees, Patt. Z5125, marked w/Wedgwood Portland Vase mark (ILLUS.)................................ **$4,888**

Wedgwood Butterfly Lustre Bowl

Bowl, 6 1/2" w., Butterfly Lustre, footed octagonal form, the exterior in pale blue lustre w/large blue & gold butterflies, the interior in deep gold lustre (ILLUS.) **$480**

Rare Fairyland Lustre Willow Bowl

Bowl, 8"w., Fairyland Lustre, footed deep octagonal shape decorated in the Willow patt., the exterior in Coral & Bronze decorated w/a printed gold Willow Ware style decoration, the interior w/a Willow patt. in the bottom & a blue leafy band around the rim, Portland Vase mark & "Z5406" (ILLUS.) **$3,450**

Woodland Elves VI Fairyland Lustre Bowl

Bowl, 8" w., Fairyland Lustre, footed octagonal form, the exterior in the Woodland Elves VI patt., the Fiddler in Tree against a midnight blue lustre background, the interior decorated w/the Ship & Mermaid patt. against a white lustre ground, some minor scratches to interior bottom (ILLUS.) **$4,600**

Lahore Pattern Fairyland Lustre Bowl

Bowl, 8" d., 5 1/2" h., Fairyland Lustre, Lahore patt., pedestal base below widely flaring bell-shaped bowl, the exterior w/colorful drapery swags & lanterns picked out in orange enamel, the interior w/the Melba Center decorated around the sides w/black elephants, camels, horses & Indian warriors against a yellow ground, marked w/Portland vase mark & "Wedgwood - Made in England" (ILLUS.)........... **$8,050**

Woodland Elves VI Fairyland Bowl

Bowl, 8 1/2" d., 4" h., Fairyland Lustre, Woodland Elves VI patt., a narrow footring supports the octagonal bowl, the exterior w/a continuous design of tree trunks in dark bluish green & all the elves in brown on a flame lustre background of orange over crimson, the interior w/the Ship & Mermaid patt. w/a flame lustre center, Pattern No. Z5360 (ILLUS.) **$7,475**

Wedgwood Dragon Lustre Bowl

Bowl, 9" d., 5 1/2" h., Dragon Lustre, a low flaring round foot below the deep flaring bell-form bowl, the exterior in mottled blue & green w/enameled gold dragons & red highlights, the interior bottom w/an Oriental medallion in blues, greens, reds & gold, Portland vase mark on the bottom (ILLUS.)... **$575**

Fine Wedgwood Fairyland Lustre Compote

Compote, 4 3/4" d., 3 1/4" h., Fairyland Lustre, deep flaring round bowl on a short flaring pedestal base, decorated on the exterior w/the Elves on a Branch patt. w/an orange sky, green foreground w/mushrooms & brown fairies, the interior decorated w/a shaded green background centered w/elves on a branch w/flying elves, butterflies & bats, Patt. Z5360 - 9, Portland Vase mark (ILLUS.) **$4,600**

Crocus pot & undertray, majolica, a tall domed top w/a molded basketweave design & pierced w/numerous holes, dark green glaze, impressed mark on undertray, ca. 1870, 6 1/2" h. (slight glaze nicks along pierced holes, chip under foot of the undertray)............................ **$499**

Egg basket & stand, Queen's Ware, each of oval shape & w/wide ribbed panels & enamel decorated bellflowers & stiff leaf borders, impressed mark, ca. 1800, 11 7/8" l. (surface wear to dish center) **$881**

Extremely Rare Fairyland Lustre Jar

Jar, cov., Fairyland Lustre, malfrey pot Shape No. 2312, bulbous ovoid body fitted w/a domed cover, the exterior includes various patterns including Demon Tree, Roc Bird, Bat in the Demon Tree, Black Toad & Dwarf, Red Monkeys & the Scorpion w/a long yellow tail & spines, a narrow dragon bead border around the base & rim of the collar, inside of collar decorated in the Pan-Fei border, the cover decorated w/Owls of Wisdom w/purple bodies & bright copper-colored faces, blue eyes & red pupils, the cover w/a Red Fei border band & the Scorpion, cover also w/a Pan-Fei border around the inside surrounding Elves on a branch in the center, Pattern No. Z-4968, very light wear to gold cover trim, 14" h. (ILLUS.) **$57,500**

Extremely Rare Fairyland Lustre Malfrey Pot

Malfrey Pot, cov., Fairyland Lustre, bulbous body w/wide low domed cover, decorated in the Bubble II patt. No. Z4968, the mottled dark blue & purple watery background decorated w/numerous fairies & bubbles, the cover depicts a large spider in a web surrounded by winged fairies, interior of cover depicts a large bubble w/fairies inside, bottom interior w/a geometric square design encircling a stylized flower, Wedgwood Portland Vase mark, also paper label of retailer "Leo. Kaplan Ltd., NYC - Guaranteed Genuine," 8" d., 7" h. (ILLUS.) **$34,500**

Malfrey Pot with Bubbles II Pattern

Malfrey pot, cov., Fairyland Lustre, Pattern Z5257, bulbous ovoid body tapering to a domed cover, decorated in the Bubbles II in the moonlight patt. on a dark blue

ground, printed marks, ca. 1920, 7" h.
(ILLUS.)... **$39,950**

Very Rare Fairyland Lustre Malfrey Pot

Malfrey pot, cov., Fairyland Lustre, Shape 2312, bulbous ovoid body tapering to a domed cover, Ghostly Woods patt. decorated w/Demon Tree, Roc bird, black toad & dwarf & scorpion w/large yellow tail & spines, the cover in the Owls of Wisdom w/purple bodies & blue-trimmed eyes, base & cover trimmed in dragon bead decoration, the inside of rim of both decorated in the Pan-Fei border, inside of cover w/light blue lustre background & two elves on a branch, base w/Portland vase mark & "Wedgwood - England - Z4968," 14" h. (ILLUS.) **$40,250**

Fairyland Lustre Malfrey Pot in Willow Pattern

Malfrey Pot, cov., Fairyland Lustre, tall tapering ovoid body w/a domed cover, decorated in the Willow patt. Z5360, flame lustre background w/an Oriental landscape, Shape No. 2311, Wedgwood Portland Vase, mark, very tiny chip repair on side, probably done during manufacture, 8 1/2" h. (ILLUS.) **$3,738**

One of a Set of Bone China Plates

Plates, 9" d., bone china, each w/a narrow scrolled foliate & diaper gilded rim border & central transfers in shades of blue of historical places, titles & printed marks, late 19th - early 20th c., one w/hairline, very light gilt rim wear, set of 23 (ILLUS. of one).. **$499**

Set of 12 Wedgwood Lustre Plates

Plates, 11" d., Lustre decoration, octagonal w/eight alternating panels of gold geometric designs alternating w/panels showing Oriental men, the figures in gold against a dark blue lustre ground, Portland Vase mark & retailer mark for William H. Plummer & Co., New York, set of 12 (ILLUS.).. **$900**

Rare Candlemas Pattern Lustre Vase

Vase, 8" h., Fairyland Lustre, Candlemas patt., wide ovoid body w/a wide, low rolled neck, Shape No. 2411, the exterior divided into four panels showing a tall white candle w/blue colorations & the head of a queen w/crown instead of a flame, the panels separated by vertical bands of blue lustre w/brown fairies hanging from a bell rope, marked w/Portland vase mark & "Wedgwood - Made in England - Z5157 - B" (ILLUS.) **$20,125**

Fairyland Lustre Vase with Goblin Pattern

Vase, 8 1/2" h., Fairyland Lustre, slightly tapering cylindrical body w/a flaring round foot & angled shoulder to the short trumpet neck, decorated in the Goblin patt. No. Z5367, brown goblins w/red-spotted wings standing & kneeling on green grass alongside dark blue water w/butterflies &

fairies flying above, gold Wedgwood Portland Vase mark, few glaze hairline cracks, small flake under foot (ILLUS.) **$7,475**

Fairyland Lustre Willow Pattern Bowl

Vase, 8 1/2" h., Fairyland Lustre, Willow patt., baluster-form body w/a short flaring neck, finely decorated w/violet tree trunks & flower spikes, green leaves & lanterns of red & yellow w/orange lustre that are surrounded by a view of sky & water of blue lustre over a rich bluish green shade, the houses in black w/torches of crimson & the conventional "Candle Lighthouse" on the bridge reflected in orange ripples, a group of violet gnomes shelter under black toadstool umbrellas at the base, the chestnut leaflets not hatched in gold print but have both Flame & Moonlight Fairyland Lustre, Pattern No. Z5228 (ILLUS.) **$6,900**

Willow Pattern Fairyland Lustre Vase

Vase, 10 1/4" h., Fairyland Lustre, flared foot tapering to a gently swelling tall cylindrical body w/a rounded shoulder centered by a short flaring neck, the exterior decorated in the Willow patt. w/violet tree trunks & flower spikes, green leaves & blue lustre over a rich bluish green ground, houses between trees in black w/touches of crimson & the conventional "Candle Lighthouse" on the bridge reflected in orange ripples, a group of violet gnomes shelters under black toadstool umbrellas at the base, chestnut leaflets not hatched in gold, marked w/Portland vase mark & "Wedgwood - Made in England - Z5228" (ILLUS., previous page).. **$8,625**

Very Rare Tall Fairyland Lustre Vase

Fairyland Lustre Imps on Bridge Vase

Vase, 10 1/2" h., Fairyland Lustre, tall tapering ovoid body w/a flaring foot & short flaring neck, decorated in the Imps on a Bridge patt., No. Z5360, fine flame lustre background w/Imps in red shaded w/violet, a boy in the foreground in brown w/green wings spotted w/orange while a Roc bird in green, Shape No. 3148, Wedgwood Portland Vase mark, some minor wear to gold trim inside of lip (ILLUS.)........................... **$7,475**

Vase, 11" h., Fairyland Lustre, footed squatty bulbous lower body tapering to a tall cylindrical neck w/flaring rim, decorated in the Imps on Bridge patt., No. Z5481, flame lustre background w/green Imps on a bridge, blue Roc bird & the boy done in black w/lavender wings, gold Portland Vase mark, Shape No. 3452 (ILLUS., top next column)... **$32,200**

Fairyland Lustre Tree Serpent Vase

Vase, 11" h., Fairyland Lustre, Serpent Tree patt., a flaring base tapering to a tall cylindrical body w/a flaring rim, the abstract tree & landscape design in bright colors against a flame lustre sky, base signed, Pattern No. Z4968 (ILLUS.) **$7,475**

Weller

This pottery was made from 1872 to 1945 at a pottery established originally by Samuel A. Weller at Fultonham, Ohio, and moved in 1882 to Zanesville. Numerous lines were produced, and listings below are by pattern or line.

Reference books on Weller include The Collectors Encyclopedia of Weller Pottery by Sharon & Bob Huxford (Collector Books, 1979) and All About Weller by Ann Gilbert McDonald (Antique Publications, 1989).

Weller Marks

Ardsley (1928)

Various shapes molded as cattails among rushes with water lilies at the bottom. Matte glaze.

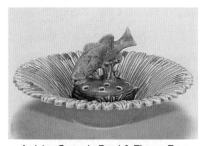

Ardsley Console Bowl & Flower Frog

Console bowl & flower frog, the widely flaring shallow round bowl molded overall w/cattails, the figural flower frong w/a large lavender blue fish above the round domed base, ink stamp marks, restoration to the fish tail & edge of bowl, bowl 12" d., 2 pcs. (ILLUS.) **$345**

Ardsley Umbrella Stand

Umbrella stand, flaring foot molded w/white water lilies, the trumpet-form body molded w/cattails, partial paper label, repaired chips, 19 1/2" h. (ILLUS.) **$316**

Ardsley Double Vase

Vase, double, 10" h., two angled clusters of cattails connected at the top by a pointed branch handle, a molded white pond lily blossom at the base, marked w/half kiln ink stamp mark (ILLUS.) **$115-130**

Aurelian (1898-1910)

Similar to Louwelsa line but with brighter colors and a glossy glaze. Features bright yellow/orange brush-applied background along with brown and yellow transparent glaze.

Weller Aurelian Ewer with Berries

Jug, footed squatty spherical body w/a short small neck w/spout, handle from rim to shoulder, decorated w/blackberries & green leaves & brown vine against a dark green shaded to golden yellow ground, artist-signed, No. 382 8, some light scratches, 5 1/4" h. (ILLUS.) **$431**

Weller Aurelian Mug with Seed Pods

Mug, flared ringed base below the tall slightly tapering sides, large C-form handle, h.p. large deep orange mountain ash seed pods w/green leaves on a long stem against a shaded dark brown & golden yellow ground, artist-signed, marked "Aurelian Weller 435," 6 1/4" h. (ILLUS.)........... **$184**

Aurelian Mug with Dark Fruits

Mug, slightly tapering cylindrical body w/a heavy C-form handle, decorated w/large very dark blue grapes w/a brown stem & green & yellow leaves against a slightly mottled dark blackish green ground, artist-signed, marked "Weller Aurelian 562 12," 6" h. (ILLUS.) **$150**

Tall Aurelian Vases with Irises

Vase, 14 3/8" h., tall ovoid body w/a rounded shoulder to the short rolled neck, h.p. deep yellow & orange-red irises on green leafy stems against the dark brown to yellow & tan ground, impressed Aurelian mark & "334," small glaze nick on edge of base, artist-signed (ILLUS.) **$1,150**

Baldin (about 1915-20)
Rustic designs with relief-molded apples and leaves on branches wrapped around each piece.

Baldin Vase with Red Apple at Base

Vase, 7" h., squatty bulbous base tapering to a tall slightly flaring cylindrical neck, twisted branch down the sides w/a red apple & green leaves at the base, unmarked (ILLUS.).. **$127**

Baldin Vase with Apples

Vase, 9 1/2" h., slightly tapering body w/a swelled shoulder & short flaring neck, molded around the top w/applies & leaves (ILLUS.) **$207**

Barcelona (1920s)

A line of simple peasant-style pieces with a golden tan background hand-painted with colorful stylized floral medallions.

Colorful Weller Barcelona Bowl

Bowl, 9" d., 2 1/8" h., wide shallow round form, h.p. center four-petal blossoms surrounded by small red blossoms & green & yellow leaves, dark green border band, original paper label (ILLUS.) **$104**

Small Weller Barcelona Vase

Vase, 6 1/2" h., flaring cylindrical lower body & angled shoulder to a wide flaring neck flanked by large loop handles, decorated w/a colorful stylized flower head in red, green, blue & yellow, marked (ILLUS.).. **$127**

Vase, 7 1/4" h., baluster-form w/a wide flat rim flanked by heavy C-form shoulder handles, Weller inkstamp mark & portion of paper label (ILLUS., top next column).... **$115**

Vase, 11 1/2" h., flat-bottomed ovoid body tapering to a short flared neck, small twisted handles at the shoulder, decorated w/a large colorful quatrefoil design, stamped mark, minor firing separation on one handle, uncrazed (ILLUS., middle next column)... **$345**

Weller Barcelona Vase

Large Weller Barcelona Vase

Bedford Glossy (ca. 1915)

Simple shapes generally molded around the top w/a band of molded blossoms in pastel colors above a dark shaded ground. Bedford Matte is a similar line with a matte finish.

Weller Bedford Glossy Vase

Vase, 8 1/4" h., slightly waisted cylindrical body w/molded alternating bluish pink & yellow blossoms around the top above a streaky dark green ground, unmarked, stilt pull on base & some minor burst glaze bubbles, overall crazing (ILLUS., previous page) **$104**

Besline (1925)
A scarce line with acid-etched decoration of Virginia Creeper vine with leaves & berries on an orange lustre ground.

Besline Urn-shaped Vase

Vase, 6 1/2" h., ovoid urn-form on a ringed pedestal base, flat rolled rim above loop handles (ILLUS.) **$345**

Blo Red (1930)
Pieces feature an orange glaze overglazed in deep red to produce a blood red mottled effect. This line shared molds with the Turkis and Nile lines.

Blo Red Vase with In-body Twist

Vase, 4 3/4" h., bulbous ovoid body w/in-body twist continuing into the wide short neck, Weller inkstamp mark (ILLUS.) **$81**

Blo Red Vase with Low Handles

Vase, 7 1/2" h., cylindrical form w/swelled angled lower body & low flared neck, low asymmetrical handles handles, tiny nick at rim, some burst glaze bubbles (ILLUS.) **$81**

Blue & Decorated Hudson (1919)
Handpainted lifelike sprays of fruit blossoms and flowers in shades of pink and blue on a rich dark blue ground.

Blue & Decorated Hudson Vase with Cherries

Vase, 9" h., slightly swelled cylindrical body tapering to a flat mouth, dark blue ground h.p. w/a green & white upper band suspending pink cherries & blue & green leaves, impressed mark (ILLUS.)
.... **$259**

Blue & Decorated Floral Cluster Vase

Vase, 9 5/8" h., a gently swelled cylindrical body w/a rounded shoulder to a short flat neck, a lighter blue shoulder band decorated w/a long trailing cluster of dark rose, pink & white blossoms & green leaves, block letter mark, crazing (ILLUS.) **$317**

Blue & Decorated Hudson Bud Vase

Vase, 10" h. bud-type, the flaring base tapering sharply to a tall slender cylindrical body, decorated around the base w/a cluster of blossoming blackberry plant, block letter mark (ILLUS.) **$184**

Tall Blue & Decorated Hudson Vase

Vase, 10 1/2" h., a disk foot below the tall cylindrical body w/a widely flaring trumpet-form top, decorated w/a long cluster of small pink & white blossoms on a green leafy stem down the side, block letter mark, light crazing (ILLUS.) **$184**

Blue Louwelsa (ca. 1905)

A high-gloss line shading from medium blue to cobalt blue with underglaze slip decorations of fruits & florals and sometimes portraits. Decorated in shades of white, cobalt and light blue slip. Since few pieces were made, they are rare and sought after today.

Vase, 9" h., simple ovoid body tapering to a short rolled neck, decorated around the upper half w/a leaf & berry leafy fine in shades of dark blue on a light blue shaded to dark blue ground, base chip (ILLUS. center with two Louwelsa vases, bottom of page) **$805**

A Blue Louwelsa & Two Louwelsa Vases

Blue Ware (before 1920)
Classical relief-molded white or cream figures on a dark blue ground.

Fancy Weller Blue Ware Jardiniere

Jardiniere, wide ovoid body on low tab feet, a wide rolled flat rim, dark blue ground w/white high-relief classical winged caryatids alternating w/floral swags above leafy scrolls & blossoms, 9 1/2" h. (ILLUS.)...................................... **$259**

Blue Ware Vase with Walking Lady

Vase, 7 1/2" h., gently tapering cylindrical shape, molded w/a walking Grecian lady holding leafy green swags, a small rose bush nearby (ILLUS.) **$184**

Bonito (1927-33)
Hand-painted florals and foliage in soft tones on cream ground. Quality of artwork greatly affects price.

Vase, 5" h., trumpet-shaped w/widely flaring top, h.p. w/a blue daisy & green leaves, artist-signed, impressed mark (ILLUS., top next column)... **$127**

Bonito Vase with Blue Daisy Decoration

Weller Bonito Urn-shaped Vase

Vase, 7" h., urn-shaped, baluster-form w/a wide flaring upper body, incurved loop handles at center of sides, h.p. w/large pansies & green leaves, artist-signed, impressed mark (ILLUS.)............................... **$127**

Brighton (1915)
Various bird or butterfly figurals colorfully decorated and with glossy glazes.

Weller Brighton Bluebird Figure

Model of a Bluebird, perched atop small leafy stump, unmarked, faint crazing, 6 5/8" h. (ILLUS., previous page) **$863**

Fine Weller Brighton Parrot on Perch

Model of parrot, green parrot w/yellow & pink bands on the wings, perched on a tall flaring & fluted perch, 7 1/2" h. (ILLUS.) **$978**

Burnt Wood (1908)
Molded designs on an unglazed light tan ground with dark brown trim. Similar to Clay-wood but no vertical bands.

Burnt Wood Mug with Owl & Elf

Mug, slightly tapering cylindrical shape w/a C-form handle, decorated w/an owl on a branch & a smiling elfin creature against a banded background, 4 3/8" h. (ILLUS.)
.... **$115**

Vase, 9" h., slender conical body w/a flaring cupped rim supported by three wing-form buttresses, incised decoration of the Magi & camels following the Christmas star, un-marked, repaired rim chip (ILLUS., top next column) **$173**

Weller Burnt Wood Vase with Magi

Chase (late 1920s)
White relief fox hunt scenes, usually on a deep blue ground.

Tall Weller Chase Vase

Vase, 11 1/2" h., a ringed foot & cylindrical sides w/a gently flaring rim, two tiny glaze inclusions at rim (ILLUS.) **$259**

Clinton Ivory (ca. 1914)
Various forms, many in Art Nouveau designs, glazed in ivory with sepia accents.

Rare Clinton Ivory Jardinieres

Three Figural Coppertone Pieces

Jardinieres & pedestals, bulbous jardinere in the Baldin patt., raised on a tall slender tree-trunk form base, signed, overall crazing, 39" h., pr. (ILLUS., previous page) **$2,300**

Coppertone (late 1920s)

Various shapes with an overall mottled bright green glaze on a "copper" glaze base. Some pieces with figural frog or fish handles. Models of frogs also included.

Coppertone Rock-form Flower Frog

Flower frog, modeled as a shaped squatty rock formation, 5 1/4" w., 2 5/8" h. (ILLUS.) **$173**

Scarce Coppertone Figural Flower Frog

Flower frog, model of lily pad bloom enclosing a seated frog, raised on a rounded footed base w/flower holes, 4 3/8" h. (ILLUS.) **$518**

Pitcher, 7 5/8" h., bulbous ovoid body w/arched spout, figural fish handle, marked, minute flake on fin (ILLUS. right with Coppertone small planter & fish vase, top of page) **$2,415**

Planter, miniature, figural frog seated holding a water lily blossom, marked, 4 1/2" h. (ILLUS. center with Coppertone fish vase and fish-handled pitcher, top of page) **$115**

Spherical Weller Coppertone Vase

Vase, 7" h., spherical shape w/closed rim & small arched side handles, unmarked (ILLUS.) **$480**

Bulbous Frog-handled Coppertone Vase

Vase, 8" h., bulbous ovoid body w/molded rim, figural frog shoulder handles, dark bronzed glaze over green, ink stamp mark, one minuscule flake (ILLUS.)........ **$1,380**

Fine Large Coppertone Vase

Vase, 8" h., bulbous ovoid body w/molded rim, figural frog shoulder handles, ink stamp mark (ILLUS.) **$2,100**

Vase, 8" h., modeled as a large fish leaping straight out of the water, on a rounded base, marked, minor flakes (ILLUS. left with small Coppertone planter & pitcher, top previous page) **$2,135**

Copra (1915)

Copra was a branch of the Hudson line and is found mainly in vases, baskets and jars. It features a smeared glaze effect with irregular, horizontal bands of dark green, brown or black over hand-painted large colorful flowers.

Tall Weller Copra Basket

Basket, four low feet support the flaring trumpet-form body w/a high arched handle, decorated w/a cluster of red & pink wild roses on a mottled green ground, impressed block letter mark, small chip on one foot, 12" h. (ILLUS.) **$115**

Cornish (1933)

Simple shapes with a mottled tan, deep rust red or dark blue ground molded near the rim with two or three long pointed leaves suspending a small cluster of blue berries.

Weller Blue Cornish Console Set

Console set: bowl & pair of short candlesticks; the 7 1/4" d., 3" h. bowl w/a wide flat bottom & upright cylindrical sides w/small rosette knob rim handles, 3 1/4" h. candlesticks w/a domed base w/small knob handles & a cylindrical socket, mottled blue, impressed script mark, the set (ILLUS.) **$196**

Ovoid Weller Cornish Vase

Vase, 7 1/4" h., large ovoid body w/tiny rosette knob shoulder handles & a short cylindrical neck, mottled rust, incised mark (ILLUS.) **$127**

Dechiwo (1908)

This was the original name for the Burnt Wood line. Since this name was hard to remember, Weller changed it to Burnt Wood in 1908. Dechiwo pieces can have a glossy or matt glaze.

Rare Green-glazed Dechiwo Vase

Vase, 6 1/2" h., a bulbous ovoid shape tapering to a thick flat molded mouth, incised w/a continuous scene of children in early 20th clothing playing beneath an upper band of green leaf clusters w/red apples at the centers, overall shaded light to dark green glossy glaze, block letter mark, a line at the rim, overall crazing (ILLUS.)... **$3,940**

Dickensware 2nd Line (early 1900s)

Various incised "sgraffito" designs, usually with a matte glaze. Quality of the artwork greatly affects price.

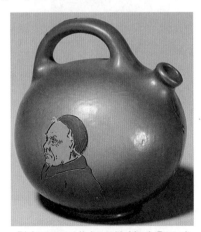

Dickensware II Jug with Monk Portrait

Jug, footed spherical body w/a top arched loop handle & small shoulder spout, decorated w/a bust portrait of a monk against a shaded green to brown ground, artist-signed, No. 300 1, 5 3/4" h. (ILLUS.) **$259**

Vase, 5" h., wide flattened ovoid form tapering to a molded rim, incised w/a scene of ducks in brown, white, green, rose & pale green impressed mark, factory flaw (ILLUS., top next column)........... **$431**

Dickensware 2nd Line Ducks Vase

Dickensware 2nd Line Pillow Vase

Vase, 8 7/8" h., pillow-type, four knob feet supporting the flattened rounded body w/a low, long oblong mouth, colorful incised design of two men in Colonial attire seated at a tavern table playing checkers, against a shaded dark green ground, signed by John Herold, incised Weller mark on base (ILLUS.).............................. **$683**

Dickensware 2nd Line Dragonfly Vase

Vase, 9" h., slightly swelled tapering cylindrical body, incised w/a large vertical dragonfly in tan & brown on a pale green matte ground, impressed mark, minor flaws (ILLUS., previous page) **$288**

Dickensware II Vase with Japanese Figures

Vase, 10 1/2" h., gently swelled ovoid body w/a rounded shoulder to a short widely flaring neck, decorated w/a Japanese peasant man bowing to a geisha, impressed & incised marks, glazed-over factory flaw (ILLUS.) **$633**

Unusual Glossy Dickensware Vase

Vase, 10 5/8" h., tall cylindrical body w/a narrow shoulder below the short cylindrical rolled neck, incised scene of a church interior w/a monk kneeling before the altar, in black, white & yellow against a dark redding brown ground, unusual glossy glaze, impressed "Dickens Ware Weller 604-7," fine overall crazing (ILLUS.) **$1,150**

Dickensware II Vase with Indian Chief

Vase, 11 1/8" h., tall ovoid body tapering to a small flaring neck, decorated w/a large bust portrait of Native American Chief Black Bear, artist-signed (ILLUS.) **$1,725**

Tall Dickensware 2nd Line Portrait Vase

Vase, 12 1/8" h., gently swelled cylindrical form w/a short flaring neck, decorated w/a large profile bust portrait of Native American Chief Jack Red Cloud, artist-signed (ILLUS.) **$1,725**
Vase, 16 1/4" h., tall ovoid body tapering to a flared rim, incised w/a colorful scene of Satan being cast out of Heaven by the Archangel Michael, all against a dark blue ground, signed by Charles Babcock Upjohn, marked on the base "X 270 1," inscribed on the side "Satan Smitten by Michael," rare (ILLUS., next page) **$3,795**

Large Rare Dickensware 2nd Line Vase

Dickensware 3rd Line (1904)
Similar to Eocean line. Various fictional characters molded and slip-painted against pale background colors. Glossy glaze.

Dickinsware Mug with Comic Man

Mug, tapering cylindrical body w/C-form handle, relief image of a skinny man wearing a floppy yellow hat, large red bow tie & blue jacket, against a dark green shaded to blue ground, light crazing, 5 1/4" h. (ILLUS.).............................. **$230**

Dickensware 3rd Line Comical Mug

Mug, two-handled, slightly waisted cylindrical form, decorated w/the head of a comical man wearing a top hat & monocle, impressed mark, fracture at rim, crazing, 3 1/2" h. (ILLUS.) **$207**

Eldora-Chelsea (pre-1920)
Pieces decorated around the upper body with a wide molded band of stylized floral rosettes in light blue and red with green leaves. The lower body molded with green-tinted vertical ribbing.

Weller Eldora-Chelsea Vase

Vase, 8 3/4" h., footed ovoid body tapering to a wide flat mouth, impressed mark, overall crazing & staining on interior (ILLUS.)......... **$104**

Eocean and Eocean Rose (1898-1925)
Early art line with various handpainted flowers on shaded grounds, usually with a clear glossy glaze. Quality of artwork varies greatly.

Squatty Weller Eocean Vase

Vase, 5 1/4" h., footed wide squatty bulbous body centered by a wide cylindrical neck w/a molded rim, decorated w/a large deep rose nasturtium blossom & green leafy vine against a very dark green shaded to cream ground, artist-signed, marked "Eocean Weller R 63 C - D 206," overall crazing (ILLUS.) **$207**

Tall Slender Weller Eocean Vase

Vase, 11 7/8" h., tall slender gently swelled cylindrical body w/a narrow shoulder to the short molded neck, decorated w/a ring of white dogwood blossoms around the shoulder against a dark green to cream ground, leans slightly (ILLUS.)........ **$288**

Tall Eocean Vase with Dogwood Blossoms

Vase, 12 1/2" h., simple ovoid body tapering to a flaring neck, decorated around the neck & shoulder w/large pink & white dogwood blossoms & green leaves on a dark blue shaded to white ground, artist-signed, factory cast hole for lamp conversion (ILLUS.) **$316**

Etched Floral (ca. 1905)
Various simple shapes decorated with incised flowers or berries outlined in black and usually against solid backgrounds in green, orange, yellow, beige, or pink.

Rare Tall Etched Floral Vase

Vase, 12 1/4" h., tall slender ovoid body w/a small flat mouth, deeply carved white & orange irises & pale green leaves against a light tan matte ground, impressed mark, overall crazing (ILLUS.) **$1,380**

Etna (1906)
Colors similar to Early Eocean line, but designs are molded in low relief and colored.

Etna Jardiniere & Pedestal with Pansies

Jardiniere & pedestal, bulbous ovoid jardiniere swelled around the top below the wide rolled rim, dark green rim shading to blue to cream, molded around the top w/red pansies on tall stems w/leaves around the base, the match pedestal w/red pansies on a dark blue shaded to cream ground, impressed mark, some minor chips, overall 24" h., 2 pcs. (ILLUS.) **$432**

Small Weller Etna Vase with Tree Decor

Vase, 4 1/2" h., a wide flattened squatty base w/a wide shoulder tapering to conical upper body, loop handles from shoulder to base of upper body, decorated w/an applied stylized dark blue tree w/thin green trunk against a grey shaded to white ground, Weller block letter mark & Etna in script, crazing (ILLUS.) **$81**

Weller Etna Vase with Large Roses

Vase, 10" h., tall slender ovoid body tapering to a short cylindrical neck, molded on the shoulder w/large deep red roses w/leafy green stem down the side, against a deep purple shaded to white shaded to pink ground, block letter mark, overall crazing (ILLUS.) **$184**

Tall Etna Vase with Thistle Decoration

Vase, 10 1/2" h., tall swelled cylindrical body w/a thin shoulder & short molded neck, decorated w/a tall thistle w/a pink blossom against a dark grey to light grey to white ground, impressed mark, ca. 1910 (ILLUS.) **$345**

Weller Etna Vase with Pink Blossoms

Vase, 11" h., ovoid body w/a bulbous neck w/closed rim, small loop handles from neck to shoulder, molded & decorated w/clusters of pink blossoms on a dark green to very pale pink ground, stamped mark, few tiny glaze nicks (ILLUS.) **$259**

Floretta (ca. 1904)

An early line with various forms molded with clusters of various fruits or flowers against a dark brown, shaded brown or sometimes a dark grey to cream ground. Usually found with a glossy glaze but sometimes with a matte glaze.

Floretta Tankard Pitcher with Grapes

Pitcher, 10 3/4" h., tankard-type, tall slightly tapering cylindrical body w/a small rim spout & D-form handle, a molded cluster of large light purple grapes against a shaded green to pink matte ground, unmarked (ILLUS.)... **$115**

Weller Floretta Vase with Grapes

Vase, 5 3/4" h., a tapering cylindrical body w/a bulbous four-lobed top w/a conforming rim, molded w/a cluster of green grapes against a dark shaded to light brown ground, marked w/Floretta Weller seal (ILLUS.) **$81**

Vase, 5 5/8" h., tapering cylindrical sides below a bulbous four-lobed top, a molded cluster of reddish purple grapes on the side against a dark green shaded to cream ground, circular Floretta Weller mark, Shape No. 10, moderate overall crazing (ILLUS., top next column)............... **$81**

Floretta Vase with Grape Cluster

Forest (mid-teens to 1928)
Realistically molded and painted forest scene.

Scarce Weller Forest Jardiniere

Jardiniere, large cylindrical form, unusual molded design of two young girls walking in a deep forest, tight high line down from rim, 10 3/4" d., 9 5/8" h. (ILLUS.).............. **$633**

Glendale (early to late 1920s)
Various relief-molded birds in their natural habitats, lifelike coloring.

Gate-form Glendale Double Bud Vase

Vase, double-bud, 4 3/4 x 8", gate-form, square shaped vases joined by openwork fence, wren & grapevine decoration (ILLUS.).. **$403**

Glendale Vase with Large Marsh Bird

Vase, 6" h., cylindrical w/narrow shoulder to a short cylindrical neck, large standing marsh bird, small chip at base (ILLUS.)..... **$374**

Glendale Vase with Marsh Bird

Vase, 6 1/2" h., footed bulbous ovoid w/flared rim, embossed w/polychrome marsh scene of marsh bird & nest (ILLUS.)...................... **$460**

Glendale Vase with Marsh Bird

Vase, 6 1/2" h., footed bulbous ovoid w/flared rim, embossed w/polychrome marsh scene of marsh bird & nest, vibrant colors (ILLUS.)................................. **$863**

Glendale Vase with Flying Bird

Vase, 6 1/2" h., ovoid body w/slightly tapering neck & a flat rim, decorated w/outdoor scene of a bird in flight (ILLUS.)................. **$460**

Glendale Bird with Nest Vase

Vase, 10" h., slender ovoid w/short rolled rim, decorated w/red & blue flowers & berries & a blue & yellow bird w/nest in tree, impressed mark (ILLUS.)................. **$748**

Greenbriar (early 1930s)
Hand-made shapes with green underglaze covered with flowing pink overglaze marbleized with maroon striping.

Greenbriar Double-gourd Vase

Vase, 7 3/4" h., slightly tapering double-gourd form body w/a wide slightly cupped neck, low asymmetrical handles down the sides, streaky green & blackish purple glaze w/overall white speckling, small grinding chip at the base, uncrazed (ILLUS.) **$69**

Greenbriar Vase with White Speckling

Vase, 7 7/8" h., footed squatty bulbous lower body w/tiny pointed handles below the tall trumpet neck, heavy white speckling on a dark purple ground w/streaked banding of green & purple around the lower body, unmarked (ILLUS.) **$58**
Vase, 7 7/8" h., footed squatty bulbous lower body w/tiny pointed handles below the tall trumpet neck, green drippy glaze over purple & speckled white on the upper body w/swirled colors on the lower body, unmarked (ILLUS., top next column) **$127**

Greenbriar Vase with Drippy Green Glaze

Greora (early 1930s)
Various shapes with a bicolor orange shaded to green glaze splashed overall with brighter green. Semigloss glaze.

Large Greora Strawberry Pot

Strawberry pot, bulbous baluster-form body w/flaring neck & half-round cupped opening around the middle of the sides, script mark & partial paper label, 8 1/4" h. (ILLUS.)... **$260**

Hobart (early to late 1920s)
Figural women, children and birds on various shaped bowls in solid pastel colors. Matte glaze.

Hobart Flying Geese Flower Frog

Flower frog, modeled as a pair of geese just taking flight, on a wide flat round base, all-white glaze, ink stamp mark, lightly crazed, 9" d., 6" h. (ILLUS., previous page) **$196**

Hudson (1917-34)
Underglaze slip-painted decoration, "parchment-vellum" transparent glaze.

Hudson Pitcher with Floral Branch

Pitcher, 6 3/4" h., wide gently rounded body w/a long pointed rim spout, long C-form handle, decorated around the sides w/a large leafy flower stem in light green & brown on a pale pink ground, glossy glaze, Weller ink stamp mark, crazing (ILLUS.) **$431**

Weller Hudson Vase with Dogwood

Vase, 6" h., gently swelled cylindrical body tapering to a flat rim, decorated w/white & pink dogwood blossoms on leafy branches against a dark blue shaded to light blue ground, artist-signed, impressed script mark (ILLUS.) **$345**

Hudson Double-Gourd Floral Vase

Vase, 6 3/8" h., double-gourd form w/curved handles from the upper body to the lower body, decorated w/large blue & pink wild roses & green leafy stems on a light green shaded to blue ground, signed by Mae Timberlake, full kiln ink stamp logo on the base (ILLUS.) **$575**

Weller Hudson Double-Gourd Vase

Vase, 6 1/2" h., spherical double-gourd shape w/a flat rim, arched handles from upper body to shoulder, decorated w/large white & blue dogwood flowers & leaves on a pale green to dark blue ground, artist-signed, impressed mark (ILLUS.) **$345**
Vase, 6 3/4" h., gently swelled cylindrical body w/a wide flat mouth, decorated w/pale yellow wild roses on leafy stems against a dark blue shaded to pale yellow ground, artist-signed, Weller script mark (ILLUS., next page) **$374**

Weller Hudson Vase with Wild Roses

Hudson Vase with Dogwood Blossoms

Vase, 6 3/4" h. swelled cylindrical body w/a flat molded rim, decorated w/large white dogwood blossoms & leafy stems on a bluish grey shaded to yellow ground, signed by Dorothy England, impressed Weller mark on base (ILLUS.)................... **$403**

Hudson Vase with Daisy Decoration

Vase, 7 1/4" h., cylindrical body tapering slightly to the flat rim, decorated w/tall white & yellow daisies on leafy green stems against a grey shaded to pink ground, impressed mark (ILLUS.)............. **$690**

Weller Hudson Vase with Lotus

Vase, 8" h., bulbous ovoid body tapering to a wide flat mouth, decorated w/white lotus blossoms & green leaves & vines on a dark green shaded to lighter green ground, impressed mark (ILLUS.)............. **$374**

Weller Hudson Vase with Dogwood

Vase, 8" h., footed ovoid body tapering to a short cylindrical neck flanked by arched handles, decorated w/large white dogwood blossoms & shaded blue & white leaves against a dark blue shaded to light blue ground, incised mark & artist-signed on the base (ILLUS.)................................. **$748**

Vase, 8 5/8" h. swelled cylindrical body w/a flat molded rim, decorated w/large yellow & white wild roses & leafy stems on a blue shaded to light green ground, signed by Hester Pillsbury, impressed Weller mark on base, light small scratch on the back **$575**

Vase, 9 3/8" h., slightly tapering tall square creamy body, a thin black rim band & a wide grey & black body band decorated w/tight scrolls in pale blue & pink, block letter mark, minor glaze bubbles, overall crazing **$317**

Weller Hudson Vase with Daisies

Vase, 9 1/2" h., slightly tapering hexagonal form w/a small rounded shoulder & short cylindrical neck, the neck & shoulder in purple shaded to pink above a fine black scalloped line above a narrow purple band trimmed w/large stylized yellow daisies all against a creamy ground, block letter mark, overall crazing (ILLUS.)........... **$230**

Vase, 9 1/2" h., tall gently swelled cylindrical body tapering at the top to a low flat rim, h.p. w/a large pale yellow & lavender iris on a tall pale green leafy stem, against a dark blue shaded to creamy matte ground, stamped mark **$575**

Hudson Vase with Trailing Floral Band

Vase, 9 5/8" h., slightly swelled cylindrical form tapering slightly to a flat rim, creamy ground h.p. around the shoulder w/narrow black bands & trailing pink, green & yellow florals, block letter mark, overall crazing (ILLUS.) **$161**

Hudson Vase with Colorful Flowers

Vase, 10" h., ovoid body tapering to a short trumpet-form neck, decorated w/large pink & yellow blossoms on tall leafy green stems, on a blue shaded to pale green ground, signed by Dorothy England (ILLUS.)... **$1,840**

Tall Handled Hudson Vase with Grapes

Vase, 10" h., urn-form, a footed bulbous lower body tapering to a very tall cylindrical neck flanked by long squared handles from the rim to the shoulder, decorated w/clusters of brown & blue grapes on a leafy stem suspended from the rim, on a pale green shaded to dark blue ground, initialed by H. Pillsbury, stamped mark (ILLUS.).. **$748**

Tall Weller Hudson Vase with Irises

Vase, 15 1/4" h., tall swelled cylindrical body tapering to a short trumpet neck, decorated w/light blue & white irises on pale green leafy stems against a dark blue shaded to pale lavender ground, artist-signed, repair to rim (ILLUS.) **$1,035**

Huge Weller Hudson Peony Vase

Vase, 23 1/8" h., very large ovoid body tapering to a short widely flaring & flattened neck, decorated w/large white, gold & pink peony blossoms on a leafy stem against a dark blue shaded to cream ground, decorated by Hester Pillsbury, ink stamp logo, a patch of bubbles & peppering on the back (ILLUS.) **$4,830**

Hudson Light (1917-34)

The same as the Hudson line except decorated in paler colors on pale backgrounds.

Hudson Light Vase with Roses

Vase, 7 1/4" h., gently swelled cylindrical form tapering to a short molded rim, decorated w/large pale yellow roses against a pale green to green ground, block letter mark (ILLUS.)... **$196**

Weller Hudson Light Vase with Pansies

Vase, 8" h., footed tapering cylindrical body w/a paneled lower body, decorated around the rim w/a circle of pale blue & pink pansies against a pale green to cream ground, impressed block letter mark, crazing (ILLUS.)............................... **$230**

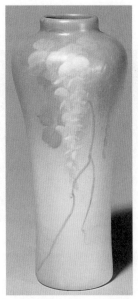

Hudson Light Vase with Hydrangeas

Vase, 9" h., tall slender ovoid body w/a short flared neck, decorated w/white & pale purple hydrangea blossoms around the shoulder against a pale blue to cream ground, unmarked (ILLUS.)........................ **$230**

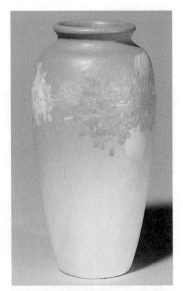

Hudson Light Tall Vase with Wisteria

Vase, 10 1/4" h., a tall slender cylindrical lower body swelled to a bulbous shoulder below the short cylindrical neck, decorated w/white wisteria blossoms & leaves against a light blue to pale pink ground, artist-signed, block Weller mark (ILLUS.) .. **$316**

Ivory (1910 to late 1920s)
Ivory-colored body with various shallow embossed designs with rubbed-on brown highlights.

Ivory Jardiniere with Rose Clusters

Jardiniere, a wide bulbous body raised on four small scroll feet, the wide molded rim flanked by looped scroll handles, the sides embossed w/short & long pendent clusters of roses, marked in block letters, 7 1/2" h. (ILLUS.) **$110**

Jewell & Cameo Jewell (about 1910-15)
Similar to the Etna line but most pieces molded with a band of raised oval 'jewels' or jew-

Weller Hudson Light Vase with Dogwood

Vase, 9 1/8" h., gently swelled cylindrical body w/a wide flat mouth, decorated around the top half w/a band of large white & pink dogwood blossoms on a very pale green to cream ground, impressed Weller mark, a few pepper spots, crazing (ILLUS.).............................. **$184**

els and cameo portraits in color against a light or
dark shaded ground.

Weller Cameo Jewel Jardiniere

Jardinere, a scalloped, molded base on a
flaring wide body w/an indented neck
band & thick molded rim, dark green to
light green ground, few glaze chips at
base, crazed, 6 7/8" h., 8" d. (ILLUS.)
.... **$150-$200**

Klyro (early to late '20s)
*Most pieces feature molded wood framing
around panels topped by double pink blossoms
and dark purple berries against a finely ribbed
ground, often trimmed in tan, brown, cream or
olive green.*

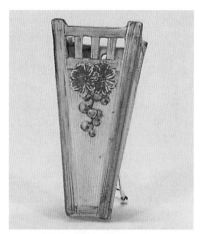

Weller Klyro Wall Pocket

Wall pocket, long tapering rectangular form
w/an openwork fence top band above a
pair of deep rose molded blossoms
above a cluster of blue berries, green
ground, overall crazing, 7 1/2" l. (ILLUS.)
.... **$115**

Knifewood (late teens)
*Pieces feature deeply molded designs of dogs,
swans, and other birds and animals or flowers in
white or cream against dark brown grounds.*

Scarce Knifewood Mug with Dogs

Tumbler, slightly flaring cylindrical shape,
etched w/two panels showing a hunting
dog in a landscape w/trees & grass, over-
all green wash, 3 1/8" h. (ILLUS.) **$259**

Knifewood Wall Pocket with Daisies

Wall pocket, bullet-shaped w/flat rim, large
Shasta daisies on green leafy stems
against a finely ribbed tan ground, light
crazing, 8 1/4" l. (ILLUS.) **$207**

L'Art Nouveau (1903-04)
*Various figural and floral-embossed Art Nou-
veau designs.*

Vase, 10 1/4" h., slender four-sided body
w/a floral-embossed four-lobed rim
above embossed panels of flowers & Art
Nouveau woman, impressed "Weller" in
small block letters (ILLUS., next page) **$546**

L'Art Nouveau Four-sided Vase

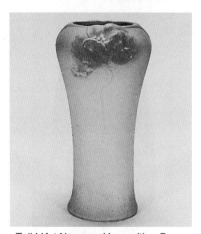

Tall L'Art Nouveau Vase with a Poppy

Vase, 11 5/8" h., tall cylindrical lower body below the wide swelled top curving to a closed rim, the rim molded w/a large orange poppy blossom, the rim & base in pale green shading to a pinkish cream ground, impressed round mark, slight discoloration above the base; (ILLUS.)..... **$230**

Vase, 12 1/2" h., tall cylindrical lower body below the wide swelled top curving to a closed rim, the rim molded w/a large orange poppy blossom, the rim & base in pale green shading to a pinkish cream ground, impressed mark (ILLUS., top next column).. **$460**

Tall L'Art Nouveau Vase with a Poppy

Lamar (1923)

A metallic luster ware in a deep red decorated with black luster scenery. Never marked except with a paper label.

Tall Lamar Vase with Slender Trees

Vase, 11 1/2" h., slender tall ovoid body tapering to a short flaring neck, deep red ground decorated w/tall slender black leafy trees, minor wear (ILLUS.) **$259**

Lasa (1920-25)

Various landscapes on a banded reddish and gold iridescent ground. Lack of scratches and abrasions important.

Vase, 5 3/4" h., swelled cylindrical body w/a wide flat molded mouth, decorated w/a mountainous landscape w/tall fir trees in the foreground, banded iridescent background, faintly marked, minor scratch (ILLUS., next page) **$575**

Lasa Vase with Mountain Landscape

Lasa Vase with Tree Decoration

Vase, 8 5/8" h., swelled cylindrical body tapering to a flaring trumpet neck, decorated w/a tall leafy tree against a banded iridescent background in shades of deep rose, gold, blue & pink, signed on the side (ILLUS.) **$547**

Vase, 9" h., swelled cylindrical body w/a low molded flat mouth, tall black silhouetted trees against a banded background in shades of red, gold & green, marked **$1,610**

Fine Lasa Vase with Palm Trees

Vase, 9 1/4" h., footed bulbous ovoid body tapering sharply to a small flat mouth, tropical scene of tall green palm trees against a banded iridescent ground in gold, deep rose, purple & blue, some minor scratches (ILLUS.) **$978**

Tall Lasa Vase with Fir Trees

Vase, 11 3/8" h., footed tall slender swelled cylindrical body, decorated w/very tall fir trees in the foreground & hills in the distance, on a banded iridescent ground, several scratches on lower body (ILLUS.) .. **$575**

Very Tall Lasa Vase with Slender Trees

Vase, 16" h., tall gently swelled cylindrical body tapering to a trumpet neck, decorated w/a continuous scene of very tall slender trees w/leafy tops, hills is the distance, signed on the side, on a banded iridescent ground, black painted notation on the bottom "$37.50," very minor scratches (ILLUS.) **$2,070**

Pair of Slender Lasa Vases

Vases, 6 1/8" h., tall slender tapering body decorated w/a very tall fir tree against a shaded iridescent ground, signed near the foot, minor scratches, pr. (ILLUS.) **$345**

Lonhuda Faience (1894-1895)

William Long, founder of the Lonhuda Pottery, joined the Weller Pottery with this line in 1894. It was a hand-decorated Standard Glaze ware very similar to Rookwood pottery of that era. After Long left Weller, they introduced the Louwelsa and Aurelian lines to take its place.

Weller Lonhuda Faience Ewer

Ewer, short squatty bulbous body tapering to a short neck w/widely rolled tri-lobed rim & delicate C-scroll handle, decorated w/deep red tulips & green leaves against a dark green shaded to a mottled yellow & orange ground, Lonhuda shield mark, initialed by decorator, overall crazing, 8 7/8" h. (ILLUS.) **$805**

Squatty Weller Lonhuda Powder Box

Powder box, cov., squatty rounded double-lobed box w/conforming domed cover, the cover decorated w/orange blossoms & green leafy stems on a shaded dark green to yellow & orange ground, mottled dark green & orange box, Lonhuda block letter & shield mark, Shape No. 209, fine overall crazing, 2 1/2" h. (ILLUS.) **$490**

Louella (ca. 1915)

This line featured pieces molded with a vertical linenfold effect and covered in a greyish tan glaze accented with dark brown trim. Most pieces were further decorated with hand-painted floral designs.

Weller Louella Vase with Flowers

Vase, 7 7/8" h., footed ovoid body tapering to a widely flaring ruffled rim, a thin rope band around the neck & molded ring handles at the sides, decorated w/white blossoms on branches w/colorful leaves, impressed Weller mark (ILLUS.).................... **$173**

Louwelsa (1896-1924)

Handpainted underglaze slip decoration on dark brown shading to yellow ground; glossy yellow glaze.

Small Louwelsa Ewer with Daffodil

Ewer, squatty bulbous body tapering to a flat base & to a slender flaring neck w/a tricorner rim & long applied strap handle, decorated w/a pale yellow daffodil & green leaves on a dark green to yellow ground, artist-signed, numbered 9 x 65 1, some glaze bubbles & small chips, 5" h. (ILLUS.) **$138**

Weller Louwelsa Ewer with Dogwood

Ewer, footed bulbous tapering ovoid body w/a slender neck & large flared tricorner rim, applied loop handle from neck to shoulder, h.p. decoration of white dogwood blossoms & light green leaves on a dark green shaded ground, No. 431, two glaze-only chips on spout, 8 1/2" h. (ILLUS.) **$138**

Weller Louwelsa Jug with Ear of Corn

Jug, squatty waisted cylindrical body w/a rounded shoulder to the small flared neck, applied loop shoulder handle, h.p. w/an ear of corn in yellow w/green leaves against a dark green to dark yellow ground, artist-signed, numbered 614-3, 5 1/2" h. (ILLUS.) **$259**

Vase, 10 1/4" h., a wide cushion base tapering sharply to a tall slender trumpet neck, decorated around the lower body w/a leaf & berry design on a very dark green ground, Shape No. 325, minor scratches (ILLUS. right with Blue Louwelsa & large Louwelsa vase, bottom of page 680)
.... **$175**

Two Large, Unusual Louwelsa Vases

Vase, 12 1/4" h., tall ovoid body tapering to a small flaring neck w/flattened rim, decorated w/a portrait of a small Benji-esque dog against a dark brown shaded to dark gold ground, signed by Lisabeth Black, marked "Louwelsa Weller K 539 2" & w/partial factory sticker, crazing (ILLUS. lower left with Indian portrait vase).......... **$1,150**

Vase, 13" h., large ovoid body tapering to a short trumpet neck, decorated w/a large golden yellow & orange iris on tall pale green leafy stems against a shaded dark green ground, rim chip (ILLUS. left with Blue Louwelsa & slender Louwelsa vase, bottom of page 680) **$345**

Vase, 13 5/8" h., wide ovoid body w/a rounded shoulder & short rolled neck, decorated w/a fine half-length portrait of a Native American chief in full regalia, signed by Anthony Dunlavy in 1901, marked "Weller Louwelsa 11 - K 227 5," crack at neck, overall crazing (ILLUS. upper right with dog portrait vase, above)... **$2,185**

Vase, 14" h., a tall flat-based ovoid body w/a rounded shoulder to the short, wide rolled neck, painted w/a large Rembrandt-style half-length portrait of a cavalier wearing a large plumed hat & lacy cravat, against a shaded light green to gold to dark brown ground, artist-signed by Levi Burgess, base drilled, early 20th c. (ILLUS., top next column).. **$823**

Vase, 15 1/8" h., large bulbous ovoid body tapering to a short flaring neck, decorated w/a dark golden yellow owl perched on a branch & ready to pounce down on two small mice below, all against a very dark brown to tan ground, signed by Ed Abel, Louwelsa Weller logo, Shape No. 506, light crazing (ILLUS., bottom next column) **$2,990**

Rare Weller Louwelsa Portrait Vase

Large Louwelsa Vase with Owl & Mice

Manhattan (early 1930s-'34)
Simple modern shapes embossed with stylized leaves or leaves and blossoms and glazed in shades of green or brown.

Unusual Weller Manhattan Vase

Vase, 6" h., gently flaring cylindrical body w/a wide flaring rim, molded around the bottom w/stylized flowers growing along a latticework fence, covered w/an iridescent metallic glaze, Weller script mark & "D 977 - TK" in blue slip (ILLUS.) **$805**

Marbleized (Bo Marblo, 1915)

Simple shapes with swirled "marbleized" clays, usually in browns and blues.

Tall Slender Weller Marbleized Vase

Vase, 10" h., a flaring ruffled foot tapering to a very tall slender body w/a tiny mouth, overall long streaks in shades of brown, orange & green, impressed Weller mark, crazing (ILLUS.) **$173**

Marengo (1926)

A line of lustre-decorated wares with orange, lavender, blue, green or pink background painted with stylized trees and landscapes in darker colors.

Cylindrical Weller Marbleized Vase

Vase, 9" h., tall slightly tapering cylindrical form, overall swirled black, grey & rose glaze, impressed Weller mark (ILLUS.) **$288**

Marengo Wall Pocket with Trees

Wall pocket, long conical shape in deep orange lustre decorated w/tall stylized trees & distant hills in dark reddish brown outlined w/white, 8 3/4" l. (ILLUS.) **$259**

Marvo (mid-1920s-'33)

Molded overall fern and leaf design on various matte background colors.

Marvo Vase with Chinese Red Glaze

Vase, 6 1/2" h., flaring ovoid body w/a wide angled shoulder to the short flaring neck, deeply molded design w/a Chinese Red Chengtu glaze, Weller inkstamp mark (ILLUS.).. **$115**

Ovoid Marvo Vase with Flaring Mouth

Vase, 7 1/4" h., ovoid body w/angled upper body to the wide flaring mouth, tan & green mottled glaze, unmarked (ILLUS.)..... **$69**

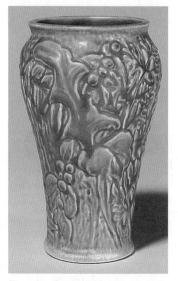

Tapering Ovoid Weller Marvo Vase

Vase, 7" h., a wide flat mouth above a tapering ovoid body, mottled tan & green glaze, Weller inkstamp mark (ILLUS.)........ **$104**

Very Tall Marvo Trumpet-form Vase

Vase, 20" h., floor-type, a flaring base tapering to a very tall trumpet-form body, relief-molded foliate decoration under matte butterscotch & green glazes, partial paper label, minor glaze rim flake (ILLUS.) **$288**

Matt Green (ca. 1904)

Various shapes with slightly shaded dark green matte glaze and molded with leaves and other natural forms.

Small Weller Matt Green Jardiniere

Jardiniere, four knob feet supporting the slightly tapering hexagonal body w/a thick molded rim, molded swirling poppy flowers & vines around the sides, tiny chip on one foot, 3 5/8" h. (ILLUS.)............ **$230**

Unusual Matt Green Vase with Thistles

Vase, 13 1/2" h., tall simple ovoid body w/a short cylindrical neck, molded overall w/thistles on leafy stems, unmarked (ILLUS.)... **$720**

Muskota (1915 - late 1920s)
Figural pieces with human figures, birds, animals or frogs. Matte glaze.

Muskota Frog & Lotus Flower Frog

Flower frog, figural frog emerging from a lotus blossom, block letter mark, crazing, 4 1/2" h. (ILLUS.) **$230**

Nile (1929)
Heavy designs covered with a fine streaky and drippy bluish green glaze shading from deep green to teal blue.

Fine Matt Green Vase with Buttresses

Vase, 9 5/8" h., ovoid body tapering to a ring-molded rim w/four buttress handles down the sides, lightly molded design around the sides, fine hairline at rim, glaze skip near base, uncrazed, unmarked (ILLUS.)... **$500**

Weller Nile Handled Vase

Vase, 6 7/8" h., bulbous ovoid body tapering to a flat mouth flanked by long loop handles to the shoulder, fine streaky glaze (ILLUS.) **$92**

Noval (about 1920)
Pieces feature a white background with narrow black bordering and applied roses or fruit. Glossy glaze.

Weller Noval Coupe-shaped Vase

Vase, 7 3/4" h., tall slender coupe-shaped body w/flaring stem mounted w/three

long black loop handles, applied red rose buds & green leaves near the rim, crazing (ILLUS.) **$92**

Roba (mid-late 1930s)
Various shapes with molded panels or swirled ridges and various molded flower sprigs on shaded blue, green or tan grounds.

Roba Three-Piece Console Set

Console set: 10 1/2" l. bowl & a pair of double candleholders; the oblong bowl w/scrolled & serpentine rim above a molded yellow blossom above green pad leafform foot, the candleholders w/a serpentine scroll base mounted w/two sockets joined by a small arched handle, white shaded to green glazes, the set (ILLUS.).... **$127**

Rochelle (1920s)
A line of Hudson pieces with a shaded dark brown ground hand-painted with various colorful flowers including roses, dogwood, tulips, lilies and grapes.

Floral-decorated Rochelle Vase

Vase, 7 1/8" h., a flared foot & gently swelled cylindrical body with a widely flaring rim, h.p. around the shoulder w/a band of stylized blossoms in white & lavender on green stems w/long leaves, signed by Sarah Reid McLaughlin, impressed Weller mark (ILLUS.).................... **$500**

Roma (1912-late '20s)
Cream-colored ground decorated with embossed floral swags, bands or fruit clusters.

Weller Roma Flowerport

Flowerpot, tapering cylindrical sides w/a wide molded fruit & leaf band below the wide rolled & gadrooned tan-tinted rim, crazing, 5 1/2" h. (ILLUS.)............................ **$92**

Weller Roma Square Planter

Planter, low square form w/concave sides molded w/rose swags & molded at each corner w/a tan lion head holding a ring, removable liner, impressed mark, 6 3/8" w., 3 3/8" h. (ILLUS.)......................... **$69**

Sabrinian (late '20s)
Seashell body with sea horse handle. Pastel colors. Matte finish. Middle period.

Sabrinian Double-Bud Vase

Vase, double-bud, 6 1/2" h., a round sea-weed-molded base supporting to tall pointed shells joined at the top by an arched handle (ILLUS.)............................ **$127**

Sicardo (1902-07)
Various shapes with iridescent glaze of metallic shadings in greens, blues, crimson, purple or coppertone decorated with vines, flowers, stars or freeform geometric lines.

Small Sicardo Vase with Daisies

Vase, 3 7/8" h., squatty cushion base below the tapering cylindrical sides w/a small flat mouth, overall abstract design of daisies & scrolling leaves, iridescent green & purple glaze, signed on the side (ILLUS.) **$633**

Squatty Sicardo Vase with Clover Leaves

Vase, 4 1/2" h., wide squatty lobed body tapering to a flat mount flanked by small knob shoulder handles, decorated overall w/stylized clover leaves & dots in a purplish iridescent glaze, signed on the side, very tiny grinding chips on bottom (ILLUS.).. **$863**

Fine Sicardo Vase with Shell-like Flowers

Vase, 7 3/8" h., tall tapering melon-lobed body w/a tiny mouth, decorated overall w/a repeating design of cockle shell-like blossoms on stems, signed on the side, deep iridescent purple & gold glaze (ILLUS.) **$3,450**

Simple Cylindrical Sicardo Vase

Vase, 10 3/4" h., simple cylindrical form w/a flat molded mouth, bluish green irides-cent glazed w/golden-copper leaf design, Shape No. 602 (ILLUS) **$518**

Silvertone (1928)
Various flowers, fruits or butterflies molded on a pale purple-blue matte pebbled ground.

Vase, 6 3/8" h., footed bulbous ovoid body w/wide flaring rim & small loop handles at shoulder, decorated w/relief-molded grape clusters & leaves, ink stamp (ILLUS., top next column) **$230**

Vase, 6 1/2" h., ovoid form tapering sharply at the shoulder to a flared neck flanked by arched handles to shoulder, decorat-ed w/large black-eyed Susans, ink stamp mark (ILLUS., middle next column)............ **$230**

Silvertone Vase with Molded Grapes

Silvertone Vase with Black-eyed Susans

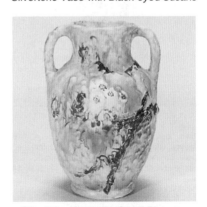

Silvertone Vase with Small Blossoms

Vase, 7 3/4" h., ovoid body tapering to a short cylindrical neck flanked by handles from rim to shoulder, molded cluster of stylized deep rose & white blossoms & green leaves w/a brown branches against a pale lavender ground, ink stamp mark, crazing (ILLUS.) **$260**

Weller Silvertone Vase with Calla Lilies

Vase, 10 1/2" h., trumpet-form, molded w/white calla lilies, ink-stamped mark (ILLUS.) **$316**

Tall Silvertone Vase with Poppies

Vase, 11 3/4" h., ovoid body tapering down to a flared base, the wide mouth w/a deeply ruffled rim, thick shoulder handles, large stylized pink poppies & green leaves w/a yellow butterfly against the pale lavender ground, inkstamp mark, some dry crazing (ILLUS.) **$432**

Souevo (1907-10)
Unglazed redware bodies with glossy black interiors. The exterior decorated with black & white American Indian geometric designs.

Vase, 3" h., squatty bulbous form tapering to a flat mouth, wide white upper band decorated w/black half-circles & arches, unmarked, some staining, couple of minor glaze nicks, uncrazed (ILLUS., top next column) **$115**

Small Weller Souevo Squatty Vase

Vase, 7" h., bulbous ovoid body w/short cylindrical neck, decorated w/Native American designs in black & white of stepped cross devices centered by a small diamond-shaped checkerboard , dark brown neck & base band, unmarked, minor rim flakes **$220**

Ovoid Signed Weller Souevo Vase

Vase, 8 1/2" h., ovoid body tapering to a flat rim, wide white body band decorated w/black abstract geometric design, impressed Weller mark, minor abrasions (ILLUS.)... **$173**

Tall Waisted Weller Souevo Vase

Vase, 11 7/8" h., tall waisted cylindrical form, decorated w/a band of triangles in white & white & vertical bands of graduated black triangles, unmarked (ILLUS., previous page) **$173**

Sydonia (1931)
Pleated blossom or fan shapes on a leaf-molded foot. Mottled blue or dark green glaze.

Weller Sydonia Footed Bowl

Bowl, 6 1/2" l., 2" h., rectangular green foot supporting a long shallow flaring & ribbed blue bowl, script mark (ILLUS.) **$58**

Pair of Blue Weller Sydonia Vases

Vases, 5 1/4" h., forked fan shape w/pleated sides, mottled blue body on green rectangular foot, marked, pr. (ILLUS.). **$75-$100**

Turada (1897)
Turada was an early ware used to produce lamps, mugs, vases and various other decorative items. The dark glossy background was glazed in shades of brown, orange, blue, olive green and claret and highlighted with applied bands of delicate ivory or white pierced scrolling. Pieces were often marked with the line name.

Velva (1933)
Simple forms with a dark green, blue or shaded tan ground decorated with a full-length rectangular panel down the side molded in low-relief with large stylized green leaves & small creamy blossoms.

Tall Weller Velva Covered Urn

Urn, cov., footed tall ovoid body w/small scroll shoulder handles, short cylindrical neck w/a fitted high domed cover w/button finial, shaded tan, impressed script mark, 11" h. (ILLUS.) **$260**

Weller Velva Ovoid Vase

Vase, 6" h., footed bulbous ovoid body tapering to a low rolled mouth, small curled handles at the sides, vertical band of stylized leaves & flowers, shaded tan ground, Weller script mark, uncrazed (ILLUS.) **$138**

White & Decorated Hudson (1917-34)
A version of the Hudson line usually with dark colored floral designs against a creamy white ground.

Decorated Hudson Vase with Berries

Vase, 8 1/2" h., slightly tapering cylindrical body w/a flat rim, decorated around the rim w/swirled green leaves & stems suspending clusters of pink & lavender berries against a white background, impressed Weller mark (ILLUS.).................... **$345**

Decorated Hudson Vase with Blossoms

Vase, 9" h., gently swelled ovoid body tapering to a flat molded mouth, decorated w/a large limb w/clusters of deep pink applied blossoms & pale green leaves on the white ground, impressed Weller mark (ILLUS.).. **$288**

Decorated Hudson Vase with Nasturtiums

Vase, 9 3/8" h., cylindrical body w/a wide flat mouth, a thin dark blue rim band above a wide band w/stylized nasturtium blossoms & leaves against a green band, impressed block Weller mark, a few blue streaks near the base (ILLUS.)................. **$288**

Woodcraft (1917)
Rustic designs simulating the appearance of stumps, logs and tree trunks. Some pieces are adorned with owls, squirrels, dogs and other animals. Matte finish.

Woodcraft (1917)

White & Decorated Hudson Vase

Vase, 9 3/8" h., bulbous bottom tapering to a cylindrical neck, decorated w/Virginia Creeper in shades of blue, pink & green against two body bands & a cream ground, unmarked (ILLUS.)........................ **$374**

Woodland Mug with Small Foxes

Mug, slightly tapering cylindrical molded tree trunk form w/three small foxes peaking out of an opening, forked tree branch handle, impressed mark, 6" h. (ILLUS.)..... **$322**

Woodcraft Planter with Mushroom Handle

Planter, wide low cylindrical log form w/molded yellow jonquils & a molded mushroom handle on one side, impress mark, minor flaws, 9 1/2" w., 5 1/8" h. (ILLUS.) **$184**

Zona Baby Ware Small Pitcher

Fine Tall Zona Vase with Scenic Panels

Vase, 10" h., slightly swelled cylindrical body w/a narrow flared blue rim, the sides divided into tall arched panels, each incised w/a design of plump birds perched in leafy grapevines w/foxes circling below, minor surface flakes (ILLUS.) **$1,035**

Woodcraft Wall Pocket with Owl

Wall pocket, long flattened trumpet form molded as a tree trunk w/molded leaves near the base & a round opening showing the head of an owl near the top, 11" l. (ILLUS.) .... **$250-$350**

Zona (1911 to 1936)

Red apples and green leaves on brown branches, all on a cream-colored ground; some pieces with molded florals or birds with various glazes. A line of children's dishes was also produced featuring hand-painted or molded animals. This is referred to as the "Zona Baby Ware."

Zona (about 1920)

Pitcher, 4" h., Baby Ware, tapering cylindrical body w/an arched rim spout & loop handle, cream ground w/a seated brown rabbit looking up at a bluebird on a leafy branch, impressed script mark (ILLUS., top next column) **$69**

Wheatley Pottery

Thomas J. Wheatley was one of the original founders of the art pottery movement in Cincinnati, Ohio, in the early 1880s. In 1879 the Cincinnati Art Pottery was formed, and after some legal problems it operated under the name T.J. Wheatley & Company. Its production featured Limoges-style handpainted decorations, and most pieces were carefully marked and often dated.

In 1882 Wheatley dissociated himself from the Cincinnati Art Pottery and opened another pottery, which was destroyed by fire in 1884. Around 1900 Wheatley finally resumed making art pottery in Cincinnati, and in 1903 he founded the Wheatley Pottery Company with a new partner, Isaac Kahn.

The new pottery from this company featured colored matte glazes over relief work designs; green, yellow and blue were the most often used colors. There were imitations of the well-known Grueby Pottery wares as well as artware, garden pottery and architectural pieces. Artwork was apparently not made much after 1907. This plant was destroyed by fire in 1910 but was rebuilt and run by Wheatley until his death in 1917. Wheatley artware was generally unmarked except for a paper label.

Wheatley Marks

Tall Green Handled Wheatley Vase

Vase, 17 3/4" h., tall slightly tapering cylindrical body w/a wide rolled rim issuing four long rope-like handles down the sides, fine matte green glaze, base marked "TWP - 606 - B," small chip low on body (ILLUS.) **$3,040**

Willow Wares

This pseudo-Chinese pattern has been used by numerous firms throughout the years. The original design is attributed to Thomas Minton about 1780, and Thomas Turner is believed to have first produced the ware during his tenure at the Caughley works. The blue underglaze transfer print pattern has never been out of production since that time. An Oriental landscape incorporating a bridge, pagoda, trees, figures and birds supposedly tells the story of lovers fleeing a cruel father who wished to prevent their marriage. The gods, having pity on them, changed them into birds, enabling them to fly away and seek their happiness together.

Blue

Ashtray, figural whale, ca. 1960, Japan.... **$40-$45**
Ashtray, round, unmarked, American **$1**

Rare Early Blue Willow Baby Feeder

Baby feeder, flat boat-shaped w/top opening, unmarked, early 19th c. (ILLUS.)
.... **$600-$700**
Bank, figural, stacked pigs, ca. 1960, Japan, 7" h. .... **$50-$55**
Batter jug, frosted glass, Hazel Atlas Glass, 9" h. .... **$100-$125**
Batter jug, Moriyama, Japan, 9 1/2" h.. **$125-$150**
Bell, modern, Enesco, Japan .... **$20-$25**
Bone dish, ca. 1890, unmarked, England **$40-$45**

Blue Willow Bone Dish

Bone dish, Buffalo Pottery, 6 1/2" l. (ILLUS.)
.... **$60-$70**
Bowl, berry, Allertons, England .... **$12-$15**
Bowl, berry, Japan .... **$6-$8**
Bowl, berry, milk glass, Hazel Atlas Glass Company .... **$12-$15**
Bowl, cereal, Royal China Co. **$11**

Doulton Blue Willow "Rose Bowl"

Bowl, flat-bottomed "rose bowl," Royal Doulton, England (ILLUS.) .... **$150-$175**

Spode Blue Willow Bowl in Stand

Bowl, round, serving-type w/fluted rim, in fitted silver plate stand w/swing handle & wooden grip, Spode, England (ILLUS.)
.... **$200-$225**

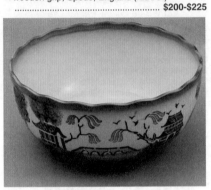

Blue Willow Stenciled Bowl

Bowl, 6 5/8" d., round w/scalloped rim, stenciled pattern (ILLUS.) .... **$75-$85**
Bowl, soup, 8" d., round, Japan .... **$18-$20**
Bowl, 12 1/4" d., serving-type w/beaded rim
.... **$50-$75**
Bowls, 8", 9 1/4" & 10 1/2" l., rectangular, stacking-type, Ridgways, set of 3.............. **$200**
Box, cov., model of a miniature piano, modern... **$5-$10**
Box, cov., tin, upright w/slanted hinged cover, rectangular w/bowed front, 6" h. (ILLUS., top next column) .... **$75-$100**
Butter dish, cov., round domed cover, Allerton, England, 8" d......................... **$100-$125**
Butter dish, ceramic insert in wood holder, 6" d.. **$50-$60**
Butter dish, cov., rectangular, for stick, Japan, 7" l. .... **$40-$50**
Butter dish, drain & cover, cov., square, Ridgways, England .... **$100-$125**
Butter dish, drain & cover, Ridgways, 3 pcs... **$200**
Butter pat, Buffalo Pottery **$2**
Butter pat, Carlton/Grindley Hotel, 3" .... **$20-$25**
Butter warmer, server & candleholder, black stand, Japan .... **$50-$60**
Cake plate, Green & Co., 8" sq................ **$40-$45**
Candle & napkin set, in box, Alladin, Denmark, the set .... **$25-$30**

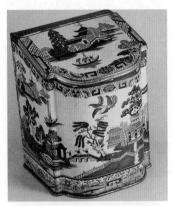

Blue Willow Tin Box with Hinged Cover

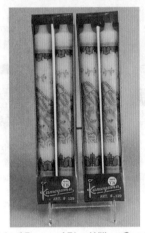

Pair of Boxes of Blue Willow Candles

Candles, sealed in original box, Kameyama, mid-20th c., pr. of boxes (ILLUS.).. **$20-$25**
Canister set: cov., "Coffee," "Flour," "Sugar," "Tea," barrel-shaped, ca. 1960s, Japan, the set .... **$175-$200**
Chamber pot, Wedgwood, 9" d. .... **$125-$150**

Modern Blue Willow Chamberstick

Chamberstick, dished base w/S-scroll rim handle, shaped center socket, Cardew Blue, modern (ILLUS.) .... **$25-$30**

Blue Willow Cracker Jar

Cracker jar, cov., silver lid & handle, Minton, England, 5" h. (ILLUS.) .... **$150-$175**
Creamer, Allerton, England....................... **$35-$40**
Creamer, cow-shaped, unmarked, England, mid-19th c............................. **$400-$500**

Blue Willow Cow-shaped Creamer

Creamer, cow-shaped, W. Kent, England, 1950s (ILLUS.)................................. **$250-$300**
Creamer, individual, Shenango China Co. **$25-$30**
Creamer, John Steventon **$3**
Cruets w/original stoppers, oil & vinegar, Japan, 6" h., the set .... **$45-$50**
Cup, farmer's mug, Japan, 4" h................. **$12-$15**
Cup & saucer, Booths, England .... **$35-$40**
Cup & saucer, Buffalo Pottery .... **$35-$40**
Cup & saucer, child's, ca. 1900, unmarked, England.. **$40-$50**

Willow Oatmeal/Bouillon Cup & Saucer

Cup & saucer, cov., oatmeal/bouillon, double-handled, Gibson, the set (ILLUS.)... **$50-$60**
Cup & saucer, demitasse, Copeland, England .... **$35-$40**
Cup & saucer, Japan................................. **$7-$10**
Cup & saucer, oversized, "For Auld Lang Syne," W. Adams, England .... **$75-$100**
Drainer, butter, ca. 1890, England, 6" sq........ **$50**

Early Blue Willow Platter Drainer

Drainer, platter, oval, impressed Davenport mark, England, 9 3/4 x 13 3/4" (ILLUS.)
.... **$200-$250**
Dresser box, cov., Gibson, 3 1/2" h. .... **$100-$125**
Egg cup, Allertons, England, 4 1/2" h....... **$45-$50**
Egg cup, Booths, England, 4" h............... **$45-$50**
Fish set, fork & knife blue Willow handles, in original box, the set.......................... **$175-$200**
Ginger jar, cov., Japan, 5" h.................... **$30-$35**
Ginger jar, cov., Mason's, 9" h. .... **$60-$75**
Gravy boat, Buffalo Pottery .... **$75-$85**

Blue Willow Gravy Boat

Gravy boat, ca. 1890, unmarked, England, 7" l. (ILLUS.) .... **$45-$50**
Gravy boat w/attached underplate, double-spouted, Ridgways, England .... **$50-$60**

Allertons Double-Spouted Gravy Boat

Gravy boat w/attached underplate, round, double-spouted, Allertons, England (ILLUS.)................................... **$125-$150**
Hot pot, electric, w/cord, Japan, 6" h. .... **$60-$75**
Juice reamer, modern, China.................. **$12-$15**

English Blue Willow Ladle with Pattern in Bowl

Knife rest, ca. 1860, unmarked, England . **$75-$85**
Ladle, pearlware, pattern inside & outside
   bowl, unmarked, England, 6" l. (ILLUS.,
   top of page).. **$125-$150**
Lamp, w/ceramic shade, Japan, 8" h. ...... **$50-$60**
Lamp, Wedgwood, England, 10" h........ **$200-$225**
Lighter, teacup-shaped, Japan................. **$35-$40**

Blue Willow Mug

Mug, barrel-shaped mold, Granger &
   Worcester, England, ca. 1850, 4 1/4" h.
   (ILLUS.)... **$200-$250**

Willow Ware Mug

Mug, Maling, England, 4 1/2" h. (ILLUS.)......... **$50**
Mustache cup & saucer, Hammersley &
   Co. .... **$90-$100**

Blue Willow Mustard Pot

Mustard pot, cov., ca. 1870, unmarked, England, 3" h. (ILLUS.) .... **$90-$100**
Napkin holder, Japan............................... **$45-$50**

Blue Willow Nut Dish

Nut dish, scalloped shape, ca. 1900, 7" l.
   (ILLUS.)... **$75-$85**
Pepper pot, ca. 1870, England, 4" h., each
   (ILLUS. of four different styles, below) **$90-$100**

Group of Early Blue Willow Pepper Pots

Willow Ware Pepper Shaker

Pepper shaker, figural Toby, "Prestopan," unmarked, Scotland, 5 1/4" h. (ILLUS.)
.... **$225-$250**
Pie bird, modern .... **$20-$25**
Pie server, Moriyama, Japan .... **$50-$60**

Buffalo China Restaurant Ware Pitcher

Pitcher, 6 3/4" h., cylindrical, restaurant ware, Buffalo China, 1920s (ILLUS.).. **$200-$250**

Blue Willow Pitcher

Pitcher, 5 1/2" h., Ridgways, England (ILLUS.).. **$50-$75**

Blue Willow "Chicago Jug"

Pitcher, 7" h., "Chicago Jug," ca. 1907, Buffalo Pottery, 3 pt. (ILLUS.) .... **$150-$175**

Buffalo Pottery Blue Willow Pitcher

Pitcher, cov., 5 1/2" h., Buffalo Pottery (ILLUS.) .... **$150-$175**
Pitcher, 6" h., scalloped rim, Allerton, England **$100**

Doulton Lambeth Stoneware Pitcher

Pitcher, 7 1/2" h., stoneware, tan & brown w/molded designs trimmed in blue, Doulton Lambeth, late 19th c. (ILLUS., previous page) .... **$175-$200**
Pitcher w/ice lip, 10" h., Japan **$100**

Blue Willow Place Card Holder

Place card holder, unmarked, England, ca. 1870s, 2 1/2" d. (ILLUS.)...................... **$85-$100**
Place mat, cloth, 12 x 16" .... **$15-$20**
Plate, bread & butter, Allertons, England .. **$10-$12**
Plate, bread & butter, Japan.......................... **$5-$7**
Plate, "Child's Day 1971," Sandman w/willow umbrella, Wedgwood, England....... **$40-$45**
Plate, dinner, Booth's, England................. **$40-$45**
Plate, dinner, Cambridge, blue pattern on clear glass.. **$40-$50**
Plate, dinner, flow blue, Royal Doulton ..... **$50-$75**
Plate, dinner, Japan .... **$10-$15**
Plate, dinner, Mandarin patt., Copeland, England .... **$35-$40**
Plate, dinner, Paden City Pottery .... **$45-$50**
Plate, dinner, restaurant ware, Jackson.... **$15-$20**
Plate, dinner, Royal China Co. .... **$5-$10**
Plate, dinner, Royal Wessex, England, modern... **$6-$9**
Plate, dinner, scalloped rim, Allertons, England .... **$30-$35**
Plate, dinner, unmarked, England, ca. 1870 .... **$35-$40**
Plate, luncheon, square, Johnson Brothers, England.. **$12-$15**
Plate, luncheon, Wedgwood, England ...... **$15-$20**
Plate, luncheon, Worcester patt. .... **$20-$25**

Plate, child's, 4 1/2" d., Japan................... **$10-$15**
Plate, 7 1/2" d., Arklow, Ireland................ **$15-$20**
Plate, grill, 10" d., Japan .... **$18-$20**

Japanese Blue Willow Grill Plate

Plate, grill, 10" d., Japan (ILLUS.)............. **$18-$20**
Plate, 10 1/4" d., paper, Fonda .... **$1-$2**
Platter, 9 x 11", gold trim, dark blue handles, Coronaware............................. **$125-$150**
Platter, 9 x 11", rectangular, Wedgwood & Co., England .... **$100-$125**
Platter, 8 1/2 x 11 1/2" l., oval, scalloped rim, Buffalo Pottery **$80-100**
Platter, 9 x 12" l., oval, American.............. **$15-$18**
Platter, 9 x 12" l., oval, Japan .... **$20-$25**
Platter, 9 x 12" l., rectangular, Allertons, England... **$100-$125**
Platter, 11 x 14" l., oval, Johnson Bros., England .... **$40-$45**
Platter, 11 x 14" l., rectangular, Buffalo Pottery... **$150-$175**
Platter, 11 x 14" l., rectangular, ca. 1880s, unmarked, England (ILLUS., bottom of page).. **$100-$150**
Platter, 11 x 14" l., rectangular, Holland ... **$20-$25**
Platter, 15 x 19" l., rectangular, well & tree, ca. 1890, unmarked, England... **$250-$275**
Platter, 20 1/2" l., oval, English, late 19th - early 20th c. .... **$250-$300**
Prestopan, figural toby-shaped, for salt, pepper, vinegar or oil, each .... **$100-$125**
Pudding mold, England, 4 1/2" h. .... **$20-$25**

Large English Victorian Blue Willow Platter

Willow Ware Punch Cup

Punch cup, pedestal foot, unmarked, England, ca. 1900, 3 1/2" h. (ILLUS.) ... **$30-$40**

Early Willow Leaf-shaped Relish Dish

Relish dish, leaf-shaped, ca. 1870, England (ILLUS.) .... **$100-$125**

Rectangular Victorian Blue Willow Relish Dish

Relish dish, rectangular w/wide flaring tab handles, late 19th c. (ILLUS.)............. **$100-$125**

Blue Willow Salt Box

Salt box, cov., ca. 1960, wooden lid, Japan, 5 x 5" (ILLUS.) .... **$125-$150**

English Blue Willow Master Salt Dip

Salt dip, master, pedestal base, unmarked, England, 2" h. (ILLUS.) .... **$100-$125**

Japanese Blue Willow Salt & Pepper

Salt & pepper shakers, footed hexagonal shape w/pointed top, Japan, 6 1/2" h., pr. (ILLUS.).. **$25-$30**
Salt & pepper shakers, Japan, pr............ **$30-$35**

Blue Willow Sauce Tureen

Sauce tureen, cov., England, ca. 1880s, 5" h. (ILLUS.) .... **$100-$125**

Blue Willow Soap Dish & Tumbler

Soap dish, oval slab-type, Burleigh, England (ILLUS. left with tumbler)............. **$45-$50**
Soup tureen, cov., ca. 1880, unmarked, England... **$275-$325**

Blue Willow Sugar Barrel

Tea set, child's, Japan, service for four (ILLUS., bottom of page)................ **$125-$150**
Tea set, child's, Japan, service for six in box .... **$200-$250**

Rare Early Blue Willow Spill Vase

Spill vase, pearlware, deeply waisted shape, unmarked, early 19th c., 4" h. (ILLUS.) .... **$175-$200**
Spoon rest, Japan .... **$35-$40**
Sugar barrel, cov., silver lid & handle, unmarked, England, ca. 1880s, 5" h. (ILLUS., top next column).. **$175**
Sugar bowl, cov., Buffalo Pottery .... **$40-$50**
Sugar bowl, cov., Japan .... **$20-$25**
Sugar bowl, cov., Ridgways, England ...... **$30-$35**
Tablecloth, Simtex................................... **$40-$45**
Tea cozy, Blue Willow fabric, modern .... **$40-$45**

Japanese Blue Willow Tea Set for Two

Tea set, Double Phoenix, Japan, service for two (ILLUS.)..................................... **$175-$200**
Tea set, stacking-type, teapot, creamer & sugar, Japan .... **$80-$100**
Tea set, ca. 1900, unmarked, England, 6" sq. **$50**
Tea tile, Minton, England, 6" sq. .... **$50-$75**
Tea towel, souvenir of Historic Charleston, 16 1/2 x 26".. **$10-$15**

Blue Willow Child's Tea Set for Four

Miniature Blue Willow Teapot

Teapot, cov., miniature, lobed ovoid body, domed inset cover w/finial, C-scroll handle, serpentine spout, gold line decoration on handle, spout, rim & finial, Windsor China, England, modern, 3 3/4" h. (ILLUS.).. **$15-$20**

Teapot, cov., enamelware, unmarked, 7" h. .... **$40-$50**

Teapot, cov., individual, Moriyama, Made in Japan, 4 1/2" h. .... **$50-$60**

Teapot, cov., Sadler, 4 3/4" h. .... **$35-$40**

"Yorkshire Relish" Tip Tray

Tip tray, "Yorkshire Relish," England, 4" d. (ILLUS.).. **$40-$50**

Blue Willow Tip Tray

Tip tray, "Schweppes Lemon Squash," England, 4 1/2" d. (ILLUS.)....................... **$30-$40**

Blue Willow Toby Jug

Toby jug, w/Blue Willow jacket, unmarked, England, 6" h. (ILLUS.) .... **$250-$300**

Toby jug, w/Blue Willow jacket, W. Kent, England, 6" h. .... **$200-$250**

Toothbrush holder, Wedgwood, England, 5 1/4" h.. **$70-$80**

Tray, round, brass, 6" d............................. **$25-$30**

Trivet, scalloped foot, Moriyama, very rare, 6".. **$50-$75**

Tumbler, clear glass, Johnson Brothers, England, 6 1/4" h. .... **$5-$7**

Tumbler, frosted glass, 5" h...................... **$10-$12**

Tumbler, tapering cylindrical shape, Burleigh (ILLUS. right with soap dish, page 721)... **$45-$50**

Buffalo Pottery Round Vegetable Bowl

Vegetable bowl, cov., round, Buffalo Pottery (ILLUS.)..................................... **$150-$175**

Vegetable bowl, cov., round, Societe Ceramique, Holland............................... **$75-$100**

Square English Covered Vegetable

Vegetable bowl, cov., square, ca. 1900, unmarked, England (ILLUS.) .... **$125-$150**

Vegetable bowl, open, individual size, oval, J. Maddock, England, 5 1/4" l....... **$25-$30**

Vegetable bowl, open, oval, Japan **$35**

Vegetable bowl, open, round, Allertons, England, 7" d.. **$60-$75**

Wall pocket, figural, in the shape of a coffeepot, Japan .... **$35-$40**

Blue Willow Wash Pitcher

Wash pitcher, bulbous ovoid body w/wide scalloped spout, sponged border, 7 3/4" h. (ILLUS.) .... **$150-$175**

Blue Willow Wash Bowl & Pitcher

Wash pitcher & bowl, Royal Doulton, the set (ILLUS.)...................................... **$400-$500**

Other Colors

Purple Willow Ware Cup

Cup, purple, handleless, unmarked, England (ILLUS.)...................................... **$50-$60**

Black Willow English Cup & Saucer

Cup & saucer, black, unmarked, England, early 20th c., the set (ILLUS.) .... **$35-$40**

Red Willow Ware Pitcher

Pitcher, 5" h., red, "Old Gustavsberg," Sweden (ILLUS.).. **$40-$50**

Plate, dinner, gaudy coloring, Buffalo Pottery, dated 1911 .... **$80-$100**

Ridgways Gaudy Willow Dinner Plate

Plate, dinner, gaudy coloring, Ridgways, England, 1920s (ILLUS.)...................... **$50-$70**

English Brown Willow Dinner Plate

Plate, 9 1/2" d., brown, unmarked, England
(ILLUS.)... **$20-$25**

Multicolored Willow Platter by Newport

Platter, 9 1/2 x 11 3/4", oval, multicolored,
Newport (ILLUS.) .... **$40-$50**
Relish dish, rectangular, red, Mason's, En-
gland, 5 3/4" l. .... **$50-$60**

Orange Willow Royal Doulton Vase

Vase, 5 1/4" h., orange, bottle-shaped w/tall
stick neck, Booth's patt., Royal Doulton
(ILLUS.)... **$40-$45**

Zeisel (Eva) Designs

*One of the most influential ceramic artists and
designers of the 20th century, Eva Zeisel began
her career in Europe as a young woman, eventually immigrating to the United States, where her*

*unique, streamlined designs met with great suc-
cess. Since the 1940s her work has been at the
forefront of commercial ceramic design, and in
recent decades she has designed in other media.
Now in her ninth decade, she continues to be
active and involved in the world of art and
design.*

Castleton - Museum Ware

Bowl, 11" d., salad, White.............................. **$160**
Bowl, 13" d., salad, French Garden.............. **$375**

Castleton - Museum Ware Coffee Set

Coffeepot, cov., tall, slender form w/C-
scroll handle (ILLUS. second from left
w/coffee set)... **$500**
Coffeepot, cov., White .... **$400-$500**
Creamer, handleless (ILLUS. second from
right w/coffee set, above)........................... **$300**
Creamer, w/handle, White **$75**
Cup & saucer, flat, Mandalay **$20**
Cup & saucer, flat, White **$45**
Cup & saucer (ILLUS. far left w/coffee set,
above).. **$150-$200**
Plate, 8 1/4" d., salad, White........................... **$30**
Plate, 8 1/4" sq., salad, White **$135**
Plate, 8 1/4" sq., salad, Wisteria **$18**
Plate, 10 1/2" d., dinner, White **$50**
Sugar, cov., handleless (ILLUS. far right
w/coffee set)... **$250**

Goss American - Wee Modern

Wee Modern Child's Plate

Child's plate (ILLUS.).................................... **$265**

Hall China Company - Kitchenware

Golden Clover Cookie Jar

Cookie jar, cov., Golden Clover (ILLUS.) **$65**

Creamer, Tri-tone... $45
Marmite, Casual Living $30

Tri-tone Nested Mixing Bowls

Mixing bowls, nested, Tri-tone, set of 5
    (ILLUS.) $250
Refrigerator jug, cov., Casual Living............. $100
Refrigerator jug, cov., Tri-tone...................... $150

Casual Living Shakers

Shakers, Casual Living, set (ILLUS.) $40
Sugar, Tri-tone $60

Tri-tone Teapot

Teapot, cov., 6-cup, Tri-tone, ca. 1954
    (ILLUS.)... $150

Hall China Casual Living Teapot

Teapot, cov., Casual Living, brown body
    (ILLUS.).. $175

Hallcraft by Hall China Co. - Tomorrow's Classic Shape

This shape was produced in plain white and with a variety of decal designs. A selection of the designs are listed here.

Black Satin
Cup & saucer, the set $30

Bouquet (blue floral decals)
Creamer, after-dinner size $55
Creamer $45
Onion soup, cov. $100
Platter, 17 1/4" oval $60

Caprice (muted floral decals)
Bowl, fruit, 5 3/4" d. $15

Hallcraft Caprice Pattern Casserole

Casserole, cov. (ILLUS.) $125

Hallcraft Caprice After-dinner Creamer

Creamer, after-dinner size (ILLUS.)................. $50
Gravy boat $40
Gravy ladle $50
Platter, 13" oval $40
Platter, 17 1/4" oval $50
Vegetable serving bowl, oval, 11 3/4" l. $45

Classic White (no decals)
Ashtray $55
Creamer $55
Cup $25
Cup & saucer, after dinner size, the set.......... $95
Gravy boat $75
Gravy ladle $100
Plate, 11" d., dinner.. $22
Saucer $7
Teapot, cov. $200

Dawn (mottled design)
Creamer, after dinner size $45

Fantasy (abstract black lines)
Creamer $45

Cup & saucer, the set...................................... $40

Hallcraft Fantasy Pattern Eggcups & Gravy Boat

Eggcup, each (ILLUS. of two, front of gravy
boat)... $100
Gravy boat (ILLUS. back with Fantasy egg
cups) $60
Plate, 6" d., bread & butter $10
Plate, 11" d., dinner $35
Platter, 15 1/8" oval... $55
Sugar bowl, cov... $55
Vegetable serving bowl, oval, 11 3/4" l. $70

Frost Flowers (blue floral)
Creamer $30
Platter, 12 7/8" oval... $40
Sugar bowl, cov... $35

Harlequin (pink & black abstract design)
Bowl, 6" d., cereal $20
Plate, 6" d., bread & butter $10
Plate, 11" d., dinner... $25
Platter, 12 7/8" oval... $45
Salt & pepper shakers, the set $65
Vegetable serving bowl, oval, 11 3/4" l. $50

Holiday (red & black modern poinsettia design)
Ashtray $30
Plate, 11" d., dinner... $25
Platter, 15 1/8" oval... $45

Mulberry (literal mulberry design)
Bowl, 6" d., cereal $20
Cup & saucer, the set.. $25
Plate, 11" d., dinner... $30

Spring (modern floral design)

Hallcraft Spring Pattern Teapot

Teapot, cov. (ILLUS.)...................................... $175

Hallcraft - Century Dinnerware
Creamer, Fern.. $45
Cup & saucer, Garden of Eden....................... $35
Gravy boat & ladle, Fern................................ $100

Fern Jug

Jug, Fern, 1 1/4 qt. (ILLUS.) $125
Plate, 10" d., dinner, Sunglow......................... $35
Platter, 15" l., White $50
Relish, divided, White $90
Sugar, cov., Fern $40

White Vegetable Bowl

Vegetable bowl, 10 1/2" d., White (ILLUS.) $80

Hollydale

Hollydale Chop Plate

Chop plate, 14" l., brown (ILLUS.).................. $80
Creamer $65
Gravy bowl, bird-shape $100
Plate, 10 1/4" d., desert yellow........................ $30
Sauce dish, bird-shape, yellow/turquoise...... $200
Sugar, cov... $90
Tureen & ladle, bird design, the set $300

Hyalyn "Z Ware"
Bowl, cereal, oxblood, commercial
grade/restaurant ware................................. $40
Carafe, autumn gold.. $200

Satin Black "Z Ware" Coffee Server

Coffee server, cov., satin black w/white lid
  (ILLUS.)... $150

"Z Ware" Autumn Gold Compote

Compote, footed, autumn gold, 5" (ILLUS.)... $350
Creamer, handleless, autumn gold,
  4 3/4" h.. $85
Mug & saucer, olive green............................ $145

Johann Haviland

Bowl, fruit, Wedding Ring patt. $25
Coffeepot, cov., Eva White............................ $175
Creamer & cov. sugar, Wedding Ring patt. $80
Creamer & sugar, Eva White, the set............ $100
Cup & saucer, Wedding Ring......................... $30
Dinnerware set, Wedding Ring, 20-pc. ser-
  vice for 4.. $250+
Plate, bread & butter, Wedding Ring patt........ $10
Plate, 10 1/4" d., dinner, Wedding Ring $25
Platter, oval, Wedding Ring patt. $60
Sauce dish & underplate, Wheat $50
Serving bowl, round, Wedding Ring patt. $40

Johann Haviland

Blue Roses Teapot

Teapot, cov., Blue Roses patt., 1950s
  (ILLUS.)... $150

Johann Haviland

Tureen/vegetable bowl, cov., White............. $175

Monmouth Dinnerware

Butter pat, Pals, 4" $40
Creamer, Blueberry....................................... $40
Creamer, Lacy Wings $50
Cup & saucer, Lacey Wings/Rosette $45

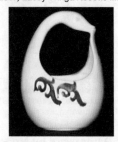

Goose-shaped Gravy Boat

Gravy boat, goose shape, Lacey Wings
  (ILLUS.) $175
Sauce dish, Pals.. $140

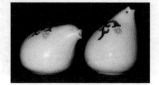

Lacey Wings Shakers

Shaker set, Lacey Wings, pr. (ILLUS.) $80
Sugar, cov., bird lid, Blueberry........................ $60

Monmouth Bird-shaped Sugar

Sugar, cov., bird lid, Lacey Wings (ILLUS.) $80

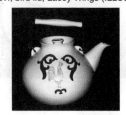

Lacey Wings Teapot with Bird Decoration

Teapot, cov., Lacey Wings patt., wire handle w/ceramic grip, Prairie Hen, w/bird decoration, ca. 1952 (ILLUS.) **$300**

Pals Teapot

Teapot, cov., Pals patt., in the form of a stylized bird w/"dancing turnips" decoration, ceramic ribbon handle, ca. 1952 (ILLUS.) .. **$400**
Vase, 7 1/2" h., perforated, Lacey Wings **$125**
Vegetable bowl, 9 1/2" d. **$75**

Norleans Dinnerware by Meito

(Pieces marked "Made in Occupied Japan" are worth 25% more.)

Fairfield Cup & Saucer

Cup & saucer, Fairfield (ILLUS.) **$25**
Cup & saucer, Livonia **$25**

Livonia Gravy Boat with Underliner

Gravy boat w/underliner, Livonia (ILLUS.) **$65**

Livonia Dinner Plate

Plate, dinner, Livonia (ILLUS.) **$25**
Plate, salad, Livonia **$20**
Service for six, Livonia, 36-piece set **$350**

Norleans Vegetable Bowl

Vegetable bowl, 12" oval, Livonia (ILLUS.) **$65**

Riverside

Riverside Bowl

Bowl, 8 1/2" d., celadon & moss yellow (ILLUS.) **$600**
Creamer **$175**
Plate, dinner, yellow & olive green **$60**

Riverside Vase in Rust

Vase, 4 1/2" h., rust (ILLUS.) **$100**

Schmid Dinnerware

Casserole, cov., bird lid, 9 1/2 x 8" **$200**

Schmid Dinnerware Coffeepot

Coffeepot, cov., Lacey Wings/Rosette (ILLUS.) **$250**

Gravy or sauce server, Lacey Wings, 7" d. .. **$175**

Sunburst Mug

Mug, Sunburst (ILLUS.)..................................... **$45**

Schmid Dinnerware Pitcher

Pitcher, 10" h., Lacey Wings & Sunburst
(ILLUS.)... **$200**
Plate, 10 1/2" d., dinner, Lacey Wings/Sun-
burst **$25**

Schmid Bird-shaped Teapot

Teapot, cov., bird-shaped, rattan handle,
Lacey Wings, 1950s (ILLUS.) **$150**

Schramberg

Ashtray, triangular, Gobelin 13 (ILLUS.,
bottom of page)... **$160**
Creamer, cov., Mondrian **$170**
Cup & saucer, Gobelin 13 .... **$75**

Gobelin 13 Covered Jar

Jar, cov., Gobelin 13, 5" (ILLUS.) **$375**

Mondrian Covered Jar

Jar, cov., terraced, Mondrian, 5" (ILLUS.)... **$1,000**
Jug, cover & undertray, hot water, Mondri-
an **$90**
Pitcher, 4 1/2" h., Mondrian **$225**
Plate, salad, matte grun (green)...................... **$40**
Plate, 7 1/2" d., dessert, Gobelin 13 .... **$60**

Mondrian Covered Sugar

Sugar, cov., Mondrian (ILLUS.) **$125**

Schramberg Triangular Ashtray

Gobelin 13 Teapot

Teapot, cov., Gobelin 13 patt., Germany, 1930s (ILLUS.).. **$900**
Tray, Mondrian, 12" **$450**

Gobelin 8 Vase

Vase, 6" h., offset oval, Gobelin 8 (ILLUS.).... **$250**

Stratoware

Stratoware Candlestick

Candlestick, brown trim (ILLUS.) **$120**
Casserole, cov., beige & brown **$150**

Stratoware Cup & Saucer

Cup & saucer, gold interior (ILLUS.) **$50**
Plate, 11 1/2" d., yellow & green **$60**

Stratoware Refrigerator Jar

Refrigerator jar, cov., blue & beige (ILLUS.)... **$200**

Stratoware Shakers

Shakers, green trim, pr. (ILLUS.)..................... **$85**

Stratoware Covered Sugar

Sugar, cov., gold & beige (ILLUS.) **$100**

Town and Country Dinnerware - for Red Wing Potteries

Pieces are unmarked and must be identified by the unique shapes. Glaze colors include rust, gray, dusk blue, peach, chartreuse, sand, Ming green, bronze and white.

Baker, oval, dusk blue, 10 3/4" l. **$85**
Baker, oval, rust, 10 3/4" l. **$85**
Bowl, 5 3/4" d., chili or cereal, bronze **$35**
Bowl, 5 3/4" d., chili or cereal, peach.............. **$25**
Bowl, 5 3/4" d., chili or cereal, sand................ **$25**
Creamer, peach **$50**
Creamer, sand **$45**

Town and Country Mustard Jar

Town and Country "Yawn" Creamer

Creamer, "yawn," bronze (ILLUS.) **$70**

Town and Country Cruets

Cruets, dusk blue & peach, set (ILLUS.)........ **$150**

Town & Country Cups & Saucers & Syrup

Cup & saucer, peach, the set (ILLUS. of two, front with rust syrup pitcher) **$45**
Cup & saucer, rust, the set **$45**

Lazy Susan Relish Set

Lazy Susan relish set w/mustard jar (ILLUS.)
.... **$600**
Mixing bowl rust **$175**
Mixing bowl dusk blue **$175**
Mustard jar, cover & ladle, dusk blue, the set (ILLUS., top of page)............................. **$250**

Town and Country Syrup Pitcher

Pitcher, syrup, chartreuse (ILLUS.) **$135**
Pitcher, jug-type, chartreuse, rust, Ming green or dusk blue, 2 pt., each **$250**

Group of Town & Country 3 Pt. Pitchers

Pitcher, jug-type, rust, Ming green, chartreuse or dusk blue, 3 pt., each (ILLUS. of each color, top of page) **$325**

Plate, 8" d., salad, chartreuse **$30**

Plate, 8" d., salad, dusk blue **$30**

Plate, 8" d., salad, sand **$30**

Plate, 10 1/2" d., dinner, bronze **$55**

Plate, 10 1/2" d., dinner, gray **$40**

Plate, 10 1/2" d., dinner, peach **$45**

Plate, 10 1/2" d., dinner, rust **$45**

Platter, 15" l., comma shape, dusk blue **$110**

Platter, 15" l., comma shape, rust **$110**

Shaker, large "schmoo," Ming green (ILLUS. right w/small "schmoo" shaker) **$75**

Shaker, large "schmoo," rust **$70**

Shaker, small "schmoo," chartreuse **$40**

Shaker, small "schmoo," rust (ILLUS. left w/large "schmoo" shaker, previous column) **$40**

Spoons, salad servers, white, the set (ILLUS., bottom of page) **$1,700**

Sugar bowl, cov., charteuse **$60**

Sugar bowl, cov., dusk blue **$60**

Sugar bowl, cov., rust **$60**

Syrup pitcher, rust (ILLUS. back with Town & Country cups & saucers, previous page) **$140**

Large & Small "Schmoo" Shakers

Bronze Town and Country Teapot

Teapot, cov., ca. 1947, bronze (ILLUS.) **$550**

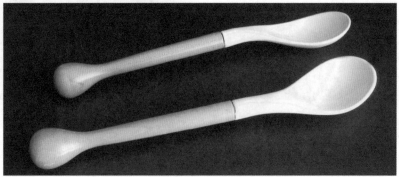

Salad Serving Spoons

Town & Country Covered Soup Tureen

Tureen, cov., soup, sand (ILLUS.) **$850**

Watt Pottery

Watt Pottery Drip Glaze Bowl

Bowl, 8 1/4" d., blue drip glaze (ILLUS.) **$25**

Watt Pottery Carafe

Carafe, ribbon handle, Nassau (ILLUS.) **$80**
Chop tray, Mountain Road, 14 1/2" **$210**
Shaker set, hourglass shape, bisque............... **$35**
Teapot, cov., rattan handle, Animal Farm
patt., ca. 1954 .... **$650**

Zsolnay

This pottery was made in Pecs, Hungary, in a factory founded in 1862 by Vilmos Zsolnay. Utilitarian earthenware was originally produced with an increase in art pottery production from as early as 1870. The highest level of production employed over 1000 workers. The Art Nouveau era produced the most collectibles and valuable pieces in today's marketplace. Examples are displayed in every major art museum worldwide.

Zsolnay is always well marked and easy to identify. One specialty was the metallic Eosin glaze. With over 10,000 different forms created over the years and dozens of glaze variations for each form, there is always something new in Zsolnay being discovered. Today the original factory size has been significantly reduced with pieces being made in a new factory.

Zsolnay Marks

Fine Zsolnay Art Nouveau Cachepot

Cachepot, Art Nouveau style, squatty bulbous body w/four open stem handles around the base w/stems continuing up the sides & ending in lily pads around the scalloped rim, Shape #5792, metallic Eosin glaze against a dull Eosins ground, ca. 1900, 6" h. (ILLUS.).................... **$9,500-$12,500**

Rare Zsolnay Gres Cachepot

Cachepot, wide squatty flat-bottomed form w/a wide flat mouth, Shape #7140, gres (stone) body molded w/a repeated band of elk, metallic green & red Eosin glaze decoration, designed by Sandor Apati Abt, round raised factory mark, ca. 1903, 4 1/4" h. (ILLUS.) .... **$12,500-$15,000**

One of a Pair of Zsolnay Candelabra

Candelabra, three-light, Romanesque style, a tapering conical foot molded w/buttons, crosses & scrolls below the paneled stem trimmed w/buttons & supporting a pair of upturned arms ending in candle sockets flanking the large center cupped candle socket, Pyrogranite w/Eosin & polychrome decorations, Shape #2732, ca. 1890, 18 1/2" h., pr. (ILLUS. of one)........................... **$8,500-$9,500**

Zsolnay Chalice

Chalice, organic form w/applied handles curving out connecting base to bowl, multi glazes, printed Zsolnay Factory mark, incised form number 5668, ca. 1900, 6" h. (ILLUS.) .... **$1,500-$2,000**

Charger, painted w/scene of peasants in folkloric costumes pressing grapes in a vineyard, design by Armin Klein, printed Zsolnay factory mark, incised form number 470, ca. 1880, 15" d. (ILLUS., top next column).. **$1,500-$2,000**

Zsolnay Armin Klein Charger

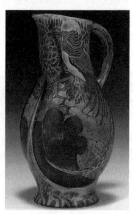

Iridescent Zsolnay Bird-decorated Ewer

Ewer, footed ovoid body tapering to a cylindrical neck pinched-in to form a long rim spout, simple applied strap handle, decorated overall w/exotic birds in shades of red, pale green & purple among branches of stylized blossoms in dark blue & red on iridescent green stems against a blue spotted & dark red iridescent ground, raised churches mark, ca. 1900, 9" h. (ILLUS.).............................. **$13,200**

Ornate Reticulated Zsolnay Ewer

Ewer, wide low domed & reticulated base divided into petal-form panels, swelled cylindrical & reticulated neck w/oval reservers below the widely rolled & pierced rim, ornate scroll-pierced dragon-form handle, decorated in blue & red enamel against a creamy yellow ground, impressed on bottom "Zsolnay Pecs 2042," remnants of paper label, 9 1/2" h. (ILLUS., previous page) **$1,265**

Zsolnay Figure

Figure of a female nude, standing figure w/one hand to her breast & the other holding a drapery behind her, deep brown iridescent glaze, molded factory seal, ca. 1900, 12 1/4" h. (ILLUS.) **$2,868**

Yellow-glazed Zsolnay Garden Seat

Garden seat, barrel-shaped, an overall drippy yellow & brown glaze, the sides

molded in relief w/bands of scrolls & flowerheads, Shape #1105, incised factory mark, ca. 1882, 18 1/2" h. (ILLUS.) .... **$1,500-$2,000**

Zsolnay Mushroom-shaped Garden Seat

Garden seat, molded as a large mushrom w/smaller mushrooms below on the molded base, majolica-glazed Pyrogranite, incised factory mark, originally had a matching table, ca. 1888, 18" h., garden seat (ILLUS.).............................. **$4,500-$6,500**

Zsolnay Tadé Sikorsky Jug

Jug, form designed by Tadé Sikorsky, shriveled glaze w/applied pierced decorations, incised Zsolnay factory mark & form number 1379, ca. 1885, 8" h. (ILLUS.) ..... **$350-$550**

Zsolnay Lamp by Lajos Mack

Lamp, figural, Art Nouveau model of a woman in the style of Lolie Fuller, w/arms upraised & flowing hair, designed by Lajos Mack, mostly gold/green Eosin glazes, round raised Zsolnay factory mark, incised form number 6324, ca. 1900, 22 1/2" h. (ILLUS.) .... **$20,000-$25,000**

Very Rare Figural Zsolnay Table Lamp

Lamp, table-model, electric, Shape #6161, figural Art Nouveau design, the base modeled as a tall tapering ribbed plant stem w/leaf handles decorated w/a green & gold iridescent Eosin glaze, the large

red flower-form top enclosing the electric socket, round raised factory mark, ca. 190, 14 1/2" h. (ILLUS.) .... **$15,000-$20,000**

Zsolany Skull & Bible Paperweight

Paperweight, figural, modeled as a closed Bible w/a skull resting on the top, dark blue lustre glaze w/green highlights, impressed mark & number 5788, thin lines radiate from one corner, 3" h. (ILLUS.) **$288**

Zsolany Pitcher with Applied Decoration

Pitcher, 7 1/2" h., bulbous fluted body w/a cylindrical neck, a wide mid-body band decorated w/domed & pierced buttons. small bottoms around the rim of the neck, the angled handle also trimmed w/buttons, a shriveled dark brown over yellow glaze, Shape #992, incised factory mark, ca. 1882 (ILLUS.)................... **$200-$300**

Pitcher, 8 1/4" h., Art Nouveau style, Shape #6102, bulbous tapering smooth melon-form body tapering to a wide arched & pointed pointed, a large figural handle in the shape of a satyr glazed in red & black, the body w/a green & gold iridescent marbled Eosin glaze, round raised factory mark & artist mark of an acorn for Lajos Mack, ca. 1900 (ILLUS.)
.... **$12,500-$14,500**

Rare Zsolany Tazza with Figural Angels on Base

Zsolany Statue of a Hussar

Rare Zsolnay Umbrella Stand

Statue, figure of a Hussar in full military uniform, high-fired white glaze, one of 30 different figures commissioned for the Hungarian pavillion at the Paris World Exposition of 1900, impressed factory mark & artist mark for Sandor Abt, ca. 1900, 13 1/2" h. (ILLUS.) .... **$2,500-$3,500**

Tazza, an oblong quatrefoil foot w/a central pedestal in a dark metallic blue Eosin glaze mounted at each point w/a figural standing angel w/a majolica glaze in gold & orange, all supporting the wide shallow dished top dish w/a metallic gold & green & blue Eosin glaze, round raised factory mark, ca. 1906, 11" d. (ILLUS., top of page) ...... **$12,500-$15,000**

Umbrella stand, tall, slightly waisted cylindrical form w/rolled rim, the sides decorated w/dark golden iridescent fish swimming in iridescent swirls of dark blue, purple & gold, impressed "Zsolnay - Pecs - 4036 - 21," ca. 1900, 26 3/4" h. (ILLUS., top next column)................................... **$14,400**

Miniature Zsolnay Vase

Vase, miniature, 4" h., wide base tapering to ring foot & long neck, richly decorated w/Hungarian folkloric designs in gold & blue/green Eosin glazes, incised Zsolnay factory mark, ca. 1912 (ILLUS., previous page) .... **$1,000-$1,250**

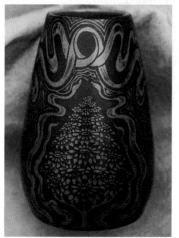

Small Zsolnay Art Nouveau Vase

Vase, 4 1/4" h., gently tapering swelled cylindrical form w/a flat rim, decorated in an Art Nouveau design w/undulating ribbons framing flowering trees, Shape # 5330, dull Eosin glaze in shades of brown & yellow, painted factory mark, a design found in many sizes & variations, ca. 1898 (ILLUS.) ..... **$1,750-$2,500**

Four-handled Zsolnay Vase

Vase, 4 7/8" h., footed bulbous body tapering to a cylindrical neck & mounted w/four large flattened gold handles, deep red ground w/a rim band of stylized flowerheads in white, dark blue & gold, Zsolnay mark & number 2293 (ILLUS.) **$690**

Zsolnay Vase with Iridescent Eosin Glaze

Vase, 6 7/8" h., bulbous ovoid lower body tapering to a pinched center below the upright squared neck, iridescent Eosin glaze w/rust over brushed gold, marked w/raised wafer logo & impressed numbers "6035 - 23" (ILLUS.) **$863**

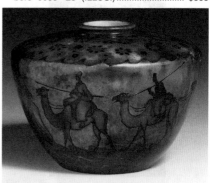

Wide Squatty Zsolnay Iridescent Vase

Vase, 8" d., in the Persian taste, broad squatty shield-shaped body w/a wide shoulder centered by a small low rolled neck, the shoulder decorated w/iridescent stylized flambé flowers on a scalloped ground, the sides painted w/an iridescent continuous caravansary & three palm trees in a desert landscape, five churches raised pad mark, ca. 1914-20 (ILLUS.) **$7,200**

Vase, 8" w., earthenware, wide ovoid base w/broad flattened shoulder centered by a short cylindrical rim, decorated w/a caravan of men on camels carrying guns & spears, in an oasis w/palm trees, below a wavy edged border of scattered flower heads, iridescent red, brown & blue glaze, ca. 1900-10, molded factory seal, impressed "8868" & "19," imperfection at edge of foot **$2,300**

Vase, 11 3/4" h., bulbous waisted form w/short bulbous applied feet, Hungarian Millennium decoration of painted stylized birds & flowers, round printed Zsolnay factory mark, incised form number 933, ca. 1882 (ILLUS.) .... **$2,500-$3,500**

Fine Reticulated Iridescent Zsolnay Vase

Vase, 12 1/2" h., in the Persian taste, footed tall slightly tapering cylindrical body w/a rounded shoulder & short cylindrical neck w/flaring rim, the central double-walled section pierced about the base & upper body w/cartouches of birds & berried vine, painted between the panels w/similar decoration, the single-walled neck w/similar reticulation, overall iridescent metallic lustre in shades of greenish gold & shades of orange & red, possibly by Henri Darilek, ca. 1905 (ILLUS.) **$6,600**

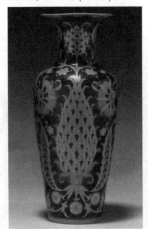

One of Two Fine Zsolnay Lustre Vases

Vases, 13 3/8" h., in the Persian taste, tall slightly tapering cylindrical body w/a rounded shoulder to the cylindrical neck

w/a widely flaring flattened rim, the dark copy lustre ground decorated front & back w/large stylized pineapples & foliage light blue & gold lustre, the sides w/matching stylized flowers, printed five churches mark, early 20th c., pr. (ILLUS. of one) **$10,800**

One of Two Zsolnay Palace Vases

Vases, 22" h., palace-type, flaring foot & tall slender ovoid body tapering to a short slightly flaring cylindrical neck, white ground w/overall ornate colorful exotic birds & flowers decoration painted underglaze on a high-fired porcelain faience, applied ornate gilt-brass lion head & ring handles, signed by Julia Zsolnay, ca. 1881 (ILLUS. of one) **$6,500-7,500**

KITCHENWARES

Eggcups

Princess Diana Commemorative Eggcup

Bucket-style, color transfer-printed portrait of Princess Diana, commemorating her death, England, 1997 (ILLUS.) **$35**

Bucket Eggcup with Vintage Auto

Bucket-style, colored transfer image of a vintage automobile, found w/a variety of boy's names printed, unmarked, England, 1999 (ILLUS.) **$15**

Gouda Pottery Eggcup

Bucket-style, squat shape in brown h.p. w/colorful stylized flowers, Gouda Pottery, Holland, ca. 1930s (ILLUS.) **$75**

British Transport System Eggcup

Hoop-style, designed for use by the British Transport System, their logo printed in red, England, ca. 1930s (ILLUS.) **$40**

Mintons Eggcup for Use On a Ship

Hoop-style, designed for use on a ship as indicated by flags decoration, gold rim band, Mintons, England, 1930 (ILLUS.) **$85**

Hoop Eggcup with Ship's Flag Design

Hoop-style, white ground w/a red & white ship's flag decoration, unmarked, England, ca. 1930 (ILLUS.) **$35**

Blue & White Royal Doulton Eggcup

Single, a dark blue wide rim band w/undulating white band above scattered stylized blue florals, Royal Doulton, England, 1930 (ILLUS.)................................ **$40**

Early Wileman Flower Decor Eggcup

Single, a dark cobalt blue ground w/gold trim framing large heart-shaped reserves printed w/red flower clusters, Wileman (pre-Shelley), England, 1884 (ILLUS.) **$175**

Fine Early Decorated Lenox Eggcup

Single, a narrow turquoise enamel rim band decorated w/tiny gold beading & flanked by think gold bands, suspends swags of blue beading, Lenox, United States, ca. 1900 (ILLUS.)... **$100**

Single, alphabet-type, printed w/"Q is for Quail," part of a line of dinnerware produced for children, Adderleys, England, 1939 (ILLUS., top next column) **$55**

Single, boldly colored Imari patt. in dark blue, red & gold, Royal Crown Derby, England, ca. 1880s (ILLUS., middle next column) **$100**

Adderleys Alphabet Eggcup

Royal Crown Derby Imari Patt. Eggcup

1930s Aynsley China Eggcup

Single, brightly colored poppies on a cream ground, Aynsley, England, ca. 1930 (ILLUS., previous page) **$45**

Portrait Eggcup of Young Elizabeth II

Single, color transfer-print portrait of Queen Elizabeth II as a young girl, part of a set that includes Princess Margaret Rose, England, ca. 1937, each (ILLUS.) **$75**

Early Mintons Bird-decorated Eggcup

Single, colorful decoration in a Cockatrice or Ho-Ho Bird design, green border, Mintons, England, ca. 1890 (ILLUS.) **$50**

Single, colorful floral decoration w/h.p. gold trim, Limoges, France, 2002 (ILLUS., top next column) **$55**

Single, colorful floral design against a blue lattice background, bone china, Cauldon, England, ca. 1920s (ILLUS., middle next column) **$85**

Single, colorful floral wreath below various Italian names printed in black, unmarked, Italy, 1987 (ILLUS. of one, bottom next column) **$20**

Modern Limoges Porcelain Eggcup

Cauldon China Floral Eggcup

Contemporary Italian Name Eggcup

Rose-decorated Aynsley Eggcup

Single, decorated w/red rose clusters below a narrow ropetwist rim band in black & white, Aynsley, England, ca. 1930s (ILLUS.)............ **$40**

Contemporary Rosenthal Eggcup

Single, embossed body h.p. w/flowers & gold wreathes & banding, Rosenthal, Germany, 1988 (ILLUS.) **$55**

Rare Figural Sarreguemines Eggcup

Single, figural, brightly colored model of a peacock w/the cup on its back, Sarreguemines, France, ca. 1935 (ILLUS.) **$155**

Scarce Figural Stan Laurel Eggcup

Single, figural, modeled as the head of Stan Laurel of the Laurel & Hardy comedy team, Germany, ca. 1930 (ILLUS.) **$150**

Cute Figural Baby Head Eggcup

Single, figural, model of a baby's head & shoulders, separate white insert for the egg, nicely detailed, unmarked, ca. 1925 (ILLUS.) **$100**

Fine Figural Boy's Head Eggcup

Single, figural, model of a boy's face w/fine detailing, unmarked, possibly France, ca. 1920 (ILLUS.) **$100**

Eggcup with Blue Branch Decoration

Single, flaring cylindrical top w/molded rim, teal blue branch decoration, unmarked, Staffordshire, England, ca. 1885 (ILLUS.)..... **$75**

Fluted Mintons Eggcup with Flowers

Single, fluted body decorated w/blue flowers on the outside & interior, Mintons, England, ca. 1890 (ILLUS.)......................... **$50**

Scarce Early Hochst Porcelain Eggcup

Single, four-lobed foot & leaf-molded stem below a gadrooned band around the base of the cup, h.p. floral decor & trim, impressed mark of the Hochst Porcelain Manufactury, Germany, ca. 1763 (ILLUS.) .. **$200**

Pink Jasper Ware Eggcup

Single, Jasper Ware, applied white classical figures on six different colored backgrounds, Dancing Hours patt., Josiah Wedgwood, England, 1994 (ILLUS. of one) **$40**

Rare Early Pierced Creamware Eggcup

Single, ornately pierced creamware bowl, unmarked, England, ca. 1820s (ILLUS.).... **$225**
Single, pink lustre base below the black-printed portrait of Lord Roberts, an English general during the Boer War, Germany, ca. 1900 (ILLUS., next page) **$55**

Eggcup with Portrait of Lord Roberts

Rare Victorian Bisque Eggcup

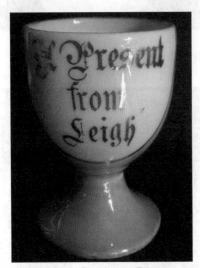

Inscribed Pink Lustre Eggcup

Wedgwood Ribbed & Floral Eggcup

Single, pink lustre base, cup printed in gold "A Present From Leigh," unmarked, England, ca. 1900 (ILLUS.)........................... **$35**

Single, pure white w/a deeply scalloped rim & embossed design on the sides, Meissen, Germany, 2002 .... **$85**

Single, rare bisque example in peach w/a pink tinge, Locke, Worcester, England, 1886 (ILLUS., top next column) **$80**

Single, ribbed lower bowl below a wide band decorated w/orange flowers & bands, Josiah Wedgwood, England, ca. 1870s (ILLUS., middle next column) **$75**

Single, tall figural style in the shape of a lady w/red hair, part of a series of ladies individually named & clothed, modern, United States (ILLUS., bottom next column) **$15**

Modern Figural Lady Eggcup

Eggcup with Band of Children at Play

Single, tan lustre base, wide border band in color showing children at play, unmarked, ca. 1920s (ILLUS.) **$50**

Rare Pair of Early French Eggcups

Single, white bowl h.p. w/flower bouquets, raised on three goat-leg supports on a triangular base, silver rim applied later, from the D.v. Mannency factory that operated from 1734 through 1774, from the estate of Amy Bess Miller, France, ca. 1760s, pr. (ILLUS.) **$550**

Eggcup from the Wembley Exhibition

Single, white decorated w/the emblem of the Wembley Exhibition of 1924, England (ILLUS.) **$55**

Early Davenport, England Eggcup

Single, white ground decorated around the cup w/thin h.p. blue stripes, Davenport, England, ca. 1850 (ILLUS.) **$95**

Eggcup with Queen Victoria Portrait

Single, white ground printed w/a black bust portrait of Queen Victoria, probably a souvenir of her funeral, pink lustre base, Germany, early 1900s (ILLUS.) **$130**

Single, white ground printed w/a Swallow-tail butterfly, one of a dated series featuring various birds, flowers & animals, embossed date, 1990, Germany (ILLUS. of first in series, next page) **$25**

Dated Eggcup with Butterfly

English Eggcup with Ribbed Body

English Wooden Puzzle Eggcup

Victorian Opalescent Glass Eggcup

Single, white opalescenet blown glass w/a thin applied blue band on the rolled rim, American-made, ca. 1880 (ILLUS.)............ **$110**

Single, white ribbed body w/a narrow gold rim band trimmed w/turquoise jewels or beads, England, ca. 1920s (ILLUS., top next column)... **$65**

Single, wooden puzzle-type, carved w/a loose ring from a single block of wood, no opening in the ring, England, ca. 1900 (ILLUS., middle next column)...................... **$45**

Single w/attached saucer base, h.p. fruit decoration, Herend, Hungary, 1988 (ILLUS., bottom next column) **$90**

Contemporary Herend Eggcup

Early Copeland-Spode Eggcup

Urn-shaped, color transfer of a bird perched on a flower, colored by hand, Copeland-Spode, England, ca. 1880 (ILLUS.).............. **$65**

Early Copeland Bone China Eggcup

Urn-shaped, h.p. floral decoration w/gold trim, bone china, Copeland, England, ca. 1880 (ILLUS.).. **$75**

The Modern Kitchen - 1920-1980

Kitchen Accessories

Egg Timers
Angel, ceramic, wearing blue robe & gold wings, w/verse "May the meals that I...," unmarked .... **$45-$65**
Baker, ceramic, Goebel (ILLUS., top next column) **$50**
Bear, ceramic, howling, USA .... **$50-$75**

Goebel Baker Egg Timer

Bear, ceramic, wearing chef's outfit, marked "Japan"... **$65-$85**
Bellhop, ceramic, Oriental, kneeling, marked "Germany"............................... **$65-$85**
Bellhop, ceramic, wearing green uniform, marked "Japan," 4 1/2" h. **$70**
Bellhop, ceramic, wearing white uniform w/buttons down leg seam, marked "Germany".. **$65-$85**
Bird, ceramic, red bird sitting by yellow post, marked "Germany"...................................... **$50**
Bird, ceramic, sitting on nest, wearing white bonnet w/green ribbon, Josef Originals sticker.. **$45**

Bird & Egg Near Stump Egg Timer

Bird, ceramic, standing next to stump w/egg at base, shades of brown w/green grassy base & leaves on stump, Japan (ILLUS.) **$50**
Black chef, ceramic, standing, marked "Llangollen" **$95**

Black Chef with Fish Egg Timer

Black chef, ceramic, standing w/large fish, timer in fish's mouth, Germany, 4 3/4" h. (ILLUS.).. **$125**

Lady Chef Egg Timer

Black lady chef, ceramic, sitting, Germany (ILLUS.).. **$95**

Bo-Peep Egg Timer

Bo-Peep, ceramic, "Bo-Peep" on base, Japan (ILLUS.).. **$95**

Boy, ceramic, playing guitar, marked "Germany," 3 1/2" h... **$50**

Boy Chef Egg Timer

Boy chef, ceramic, sitting w/raised arm, Germany (ILLUS.).. **$65**

Goebel Egg Timer with Boy & Girl

Boy & girl, ceramic, flanking timer on oblong base, boy w/white pants, dark blue coat & yellow cap, girl in red dress w/white apron & large dark blue hat, Goebel, Germany (ILLUS.) **$95**

Cat, ceramic, black cat w/white-tipped tail sitting by fireplace, "Ireland" painted on front, marked "Manorware, England" .... **$25-$35**

Cat, ceramic, white & black cat, marked "Germany"... **$65-$85**

Chef, ceramic, holding egg, Germany....... **$45-$65**

Chef, ceramic, holding knife, Japan.......... **$45-$65**

Chef, ceramic plate w/hole to hold timer, which removes to change, Japan **$50**

Chef, ceramic, w/black shoes & hair, marked "Germany"............................... **$45-$65**

Chefs, ceramic, man & woman, Goebel, Germany, 4" h.. **$100**

Chicken, ceramic, multicolored, marked
"Germany"... **$75-$95**
Chicken, ceramic, white w/black wings &
tail feathers, marked "Germany" **$50**

Goebel Chimney Sweep Egg Timer

Chimney sweep, ceramic, Goebel, Germa-
ny (ILLUS.)... **$50**

Clown Egg Timer

Clown, ceramic, Germany (ILLUS.) **$95**
Clown, ceramic, w/ball on head, marked
"Japan"... **$45-$65**
Colonial man in knickers, ruffled shirt, ce-
ramic, Japan, 4 3/4" h. **$75**
Dog, ceramic, black Poodle, sitting, Germa-
ny **$75**

Green Dog Egg Timer

Dog, ceramic, green, looking at his tail
(ILLUS.)... **$75**

Dog Egg Timer

Dog, ceramic, sitting, white w/brown tail &
ears, timer in head, Germany (ILLUS.)........ **$75**
Dog, ceramic, white & brown dog w/red collar sitting by post, marked "Germany"... **$65-$85**
Dogs, ceramic, Scotties, brown, standing
facing each other holding timer in paws,
marked "Germany"...................................... **$95**
Dutch boy, ceramic, standing by green
post, Japan, tall.. **$35**
Dutch boy, ceramic, white w/red scarf
around neck, kneeling, Japan **$35**
Dutch girl, ceramic, all white w/blue trim at
waist & neckline, kneeling.................... **$50-$75**

Dutch Girl Egg Timer

Dutch girl, ceramic, white w/blue apron &
trim, Germany (ILLUS.) **$50**
Friar Tuck, ceramic, double-type, modeled
by Helmut White, timer marked w/3-, 4- &
5-minute intervals, Goebel, Germany,
1956... **$65**

Rabbit, ceramic, sitting, white w/red jacket, holding ear of corn that supports the timer, Germany **$50**

Santa Claus, ceramic, standing by wrapped gift, label reads "SONSCO," marked "Japan" .... **$50-$75**

Sea gull, ceramic, lustre, white w/brown-tipped spread wings & tail, purple base, Germany **$75**

Swami Egg Timer

Swami, ceramic, standing wearing turban, Germany (ILLUS.) **$110**

Swiss woman, ceramic, w/multicolored striped apron, marked "Germany" **$50**

Victorian lady, ceramic, wearing green & pink gown, marked "Germany" **$50**

Welsh woman, ceramic, marked "Japan" **$35**

Windmill, ceramic, all green, goose sitting atop windmill, marked "Germany" **$50**

Windmill, ceramic, brown, black & yellow, w/dog standing on base, marked "Japan" .. **$100**

Pie Birds

Advertising, "Paulden's Crockery Department Stretford Road," ceramic, white, England **$45**

Bird, ceramic, black on white base, yellow feet & beak, Nutbrown, England **$25**

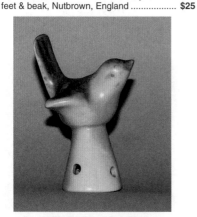

Half-doll Style Pie Bird

Bird, ceramic, half-doll style, blue & yellow on conical base, USA (ILLUS.) **$350**

Rowe Pottery Pie Bird

Bird, ceramic, two-piece w/detachable base, 1992, Rowe Pottery (ILLUS.) **$25**

English White Pie Bird

Bird, ceramic, white w/wide mouth, England (ILLUS.) .... **$50-$60**

White & Blue Pie Bird

Bird, ceramic, white w/yellow beak, blue trim on tail & base, made in California, 1950s (ILLUS.) .... **$300-$500**

Rare Pie Boy Pie Bird

"Pie Boy," ceramic, white w/black & green trim, Squire Pottery of California, USA, rare (ILLUS.) .... **$350-$500**

Marion Drake Rooster Pie Bird

Rooster, ceramic, Marion Drake, white w/black, red & yellow trim on brown base (ILLUS.)... **$50**

Rare Brown "Patrick" Pie Bird

Rooster "Patrick," ceramic, tan w/brown trim, California Cleminsons, USA, rare (ILLUS.).. **$175**

Seal, black, ceramic, Japan **$125**

American Pottery Pie Bird

Songbird, ceramic, blue & yellow, American Pottery Company, 1940-50 (ILLUS.)
.... **$40-$50**

"Patch" Pie Bird

Songbird, ceramic, "Patch," white, yellow, green & pink, Morton Pottery (ILLUS.).. **$35-$50**

Welsh Woman Pie Bird

Welsh woman, ceramic, brown w/large black hat, 1969, commemorating investiture of Prince Charles (ILLUS.)................ **$200+**

Reamers

Ceramic, boat-shaped, pale green w/pink, blue & white flowers, cream reamer cone, handle & inside bowl, Shelley - England, 7" h. .... **$225-$250**

Boat-shaped Leaf-decorated Reamer

Ceramic, boat-shaped, white w/gilt line trim, decorated w/rust-colored leaves & navy blue, small loop handle, 3 1/2" h. (ILLUS.) .... **$45-$65**

Bucket-style Handled Reamer

Ceramic, bucket-style, two-piece, tan w/embossed cherub, flowers & decorative panels, green trim, rattan handle, marked "Made In Japan, Pat. 49541," 7 3/4" h. (ILLUS.) .... **$60-$85**

Manx Cat Creamer-Style Reamer

Ceramic, creamer-style, two-piece, beige w/image of black cat & "Manx Cat From The Isle of Man," reamer on lid, marked

"Crown Devon, Made in England," 3 1/2" h. (ILLUS.) .... **$75-$85**

"Sourpuss" Clown Ceramic Reamer

Ceramic, figural clown head reamer in saucer base, white w/black & pink & marked "Sourpuss," 4 3/4" d. (ILLUS.)............. **$90-$125**

Oriental Man's Head Reamer

Ceramic, figural Oriental man's head, two-piece, w/collar as base, hat as lid/reamer, light blue w/dark grey highlights, incised "9496," 5 3/4" h. (ILLUS.)................. **$125-$150**

Reamer in the Form of Amish Man

Ceramic, figure of Amish man, three-piece, black pants, green shirt, yellow cone top & hat, marked "JCC, NRCA, PA-1996," 5 1/2" h. .... **$40-$50**

Ceramic, model of pansy blossom, two-piece, decorated w/a yellow & purple pansy, white top w/ruffled rim, 4" h. ...... **$60-$75**

White Pear Ceramic Reamer

Ceramic, model of pear, three-piece, white w/black & gold trim, marked "Handpainted Made in Japan," 5" h. (ILLUS.)......... **$45-$55**

Two-piece Pitcher Reamer with Clown Head

Ceramic, pitcher-shaped, figural clown head reamer top w/green cone, two-piece w/colorful stylized orange & yellow flowers on the base, 6" h. (ILLUS.) .... **$55-$65**

Flowered Universal Cambridge Reamer

Ceramic, pitcher-shaped, two-piece, cream w/yellow & purple flowers & green leaves, marked "Universal Cambridge, Ovenproof, Made in USA," 9 1/2" h. (ILLUS.)
.... **$150-$175**

Ceramic Two-piece Pitcher Reamer

Ceramic, pitcher-shaped, two-piece, tall footed light pink body w/green trim, colorful pink, yellow & blue flower sprig, marked "Pantry BAK-IN by Ware, Crooksville," 8 1/4" h. (ILLUS.)......... **$100-$125**

Pitcher-style Clown Head Reamer

Ceramic, pitcher-style, figural clown head yellow reamer top, base decorated w/yellow & purple flowers, yellow cone & lustre trim, marked "Made in Japan," 6" h. (ILLUS.)....................................... **$75-$95**

Green One-Piece Ceramic Reamer

Ceramic, pitcher-style, one-piece, green, Art Deco design, w/spring-loaded cone, Ade-O-Matic, Genuine Coorsite Porcelain, 9" h. (ILLUS.)............................ **$150-$175**

APPENDIX I

CERAMICS CLUBS & ASSOCIATIONS

ABC Plates
ABC Collectors' Circle
67 Stevens Ave.
Old Bridge, NJ 08857-2244

Abingdon Pottery Club
210 Knox Hwy. 5
Abingdon, IL 61410-9332

American Art Pottery Association
P.O. Box 834
Westport, MA 02790-0697
www.amartpot.org

American Ceramic Circle
520 16th St.
New York, NY 11215

Amphora Collectors Club
129 Bathurst St.
Toronto, Ontario
Canada M5V 2R2

Arkansas Pottery

National Society of Arkansas Pottery
Collectors
2006 Beckenham Cove
Little Rock, AR 72212
www.flash.net/~gemoore/nsapc.htm

Pottery Lovers Reunion
4969 Hudson Dr.
Stow, OH 44224

Bauer Pottery
www.bauerpottery.com

Belleek Collectors International Society
9893 Georgetown Pike, Ste. 525
Great Falls, VA 22066
www.belleek:ie/collectors.com

Blue & White Pottery Club
224 12th St. NW
Cedar Rapids, IA 52405

Blue Ridge Collectors Club
208 Harris St.
Erwin, TN 37650
(423) 743-9337

Carlton Ware Collectors International
Carlton Works
P.O. Box 161
Sevenoaks, Kent, England
TN15 6GA
e-mail: cwciclub@aol.com

Ceramic Arts Studio Collectors
P.O. Box 46
Madison, WI 53701-0046
www.ceramicartsstudio.com

Chintz Connection
P.O. Box 222
Riverdale, MD 20738-0222

Clarice Cliff Collectors Club
Fantasque House
Tennis Drive, The Park
Nottingham NG7 1AE
UNITED KINGDOM
www.claricecliff.com

Currier & Ives Dinnerware
Collectors Club
29470 Saxon Rd.
Toulon, IL 61438
www.royalchinaclub.com

Czechoslovakian Collectors Assoc.
P.O. Box 137
Hopeland, PA 17533

The Dedham Pottery Collectors Society
248 Highland St.
Dedham, MA 02026-5833
www.dedhampottery.com

Delftware Collectors Association
P.O. Box 670673
Marietta, GA 30066
www.delftware.org

Doulton & Royal Doulton
Northern California Doulton
Collectors Club
P.O. Box 214
Moraga, CA 94556
www.royaldoultonwest.com

Royal Doulton International
Collectors Club
701 Cottontail Lane
Somerset, NJ 08873
www.royal-doulton.com

Fiesta Collector's Club
P.O. Box 471
Valley City, OH 44280-0471
www.chinaspecialties.com/fiesta.html

Flow Blue International Collector's Club
P.O. Box 6664
Leawood, KS 66206
www.flowblue.org

Franciscan Pottery Collectors Society
500 S. Farrell Dr., #S-114
Palm Springs, CA 92264
www.gmcb.com/franciscan

Frankoma Family Collectors Association
P.O. Box 32571
Oklahoma City, OK 73123
www.frankoma.org

Gonder Collectors Club
3735 E. Rousay Dr.
Queen Creek, AZ 85242
e-mail: GonderNut@aol.com

Goss & Crested China Club
62 Murray Rd.
Horndean
Waterlooville, Hants. PO8 9JL
United Kingdom
www.gosschina.com

Gouda Pottery
See Delftware Collectors Association

Haeger Pottery Collectors of America
5021 Toyon Way
Antioch, CA 94509-8426

Hall China Collector's Club
P.O. Box 360488
Cleveland, OH 44136-0488
www.chinaspecialties.com/hallnews.html

Haviland Collectors International
Foundation
P.O. Box 271383
Fort Collins, CO 80527
www.havilandcollectors.com

Head Vases (Head Hunters Newsletter)
P.O. Box 83H
Scarsdale, NY 10583-8583

Hull Pottery Association
112 Park DeVille Dr.
Columbia, MO 65203
www.hullpotteryassociation.org
<http://hullpotteryassociation.org>

Homer Laughlin China Collectors
P.O. Box 1093
Corbin, KY 40702-1093
www.hlcca.org

Illinois Pottery
Collectors of Illinois Pottery
& Stoneware
308 N. Jackson St.
Clinton, IL 61727-1320

Ironstone China

White Ironstone China Association
P.O. Box 855
Fairport, NY 14450-0855
www.whiteironstonechina.com

Jewel Tea Autumn Leaf
National Autumn Leaf Collectors Club
P.O. Box 7929
Moreno Valley, CA 92552-7929
www.nalcc.org

Majolica International Society
1275 First Ave., PBO 103
New York, NY 10021-5601
www.majolicasociety.com

McCoy Pottery Collectors' Society
14 North Morris St.
Dover, NJ 07801
www.mccoypotterycollectorssociety.org

McCoy Pottery Collectors Connection
2210 Sherwin Dr.
Twinsburg, OH 44087
www.ohiopottery.com/mccoy

Moorcroft Collectors Club
Sandbach Road
Burslem, Stoke-on-Trent ST6 2DG
United Kingdom
www.moorcroft.com

Nippon Porcelain
International Nippon Collectors Club
1387 Lance Court
Carol Stream, IL 60188
www.nipponcollectorsclub.com

Lakes & Plains Nippon Collectors' Club
P.O. Box 230
Peotone, IL 60468-0230

New England Nippon Collectors Club
64 Burt Rd.
Springfield, MA 01118-1848

Sunshine State Nippon Collectors' Club
P.O. Box 425
Frostproof, FL 33843-0425

Noritake Collectors' Society
1237 Federal Ave. E.
Seattle, WA 98102-4329
www.noritakecollectors.com

North Dakota Pottery Collectors Society
P.O. Box 14
Beach, ND 58621-0014

Old Ivory China

Society for Old Ivory & Ohme Porcelains
700 High St.
Hicksville, OH 43526

Pewabic Pottery
10125 E. Jefferson Ave.
Detroit, MI 48214
www.pewabic.com

Phoenix Bird Collectors of America
1107 Deerfield St.
Marshall, MI 49068

Pickard Collectors Club
300 E. Grove St.
Bloomington, IL 61701-5232

Porcelier Collectors Club
21 Tamarac Swamp Road
Wallingford, CT 06492-5529

Purinton Pottery
Purinton News & Views Newsletter
P.O. Box 153
Connellsville, PA 15425

Quimper Club International
5316 Seascape Lane
Plano, TX 75093
www.quimperclub.org

Red Wing Collectors Society, Inc.
P.O. Box 50
Red Wing, MN 55066-0050
www.redwingcollectors.org

Royal Bayreuth International Collectors'
Society
P.O. Box 325
Orrville, OH 44667-0325

R.S. Prussia
International Association of
R.S. Prussia Collectors Inc.
P.O. Box 185
Lost Nation, IA 55254
www.rsprussia.com

Shelley China
National Shelley China Club
591 W. 67th Ave.
Anchorage, AK 99518-1555
www.nationalshelleychinaclub.com

Southern Folk Pottery Collectors Society
220 Washington St.
Bennett, NC 27208

Staffordshire
The Transfer Ware Collectors Club
734 Torreya Court
Palo Alto, CA 94303
www.transcollectorsclub.org

Stangl/Fulper Collectors Association
P.O. Box 538
Flemington, NJ 08822
www.stanglfulper.com

Stoneware
American Stoneware Collectors Society
P.O. Box 281
Point Pleasant Beach, NJ 08742-0281

Susie Cooper Collectors Group
P.O. Box 7436
London N12 7QF
United Kingdom

Tea Leaf Club International
Maxine Johnson, Membership
P.O. Box 377
Belton, MO 64012
www.TeaLeafClub.com

Torquay Pottery
North American Torquay Society
214 N. Ronda Rd.
McHenry, IL 60050
www.torquayus.org

Uhl Collectors Society, Inc.
3704 W. Old Road 64
Huntingburg, IN 47542
www.uhlcollectors.org

Van Briggle Collectors Society
600 S. 21st St.
Colorado Springs, CO 80904
www.vanbriggle.com

Wade Watch, Ltd.
8199 Pierson Court
Arvada, CO 80005
www.wadewatch.com

Watt Collectors Association
1431 4th St. SW
P.M.B. 221
Mason City, IA 50401
server34.hypermart.net
wattcollectors/watt.htm

Wedgwood International Seminar
22 De Savry Crescent
Toronto, Ontario
Canada M45 2L2
www.w-i-s.org

Wedgwood Society of Boston, Inc.
P.O. Box 215
Dedham, MA 02027-0215
htlp://www.angelfire.com/ma/wsb/
index.html

The Wedgwood Society of New York
5 Dogwood Ct.
Glen Head, NY 11545-2740
www.wsny.org

Wedgwood Society of Washington, DC
3505 Stringfellow Court
Fairfax, VA 22033

Willow Wares
International Willow Collectors
503 Chestnut St.
Perkasie, PA 18944
www.willowcollectors.org

Wisconsin Pottery Association
P.O. Box 8213
Madison, WI 53708-8213
www.wisconsinpottery.org

Eva Zeisel Collectors Club
695 Monterey Blvd. #203
San Francisco, CA 94127
www.evazeisel.org

APPENDIX II
Museums & Libraries with Ceramic Collections

CERAMICS (AMERICAN)

Everson Museum of Art of Syracuse &
Onondaga County
401 Harrison St.
Syracuse, NY 13202-3019
www.everson.org

Museum of Ceramics at East Liverpool
400 E. 5th St.
East Liverpool, OH 43920-3134
www.ohiohistory.org/places/ceramics

CERAMICS (AMERICAN ART POTTERY)

Cincinnati Art Museum
953 Eden Park
Cincinnati, OH 45202
www.cincinnatiartmuseum.com

Newcomb College Art Gallery
Woldenberg Art Center
Newcomb College/Tulane University
1229 Broadway
New Orleans, LA 70118
www.newcomb.tulane.edu

Zanesville Art Center
620 Military Rd.
Zanesville, OH 43701
www.zanesville.com

OTHER CERAMICS:
BENNINGTON

The Bennington Museum
West Main St.
Bennington, VT 05201

www.benningtonmuseum.com

CATALINA ISLAND POTTERY

Catalina Island Museum
P.O. Box 366
Avalon, CA 90704
www.catalina.com/museum

CHINESE EXPORT PORCELAIN

Peabody Essex Museum
East India Square
Salem, MA 01970
www.pem.org

CLEWELL POTTERY

Jesse Besser Museum
491 Johnson St.
Alpena, MI 49707
www.ogdennews.com/upnorth/
museum/home.htm

COWAN POTTERY

Cowan Pottery Museum at the Rocky River
Public Library
1600 Hampton Rd.
Rocky River, OH 44116-2699
www.rrpl.org/rrpl_cowan.stm

DEDHAM

Dedham Historical Society
612 High St.
Dedham, MA 02027-0125
www.dedhamhistorical.org

GEORGE OHR

Ohr/O'Keefe Museum of Art
136 G.E. Ohr St.
Biloxi, MS 39530
www.georgeohr.org

PENNSYLVANIA GERMAN

Hershey Museum
170 W. Hersheypark Dr.
Hershey, PA 17033

ROSEVILLE POTTERY

Roseville Historical Society
91 Main St.
Roseville, OH 43777
www.netpluscom.com/~pchs/
rosevill.htm

SOUTHERN FOLK POTTERY

Museum of Southern Stoneware
River Market Antiques Mall
3226 Hamilton Rd.
Columbus, GA 31904

WEDGWOOD

Birmingham Museum of Art
2000 Eighth Ave. No.
Birmingham, AL 35203
www.artsbma.org

GENERAL COLLECTIONS:

The Bayou Bend Collection
#1 Westcott
Houston, TX 77007
www.bayoubend.uh.edu

Greenfield Village and Henry Ford
Museum
20900 Oakwood Blvd.
Dearborn, MI 48124-4088

Museum of Early Southern
Decorative Arts
924 Main St.
Winston Salem, NC 27101

Abby Aldrich Rockefeller Folk
Art Collection
England St.
Williamsburg, VA 23185

The Margaret Woodbury Strong Museum
700 Allen Creek Rd.
Rochester, NY 14618

Henry Francis DuPont Winterthur Museum
Winterthur, DE 19735
www.winterthur.org

APPENDIX III
References to Pottery and Porcelain Marks

*DeBolt's Dictionary of American Pottery
Marks—Whiteware & Porcelain*
Gerald DeBolt
Collector Books,
Paducah, Kentucky, 1994

*Encyclopaedia of British Pottery and
Porcelain Marks*
Geoffrey A. Godden
Bonanza Books,
New York, New York, 1964

*Encyclopedia of Marks on American,
English, and European Earthenware,
Ironstone and Stoneware*
Arnold A. and Dorthy E. Kowalsky
Schiffer Publishing, Ltd.
Atglen, PA, 1999

*Kovel's New Dictionary of Marks, Pottery &
Porcelain, 1850 to the Present*
Ralph & Terry Kovel

Crown Publishers,
New York, New York, 1986

*Lehner's Encyclopedia of U.S. Marks on
Pottery, Porcelain & Clay*
Lois Lehner
Collector Books,
Paducah, Kentucky, 1988

*Marks on German, Bohemian and Austrian
Porcelain, 1710 to the Present*
Robert E. Röntgen
Schiffer Publishing, Ltd.,
Atglen, Pennsylvania

Pictorial Guide to Pottery & Porcelain Marks
Chad Lage
Collector Books
Paducahy, Kentucky, 2004

APPENDIX IV
English Registry Marks

Since the early 19th century, the English have used a number of markings on most ceramics wares that can be very helpful in determining the approximate date a piece was produced.

The registry mark can be considered an equivalant of the American patent number. This English numbering system continues in use today.

Beginning in 1842 and continuing until 1883, most pottery and porcelain pieces were printed or stamped with a diamond-shaped registry mark, which was coded with numbers and letters indicating the type of material, parcel number of the piece and, most helpful, the day, month and year that the design or pattern was registered at the Public Record Office. Please note that a piece may have been produced a few years after the registration date itself.

Chart A shows the format of the diamond registry mark used between 1842 and 1867. Accompanying it are listings of the corresponding month and year letters used during that period. In a second chart, Chart B, we show the version of the diamond mark used between 1868 and 1883, which depicts a slightly different arrangement. Keep in mind that this diamond registry mark was also used on metal, wood and glasswares. It is important to note that the top bubble with the Roman numeral indicates the material involved; pottery and porcelain will always be Numeral IV.

After 1884, the diamond mark was discontinued and instead just a registration number was printed on pieces. The abbreviation "Rd" for "Registration" appears before the number. We list here these design registry numbers by year with the number indicating the first number that was used in that year. For instance, design number 494010 would have been registered sometime in 1909.

CHART A	CHART B

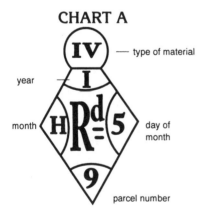

**Registration for
April 5, 1846**

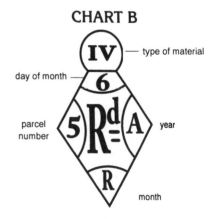

**Registration for
August 6, 1871**

LIST
Month of the Year of Registration

C—January

G—February

W—March

H—April

E—May

M—June

I—July

R—August

D—December

B—October

K—November

A—December

LIST
Year of Registration—1842-1867

1842—X	1851—P	1860—Z
1843—H	1852—D	1861—R
1844—C	1853—Y	1862—O
1845—A	1854—J	1863—G
1846—I	1855—E	1864—N
1847—F	1856—L	1865—W
1848—U	1857—K	1866—Q
1849—S	1858—B	1867—T
1850—V	1859—M	

LIST 3

Year of Registration — 1868-1883

1868—X	1874—U	1879—Y
1869—H	1875—S	1880—J
1870—C	1876—V	1881—E
1871—A	1877—P	1882—L
1872—I	1878—D	1883—K
1873—F		

LIST 4

DESIGN REGISTRY NUMBERS — 1884-1951

Jan. 1884—1	1907—493900	1929—742725
1885—20000	1908—518640	1930—751160
1886—40800	1909—535170	1931—760583
1887—64700	Sep. 1909—548919	1932—769670
1888—91800	Oct. 1909—548920	1933—779292
1889—117800	Jan. 1911—575817	1934—789019
1890—142300	1912—594195	1935—799097
1891—164000	1913—612431	1936—808794
1892—186400	1914—630190	1937—817293
1893—206100	1915—644935	1938—825231
1894—225000	1916—635521	1939—832610
1895—248200	1917—658988	1940—837520
1896—268800	1918—662872	1941—838590
1897—291400	1919—666128	1942—839230
Jan. 1898—311677	1920—673750	1943—839980
1899—332200	1921—680147	1944—841040
1900—351600	1922—687144	1945—842670
1901—368186	1923—694999	Jan. 1946—845550
1902—385180	1924—702671	1947—849730
1903—403200	1925—710165	1948—853260
1904—424400	1926—718057	1949—856999
1905—447800	1927—726330	1950—860854
1906—471860	1928—734370	1951—863970

GLOSSARY OF SELECTED CERAMICS TERMS

Abino Ware—A line produced by the Buffalo Pottery of Buffalo, New York. Introduced in 1911, this limited line featured mainly sailing ship scenes with a windmill on shore.

Agate Ware—An earthenware pottery featuring a mixture of natural colored clays giving a marbled effect. Popular in England in the 18th century.

Albany slip—A dark brown slip glaze used to line the interiors of most salt-glazed stoneware pottery. Named for a fine clay found near Albany, New York.

Albino line—A version of Griffen, Smith and Hill's Shell & Seaweed majolica pattern with an off-white overall color sometimes trimmed with gold or with pink or blue feathering.

Albion Ware—A line of majolica developed by Edwin Bennett in the 1890s. It featured colored liquid clays over a green clay body decorated with various scenes. Popular for jardinieres and pedestals.

Bas relief—Literally "low relief," referring to lightly molded decorations on ceramic pieces.

Bisquit—Unglazed porcelain left undecorated or sometimes trimmed with pastel colors. Also known as bisque.

Bocage—A background of flowering trees or vines often used as a backdrop for figural groups, which were meant to be viewed from the front only.

Bone china—A porcelain body developed in England using the white ashes of bone. It has been the standard English porcelain ware since the early 19th century.

Coleslaw—A type of decoration used on ceramic figurines to imitate hair or fur. It is finely crumbled clay applied to the unfired piece and resembling coleslaw cabbage.

Crackled glaze—A glaze with an intentional network of fine lines produced by uneven contracting of the glaze after firing. First popular on Chinese wares.

Crazing—The fine network of cracks in a glaze produced by uneven contracting of the glaze after firing or later reheating of a piece during usage. An unintentional defect usually found on eatherwares.

Creamware—A light-colored fine earthenware developed in England in the late 18th century and used by numerous potters into the 19th century. Josiah Wedgwood marketed his version as Queensware.

Crystalline glaze—A glaze containing fine crystals resulting from the presence of mineral salts in the mixture. It was a popular glaze on American art pottery of the late 19th century and early 20th century.

Eared handles—Handles applied to ceramic pieces such as crocks. They are crescent or ear-shaped, hence the name.

Earthenware—A class of fine-grained porous pottery fired at relatively low temperature and then glazed. It produces a light and easily molded ware that was widely used by the potteries of Staffordshire, England in the late 18th and early 19th century.

Faience—A form of fine earthenware featuring a tin glaze and originally inspired by Chinese porcelain. It includes early Dutch Delft ware and similar wares made in France, Germany and other areas of Europe.

Fairyland Lustre—A special line of decorated wares developed by Susannah "Daisy" Makeig-Jones for the Josiah Wedgwood firm early in the 20th century. It featured fantastic or dreamlike scenes with fairies and elves in various colors and with a mother-of-pearl lustre glaze. Closely related to Dragon Lustre featuring designs with dragons.

Flambé glaze—A special type of glaze featuring splashed or streaked deep reds and purple, often dripping over another base color. Popular with some American art pottery makers but also used on porcelain wares.

Flint Enamel glaze—A version of the well-known brown mottled Rockingham pottery glaze. It was developed by Lyman Fenton & Co. of Bennington, Vermont and patented in 1849. It featured streaks and flecks of green, orange, yellow and blue mixed with the mottled brown glaze.

Glaze—The general term for vitreous (glass-like) coating fired onto pottery and porcelain to produce an impervious surface and protect underglaze decoration.

Hard-paste—Refers to true porcelain, a fine, white clay body developed by the Chinese and containing kaolin and petuntse or china stone. It is fired at a high temperature and glazed with powdered feldspar to produce a smooth, shiny glaze.

Lead glaze—A shiny glaze most often used on cheap redware pottery and produced using a dry powdered or liquid lead formula. Since it would be toxic, it was generally used on the exterior of utilitarian wares only

Lithophane—A panel of thin porcelain delicately molded with low-relief pattern or scenes that show up clearly when held to light. It was developed in Europe in the 19th century and was used for decorative panels or lamp shades and was later used in the bottom of some German and Japanese steins, mugs or cups.

Majolica—A type of tin-glazed earthenware pottery developed in Italy and named for the island of Majorca. It was revived in Europe and America in the late 19th century and usually featured brightly colored shiny glazes

Married—A close match or a duplicate of the original missing section or piece, such as a lid.

Mission Ware—A decorative line of pottery developed by the Niloak Pottery of Benton, Arkansas. It featured variously colored clays swirled together and was used to produce such decorative pieces as vases and candlesticks.

Moriage—Japanese term for the slip-trailed relief decorations used on various forms of porcelain and pottery. Flowers, beading and dragon decoration are typical examples.

Pâte-sur-pâte—French for "paste on paste," this refers to a decorative technique where layers of porcelain slip in white are layered on a darker background. Used on artware produced by firms like Minton, Ltd. of England.

Pearlware—A version of white colored creamware developed in England and widely used for inexpensive eathenwares

in the late 18th and early 19th century. It has a pearly glaze, hence the name.

Pillow vase—a form of vase designed to resemble a flattened round or oblong pillow. Generally an upright form with flattened sides. A similar form is the Moon vase or flask, meant to resemble a full moon.

Porcelain—The general category of translucent, vitrified ceramics first developed by the Chinese and later widely produced in Europe and America. Hard-paste is true porcelain, while soft-paste is an artificial version developed to imitate hard-paste using other ingredients.

Pottery—The very general category of ceramics produced from various types of clay. It includes redware, yellowware, stoneware and various earthenwares. It is generally fired at a much lower temperature than porcelain.

PUG—An abbreviation for "printed under glaze," referring to colored decorations on pottery. Most often it is used in reference to decorations found on Mettlach pottery steins.

Relief-molding—A decorative technique, sometimes erroneously referred to as "blown-out," whereby designs are raised in bold relief against a background. The reverse side of such decoration is hollowed-out, giving the impression the design was produced by blowing from the inside. Often used in reference to certain Nippon porcelain wares.

Rocaille—A French term meaning "rockwork." It generally refers to a decoration used for the bases of ceramic figurines.

Salt-glazed stoneware—A version of stoneware pottery where common rock salt is thrown in the kiln during firing and produces hard, shiny glaze like a thin coating of glass. A lightly pitted orange peel surface is sometimes the result of this technique.

Sanded—A type of finish usually on pottery wares. Unfired pieces are sprinkled or rolled in fine sand, which, when fired, gives the piece a sandy, rough surface texture.

Sang-de-boeuf—Literally French for "ox blood," it refers to a deep red glaze produced with copper oxide. It was first produced by the Chinese and imitated by European and American potters in the late 19th and early 20th century.

Sgrafitto—An Italian-inspired term for decorative designs scratched or cut through a layer of slip before firing. Generally used on earthenware forms and especially with the Pennsylvania-German potters of America.

Slip—The liquid form of clay, often used to decorate earthenware pieces in a process known as slip-trailing or slip-quilling.

Soft-paste—A term used to describe a certain type of porcelain body developed in Europe and England from the 16th to late 18th centuries. It was used to imitate true hard-paste porcelain developed by the Chinese but was produced using a white clay mixed with a grit or flux of bone ash or talc and fired at fairly low temperatures. The pieces are translucent, like hard-paste porcelain, but are not as durable. It should not be used when referring to earthenwares such as creamware or pearlware.

Sprigging—A term used to describe the ornamenting of ceramic pieces with applied relief decoration, such as blossoms, leaves or even figures.

Standard glaze—The most common form of glazing used on Rookwood Pottery pieces. It is a clear, shiny glaze usually on pieces decorated with florals or portraits against a dark shaded backhground.

Stoneware—A class of hard, high-fired pottery usually made from dense grey clay and most often decorated with a salt glaze. American 19th century stoneware was often decorated with slip-quilled or hand-brushed cobalt blue decorations.

Tapestry ware—A form of late 19th century porcelain where the piece is impressed with an overall linen cloth texture before firing. The Royal Bayreuth firm is especially known for their fine "Rose Tapestry" line wherein the finely textured ground is decorated with colored roses.

Tin glaze—A form of pottery glaze made opaque by the addition of tin oxide. It was used most notably on early Dutch Delft as well as other early faience and majolica wares.

Underglaze-blue—A cobalt blue produced with metallic oxides applied to an unfired clay body. Blue was one of the few colors that did not run or smear when fired at a high temperature. It was used by the Chinese on porcelain and later copied by firms such as Meissen.

INDEX

ABC Plates..31
Abingdon 38
American Painted Porcelain........................42
Amphora - Teplitz 47
Austrian...56
Autumn Leaf, see Jewel Tea Autumn Leaf
Bauer...57
Bavarian..58
Beatrix Potter Figurines 59
Belleek, American.......................................64
Belleek, Irish 65
Bennington 86
Berlin (KPM)..87
Betty Lou Nichols 89
Bisque...92
Blue Ridge Dinnerwares.............................94
Blue & White Pottery 98
Boch Freres 111
Brayton Laguna Pottery 112
Buffalo Pottery..118
Caliente Pottery..127
Cambridge Art Pottery 130
Canton 130
Capo-di-Monte 133
Carlton Ware 134
Catalina Island Pottery.............................135
Ceramic Arts Studio of Madison...............136
Chinese Export 144
Chintz China 146
Clarice Cliff Designs 146
Cleminson Clay..148
Clewell Wares 153
Clifton Pottery...154
Cowan Pottery...155
deLee Art 167
Delft...170
Derby & Royal Crown Derby 172
Doulton & Royal Doulton...........................173
    Animals & Birds 174
    Bunnykins Figurines..........................176
    Burslem Wares 179
    Character Jugs 185
    Figurines 186
    Flambé Glazes..................................189
    Miscellaneous...................................193

Kingsware 196
Lambeth Art Wares............................200
    Series Wares..................................215
    Coaching Days Series 217
    Dickens Ware Series 220
    Barlow Family 224
    Tinworth 226
Dresden...227
East Liverpool.....................................228
Fiesta 239
Florence Ceramics 243
    Figures 244
    Other Items 247
Flow Blue 247
Franciscan Ware.................................278
Frankoma 283
Fulper Pottery 290
Gallé Pottery 295
Gaudy Dutch..297
Gaudy Welsh..297
Geisha Girl Wares 297
Gonder 301
Grueby Pottery 305
Hadley Pottery 308
Hall China..310
Hampshire Pottery...............................319
Harker Pottery 320
Harris Strong Designs 329
Haviland 331
Historical & Commemorative Wares.........337
Hull 338
Imari 343
Ironstone China 344
    General..344
    Tea Leaf...350
    Tea Leaf Variants 357
Jewel Tea Autumn Leaf Pattern................361
Jugtown Pottery 362
Lenox 363
Limoges 364
Liverpool 371
Longwy 372
Lotus Ware..374
Majolica...375
    Etruscan...375

General...................................378
McCoy....................................385
Meissen.................................388
Mettlach................................393
Minton...................................396
Mocha...................................401
Monmouth-Western..................402
Moorcroft..............................412
Morton Potteries....................415
Mulberry...............................421
Newcomb College Pottery.......427
Nicodemus.............................430
Niloak Pottery........................431
Nippon..................................432
Noritake................................440
North Dakota School of Mines.....447
Ohr (George) Pottery..............449
Old Sleepy Eye.......................450
Owens Pottery........................450
Oyster Plates.........................453
Paul Revere Pottery................456
Peters & Reed........................457
Pickared China.......................459
Pierce (Howard) Porcelains........460
Quimper................................462
R.S. Prussia & Related Wares.....470
       R.S. Germany..................470
       R.S. Prussia...................470
Red Wing...............................475
Redware................................494
Rockingham Wares..................497
Rogers (John) Groups...............498
Rookwood...............................500
Rose Medallion & Rose Canton....510
Rosenthal..............................512
Roseville...............................512
Royal Bayreuth.......................564
       Corinthian.....................564
       Devil & Cards................564
       Mother-of-Pearl..............565
       Old Ivory......................565
       Rose Tapestry................565
       Sand Babies..................567
       Snow Babies..................567
       Sunbonnet Babies...........567
       Tomato Items................567
       Miscellaneous...............567

Royal Copley.........................576
Royal Crown Derby, see Derby & Royal
    Crown Derby
Royal Doulton, see Doulton & Royal Doulton
Royal Dux..............................582
Royal Vienna..........................584
Royal Worcester......................586
Rozart Pottery........................593
Satsuma................................595
Schoop (Hedi).........................597
Sèvres & Sèvres-Style..............600
Shawnee................................606
Shelley.................................614
Slipware...............................618
Spatterware...........................619
Spongeware............................622
Staffordshire Figures...............625
Staffordshire Transfer Wares......627
Stangl..................................629
Steins..................................629
Stoneware.............................635
Tea Leaf Ironstone, see Ironstone
Teco Pottery..........................643
Teplitz - Amphora, see Amphora
Tiffany Pottery.......................646
Tiles....................................646
Toby Mugs & Jugs...................649
Van Briggle............................650
Vernon Kilns..........................651
Warwick................................658
Watt Pottery..........................660
Wedgwood.............................665
       Basalt..........................665
       Caneware.......................666
       Jasperware.....................666
       Rosso Antico...................670
       Miscellaneous.................670
Weller..................................676
Wheatley Pottery....................713
Willow Wares.........................714
Zeisel (Eva) Designs................724
Zsolnay.................................733
Kitchenwares.........................739
       Eggcups.........................739
       Egg Timers......................748
       Pie Birds.......................751
       Reamers.........................753

More Pottery Price Guides

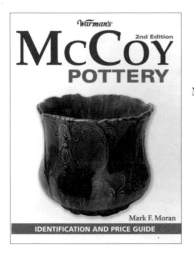
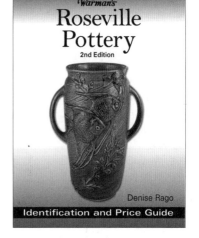